The Journal *of* Artificial Intelligence Research

Volume 13

July 2000 – December 2000

Morgan Kaufmann Publishers
San Francisco, California

Sponsoring Editor   Denise E. M. Penrose
Editorial Coordinator   Emilia Thiuri
Production Manager   Vince Gleason
Printer   The Printing House

Editorial Offices
Morgan Kaufmann Publishers
340 Pine Street, Sixth Floor
San Francisco, CA 94104
http://www.mkp.com

ISBN 1-55860-807-9
ISSN 1076-9757

Journal of Artificial Intelligence Research

Contents

Preface

The Journal of Artificial Intelligence Research (JAIR) began electronic publication in August 1993, and so is now well into the second half of its first decade. A retrospective on JAIR's first half decade appears in the Summer 1999 issue of *AI Magazine*. This volume includes all of the articles published in JAIR from July 2000 through December 2000, exactly as they appear online.

Some of the articles mention "online appendices". These appendices can be retrieved electronically via anonymous FTP from JAIR's internet distribution sites at Carnegie Mellon and the University of Genoa.[1] World-Wide Web users can also access these appendices via the URL:

http://www.jair.org

JAIR could of course not be possible without the quality research of the authors contributing to this volume. But it is important to acknowledge the equally crucial contributions of the editors, editorial board, advisory board, and auxiliary reviewers. These dedicated individuals have made it possible to provide the AI research community with a rapid yet rigorously evaluated publication medium, and their service is much appreciated.

JAIR was established by AI Access Foundation, a nonprofit public benefit corporation whose purpose is to facilitate the dissemination of scientific results in Artificial Intelligence. The directors of AI Access Foundation and JAIR's editors, advisory board, editorial board, and staff all serve on an unpaid volunteer basis, and their work is made possible by the research institutions and universities who support them. Our electronic distribution sites are supported by USC's Information Sciences Institute, NASA's Ames Research Center, the University of Washington, the University of Michigan, Carnegie Mellon University, and the University of Genoa. A brief essay on the role of community support for an academic journal such as JAIR can be found in the January/February 1998 issue of *IEEE Intelligent Systems*.

I would also like to thank Deborah Stark, who has completed over three years as production supervisor, sustaining the journal's operation. JAIR's founding Editor, Steve Minton, continues as Managing Editor to contribute toward running the journal and supporting the editorial process. Finally, JAIR is very grateful to Mike Morgan and Morgan Kaufmann Publishers for making the project possible.

– Michael P. Wellman, Executive Editor

---

1. ftp://ftp.cs.cmu.edu/project/jair or ftp://ftp.mrg.dist.unige.it/pub/jair/pub.

How to Cite Articles Published in JAIR

The articles published in this volume are identical to the articles that appear online. Thus, in citing JAIR articles, there is no need to make a distinction between the electronic and print publications. For instance, an appropriate bibliographic entry for the article by Gordon in this volume[1] would be:

> Gordon, D. F. (2000). Asimovian adaptive agents. *Journal of Artificial Intelligence Research*, *13*, 95-153.

The only distinction between the electronic and print versions is the date they become available. Each article in this volume includes a publication date (month/year), which is listed at the top of the article's first page. This is the date that the article was published electronically, and the appropriate date to use in any citations.

For situations calling for explicit reference to the electronic or print volume, please note that the publisher of the electronic version is AI Access Foundation of El Segundo, California, and the publisher of the printed version is Morgan Kaufmann Publishers of San Francisco, California. Questions about JAIR may be directed to jair-ed@isi.edu.

---

1. We are proud to note that this article received the prestigious Berman publication award from the US Naval Research Laboratories.

Journal of Artificial Intelligence Research 13 (2000) 1-31   Submitted 8/99; published 8/00

Space Efficiency of Propositional Knowledge Representation Formalisms

Marco Cadoli   CADOLI@DIS.UNIROMA1.IT
Dipartimento di Informatica e Sistemistica
Università di Roma "La Sapienza"
Via Salaria 113, I-00198, Roma, Italy

Francesco M. Donini   DONINI@DIS.UNIROMA1.IT
Politecnico di Bari
Dipartimento di di Elettrotecnica ed Elettronica
Via Orabona 4, I-70125, Bari, Italy

Paolo Liberatore   LIBERATO@DIS.UNIROMA1.IT
Marco Schaerf   SCHAERF@DIS.UNIROMA1.IT
Dipartimento di Informatica e Sistemistica
Università di Roma "La Sapienza"
Via Salaria 113, I-00198, Roma, Italy

Abstract

We investigate the *space efficiency* of a Propositional Knowledge Representation (PKR) formalism. Intuitively, the space efficiency of a formalism F in representing a certain piece of knowledge α, is the size of the shortest formula of F that represents α. In this paper we assume that knowledge is either a set of propositional interpretations (models) or a set of propositional formulae (theorems). We provide a formal way of talking about the relative ability of PKR formalisms to compactly represent a set of models or a set of theorems. We introduce two new compactness measures, the corresponding classes, and show that the relative space efficiency of a PKR formalism in representing models/theorems is directly related to such classes. In particular, we consider formalisms for nonmonotonic reasoning, such as circumscription and default logic, as well as belief revision operators and the stable model semantics for logic programs with negation. One interesting result is that formalisms with the same time complexity do not necessarily belong to the same space efficiency class.

1. Introduction

During the last years a large number of formalisms for knowledge representation (KR) have been proposed in the literature. Such formalisms have been studied from several perspectives, including semantical properties, and computational complexity. Here we investigate *space efficiency*, a property that has to do with the minimal size needed to represent a certain piece of knowledge in a given formalism. This study is motivated by the fact that the same piece of knowledge can be represented by two formalisms using a different amount of space. Therefore, all else remaining the same, a formalism could be preferred over another one because it needs less space to store information.

The definition of space efficiency, however, is not simple. Indeed, a formalism may allow several different ways to represent the same piece of knowledge. For example, let us assume that we want to represent the piece of knowledge "today is Monday". In Propositional

Logic we may decide to use a single propositional variable *monday*. The fact that today is Monday can be represented by the formula *monday*, but also by the formula $\neg\neg monday$, as well as *monday* $\land$ (*rain* $\lor$ $\neg rain$), because all formulae of the Propositional Logic that are logically equivalent to *monday* represent exactly the same information.

In Propositional Logic, we should consider the shortest of the equivalent formulae used to represent the information we have. The same principle can be applied to a generic formalism: if it allows several formulae to represent the same information, then we only take into account the shortest one. Therefore, we say that the space efficiency of a formalism F in representing a certain piece of knowledge α is the size of the shortest formula of F that represents α. Space efficiency —also called *succinctness* or *compactness*— of a formalism is a measure of its ability in representing knowledge in a small amount of space.

In this paper we focus on propositional KR (PKR) formalisms. We do not give a formal definition of which formalisms are propositional and which one are not: intuitively, in a propositional formalism, quantifications are not allowed, and thus the formulae are syntactically bounded to be formed only using propositional connectives, plus some other kind of nonclassical connectives (for instance, negation in logic programs, etc.).

So far, we have not discussed what knowledge represents. A possible way to think of a piece of knowledge is that it represents all facts that can be inferred from it. In other words, knowing something is the same as knowing everything that can be logically implied. The second way — which is in some cases more natural — is to think of a piece of knowledge as the set of states of the world that we consider possible.

In a more formal way, we say that knowledge is represented either by a set of propositional interpretations (those describing states of the world we consider plausible) or a set of formulae (those implied from what we know). Consequently, we focus on both reasoning problems of model checking and theorem proving. The following example shows that we can really think of knowledge in both ways.

Example 1 *We want to eat in a fast food, and want to have either a sandwich or a salad (but not both), and either water or coke (but not both).*

In Propositional Logic, each choice can be represented as a model, and the following models represent all possible choices (models are represented by writing down only the letters mapped to true).

$$A = \{\{sandwich, water\}, \{sandwich, coke\}, \{salad, water\}, \{salad, coke\}\}$$

For representing the set of choices we can use formulae instead of models. In this case, we write down a set of formulae whose models represent exactly the allowed choices, as follows.

$$\begin{aligned} C \quad = \quad & (sandwich \lor salad) \land (\neg sandwich \lor \neg salad) \land (sandwich \to \neg salad) \land \\ & (water \lor coke) \land (\neg water \lor \neg coke) \land (\neg coke \to water) \end{aligned}$$

Actually, we can get rid of redundancies, and end up with the following formula.

$$F = (sandwich \lor salad) \land (\neg sandwich \lor \neg salad) \land (water \lor coke) \land (\neg water \lor \neg coke)$$

2

More formally, F represents the set of models A, because for each interpretation I, I ∈ A holds if and only if I ⊨ F. The formula F also represents the set of formulae C, because Cn(F) = Cn(C), where Cn(.) is the function that gives the set of all conclusions that can be drawn from a propositional formula.

1.1 State of the Art

A question that has been deeply investigated, and is related to space efficiency, is the possibility of translating a formula expressed in one formalism into a formula expressed in another formalism (under the assumption, of course, that these formulae represent the same knowledge).

In most cases, the analysis is about the possibility of translating formulae from different formalisms to Propositional Logic (PL). For example, Ben-Eliyahu and Dechter (1991, 1994) proposed a translation from default logic to PL, and a translation from disjunctive logic programs to PL, while Winslett (1989) introduced a translation from revised knowledge bases to PL, and Gelfond, Przymusinska, and Przymusinskyi (1989) defined a translation from circumscription to PL.

All the above translations, as well as many other ones in the literature, lead to an exponential increase of the size of the formula, in the worst case. When the best known translation yields a formula in the target formalism which has exponential size w.r.t. the formula in the source formalism, a natural question arising is whether such exponential blow up is due to the specific translation, or is intrinsic of the problem. For example, although all proposed translations from default logic to PL lead to the exponential blow up, we cannot conclude that all possible translations suffer from this problem: it could be that a polynomial translation exists, but it has not discovered so far.

Some works have focussed on the question of whether this kind of exponential increase in the size is intrinsic or not. Cadoli, Donini, and Schaerf (1996) have shown that many interesting fragments of default logic and circumscription cannot be expressed by polynomial-time fragments of PL without super-polynomially increasing the size of formulae. It has been proved that such a super-polynomial increase of size is necessary when translating unrestricted propositional circumscription (Cadoli, Donini, Schaerf, & Silvestri, 1997) and most operators for belief revision into PL (Cadoli, Donini, Liberatore, & Schaerf, 1999; Liberatore, 1995).

Gogic and collegues (1995) analyzed the relative succinctness of several PKR formalisms in representing sets of models. Among other results, they showed that skeptical default logic can represent sets of models more succinctly than circumscription.

Kautz, Kearns, and Selman (1995) and Khardon and Roth (1996, 1997) considered representations of knowledge bases based on the notion of *characteristic model*, comparing them to other representations, e.g., based on clauses. They showed that the representation of knowledge bases with their characteristic models is sometimes exponentially more compact than other ones, and that the converse is true in other cases.

However, all the above results are based on specific proofs, tailored to a specific reduction, and do not help us to define equivalence classes for the space efficiency of KR formalisms. In a recent paper (Cadoli, Donini, Liberatore, & Schaerf, 1996b), a new complexity measure for decision problems, called *compilability*, has been introduced. In the present paper we show how this new measure can be directly used to characterize the space efficiency of PKR formalisms. We emphasize methodological aspects, expressing in a more general context many of the results presented before.

1.2 Goal

The notion of polynomial time complexity has a great importance in KR (as well as many other fields of computer science), as problems that can be solved in polynomial time are to be considered easy, from a computational point of view.

The notion of *polynomial many-one reducibility* also has a very intuitive meaning when applied to KR: if there exists a polynomial many-one reduction from one formalism to another one, then the time complexity of reasoning in the two formalisms is comparable. This allows to say, e.g., that inference in PL is coNP-complete, i.e. it is one of the hardest problems among those in the complexity class coNP.

As a result, we have a formal tool for comparing the difficulty of reasoning in two formalisms. What is missing is a way for saying that one formalism is able to represent the same information in less space.

Example 2 *We consider again the lunch scenario of the previous example. We show that we can reduce the size of the representation using circumscription instead of Propositional Logic. In PL, the knowledge of the previous example was represented by the formula F:*

$$F = (sandwich \lor salad) \land (\neg sandwich \lor \neg salad) \land (water \lor coke) \land (\neg water \lor \neg coke)$$

The set of models of this formula is A, and the models of A are exactly the minimal models of the formula F_c defined as follows.

$$F_c = (sandwich \lor salad) \land (water \lor coke)$$

By the definition of circumscription (McCarthy, 1980) it holds that F is equivalent to $CIRC(F_c; \{sandwich, salad, water, coke\}, \emptyset, \emptyset)$. Note that F_c is shorter than F. If this result can be proved to hold for arbitrary sets of models, we may conclude that circumscription is more space efficient than Propositional Logic in representing knowledge expressed as sets of models.

Our goal is to provide a formal way of talking about the relative ability of PKR formalisms to compactly represent information, where the information is either a set of models or a set of theorems. In particular, we would like to be able to say that a specific PKR formalism provides "one of the most compact ways to represent models/theorems" among the PKR formalisms of a specific class.

1.3 Results

We introduce two new compactness measures (*model* and *theorem compactness*) and the corresponding classes (model-C and thm-C, where C is a complexity class like P, NP, coNP, etc.). Such classes form two hierarchies that are isomorphic to the polynomial-time hierarchy (Stockmeyer, 1976). We show that the relative space efficiency of a PKR formalism is directly related to such classes. In particular, the ability of a PKR formalism to compactly represent sets of models/theorems is directly related to the class of the model/theorem hierarchy it belongs to. Problems higher up in the model/theorem hierarchy can represent sets of models/theorems more compactly than formalisms that are in lower classes.

This classification is obtained through a general framework and not by making direct comparisons and specific translations between the various PKR formalisms. Furthermore, our approach also allows for a simple and intuitive notion of completeness for both model and theorem hierarchies. This notion precisely characterizes both the relation between formalisms at different levels, and the relations between formalisms at the same level. An interesting result is that two PKR formalisms in which model checking or inference belong to the same time complexity class may belong to different compactness classes. This may suggest a criterion for choosing between two PKR formalisms in which reasoning has the same time complexity—namely, choose the more compact one. Also, two PKR formalisms may belong to the same theorem compactness class, yet to different model compactness classes. This stresses the importance of clarifying whether one wants to represent models or theorems when choosing a PKR formalism.

1.4 Outline

In the next section we introduce the notation and the assumptions that we adopt in this work. In Section 3 (Compilability) we briefly recall some notions on non-uniform computation that are important for what follows and we recall the basic definitions of compilability classes (Cadoli et al., 1996b). In Section 4 (Reductions) we describe the constraints we impose on reductions, while in Section 5 (Space Efficiency) we introduce our compactness classes. In Section 6 (Applications) we actually compare many known PKR formalisms using our framework. Finally, in Section 7 (Related Work and Conclusions) we compare our work with other proposals presented in the literature and draw some conclusions.

2. Notations and Assumptions

In this section we define what knowledge bases and formalisms are. Since we want to consider formalisms that are very different both in syntax and in semantics, we need very general definitions. Let us consider, as a base case, the formalism of propositional calculus. Formally, we can assume that it is composed of three parts:

1. a *syntax*, which is used to define the well-formed formulae;

2. a *proof theory*, which allows for saying when a formula follows from another one; and

3. a *model-theoretic semantics*, which establishes when a model satisfies a formula.

The syntax is defined from a finite alphabet of propositional symbols $L = \{a, b, c, \ldots\}$, possibly with subscripts, and the usual set of propositional connectives $\land$, $\lor$, $\neg$.

In terms of knowledge representation, the proof theory can be seen as a way for extracting knowledge from a knowledge base. For example, if our knowledge base is $a \land c$, then the fact $a \lor b$ holds. We can thus say that the formula $a \lor b$ is part of the knowledge represented by $a \land c$.

In some cases, we want knowledge bases to represent models rather than sets of formulas. An *interpretation* for an alphabet of propositional variables L is a mapping from L in {true, false}. The *model-theoretic semantics* of the propositional calculus is the usual way of extending an interpretation for L to well-formed formulas.

Let us now extend such definition to generic formalisms: a formalism is composed of a syntax, a proof theory, and a model-theoretic semantics.

We remark that each formalism has its own syntax: for instance, default logic includes a ternary connective $\dashv$ for denoting default rules, while logic programming has a special unary connective $not()$, and so on. A knowledge base of a formalism F is simply a well-formed formula, according to the syntax of the formalism.

Each formalism has its own proof theory as well. The proof theory of a formalism F is a binary relation $\vdash_F$ on the set of knowledge bases and formulae. Intuitively, $FB \vdash_F \phi$ means that ϕ is a consequence of the knowledge base KB, according to the rules of the formalism F. As a result, the set of formulae ϕ that are implied by a knowledge base KB is exactly the knowledge represented by KB.

The base of a comparison between two different formalisms is a concept of equivalence, allowing for saying that two knowledge bases (of two different formalisms) represent the same piece of knowledge. Since the knowledge represented by a knowledge base is the set of formulas it implies, we have to assume that the syntax of these formulae is the same for all formalisms. Namely, we always assume that the formulae implied by a knowledge base are well-formed formulae of the propositional calculus. In other words, each formalism has a syntax for the knowledge bases: however, we assume that the proof theory relates knowledge bases (formulae in the syntax of the formalism) with propositional formulae. So, while writing $KB \vdash_F \phi$, we assume that KB is a knowledge base in the syntax of F, while ϕ is a propositional formula.

This allows for saying that two knowledge bases KB_1 and KB_2, expressed in two different formalisms F_1 and F_2, represent the same piece of knowledge: this is true when, for any propositional formula ϕ it holds $KB_1 \vdash_{F_1} \phi$ if and only if $KB_2 \vdash_{F_2} \phi$.

The *model-theoreric semantics of a formalism* is a relation $\models_F$ between propositional models and knowledge bases. In this case, we assume a fixed alphabet L, thus the set of all interpretations is common to all formalisms. When a model M and a knowledge base KB are in the relation, we write $M \models_F KB$. Intuitively, this means that the model M supports the piece of knowledge represented by KB.

We remark that some formalisms, e.g. credolous default logic (Reiter, 1980), have a proof theory, but do not have a model-theoretic semantics. It is also possible to conceive formalisms with a model-theoretic semantics but no proof theory. When both of them are defined, we assume that they are related by the following formula:

$$KB \vdash_F \phi \quad \text{iff} \quad \forall I \, . \, I \models KB \text{ implies } I \models \phi$$

Regarding the proof theory of formalisms, we only consider formulae that are shorter than the knowledge base, that is, we assume that the knowledge represented by a knowlegde base KB is the set of formulae ϕ such that $KB \vdash_F \phi$, and the size of ϕ is at most the size of KB. This is done for two reasons: first, formulas that are larger than KB are likely to contain large parts that are actually independent from KB; second, we can give technicals result in a very simple way by using the compilability classes introduced in the next section.

Assumption 1 *We consider only formulae whose size is less than or equal to that of the knowledge base.*

All formalisms we consider satisfy the right-hand side distruibutivity of conjunction, that is, $KB \vdash_F \phi \wedge \mu$ if and only if $KB \vdash_F \phi$ and $KB \vdash_F \mu$. The assumption on the size of ϕ is not restrictive in this case, if ϕ is a CNF formula.

3. Compilability Classes

We assume the reader is familiar with basic complexity classes, such as P, NP and (uniform) classes of the polynomial hierarchy (Stockmeyer, 1976; Garey & Johnson, 1979). Here we just briefly introduce non-uniform classes (Johnson, 1990). In the sequel, C, C', etc. denote arbitrary classes of the polynomial hierarchy.

We assume that the input instances of problems are strings built over an alphabet Σ. We denote with ϵ the empty string and assume that the alphabet Σ contains a special symbol # to denote blanks. The *length* of a string $x \in \Sigma^*$ is denoted by $|x|$.

Definition 1 *An advice A is a function that takes an integer and returns a string.*

Advices are important in complexity theory because definitions and results are often based on special Turing machines that can determine the result of an oracle "for free", that is, in constant time.

Definition 2 *An* advice-taking *Turing machine is a Turing machine enhanced with the possibility to determine $A(|x|)$ in constant time, where x is the input string.*

Of course, the fact that $A(|x|)$ can be determined in constant time (while A can be an intractable or even undecidable function) makes all definitions based on advice-taking Turing machine different from the same ones based on regular Turing machine. For example, an advice-taking Turing machine can calculate in polynomial time many functions that a regular Turing machine cannot (including some untractable ones).

Note that the advice is only a function of the *size* of the input, not of the input itself. Hence, advice-taking Turing machines are closely related to non-uniform families of circuits (Boppana & Sipser, 1990). Clearly, if the advice were allowed to access the whole instance, it would be able to determine the solution of any problem in constant time.

Definition 3 *An advice-taking Turing machine uses polynomial advice if there exists a polynomial p such that the advice oracle A satisfies $|A(n)| \leq p(n)$ for any nonnegative integers n.*

The non-uniform complexity classes are based on advice-taking Turing machines. In this paper we consider a simplified definition, based on classes of the polynomial hierarchy.

Definition 4 *If* C *is a class of the polynomial hierarchy, then* C/poly *is the class of languages defined by Turing machines with the same time bounds as* C, *augmented by polynomial advice.*

Any class C/poly is also known as *non-uniform* C, where non-uniformity is due to the presence of the advice. Non-uniform and uniform complexity classes are related: Karp and Lipton (1980) proved that if $NP \subseteq P/poly$ then $\Pi_2^p = \Sigma_2^p = PH$, i.e., the polynomial hierarchy collapses at the second level, while Yap (1983) generalized their results, in particular by showing that if $NP \subseteq coNP/poly$ then $\Pi_3^p = \Sigma_3^p = PH$, i.e., the polynomial hierarchy collapses at the third level. An inprovement of this results has been given by Köbler and Watanabe (1998): they proved that $\Pi_k^p \subseteq \Sigma_k^p/poly$ implies that the polynomial hierarchy collapses to $ZPP(\Sigma_{k+1}^p)$. The collapse of the polynomial hierarchy is considered very unlikely by most researchers in structural complexity.

We now summarize some definitions and results proposed to formalize the compilability of problems (Cadoli et al., 1996b), adapting them to the context and terminology of PKR formalisms. We remark that it is not the aim of this paper to give a formalization of compilability of problems, or to analyze problems from this point of view. Rather, we show how to *use* the compilability classes as a technical tool for proving results on the relative efficiency of formalisms in representing knowledge in little space.

Several papers in the literature focus on the problem of reducing the complexity of problems via a preprocessing phase (Kautz & Selman, 1992; Kautz et al., 1995; Khardon & Roth, 1997). This motivates the introduction of a measure of complexity of problems assuming that such preprocessing is allowed. Following the intuition that a knowledge base is known well before questions are posed to it, we divide a reasoning problem into two parts: one part is *fixed* or *accessible off-line* (the knowledge base), and the second one is *varying*, or *accessible on-line* (the interpretation/formula). Compilability aims at capturing the *on-line complexity* of solving a problem composed of such inputs, i.e., complexity with respect to the second input when the first one can be preprocessed in an arbitrary way. In the next section we show the close connection between compilability and the space efficiency of PKR formalisms.

A function f is called *poly-size* if there exists a polynomial p such that for all strings x it holds $|f(x)| \leq p(|x|)$. An exception to this definition is when x represents a number: in this case, we impose $|f(x)| \leq p(x)$. As a result, we can say that the function A used in advice-taking turing machine is a polysize function.

A function g is called *poly-time* if there exists a polynomial q such that for all x, $g(x)$ can be computed in time less than or equal to $q(|x|)$. These definitions easily extend to binary functions as usual.

We define a *language of pairs* S as a subset of $\Sigma^* \times \Sigma^*$. This is necessary to represent the two inputs to a PKR reasoning problem, i.e., the knowledge base (KB), and the formula or interpretation. As an example, the problem of Inference in Propositional Logic (PLI) is defined as follows.

$$PLI = \{\langle x, y \rangle \mid x \text{ is a set of propositional formulae (the KB)}, y \text{ is a formula, and } x \vdash y\}$$

It is well known that PLI is coNP-complete, i.e., it is one of the "hardest" problems among those belonging to coNP. Our goal is to prove that PLI is the "hardest" theorem-proving problem among those in coNP that can be solved by preprocessing the first input in an arbitrary way, i.e., the KB. To this end, we introduce a new hierarchy of classes, the *non-uniform compilability classes*, denoted as $\|\!\leadsto\!C$, where C is a generic uniform complexity class, such as P, NP, coNP, or Σ_2^p.

Definition 5 ($\|\!\leadsto\!C$ classes) *A language of pairs $S \subseteq \Sigma^* \times \Sigma^*$ belongs to $\|\!\leadsto\!C$ iff there exists a binary poly-size function f and a language of pairs $S' \in C$ such that for all $\langle x, y \rangle \in S$ it holds:*

$$\langle f(x, |y|), y \rangle \in S' \text{ iff } \langle x, y \rangle \in S$$

Notice that the poly-size function f takes as input both x (the KB) and the size of y (either the formula or the interpretation). This is done for technical reason, that is, such assumption allows obtaining results that are impossible to prove if the function f only takes x as input (Cadoli et al., 1996b). Such assuption is useful for proving negative results, that is, theorems of impossibility of compilation: indeed, if it is impossible to reduce the complexity of a problem using a function that takes both x and $|y|$ as input, then such reduction is also impossible using a function taking x only as its argument.

Theorem 1 (Cadoli, Donini, Liberatore, & Schaerf, 1997, Theorem 6) *Let C be a class in the polynomial hierarchy and $S \subseteq \Sigma^* \times \Sigma^*$. A problem S belongs to $\|\!\leadsto\!C$ if and only if there exists a poly-size function f and a language of pairs S', such that for all $\langle x, y \rangle \in \Sigma^* \times \Sigma^*$ it holds that:*

1. for all y such that $|y| \leq k$, $\langle f(x, k), y \rangle \in S'$ if and only if $\langle x, y \rangle \in S$;

2. $S' \in C$.

Clearly, any problem whose time complexity is in C is also in $\|\!\leadsto\!C$: just take $f(x, |y|) = x$ and $S' = S$. What is interesting is that some problem in C may belong to $\|\!\leadsto\!C'$ with $C' \subset C$, e.g.,, some problems in NP are in $\|\!\leadsto\!P$. This is true for example for some problems in belief revision (Cadoli et al., 1999). In the rest of this paper, however, we mainly focus on "complete" problems, defined below. A pictorial representation of the class $\|\!\leadsto\!C$ is in Figure 1, where we assume that $S' \in C$.

For the problem PLI no method proving that it belongs to $\|\!\leadsto\!P$ is known. In order to show that it (probably) does not belong to $\|\!\leadsto\!P$, we define a notion of reduction and completeness.

Definition 6 (Non-uniform comp-reducibility) *Given two problems A and B, A is non-uniformly comp-reducible to B (denoted as $A \leq_{nu-comp} B$) iff there exist two poly-size binary functions f_1 and f_2, and a polynomial-time binary function g such that for every pair $\langle x, y \rangle$ it holds that $\langle x, y \rangle \in A$ if and only if $\langle f_1(x, |y|), g(f_2(x, |y|), y) \rangle \in B$.*

The $\leq_{nu-comp}$ reductions can be represented as depicted in Figure 2. Such reductions satisfy all important properties of a reduction.

Theorem 2 (Cadoli et al., 1996b, Theorem 5) *The reductions $\leq_{nu-comp}$ satisfy transitivity and are compatible (Johnson, 1990) with the class $\|\!\leadsto\!C$ for every complexity class C.*

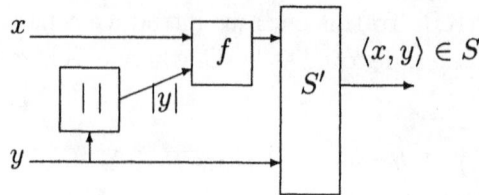

Figure 1: A representation of $\Vdash\!\!\rightarrow$C.

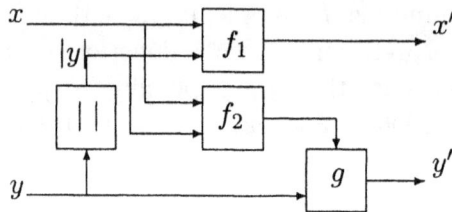

Figure 2: The nu-comp-C reductions.

Therefore, it is possible to define the notions of *hardness* and *completeness* for $\Vdash\!\!\rightarrow$C for every complexity class C.

Definition 7 ($\Vdash\!\!\rightarrow$C-completeness) *Let S be a language of pairs and C a complexity class. S is $\Vdash\!\!\rightarrow$C-hard iff for all problems $A \in \Vdash\!\!\rightarrow$C we have that $A \leq_{nu-comp} S$. Moreover, S is $\Vdash\!\!\rightarrow$C-complete if S is in $\Vdash\!\!\rightarrow$C and is $\Vdash\!\!\rightarrow$C-hard.*

We now have the right complexity class to completely characterize the problem PLI. In fact PLI is $\Vdash\!\!\rightarrow$coNP-complete (Cadoli et al., 1996b, Theorem 7). Furthermore, the hierarchy formed by the compilability classes is proper if and only if the polynomial hierarchy is proper (Cadoli et al., 1996b; Karp & Lipton, 1980; Yap, 1983) — a fact widely conjectured to be true.

Informally, we may say that $\Vdash\!\!\rightarrow$NP-hard problems are "not compilable to P", as from the above considerations we know that if there exists a preprocessing of their fixed part that makes them on-line solvable in polynomial time, then the polynomial hierarchy collapses. The same holds for $\Vdash\!\!\rightarrow$coNP-hard problems. In general, a problem which is $\Vdash\!\!\rightarrow$C-complete for a class C can be regarded as the "toughest" problem in C, even after arbitrary preprocessing of the fixed part. On the other hand, a problem in $\Vdash\!\!\rightarrow$C is a problem that, after preprocessing of the fixed part, becomes a problem in C (i.e., it is "compilable to C").

We close the section by giving another example of use of the compilability classes through the well-known formalism of Circumscription (McCarthy, 1980). Let x be any propositional formula. The *minimal* models of x are the truth assignments satisfying x having as few positive values as possible (w.r.t. set containment). The problem we consider is: check whether a given model is a minimal model of a propositional formula. This problem, called Minimal Model checking (MMC), can be reformulated as the problem of model checking in Circumscription, which is known to be co-NP-complete (Cadoli, 1992).

If we consider the knowledge base x as given off-line, and the truth assignment y as given on-line, we obtain the following definition:

$$\text{MMC} = \{\langle x, y \rangle \mid y \text{ is a minimal model of } x \}$$

This problem can be shown to be $\|{\sim}$coNP-complete (Cadoli et al., 1996b, Theorem 13). Hence, it is very unlikely that it can be in $\|{\sim}$P; that is, it is very unlikely that there exists some off-line processing of the knowledge base, yielding (say) some data structure x', such that given y, it can now checked in polynomial time whether y is a minimal model of x. This, of course, unless x' has exponential size. This observation applies also when x' is a knowledge base in Propositional Logic, and led to the interpretation that Circumscription is more compact, or succint, than PL (Cadoli, Donini, & Schaerf, 1995; Gogic et al., 1995). Our framework allows to generalize these results for all PKR formalisms, as shown in the sequel.

4. Reductions among KR Formalisms

We now define the forms of reduction between PKR formalisms that we analyze in the following sections. A formula can always be represented as a string over an alphabet Σ, hence from now on we consider translations as functions transforming strings.

Let F_1 and F_2 be two PKR formalisms. There exists a *poly-size reduction* from F_1 to F_2, denoted as $f : F_1 \mapsto F_2$, if f is a poly-size function such that for any given knowledge base KB in F_1, $f(KB)$ is a knowledge base in F_2. Clearly, reductions should be restricted to produce a meaningful output. In particular, we now discuss reductions that preserve the models of the original theory.

The semantic approach by Gogic and collegues (1995) is that the models of the two knowledge bases must be exactly the same. In other words, if a knowledge base KB of the formalism F_1 is translated into a knowledge base KB' of the formalism F_2, then $M \models_{F_1} KB$ if and only if $M \models_{F_2} KB'$. This approach can be summarized by: a reduction between formalisms F_1 and F_2 is a way to translate knowledge bases of F_1 into knowledge bases of F_2, preserving their sets of models. While this semantics is intuitively grounded, it is very easy to show examples in which two formalisms that we consider equally space-efficient cannot be translated to each other. Let us consider for instance a variant of the propositional calculus in which the syntax is that formulas must be of the form $x_1 \wedge F$, where F is a regular formula over the variables $x_2, \ldots$. Clearly, this formalism is able to represent knowledge in the same space than the propositional calculus (apart a polynomial factor). However, according to the definition, this formalism cannot be translated to propositional calculus: there is no knowledge base that is equivalent to $KB = \neg x_1$. Indeed, the only model of KB is $\emptyset$, while any model of any consistent knowledge base of the modified propositional calculus contains x_1.

We propose a more general approach that can deal also with functions f that change the language of the KB. To this end, we allow for a translation g_{KB} from models of KB to models of $f(KB)$. We stress that, to be as general as possible, the translation may depend on KB — i.e., different knowledge bases may have different translations of their models. We want this translation easy to compute, since otherwise the computation of g_{KB} could hide the complexity of reasoning in the formalism. However, observe that to this end, it is not sufficient to impose that g_{KB} is computable in polynomial time. In fact, once KB is fixed, its models could be trivially translated to models of $f(KB)$ in constant time, using a lookup table. This table would be exponentially large, though; and this is what we want to forbid. Hence, we impose that g_{KB} is a *circuit* of polynomial-size wrt KB. We still use a functional notation $g_{KB}(M)$ to denote the result of applying a model M to the circuit g_{KB}. A formal definition follows.

Definition 8 (Model Preservation) *A poly-size reduction $f : F_1 \mapsto F_2$ satisfies* model-preservation *if there exists a polynomial p such that, for each knowledge base KB in F_1 there exists a circuit g_{KB} whose size is bounded by $p(|KB|)$, and such that for every interpretation M of the variables of KB it holds that $M \models_{F_1} KB$ iff $g_{KB}(M) \models_{F_2} f(KB)$.*

The rationale of model-preserving reduction is that the knowledge base KB of the first formalism F_1 can be converted into a knowledge base $f(KB)$ in the second one F_2, and this reduction should be such that each model M in F_1 can be easily translated into a model $g_{KB}(M)$ in F_2.

We require g to depend on KB, because the transformation f, in general, could take the actual form of KB into account. This happens in the following example of a model-preserving translation.

Example 3 *We reduce a fragment of skeptical default logic (Kautz & Selman, 1991) to circumscription with varying letters, using the transformation introduced by Etherington (1987). Let $\langle D, W \rangle$ be a prerequisite-free normal (PFN) default theory, i.e., all defaults are of the form $\frac{:\gamma}{\gamma}$, where γ is a generic formula. Let Z be the set of letters occurring in $\langle D, W \rangle$. Define P_D as the set of letters $\{a_\gamma | \frac{:\gamma}{\gamma} \in D\}$. The function f can be defined in the following way: $f(\langle D, W \rangle) = CIRC(T; P_D; Z)$, where $T = W \cup \{a_\gamma \equiv \neg\gamma | a_\gamma \in P_D\}$, P_D are the letters to be minimized, and Z (the set of letters occurring in $\langle D, W \rangle$) are varying letters. We show that f is a model-preserving poly-size reduction. In fact, given a set of PFN defaults D let g_D be a function such that for each interpretation M for Z, $g_D(M) = M \cup \{a_\gamma \in P_D | M \models \neg\gamma\}$. Clearly, f is poly-size, g_D can be realized by a circuit whose size is polynomial in $|D|$, and M is a model of at least one extension of $\langle D, W \rangle$ iff $g_D(M) \models CIRC(T; P_D; Z)$. The dependence of g only on D stresses the fact that, in this case, the circuit g does not depend on the whole knowledge base $\langle D, W \rangle$, but just on D.*

Clearly, when models are preserved, theorems are preserved as well. A weaker form of reduction is the following one, where only theorems are preserved. Also in this case we allow theorems of KB to be translated by a "simple" circuit g_{KB} to theorems of KB.

Definition 9 (Theorem Preservation) *A poly-size reduction $f : F_1 \mapsto F_2$ satisfies* theorem-preservation *if there exists a polynomial p such that, for each knowledge base KB in F_1, there exists a circuit g_{KB} whose size is bounded by $p(|KB|)$, and such that for every formula φ on the variables of KB, it holds that $KB \vdash_{F_1} \varphi$ iff $f(KB) \vdash_{F_2} g_{KB}(\varphi)$.*

The theorem-preserving reduction has a property similar to that of the model-preserving reduction, when the knowledge bases are used to represent theorems rather than models. Namely, a knowledge base KB is translated into another knowledge base $f(KB)$ which can be used to represent the same set of theorems. More precisely, we have that each theorem φ of KB is represented by a theorem $g_{KB}(\varphi)$ of $f(KB)$.

Winslett (1989) has shown an example of a reduction from updated knowledge bases to PL that is theorem-preserving but not model-preserving. Using Winslett's reduction, one could use the same machinery for propositional reasoning in the KB, both before and after the update (plus the reduction). Also the reduction shown in the previous Example 3 is theorem-preserving, this time g being the identity circuit.

We remark that our definitions of reduction are more general than those proposed by Gogic and colleagues (1995). In fact, these authors consider only a notion analogous to Definition 8. and only for the case when g is the identity — i.e., models in the two formalisms should be identical. By allowing a simple translation g between models Definition 8 covers more general forms of reductions preserving models, like the one of Example 3.

5. Comparing the Space Efficiency of PKR Formalisms

In this section we show how to use the compilability classes defined in Section 3 to compare the succinctness of PKR formalisms.

Let F_1 and F_2 be two formalisms representing sets of models. We prove that any knowledge base α in F_1 can be reduced, via a poly-size reduction, to a knowledge base β in F_2 satisfying model-preservation if and only if the compilability class of the problem of *model checking* (first input: KB, second input: interpretation) in F_2 is higher than or equal to the compilability class of the problem of model checking in F_1.

Similarly, we prove that theorem-preserving poly-size reductions exist if and only if the compilability class of the problem of *inference* (first input: KB, second input: formula, cf. definition of the problem PLI) in F_1 is higher than or equal to the compilability class of the problem of inference in F_2.

In order to simplify the presentation and proof of the theorems we introduce some definitions.

Definition 10 (Model hardness/completeness) *Let F be a PKR formalism and C be a complexity class. If the problem of model checking for F belongs to the compilability class $\|\!\sim\!C$, where the model is the varying part of the instances, we say that F is in* model-C. *Similarly, if model checking is $\|\!\sim\!C$-complete (hard), we say that F is* model-C-complete *(hard).*

Definition 11 (Theorem hardness/completeness) *Let F be a PKR formalism and C be a complexity class. If the problem of inference for the formalism F belongs to the compilability class $\|\!\sim\!C$, whenever the formula is the varying part of the instance, we say that F is in* thm-C. *Similarly, if inference is $\|\!\sim\!C$-complete (hard), we say that F is* thm-C-complete *(hard).*

These definitions implicitly define two hierarchies, which parallel the polynomial hierarchy (Stockmeyer, 1976): the model hierarchy (model-P,model-NP,model-Σ_2^p,etc.) and the theorem hierarchy (thm-P,thm-NP,thm-Σ_2^p,etc.). The higher a formalism is in the model hierarchy, the more its efficiency in representing models is — and analogously for theorems. As an example (Cadoli et al., 1996, Thm. 6), we characterize model and theorem classes of Propositional Logic.

Theorem 3 PL *is in* model-P *and it is* thm-coNP-*complete*.

We can now formally establish the connection between succinctness of representations and compilability classes. In the following theorems, the complexity classes C, C_1, C_2 belong to the polynomial hierarchy (Stockmeyer, 1976). In Theorems 5 and 7 we assume that the polynomial hierarchy does not collapse.

We start by showing that the existence of model-preserving reductions from a formalism to another one can be easily obtained if their levels in the model hierarchy satisfy a simple condition.

Theorem 4 *Let F_1 and F_2 be two PKR formalisms. If F_1 is in* model-C *and F_2 is* model-C-*hard, then there exists a poly-size reduction $f : F_1 \mapsto F_2$ satisfying model preservation.*

Proof. Recall that since F_1 is in model-C, model checking in F_1 is in $\|\hookrightarrow$C, and since F_2 is model-C-hard, model checking in F_1 is non-uniformly comp-reducible to model checking in F_2. That is, (adapting Def. 6) there exist two poly-size binary functions f_1 and f_2, and a polynomial-time binary function g such that for every pair $\langle KB, M \rangle$ it holds that

$$M \models_{F_1} KB \text{ if and only if } g(f_2(KB, |M|), M) \models_{F_2} f_1(KB, |M|)$$

(note that g is the poly-time function appearing in Def. 6, different from g_{KB} which is the poly-size circuit appearing in Def. 8).

Now observe that $|M|$ can be computed from KB by simply counting the letters appearing in KB; let f_3 be such a counting function, i.e., $|M| = f_3(KB)$. Clearly, f_3 is poly-size. Define the reduction f as $f(KB) = f_1(KB, f_3(KB))$. Since poly-size functions are closed under composition, f is poly-size. Now we show that f is a model-preserving reduction. By Definition 8, we need to prove that there exists a polynomial p such that for each knowledge base KB in F_1, there exists a poly-size circuit g_{KB} such that for every interpretation M of the variables of KB it holds that $M \models_{F_1} KB$ iff $g_{KB}(M) \models_{F_2} f(KB)$.

We proceed as follows: Given a KB in F_1, we compute $z = f_2(KB, |M|) = f_2(KB, f_3(KB))$. Since f_2 and f_3 are poly-size, z has size polynomial with respect to $|KB|$. Define the circuit $g_{KB}(M)$ as the one computing $g(z, M) = g(f_2(KB, f_3(KB)), M)$. Since g is a poly-time function over both inputs, and z is poly-size in KB, there exists a representation of $g(z, M)$ as a circuit g_{KB} whose size is polynomial wrt KB. From this construction, $M \models_{F_1} KB$ iff $g_{KB}(M) \models_{F_2} f(KB)$. Hence, the thesis follows. $\square$

The following theorem, instead, gives a simple method to prove that there is no model-preserving reduction from one formalism to another one.

Theorem 5 *Let F_1 and F_2 be two PKR formalisms. If the polynomial hierarchy does not collapse, F_1 is* model-C_1-*hard, F_2 is in* model-C_2, *and $C_2 \subset C_1$, then there is no poly-size reduction $f : F_1 \mapsto F_2$ satisfying model preservation.*

Proof. We show that if such a reduction exists, then $C_1/poly \subseteq C_2/poly$ which implies that the polynomial hierarchy collapses at some level (Yap, 1983). Let A be a complete problem for class C_1 — e.g., if C_1 is Σ_3^p then A may be validity of $\exists\forall\exists$-quantified boolean formulae (Stockmeyer, 1976). Define the problem ϵA as follows.

$$\epsilon A = \{\langle x, y \rangle \mid x = \epsilon \text{ (the empty string) and } y \in A\}$$

We already proved (Cadoli et al., 1996b, Thm. 6) that ϵA is $\Vdash C_1$-complete. Since model checking in F_1 is model-C_1-hard, ϵA is non-uniformly comp-reducible to model checking in F_1. That is, (adapting Def. 6) there exist two poly-size binary functions f_1 and f_2, and a polynomial-time binary function g such that for every pair $\langle \epsilon, y \rangle$, it holds $\langle \epsilon, y \rangle \in \epsilon A$ if and only if $g(f_2(\epsilon, |y|), y) \models_{F_1} f_1(\epsilon, |y|)$. Let $|y| = n$. Clearly, the knowledge base $f_1(\epsilon, |y|)$ depends only on n, i.e., there is exactly one knowledge base for each integer. Call it KB_n. Moreover, $f_2(\epsilon, |y|) = f_2(\epsilon, n)$ also depends on n only: call it O_n (for Oracle). Observe that both KB_n and O_n have polynomial size with respect to n.

If there exists a poly-size reduction $f : F_1 \mapsto F_2$ satisfying model preservation, then given the knowledge base KB_n there exists a poly-size circuit h_n such that $g(O_n, y) \models_{F_1} KB_n$ if and only if $h_n(g(O_n, y)) \models_{F_2} f(KB_n)$.

Therefore, the $\Vdash C_1$-complete problem ϵA can be non-uniformly reduced to a problem in $\Vdash C_2$ as follows: Given y, from its size $|y| = n$ one obtains (with a preprocessing) $f(KB_n)$ and O_n. Then one checks whether the interpretation $h_n(g(O_n, y))$ (computable in polynomial time given n, y and O_n) is a model in F_2 for $f(KB_n)$. From the fact that model checking in F_2 is in $\Vdash C_2$, we have that $\Vdash C_1 \subseteq \Vdash C_2$. We proved in a previous paper that such result implies that $C_1/\text{poly} \subseteq C_2/\text{poly}$ (Cadoli et al., 1996b, Thm. 9), which in turns implies that the polynomial hierarchy collapses (Yap, 1983). $\qquad \square$

The above theorems show that the hierarchy of classes model-C exactly characterizes the space efficiency of a formalism in representing sets of models. In fact, two formalisms at the same level in the model hierarchy can be reduced into each other via a poly-size reduction (Theorem 4), while there is no poly-size reduction from a formalism (F_1) higher up in the hierarchy into one (F_2) in a lower class (Theorem 5). In the latter case we say that F_1 is *more space-efficient* than F_2.

Analogous results (with similar proofs) hold for poly-size reductions preserving theorems. Namely, the next theorem shows how to infer the existence of theorem-preserving reductions, while the other one gives a way to prove that there is no theorem-preserving reduction from one formalism to another one.

Theorem 6 *Let F_1 and F_2 be two PKR formalisms. If F_1 is in thm-C and F_2 is thm-C-hard, then there exists a poly-size reduction $f : F_1 \mapsto F_2$ satisfying theorem preservation.*

Proof. Recall that since F_1 is in thm-C, inference in F_1 is in $\Vdash C$, and since F_2 is thm-C-hard, inference in F_1 is non-uniformly comp-reducible to inference in F_2. That is, (adapting Def. 6) there exist two poly-size binary functions f_1 and f_2, and a polynomial-time binary function g_1 such that for every pair $\langle KB, \varphi \rangle$ it holds that

$$KB \vdash_{F_1} \varphi \text{ if and only if } f_1(KB, |\varphi|) \vdash_{F_2} g(f_2(KB, |\varphi|), \varphi)$$

(here we distinguish the poly-time function g appearing in Def. 6 and the poly-size circuit g_{KB} appearing in Def. 9).

Using Theorem 1 we can replace $|\varphi|$ with an upper bound in the above formula. From Assumption 1, we know that the size of φ is less than or equal to the size of KB; therefore we replace $|\varphi|$ with $|KB|$. The above formula now becomes

$$KB \vdash_{F_1} \varphi \text{ if and only if } f_1(KB, |KB|) \vdash_{F_2} g(f_2(KB, |KB|), \varphi)$$

Define the reduction f as $f(KB) = f_1(KB, f_3(KB))$, where f_3 is the poly-size function that computes the size of its input. Since poly-size functions are closed under composition, f is poly-size.

Now, we show that f is a theorem-preserving reduction, i.e., f satisfies Def. 9. This amounts to proving that for each knowledge base KB in F_1 there exists a circuit g_{KB}, whose size is poynomial wrt KB, such that for every formula φ on the variables of KB it holds that $KB \vdash_{F_1} \varphi$ iff $f(KB) \vdash_{F_2} g_{KB}(\varphi)$.

We proceed as in the proof of Theorem 4: Given a KB in F_1, let $z = f_2(KB, f_3(KB))$. Since f_2 and f_3 are poly-size, z has polynomial size with respect to $|KB|$. Define $g_{KB}(\varphi) = g(z, \varphi) = g(f_2(KB, f_3(KB)), \varphi)$. Clearly, g_{KB} can be represented by a circuit of polynomial size wrt KB. From this construction, $KB \vdash_{F_1} \varphi$ iff $f(KB) \vdash_{F_2} g_{KB}(\varphi)$. Hence, the claim follows. □

Theorem 7 *Let F_1 and F_2 be two PKR formalisms. If the polynomial hierarchy does not collapse, F_1 is thm-C_1-hard, F_2 is in thm-C_2, and $C_2 \subset C_1$, then there is no poly-size reduction $f : F_1 \mapsto F_2$ satisfying theorem preservation.*

Proof. We show that if such a reduction exists, then $C_1/poly \subseteq C_2/poly$ and the polynomial hierarchy collapses at some level (Yap, 1983). Let A be a complete problem for class C_1. Define the problem ϵA as in the proof of Theorem 5: this problem is $\| {\sim} C_1$-complete (Cadoli et al., 1996b, Thm. 6). Since inference in F_1 is thm-C_1-hard, ϵA is non-uniformly compreducible to inference in F_1. That is, (adapting Def. 6) there exist two poly-size binary functions f_1 and f_2, and a polynomial-time binary function g such that for every pair $\langle \epsilon, y \rangle$, $\langle \epsilon, y \rangle \in \epsilon A$ if and only if $f_1(\epsilon, |y|) \vdash_{F_1} g(f_2(\epsilon, |y|), y)$. Let $|y| = n$. Clearly, the knowledge base $f_1(\epsilon, |y|)$ depends just on n, i.e., there is one knowledge base for each integer. Call it KB_n. Moreover, also $f_2(\epsilon, |y|) = f_2(\epsilon, n)$ depends just on n: call it O_n (for Oracle). Observe that both KB_n and O_n have polynomial size with respect to n.

If there exists a poly-size reduction $f : F_1 \mapsto F_2$ satisfying theorem preservation, then given the knowledge base KB_n there exists a poly-time function h_n such that $KB_n \vdash_{F_1} g(O_n, y)$ if and only if $f(KB_n) \vdash_{F_2} h_n(g(O_n, y))$.

Therefore, the $\| {\sim} C_1$-complete problem ϵA can be non-uniformly reduced to a problem in $\| {\sim} C_2$ as follows: Given y, from its size $|y| = n$ one obtains (with an arbitrary preprocessing) $f(KB_n)$ and O_n. Then one checks whether the formula $h_n(g(O_n, y))$ (computable in poly-time given y and O_n) is a theorem in F_2 of $f(KB_n)$. From the fact that inference in F_2 is in $\| {\sim} C_2$, we have that $\| {\sim} C_1 \subseteq \| {\sim} C_2$. It follows that $C_1/poly \subseteq C_2/poly$ (Cadoli et al., 1996b, Thm. 9), which implies that the polynomial hierarchy collapses (Yap, 1983). □

Theorems 4-7 show that compilability classes characterize very precisely the relative capability of PKR formalisms to represent sets of models or sets of theorems. For example, as a consequence of Theorems 3 and 7 there is no poly-size reduction from PL to the syntactic restriction of PL allowing only Horn clauses that preserves the theorems, unless the polynomial hierarchy collapses. Kautz and Selman (1992) proved non-existence of such a reduction for a problem strictly related to PLI using a specific proof.

6. Applications

This section is devoted to the application of the theorems presented in the previous section. Using Theorems 4-7 and results previously known from the literature, we are able to asses model- and theorem-compactness of some PKR formalisms.

We assume that definitions of Propositional Logic, default logic (Reiter, 1980), and circumscription (McCarthy, 1980) are known. Definitions of WIDTIO, SBR, GCWA, and stable model semantics are in the appropriate subsections.

In the following proofs we refer to the problem $\exists\forall 3$QBF, that is, the problem of verifying whether a quantified Boolean formula $\exists X \forall Y . \neg F$ is valid, where X and Y are disjoint sets of variables, and F is a set of clauses on the alphabet $X \cup Y$, each composed of three literals. As an example, a simple formula belonging to this class is: $\exists x_1, x_2 \forall y_1, y_2 \ \neg((x_1 \vee y_2) \wedge (\neg x_1 \vee \neg x_2 \vee \neg y_1) \wedge (\neg y_1 \vee \neg x_2 \vee \neg y_2) \wedge (\neg x_1 \vee \neg x_2))$.

The problem of deciding validity of a $\exists\forall 3$QBF is complete for the class Σ_2^p. As a consequence, the corresponding problem $*\exists\forall 3$QBF, that is deciding whether an input composed of any string $(*)$ as the fixed part and a quantified Boolean formula $\exists X \forall Y . \neg F$ as the varying one, is complete for the class $\|\!\!\sim\!\Sigma_2^p$ (Liberatore, 1998). Notice that in most of the hardness proofs we show in the sequel we use problems without any meaningful fixed part.

6.1 Stable Model Semantics

Stable model semantics (**SM**) was introduced by Gelfond and Lifschitz (1988) as a tool to provide a semantics for logic programs with negation. their original proposal is now one of the standard semantics for logic programs. We now recall the definition of propositional stable model.

Let P be a propositional, general logic program. Let M be a subset (i.e., an interpretation) of the atoms of P. Let P^M be the program obtained from P in the following way: if a clause C of P contains in its body a negated atom $\neg A$ such that $A \in M$ then C is deleted; if a body of a clause contains a negated atom $\neg A$ such that $A \notin M$ then $\neg A$ is deleted from the body of the clause. If M is a least Herbrand model of P^M then M is a stable model of P.

For the formalism SM, we consider the program P as the knowledge base. We write $P \models_{\text{SM}} Q$ to denote that query Q is implied by a logic program P under Stable Model semantics.

In order to prove our result, we need to define the kernel of a graph.

Definition 12 (Kernel) *Let $G = (V, E)$ be a graph. A kernel of G is a set $K \subseteq V$ such that, denoting $H = V - K$, it holds:*

  1. *H is a vertex cover of G*

  2. *for all $j \in H$, there exists an $i \in K$ such that $(i, j) \in E$.*

We can now state the theorem on the compilability class of inference in the stable model semantics, and the corresponding theorem compactness class.

Theorem 8 *The problem of inference for the Stable Model semantics is $\|\!\!\sim\!$coNP-complete, thus Stable Model Semantics is* thm-coNP *complete.*

Proof. Membership in the class follows from the fact that the problem is coNP-complete (Marek & Truszczyński, 1991). For the hardness, we adapt the proof of Marek and Truszczyński (1991) showing that deciding whether a query is true in all stable models is coNP-hard.

Let ϵKERNEL be the language $\{\epsilon, G\}$ such that G is a graph with at least one kernel. Let $|G| = n$, and observe that G cannot have more vertices than its size n.

We show that for each n, there exists a logic program P_n such that for every graph G with at most n vertices, there exists a query Q_G such that G has a kernel iff $P_n \not\models_{SM} Q_G$.

Let the alphabet of P_n be composed by the following $2n^2 + n$ propositional letters: $\{a_i | i \in \{1..n\}\ \} \cup \{r_{ij}, s_{ij} | i, j \in \{1..n\}\ \}$.

The program P_n is defined as:

$$\left. \begin{array}{rcl} a_j & :- & \neg a_i, r_{ij} \\ s_{ij} & :- & \neg r_{ij} \\ r_{ij} & :- & \neg s_{ij} \end{array} \right\} \text{ for } i, j \in \{1..n\}$$

Given a graph $G = (V, E)$, the query Q_G is defined as

$$Q_G = (\bigvee_{(i,j) \in E} \neg r_{ij}) \vee (\bigvee_{(i,j) \notin E} r_{ij})$$

The reduction from ϵKERNEL to SM is defined as: $f_1(x, n) = P_n$, i.e., f_1 depends only on its second argument, $f_2(x, n) = \epsilon$, i.e., f_2 is a constant function, and $g = Q_y$, i.e., given a graph G, the circuit g computes the query Q_G.

As a result, this is a $\|\!\leadsto$ reduction. We now show that this reduction is correct, i.e., $\langle \epsilon, G \rangle \in \epsilon$KERNEL ($G$ has a kernel) iff $P_n \not\models_{SM} Q_G$.

If-part. Suppose $P_n \not\models_{SM} Q_G$. Then, there exists a stable model M of P_n such that $M \models \neg Q_G$. Observe that $\neg Q_G$ is equivalent to the conjunction of all r_{ij} such that $(i, j) \in E$, and all $\neg r_{ij}$ such that $(i, j) \notin E$. Simplifying P_n with $\neg Q_G$ we obtain the clauses:

$$a_j :- \neg a_i, \text{ for } (i, j) \in E \tag{1}$$

Observe that M contains all s_{ij} such that $(i, j) \notin E$, and in order to be stable, — i.e., to support atoms r_{ij} such that $(i, j) \in E$ — M contains no atom s_{ij} such that $(i, j) \in E$.

Let $H = \{j | a_j \in M\}$, $K = \{i | a_i \notin M\}$. Now H is a vertex cover of G, since for each edge $(i, j) \in E$, M should satisfy the corresponding clause (1) $a_j\ :- \neg a_i$, hence either $a_i \in M$, or $a_j \in M$. Moreover, for each j in H, the atom a_j is in M, and since M is a stable model, there exists a clause $a_j\ :- \neg a_i$ such that $a_i \notin M$, that is, $i \in K$. Therefore, K is a kernel of G.

Only-if part. Suppose $G = (V, E)$ has a kernel K, and let $H = V - K$. Let M be the interpretation

$$M = \{r_{ij} | (i, j) \in E\} \cup \{s_{ij} | (i, j) \notin E\} \cup \{a_j | j \in H\}$$

Obviously, $M \not\models Q_G$. We now show that M is a stable model of P_n, i.e., M is a least Herbrand model of P_n^M. In fact, P_n^M contains the following clauses:

$$\begin{array}{llr} s_{ij} & \text{for } (i, j) \notin E & (2) \\ r_{ij} & \text{for } (i, j) \in E & (3) \\ a_j\ :- r_{ij} & \text{for } i \in K & (4) \end{array}$$

Clauses in the last line are obtained from clauses in P_n of the form a_j :– $\neg a_i, r_{ij}$, where the clauses such that $i \in H$ (hence $a_i \in M$) are deleted, while in the other clauses the negated atom $\neg a_i$ is deleted, since $i \in K$, hence $a_i \notin M$. Now for each $a_j \in M$, the vertex j is in H, hence there is an edge $(i,j) \in E$, and $i \in K$. Hence clauses (4) and (3) are in P_n^M, hence in the least Herbrand model of P_n^M there are exactly all a_j such that $j \in H$. $\qquad\square$

6.2 Minimal Model Reasoning

One of the most successful form of non-monotonic reasoning is based on the selection of minimal models. Among the various formalisms based on minimal model semantics we consider here Circumscription (McCarthy, 1980) and the Generalized Closed World Assumption (GCWA) (Minker, 1982), which is a formalism to represent knowledge in a closed world.

We assume that the reader is familiar with Circumscription, we briefly present the definition of GCWA. The model semantics for GCWA is defined as (a is a letter):

$$M \models_{GCWA} KB \text{ iff } M \models KB \cup \{\neg a \mid \text{for any positive clause } \gamma, \text{ if } KB \not\vdash \gamma \text{ then } KB \not\vdash \gamma \vee a\}$$

We can now present the results for these two formalisms.

Theorem 9 *The problem of model checking for Circumscription is $\|\!\sim$coNP-complete, thus Circumscription is* model-coNP-*complete.*

This result is a trivial corollary of a theorem already proved (Cadoli et al., 1997, Theorem 6). In fact, that proof implicitly shows that model checking for circumscription is $\|\!\sim$coNP-complete.

Theorem 10 *The problem of model checking for GCWA is in $\|\!\sim$P, thus GCWA is in* model-P.

Proof. As already pointed out (Cadoli et al., 1997), it is possible to rewrite $GCWA(T)$ into a propositional formula F such that, for any given model M, $M \models GCWA(T)$ if and only if $M \models F$. Moreover, the size of F is polynomially bounded by the size of T. As a consequence, the model compactness for GCWA is in the same class of PL. By Theorem 3 the thesis follows. $\qquad\square$

Theorem 11 *The problem of inference for Circumscription is $\|\!\sim\Pi_2^p$-complete, thus Circumscription is* thm-Π_2^p-*complete.*

This result is a trivial corollary of a theorem published in a previous paper (Cadoli et al., 1997, Theorem 7) which implicitly shows that inference for circumscription is $\|\!\sim\Pi_2^p$-complete.

Theorem 12 *The problem of inference for GCWA is $\|\!\sim$coNP-complete, thus GCWA is* thm-coNP-*complete.*

Proof. As already pointed out in the proof of Theorem 10, it is possible to rewrite $GCWA(T)$ into a formula F that is equivalent to it. As a consequence, a formula α is a theorem of $GCWA(T)$ if and only if it is a theorem of F. Thus, GCWA has at most the theorem compexity of PL. Since GCWA is a generalization of PL, it follows that GCWA is in the same theorem compactness class of PL. Hence, GCWA is thm-coNP-complete. $\qquad\square$

6.3 Default Logic

In this subsection we present the results for default logic, in its two variants (credulous and skeptical). For more details on these two main variants of default logic, we refer the reader to the paper by Kautz and Selman (1991). Notice that model-compactness is only applicable to skeptical default logic.

Theorem 13 *The problem of model checking for skeptical default logic is* $\|\!\sim\!\Sigma_2^p$ *complete, thus skeptical default logic is* model-Σ_2^p *complete.*

Proof. The proof of membership is straightforward: since model checking for skeptical default logic is in Σ_2^p (Liberatore & Schaerf, 1998), it follows that it is also in $\|\!\sim\!\Sigma_2^p$.

The proof of $\|\!\sim\!\Sigma_2^p$-hardness is similar to the proof of Σ_2^p-hardness (Liberatore & Schaerf, 1998). The reduction is from the problem $*\exists\forall$3QBF. Let $\langle\alpha,\beta\rangle$ be an instance of $*\exists\forall$3QBF, where $\beta = \exists X\forall Y.\neg F$ represents a valid $\exists\forall$3QBF formula, and α is any string.

Let n be the size of the formula F. This implies that the variables in the formula are at most n. Let $\Gamma = \{\gamma_1, \ldots, \gamma_k\}$ be the set of all the clauses of three literals over this alphabet. The number of clauses of three literals over an alphabet of n variables is less than $O(n^3)$, thus bounded by a polynomial in n.

We prove that $\exists X\forall Y.\neg F$ is valid if and only if M is a model of some extension of $\langle W, D\rangle$, where

$$
\begin{aligned}
W &= \emptyset \\
D &= \bigcup_{\gamma_i \in \Gamma}\left\{\frac{:c_i}{c_i}, \frac{:\neg c_i}{\neg c_i}\right\} \cup \bigcup_{x_i \in X}\left\{\frac{:w \wedge (w \to x_i)}{w \to x_i}, \frac{:w \wedge (w \to \neg x_i)}{w \to \neg x_i}\right\} \cup \left\{\frac{:w \wedge \bigwedge_{\gamma_i \in \Gamma} c_i \to \gamma_i}{w}\right\} \\
M &= \{c_i \mid \gamma_i \in F\}
\end{aligned}
$$

The set $\{c_i \mid 1 \le i \le k\}$ is a set of new variables, one-to-one with the elements of Γ. Note that W and D only depends on the size n of F, while M depends on F. As a result, this is a $\le_{nu-comp}$ reduction.

We now prove that the formula is valid if and only if M is a model of some extension of the default theory $\langle W, D\rangle$. This is similar to an already published proof (Liberatore & Schaerf, 1998). Consider an evaluation C_1 of the variables $\{c_i\}$ and an evaluation X_1 of the variables X. Let D' be the following set of defaults.

$$
D' = \bigcup_{c_i \in C_1}\left\{\frac{:c_i}{c_i}\right\} \bigcup_{c_i \notin C_1}\left\{\frac{:\neg c_i}{\neg c_i}\right\} \cup \bigcup_{x_i \in X_1}\left\{\frac{:w \wedge (w \to x_i)}{w \to x_i}\right\} \bigcup_{x_i\neg \in X_1}\left\{\frac{:w \wedge (w \to \neg x_i)}{w \to \neg x_i}\right\}
$$

This set of defaults has been chosen so that the set R of its consequences corresponds to the sets C_1 and X_1. Namely, we have:

$$
\begin{aligned}
c_i \in C_1 &\quad\text{iff}\quad R \models c_i \\
c_i \notin C_1 &\quad\text{iff}\quad R \models \neg c_i \\
x_i \in X_1 &\quad\text{iff}\quad R \models w \to x_i \\
x_i \notin X_1 &\quad\text{iff}\quad R \models w \to \neg x_i
\end{aligned}
$$

Now, we prove that the consequences of this set of defaults are an extension of the default theory if and only if the QBF formula is valid. Since all defaults are semi-normal, we have to prove that:

1. the set of consequences of D' is consistent; and

2. no other default is applicable, that is, there is no other default whose precondition is consistent with R.

Consistency of R follows by construction: assigning c_i to true for each $c_i \in C_1$, etc., we obtain a model of R.

We have then to prove that no other default is applicable. If $c_i \in C_1$, the default $\frac{:\neg c_i}{\neg c_i}$ is not applicable, and vice versa, if $\neg c_i \in C_1$, then $\frac{:c_i}{c_i}$ is not applicable. Moreover, none of the defaults $\frac{:w\wedge(w\rightarrow x_i)}{w\rightarrow x_i}$, is applicable if $x_i \notin X_1$, because in this case $w \rightarrow \neg x_i \in R$, thus $\neg w$ would follow (while w is a justification of the default). A similar statement holds for $\frac{:w\wedge(w\rightarrow\neg x_i)}{w\rightarrow\neg x_i}$ if $x_i \in X_1$.

As a result, the only applicable default may be the last one, $\frac{:w\wedge\bigwedge_{\gamma_i\in\Gamma}c_i\rightarrow\gamma_i}{w}$ (recall that F is negated). This default is applicable if and only if, for the given evaluation of the c_i's and x_i's, the set of clauses is satisfiable. This amount to say: "there is an extension in which the last default is not applicable if and only if the QBF formula is valid". Now, if the last default is applicable, then M is not a model of the extension because w is the consequence of the last default while $w \not\models M$. The converse also holds: if the last default is not applicable then M is a model of the default theory.

As a result, the QBF is valid if and only if M is a model of the given default theory. $\square$

Theorem 14 *The inference problem for skeptical default logic is $\|\!\sim\!\Pi_2^p$ complete, thus skeptical default logic is* thm-Π_2^p *complete.*

Proof. Since inference in skeptical default logic is in Π_2^p, it is also in $\|\!\sim\!\Pi_2^p$. $\|\!\sim\!\Pi_2^p$-hardness comes from a simple reduction from circumscription. Indeed, the circumscription of a formula T is equivalent to the conjunction of the extensions of the default theory $\langle T, D \rangle$, where (Etherington, 1987):

$$D = \bigcup \left\{ \frac{: \neg x_i}{\neg x_i} \right\}$$

As a result, $CIRC(T) \models Q$ if and only if Q is implied by $\langle T, D \rangle$ under skeptical semantics. Since $\langle T, D \rangle$ only depends on T (and not on Q) this is a $\leq_{nu-comp}$ reduction. Since inference for circumscription is $\|\!\sim\!\Pi_2^p$-complete (see Theorem 11), it follows that skeptical default logic is $\|\!\sim\!\Pi_2^p$-hard. $\square$

Theorem 15 *The inference problem for credulous default logic is $\|\!\sim\!\Sigma_2^p$ complete, thus credulous default logic is* thm-Σ_2^p *complete.*

Proof. The proof is very similar to the proof for model checking of skeptical default logic. Indeed, both problems are $\Vdash \Sigma_2^p$ complete. Since the problem is in Σ_2^p, as proved by Gottlob (1992), it is also in $\Vdash \Sigma_2^p$. Thus, what we have to prove is that is hard for that class.

We prove that the $*\exists\forall$3QBF problem can be reduced to the problem of verifying whether a formula is implied by some extensions of a default theory (that is, inference in credulous default logic).

Namely, a formula $\forall X \exists Y. \neg F$ is valid if and only if Q is derived by some extension of the default theory $\langle D, W \rangle$, where W and D are defined as follows (Γ is the set of all the clauses of three literals over the alphabet of F, and C is a set of new variables, one-to-one with Γ).

$$W = \emptyset$$

$$D = \bigcup_{c_i \in C} \left\{ \frac{: c_i}{c_i}, \frac{: \neg c_i}{\neg c_i} \right\} \cup \bigcup_{x_i \in X} \left\{ \frac{: x_i}{x_i}, \frac{: \neg x_i}{\neg x_i} \right\} \cup \left\{ \frac{\neg(\bigwedge_{c_i \in C} c_i \rightarrow \gamma_i) :}{w} \right\}$$

$$Q = \bigwedge_{\gamma_i \in F} c_i \wedge \bigwedge_{\gamma_i \notin F} \neg c_i \wedge w$$

Informally, the proof goes as follows: for each truth evaluation of the variables in C and X there is a set of defaults which are both justified and consistent. A simple necessary and sufficient condition for the consequences of this set of defaults to be an extension is the following. If, in this evaluation, the formula

$$\neg \bigwedge_{c_i = \text{true}} \gamma_i$$

is valid, then the last default is applicable, thus the extension also contains w. The converse also holds: if the formula is not valid in the evaluation, then the variable w is not in the extension.

As a result, there exists an extension in which Q holds if and only if there exists an extension in which each c_i is true if and only if $\gamma_i \in F$, and such that w also holds. When the variables c_i have the given value, the above formula is equivalent to $\neg F$. As a result, such an extension exists if and only if there exists a truth evaluation of the variables X in which $\neg F$ is valid. $\square$

6.4 Belief Revision

Many formalisms for belief revision have been proposed in the literature, here we focus on two of them: WIDTIO (When In Doubt Throw it Out) and SBR (Skeptical Belief Revision). Let K be a set of propositional formulae, representing an agent's knowledge about the world. When a new formula A is added to K, the problem of the possible inconsistency between K and A arises. The first step is to define the set of sets of formulae $W(K, A)$ in the following way:

$$W(K, A) = \{K' \mid K' \text{ is a maximal consistent subset } \text{ of } K \cup \{A\} \text{ containing } A \}$$

Any set of formulae $K' \in W(K, A)$ is a maximal choice of formulae in K that are consistent with A and, therefore, we may retain when incorporating A. The definition of this set leads to two different revision operators: SBR and WIDTIO.

SBR Skeptical Belief Revision (Fagin, Ullman, & Vardi, 1983; Ginsberg, 1986). The revised theory is defined as a set of theories: $K * A \doteq \{K' \mid K' \in W(K, A)\}$. Inference in the revised theory is defined as inference in each of the theories:

$$K * A \vdash_{SBR} Q \quad \text{iff} \quad \text{for all } K' \in W(K, A) \text{ , we have that } K' \vdash Q$$

The model semantics is defined as:

$$M \models_{SBR} K * A \quad \text{iff} \quad \text{there exists a } K' \in W(K, A) \text{ such that } M \models K'$$

WIDTIO When In Doubt Throw It Out (Winslett, 1990). A simpler (but somewhat drastical) approach is the so-called WIDTIO, where we retain only the formulae of K that belong to all sets of $W(K, A)$. Thus, inference is defined as:

$$K * A \vdash_{WIDTIO} Q \quad \text{iff} \quad \bigcap W(K, A) \vdash Q$$

The model semantics of this formalism is defined as:

$$M \models_{WIDTIO} K * A \quad \text{iff} \quad M \models \bigcap W(K, A)$$

The results on model compactness have been shown by Liberatore and Schaerf (2000). Here we recall them.

Theorem 16 (Liberatore & Schaerf, 2000, Theorem 11) *The problem of model checking for WIDTIO is in* $\|\!\sim\!P$, *thus WIDTIO is in* model-P.

Theorem 17 (Liberatore & Schaerf, 2000, Theorem 5) *The problem of model checking for Skeptical Belief Revision is* $\|\!\sim\!coNP$-complete, *thus Skeptical Belief Revision is* model-coNP-complete.

The results on theorem compactness are quite simple and we provide here the proofs.

Theorem 18 *The problem of inference for WIDTIO is* $\|\!\sim\!coNP$-complete, *thus WIDTIO is* thm-coNP-complete.

Proof. Membership in the class thm-coNP immediately follows from the definition. In fact, we can rewrite $K * A$ into a propositional formula by computing the set $W(K, A)$ and then constructing their intersection. By construction their intersection has size less than or equal to the size of $K \cup A$. As a consequence, after preprocessing, deciding whether a formula Q follows from $K * A$ is a problem in coNP. Hardness follows from the obvious fact that PL can be reduced to WIDTIO and PL is thm-coNP-complete (see Theorem 3). $\qquad\square$

Theorem 19 *The problem of inference for Skeptical Belief Revision is* $\|\!\sim\!\Pi_2^p$-complete, *thus Skeptical Belief Revision is* thm-Π_2^p-complete.

	Time Complexity	Space Efficiency
Propositional Logic	P –	model-P –
WIDTIO	Σ_2^p-complete (Liberatore & Schaerf, 1996)	model-P Th. 16
Skeptical Belief Revision	coNP-complete (Liberatore & Schaerf, 1996)	model-coNP-complete Th. 17
Circumscription	coNP-complete (Cadoli, 1992)	model-coNP-complete Th. 9
GCWA	coNP-hard, in $\Delta_2^p[\log n]$ (Eiter & Gottlob, 1993)	model-P Th. 10
Skeptical Default Reasoning	Σ_2^p-complete (Liberatore & Schaerf, 1998)	model-Σ_2^p-complete Th. 13
Credulous Default Reasoning	N/A	N/A
Stable Model Semantics	P –	model-P –

Table 1: Complexity of model checking and Space Efficiency of Model Representations

Proof. Membership follows from the complexity results of Eiter and Gottlob (1992), where they show that deciding whether $K * A \vdash_{SBR} Q$ is a Π_2^p-complete problem. Hardness follows easily from Theorem 17. In fact, $M \models_{SBR} K * A$ iff $K * A \not\vdash_{SBR} \neg form(M)$, where $form(M)$ is the formula that represents the model M. As a consequence, model checking can be reduced to the complement of inference. Thus inference is $\|\sim\Pi_2^p$-complete. $\square$

6.5 Discussion

Tables 1 and 2 summarize the results on space efficiency of PKR formalisms and where they were proved (a dash "–" denotes a folklore result).

First of all, notice that space efficiency is not always related to time complexity. As an example, we compare in detail WIDTIO and circumscription. From the table it follows that model checking is harder for WIDTIO than for circumscription, and that inference has the same complexity in both cases. Nevertheless, since circumscription is thm-Σ_2^p-complete and WIDTIO is thm-coNP-complete (and thus in thm-Σ_2^p), there exists a poly-size reduction from WIDTIO to circumscription satisfying theorem preservation. The converse does not hold: since circumscription is thm-Σ_2^p-complete and WIDTIO is thm-coNP, unless the Polynomial Hierarchy does not collapse there is no theorem-preserving poly-size reduction from the former formalism to the latter. Hence, circumscription is a more compact formalism than WIDTIO to represent theorems. Analogous considerations can be done for models. Intuitively, this is due to the fact that for WIDTIO both model checking and inference require a lot of work on the revised knowledge base alone—computing the intersection of

	Time Complexity	Space Efficiency
Propositional Logic	coNP-complete (Cook, 1971)	thm-coNP-complete (Cadoli et al., 1996)
WIDTIO	Π_2^p-complete (Eiter & Gottlob, 1992) & (Nebel, 1998)	thm-coNP-complete Th. 18
Skeptical Belief Revision	Π_2^p-complete (Eiter & Gottlob, 1992)	thm-Π_2^p-complete Th. 19
Circumscription	Π_2^p-complete (Eiter & Gottlob, 1993)	thm-Π_2^p-complete Th. 11
GCWA	Π_2^p-complete (Eiter & Gottlob, 1993) & (Nebel, 1998)	thm-coNP-complete Th. 12
Skeptical Default Reasoning	Π_2^p-complete (Gottlob, 1992)	thm-Π_2^p-complete Th. 14
Credulous Default Reasoning	Σ_2^p-complete (Gottlob, 1992)	thm-Σ_2^p-complete Th. 15
Stable Model Semantics	coNP-complete (Marek & Truszczyński, 1991)	thm-coNP-complete Th. 8

Table 2: Complexity of inference and Space Efficiency of Theorem Representations

all elements of $W(K, A)$. Once this is done, one is left with model checking and inference in PL. Hence, WIDTIO has the same space efficiency as PL, which is below circumscription.

Figures 3 and 4 contain the same information of Tables 1 and 2, but highlight existing reductions. Each figure contains two diagrams, the left one showing the existence of polynomial-time reductions among formalisms, the right one showing the existence of poly-size reductions. An arrow from a formalism to another denotes that the former can be reduced to the latter one. We use a bidirectional arrow to denote arrows in both directions and a dashed box to enclose formalisms that can be reduced one into another. Note that some formalisms are more appropriate in representing sets of models, while others perform better on sets of formulae. An interesting relation exists between skeptical default reasoning and circumscription. While there is no model-preserving poly-size reduction from circumscription to skeptical default reasoning (Gogic et al., 1995), a theorem-preserving poly-size reduction exists, as shown by Theorem 14.

7. Related Work and Conclusions

The idea of comparing the compactness of KR formalisms in representing information is not novel in AI. It is well known that first-order circumscription can be represented in second-order logic (Schlipf, 1987). Kolaitis and Papadimitriou (1990) discuss several computational aspects of circumscription. Among many interesting results they show a reduction from a restricted form of first-order circumscription into first-order logic. The proposed reduction will increase the size of the original formula by an exponential factor. It is left as an open problem to show whether this increase is intrinsic, because of the different compactness properties of the two formalisms, or there exists a more space-efficient reduction. When a

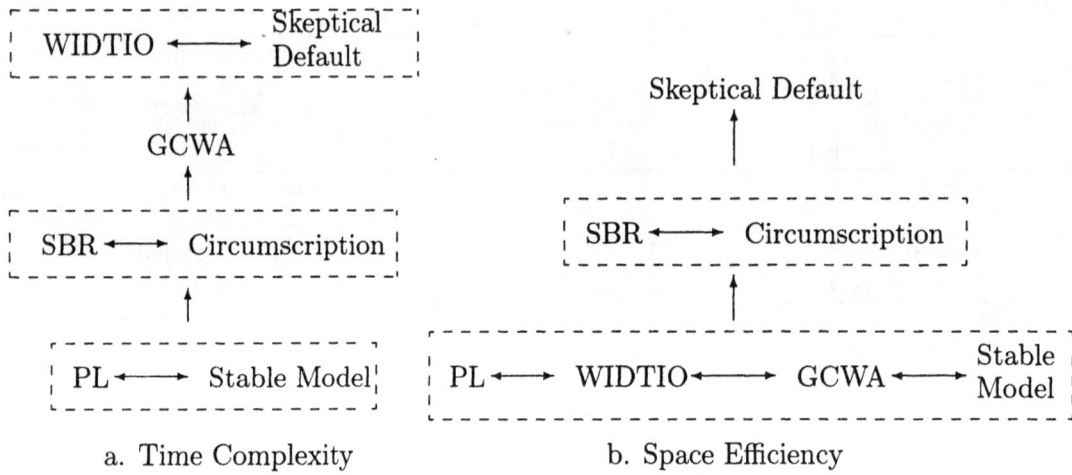

a. Time Complexity   b. Space Efficiency

Figure 3: Complexity of Model Checking vs. Space Efficiency of Model Representation

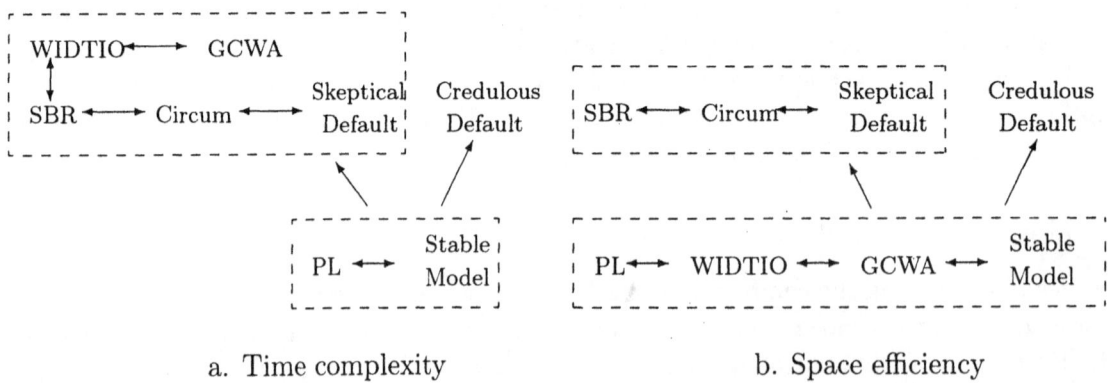

a. Time complexity   b. Space efficiency

Figure 4: Complexity of Inference vs. Space Efficiency of Theorem Representation

first-order language is used, more results on compactness and existence of reductions are reported by Schlipf (1995).

Khardon and Roth (1996, 1997), and Kautz, Kearns and Selman (1995) propose model-based representations of a KB in Propositional Logic, and compare it with formula-based representations. Although their results are significant for comparing representations within PL, they refer only to this formalism, hence they are not applicable to our comparison between *different* PKR formalisms. The same comment applies also to the idea of representing a KB with an efficient basis by Moses and Tennenholz (1996), since it refers only to one PKR formalism, namely, PL.

An active area of research studies the connections of the various non-monotonic logics. In particular, there are several papers discussing the existence of translations that are polynomial in time and satisfy other intuitive requirements such as *modularity* and *faithfulness*. Janhunen (1998), improving on results of Imielinski (1987) and Gottlob (1995), shows that default logic is the most expressive, among the non-monotonic logics examined, since both circumscription and autoepistemic logic can be modularly and faithfully embedded in default logic, but not the other way around. While these results are of interest and help to fully understand the relation among many knowledge representation formalisms, they are not directly related to ours. In fact, we allow for translations that are more general than polynomial time, while in all of the above papers they only consider translations that use polynomial time and also satisfy additional requirements.

The first result on compactness of representations for a propositional language is presented, to the best of our knowledge, by Kautz and Selman (1992). They show that, unless there is a collapse in the polynomial hierarchy, the size of the smallest representation of the least Horn upper bound of a propositional theory is superpolynomial in the size of the original theory. These results are also presented in a different form in the more comprehensive paper (Selman & Kautz, 1996). The technique used in the proof has been then used by us and other researchers to prove several other results on the relative complexity of propositional knowledge representation formalisms (Cadoli et al., 1996, 1997, 1999; Gogic et al., 1995).

In a recent paper (Cadoli et al., 1996b) we introduced a new complexity measure, i.e., *compilability*. In this paper we have shown how this measure is inherently related to the succinctness of PKR formalisms. We analyzed PKR formalisms with respect to two succinctness measures: succinctness in representing sets of models and succinctness in representing sets of theorems.

The main advantage of our framework is the machinery necessary for a formal way of talking about the relative ability of PKR formalisms to compactly represent information. In particular, we were able to formalize the intuition that a specific PKR formalism provides "one of the most compact ways to represent models/theorems" among the PKR formalisms of a specific class.

In our opinion, the proposed framework improves over the state of the art in two different aspects:

1. All the proofs presented in the previous papers only compare pairs of PKR formalisms, for example propositional circumscription and Propositional Logic (Cadoli et al., 1997). These results do not allow for a precise classification of the level of

compactness of the considered formalisms. Rephrasing and adapting these results in our framework allows us to infer that circumscription is model-coNP-complete and thm-Π_2^p-complete. As a consequence, we also have that it is more space-efficient of the WIDTIO belief revision formalism in representing sets of models or sets of theorems.

2. Using the proposed framework it is now possible to find criteria for adapting existent polynomial reductions showing C-hardness into reductions that show model-C or thm-C-hardness, where C is a class in the polynomial hierarchy (Liberatore, 1998).

Acknowledgments

This paper is an extended and revised version of a paper by the same authors appeared in the proceedings of the fifth international conference on the principles of knowledge representation and reasoning (KR'96) (Cadoli, Donini, Liberatore, & Schaerf, 1996a). Partial supported has been given by ASI (Italian Space Agency) and CNR (National Research Council of Italy).

References

Ben-Eliyahu, R., & Dechter, R. (1991). Default logic, propositional logic and constraints. In *Proceedings of the Ninth National Conference on Artificial Intelligence (AAAI'91)*, pp. 379–385.

Ben-Eliyahu, R., & Dechter, R. (1994). Propositional semantics for disjunctive logic programs. *Annals of Mathematics and Artificial Intelligence, 12*, 53–87.

Boppana, R., & Sipser, M. (1990). The complexity of finite functions. In van Leeuwen, J. (Ed.), *Handbook of Theoretical Computer Science*, Vol. A, chap. 14, pp. 757–804. Elsevier Science Publishers (North-Holland), Amsterdam.

Cadoli, M. (1992). The complexity of model checking for circumscriptive formulae. *Information Processing Letters, 44*, 113–118.

Cadoli, M., Donini, F., Liberatore, P., & Schaerf, M. (1996a). Comparing space efficiency of propositional knowledge representation formalisms. In *Proceedings of the Fifth International Conference on the Principles of Knowledge Representation and Reasoning (KR'96)*, pp. 364–373.

Cadoli, M., Donini, F. M., Liberatore, P., & Schaerf, M. (1996b). Feasibility and unfeasibility of off-line processing. In *Proceedings of the Fourth Israeli Symposium on Theory of Computing and Systems (ISTCS'96)*, pp. 100–109. IEEE Computer Society Press. URL = ftp://ftp.dis.uniroma1.it/PUB/AI/papers/cado-etal-96.ps.gz.

Cadoli, M., Donini, F. M., Liberatore, P., & Schaerf, M. (1997). Preprocessing of intractable problems. Tech. rep. DIS 24-97, Dipartimento di Informatica e Sistemistica, Università di Roma "La Sapienza". URL = http://ftp.dis.uniroma1.it/PUB/AI/papers/cado-etal-97-d-REVISED.ps.gz.

Cadoli, M., Donini, F. M., Liberatore, P., & Schaerf, M. (1999). The size of a revised knowledge base. *Artificial Intelligence*, *115*(1), 25–64.

Cadoli, M., Donini, F. M., & Schaerf, M. (1995). On compact representations of propositional circumscription. In *Proceedings of the Twelfth Symposium on Theoretical Aspects of Computer Science (STACS'95)*, pp. 205–216. Extended version as RAP.14.95 DIS, Univ. of Roma "La Sapienza", July 1995.

Cadoli, M., Donini, F. M., & Schaerf, M. (1996). Is intractability of non-monotonic reasoning a real drawback?. *Artificial Intelligence*, *88*(1–2), 215–251.

Cadoli, M., Donini, F. M., Schaerf, M., & Silvestri, R. (1997). On compact representations of propositional circumscription. *Theoretical Computer Science*, *182*, 183–202.

Cook, S. A. (1971). The complexity of theorem-proving procedures. In *Proceedings of the Third ACM Symposium on Theory of Computing (STOC'71)*, pp. 151–158.

Eiter, T., & Gottlob, G. (1992). On the complexity of propositional knowledge base revision, updates and counterfactuals. *Artificial Intelligence*, *57*, 227–270.

Eiter, T., & Gottlob, G. (1993). Propositional circumscription and extended closed world reasoning are Π_2^p-complete. *Theoretical Computer Science*, *114*, 231–245.

Etherington, D. V. (1987). *Reasoning with incomplete information*. Morgan Kaufmann, Los Altos, Los Altos, CA.

Fagin, R., Ullman, J. D., & Vardi, M. Y. (1983). On the semantics of updates in databases. In *Proceedings of the Second ACM SIGACT SIGMOD Symposium on Principles of Database Systems (PODS'83)*, pp. 352–365.

Garey, M. R., & Johnson, D. S. (1979). *Computers and Intractability: A Guide to the Theory of NP-Completeness*. W.H. Freeman and Company, San Francisco, Ca.

Gelfond, M., & Lifschitz, V. (1988). The stable model semantics for logic programming. In *Proceedings of the Fifth Logic Programming Symposium*, pp. 1070–1080. The MIT Press.

Gelfond, M., Przymusinska, H., & Przymusinsky, T. (1989). On the relationship between circumscription and negation as failure. *Artificial Intelligence*, *38*, 49–73.

Ginsberg, M. L. (1986). Conterfactuals. *Artificial Intelligence*, *30*, 35–79.

Gogic, G., Kautz, H. A., Papadimitriou, C., & Selman, B. (1995). The comparative linguistics of knowledge representation. In *Proceedings of the Fourteenth International Joint Conference on Artificial Intelligence (IJCAI'95)*, pp. 862–869.

Gottlob, G. (1992). Complexity results for nonmonotonic logics. *Journal of Logic and Computation*, *2*, 397–425.

Gottlob, G. (1995). Translating default logic into standard autoepistemic logic. *Journal of the ACM*, *42*, 711–740.

Imielinski, T. (1987). Results on translating defaults to circumscription. *Artificial Intelligence*, *32*, 131–146.

Janhunen, T. (1998). On the intertranslatability of autoepistemic, default and priority logics, and parallel circumscription. In *Proceedings of the Sixth European Workshop on Logics in Artificial Intelligence (JELIA '98)*, No. 1489 in Lecture Notes in Artificial Intelligence, pp. 216–232. Springer-Verlag.

Johnson, D. S. (1990). A catalog of complexity classes. In van Leeuwen, J. (Ed.), *Handbook of Theoretical Computer Science*, Vol. A, chap. 2, pp. 67–161. Elsevier Science Publishers (North-Holland), Amsterdam.

Karp, R. M., & Lipton, R. J. (1980). Some connections between non-uniform and uniform complexity classes. In *Proceedings of the Twelfth ACM Symposium on Theory of Computing (STOC'80)*, pp. 302–309.

Kautz, H. A., Kearns, M. J., & Selman, B. (1995). Horn approximations of empirical data. *Artificial Intelligence*, *74*, 129–145.

Kautz, H. A., & Selman, B. (1991). Hard problems for simple default logics. *Artificial Intelligence*, *49*, 243–279.

Kautz, H. A., & Selman, B. (1992). Forming concepts for fast inference. In *Proceedings of the Tenth National Conference on Artificial Intelligence (AAAI'92)*, pp. 786–793.

Khardon, R., & Roth, D. (1996). Reasoning with models. *Artificial Intelligence*, *87*, 187–213.

Khardon, R., & Roth, D. (1997). Defaults and relevance in model-based reasoning. *Artificial Intelligence*, *97*, 169–193.

Köbler, J., & Watanabe, O. (1998). New collapse consequences of NP having small circuits. *SIAM Journal on Computing*, *28*(1), 311–324.

Kolaitis, P. G., & Papadimitriou, C. H. (1990). Some computational aspects of circumscription. *Journal of the ACM*, *37*(1), 1–14.

Liberatore, P. (1995). Compact representation of revision of Horn clauses. In Yao, X. (Ed.), *Proceedings of the Eighth Australian Joint Artificial Intelligence Conference (AI'95)*, pp. 347–354. World Scientific.

Liberatore, P. (1998). *Compilation of intractable problems and its application to Artificial Intelligence*. Ph.D. thesis, Dipartimento di Informatica e Sistemistica, Università di Roma "La Sapienza". URL = ftp://ftp.dis.uniroma1.it/pub/AI/papers/libe-98-c.ps.gz.

Liberatore, P., & Schaerf, M. (1996). The complexity of model checking for belief revision and update. In *Proceedings of the Thirteenth National Conference on Artificial Intelligence (AAAI'96)*, pp. 556–561.

Liberatore, P., & Schaerf, M. (1998). The complexity of model checking for propositional default logics. In *Proceedings of the Thirteenth European Conference on Artificial Intelligence (ECAI'98)*, pp. 18–22.

Liberatore, P., & Schaerf, M. (2000). The compactness of belief revision and update operators. Tech. rep., Dipartimento di Informatica e Sistemistica, Università di Roma "La Sapienza".

Marek, W., & Truszczyński, M. (1991). Autoepistemic logic. *Journal of the ACM*, *38*(3), 588–619.

McCarthy, J. (1980). Circumscription - A form of non-monotonic reasoning. *Artificial Intelligence*, *13*, 27–39.

Minker, J. (1982). On indefinite databases and the closed world assumption. In *Proceedings of the Sixth International Conference on Automated Deduction (CADE'82)*, pp. 292–308.

Moses, Y., & Tennenholtz, M. (1996). Off-line reasoning for on-line efficiency: knowledge bases. *Artificial Intelligence*, *83*, 229–239.

Nebel, B. (1998). How hard is it to revise a belief base?. In Dubois, D., & Prade, H. (Eds.), *Belief Change - Handbook of Defeasible Reasoning and Uncertainty Management Systems, Vol. 3*. Kluwer Academic.

Reiter, R. (1980). A logic for default reasoning. *Artificial Intelligence*, *13*, 81–132.

Schlipf, J. S. (1987). Decidability and definability with circumscription. *Annals of Pure and Applied Logic*, *35*, 173–191.

Schlipf, J. S. (1995). A survey of complexity and undecidability results for logic programming. *Annals of Mathematics and Artificial Intelligence*, *15*, 257–288.

Selman, B., & Kautz, H. A. (1996). Knowledge compilation and theory approximation. *Journal of the ACM*, *43*, 193–224.

Stockmeyer, L. J. (1976). The polynomial-time hierarchy. *Theoretical Computer Science*, *3*, 1–22.

Winslett, M. (1989). Sometimes updates are circumscription. In *Proceedings of the Eleventh International Joint Conference on Artificial Intelligence (IJCAI'89)*, pp. 859–863.

Winslett, M. (1990). *Updating Logical Databases*. Cambridge University Press.

Yap, C. K. (1983). Some consequences of non-uniform conditions on uniform classes. *Theoretical Computer Science*, *26*, 287–300.

Halpern, J.Y. & Moses, Y. (1992). The complexity of modal logic for propositional databases. In Proceedings of the Tenth European Conference on Artificial Intelligence (ECAI'92), pp. ...

Imielinski, T. & Schmid, M. (1993). The complexness of belief revision and update, ...

Marek, W. & Truszczyński, M. (1991). Autoepistemic logic. Journal of the ACM, 38(3), 588–619.

McCarthy, J. (1980). Circumscription: A form of non-monotonic reasoning. Artificial Intelligence, 13, 27–39, ...

Journal of Artificial Intelligence Research 13 (2000) 33–94   Submitted 9/99; published 8/00

Value-Function Approximations for Partially Observable Markov Decision Processes

Milos Hauskrecht   MILOS@CS.BROWN.EDU

Computer Science Department, Brown University
Box 1910, Brown University, Providence, RI 02912, USA

Abstract

Partially observable Markov decision processes (POMDPs) provide an elegant mathematical framework for modeling complex decision and planning problems in stochastic domains in which states of the system are observable only indirectly, via a set of imperfect or noisy observations. The modeling advantage of POMDPs, however, comes at a price — exact methods for solving them are computationally very expensive and thus applicable in practice only to very simple problems. We focus on efficient approximation (heuristic) methods that attempt to alleviate the computational problem and trade off accuracy for speed. We have two objectives here. First, we survey various approximation methods, analyze their properties and relations and provide some new insights into their differences. Second, we present a number of new approximation methods and novel refinements of existing techniques. The theoretical results are supported by experiments on a problem from the agent navigation domain.

1. Introduction

Making decisions in dynamic environments requires careful evaluation of the cost and benefits not only of the immediate action but also of choices we may have in the future. This evaluation becomes harder when the effects of actions are stochastic, so that we must pursue and evaluate many possible outcomes in parallel. Typically, the problem becomes more complex the further we look into the future. The situation becomes even worse when the outcomes we can observe are imperfect or unreliable indicators of the underlying process and special actions are needed to obtain more reliable information. Unfortunately, many real-world decision problems fall into this category.

Consider, for example, a problem of patient management. The patient comes to the hospital with an initial set of complaints. Only rarely do these allow the physician (decision-maker) to diagnose the underlying disease with certainty, so that a number of disease options generally remain open after the initial evaluation. The physician has multiple choices in managing the patient. He/she can choose to do nothing (wait and see), order additional tests and learn more about the patient state and disease, or proceed to a more radical treatment (e.g. surgery). Making the right decision is not an easy task. The disease the patient suffers can progress over time and may become worse if the window of opportunity for a particular effective treatment is missed. On the other hand, selection of the wrong treatment may make the patient's condition worse, or may prevent applying the correct treatment later. The result of the treatment is typically non-deterministic and more outcomes are possible. In addition, both treatment and investigative choices come with different costs. Thus, in a course of patient management, the decision-maker must carefully evaluate the costs and benefits of both current and future choices, as well as their interaction and ordering. Other decision problems with similar characteristics — complex temporal cost-benefit tradeoffs, stochasticity, and partial observability of the underlying controlled process — include robot navigation, target tracking, machine mantainance and replacement, and the like.

Sequential decision problems can be modeled as *Markov decision processes (MDPs)* (Bellman, 1957; Howard, 1960; Puterman, 1994; Boutilier, Dean, & Hanks, 1999) and their extensions. The model of choice for problems similar to patient management is the *partially observable Markov decision process (POMDP)* (Drake, 1962; Astrom, 1965; Sondik, 1971; Lovejoy, 1991b). The POMDP represents two sources of uncertainty: stochasticity of the underlying controlled process (e.g. disease dynamics in the patient management problem), and imperfect observability of its states via a set of noisy observations (e.g. symptoms, findings, results of tests). In addition, it lets us model in a uniform way both control and information-gathering (investigative) actions, as well as their effects and cost-benefit trade-offs. Partial observability and the ability to model and reason with information-gathering actions are the main features that distinguish the POMDP from the widely known *fully observable Markov decision process* (Bellman, 1957; Howard, 1960).

Although useful from the modeling perspective, POMDPs have the disadvantage of being hard to solve (Papadimitriou & Tsitsiklis, 1987; Littman, 1996; Mundhenk, Goldsmith, Lusena, & Allender, 1997; Madani, Hanks, & Condon, 1999), and optimal or ϵ-optimal solutions can be obtained in practice only for problems of low complexity. A challenging goal in this research area is to exploit additional structural properties of the domain and/or suitable approximations (heuristics) that can be used to obtain good solutions more efficiently.

We focus here on heuristic approximation methods, in particular approximations based on value functions. Important research issues in this area are the design of new and efficient algorithms, as well as a better understanding of the existing techniques and their relations, advantages and disadvantages. In this paper we address both of these issues. First, we survey various value-function approximations, analyze their properties and relations and provide some insights into their differences. Second, we present a number of new methods and novel refinements of existing techniques. The theoretical results and findings are also supported empirically on a problem from the agent navigation domain.

2. Partially Observable Markov Decision Processes

A *partially observable Markov decision process (POMDP)* describes a stochastic control process with partially observable (hidden) states. Formally, it corresponds to a tuple (S, A, Θ, T, O, R) where S is a set of states, A is a set of actions, Θ is a set of observations, $T : S \times A \times S \rightarrow [0, 1]$ is a set of transition probabilities that describe the dynamic behavior of the modeled environment, $O : S \times A \times \Theta \rightarrow [0, 1]$ is a set of observation probabilities that describe the relationships among observations, states and actions, and $R : S \times A \times S \rightarrow \mathbb{R}$ denotes a reward model that assigns rewards to state transitions and models payoffs associated with such transitions. In some instances the definition of a POMDP also includes an *a priori* probability distribution over the set of initial states S.

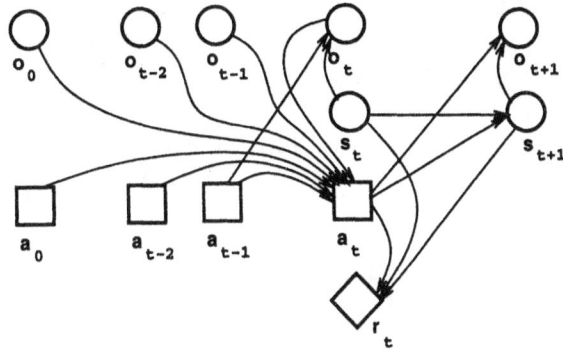

Figure 1: Part of the influence diagram describing a POMDP model. Rectangles correspond to decision nodes (actions), circles to random variables (states) and diamonds to reward nodes. Links represent the dependencies among the components. s_t, a_t, o_t and r_t denote state, action, observation and reward at time t. Note that an action at time t depends only on past observations and actions, not on states.

2.1 Objective Function

Given a POMDP, the goal is to construct a *control policy* that maximizes an *objective (value) function*. The objective function combines partial (stepwise) rewards over multiple steps using various kinds of decision models. Typically, the models are cumulative and based on expectations. Two models are frequently used in practice:

- a *finite-horizon* model in which we maximize $E(\sum_{t=0}^{T} r_t)$, where r_t is a reward obtained at time t.

- an *infinite-horizon discounted* model in which we maximize $E(\sum_{t=0}^{\infty} \gamma^t r_t)$, where $0 < \gamma < 1$ is a discount factor.

Note that POMDPs and cumulative decision models provide a rich language for modeling various control objectives. For example, one can easily model goal-achievement tasks (a specific goal must be reached) by giving a large reward for a transition to that state and zero or smaller rewards for other transitions.

In this paper we focus primarily on discounted infinite-horizon model. However, the results can be easily applied also to the finite-horizon case.

2.2 Information State

In a POMDP the process states are hidden and we cannot observe them while making a decision about the next action. Thus, our action choices are based only on the information available to us or on quantities derived from that information. This is illustrated in the influence diagram in Figure 1, where the action at time t depends only on previous observations and actions, not on states. Quantities summarizing all information are called *information states*. *Complete information states* represent a trivial case.

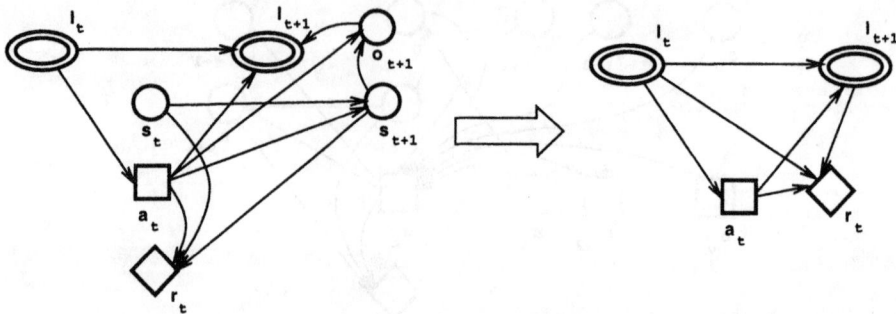

Figure 2: Influence diagram for a POMDP with information states and corresponding information-state MDP. Information states (I_t and I_{t+1}) are represented by double-circled nodes. An action choice (rectangle) depends only on the current information state.

Definition 1 *(Complete information state). The complete information state at time t (denoted I_t^C) consists of:*

- *a prior belief b_0 on states in S at time 0;*

- *a complete history of actions and observations $\{o_0, a_0, o_1, a_1, \cdots, o_{t-1}, a_{t-1}, o_t\}$ starting from time $t = 0$.*

A sequence of information states defines a controlled Markov process that we call an *information-state Markov decision process* or *information-state MDP*. The policy for the information-state MDP is defined in terms of a control function $\mu : \mathcal{I} \to A$ mapping information state space to actions. The new information state (I_t) is a deterministic function of the previous state (I_{t-1}), the last action (a_{t-1}) and the new observation (o_t):

$$I_t = \tau(I_{t-1}, o_t, a_{t-1}).$$

$\tau : \mathcal{I} \times \Theta \times A \to \mathcal{I}$ is the *update function* mapping the information state space, observations and actions back to the information space.[1] It is easy to see that one can always convert the original POMDP into the information-state MDP by using complete information states. The relation between the components of the two models and a sketch of a reduction of a POMDP to an information-state MDP, are shown in Figure 2.

2.3 Bellman Equations for POMDPs

An information-state MDP for the infinite-horizon discounted case is like a fully-observable MDP and satisfies the standard fixed-point (Bellman) equation:

$$V^*(I) = \max_{a \in A} \left\{ \rho(I, a) + \gamma \sum_{I'} P(I'|I, a) V^*(I') \right\}. \tag{1}$$

---

1. In this paper, τ denotes the generic update function. Thus we use the same symbol even if the information state space is different.

Here, $V^*(I)$ denotes the optimal value function maximizing $E(\sum_{t=0}^{\infty} \gamma^t r_t)$ for state I. $\rho(I, a)$ is the expected one-step reward and equals

$$\rho(I, a) = \sum_{s \in S} \rho(s, a) P(s|I) = \sum_{s \in S} \sum_{s' \in S} R(s, a, s') P(s'|s, a) P(s|I).$$

$\rho(s, a)$ denotes an expected one-step reward for state s and action a.

Since the next information state $I' = \tau(I, o, a)$ is a deterministic function of the previous information state I, action a, and the observation o, the Equation 1 can be rewritten more compactly by summing over all possible observations Θ:

$$V^*(I) = \max_{a \in A} \left\{ \sum_{s \in S} \rho(s, a) P(s|I) + \gamma \sum_{o \in \Theta} P(o|I, a) V^*(\tau(I, o, a)) \right\}. \tag{2}$$

The optimal policy (control function) $\mu^* : \mathcal{I} \to A$ selects the value-maximizing action

$$\mu^*(I) = \arg\max_{a \in A} \left\{ \sum_{s \in S} \rho(s, a) P(s|I) + \gamma \sum_{o \in \Theta} P(o|I, a) V^*(\tau(I, o, a)) \right\}. \tag{3}$$

The value and control functions can be also expressed in terms of *action-value functions (Q-functions)*

$$V^*(I) = \max_{a \in A} Q^*(I, a) \qquad \mu^*(I) = \arg\max_{a \in A} Q^*(I, a),$$

$$Q^*(I, a) = \sum_{s \in S} \rho(s, a) P(s|I) + \gamma \sum_{o \in \Theta} P(o|I, a) V^*(\tau(I, o, a)). \tag{4}$$

A Q-function corresponds to the expected reward for chosing a fixed action (a) in the first step and acting optimally afterwards.

2.3.1 SUFFICIENT STATISTICS

To derive Equations 1—3 we implicitly used complete information states. However, as remarked earlier, the information available to the decision-maker can be also summarized by other quantities. We call them *sufficient information states*. Such states must preserve the necessary information content and also the Markov property of the information-state decision process.

Definition 2 (*Sufficient information state process*). *Let $\mathcal{I}$ be an information state space and $\tau : \mathcal{I} \times A \times \Theta \to \mathcal{I}$ be an update function defining an information process $I_t = \tau(I_{t-1}, a_{t-1}, o_t)$. The process is sufficient with regard to the optimal control when, for any time step t, it satisfies*

$$P(s_t|I_t) = P(s_t|I_t^C)$$

$$P(o_t|I_{t-1}, a_{t-1}) = P(o_t|I_{t-1}^C, a_{t-1}),$$

where I_t^C and I_{t-1}^C are complete information states.

It is easy to see that Equations 1 — 3 for complete information states must hold also for sufficient information states. The key benefit of sufficient statistics is that they are often easier to manipulate and store, since unlike complete histories, they may not expand with time. For example, in the standard POMDP model it is sufficient to work with belief states that assign probabilities to every possible process state (Astrom, 1965).[2] In this case the Bellman equation reduces to:

$$V(b) = \max_{a \in A} \left\{ \sum_{s \in S} \rho(s,a)b(s) + \gamma \sum_{o \in \Theta} \sum_{s \in S} P(o|s,a)b(s)V(\tau(b,o,a)) \right\}, \tag{5}$$

where the next-step belief state b' is

$$b'(s) = \tau(b,o,a)(s) = \beta P(o|s,a) \sum_{s' \in S} P(s|a,s')b(s').$$

$\beta = 1/P(o|b,a)$ is a normalizing constant. This defines a *belief-state MDP* which is a special case of a continuous-state MDP. Belief-state MDPs are also the primary focus of our investigation in this paper.

2.3.2 Value-Function Mappings and their Properties

The Bellman equation 2 for the belief-state MDP can be also rewritten in the value-function mapping form. Let $\mathcal{V}$ be a space of real-valued bounded functions $V : \mathcal{I} \to \mathbb{R}$ defined on the belief information space $\mathcal{I}$, and let $h : \mathcal{I} \times A \times B \to \mathbb{R}$ be defined as

$$h(b,a,V) = \sum_{s \in S} \rho(s,a)b(s) + \gamma \sum_{o \in \Theta} \sum_{s \in S} P(o|s,a)b(s)V(\tau(b,o,a)).$$

Now by defining the value function mapping $H : \mathcal{V} \to \mathcal{V}$ as $(HV)(b) = \max_{a \in A} h(b,a,V)$, the Bellman equation 2 for all information states can be written as $V^* = HV^*$. It is well known that H (for MDPs) is an isotone mapping and that it is a contraction under the supremum norm (see (Heyman & Sobel, 1984; Puterman, 1994)).

Definition 3 *The mapping H is isotone, if $V, U \in \mathcal{V}$ and $V \leq U$ implies $HV \leq HU$.*

Definition 4 *Let $\|.\|$ be a supremum norm. The mapping H is a contraction under the supremum norm, if for all $V, U \in \mathcal{V}$, $\|HV - HU\| \leq \beta\|V - U\|$ holds for some $0 \leq \beta < 1$.*

2.4 Value Iteration

The optimal value function (Equation 2) or its approximation can be computed using *dynamic programming* techniques. The simplest approach is the *value iteration* (Bellman, 1957) shown in Figure 3. In this case, the optimal value function V^* can be determined in the limit by performing a sequence of value-iteration steps $V_i = HV_{i-1}$, where V_i is the ith approximation of the value function (ith value function).[3] The sequence of estimates

---

2. Models in which belief states are not sufficient include POMDPs with observation and action channel lags (see Hauskrecht (1997)).

3. We note that the same update $V_i = HV_{i-1}$ can be applied to solve the finite-horizon problem in a standard way. The difference is that V_i now stands for the i-steps-to-go value function and V_0 represents the value function (rewards) for end states.

Value iteration $(POMDP, \epsilon)$
    initialize V for all $b \in \mathcal{I}$;
    repeat
            $V' \leftarrow V$;
            update $V \leftarrow HV'$ for all $b \in \mathcal{I}$;
    until $\sup_b | V(b) - V'(b) | \le \epsilon$
    return V;

Figure 3: Value iteration procedure.

converges to the unique fixed-point solution which is the direct consequence of Banach's theorem for contraction mappings (see, for example, Puterman (1994)).

In practice, we stop the iteration well before it reaches the limit solution. The stopping criterion we use in our algorithm (Figure 3) examines the maximum difference between value functions obtained in two consecutive steps — the so-called Bellman error (Puterman, 1994; Littman, 1996). The algorithm stops when this quantity falls below the threshold ϵ. The accuracy of the approximate solution (ith value function) with regard to V^* can be expressed in terms of the Bellman error ϵ.

Theorem 1 *Let* $\epsilon = \sup_b |V_i(b) - V_{i-1}(b)| = \|V_i - V_{i-1}\|$ *be the magnitude of the Bellman error. Then* $\|V_i - V^*\| \le \frac{\gamma\epsilon}{1-\gamma}$ *and* $\|V_{i-1} - V^*\| \le \frac{\epsilon}{1-\gamma}$ *hold.*

Then, to obtain the approximation of V^* with precision δ the Bellman error should fall below $\frac{\delta(1-\gamma)}{\gamma}$.

2.4.1 PIECEWISE LINEAR AND CONVEX APPROXIMATIONS OF THE VALUE FUNCTION

The major difficulty in applying the value iteration (or dynamic programming) to belief-state MDPs is that the belief space is infinite and we need to compute an update $V_i = HV_{i-1}$ for all of it. This poses the following threats: the value function for the ith step may not be representable by finite means and/or computable in a finite number of steps.

To address this problem Sondik (Sondik, 1971; Smallwood & Sondik, 1973) showed that one can guarantee the computability of the ith value function as well as its finite description for a belief-state MDP by considering only piecewise linear and convex representations of value function estimates (see Figure 4). In particular, Sondik showed that for a piecewise linear and convex representation of V_{i-1}, $V_i = HV_{i-1}$ is computable and remains piecewise linear and convex.

Theorem 2 *(Piecewise linear and convex functions). Let* V_0 *be an initial value function that is piecewise linear and convex. Then the ith value function obtained after a finite number of update steps for a belief-state MDP is also finite, piecewise linear and convex, and is equal to:*

$$V_i(b) = \max_{\alpha_i \in \Gamma_i} \sum_{s \in S} b(s)\alpha_i(s),$$

where b and α_i are vectors of size $|S|$ and Γ_i is a finite set of vectors (linear functions) α_i.

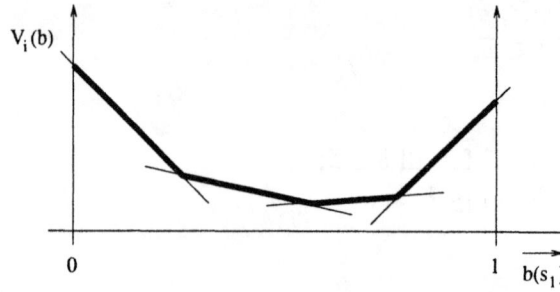

Figure 4: A piecewise linear and convex function for a POMDP with two process states $\{s_1, s_2\}$. Note that $b(s_1) = 1 - b(s_2)$ holds for any belief state.

The key part of the proof is that we can express the update for the ith value function in terms of linear functions Γ_{i-1} defining V_{i-1}:

$$V_i(b) = \max_{a \in A} \left\{ \sum_{s \in S} \rho(s,a) b(s) + \gamma \sum_{o \in \Theta} \max_{\alpha_{i-1} \in \Gamma_{i-1}} \sum_{s' \in S} \left[\sum_{s \in S} P(s', o|s, a) b(s) \right] \alpha_{i-1}(s') \right\}. \qquad (6)$$

This leads to a piecewise linear and convex value function V_i that can be represented by a finite set of linear functions α_i, one linear function for every combination of actions and permutations of α_{i-1} vectors of size $|\Theta|$. Let $W = (a, \{o_1, \alpha_{i-1}^{j_1}\}, \{o_2, \alpha_{i-1}^{j_2}\}, \cdots \{o_{|\Theta|}, \alpha_{i-1}^{j_{|\Theta|}}\})$ be such a combination. Then the linear function corresponding to it is defined as

$$\alpha_i^W(s) = \rho(s,a) + \gamma \sum_{o \in \Theta} \sum_{s' \in S} P(s', o|s, a) \alpha_{i-1}^{j_o}(s'). \qquad (7)$$

Theorem 2 is the basis of the dynamic programming algorithm for finding the optimal solution for the finite-horizon models and the value-iteration algorithm for finding near-optimal approximations of V^* for the discounted, infinite-horizon model. Note, however, that this result does not imply piecewise linearity of the optimal (fixed-point) solution V^*.

2.4.2 ALGORITHMS FOR COMPUTING VALUE-FUNCTION UPDATES

The key part of the value-iteration algorithm is the computation of value-function updates $V_i = HV_{i-1}$. Assume an ith value function V_i that is represented by a finite number of linear segments (α vectors). The total number of all its possible linear functions is $|A||\Gamma_{i-1}|^{|\Theta|}$ (one for every combination of actions and permutations of α_{i-1} vectors of size $|\Theta|$) and they can be enumerated in $O(|A||S|^2|\Gamma_{i-1}|^{|\Theta|})$ time. However, the complete set of linear functions is rarely needed: some of the linear functions are dominated by others and their omission does not change the resulting piecewise linear and convex function. This is illustrated in Figure 5.

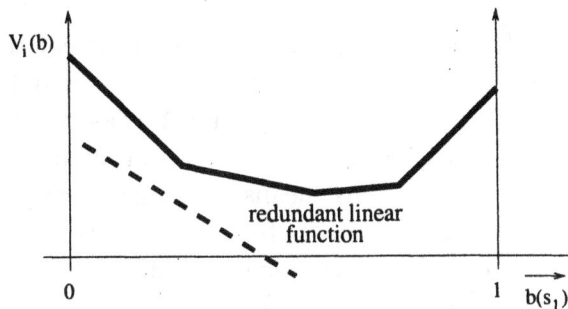

Figure 5: Redundant linear function. The function does not dominate in any of the regions of the belief space and can be excluded.

A linear function that can be eliminated without changing the resulting value function solution is called *redundant*. Conversely, a linear function that singlehandedly achieves the optimal value for at least one point of the belief space is called *useful*.[4]

For the sake of computational efficiency it is important to make the size of the linear function set as small as possible (keep only useful linear functions) over value-iteration steps. There are two main approaches for computing useful linear functions. The first approach is based on a generate-and-test paradigm and is due to Sondik (1971) and Monahan (1982). The idea here is to enumerate all possible linear functions first, then test the usefulness of linear functions in the set and prune all redundant vectors. Recent extensions of the method interleave the generate and test stages and do early pruning on a set of partially constructed linear functions (Zhang & Liu, 1997a; Cassandra, Littman, & Zhang, 1997; Zhang & Lee, 1998).

The second approach builds on Sondik's idea of computing a useful linear function for a single belief state (Sondik, 1971; Smallwood & Sondik, 1973), which can be done efficiently. The key problem here is to locate all belief points that seed useful linear functions and different methods address this problem differently. Methods that implement this idea are Sondik's one- and two-pass algorithms (Sondik, 1971), Cheng's methods (Cheng, 1988), and the Witness algorithm (Kaelbling, Littman, & Cassandra, 1999; Littman, 1996; Cassandra, 1998).

2.4.3 Limitations and Complexity

The major difficulty in solving a belief-state MDP is that the complexity of a piecewise linear and convex function can grow extremely fast with the number of update steps. More specifically, the size of a linear function set defining the function can grow exponentially (in the number of observations) during a single update step. Then, assuming that the initial value function is linear, the number of linear functions defining the ith value function is $O(|A|^{|\Theta|^{i-1}})$.

---

4. In defining redundant and useful linear functions we assume that there are no linear function duplicates, i.e. only one copy of the same linear function is kept in the set Γ_i.

The potential growth of the size of the linear function set is not the only bad news. As remarked earlier, a piecewise linear convex value function is usually less complex than the worst case because many linear functions can be pruned away during updates. However, it turned out that the task of identifying all useful linear functions is computationally intractable as well (Littman, 1996). This means that one faces not only the potential super-exponential growth of the number of useful linear functions, but also inefficiencies related to the identification of such vectors. This is a significant drawback that makes the exact methods applicable only to relatively simple problems.

The above analysis suggests that solving a POMDP problem is an intrinsically hard task. Indeed, finding the optimal solution for the finite-horizon problem is PSPACE-hard (Papadimitriou & Tsitsiklis, 1987). Finding the optimal solution for the discounted infinite-horizon criterion is even harder. The corresponding decision problem has been shown to be undecidable (Madani et al., 1999), and thus the optimal solution may not be computable.

2.4.4 STRUCTURAL REFINEMENTS OF THE BASIC ALGORITHM

The standard POMDP model uses a flat state space and full transition and reward matrices. However, in practice, problems often exhibit more structure and can be represented more compactly, for example, using graphical models (Pearl, 1988; Lauritzen, 1996), most often dynamic belief networks (Dean & Kanazawa, 1989; Kjaerulff, 1992) or dynamic influence diagrams (Howard & Matheson, 1984; Tatman & Schachter, 1990).[5] There are many ways to take advantage of the problem structure to modify and improve exact algorithms. For example, a refinement of the basic Monahan algorithm to compact transition and reward models has been studied by Boutilier and Poole (1996). A hybrid framework that combines MDP-POMDP problem-solving techniques to take advantage of perfectly and partially observable components of the model and the subsequent value function decomposition was proposed by Hauskrecht (1997, 1998, 2000). A similar approach with perfect information about a region (subset of states) containing the actual underlying state was discussed by Zhang and Liu (1997b, 1997a). Finally, Castañon (1997) and Yost (1998) explore techniques for solving large POMDPs that consist of a set of smaller, resource-coupled but otherwise independent POMDPs.

2.5 Extracting Control Strategy

Value iteration allow us to compute an ith approximation of the value function V_i. However, our ulimate goal is to find the optimal control strategy $\mu^* : \mathcal{I} \to A$ or its close approximation. Thus our focus here is on the problem of extraction of control strategies from the results of value iteration.

2.5.1 LOOKAHEAD DESIGN

The simplest way to define the control function $\mu : \mathcal{I} \to A$ from the value function V_i is via greedy one-step lookahead:

$$\mu(b) = \arg\max_{a \in A} \left\{ \sum_{s \in S} \rho(s, a) b(s) + \gamma \sum_{o \in \Theta} P(o|b, a) V_i(\tau(b, o, a)) \right\}.$$

5. See the survey by Boutilier, Dean and Hanks (1999) for different ways to represent structured MDPs.

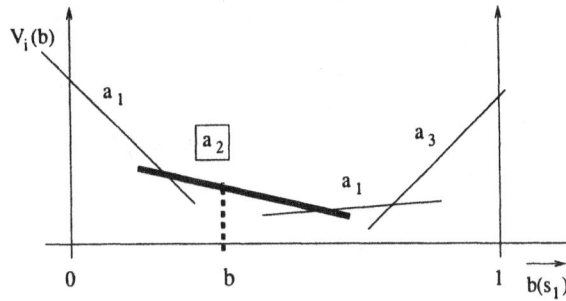

Figure 6: Direct control design. Every linear function defining V_i is associated with an action. The action is selected if its linear function (or Q-function) is maximal.

As V_i represents only the ith approximation of the optimal value function, the question arises how good the resulting controller really is.[6] The following theorem (Puterman, 1994; Williams & Baird, 1994; Littman, 1996) relates the accuracy of the (lookahead) controller and the Bellman error.

Theorem 3 *Let $\epsilon = \|V_i - V_{i-1}\|$ be the magnitude of the Bellman error. Let V_i^{LA} be the expected reward for the lookahead controller designed for V_i. Then $\|V_i^{LA} - V^*\| \leq \frac{2\epsilon\gamma}{1-\gamma}$.*

The bound can be used to construct the value-iteration routine that yields a lookahead strategy with a minimum required precision. The result can be also extended to the k-step lookahead design in a straightforward way; with k steps, the error bound becomes $\|V_i^{LA(k)} - V^*\| \leq \frac{2\epsilon\gamma^k}{(1-\gamma)}$.

2.5.2 DIRECT DESIGN

To extract the control action via lookahead essentially requires computing one full update. Obviously, this can lead to unwanted delays in reaction times. In general, we can speed up the response by remembering and using additional information. In particular, every linear function defining V_i is associated with the choice of action (see Equation 7). The action is a byproduct of methods for computing linear functions and no extra computation is required to find it. Then the action corresponding to the best linear function can be selected directly for any belief state. The idea is illustrated in Figure 6.

The bound on the accuracy of the direct controller for the infinite-horizon case can be once again derived in terms of the magnitude of the Bellman error.

Theorem 4 *Let $\epsilon = \|V_i - V_{i-1}\|$ be the magnitude of the Bellman error. Let V_i^{DR} be an expected reward for the direct controller designed for V_i. Then $\|V_i^{DR} - V^*\| \leq \frac{2\epsilon}{1-\gamma}$.*

The direct action choice is closely related to the notion of action-value function (or Q-function). Analogously to Equation 4, the ith Q-function satisfies

$$V_i(b) = \max_{a \in A} Q_i(b, a),$$

---

6. Note that the control action extracted via lookahead from V_i is optimal for $(i + 1)$ steps-to-go and the finite-horizon model. The main difference here is that V_i is the optimal value function for i steps to go.

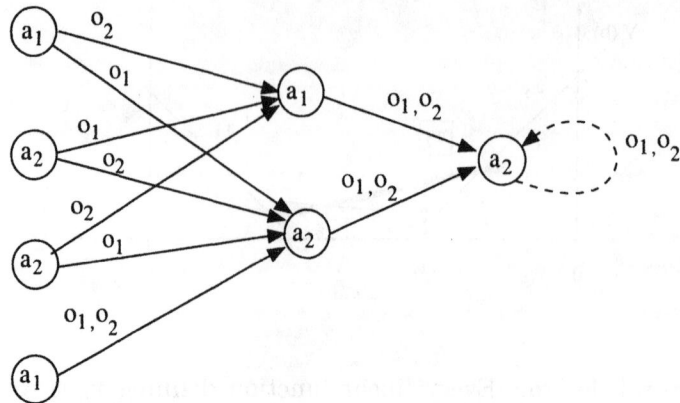

Figure 7: A policy graph (finite-state machine) obtained after two value iteration steps. Nodes correspond to linear functions (or states of the finite-state machine) and links to dependencies between linear functions (transitions between states). Every linear function (node) is associated with an action. To ensure that the policy can be also applied to the infinite-horizon problem, we add a cycle to the last state (dashed line).

$$Q_i(b,a) = R(b,a) + \gamma \sum_{o \in \Theta} P(o|b,a) V_{i-1}(\tau(b,a,o)).$$

From this perspective, the direct strategy selects the action with the best (maximum) Q-function for a given belief state.[7]

2.5.3 FINITE-STATE MACHINE DESIGN

A more complex refinement of the above technique is to remember, for every linear function in V_i, not only the action choice but also the choice of a linear function for the previous step and to do this for all observations (see Equation 7). As the same idea can be applied recursively to the linear functions for all previous steps, we can obtain a relatively complex dependency structure relating linear functions in $V_i, V_{i-1}, \cdots V_0$, observations and actions that itself represents a control strategy (Kaelbling et al., 1999).

To see this, we model the structure in graphical terms (Figure 7). Here different nodes represent linear functions, actions associated with nodes correspond to optimizing actions, links emanating from nodes correspond to different observations, and successor nodes correspond to linear functions paired with observations. Such graphs are also called *policy graphs* (Kaelbling et al., 1999; Littman, 1996; Cassandra, 1998). One interpretation of the dependency structure is that it represents a collection of finite-state machines (FSMs) with many possible initial states that implement a POMDP controller: nodes correspond to states of the controller, actions to controls (outputs), and links to transitions conditioned on inputs

---

7. Williams and Baird (1994) also give results relating the accuracy of the direct Q-function controller to the Bellman error of Q-functions.

(observations). The start state of the FSM controller is chosen greedily by selecting the linear function (controller state) optimizing the value of an initial belief state.

The advantage of the finite-state machine representation of the strategy is that for the first i steps it works with observations directly; belief-state updates are not needed. This contrasts with the other two policy models (lookahead and direct models), which must keep track of the current belief state and update it over time in order to extract appropriate control. The drawback of the approach is that the FSM controller is limited to i steps that correspond to the number of value iteration steps performed. However, in the infinite-horizon model the controller is expected to run for an infinite number of steps. One way to remedy this deficiency is to extend the FSM structure and to create cycles that let us visit controller states repeatedly. For example, adding a cycle transition to the end state of the FSM controller in Figure 7 (dashed line) ensures that the controller is also applicable to the infinite-horizon problem.

2.6 Policy Iteration

An alternative method for finding the solution for the discounted infinite-horizon problem is *policy iteration* (Howard, 1960; Sondik, 1978). Policy iteration searches the policy space and gradually improves the current control policy for one or more belief states. The method consists of two steps performed iteratively:

- *policy evaluation*: computes expected value for the current policy;

- *policy improvement*: improves the current policy.

As we saw in Section 2.5, there are many ways to represent a control policy for a POMDP. Here we restrict attention to a finite-state machine model in which observations correspond to inputs and actions to outputs (Platzman, 1980; Hansen, 1998b; Kaelbling et al., 1999).[8]

2.6.1 FINITE-STATE MACHINE CONTROLLER

A finite-state machine (FSM) controller $C = (M, \Theta, A, \phi, \eta, \psi)$ for a POMDP is described by a set of memory states M of the controller, a set of observations (inputs) Θ, a set of actions (outputs) A, a transition function $\phi : M \times \Theta \to M$ mapping states of the FSM to next memory states given the observation, and an output function $\eta : M \to A$ mapping memory states to actions. A function $\psi : \mathcal{I}_0 \to M$ selects the initial memory state given the initial information state. The initial information state corresponds either to a prior or a posterior belief state at time t_0 depending on the availability of an initial observation.

2.6.2 POLICY EVALUATION

The first step of the policy iteration is policy evaluation. The most important property of the FSM model is that the value function for a specific FSM strategy can be computed efficiently in the number of controller states M. The key to efficient computability is the

---

8. A policy-iteration algorithm in which policies are defined over the regions of the belief space was described first by Sondik (1978).

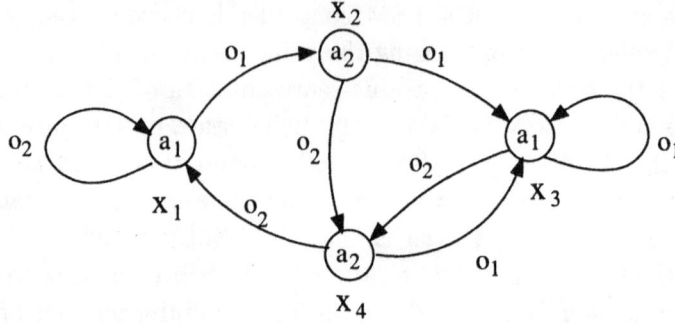

Figure 8: An example of a four-state FSM policy. Nodes represent states, links transitions between states (conditioned on observations). Every memory state has an associated control action (output).

fact that the value function for executing an FSM strategy from some memory state x is linear (Platzman, 1980).[9]

Theorem 5 *Let C be a finite-state machine controller with a set of memory states M. The value function for applying C from a memory state $x \in M$, $V^C(x, b)$, is linear. Value functions for all $x \in M$ can be found by solving a system of linear equations with $|S||M|$ variables.*

We illustrate the main idea by an example. Assume an FSM controller with four memory states $\{x_1, x_2, x_3, x_4\}$, as in Figure 8, and a stochastic process with two hidden states $S = \{s_1, s_2\}$. The value of the policy for an augmented state space $S \times M$ satisfies a system of linear equations

$$V(x_1, s_1) = \rho(s_1, \eta(x_1)) + \gamma \sum_{o \in \Theta} \sum_{s \in S} P(o, s|s_1, \eta(x_1))V(\phi(x_1, o), s)$$

$$V(x_1, s_2) = \rho(s_2, \eta(x_1)) + \gamma \sum_{o \in \Theta} \sum_{s \in S} P(o, s|s_2, \eta(x_1))V(\phi(x_1, o), s)$$

$$V(x_2, s_1) = \rho(s_1, \eta(x_2)) + \gamma \sum_{o \in \Theta} \sum_{s \in S} P(o, s|s_1, \eta(x_2))V(\phi(x_2, o), s)$$

$$\cdots$$

$$V(x_4, s_2) = \rho(s_2, \eta(x_4)) + \gamma \sum_{o \in \Theta} \sum_{s \in S} P(o, s|s_2, \eta(x_4))V(\phi(x_4, o), s),$$

where $\eta(x)$ is the action executed in x and $\phi(x, o)$ is the state to which one transits after seeing an input (observation) o. Assuming we start the policy from the memory state x_1, the value of the policy is:

$$V^C(x_1, b) = \sum_{s \in S} V(x_1, s)b(s).$$

---

9. The idea of linearity and efficient computability of the value functions for a fixed FSM-based strategy has been addressed recently in different contexts by a number of researchers (Littman, 1996; Cassandra, 1998; Hauskrecht, 1997; Hansen, 1998b; Kaelbling et al., 1999). However, the origins of the idea can be traced to the earlier work by Platzman (1980).

Thus the value function is linear and can be computed efficiently by solving a system of linear equations.

Since in general the FSM controller can start from any memory state, we can always choose the initial memory state greedily, maximizing the expected value of the result. In such a case the optimal choice function ψ is defined as:

$$\psi(b) = \arg \max_{x \in M} V^C(x, b),$$

and the value for the FSM policy C and belief state b is:

$$V^C(b) = \max_{x \in M} V^C(x, b) = V^C(\psi(b), b).$$

Note that the resulting value function for the strategy C is piecewise linear and convex and represents expected rewards for following C. Since no strategy can perform better that the optimal strategy, $V^C \leq V^*$ must hold.

2.6.3 POLICY IMPROVEMENT

The policy-iteration method, searching the space of controllers, starts from an arbitrary initial policy and improves it gradually by refining its finite-state machine (FSM) description. In particular, one keeps modifying the structure of the controller by adding or removing controller states (memory) and transitions. Let C and C' be an old and a new FSM controller. In the improvement step we must satisfy

$$V^{C'}(b) \geq V^C(b) \text{ for all } b \in \mathcal{I};$$

$$\exists b \in \mathcal{I} \text{ such that } V^{C'}(b) > V^C(b).$$

To guarantee the improvement, Hansen (1998a, 1998b) proposed a policy-iteration algorithm that relies on exact value function updates to obtain a new improved policy structure.[10] The basic idea of the improvement is based on the observation that one can switch back and forth between the FSM policy description and the piecewise-linear and convex representation of a value function. In particular:

- the value function for an FSM policy is piecewise-linear and convex and every linear function describing it corresponds to a memory state of a controller;

- individual linear functions comprising the new value function after an update can be viewed as new memory states of an FSM policy, as described in Section 2.5.3.

This allows us to improve the policy by adding new memory states corresponding to linear functions of the new value function obtained after the exact update. The technique can be refined by removing some of the linear functions (memory states) whenever they are fully dominated by one of the other linear functions.

---

10. A policy-iteration algorithm that exploits exact value function updates but works with policies defined over the belief space was used earlier by Sondik (1978).

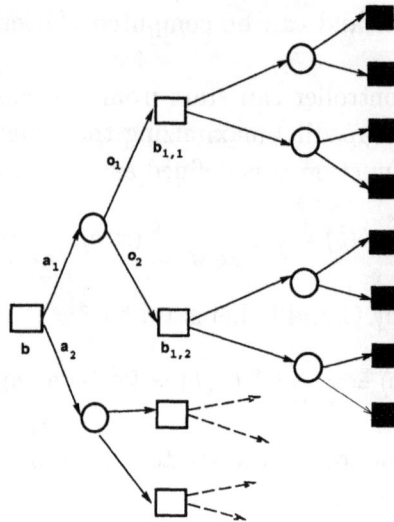

Figure 9: A two-step decision tree. Rectangles correspond to the decision nodes (moves of the decision-maker) and circles to chance nodes (moves of the environment). Black rectangles represent leaves of the tree. The reward for a specific path is associated with every leaf of the tree. Decision nodes are associated with information states obtained by following action and observation choices along the path from the root of the tree. For example, $b_{1,1}$ is a belief state obtained by performing action a_1 from the initial belief state b and observing observation o_1.

2.7 Forward (Decision Tree) Methods

The methods discussed so far assume no prior knowledge of the initial belief state and treat all belief states as equally likely. However, if the initial state is known and fixed, methods can often be modified to take advantage of this fact. For example, for the finite-horizon problem, only a finite number of belief states can be reached from a given initial state. In this case it is very often easier to enumerate all possible histories (sequences of actions and observations) and represent the problem using stochastic decision trees (Raiffa, 1970). An example of a two-step decision tree is shown in Figure 9.

The algorithm for solving the stochastic decision tree basically mimics value-function updates, but is restricted only to situations that can be reached from the initial belief state. The key difficulty here is that the number of all possible trajectories grows exponentially with the horizon of interest.

2.7.1 COMBINING DYNAMIC-PROGRAMMING AND DECISION-TREE TECHNIQUES

To solve a POMDP for a fixed initial belief state, we can apply two strategies: one constructs the decision tree first and then solves it, the other solves the problem in a backward fashion via dynamic programming. Unfortunately, both these techniques are inefficient, one suffering from exponential growth in the decision tree size, the other from super-exponential growth in the value function complexity. However, the two techniques can be combined in a way that at least partially eliminates their disadvantages. The idea is based on the fact that the two techniques work on the solution from two different sides (one forward and the other backward) and the complexity for each of them worsens gradually. Then the solution is to compute the complete kth value function using dynamic programming (value iteration) and cover the remaining steps by forward decision-tree expansion.

Various modifications of the above idea are possible. For example, one can often replace exact dynamic programming with two more efficient approximations providing upper and lower bounds of the value function. Then the decision tree must be expanded only when the bounds are not sufficient to determine the optimal action choice. A number of search techniques developed in the AI literature (Korf, 1985) combined with branch-and-bound pruning (Satia & Lave, 1973) can be applied to this type of problem. Several researchers have experimented with them to solve POMDPs (Washington, 1996; Hauskrecht, 1997; Hansen, 1998b). Other methods applicable to this problem are based on Monte-Carlo sampling (Kearns, Mansour, & Ng, 1999; McAllester & Singh, 1999) and real-time dynamic programming (Barto, Bradtke, & Singh, 1995; Dearden & Boutilier, 1997; Bonet & Geffner, 1998).

2.7.2 CLASSICAL PLANNING FRAMEWORK

POMDP problems with fixed initial belief states and their solutions are closely related to work in classical planning and its extensions to handle stochastic and partially observable domains, particularly the work on BURIDAN and C-BURIDAN planners (Kushmerick, Hanks, & Weld, 1995; Draper, Hanks, & Weld, 1994). The objective of these planners is to maximize the probability of reaching some goal state. However, this task is similar to the discounted reward task in terms of complexity, since a discounted reward model can be converted into a goal-achievement model by introducing an absorbing state (Condon, 1992).

3. Heuristic Approximations

The key obstacle to wider application of the POMDP framework is the computational complexity of POMDP problems. In particular, finding the optimal solution for the finite-horizon case is PSPACE-hard (Papadimitriou & Tsitsiklis, 1987) and the discounted infinite-horizon case may not even be computable (Madani et al., 1999). One approach to such problems is to approximate the solution to some ϵ-precision. Unfortunately, even this remains intractable and in general POMDPs cannot be approximated efficiently (Burago, Rougemont, & Slissenko, 1996; Lusena, Goldsmith, & Mundhenk, 1998; Madani et al., 1999). This is also the reason why only very simple problems can be solved optimally or near-optimally in practice.

To alleviate the complexity problem, research in the POMDP area has focused on various heuristic methods (or approximations without the error parameter) that are more efficient.[11] Heuristic methods are also our focus here. Thus, when referring to approximations, we mean heuristics, unless specifically stated otherwise.

---

11. The quality of a heuristic approximation can be tested using the Bellman error, which requires one exact update step. However, heuristic methods per se do not contain a precision parameter.

The many approximation methods and their combinations can be divided into two often very closely related classes: *value-function approximations* and *policy approximations*.

3.1 Value-Function Approximations

The main idea of the value-function approximation approach is to approximate the optimal value function $V : \mathcal{I} \rightarrow I\!R$ with a function $\widehat{V} : \mathcal{I} \rightarrow I\!R$ defined over the same information space. Typically, the new function is of lower complexity (recall that the optimal or near-optimal value function may consist of a large set of linear functions) and is easier to compute than the exact solution. Approximations can be often formulated as dynamic programming problems and can be expressed in terms of approximate value-function updates $\widehat{H}$. Thus, to understand the differences and advantages of various approximations and exact methods, it is often sufficient to analyze and compare their update rules.

3.1.1 VALUE-FUNCTION BOUNDS

Although heuristic approximations have no guaranteed precision, in many cases we are able to say whether they overestimate or underestimate the optimal value function. The information on bounds can be used in multiple ways. For example, upper- and lower-bounds can help in narrowing the range of the optimal value function, elimination of some of the suboptimal actions and subsequent speed-ups of exact methods. Alternatively, one can use knowledge of both value-function bounds to determine the accuracy of a controller generated based on one of the bounds (see Section 3.1.3). Also, in some instances, a lower bound alone is sufficient to guarantee the control choice that always achieves an expected reward at least as high as the one given by that bound (Section 4.7.2).

The bound property of different methods can be determined by examining the updates and their bound relations.

Definition 5 *(Upper bound). Let H be the exact value-function mapping and $\widehat{H}$ its approximation. We say that $\widehat{H}$ upper-bounds H for some V when $(\widehat{H}V)(b) \geq (HV)(b)$ holds for every $b \in \mathcal{I}$.*

An analogous definition can be constructed for the lower bound.

3.1.2 CONVERGENCE OF APPROXIMATE VALUE ITERATION

Let $\widehat{H}$ be a value-function mapping representing an approximate update. Then the approximate value iteration computes the ith value function as $\widehat{V}_i = \widehat{H}\widehat{V}_{i-1}$. The fixed-point solution $\widehat{V}^* = \widehat{H}\widehat{V}^*$ or its close approximation would then represent the intended output of the approximation routine. The main problem with the iteration method is that in general it can converge to unique or multiple solutions, diverge, or oscillate, depending on $\widehat{H}$ and the initial function $\widehat{V}_0$. Therefore, unique convergence cannot be guaranteed for an arbitrary mapping $\widehat{H}$ and the convergence of a specific approximation method must be proved.

Definition 6 *(Convergence of $\widehat{H}$). The value iteration with $\widehat{H}$ converges for a value function V_0 when $\lim_{n \rightarrow \infty}(\widehat{H}^n V_0)$ exists.*

Definition 7 *(Unique convergence of $\widehat{H}$).* *The value iteration converges uniquely for $\mathcal{V}$ when for every $V \in \mathcal{V}$, $\lim_{n \to \infty}(\widehat{H}^n V)$ exists and for all pairs $V, U \in \mathcal{V}$, $\lim_{n \to \infty}(\widehat{H}^n V) = \lim_{n \to \infty}(\widehat{H}^n U)$.*

A sufficient condition for the unique convergence is to show that $\widehat{H}$ be a contraction. The contraction and the bound properties of $\widehat{H}$ can be combined, under additional conditions, to show the convergence of the iterative approximation method to the bound. To address this issue we present a theorem comparing fixed-point solutions of two value-function mappings.

Theorem 6 *Let H_1 and H_2 be two value-function mappings defined on $\mathcal{V}_1$ and $\mathcal{V}_2$ such that*

1. *H_1, H_2 are contractions with fixed points V_1^*, V_2^*;*

2. *$V_1^* \in \mathcal{V}_2$ and $H_2 V_1^* \geq H_1 V_1^* = V_1^*$;*

3. *H_2 is an isotone mapping.*

Then $V_2^* \geq V_1^*$ holds.

Note that this theorem does not require that $\mathcal{V}_1$ and $\mathcal{V}_2$ cover the same space of value functions. For example, $\mathcal{V}_2$ can cover all possible value functions of a belief-state MDP, while $\mathcal{V}_1$ can be restricted to a space of piecewise linear and convex value functions. This gives us some flexibility in the design of iterative approximation algorithms for computing value-function bounds. An analogous theorem also holds for the lower bound.

3.1.3 CONTROL

Once the approximation of the value-function is available, it can be used to generate a control strategy. In general, control solutions correspond to options presented in Section 2.5 and include lookahead, direct (Q-function) and finite-state machine designs.

A drawback of control strategies based on heuristic approximations is that they have no precision guarantee. One way to find the accuracy of such strategies is to do one exact update of the value function approximation and adopt the result of Theorems 1 and 3 for the Bellman error. An alternative solution to this problem is to bound the accuracy of such controllers using the upper- and the lower-bound approximations of the optimal value function. To illustrate this approach, we present and prove (in the Appendix) the following theorem that relates the quality of bounds to the quality of a lookahead controller.

Theorem 7 *Let $\widehat{V}_U$ and $\widehat{V}_L$ be upper and lower bounds of the optimal value function for the discounted infinite-horizon problem. Let $\epsilon = \sup_b |\widehat{V}_U(b) - \widehat{V}_L(b)| = \|\widehat{V}_U - \widehat{V}_L\|$ be the maximum bound difference. Then the expected reward for a lookahead controller $\widehat{V}^{LA}$, constructed for either $\widehat{V}_U$ or $\widehat{V}_L$, satisfies $\|\widehat{V}^{LA} - V^*\| \leq \frac{\epsilon(2-\gamma)}{(1-\gamma)}$.*

3.2 Policy Approximation

An alternative to value-function approximation is policy approximation. As shown earlier, a strategy (controller) for a POMDP can be represented using a finite-state machine (FSM) model. The policy iteration searches the space of all possible policies (FSMs) for the optimal or near-optimal solution. This space is usually enormous, which is the bottleneck of the method. Thus, instead of searching the complete policy space, we can restrict our attention only to its subspace that we believe to contain the optimal solution or a good approximation. Memoryless policies (Platzman, 1977; White & Scherer, 1994; Littman, 1994; Singh, Jaakkola, & Jordan, 1994), policies based on truncated histories (Platzman, 1977; White & Scherer, 1994; McCallum, 1995), or finite-state controllers with a fixed number of memory states (Platzman, 1980; Hauskrecht, 1997; Hansen, 1998a, 1998b) are all examples of a policy-space restriction. In the following we consider only the finite-state machine model (see Section 2.6.1), which is quite general; other models can be viewed as its special cases.

States of an FSM policy model represent the memory of the controller and, in general, summarize information about past activities and observations. Thus, they are best viewed as approximations of the information states, or as *feature states*. The transition model of the controller (ϕ) then approximates the update function of the information-state MDP (τ) and the output function of an FSM (η) approximates the control function (μ) mapping information states to actions. The important property of the model, as shown Section 2.6.2, is that the value function for a fixed controller and fixed initial memory state can be obtained efficiently by solving a system of linear equations (Platzman, 1980).

To apply the policy approximation approach we first need to decide (1) how to restrict a space of policies and (2) how to judge the policy quality.

A restriction frequently used is to consider only controllers with a fixed number of states, say k. Other structural restrictions further narrowing the space of policies can restrict either the output function (choice of actions at different controller states), or the transitions between the current and next states. In general, any heuristic or domain-related insight may help in selecting the right biases.

Two different policies can yield value functions that are better in different regions of the belief space. Thus, in order to decide which policy is the best, we need to define the importance of different regions and their combinations. There are multiple solutions to this. For example, Platzman (1980) considers the worst-case measure and optimizes the worst (minimal) value for all initial belief states. Let $\mathcal{C}$ be a space of FSM controllers satisfying given restrictions. Then the quality of a policy under the worst case measure is:

$$\max_{C \in \mathcal{C}} \min_{b \in \mathcal{I}} \max_{x \in M_C} V^C(x, b).$$

Another option is to consider a distribution over all initial belief states and maximize the expectation of their value function values. However, the most common objective is to choose the policy that leads to the best value for a single initial belief state b_0:

$$\max_{C \in \mathcal{C}} \max_{x \in M_C} V^C(x, b_0).$$

Finding the optimal policy for this case reduces to a combinatorial optimization problem. Unfortunately, for all but trivial cases, even this problem is computationally intractable. For example, the problem of finding the optimal policy for a memoryless case (only current observations are considered) is NP-hard (Littman, 1994). Thus, various heuristics are typically applied to alleviate this difficulty (Littman, 1994).

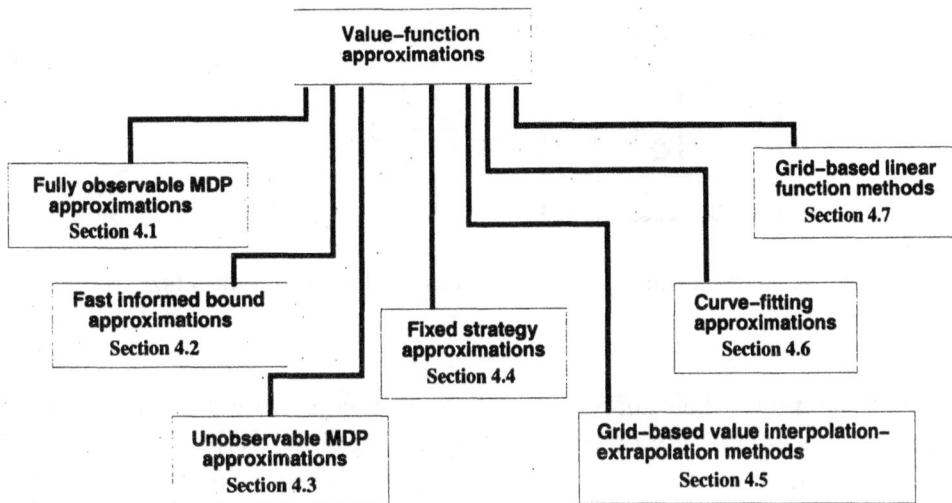

Figure 10: Value-function approximation methods.

3.2.1 RANDOMIZED POLICIES

By restricting the space of policies we simplify the policy optimization problem. On the other hand, we simultaneously give up an opportunity to find the best optimal policy, replacing it with the best restricted policy. Up to this point, we have considered only deterministic policies with a fixed number of internal controller states, that is, policies with deterministic output and transition functions. However, finding the best deterministic policy is not always the best option: *randomized policies*, with randomized output and transition functions, usually lead to the far better performance. The application of randomized (or stochastic) policies to POMDPs was introduced by Platzman (1980). Essentially, any deterministic policy can be represented as a randomized policy with a single action and transition, so that the best randomized policy is no worse than the best deterministic policy. The difference in control performance of two policies shows up most often in cases when the number of states of the controller is relatively small compared to that in the optimal strategy.

The advantage of stochastic policies is that their space is larger and parameters of the policy are continuous. Therefore the problem of finding the optimal stochastic policy becomes a non-linear optimization problem and a variety of optimization methods can be applied to solve it. An example is the gradient-based approach (see Meuleau et al., 1999).

4. Value-Function Approximation Methods

In this section we discuss in more depth value-function approximation methods. We focus on approximations with belief information space.[12] We survey known techniques, but also include a number of new methods and modifications of existing methods. Figure 10 summarizes the methods covered. We describe the methods by means of update rules they

---

12. Alternative value-function approximations may work with complete histories of past actions and observations. Approximation methods used by White and Scherer (1994) are an example.

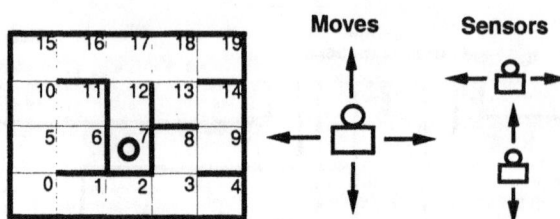

Figure 11: Test example. The maze navigation problem: Maze20.

implement, which simplifies their analysis and theoretical comparison. We focus on the following properties: the complexity of the dynamic-programming (value-iteration) updates; the complexity of value functions each method uses; the ability of methods to bound the exact update; the convergence of value iteration with approximate update rules; and the control performance of related controllers. The results of the theoretical analysis are illustrated empirically on a problem from the agent-navigation domain. In addition, we use the agent navigation problem to illustrate and give some intuitions on other characteristics of methods with no theoretical underpinning. Thus, these results should not be generalized to other problems or used to rank different methods.

AGENT-NAVIGATION PROBLEM

Maze20 is a maze-navigation problem with 20 states, six actions and eight observations. The maze (Figure 11) consists of 20 partially connected rooms (states) in which a robot operates and collects rewards. The robot can move in four directions (north, south, east and west) and can check for the presence of walls using its sensors. But, neither "move" actions nor sensor inputs are perfect, so that the robot can end up moving in unintended directions. The robot moves in an unintended direction with probability of 0.3 (0.15 for each of the neighboring directions). A move into the wall keeps the robot in the same position. Investigative actions help the robot to navigate by activating sensor inputs. Two such investigative actions allow the robot to check inputs (presence of a wall) in the north-south and east-west directions. Sensor accuracy in detecting walls is 0.75 for a two-wall case (e.g. both north and south wall), 0.8 for a one-wall case (north or south) and 0.89 for a no-wall case, with smaller probabilities for wrong perceptions.

The control objective is to maximize the expected discounted rewards with a discount factor of 0.9. A small reward is given for every action not leading to bumping into the wall (4 points for a move and 2 points for an investigative action), and one large reward (150 points) is given for achieving the special target room (indicated by the circle in the figure) and recognizing it by performing one of the move actions. After doing that and collecting the reward, the robot is placed at random in a new start position.

Although the Maze20 problem is of only moderate complexity with regard to the size of state, action and observation spaces, its exact solution is beyond the reach of current exact methods. The exact methods tried on the problem include the Witness algorithm (Kaelbling et al., 1999), the incremental pruning algorithm (Cassandra et al., 1997)[13] and

---

13. Many thanks to Anthony Cassandra for running these algorithms.

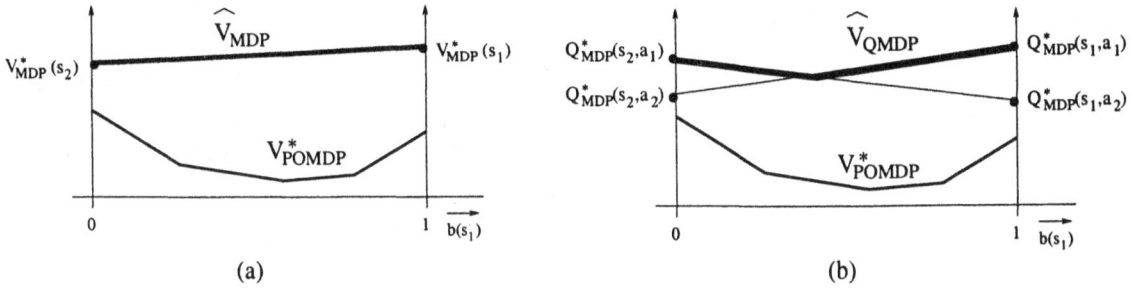

Figure 12: Approximations based on the fully observable version of a two state POMDP (with states s_1, s_2): (a) the MDP approximation; (b) the QMDP approximation. Values at extreme points of the belief space are solutions of the fully observable MDP.

policy iteration with an FSM model (Hansen, 1998b). The main obstacle preventing these algorithms from obtaining the optimal or close-to-optimal solution was the complexity of the value function (the number of linear functions needed to describe it) and subsequent running times and memory problems.

4.1 Approximations with Fully Observable MDP

Perhaps the simplest way to approximate the value function for a POMDP is to assume that states of the process are fully observable (Astrom, 1965; Lovejoy, 1993). In that case the optimal value function V^* for a POMDP can be approximated as:

$$\widehat{V}(b) = \sum_{s \in S} b(s) V^*_{MDP}(s), \tag{8}$$

where $V^*_{MDP}(s)$ is the optimal value function for state s for the fully observable version of the process. We refer to this approximation as to the *MDP approximation*. The idea of the approximation is illustrated in Figure 12a. The resulting value function is linear and is fully defined by values at extreme points of the belief simplex. These correspond to the optimal values for the fully observable case. The main advantage of the approximation is that the fully observable MDP (FOMDP) can be solved efficiently for both the finite-horizon problem and discounted infinite-horizon problems.[14] The update step for the (fully observable) MDP is:

$$V^{MDP}_{i+1}(s) = \max_a \left\{ \rho(s, a) + \gamma \sum_{s' \in S} P(s'|s, a) V^{MDP}_i(s') \right\}.$$

---

14. The solution for the finite-state fully observable MDP and discounted infinite-horizon criterion can be found efficiently by formulating an equivalent linear programming task (Bertsekas, 1995)

4.1.1 MDP Approximation

The MDP-approximation approach (Equation 8) can be also described in terms of value-function updates for the belief-space MDP. Although this step is strictly speaking redundant here, it simplifies the analysis and comparison of this approach to other approximations.

Let $\widehat{V}_i$ be a linear value function described by a vector α_i^{MDP} corresponding to values of $V_i^{MDP}(s')$ for all states $s' \in S$. Then the $(i+1)$th value function $\widehat{V}_{i+1}$ is

$$\widehat{V}_{i+1}(b) = \sum_{s \in S} b(s) \max_{a \in A} \left[\rho(s,a) + \gamma \sum_{s' \in S} P(s'|s,a)\alpha_i^{MDP}(s') \right]$$

$$= (H_{MDP}\widehat{V}_i)(b).$$

$\widehat{V}_{i+1}$ is described by a linear function with components

$$\alpha_{i+1}^{MDP}(s) = V_{i+1}^{MDP}(s) = \max_a \left\{ \rho(s,a) + \gamma \sum_{s \in S} P(s'|s,a)\alpha_i^{MDP}(s') \right\}.$$

The MDP-based rule H_{MDP} can be also rewritten in a more general form that starts from an arbitrary piecewise linear and convex value function V_i, represented by a set of linear functions Γ_i:

$$\widehat{V}_{i+1}(b) = \sum_{s \in S} b(s) \max_{a \in A} \left\{ \rho(s,a) + \gamma \sum_{s' \in S} P(s'|s,a) \max_{\alpha_i \in \Gamma_i} \alpha_i(s') \right\}.$$

The application of the H_{MDP} mapping always leads to a linear value function. The update is easy to compute and takes $O(|A||S|^2 + |\Gamma_i||S|)$ time. This reduces to $O(|A||S|^2)$ time when only MDP-based updates are strung together. As remarked earlier, the optimal solution for the infinite-horizon, discounted problem can be solved efficiently via linear programming.

The update for the MDP approximation upper-bounds the exact update, that is, $H\widehat{V}_i \leq H_{MDP}\widehat{V}_i$. We show this property later in Theorem 9, which covers more cases. The intuition is that we cannot get a better solution with less information, and thus the fully observable MDP must upper-bound the partially observable case.

4.1.2 Approximation with Q-Functions (QMDP)

A variant of the approximation based on the fully observable MDP uses Q-functions (Littman, Cassandra, & Kaelbling, 1995):

$$\widehat{V}(b) = \max_{a \in A} \sum_{s \in S} b(s) Q_{MDP}^*(s,a),$$

where

$$Q_{MDP}^*(s,a) = \rho(s,a) + \gamma \sum_{s' \in S} P(s'|s,a) V_{MDP}^*(s')$$

is the optimal action-value function (Q-function) for the fully observable MDP. The QMDP approximation $\widehat{V}$ is piecewise linear and convex with $|A|$ linear functions, each corresponding to one action (Figure 12b). The QMDP update rule (for the belief state MDP) for $\widehat{V}_i$ with linear functions $\alpha_i^k \in \Gamma_i$ is:

$$\widehat{V}_{i+1}(b) = \max_{a \in A} \sum_{s \in S} b(s) \left[\rho(s, a) + \gamma \sum_{s' \in S} P(s'|s, a) \max_{\alpha_i \in \Gamma_i} \alpha_i(s') \right]$$

$$= (H_{QMDP} \widehat{V}_i)(b).$$

H_{QMDP} generates a value function with $|A|$ linear functions. The time complexity of the update is the same as for the MDP-approximation case – $O(|A||S|^2 + |\Gamma_i||S|)$, which reduces to $O(|A||S|^2)$ time when only QMDP updates are used. H_{QMDP} is a contraction mapping and its fixed-point solution can be found by solving the corresponding fully observable MDP.

The QMDP update upper-bounds the exact update. The bound is tighter than the MDP update; that is, $H\widehat{V}_i \leq H_{QMDP}\widehat{V}_i \leq H_{MDP}\widehat{V}_i$, as we prove later in Theorem 9. The same inequalities hold for both fixed-point solutions (through Theorem 6).

To illustrate the difference in the quality of bounds for the MDP approximation and the QMDP method, we use our Maze20 navigation problem. To measure the quality of a bound we use the mean of value-function values. Since all belief states are equally important we assume that they are uniformly distributed. We approximate this measure using the average of values for a fixed set of $N = 2000$ belief points. The points in the set were selected uniformly at random at the beginning. Once the set was chosen, it was fixed and remained the same for all tests (here and later). Figure 13 shows the results of the experiment; we include also results for the fast informed bound method that is presented in the next section.[15] Figure 13 also shows the running times of the methods. The methods were implemented in Common Lisp and run on Sun Ultra 1 workstation.

4.1.3 CONTROL

The MDP and the QMDP value-function approximations can be used to construct controllers based on one-step lookahead. In addition, the QMDP approximation is also suitable for the direct control strategy, which selects an action corresponding to the best (highest value) Q-function. Thus, the method is a special case of the Q-function approach discussed in Section 3.1.3.[16] The advantage of the direct QMDP method is that it is faster than both lookahead designs. On other the hand, lookahead tends to improve the control performance. This is shown in Figure 14, which compares the control performance of different controllers on the Maze20 problem.

The quality of a policy $\widehat{\pi}$, with no preference towards a particular initial belief state, can be measured by the mean of value-function values for $\widehat{\pi}$ and uniformly distributed initial belief states. We approximate this measure using the average of discounted rewards for

---

15. The confidence interval limits for probability level 0.95 range in $\pm(0.45, 0.62)$ from their respective average scores and this holds for all bound experiments in the paper. As these are relatively small we do not include them in our graphs.

16. As pointed out by Littman et al. (1995), in some instances, the direct QMDP controller never selects investigative actions, that is, actions that try to gain more information about the underlying process state. Note, however, that this observation is not true in general and the QMDP-based controller with direct action selection may select investigative actions, even though in the fully observable version of the problem investigative actions are never chosen.

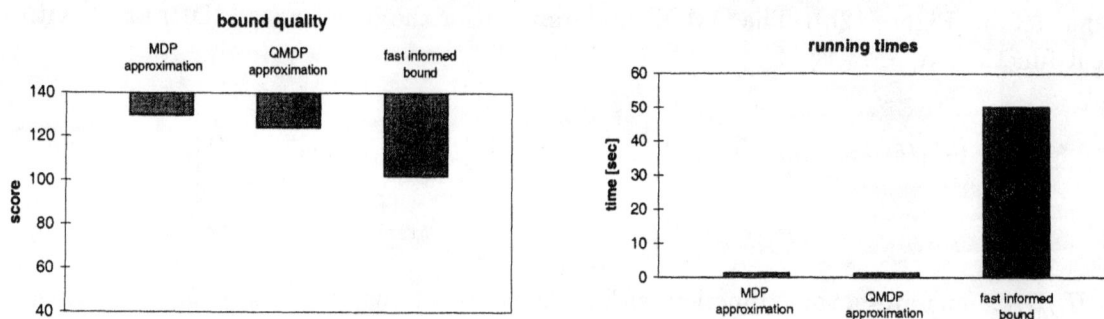

Figure 13: Comparison of the MDP, QMDP and fast informed bound approximations: bound quality (left); running times (right). The bound-quality score is the average value of the approximation for the set of 2000 belief points (chosen uniformly at random). As the methods upper-bound the optimal value function, we flip the bound-quality graph so that longer bars indicate better approximations.

2000 control trajectories obtained for the fixed set of $N = 2000$ initial belief states (selected uniformly at random at the beginning). The trajectories were obtained through simulation and were 60 steps long.[17]

To validate the comparison along the averaged performance scores, we must show that these scores are not the result of randomness and that methods are indeed statistically significantly different. To do this we rely on pairwise significance tests.[18] To summarize the obtained results, the score differences of 1.54, 2.09 and 2.86 between any two methods (here and also later in the paper) are sufficient to reject the method with a lower score being the better performer at significance levels 0.05, 0.01 and 0.001 respectively.[19] Error-bars in Figure 14 reflect the critical score difference for the significance level 0.05.

Figure 14 also shows the average reaction times for different controllers during these experiments. The results show the clear dominance of the direct QMDP controller, which need not do a lookahead in order to extract an action, compared to the other two MDP-based controllers.

4.2 Fast Informed Bound Method

Both the MDP and the QMDP approaches ignore partial observability and use the fully observable MDP as a surrogate. To improve these approximations and account (at least to

---

17. The length of the trajectories (60 steps) for the Maze20 problem was chosen to ensure that our estimates of (discounted) cumulative rewards are not far from the actual rewards for an infinite number of steps.

18. An alternative way to compare two methods is to compute confidence limits for their scores and inspect their overlaps. However, in this case, the ability to distinguish two methods can be reduced due to fluctuations of scores for different initializations. For Maze20, confidence interval limits for probability level 0.95 range in $\pm(1.8, 2.3)$ from their respective average scores. This covers all control experiments here and later. Pairwise tests eliminate the dependency by examining the differences of individual values and thus improve the discriminative power.

19. The critical score differences listed cover the worst case combination. Thus, there may be some pairs for which the smaller difference would suffice.

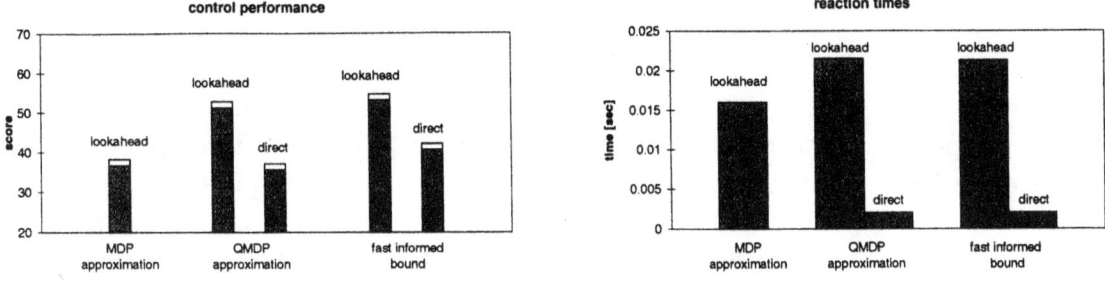

Figure 14: Comparison of control performance of the MDP, QMDP and fast informed bound methods: quality of control (left); reaction times (right). The quality-of-control score is the average of discounted rewards for 2000 control trajectories obtained for the fixed set of 2000 initial belief states (selected uniformly at random). Error-bars show the critical score difference value (1.54) at which any two methods become statistically different at significance level 0.05.

some degree) for partial observability we propose a new method – *the fast informed bound method*. Let $\widehat{V}_i$ be a piecewise linear and convex value function represented by a set of linear functions Γ_i. The new update is defined as

$$
\begin{aligned}
\widehat{V}_{i+1}(b) &= \max_{a \in A} \left\{ \sum_{s \in S} \rho(s,a)b(s) + \gamma \sum_{o \in \Theta} \sum_{s \in S} \max_{\alpha_i \in \Gamma_i} \sum_{s' \in S} P(s',o|s,a)b(s)\alpha_i(s') \right\} \\
&= \max_{a \in A} \left\{ \sum_{s \in S} b(s) \left[\rho(s,a) + \gamma \sum_{o \in \Theta} \max_{\alpha_i \in \Gamma_i} \sum_{s' \in S} P(s',o|s,a)\alpha_i(s') \right] \right\} \\
&= (H_{FIB}\widehat{V}_i)(b).
\end{aligned}
$$

The fast informed bound update can be obtained from the exact update by the following derivation:

$$
\begin{aligned}
(H\widehat{V}_i)(b) &= \max_{a \in A} \left\{ \sum_{s \in S} \rho(s,a)b(s) + \gamma \sum_{o \in \Theta} \max_{\alpha_i \in \Gamma_i} \sum_{s' \in S} \sum_{s \in S} P(s',o|s,a)b(s)\alpha_i(s') \right\} \\
&\leq \max_{a \in A} \left\{ \sum_{s \in S} \rho(s,a)b(s) + \gamma \sum_{o \in \Theta} \sum_{s \in S} \max_{\alpha_i \in \Gamma_i} \sum_{s' \in S} P(s',o|s,a)b(s)\alpha_i(s') \right\} \\
&= \max_{a \in A} \sum_{s \in S} b(s) \left[\rho(s,a) + \gamma \sum_{o \in \Theta} \max_{\alpha_i \in \Gamma_i} \sum_{s' \in S} P(s',o|s,a)\alpha_i(s') \right] \\
&= \max_{a \in A} \sum_{s \in S} b(s)\alpha_{i+1}^a(s) \\
&= (H_{FIB}\widehat{V}_i)(b).
\end{aligned}
$$

The value function $\widehat{V}_{i+1} = H_{FIB}\widehat{V}_i$ one obtains after an update is piecewise linear and convex and consists of at most $|A|$ different linear functions, each corresponding to one action

$$\alpha_{i+1}^a(s) = \rho(s,a) + \gamma \sum_{o \in \Theta} \max_{\alpha_i \in \Gamma_i} \sum_{s' \in S} P(s',o|s,a)\alpha_i(s').$$

The H_{FIB} update is efficient and can be computed in $O(|A||S|^2|\Theta||\Gamma_i|)$ time. As the method always outputs $|A|$ linear functions, the computation can be done in $O(|A|^2|S|^2|\Theta|)$ time, when many H_{FIB} updates are strung together. This is a significant complexity reduction compared to the exact approach: the latter can lead to a function consisting of $|A||\Gamma_i|^{|\Theta|}$ linear functions, which is exponential in the number of observations and in the worst case takes $O(|A||S|^2|\Gamma_i|^{|\Theta|})$ time.

As H_{FIB} updates are of polynomial complexity one can find the approximation for the finite-horizon case efficiently. The open issue remains the problem of finding the solution for the infinite-horizon discounted case and its complexity. To address it we establish the following theorem.

Theorem 8 *A solution for the fast informed bound approximation can be found by solving an MDP with $|S||A||\Theta|$ states, $|A|$ actions and the same discount factor γ.*

The full proof of the theorem is deferred to the Appendix. The key part of the proof is the construction of an equivalent MDP with $|S||A||\Theta|$ states representing H_{FIB} updates. Since a finite-state MDP can be solved through linear program conversion, the fixed-point solution for the fast informed bound update is computable efficiently.

4.2.1 FAST INFORMED BOUND VERSUS FULLY-OBSERVABLE MDP APPROXIMATIONS

The fast informed update upper-bounds the exact update and is tighter than both the MDP and the QMDP approximation updates.

Theorem 9 *Let $\widehat{V}_i$ corresponds to a piecewise linear convex value function defined by Γ_i linear functions. Then $H\widehat{V}_i \leq H_{FIB}\widehat{V}_i \leq H_{QMDP}\widehat{V}_i \leq H_{MDP}\widehat{V}_i$.*

The key trick in deriving the above result is to swap max and sum operators (the proof is in the Appendix) and thus obtain both to the upper-bound inequalities and the subsequent reduction in the complexity of update rules compared to the exact update. This is also shown in Figure 15. The UMDP approximation, also included in Figure 15, is discussed later in Section 4.3. Thus, the difference among the methods boils down to simple mathematical manipulations. Note that the same inequality relations as derived for updates hold also for their fixed-point solutions (through Theorem 6).

Figure 13a illustrates the improvement of the bound over MDP-based approximations on the Maze20 problem. Note, however, that this improvement is paid for by the increased running-time complexity (Figure 13b).

4.2.2 CONTROL

The fast informed bound always outputs a piecewise linear and convex function, with one linear function per action. This allows us to build a POMDP controller that selects an action associated with the best (highest value) linear function directly. Figure 14 compares the control performance of the direct and the lookahead controllers to the MDP and the QMDP controllers. We see that the fast informed bound leads not only to tighter bounds but also

UMDP update:
$$V_{i+1}(b) = \max_{a \in A} \left\{ \sum_{s \in S} b(s)\rho(s,a) + \gamma \max_{\alpha_i \in \Gamma_i} \sum_{s \in S} \sum_{s' \in S} P(s'|s,a)b(s)\alpha_i(s') \right\}$$

$\leq$

exact update:
$$V_{i+1}(b) = \max_{a \in A} \left\{ \sum_{s \in S} b(s)\rho(s,a) + \gamma \sum_{o \in \Theta} \max_{\alpha_i \in \Gamma_i} \sum_{s \in S} \sum_{s' \in S} P(s',o|s,a)b(s)\alpha_i(s') \right\}$$

$\leq$

fast informed bound update:
$$V_{i+1}(b) = \max_{a \in A} \left\{ \sum_{s \in S} b(s) \left[\rho(s,a) + \gamma \sum_{o \in \Theta} \max_{\alpha_i \in \Gamma_i} \sum_{s' \in S} P(s',o|s,a)\alpha_i(s') \right] \right\}$$

$\leq$

QMDP approx. update:
$$V_{i+1}(b) = \max_{a \in A} \left\{ \sum_{s \in S} b(s) \left[\rho(s,a) + \gamma \sum_{s' \in S} P(s'|s,a) \max_{\alpha_i \in \Gamma_i} \alpha_i(s') \right] \right\}$$

$\leq$

MDP approx. update:
$$V_{i+1}(b) = \sum_{s \in S} b(s) \max_{a \in A} \left[\rho(s,a) + \gamma \sum_{s' \in S} P(s'|s,a) \max_{\alpha_i \in \Gamma_i} \alpha_i(s') \right]$$

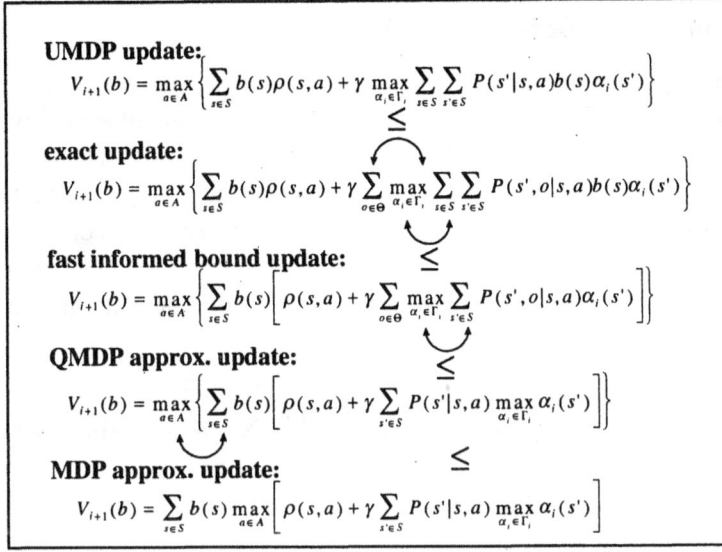

Figure 15: Relations between the exact update and the UMDP, the fast informed bound, the QMDP and the MDP updates.

to improved control on average. However, we stress that currently there is no theoretical underpinning for this observation and thus it may not be true for all belief states and any problem.

4.2.3 EXTENSIONS OF THE FAST INFORMED BOUND METHOD

The main idea of the fast informed bound method is to select the best linear function for every observation and every current state separately. This differs from the exact update where we seek a linear function that gives the best result for every observation and the combination of all states. However, we observe that there is a great deal of middle ground between these two extremes. Indeed, one can design an update rule that chooses optimal (maximal) linear functions for disjoint sets of states separately. To illustrate this idea, assume a partitioning $\mathcal{S} = \{S_1, S_2, \cdots, S_m\}$ of the state space S. The new update for $\mathcal{S}$ is:

$$\widehat{V}_{i+1}(b) = \max_{a \in A} \left\{ \sum_{s \in S} \rho(s,a)b(s) + \gamma \sum_{o \in \Theta} \left[\max_{\alpha_i \in \Gamma_i} \sum_{s \in S_1} \sum_{s' \in S} P(s',o|s,a)b(s)\alpha_i(s') + \right. \right.$$
$$\max_{\alpha_i \in \Gamma_i} \sum_{s \in S_2} \sum_{s' \in S} P(s',o|s,a)b(s)\alpha_i(s') + \cdots +$$
$$\left. \left. \max_{\alpha_i \in \Gamma_i} \sum_{s \in S_m} \sum_{s' \in S} P(s',o|s,a)b(s)\alpha_i(s') \right] \right\}$$

It is easy to see that the update upper-bounds the exact update. Exploration of this approach and various partitioning heuristics remains an interesting open research issue.

4.3 Approximation with Unobservable MDP

The MDP-approximation assumes full observability of POMDP states to obtain simpler and more efficient updates. The other extreme is to discard all observations available to the decision maker. An MDP with no observations is called *unobservable MDP (UMDP)* and one may choose its value-function solution as an alternative approximation.

To find the solution for the unobservable MDP, we derive the corresponding update rule, H_{UMDP}, similarly to the update for the partially observable case. H_{UMDP} preserves piecewise linearity and convexity of the value function and is a contraction. The update equals:

$$
\begin{aligned}
\widehat{V}_{i+1}(b) &= \max_{a \in A} \left\{ \sum_{s \in S} \rho(s,a)b(s) + \gamma \max_{\alpha_i \in \Gamma_i} \sum_{s \in S} \sum_{s' \in S} P(s'|s,a)b(s)\alpha_i(s') \right\} \\
&= (H_{UMDP}\widehat{V}_i)(b),
\end{aligned}
$$

where Γ_i is a set of linear functions describing $\widehat{V}_i$. $\widehat{V}_{i+1}$ remains piecewise linear and convex and it consists of at most $|\Gamma_i||A|$ linear functions. This is in contrast to the exact update, where the number of possible vectors in the next step can grow exponentially in the number of observations and leads to $|A||\Gamma_i|^{|\Theta|}$ possible vectors. The time complexity of the update is $O(|A||S|^2|\Gamma_i|)$. Thus, starting from $\widehat{V}_0$ with one linear function, the running-time complexity for k updates is bounded by $O(|A|^k|S|^2)$. The problem of finding the optimal solution for the unobservable MDP remains intractable: the finite-horizon case is NP-hard(Burago et al., 1996), and the discounted infinite-horizon case is undecidable (Madani et al., 1999). Thus, it is usually not very useful approximation.

The update H_{UMDP} lower-bounds the exact update, an intuitive result reflecting the fact that one cannot do better with less information. To provide some insight into how the two updates are related, we do the following derivation, which also proves the bound property in an elegant way:

$$
\begin{aligned}
(H\widehat{V}_i)(b) &= \max_{a \in A} \left\{ \sum_{s \in S} \rho(s,a)b(s) + \gamma \sum_{o \in \Theta} \max_{\alpha_i \in \Gamma_i} \sum_{s' \in S} \sum_{s \in S} P(s',o|s,a)b(s)\alpha_i(s') \right\} \\
&\geq \max_{a \in A} \left\{ \sum_{s \in S} \rho(s,a)b(s) + \gamma \max_{\alpha_i \in \Gamma_i} \sum_{o \in \Theta} \sum_{s \in S} \sum_{s' \in S} P(s',o|s,a)b(s)\alpha_i(s') \right\} \\
&= \max_{a \in A} \left\{ \sum_{s \in S} \rho(s,a)b(s) + \gamma \max_{\alpha_i \in \Gamma_i} \sum_{s \in S} \sum_{s' \in S} P(s'|s,a)b(s)\alpha_i(s') \right\} \\
&= (H_{UMDP}\widehat{V}_i)(b).
\end{aligned}
$$

We see that the difference between the exact and UMDP updates is that the max and the sum over next-step observations are exchanged. This causes the choice of α vectors in H_{UMDP} to become independent of the observations. Once the sum and max operations are exchanged, the observations can be marginalized out. Recall that the idea of swaps leads to a number of approximation updates; see Figure 15 for their summary.

4.4 Fixed-Strategy Approximations

A finite-state machine (FSM) model is used primarily to define a control strategy. Such a strategy does not require belief state updates since it directly maps sequences of observations to sequences of actions. The value function of an FSM strategy is piecewise linear and convex and can be found efficiently in the number of memory states (Section 2.6.1). While in the policy iteration and policy approximation contexts the value function for a specific strategy is used to quantify the goodness of the policy in the first place, the value function alone can be also used as a substitute for the optimal value function. In this case, the value function (defined over the belief space) equals

$$V^C(b) = \max_{x \in M} V^C(x, b),$$

where $V^C(x, b) = \sum_{s \in S} V^C(x, s) b(s)$ is obtained by solving a set of $|S||M|$ linear equations (Section 2.6.2). As remarked earlier, the value for the fixed strategy lower-bounds the optimal value function, that is $V^C \leq V^*$.

To simplify the comparison of the fixed-strategy approximation to other approximations, we can rewrite its solution also in terms of fixed-strategy updates

$$
\begin{aligned}
\widehat{V}_{i+1}(b) &= \max_{x \in M} \left\{ \sum_{s \in S} \rho(s, \eta(x)) b(s) + \gamma \sum_{o \in \Theta} \sum_{s \in S} \sum_{s' \in S} P(o, s'|s, \eta(x)) b(s) \alpha_i(\phi(x, o), s') \right\}, \\
&= \max_{x \in M} \left\{ \sum_{s \in S} b(s) \left[\rho(s, \eta(x)) + \gamma \sum_{o \in \Theta} \sum_{s' \in S} P(o, s'|s, \eta(x)) \alpha_i(\phi(x, o), s') \right] \right\} \\
&= (H_{FSM} \widehat{V}_i)(b).
\end{aligned}
$$

The value function $\widehat{V}_i$ is piecewise linear and convex and consists of $|M|$ linear functions $\alpha_i(x, .)$. For the infinite-horizon discounted case $\alpha_i(x, s)$ represents the ith approximation of $V^C(x, s)$. Note that the update can be applied to the finite-horizon case in a straightforward way.

4.4.1 QUALITY OF CONTROL

Assume we have an FSM strategy and would like to use it as a substitute for the optimal control policy. There are three different ways in which we can use it to extract the control. The first is to simply execute the strategy represented by the FSM. There is no need to update belief states in this case. The second possibility is to choose linear functions corresponding to different memory states and their associated actions repeatedly in every step. We refer to such a controller as a *direct* (DR) controller. This approach requires updating of belief states in every step. On the other hand its control performance is no worse than that of the FSM control. The final strategy discards all the information about actions and extracts the policy by using the value function $\widehat{V}(b)$ and one-step lookahead. This method (LA) requires both belief state updates and lookaheads and leads to the worst reactive time. Like DR, however, this strategy is guaranteed to be no worse than the FSM controller. The following theorem relates the performances of the three controllers.

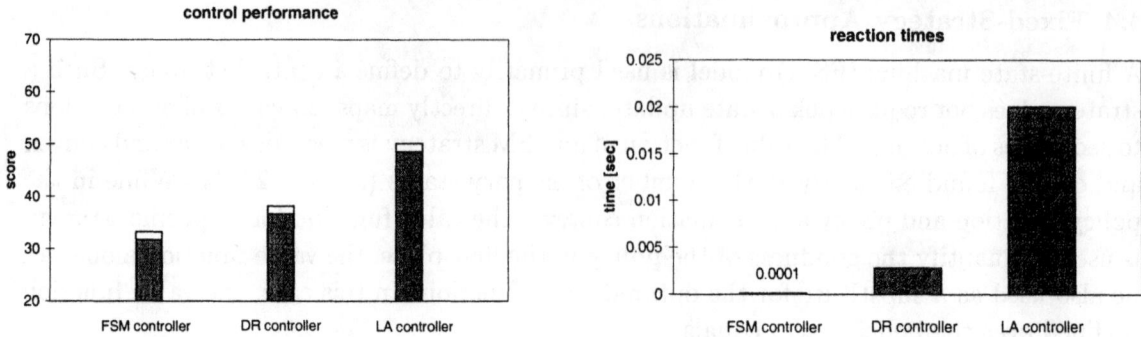

Figure 16: Comparison of three different controllers (FSM, DR and LA) for the Maze20 problem and a collection of one-action policies: control quality (left) and response time (right). Error-bars in the control performance graph indicate the critical score difference at which any two methods become statistically different at significance level 0.05.

Theorem 10 *Let C_{FSM} be an FSM controller. Let C_{DR} and C_{LA} be the direct and the one-step-lookahead controllers constructed based on C_{FSM}. Then $V^{C_{FSM}}(b) \leq V^{C_{DR}}(b)$ and $V^{C_{FSM}}(b) \leq V^{C_{LA}}(b)$ hold for all belief states $b \in \mathcal{I}$.*

Though we can prove that both the direct controller and the lookahead controller are always better than the underlying FSM controller (see Appendix for the full proof of the theorem), we cannot show the similar property between the first two controllers for all initial belief states. However, the lookahead approach typically tends to dominate, reflecting the usual trade-off between control quality and response time. We illustrate this trade-off on our running Maze20 example and a collection of $|A|$ one-action policies, each generating a sequence of the same action. Control quality and response time results are shown in Figure 16. We see that the controller based on the FSM is the fastest of the three, but it is also the worst in terms of control quality. On the other hand, the direct controller is slower (it needs to update belief states in every step) but delivers better control. Finally, the lookahead controller is the slowest and has the best control performance.

4.4.2 Selecting the FSM Model

The quality of a fixed-strategy approximation depends strongly on the FSM model used. The model can be provided a priori or constructed automatically. Techniques for automatic construction of FSM policies correspond to a search problem in which either the complete or a restricted space of policies is examined to find the optimal or the near-optimal policy for such a space. The search process is equivalent to policy approximations or policy-iteration techniques discussed earlier in Sections 2.6 and 3.2.

4.5 Grid-Based Approximations with Value Interpolation-Extrapolation

A value function over a continuous belief space can be approximated by a finite set of grid points G and an *interpolation-extrapolation rule* that estimates the value of an arbitrary point of the belief space by relying only on the points of the grid and their associated values.

Definition 8 *(Interpolation-extrapolation rule) Let $f : \mathcal{I} \to \mathbb{R}$ be a real-valued function defined over the information space $\mathcal{I}$, $G = \{b_1^G, b_2^G, \cdots b_k^G\}$ be a set of grid points and $\Psi^G = \{(b_1^G, f(b_1^G)), (b_2^G, f(b_2^G)), \cdots, (b_k^G, f(b_k^G))\}$ be a set of point-value pairs. A function $R_G : \mathcal{I} \times (\mathcal{I} \times \mathbb{R})^{|G|} \to \mathbb{R}$ that estimates f at any point of the information space $\mathcal{I}$ using only values associated with grid points is called an interpolation-extrapolation rule.*

The main advantage of an interpolation-extrapolation model in estimating the true value function is that it requires us to compute value updates only for a finite set of grid points G. Let $\widehat{V}_i$ be the approximation of the ith value function. Then the approximation for the $(i+1)$th value function $\widehat{V}_{i+1}$ can be obtained as

$$\widehat{V}_{i+1}(b) = R_G(b, \Psi_{i+1}^G),$$

where values associated with every grid point $b_j^G \in G$ (and included in Ψ_{i+1}^G) are:

$$\varphi_{i+1}(b_j^G) = (H\widehat{V}_i)(b_j^G) = \max_{a \in A} \left\{ \rho(b, a) + \gamma \sum_{o \in \Theta} P(o|b, a)\widehat{V}_i(\tau(b_j^G, o, a)) \right\}. \tag{9}$$

The grid-based update can also be described in terms of a value-function mapping H_G: $\widehat{V}_{i+1} = H_G\widehat{V}_i$. The complexity of such an update is $O(|G||A||S|^2|\Theta|C_{\mathrm{Eval}}(R_G, |G|))$ where $C_{\mathrm{Eval}}(R_G, |G|)$ is the computational cost of evaluating the interpolation-extrapolation rule R_G for $|G|$ grid points. We show later (Section 4.5.3), that in some instances, the need to evaluate the interpolation-extrapolation rule in every step can be eliminated.

4.5.1 A Family of Convex Rules

The number of all possible interpolation-extrapolation rules is enormous. We focus on a set of *convex rules* that is a relatively small but very important subset of interpolation-extrapolation rules.[20]

Definition 9 *(Convex rule) Let f be some function defined over the space $\mathcal{I}$, $G = \{b_1^G, b_2^G, \cdots b_k^G\}$ be a set of grid points, and $\Psi^G = \{(b_1^G, f(b_1^G)), (b_2^G, f(b_2^G)), \cdots, (b_k^G, f(b_k^G))\}$ be a set of point-value pairs. The rule R_G for estimating f using Ψ^G is called convex when for every $b \in \mathcal{I}$, the value $\widehat{f}(b)$ is:*

$$\widehat{f}(b) = R_G(b, \Psi^G) = \sum_{j=1}^{|G|} \lambda_j^b f(b_j),$$

such that $0 \leq \lambda_j^b \leq 1$ for every $j = 1, \cdots, |G|$, and $\sum_{j=1}^{|G|} \lambda_j^b = 1$.

---

20. We note that convex rules used in our work are a special case of averagers introduced by Gordon (1995). The difference is minor; the definition of an averager includes a constant (independent of grid points and their values) that is added to the convex combination.

The key property of convex rules is that their corresponding grid-based update H_G is a contraction in the max norm (Gordon, 1995). Thus, the approximate value iteration based on H_G converges to the unique fixed-point solution. In addition, H_G based on convex rules is isotone.

4.5.2 EXAMPLES OF CONVEX RULES

The family of convex rules includes approaches that are very commonly used in practice, like *nearest neighbor, kernel regression, linear point interpolations* and many others.

Take, for example, the *nearest-neighbor* approach. The function for a belief point b is estimated using the value at the grid point closest to it in terms of some distance metric M defined over the belief space. Then, for any point b, there is exactly one nonzero parameter $\lambda_j^b = 1$ such that $\| b - b_j^G \|_M \leq \| b - b_i^G \|_M$ holds for all $i = 1, 2, \cdots, k$. All other λs are zero. Assuming the Euclidean distance metric, the nearest-neighbor approach leads to a piecewise constant approximation, in which regions with equal values correspond to regions with a common nearest grid point.

The nearest neighbor estimates the function value by taking into an account only one grid point and its value. *Kernel regression* expands upon this by using more grid points. It adds up and weights their contributions (values) according to their distance from the target point. For example, assuming Gaussian kernels, the weight for a grid point b_j^G is

$$\lambda_j^b = \beta \exp^{-\|b - b_j^G\|_M^2 / 2\sigma^2},$$

where β is a normalizing constant ensuring that $\sum_{j=1}^{|G|} \lambda_j^b = 1$ and σ is a parameter that flattens or narrows weight functions. For the Euclidean metric, the above kernel-regression rule leads to a smooth approximation of the function.

Linear point interpolations are a subclass of convex rules that in addition to constraints in Definition 9 satisfy

$$b = \sum_{j=1}^{|G|} \lambda_j^b b_j^G.$$

That is, a belief point b is a convex combination of grid points and the λs are the corresponding coefficients. Because the optimal value function for the POMDP is convex, the new constraint is sufficient to prove the upper-bound property of the approximation. In general, there can be many different linear point-interpolations for a given grid. A challenging problem here is to find the rule with the best approximation. We discuss these issues in Section 4.5.7.

4.5.3 CONVERSION TO A GRID-BASED MDP

Assume that we would like to find the approximation of the value function using our grid-based convex rule and grid-based update (Equation 9). We can view this process also as a process of finding a sequence of values $\varphi_1(b_j^G), \varphi_2(b_j^G), \cdots, \varphi_i(b_j^G), \cdots$ for all grid-points $b_j^G \in G$. We show that in some instances the sequence of values can be computed without applying an interpolation-extrapolation rule in every step. In such cases, the problem can be converted into a fully observable MDP with states corresponding to grid-points G.[21] We call this MDP a *grid-based MDP*.

Theorem 11 *Let G be a finite set of grid points and R_G be a convex rule such that parameters λ_j^b are fixed. Then the values of $\varphi(b_j^G)$ for all $b_j^G \in G$ can be found by solving a fully observable MDP with $|G|$ states and the same discount factor γ.*

Proof For any grid point b_j^G we can write:

$$
\begin{aligned}
\varphi_{i+1}(b_j^G) &= \max_{a \in A} \left\{ \rho(b_j^G, a) + \gamma \sum_{o \in \Theta} P(o|b_j^G, a) \widehat{V}_i^G(\tau(b_j^G, a, o)) \right\} \\
&= \max_{a \in A} \left\{ \rho(b_j^G, a) + \gamma \sum_{o \in \Theta} P(o|b_j^G, a) \left[\sum_{k=1}^{|G|} \lambda_{j,k}^{o,a} \varphi_i(b_k^G) \right] \right\} \\
&= \max_{a \in A} \left\{ \left[\rho(b_j^G, a) \right] + \gamma \sum_{k=1}^{|G|} \varphi_i^G(b_k^G) \left[\sum_{o \in \Theta} P(o|b_j^G, a) \lambda_{j,k}^{o,a} \right] \right\}
\end{aligned}
$$

Now denoting $[\sum_{o \in \Theta} P(o|b_j, a)^G \lambda_{j,k}^{o,a}]$ as $P(b_k^G|b_j^G, a)$, we can construct a fully observable MDP problem with states corresponding to grid points G and the same discount factor γ. The update step equals:

$$
\varphi_{i+1}(b_j^G) = \max_{a \in A} \left\{ \rho(b_j^G, a) + \gamma \sum_{k=1}^{|G|} P(b_k^G|b_j^G, a) \varphi_i^G(b_k^G) \right\}.
$$

The prerequisite $0 \leq \lambda_j^b \leq 1$ for every $j = 1, \cdots, |G|$ and $\sum_{j=1}^{|G|} \lambda_j^b = 1$ guarantees that $P(b_k^G|b_j^G, a)$ can be interpreted as true probabilities. Thus, one can compute values $\varphi(b_j^G)$ by solving the equivalent fully-observable MDP. □

4.5.4 SOLVING GRID-BASED APPROXIMATIONS

The idea of converting a grid-based approximation into a grid-based MDP is a basis of our simple but very powerful approximation algorithm. Briefly, the key here is to find the parameters (transition probabilities and rewards) of a new MDP model and then solve it. This process is relatively easy if the parameters λ used to interpolate-extrapolate the value of a non-grid point are fixed (the assumption of Theorem 11). In such a case, we can determine parameters of the new MDP efficiently in one step, for any grid set G. The nearest neighbor or the kernel regression are examples of rules with this property. Note that this leads to polynomial-time algorithms for finding values for all grid points (recall that an MDP can be solved efficiently for both finite and discounted, infinite-horizon criteria).

The problem in solving grid-based approximation arises only when the parameters λ used in the interpolation-extrapolation are not fixed and are subject to the optimization itself. This happens, for example, when there are multiple ways of interpolating a value

---

21. We note that a similar result has been also proved independently by Gordon (1995).

at some point of the belief space and we would like to find the best interpolation (leading to the best values) for all grid points in G. In such a case, the corresponding "optimal" grid-based MDP cannot be found in a single step and iterative approximation, solving a sequence of grid-based MDPs, is usually needed. The worst-case complexity of this problem remains an open question.

4.5.5 CONSTRUCTING GRIDS

An issue we have not touched on so far is the selection of grids. There are multiple ways to select grids. We divide them into two classes – regular and non-regular grids.

Regular grids (Lovejoy, 1991a) partition the belief space evenly into equal-size regions.[22] The main advantage of regular grids is the simplicity with which we can locate grid points in the neighborhood of any belief point. The disadvantage of regular grids is that they are restricted to a specific number of points, and any increase in grid resolution is paid for in an exponential increase in the grid size. For example, a sequence of regular grids for a 20-dimensional belief space (corresponds to a POMDP with 20 states) consists of 20, 210, 1540, 8855, 42504, $\cdots$ grid points.[23] This prevents one from using the method with higher grid resolutions for problems with larger state spaces.

Non-regular grids are unrestricted and thus provide for more flexibility when grid resolution must be increased adaptively. On the other hand, due to irregularities, methods for locating grid points adjacent to an arbitrary belief point are usually more complex when compared to regular grids.

4.5.6 LINEAR POINT INTERPOLATION

The fact that the optimal value function V^* is convex for a belief-state MDPs can be used to show that the approximation based on linear point interpolation always upper-bounds the exact solution (Lovejoy, 1991a, 1993). Neither kernel regression nor nearest neighbor can guarantee us any bound.

Theorem 12 (*Upper bound property of a grid-based point interpolation update*). *Let $\widehat{V}_i$ be a convex value function. Then $H\widehat{V}_i \leq H_G\widehat{V}_i$.*

The upper-bound property of H_G update for convex value functions follows directly from Jensen's inequality. The convergence to an upper-bound follows from Theorem 6.

Note that the point-interpolation update imposes an additional constraint on the choice of grid points. In particular, it is easy to see that any valid grid must also include extreme points of the belief simplex (extreme points correspond to $(1, 0, 0, \cdots), (0, 1, 0, \cdots)$,

---

22. Regular grids used by Lovejoy (1991a) are based on Freudenthal triangulation (Eaves, 1984). Essentially, this is the same idea as used to partition evenly the n-dimensional subspace of $I\!\!R^n$. In fact, an affine transform allows us to map isomorphically grid points in the belief space to grid points in the n-dimensional space (Lovejoy, 1991a).

23. The number of points in the regular grid sequence is given by (Lovejoy, 1991a):

$$|G| = \frac{(M + |S| - 1)!}{M!(|S| - 1)!},$$

where $M = 1, 2, \cdots$ is a grid refinement parameter.

etc.). Without extreme points one would be unable to cover the whole belief space via interpolation. Nearest neighbor and kernel regression impose no restrictions on the grid.

4.5.7 FINDING THE BEST INTERPOLATION

In a general, there are multiple ways to interpolate a point of a belief space. Our objective is to find the best interpolation, that is, the one that leads to the tightest upper bound of the optimal value function.

Let b be a belief point and $\{(b_j, f(b_j))|b_j \in G\}$ a set of grid-value pairs. Then the best interpolation for point b is:

$$\widehat{f}(b) = \min_{\overline{\lambda}} \sum_{j=1}^{|G|} \lambda_j f(b_j)$$

subject to $0 \leq \lambda_j \leq 1$ for all $j = 1, \cdots, |G|$, $\sum_{j=1}^{|G|} \lambda_j = 1$, and $b = \sum_{j=1}^{|G|} \lambda_j b_j^G$.

This is a linear optimization problem. Although it can be solved in polynomial time (using linear programming techniques), the computational cost of doing this is still relatively large, especially considering the fact that the optimization must be repeated many times. To alleviate this problem we seek more efficient ways of finding the interpolation, sacrificing the optimality.

One way to find a (suboptimal) interpolation quickly is to apply regular grids proposed by Lovejoy (1991a). In this case the value at a belief point is approximated using the convex combination of grid points closest to it. The approximation leads to piecewise linear and convex value functions. As all interpolations are fixed here, the problem of finding the approximation can be converted into an equivalent grid-based MDP and solved as a finite-state MDP. However, as pointed in the previous section, the regular grids must use a specific number of grid points and any increase in the resolution of a grid is paid for by an exponential increase in the grid size. This feature makes the method less attractive when we have a problem with a large state space and we need to achieve high grid resolution.[24]

In the present work we focus on non-regular (or arbitrary) grids. We propose an interpolation approach that searches a limited space of interpolations and is guaranteed to run in time linear in the size of the grid. The idea of the approach is to interpolate a point b of a belief space of dimension $|S|$ with a set of grid points that consists of an arbitrary grid point $b' \in G$ and $|S| - 1$ extreme points of the belief simplex. The coefficients of this interpolation can be found efficiently and we search for the best such interpolation. Let $b' \in G$ be a grid point defining one such interpolation. Then the value at point b satisfies

$$\widehat{V}_i(b) = \min_{b' \in G} \widehat{V}_i^{b'}(b),$$

where $\widehat{V}_i^{b'}$ is the value of the interpolation for the grid point b'. Figure 17 illustrates the resulting approximation. The function is characterized by its "sawtooth" shape, which is influenced by the choice of the interpolating set.

To find the best value-function solution or its close approximation we can apply a value iteration procedure in which we search for the best interpolation after every update step.

---

24. One solution to this problem may be to use adaptive regular grids in which grid resolution is increased only in some parts of the belief space. We leave this idea for future work.

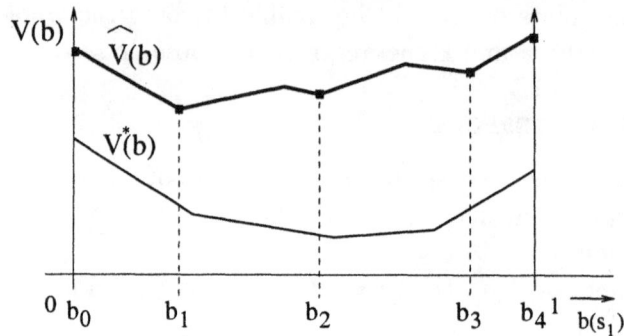

Figure 17: Value-function approximation based on the linear-time interpolation approach (a two-dimensional case). Interpolating sets are restricted to a single internal point of the belief space.

The drawback of this approach is that interpolations may remain unchanged for many update steps, thus slowing down the solution process. An alternative approach is to solve a sequence of grid-based MDPs instead. In particular, at every stage we find the best (minimum value) interpolations for all belief points reachable from grid points in one step, fix coefficients of these interpolations (λs), construct a grid-based MDP and solve it (exactly or approximately). This process is repeated until no further improvement (or no improvement larger than some threshold) is seen in values at different grid points.

4.5.8 IMPROVING GRIDS ADAPTIVELY

The quality of an approximation (bound) depends strongly on the points used in the grid. Our objective is to provide a good approximation with the smallest possible set of grid points. However, this task is impossible to achieve, since it cannot be known in advance (before solving) what belief points to pick. A way to address this problem is to build grids incrementally, starting from a small set of grid points and adding others adaptively, but only in places with a greater chance of improvement. The key part of this approach is a heuristic for choosing grid points to be added next.

One heuristic method we have developed attempts to maximize improvements in bound values via stochastic simulations. The method builds on the fact that every interpolation grid must also include extreme points (otherwise we cannot cover the entire belief space). As extreme points and their values affect the other grid points, we try to improve their values in the first place. In general, a value at any grid point b improves more the more precise values are used for its successor belief points, that is, belief states that correspond to $\tau(b, a^*, o)$ for a choice of observation o. a^* is the current optimal action choice for b. Incorporating such points into the grid then makes a larger improvement in the value at the initial grid point b more likely. Assuming that our initial point is an extreme point, we have a heuristic that tends to improve a value for that point. Naturally, one can proceed further with this selection by incorporating the successor points for the first-level successors into the grid as well, and so forth.

generate new grid points $(G, \widehat{V}^G)$

    set $G_{new} = \{\}$

    for all extreme points b **do**

        repeat until $b \notin G \cup G_{new}$

            set $a^* = \arg\max_a \left\{ \rho(b,a) + \gamma \sum_{o \in \Theta} P(o|b,a) \widehat{V}^G(\tau(b,a,o)) \right\}$

            select observation o according to $P(o|b, a^*)$

            update $b = \tau(b, a^*, o)$

        add b into G_{new}

    return G_{new}

Figure 18: Procedure for generating additional grid points based on our bound improvement heuristic.

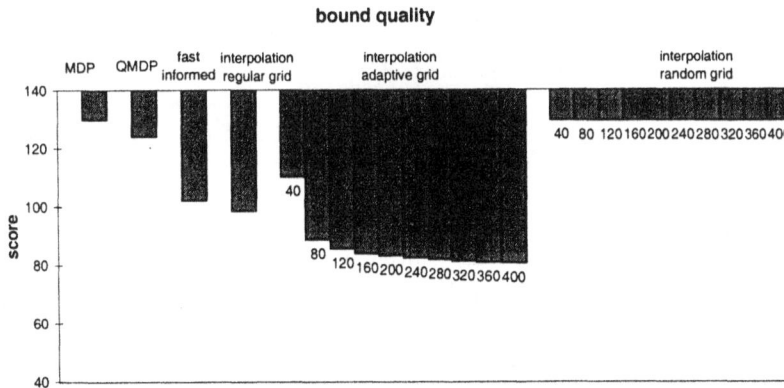

Figure 19: Improvement in the upper bound quality for grid-based point-interpolations based on the adaptive-grid method. The method is compared to randomly refined grid and the regular grid with 210 points. Other upper-bound approximations (the MDP, QMDP and fast informed bound methods) are included for comparison.

To capture this idea, we generate new grid points via simulation, starting from one of the extremes of the belief simplex and continuing until a belief point not currently in the grid is reached. An algorithm that implements the bound improvement heuristic and expands the current grid G with a set of $|S|$ new grid points while relying on the current value-function approximation $\widehat{V}^G$ is shown in Figure 18.

Figure 19 illustrates the performance (bound quality) of our adaptive grid method on the Maze20 problem. Here we use the combination of adaptive grids with our linear-time interpolation approach. The method gradually expands the grid in 40 point increments up to 400 grid points. Figure 19 also shows the performance of the random-grid method in which

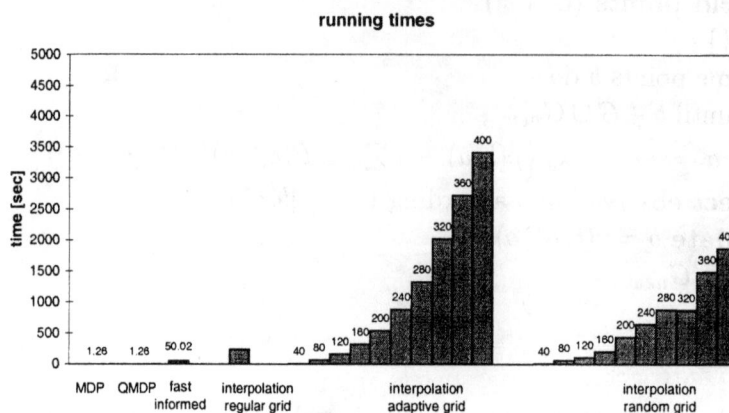

Figure 20: Running times of grid-based point-interpolation methods. Methods tested include the adaptive grid, the random grid, and the regular grid with 210 grid points. Running times for the adaptive-grid are cumulative, reflecting the dependencies of higher grid resolutions on the lower-level resolutions. The running time results for the MDP, QMDP, and fast informed bound approximations are shown for comparison.

new points of the grid are selected iniformly at random (results for 40 grid point increments are shown). In addition, the figure gives results for the regular grid interpolation (based on Lovejoy (1991a)) with 210 belief points and other upper-bound methods: the MDP, the QMDP and the fast informed bound approximations.

We see a dramatic improvement in the quality of the bound for the adaptive method. In contrast to this, the uniformly sampled grid (random-grid approach) hardly changes the bound. There are two reasons for this: (1) uniformly sampled grid points are more likely to be concentrated in the center of the belief simplex; (2) the transition matrix for the Maze20 problem is relatively sparse, the belief points one obtains from the extreme points in one step are on the boundary of the simplex. Since grid points in the center of the simplex are never used to interpolate belief states reachable from extremes in one step they cannot improve values at extremes and the bound does not change.

One drawback of the adaptive method is its running time (for every grid size we need to solve a sequence of grid-based MDPs). Figure 20 compares running times of different methods on the Maze20 problem. As grid-expansion of the adaptive method depends on the value function obtained for previous steps, we plot its cumulative running times. We see a relatively large increase in running time, especially for larger grid sizes, reflecting the trade-off between the bound quality and running time. However, we note that the adaptive-grid method performs quite well in the initial few steps, and with only 80 grid points outperforms the regular grid (with 210 points) in bound quality.

Finally, we note that other heuristic approaches to constructing adaptive grids for point interpolation are possible. For example, a different approach that refines the grid by ex-

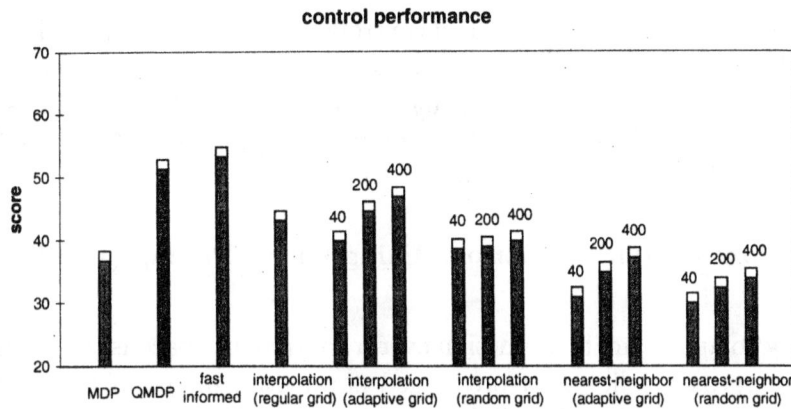

Figure 21: Control performance of lookahead controllers based on grid-based point inter- polation and nearest neighbor methods and varying grid sizes. The results are compared to the MDP, the QMDP and the fast informed bound controllers.

amining differences in values at current grid points has recently been proposed by Brafman (1997).

4.5.9 CONTROL

Value functions obtained for different grid-based methods define a variety of controllers. Fig- ure 21 compares the performances of lookahead controllers based on the point-interpolation and nearest-neighbor methods. We run two versions of both approaches, one with the adap- tive grid, the other with the random grid, and we show results obtained for 40, 200 and 400 grid points. In addition, we compare their performances to the interpolation with regular grids (with 210 grid points), the MDP, the QMDP and the fast informed bound approaches.

Overall, the performance of the interpolation-extrapolation techniques we tested on the Maze20 problem was a bit disappointing. In particular, better scores were achieved by the simpler QMDP and fast informed bound methods. We see that, although heuristics improved the bound quality of approximations, they did not lead to the similar improvement over the QMDP and the fast informed bound methods in terms of control. This result shows that a bad bound (in terms of absolute values) does not always imply bad control performance. The main reason for this is that the control performance is influenced mostly by relative rather than absolute value-function values (or, in other words, by the shape of the function). All interpolation-extrapolation techniques we use (except regular grid interpolation) approximate the value function with functions that are not piecewise linear and convex; the interpolations are based on the linear-time interpolation technique with a sawtooth-shaped function, and the nearest-neighbor leads to a piecewise-constant function. This does not allow them to match the shape of the optimal function correctly. The other factor that affects the performance is a large sensitivity of methods to the selection of grid points, as documented, for example, by the comparison of heuristic and random grids.

In the above tests we focused on lookahead controllers only. However, an alternative way to define a controller for grid-based interpolation-extrapolation methods is to use Q-function approximations instead of value functions, and either direct or lookahead designs.[25] Q-function approximations can be found by solving the same grid-based MDP, and by keeping values (functions) for different actions separate at the end.

4.6 Approximations of Value Functions Using Curve Fitting (Least-Squares Fit)

An alternative way to approximate a function over a continuous space is to use curve-fitting techniques. This approach relies on a predefined parametric model of the value function and a set of values associated with a finite set of (grid) belief points G. The approach is similar to interpolation-extrapolation techniques in that it relies on a set of belief-value pairs. The difference is that the curve fitting, instead of remembering all belief-value pairs, tries to summarize them in terms of a given parametric function model. The strategy seeks the best possible match between model parameters and observed point values. The best match can be defined using various criteria, most often the least-squares fit criterion, where the objective is to minimize

$$Error(f) = \frac{1}{2} \sum_j [y_j - f(b_j)]^2 .$$

Here b_j and y_j correspond to the belief point and its associated value. The index j ranges over all points of the sample set G.

4.6.1 Combining Dynamic Programming and Least-Squares Fit

The least-squares approximation of a function can be used to construct a dynamic-programming algorithm with an update step: $\widehat{V}_{i+1} = H_{LSF} \widehat{V}_i$. The approach has two steps. First, we obtain new values for a set of sample points G:

$$\varphi_{i+1}(b) = (H\widehat{V}_i)(b) = \max_{a \in A} \left\{ \sum_{s \in S} \rho(s,a)b(s) + \gamma \sum_{o \in \Theta} \sum_{s \in S} P(o|s,a)b(s)\widehat{V}_i(\tau(b,a,o)) \right\}.$$

Second, we fit the parameters of the value-function model $\widehat{V}_{i+1}$ using new sample-value pairs and the square-error cost function. The complexity of the update is $O(|G||A||S|^2|\Theta|C_{\text{Eval}}(\widehat{V}_i) + C_{\text{Fit}}(\widehat{V}_{i+1},|G|))$ time, where $C_{\text{Eval}}(\widehat{V}_i)$ is the computational cost of evaluating $\widehat{V}_i$ and $C_{\text{Fit}}(\widehat{V}_{i+1},|G|)$ is the cost of fitting parameters of $\widehat{V}_{i+1}$ to $|G|$ belief-value pairs.

The advantage of the approximation based on the least-squares fit is that it requires us to compute updates only for the finite set of belief states. The drawback of the approach is that, when combined with the value-iteration method, it can lead to instability and/or divergence. This has been shown for MDPs by several researchers (Bertsekas, 1994; Boyan & Moore, 1995; Baird, 1995; Tsitsiklis & Roy, 1996).

---

25. This is similar to the QMDP method, which allows both lookahead and greedy designs. In fact, QMDP can be viewed as a special case of the grid-based method with Q-function approximations, where grid points correspond to extremes of the belief simplex.

4.6.2 ON-LINE VERSION OF THE LEAST-SQUARES FIT

The problem of finding a set of parameters with the best fit can be solved by any available optimization procedure. This includes the on-line (or instance-based) version of the gradient descent method, which corresponds to the well-known delta rule (Rumelhart, Hinton, & Williams, 1986).

Let f denote a parametric value function over the belief space with adjustable weights $\overline{w} = \{w_1, w_2, \cdots, w_k\}$. Then the on-line update for a weight w_i is computed as:

$$w_i \leftarrow w_i - \alpha_i (f(b_j) - y_j) \frac{\partial f}{\partial w_i}|_{b_j},$$

where α_i is a learning constant, and b_j and y_j are the last-seen point and its value. Note that the gradient descent method requires the function to be differentiable with regard to adjustable weights.

To solve the discounted infinite-horizon problem, the stochastic (on-line) version of a least-squares fit can be combined with either parallel (synchronous) or incremental (Gauss-Seidel) point updates. In the first case, the value function from the previous step is fixed and a new value function is computed from scratch using a set of belief point samples and their values computed through one-step expansion. Once the parameters are stabilized (by attenuating learning rates), the newly acquired function is fixed, and the process proceeds with another iteration. In the incremental version, a single value-function model is at the same time updated and used to compute new values at sampled points. Littman et al. (1995) and Parr and Russell (1995) implement this approach using asynchronous reinforcement learning backups in which sample points to be updated next are obtained via stochastic simulation. We stress that all versions are subject to the threat of instability and divergence, as remarked above.

4.6.3 PARAMETRIC FUNCTION MODELS

To apply the least-squares approach we must first select an appropriate value function model. Examples of simple convex functions are linear or quadratic functions, but more complex models are possible as well.

One interesting and relatively simple approach is based on the least-squares approximation of linear action-value functions (Q-functions) (Littman et al., 1995). Here the value function $\widehat{V}_{i+1}$ is approximated as a piecewise linear and convex combination of $\widehat{Q}_{i+1}$ functions:

$$\widehat{V}_{i+1}(b) = \max_{a \in A} \widehat{Q}_{i+1}(b, a),$$

where $\widehat{Q}_{i+1}(b, a)$ is the least-squares fit of a linear function for a set of sample points G. Values at points in G are obtained as

$$\varphi_{i+1}^a(b) = \rho(b, a) + \gamma \sum_{o \in \Theta} P(o|b, a) \widehat{V}_i(\tau(b, o, a)).$$

The method leads to an approximation with $|A|$ linear functions and the coefficients of these functions can be found efficiently by solving a set of linear equations. Recall that other two approximations (the QMDP and the fast informed bound approximations) also work with

$|A|$ linear functions. The main differences between the methods are that the QMDP and fast informed bound methods update linear functions directly, and they guarantee upper bounds and unique convergence.

A more sophisticated parametric model of a convex function is the *softmax model* (Parr & Russell, 1995):

$$\widehat{V}(b) = \left[\sum_{\alpha \in \Gamma} \left[\sum_{s \in S} \alpha(s)b(s) \right]^k \right]^{\frac{1}{k}},$$

where Γ is the set of linear functions α with adaptive parameters to fit and k is a "temperature" parameter that provides a better fit to the underlying piecewise linear convex function for larger values. The function represents a soft approximation of a piecewise linear convex function, with the parameter k smoothing the approximation.

4.6.4 CONTROL

We tested the control performance of the least-squares approach on the linear Q-function model (Littman et al., 1995) and the softmax model (Parr & Russell, 1995). For the softmax model we varied the number of linear functions, trying cases with 10 and 15 linear functions respectively. In the first set of experiments we used parallel (synchronous) updates and samples at a fixed set of 100 belief points. We applied stochastic gradient descent techniques to find the best fit in both cases. We tested the control performance for value-function approximations obtained after 10, 20 and 30 updates, starting from the QMDP solution. In the second set of experiments, we applied the incremental stochastic update scheme with Gauss-Seidel-style updates. The results for this method were acquired after every grid point was updated 150 times, with learning rates decreasing linearly in the range between 0.2 and 0.001. Again we started from the QMDP solution. The results for lookahead controllers are summarized in Figure 22, which also shows the control performance of the direct Q-function controller and, for comparison, the results for the QMDP method.

The linear-Q function model performed very well and the results for the lookahead design were better than the results for the QMDP method. The difference was quite apparent for direct approaches. In general, the good performance of the method can be attributed to the choice of a function model that let us match the shape of the optimal value function reasonably well. In contrast, the softmax models (with 10 and 15 linear functions) did not perform as expected. This is probably because in the softmax model all linear functions are updated for every sample point. This leads to situations in which multiple linear functions try to track a belief point during its update. Under these circumstances it is hard to capture the structure of the optimal value function accurately. The other negative feature is that the effects of on-line changes of all linear functions are added in the softmax approximation, and thus could bias incremental update schemes. In the ideal case, we would like to identify one vector α responsible for a specific belief point and update (modify) only that vector. The linear Q-function approach avoids this problem by always updating only a single linear function (corresponding to an action).

control performance

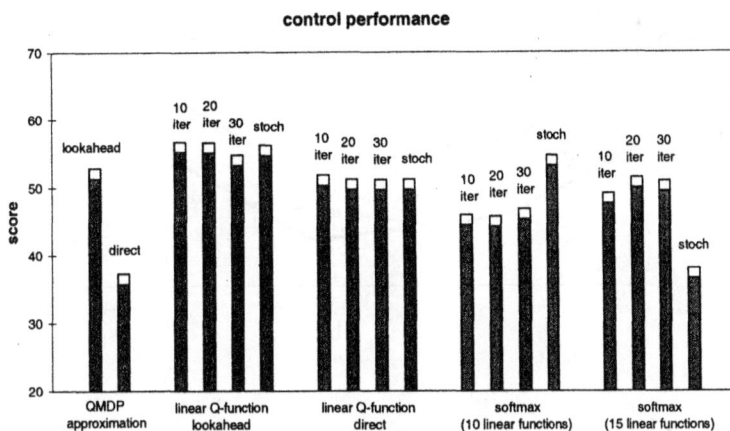

Figure 22: Control performance of least-squares fit methods. Models tested include: linear Q-function model (with both direct and lookahead control) and softmax models with 10 and 15 linear functions (lookahead control only). Value functions obtained after 10, 20 and 30 synchronous updates and value functions obtained through the incremental stochastic update scheme are used to define different controllers. For comparison, we also include results for two QMDP controllers.

4.7 Grid-Based Approximations with Linear Function Updates

An alternative grid-based approximation method can be constructed by applying Sondik's approach for computing derivatives (linear functions) to points of the grid (Lovejoy, 1991a, 1993). Let $\widehat{V}_i$ be a piecewise linear convex function described by a set of linear functions Γ_i. Then a new linear function for a belief point b and an action a can be computed efficiently as (Smallwood & Sondik, 1973; Littman, 1996)

$$\alpha_{i+1}^{b,a}(s) = \rho(s,a) + \gamma \sum_{o \in \Theta} \sum_{s' \in S} P(s',o|s,a)\alpha_i^{\iota(b,a,o)}(s'), \tag{10}$$

where $\iota(b,a,o)$ indexes a linear function α_i in a set of linear functions Γ_i (defining $\widehat{V}_i$) that maximizes the expression

$$\sum_{s' \in S} \left[\sum_{s \in S} P(s',o|s,a)b(s) \right] \alpha_i(s')$$

for a fixed combination of b, a, o. The optimizing function for b is then acquired by choosing the vector with the best overall value from all action vectors. That is, assuming Γ_{i+1}^b is a set of all candidate linear functions, the resulting functions satisfies

$$\alpha_{i+1}^{b,*} = \arg \max_{\alpha_{i+1}^b \in \Gamma_{i+1}^b} \sum_{s \in S} \alpha_{i+1}^b(s)b(s).$$

A collection of linear functions obtained for a set of belief points can be combined into a piecewise linear and convex value function. This is the idea behind a number of exact

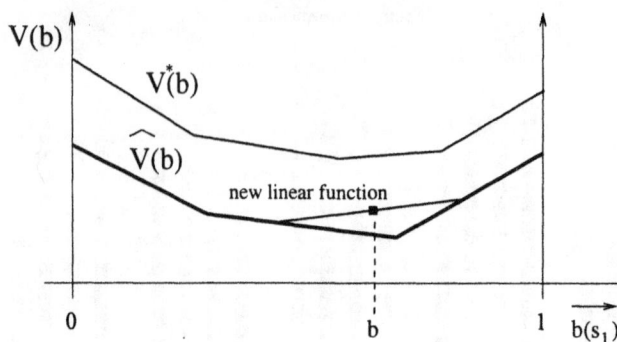

Figure 23: An incremental version of the grid-based linear function method. The piecewise linear lower bound is improved by a new linear function computed for a belief point b using Sondik's method.

algorithms (see Section 2.4.2). However, in the exact case, a set of points that cover all linear functions defining the new value function must be located first, which is a hard task in itself. In contrast, the approximation method uses an incomplete set of belief points that are fixed or at least easy to locate, for example via random or heuristic selection. We use H_{GL} to denote the value-function mapping for the grid approach.

The advantage of the grid-based method is that it leads to more efficient updates. The time complexity of the update is polynomial and equals $O(|G||A||S|^2|\Theta|)$. It yields a set of $|G|$ linear functions, compared to $|A||\Gamma_i|^{|\Theta|}$ possible functions for the exact update.

Since the set of grid-points is incomplete, the resulting approximation lower-bounds the value function one would obtain by performing the exact update (Lovejoy, 1991a).

Theorem 13 *(Lower-bound property of the grid-based linear function update). Let $\widehat{V}_i$ be a piecewise linear value function and G a set of grid points used to compute linear function updates. Then $H_{GL}\widehat{V}_i \leq H\widehat{V}_i$.*

4.7.1 Incremental Linear-Function Approach

The drawback of the grid-based linear function method is that H_{GL} is not a contraction for the discounted infinite-horizon case, and therefore the value iteration method based on the mapping may not converge (Lovejoy, 1991a). To remedy this problem, we propose an incremental version of the grid-based linear function method. The idea of this refinement is to prevent instability by gradually improving the piecewise linear and convex lower bound of the value function.

Assume that $\widehat{V}_i \leq V^*$ is a convex piecewise linear lower bound of the optimal value function defined by a linear function set Γ_i, and let α_b be a linear function for a point b that is computed from $\widehat{V}_i$ using Sondik's method. Then one can construct a new improved value function $\widehat{V}_{i+1} \geq \widehat{V}_i$ by simply adding the new linear function α^b into Γ_i. That is: $\Gamma_{i+1} = \Gamma_i \cup \alpha_b$. The idea of the incremental update, illustrated in Figure 23, is similar to incremental methods used by Cheng (1988) and Lovejoy (1993). The method can be

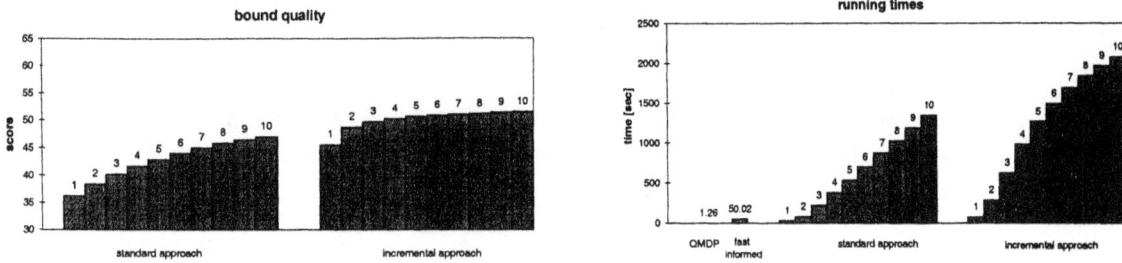

Figure 24: Bound quality and running times of the standard and incremental version of the grid-based linear-function method for the fixed 40-point grid. Cumulative running times (including all previous update cycles) are shown for both methods. Running times of the QMDP and the fast informed bound methods are included for comparison.

extended to handle a set of grid points G in a straightforward way. Note also that after adding one or more new linear functions to Γ_i, some of the previous linear functions may become redundant and can be removed from the value function. Techniques for redundancy checking are the same as are applied in the exact approaches (Monahan, 1982; Eagle, 1984).

The incremental refinement is stable and converges for a fixed set of grid points. The price paid for this feature is that the linear function set Γ_i can grow in size over the iteration steps. Although the growth is at most linear in the number of iterations, compared to the potentially exponential growth of exact methods, the linear function set describing the piecewise linear approximation can become huge. Thus, in practice we usually stop incremental updates well before the method converges. The question that remains open is the complexity (hardness) of the problem of finding the fixed-point solution for a fixed set of grid points G.

Figure 24 illustrates some of the trade-offs involved in applying incremental updates compared to the standard fixed-grid approach on the Maze20 problem. We use the same grid of 40 points for both techniques and the same initial value function. Results for 1-10 update cycles are shown. We see that the incremental method has longer running times than the standard method, since the number of linear functions can grow after every update. On the other hand, the bound quality of the incremental method improves more rapidly and it can never become worse after more update steps.

4.7.2 MINIMUM EXPECTED REWARD

The incremental method improves the lower bound of the value function. The value function, say $\widehat{V}_i$, can be used to create a controller (with either the lookahead or direct-action choice). In the general case, we cannot say anything about the performance quality of such controllers with regard to $\widehat{V}_i$. However, under certain conditions the performance of both controllers is guaranteed never to fall below $\widehat{V}_i$. The following theorem (proved in the Appendix) establishes these conditions.

Theorem 14 *Let $\widehat{V}_i$ be a value function obtained via the incremental linear function method, starting from $\widehat{V}_0$, which corresponds to some fixed strategy C_0. Let $C_{LA,i}$ and $C_{DR,i}$ be two* *controllers based on $\widehat{V}_i$: the lookahead controller and the direct action controller, and $V^{C_{LA,i}}$, $V^{C_{DR,i}}$ be their respective value functions. Then $\widehat{V}_i \leq V^{C_{LA,i}}$ and $\widehat{V}_i \leq V^{C_{DR,i}}$ hold.*

We note that the same property holds for the incremental version of exact value iteration. That is, both the lookahead and the direct controllers perform no worse than V_i obtained after i incremental updates from some V_0 corresponding to a FSM controller C_0.

4.7.3 SELECTING GRID POINTS

The incremental version of the grid-based linear-function approximation is flexible and works for an arbitrary grid.[26] Moreover, the grid need not be fixed and can be changed on line. Thus, the problem of finding grids reduces to the problem of selecting belief points to be updated next. One can apply various strategies to do this. For example, one can use a fixed set of grid points and update them repeatedly, or one can select belief points on line using various heuristics.

The incremental linear function method guarantees that the value function is always improved (all linear functions from previous steps are kept unless found to be redundant). The quality of a new linear function (to be added next) depends strongly on the quality of linear functions obtained in previous steps. Therefore, our objective is to select and order points with better chances of larger improvement. To do this we have designed two heuristic strategies for selecting and ordering belief points.

The first strategy attempts to optimize updates at extreme points of the belief simplex by ordering them heuristically. The idea of the heuristic is based on the fact that states with higher expected rewards (e.g. some designated goal states) backpropagate their effects (rewards) locally. Therefore, it is desirable that states in the neighborhood of the highest reward state be updated first, and the distant ones later. We apply this idea to order extreme points of the belief simplex, relying on the current estimate of the value function to identify the highest expected reward states and on a POMDP model to determine the neighbor states.

The second strategy is based on the idea of stochastic simulation. The strategy generates a sequence of belief points more likely to be reached from some (fixed) initial belief point. The points of the sequence are then used in reverse order to generate updates. The intent of this heuristic is to "maximize" the improvement of the value function at the initial fixed point. To run this heuristic, we need to find an initial belief point or a set of initial belief points. To address this problem, we use the first heuristic that allows us to order the extreme points of the belief simplex. These points are then used as initial beliefs for the simulation part. Thus, we have a two-tier strategy: the top-level strategy orders extremes of the belief simplex, and the lower-level strategy applies stochastic simulation to generate a sequence of belief states more likely reachable from a specific extreme point.

We tested the order heuristics and the two-tier heuristics on our Maze20 problem, and compared them also to two simple point selection strategies: the fixed-grid strategy, in which a set of 40 grid points was updated repeatedly, and the random-grid strategy, in which points were always chosen uniformly at random. Figure 25 shows the bound quality

---

26. There is no restriction on the grid points that must be included in the grid, such as was required for example in the linear point-interpolation scheme, which had to use all extreme points of the belief simplex.

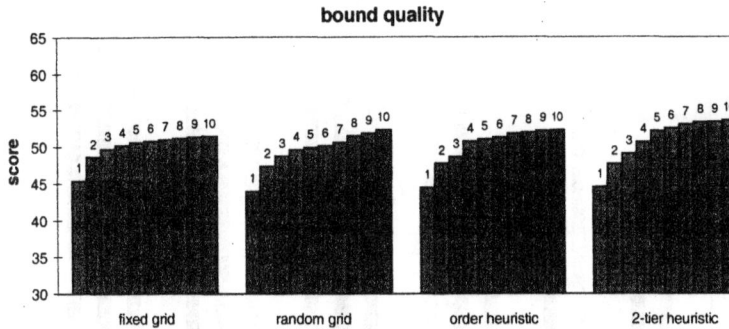

Figure 25: Improvements in the bound quality for the incremental linear-function method and four different grid-selection heuristics. Each cycle includes 40 grid-point updates.

of the methods for 10 update cycles (each cycle consists of 40 grid point updates) on the Maze20 problem. We see that the differences in the quality of value-function approximations for different strategies (even the very simple ones) are relatively small. We note that we observed similar results also for other problems, not just Maze20.

The relatively small improvement of our heuristics can be explained by the fact that every new linear function influences a larger portion of the belief space and thus the method should be less sensitive to a choice of a specific point.[27] However, another plausible explanation is that our heuristics were not very good and more accurate heuristics or combinations of heuristics could be constructed. Efficient strategies for locating grid points used in some of the exact methods, e.g. the Witness algorithm (Kaelbling et al., 1999) or Cheng's methods (Cheng, 1988) can potentially be applied to this problem. This remains an open area of research.

4.7.4 CONTROL

The grid-based linear-function approach leads to a piecewise linear and convex approximation. Every linear function comes with a natural action choice that lets us choose the action greedily. Thus we can run both the lookahead and the direct controllers. Figure 26 compares the performance of four different controllers for the fixed grid of 40 points, combining standard and incremental updates with lookahead and direct greedy control after 1, 5 and 10 update cycles. The results (see also Figure 24) illustrate the trade-offs between the computational time of obtaining the solution and its quality. We see that the incremental approach and the lookahead controller design tend to improve the control performance. The prices paid are worse running and reaction times, respectively.

---

27. The small sensitivity of the incremental method to the selection of grid points would suggest that one could, in many instances, replace exact updates with simpler point selection strategies. This could increase the speed of exact value-iteration methods (at least in their initial stages), which suffer from inefficiencies associated with locating a complete set of grid points to be updated in every step. However, this issue needs to be investigated.

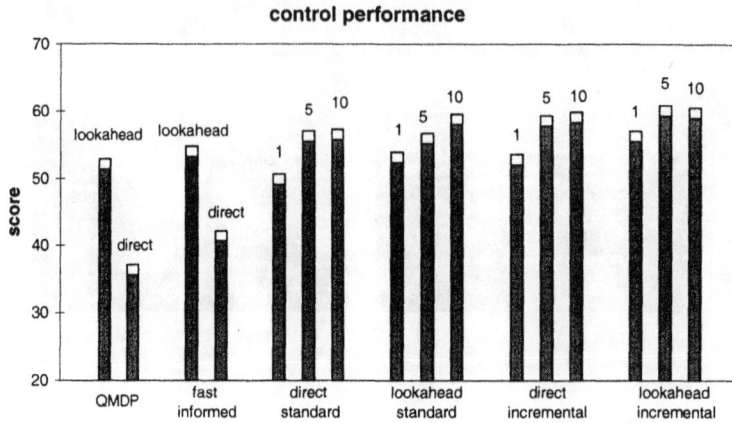

Figure 26: Control performance of four different controllers based on grid-based linear function updates after 1, 5 and 10 update cycles for the same 40-point grid. Controllers represent combinations of two update strategies (standard and incremental) and two action-extraction techniques (direct and lookahead). Running times for the two update strategies were presented in Figure 24. For comparison we include also performances of the QMDP and the fast informed bound methods (with both direct and lookahead designs).

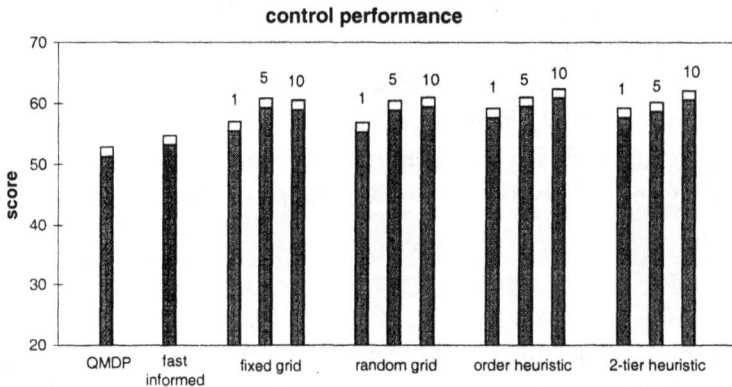

Figure 27: Control performances of lookahead controllers based on the incremental linear-function approach and different point-selection heuristics after 1, 5 and 10 improvement cycles. For comparison, scores for the QMDP and the fast informed bound approximations are shown as well.

Figure 27 illustrates the effect of point selection heuristics on control. We compare the results for lookahead control only, using approximations obtained after 1, 5 and 10 improvement cycles (each cycle consists of 40 grid point updates). The test results show that, as for the bound quality, there are no big differences among various heuristics, suggesting a small sensitivity of control to the selection of grid points.

4.8 Summary of Value-Function Approximations

Heuristic value-function approximations methods allow us to replace hard-to-compute exact methods and trade off solution quality for speed. There are numerous methods we can employ, each with different properties and different trade-offs of quality versus speed. Tables 1 and 2 summarize main theoretical properties of the approximation methods covered in this paper. The majority of these methods are of polynomial complexity or at least have efficient (polynomial) Bellman updates. This makes them good candidates for more complex POMDP problems that are out of reach of exact methods.

All of the methods are heuristic approximations in that they do not give solutions of a guaranteed precision. Despite this fact we proved that solutions of some of the methods are no worse than others in terms of value function quality (see Figure 15). This was one of the main contributions of the paper. However, there are currently minimal theoretical results relating these methods in terms of control performance; the exception are some results for FSM-controllers and FSM-based approximations. The key observation here is that for the quality of control (lookahead control) it is more important to approximate the shape (derivatives) of the value function correctly. This is also illustrated empirically on grid-based interpolation-extrapolation methods in Section 4.5.9 that are based on non-convex value functions. The main challenges here are to find ways of analyzing and comparing control performance of different approximations also theoretically and to identify classes of POMDPs for which certain methods dominate the others.

Finally, we note that the list of methods is not complete and other value-function approximation methods or the refinements of existing methods are possible. For example, White and Scherer (1994) investigate methods based on truncated histories that lead to upper and lower bound estimates of the value function for complete information states (complete histories). Also, additional restrictions on some of the methods can change the properties of a more generic method. For example, it is possible that under additional assumptions we will be able to ensure convergence of the least-squares fit approximation.

5. Conclusions

POMDPs offers an elegant mathematical framework for representing decision processes in stochastic partially observable domains. Despite their modeling advantages, however, POMDP problems are hard to solve exactly. Thus, the complexity of problem solving-procedures becomes the key aspect in the sucessful application of the model to real-world problems, even at the expense of the optimality. As recent complexity results for the approximability of POMDP problems are not encouraging (Lusena et al., 1998; Madani et al., 1999), we focus on heuristic approximations, in particular approximations of value functions.

Method	Bound	Isotonicity	Contraction
MDP approximation	upper	√	√
QMDP approximation	upper	√	√
Fast informed bound	upper	√	√
UMDP approximation	lower	√	√
Fixed-strategy method	lower	√	√
Grid-based interpolation-extrapolation	-	-	-
Nearest neighbor	-	√	√
Kernel regression	-	√	√
Linear point interpolation	upper	√	√
Curve-fitting (least-squares fit)	-	-	-
linear Q-function	-	-	-
Grid-based linear function method	lower	-	-
Incremental version (start from a lower bound)	lower	√	- *

Table 1: Properties of different value-function approximation methods: bound property, isotonicity and contraction property of the underlying mappings for $0 \leq \gamma < 1$. (*) Although incremental version of the grid-based linear-function method is not a contraction it always converges.

Method	Finite-horizon	Discounted infinite-horizon
MDP approximation	P	P
QMDP approximation	P	P
Fast informed bound	P	P
UMDP approximation	NP-hard	undecidable
Fixed-strategy method	P	P
Grid-based interpolation-extrapolation	varies	NA
Nearest neighbor	P	P
Kernel regression	P	P
Linear point interpolation	P	varies
Fixed interpolation	P	P
Best interpolation	P	?
Curve-fitting (least-squares fit)	varies	NA
linear Q-function	P	NA
Grid-based linear function method	P	NA
Incremental version	NA	?

Table 2: Complexity of value-function approximation methods for finite-horizon problem and discounted infinite-horizon problem. The objective for the discounted infinite-horizon case is to find the corresponding fixed-point solution. The complexity results take into account, in addition to components of POMDPs, also all other approximation specific parameters, e.g., the size of the grid G in grid-based methods. ? indicates open instances and NA methods that are not applicable to one of the problems (e.g. because of possible divergence).

5.1 Contributions

The paper surveys new and known value-function approximation methods for solving POMDPs. We focus primarily on the theoretical analysis and comparison of the methods, with findings and results supported experimentally on a problem of moderate size from the agent navigation domain. We analyze the methods from different perspectives: their computational complexity, capability to bound the optimal value function, convergence properties of iterative implementations, and the quality of derived controllers. The analysis includes new theoretical results, deriving the properties of individual approximations, and their relations to exact methods. In general, the relations between and trade-offs among different methods are not well understood. We provide some new insights on these issues by analyzing their corresponding updates. For example, we showed that the differences among the exact, the MDP, the QMDP, the fast-informed bound, and the UMDP methods boil down to simple mathematical manipulations and their subsequent effect on the value-function approximation. This allowed us to determine relations among different methods in terms of quality of their respective value functions which is one of the main results of the paper.

We also presented a number of new methods and heuristic refinements of some existing techniques. The primary contributions in this area include the fast-informed bound, grid-based point interpolation methods (including adaptive grid approaches based on stochastic sampling), and the incremental linear-function method. We also showed that in some instances the solutions can be obtained more efficiently by converting the original approximation into an equivalent finite-state MDP. For example, grid-based approximations with convex rules can be often solved via conversion into a grid-based MDP (in which grid points correspond to new states), leading to the polynomial-complexity algorithm for both the finite and the discounted infinite-horizon cases (Section 4.5.3). This result can dramatically improve the run-time performance of the grid-based approaches. A similar conversion to the equivalent finite-state MDP, allowing a polynomial-time solution for the discounted infinite-horizon problem, was shown for the fast informed bound method (Section 4.2).

5.2 Challenges and Future Directions

Work on POMDPs and their approximations is far from complete. Some complexity results remain open, in particular, the complexity of the grid-based approach seeking the best interpolation, or the complexity of finding the fixed-point solution for the incremental version of the grid-based linear-function method. Another interesting issue that needs more investigation is the convergence of value iteration with least-squares approximation. Although the method can be unstable in the general case, it is possible that under certain restrictions it will converge.

In the paper we use a single POMDP problem (Maze20) only to support theoretical findings or to illustrate some intuitions. Therefore, the results not supported theoretically (related mostly to control) cannot be generalized and used to rank different methods, since their performance may vary on other problems. In general, the area of POMDPs and POMDP approximations suffers from a shortage of larger-scale experimental work with multiple problems of different complexities and a broad range of methods. Experimental work is especially needed to study and compare different methods with regard to control quality. The main reason for this is that there are only few theoretical results relating the control performance. These studies should help focus theoretical exploration by discovering interesting cases and possibly identifying classes of problems for which certain approximations are more or less suitable. Our preliminary experimental results show that there are significant differences in control performance among different methods and that not all of them may be suitable to approximate the control policies. For example, the grid-based nearest-neighbor approach with piecewise-constant approximation is typically inferior to and outperformed by other simpler (and more efficient) value-function methods.

The present work focused on heuristic approximation methods. We investigated general (flat) POMDPs and did not take advantage of any additional structural refinements. However, real-world problems usually offer more structure that can be exploited to devise new algorithms and perhaps lead to further speed-ups. It is also possible that some of the restricted versions of POMDPs (with additional structural assumptions) can be solved or approximated efficiently, even though the general complexity results for POMDPs or their ϵ-approximations are not very encouraging (Papadimitriou & Tsitsiklis, 1987; Littman, 1996; Mundhenk et al., 1997; Lusena et al., 1998; Madani et al., 1999). A challenge here is to identify models that allow efficient solutions and are at the same time interesting enough from the point of application.

Finally, a number of interesting issues arise when we move to problems with large state, action, and observation spaces. Here, the complexity of not only value-function updates but also belief state updates becomes an issue. In general, partial observability of hidden process states does not allow us to factor and decompose belief states (and their updates), even when transitions have a great deal of structure and can be represented very compactly. Promising directions to deal with these issues include various Monte-Carlo approaches (Isard & Blake, 1996; Kanazawa, Koller, & Russell, 1995; Doucet, 1998; Kearns et al., 1999)), methods for approximating belief states via decomposition (Boyen & Koller, 1998, 1999), or a combination of the two approaches (McAllester & Singh, 1999).

Acknowledgements

Anthony Cassandra, Thomas Dean, Leslie Kaelbling, William Long, Peter Szolovits and anonymous reviewers provided valuable feedback and comments on this work. This research was supported by grant RO1 LM 04493 and grant 1T15LM07092 from the National Library of Medicine, by DOD Advanced Research Project Agency (ARPA) under contract number N66001-95-M-1089 and DARPA/Rome Labs Planning Initiative grant F30602-95-1-0020.

Appendix A. Theorems and proofs

A.1 Convergence to the Bound

Theorem 6 *Let H_1 and H_2 be two value-function mappings defined on $\mathcal{V}_1$ and $\mathcal{V}_2$ s.t.*

1. *H_1, H_2 are contractions with fixed points V_1^*, V_2^*;*

2. *$V_1^* \in \mathcal{V}_2$ and $H_2 V_1^* \geq H_1 V_1^* = V_1^*$;*

3. *H_2 is an isotone mapping.*

Then $V_2^* \geq V_1^*$ holds.

Proof By applying H_2 to condition 2 and expanding the result with condition 2 again we get: $H_2^2 V_1^* \geq H_2 V_1^* \geq H_1 V_1^* = V_1^*$. Repeating this we get in the limit $V_2^* \geq \cdots \geq H_2^n V_1^* \geq \cdots H_2^2 V_1^* \geq H_2 V_1^* \geq H_1 V_1^* = V_1^*$, which proves the result. $\square$

A.2 Accuracy of a Lookahead Controller Based on Bounds

Theorem 7 *Let $\widehat{V}_U$ and $\widehat{V}_L$ be upper and lower bounds of the optimal value function for the discounted infinite-horizon problem. Let $\epsilon = \sup_b |\widehat{V}_U(b) - \widehat{V}_L(b)| = \|\widehat{V}_U - \widehat{V}_L\|$ be the maximum bound difference. Then the expected reward for a lookahead controller $\widehat{V}^{LA}$, constructed for either $\widehat{V}_U$ or $\widehat{V}_L$, satisfies $\|\widehat{V}^{LA} - V^*\| \leq \frac{\epsilon(2-\gamma)}{(1-\gamma)}$.*

Proof Let $\widehat{V}$ denotes either an upper or lower bound approximation of V^* and H^{LA} be the value function mapping corresponding to the lookahead policy for $\widehat{V}$. Note, that since the lookahead policy always optimizes its actions with regard to $\widehat{V}$, $H\widehat{V} = H^{LA}\widehat{V}$ must hold. The error of $\widehat{V}^{LA}$ can be bounded using the triangle inequality

$$\|\widehat{V}^{LA} - V^*\| \leq \|\widehat{V}^{LA} - \widehat{V}\| + \|\widehat{V} - V^*\|.$$

The first component satisfies:

$$
\begin{aligned}
\|\widehat{V}^{LA} - \widehat{V}\| &= \|H^{LA}\widehat{V}^{LA} - \widehat{V}\| \\
&\leq \|H^{LA}\widehat{V}^{LA} - H\widehat{V}\| + \|H\widehat{V} - \widehat{V}\| \\
&= \|H^{LA}\widehat{V}^{LA} - H^{LA}\widehat{V}\| + \|H\widehat{V} - \widehat{V}\| \\
&\leq \gamma\|\widehat{V}^{LA} - \widehat{V}\| + \epsilon
\end{aligned}
$$

The inequality: $\|H\widehat{V} - \widehat{V}\| \leq \epsilon$ follows from the isotonicity of H and the fact that $\widehat{V}$ is either an upper or a lower bound. Rearranging the inequalities, we obtain: $\|\widehat{V}^{LA} - \widehat{V}\| = \frac{\epsilon}{(1-\gamma)}$.
The bound on the second term $\|\widehat{V} - V^*\| \leq \epsilon$ is trivial.
Therefore, $\|\widehat{V}^{LA} - V^*\| \leq \epsilon[\frac{1}{(1-\gamma)} + 1] = \epsilon\frac{(2-\gamma)}{(1-\gamma)}$. $\square$

A.3 MDP, QMDP and the Fast Informed Bounds

Theorem 8 *A solution for the fast informed bound approximation can be found by solving an MDP with $|S||A||\Theta|$ states, $|A|$ actions and the same discount factor γ.*

Proof Let α_i^a be a linear function for action a defining $\widehat{V}_i$. Let $\alpha_i(s, a)$ denote parameters of the function. The parameters of $\widehat{V}_{i+1}$ satisfy:

$$\alpha_{i+1}(s, a) = \rho(s, a) + \gamma \sum_{o \in \Theta} \max_{a' \in A} \sum_{s' \in S} P(s', o|s, a)\alpha_i(s', a').$$

Let

$$\alpha_{i+1}(s, a, o) = \max_{a' \in A} \sum_{s' \in S} P(s', o|s, a)\alpha_i(s', a').$$

Now, we can rewrite $\alpha_{i+1}(s,a,o)$ for every s,a,o as:

$$\alpha_{i+1}(s,a,o) = \max_{a' \in A} \left\{ \sum_{s' \in S} P(s',o|s,a) \left[\rho(s',a') + \gamma \sum_{o' \in \Theta} \alpha_i(s',a',o') \right] \right\}$$

$$= \max_{a' \in A} \left\{ \left[\sum_{s' \in S} P(s',o|s,a)\rho(s',a') \right] + \gamma \left[\sum_{o' \in \Theta} \sum_{s' \in S} P(s',o|s,a)\alpha_i(s',a',o') \right] \right\}$$

These equations define an MDP with state space $S \times A \times \Theta$, action space A and discount factor γ. Thus, a solution for the fast informed bound update can be found by solving an equivalent finite-state MDP. $\square$

Theorem 9 *Let $\widehat{V}_i$ corresponds to a piecewise linear convex value function defined by Γ_i linear functions. Then $H\widehat{V}_i \leq H_{FIB}\widehat{V}_i \leq H_{QMDP}\widehat{V}_i \leq H_{MDP}\widehat{V}_i$.*

Proof

$$\max_{a \in A} \left\{ \sum_{s \in S} \rho(s,a)b(s) + \gamma \sum_{o \in \Theta} \max_{\alpha_i \in \Gamma_i} \sum_{s' \in S} \sum_{s \in S} P(s',o|s,a)b(s)\alpha_i(s') \right\}$$

$$= (HV_i)(b)$$

$$\leq \max_{a \in A} \sum_{s \in S} b(s) \left[\rho(s,a) + \gamma \sum_{o \in \Theta} \max_{\alpha_i \in \Gamma_i} \sum_{s' \in S} P(s',o|s,a)\alpha_i(s') \right]$$

$$= (H_{FIB}V_i)(b)$$

$$\leq \max_{a \in A} \sum_{s \in S} b(s) \left[\rho(s,a) + \gamma \sum_{s' \in S} P(s'|s,a) \max_{\alpha_i \in \Gamma_i} \alpha_i(s') \right]$$

$$= (H_{QMDP}\widehat{V}_i)(b)$$

$$\leq \sum_{s \in S} b(s) \max_{a \in A} \left[\rho(s,a) + \gamma \sum_{s' \in S} P(s'|s,a) \max_{\alpha_i \in \Gamma_i} \alpha_i(s') \right]$$

$$= (H_{MDP}\widehat{V}_i)(b) \quad \square$$

A.4 Fixed-Strategy Approximations

Theorem 10 *Let C_{FSM} be an FSM controller. Let C_{DR} and C_{LA} be the direct and the one-step-lookahead controllers constructed based on C_{FSM}. Then $V^{C_{FSM}}(b) \leq V^{C_{DR}}(b)$ and $V^{C_{FSM}}(b) \leq V^{C_{LA}}(b)$ hold for all belief states $b \in \mathcal{I}$.*

Proof The value function for the FSM controller C_{FSM} satisfies:

$$V^{C_{FSM}}(b) = \max_{x \in M} V(x,b) = V(\psi(b),b)$$

where

$$V(x,b) = \rho(b,\eta(x)) + \gamma \sum_{o \in \Theta} P(o|b,\eta(x))V(\phi(x,o),\tau(b,\eta(x),o)).$$

The direct controller C_{DR} selects the action greedily in every step, that is, it always chooses according to $\psi(b) = \arg\max_{x\in M} V(x,b)$. The lookahead controller C_{LA} selects the action based on $V(x,b)$ one step away:

$$\eta^{LA}(b) = \arg\max_{a\in A}\left[\rho(b,a) + \gamma\sum_{o\in\Theta} P(o|b,a)\max_{x'\in M} V(x',\tau(b,a,o))\right].$$

By expanding the value function for C_{FSM} for one step we get:

$$V^{C_{FSM}}(b) = \max_{x\in M} V(x,b)$$

$$= \max_{x\in M}\left[\rho(b,\eta(x)) + \gamma\sum_{o\in\Theta} P(o|b,\eta(x))V(\phi(x,o),\tau(b,\eta(x),o))\right] \tag{1}$$

$$= \rho(b,\eta(\psi(b))) + \gamma\sum_{o\in\Theta} P(o|b,\eta(\psi(b)))V(\phi(x,o),\tau(b,\eta(\psi(b)),o))$$

$$\leq \rho(b,\eta(\psi(b))) + \gamma\sum_{o\in\Theta} P(o|b,\eta(\psi(b)))\max_{x'\in M} V(x',\tau(b,\eta(\psi(b)),o)) \tag{2}$$

$$\leq \max_{a\in A}\left[\rho(b,a) + \gamma\sum_{o\in\Theta} P(o|b,a)\max_{x'\in M} V(x',\tau(b,a,o))\right]$$

$$= \rho(b,\eta^{LA}(b)) + \gamma\sum_{o\in\Theta} P(o|b,\eta^{LA}(b))\max_{x'\in M} V(x',\tau(b,\eta^{LA}(b),o)) \tag{3}$$

Iteratively expanding $\max_{x'\in M} V(x,.)$ in 2 and 3 with expression 1 and substituing improved (higher value) expressions 2 and 3 back we obtain value functions for both the direct and the lookahead controllers. (Expansions of 2 lead to the value for the direct controller and expansions of 3 to the value for the lookahead controller.) Thus $V^{C_{FSM}} \leq V^{C_{DR}}$ and $V^{C_{FSM}} \leq V^{C_{LA}}$ must hold. Note, however, that action choices $\psi(b)$ and $\psi^{LA}(b)$ in expressions 2 and 3 can be different leading to different next step belief states and subsequently to different expansion sequences. Therefore, the above result does not imply that $V^{DR}(b) \leq V^{LA}(b)$ for all $b \in \mathcal{I}$. □

A.5 Grid-Based Linear-Function Method

Theorem 14 *Let $\widehat{V}_i$ be a value function obtained via the incremental linear function method, starting from $\widehat{V}_0$, which corresponds to some fixed strategy C_0. Let $C_{LA,i}$ and $C_{DR,i}$ be two controllers based on $\widehat{V}_i$: the lookahead controller and the direct action controller, and $V^{C_{LA,i}}$, $V^{C_{DR,i}}$ be their respective value functions. Then $\widehat{V}_i \leq V^{C_{LA,i}}$ and $\widehat{V}_i \leq V^{C_{DR,i}}$ hold.*

Proof By initializing the method with a value function for some FSM controller C_0, the incremental updates can be interpreted as additions of new states to the FSM controller (a new linear function corresponds to a new state of the FSM). Let C_i be a controller after step i. Then $V^{C_{FSM,i}} = \widehat{V}_i$ holds and the inequalities follow from Theorem 10. □

References

Astrom, K. J. (1965). Optimal control of Markov decision processes with incomplete state estimation. *Journal of Mathematical Analysis and Applications, 10*, 174–205.

Baird, L. C. (1995). Residual algorithms: Reinforcement learning with function approximation. In *Proceedings of the Twelfth International Conference on Machine Learning*, pp. 30–37.

Barto, A. G., Bradtke, S. J., & Singh, S. P. (1995). Learning to act using real-time dynamic programming. *Artificial Intelligence, 72*, 81–138.

Bellman, R. E. (1957). *Dynamic programming*. Princeton University Press, Princeton, NJ.

Bertsekas, D. P. (1994). A counter-example to temporal differences learning. *Neural Computation, 7*, 270–279.

Bertsekas, D. P. (1995). *Dynamic programming and optimal control*. Athena Scientific.

Bonet, B., & Geffner, H. (1998). Learning sorting and classification with POMDPs. In *Proceedings of the Fifteenth International Conference on Machine Learning*.

Boutilier, C., Dean, T., & Hanks, S. (1999). Decision-theoretic planning: Structural assumptions and computational leverage. *Artificial Intelligence, 11*, 1–94.

Boutilier, C., & Poole, D. (1996). Exploiting structure in policy construction. In *Proceedings of the Thirteenth National Conference on Artificial Intelligence*, pp. 1168–1175.

Boyan, J. A., & Moore, A. A. (1995). Generalization in reinforcement learning: safely approximating the value function. In *Advances in Neural Information Processing Systems 7*. MIT Press.

Boyen, X., & Koller, D. (1998). Tractable inference for complex stochastic processes. In *Proceedings of the Fourteenth Conference on Uncertainty in Artificial Intelligence*, pp. 33–42.

Boyen, X., & Koller, D. (1999). Exploiting the architecture of dynamic systems. In *Proceedings of the Sixteenth National Conference on Artificial Intelligence*, pp. 313–320.

Brafman, R. I. (1997). A heuristic variable grid solution method for POMDPs. In *Proceedings of the Fourteenth National Conference on Artificial Intelligence*, pp. 727–233.

Burago, D., Rougemont, M. D., & Slissenko, A. (1996). On the complexity of partially observed Markov decision processes. *Theoretical Computer Science, 157*, 161–183.

Cassandra, A. R. (1998). *Exact and approximate algorithms for partially observable Markov decision processes*. Ph.D. thesis, Brown University.

Cassandra, A. R., Littman, M. L., & Zhang, N. L. (1997). Incremental pruning: a simple, fast, exact algorithm for partially observable Markov decision processes. In *Proceedings of the Thirteenth Conference on Uncertainty in Artificial Intelligence*, pp. 54–61.

Castañon, D. (1997). Approximate dynamic programming for sensor management. In *Proceedings of Conference on Decision and Control*.

Cheng, H.-T. (1988). *Algorithms for partially observable Markov decision processes*. Ph.D. thesis, University of British Columbia.

Condon, A. (1992). The complexity of stochastic games. *Information and Computation*, *96*, 203–224.

Dean, T., & Kanazawa, K. (1989). A model for reasoning about persistence and causation. *Computational Intelligence*, *5*, 142–150.

Dearden, R., & Boutilier, C. (1997). Abstraction and approximate decision theoretic planning. *Artificial Intelligence*, *89*, 219–283.

Doucet, A. (1998). On sequential simulation-based methods for Bayesian filtering. Tech. rep. CUED/F-INFENG/TR 310, Department of Engineering, Cambridge University.

Drake, A. (1962). *Observation of a Markov process through a noisy channel*. Ph.D. thesis, Massachusetts Institute of Technology.

Draper, D., Hanks, S., & Weld, D. (1994). Probabilistic planning with information gathering and contingent execution. In *Proceedings of the Second International Conference on AI Planning Systems*, pp. 31–36.

Eagle, J. N. (1984). The optimal search for a moving target when search path is constrained. *Operations Research*, *32*, 1107–1115.

Eaves, B. (1984). *A course in triangulations for soving differential equations with deformations*. Springer-Verlag, Berlin.

Gordon, G. J. (1995). Stable function approximation in dynamic programming. In *Proceedings of the Twelfth International Conference on Machine Learning*.

Hansen, E. (1998a). An improved policy iteration algorithm for partially observable MDPs. In *Advances in Neural Information Processing Systems 10*. MIT Press.

Hansen, E. (1998b). Solving POMDPs by searching in policy space. In *Proceedings of the Fourteenth Conference on Uncertainty in Artificial Intelligence*, pp. 211–219.

Hauskrecht, M. (1997). *Planning and control in stochastic domains with imperfect information*. Ph.D. thesis, Massachusetts Institute of Technology.

Hauskrecht, M., & Fraser, H. (1998). Planning medical therapy using partially observable Markov decision processes. In *Proceedings of the Ninth International Workshop on Principles of Diagnosis (DX-98)*, pp. 182–189.

Hauskrecht, M., & Fraser, H. (2000). Planning treatment of ischemic heart disease with partially observable Markov decision processes. *Artificial Intelligence in Medicine*, *18*, 221–244.

Heyman, D., & Sobel, M. (1984). *Stochastic methods in operations research: stochastic optimization*. McGraw-Hill.

Howard, R. A. (1960). *Dynamic Programming and Markov Processes*. MIT Press, Cambridge.

Howard, R. A., & Matheson, J. (1984). Influence diagrams. *Principles and Applications of Decision Analysis, 2*.

Isard, M., & Blake, A. (1996). Contour tracking by stochastic propagation of conditional density. In *Proccedings of Europian Conference on Computer Vision*, pp. 343–356.

Kaelbling, L. P., Littman, M. L., & Cassandra, A. R. (1999). Planning and acting in partially observable stochastic domains. *Artificial Intelligence, 101*, 99–134.

Kanazawa, K., Koller, D., & Russell, S. J. (1995). Stochastic simulation algorithms for dynamic probabilistic networks. In *Proceedings of the Eleventh Conference on Uncertainty in Artificial Intelligence*, pp. 346–351.

Kearns, M., Mansour, Y., & Ng, A. Y. (1999). A sparse sampling algorithm for near optimal planning in large Markov decision processes. In *Proceedings of the Sixteenth International Joint Conference on Artificial Intelligence*, pp. 1324–1331.

Kjaerulff, U. (1992). A computational scheme for reasoning in dynamic probabilistic networks. In *Proceedings of the Eighth Conference on Uncertainty in Artificial Intelligence*, pp. 121–129.

Korf, R. (1985). Depth-first iterative deepening: an optimal admissible tree search. *Artificial Intelligence, 27*, 97–109.

Kushmerick, N., Hanks, S., & Weld, D. (1995). An algorithm for probabilistic planning. *Artificial Intelligence, 76*, 239–286.

Lauritzen, S. L. (1996). *Graphical models*. Clarendon Press.

Littman, M. L. (1994). Memoryless policies: Theoretical limitations and practical results. In Cliff, D., Husbands, P., Meyer, J., & Wilson, S. (Eds.), *From Animals to Animats 3: Proceedings of the Third International Conference on Simulation of Adaptive Behavior*. MIT Press, Cambridge.

Littman, M. L. (1996). *Algorithms for sequential decision making*. Ph.D. thesis, Brown University.

Littman, M. L., Cassandra, A. R., & Kaelbling, L. P. (1995). Learning policies for partially observable environments: scaling up. In *Proceedings of the Twelfth International Conference on Machine Learning*, pp. 362–370.

Lovejoy, W. S. (1991a). Computationally feasible bounds for partially observed Markov decision processes. *Operations Research, 39*, 192–175.

Lovejoy, W. S. (1991b). A survey of algorithmic methods for partially observed Markov decision processes. *Annals of Operations Research, 28,* 47–66.

Lovejoy, W. S. (1993). Suboptimal policies with bounds for parameter adaptive decision processes. *Operations Research, 41,* 583–599.

Lusena, C., Goldsmith, J., & Mundhenk, M. (1998). Nonapproximability results for Markov decision processes. Tech. rep., University of Kentucky.

Madani, O., Hanks, S., & Condon, A. (1999). On the undecidability of probabilistic planning and infinite-horizon partially observable Markov decision processes. In *Proceedings of the Sixteenth National Conference on Artificial Intelligence.*

McAllester, D., & Singh, S. P. (1999). Approximate planning for factored POMDPs using belief state simplification. In *Proceedings of the Fifteenth Conference on Uncertainty in Artificial Intelligence,* pp. 409–416.

McCallum, R. (1995). Instance-based utile distinctions for reinforcement learning with hidden state. In *Proceedings of the Twelfth International Conference on Machine Learning.*

Monahan, G. E. (1982). A survey of partially observable Markov decision processes: theory, models, and algorithms. *Management Science, 28,* 1–16.

Mundhenk, M., Goldsmith, J., Lusena, C., & Allender, E. (1997). Encyclopaedia of complexity results for finite-horizon Markov decision process problems. Tech. rep., CS Dept TR 273-97, University of Kentucky.

Papadimitriou, C. H., & Tsitsiklis, J. N. (1987). The complexity of Markov decision processes. *Mathematics of Operations Research, 12,* 441–450.

Parr, R., & Russell, S. (1995). Approximating optimal policies for partially observable stochastic domains. In *Proceedings of the Fourteenth International Joint Conference on Artificial Intelligence,* pp. 1088–1094.

Pearl, J. (1988). *Probabilistic reasoning in intelligent systems.* Morgan Kaufman.

Platzman, L. K. (1977). *Finite memory estimation and control of finite probabilistic systems.* Ph.D. thesis, Massachusetts Institute of Technology.

Platzman, L. K. (1980). A feasible computational approach to infinite-horizon partially-observed Markov decision problems. Tech. rep., Georgia Institute of Technology.

Puterman, M. L. (1994). *Markov decision processes: discrete stochastic dynamic programming.* John Wiley, New York.

Raiffa, H. (1970). *Decision analysis. Introductory lectures on choices under uncertainty.* Addison-Wesley.

Rumelhart, D., Hinton, G. E., & Williams, R. J. (1986). Learning internal representations by error propagation. In *Parallel Distributed Processing,* pp. 318–362.

Satia, J., & Lave, R. (1973). Markovian decision processes with probabilistic observation of states. *Management Science, 20,* 1–13.

Singh, S. P., Jaakkola, T., & Jordan, M. I. (1994). Learning without state-estimation in partially observable Markovian decision processes. In *Proceedings of the Eleventh International Conference on Machine Learning*, pp. 284–292.

Smallwood, R. D., & Sondik, E. J. (1973). The optimal control of partially observable processes over a finite horizon. *Operations Research, 21,* 1071–1088.

Sondik, E. J. (1971). *The optimal control of partially observable Markov decision processes.* Ph.D. thesis, Stanford University.

Sondik, E. J. (1978). The optimal control of partially observable processes over the infinite horizon: Discounted costs. *Operations Research, 26,* 282–304.

Tatman, J., & Schachter, R. D. (1990). Dynamic programming and influence diagrams. *IEEE Transactions on Systems, Man and Cybernetics, 20,* 365–379.

Tsitsiklis, J. N., & Roy, B. V. (1996). Feature-based methods for large-scale dynamic programming. *Machine Learning, 22,* 59–94.

Washington, R. (1996). Incremental Markov model planning. In *Proceedings of the Eight IEEE International Conference on Tools with Artificial Intelligence*, pp. 41–47.

White, C. C., & Scherer, W. T. (1994). Finite memory suboptimal design for partially observed Markov decision processes. *Operations Research, 42,* 439–455.

Williams, R. J., & Baird, L. C. (1994). Tight performance bounds on greedy policies based on imperfect value functions. In *Proceedings of the Tenth Yale Workshop on Adaptive and Learning Systems* Yale University.

Yost, K. A. (1998). *Solution of large-scale allocation problems with partially observable outcomes.* Ph.D. thesis, Naval Postgraduate School, Monterey, CA.

Zhang, N. L., & Lee, S. S. (1998). Planning with partially observable Markov decision processes: Advances in exact solution method. In *Proceedings of the Fourteenth Conference on Uncertainty in Artificial Intelligence*, pp. 523–530.

Zhang, N. L., & Liu, W. (1997a). A model approximation scheme for planning in partially observable stochastic domains. *Journal of Artificial Intelligence Research, 7,* 199–230.

Zhang, N. L., & Liu, W. (1997b). Region-based approximations for planning in stochastic domains. In *Proceedings of the Thirteenth Conference on Uncertainty in Artificial Intelligence*, pp. 472–480.

Journal of Artificial Intelligence Research 13 (2000) 95-153   Submitted 1/00; published 9/00

Asimovian Adaptive Agents

Diana F. Gordon   GORDON@AIC.NRL.NAVY.MIL

Navy Center for Applied Research in Artificial Intelligence
Naval Research Laboratory, Code 5515
Washington, D.C. 20375-5337 USA

Abstract

The goal of this research is to develop agents that are adaptive *and* predictable *and* timely. At first blush, these three requirements seem contradictory. For example, adaptation risks introducing undesirable side effects, thereby making agents' behavior less predictable. Furthermore, although formal verification can assist in ensuring behavioral predictability, it is known to be time-consuming.

Our solution to the challenge of satisfying all three requirements is the following. Agents have finite-state automaton plans, which are adapted online via evolutionary learning (perturbation) operators. To ensure that critical behavioral constraints are always satisfied, agents' plans are first formally verified. They are then *re*verified after every adaptation. If reverification concludes that constraints are violated, the plans are repaired. The main objective of this paper is to improve the efficiency of reverification after learning, so that agents have a sufficiently rapid response time. We present two solutions: positive results that certain learning operators are a priori guaranteed to preserve useful classes of behavioral assurance constraints (which implies that no reverification is needed for these operators), and efficient incremental reverification algorithms for those learning operators that have negative a priori results.

1. Introduction

Agents are becoming increasingly prevalent and effective. Robots and softbots, working individually or in concert, can relieve people of a great deal of labor-intensive tedium in their jobs as well as in their day-to-day lives. Designers can furnish agents with plans to perform desired tasks. Nevertheless, a designer cannot possibly foresee all circumstances that will be encountered by the agent. Therefore, in addition to supplying an agent with plans, it is essential to also enable the agent to learn and modify its plans to adapt to unforeseen circumstances. The introduction of learning, however, often makes the agent's behavior significantly harder to predict.[1] The goal of this research is to verify the behavior of adaptive agents. In particular, our objective is to develop efficient methods for determining whether the behavior of learning agents remains within the bounds of prespecified constraints (called "properties") after learning. This includes verifying that properties are preserved for single adaptive agents as well as verifying that global properties are preserved for multiagent systems in which one or more agents may adapt.

An example of a property is Asimov's First Law (Asimov, 1950). This law, which has also been studied by Weld and Etzioni (1994), states that an agent may not harm a

---

1. Even adding a simple, elegant learning mechanism such as chunking in Soar can substantially reduce system predictability (Soar project members, personal communication).

human or allow a human to come to harm. The main contribution of Weld and Etzioni is a " 'call to arms:' before we release autonomous agents into real-world environments, we need some credible and computationally tractable means of making them obey Asimov's First Law...how do we stop our artifacts from causing us harm in the process of obeying our orders?" Of course, this law is too general for direct implementation and needs to be operationalized into specific properties testable on a system, such as "Never delete a user's file." This paper addresses Weld and Etzioni's call to arms in the context of adaptive agents. To respond to the call to arms, we are working toward "Asimovian" adaptive agents, which we define to be adaptive agents that can verify, in a reasonably efficient manner, whether user-defined properties are preserved after adaptation.[2] Such agents will either constrain their adaptation methods, or repair themselves in such a way as to preserve these properties.

The verification method assumed here, *model checking*, consists of building a finite model of a system and checking whether the desired property holds in that model. In the context of this paper, model checking determines whether $S \models P$ for plan S and property P, i.e., whether plan S "models" (satisfies) property P. The output is either "yes" or "no" and, if "no," one or more counterexamples are provided. Model checking has proven to be very effective for safety-critical applications, e.g., a model checker uncovered a potentially disastrous error in a system designed to make buildings more earthquake resistant. This error would have unleashed a structural force to worsen earthquake vibrations, rather than dampen them (Elseaidy et al., 1994).

Essentially, model checking is brute force search through the set of all reachable states of the plan to check if the property holds. If the plan has a finite number of states, this process terminates. Model checking global properties of a multiagent plan has time complexity that is exponential in the number of agents.[3] With a large number of agents, this is could be a serious problem. In fact, even model checking a single agent plan with a huge number of states can be computationally prohibitive. A great deal of research in the verification community is currently focused on reduction techniques for handling very large state spaces (Clarke & Wing, 1997). One of the largest systems model checked to date using these reduction techniques had 10^{120} states (Burch et al., 1994). Nevertheless, the applicability of many of these reduction techniques is restricted and few are completely automated. Furthermore, none of them are tailored for efficient *reverification* after learning has altered the system. Some methods in the literature are designed for software that changes. One that emphasizes efficiency, as ours does, is Sokolsky and Smolka's (1994). However none of them, including Sokolsky and Smolka's method, are applicable to multiagent systems in which a single agent could adapt, thereby altering the global behavior of the overall system. In contrast, our approach addresses the timeliness of adaptive multiagent systems.

Consider how reverification fits into our overall adaptive agents framework. In this framework (see Figure 1), there are one or more agents with "anytime" plans (Grefenstette & Ramsey, 1992), i.e., plans that are continually executed in response to internal and external environmental conditions. Each agent's plan is assumed to be in the form of a finite-state automaton (FSA). FSAs have been shown to be effective representations of

---

2. They are also called *APT agents* because they are adaptive, predictable and timely.

3. The states in a multiagent plan are formed by taking the Cartesian product of states in the individual agent plans (see Section 3).

OFFLINE:

plan

(1) Develop initial agent plan(s)
(2) If SIT_{1plan} or $SIT_{multplans}$, form multiagent plan
(3) Verify (multi)agent plan
(4) Repair plan(s) if properties not satisfied

ONLINE:

agent's plan

(5) Learning modifies (multi)agent plan

new plan

(6) If $SIT_{multplans}$, re-form multiagent plan
(7) Rapidly reverify (multi)agent plan
(8) Choose another learning operator or repair plan(s) if properties not satisfied

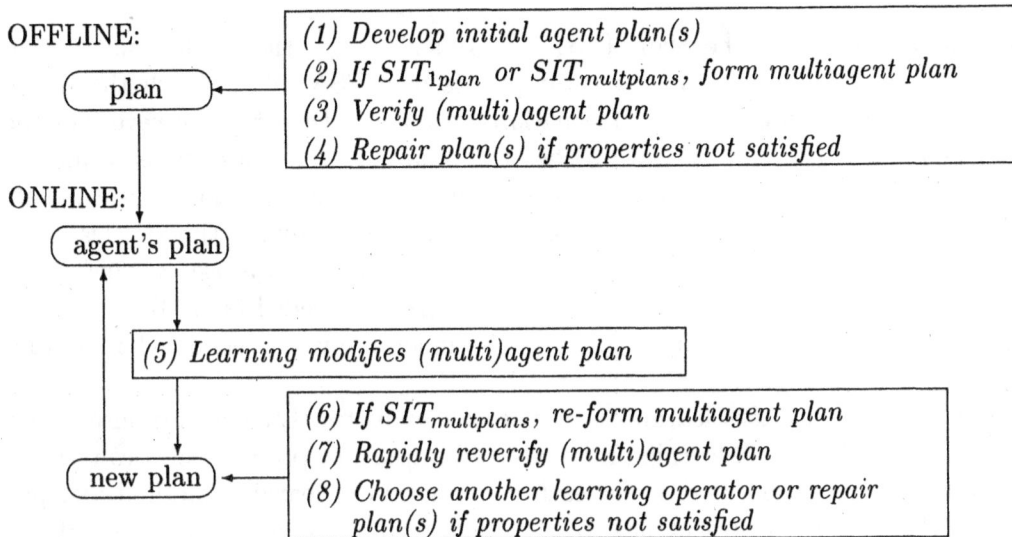

Figure 1: Verifiable adaptive agents.

reactive agent plans/strategies (Burkhard, 1993; Kabanza, 1995; Carmel & Markovitch, 1996; Fogel, 1996).

Let us begin with step 1 in Figure 1. There are at least a couple of ways that the FSA plans could be formed initially. For one, a human plan designer could engineer the initial plans. This may require considerable effort and knowledge. An appealing alternative is to evolve (i.e., learn using evolutionary algorithms) the initial plans in a simulated environment. Fogel (1996) outlines a procedure for evolving FSAs that is effective for a number of problems, including an iterated version of the Prisoner's Dilemma.

Human plan engineers or evolutionary algorithms can develop plans that satisfy an agent's goals to a high degree. However, to provide strict behavioral guarantees, formal verification is also required. Therefore we assume that prior to fielding the agents, the (multi)agent plan has been verified offline to determine whether it satisfies critical properties (steps 2 and 3). If not, the plan is repaired (step 4). Plan repair is not addressed in this paper, although it is an important topic for future research. Steps 2 through 4 require some clarification. If there is a single agent, then it has one FSA plan and that is all that is verified and repaired, if needed. We call this SIT_{1agent}. (This notation, as well as other notation used in the paper, is included in the glossary of Appendix A.) If there are multiple agents that cooperate, we consider two possibilities. In SIT_{1plan}, every agent uses the same multiagent plan, which is a "product" of the individual agent plans. This multiagent plan is formed and verified to see if it satisfies global multiagent coordination properties. The multiagent plan is repaired if verification produces any errors, i.e., failure of the plan to satisfy a property. In $SIT_{multplans}$, each agent independently uses its own individual plan. To verify global properties, one of the agents takes the product of these individual plans to form a multiagent plan. This multiagent plan is what is verified. For $SIT_{multplans}$, one or more individual plans are repaired if the property is not satisfied.

After the initial plan(s) have been verified and repaired, the agents are fielded. While fielded (online), the agents apply learning (e.g., evolutionary operators) to their plan(s) as needed (step 5). Learning may be required to adapt the plan to handle unexpected situations or to fine-tune the plan. If SIT_{1agent} or SIT_{1plan}, the single (multi)agent plan is adapted. If $SIT_{multplans}$, an agent adapts its own FSA, after which the multiagent (product) plan is *re*-formed. For all situations, one agent then rapidly *re*verifies the new (multi)agent plan to ensure it still satisfies the required properties (steps 6 and 7). Reformation of the multiagent plan and reverification are required to be as time-efficient as possible because they are performed online, perhaps in a highly time-critical situation. Whenever (re)verification fails, it produces a counterexample that is used to guide the choice of an alternative learning operator or other plan repair as needed (step 8). This process of executing, adapting, and reverifying plans cycles indefinitely as needed. The main focus of this paper is steps 6 and 7.

Rapid reverification after learning is a key to achieving timely agent responses. Our long-term goal is to examine all learning methods and important property classes to determine the quickest reverification method for each combination of learning method and property class. In this paper we present new results that certain useful learning operators are a priori guaranteed to be "safe" with respect to important classes of properties. In other words, if the property holds for the plan prior to learning, then it is guaranteed to still hold after learning.[4] If an agent uses these learning operators, it will be guaranteed to preserve the properties with *no re*verification required, i.e., steps 6 through 8 in Figure 1 need not be executed. This is the best one could hope for in an online situation where rapid response time is critical. For other learning operators and property classes our a priori results are negative. However, for the cases in which we have negative results, we present novel *incremental* reverification algorithms. These methods localize the reverification in order to save time over total reverification from scratch.[5] We also present a novel algorithm for efficiently re-forming a multiagent plan, for the situation ($SIT_{multplans}$) in which there are multiple agents, each learning independently.

The novelty of our approach is not in machine learning or verification per se, but rather the synthesis of the two. There are numerous important potential applications of our approach. For example, if antiviruses evolve more effective behaviors to combat viruses, we need to ensure that they do not evolve undesirable virus-like behavior. Another example is data mining agents that can flexibly adapt their plans to dynamic computing environments but whose behavior is adequately constrained for operation within secure or proprietary domains. A third example is planetary rovers that adapt to unforeseen conditions while remaining within critical mission parameters. Yet another example is automated factories that adapt to equipment failures but continue operation within essential tolerances and other specifications. Also, there are ongoing discussions at the Universities Space Research Association about launching orbiting unmanned vehicles to run laboratory experiments. The experiments would be semiautomated, and would thus require both adaptation and behavioral assurances.

The last important application that we will mention is in the domain of power grid and telecommunications networks. The following is an event that occurred (*The New York Times*, September 21, 1991, Business Section). In 1991 in New York, local electric utilities had a demand overload. In attempting to assist in solving the regional shortfall, AT&T put its own generators on the local power grid. This was a manual adaptation, but such

---

4. This idea of property-preserving learning transformations was first introduced by Gordon (1998).

5. Incremental methods are often used in computer science for improving the time-efficiency of software.

adaptations are expected to become increasingly automated in the future. As a result of AT&T's actions, there was a local power overload and AT&T lost its own power, which resulted in a breakdown of the AT&T regional communications network. The regional network breakdown propagated to create a national breakdown in communications systems. This breakdown also triggered failures of many other control networks across the country, such as the air traffic control network. Air travel nationwide was shut down. In the future, it is reasonable to expect that some network controllers will be implemented using multiple, distributed cooperating software agents. This example dramatically illustrates the potential vulnerability of our national resources unless these agents satisfy *all* of the following criteria: continuous execution/monitoring, flexible adaptation to failures, safety/reliability, and timely responses. Our approach ensures that agents satisfy all of these.

This paper is organized as follows. Section 2 provides an illustrative example that is used throughout the paper. Section 3 has the necessary background definitions of FSAs, property types, formal verification, and machine learning operators. A priori results for specific machine learning operators are in Section 4. These learning operators alter automaton edges and the *transition conditions* associated with edges. A transition condition specifies the condition under which a state-to-state transition may be made. We present positive a priori results for some of these operators, where a "positive a priori result" means that the learning operator preserves a specified class of properties. On the other hand, counterexamples are presented to show that some of the learning operators do not necessarily preserve these properties. Section 5 extends the a priori results for the multiagent situation $SIT_{multplans}$.

For all cases where we obtain negative a priori results, Section 6 provides incremental algorithms for re-forming the multiagent plan and reverifying it, along with a worst-case complexity analysis and empirical time complexity results. The empirical results show as much as a $\frac{1}{2}$-billion-fold speedup for one of the incremental algorithms over standard verification. The paper concludes with a discussion of related work and ideas for future research.

2. Illustrative Example

We begin with a multiagent example for SIT_{1plan} or $SIT_{multplans}$ that is used throughout the paper to illustrate the definitions and ideas. The section starts by addressing $SIT_{multplans}$, where multiple agents have their own independent plans. Later in the section we address SIT_{1plan}, where each agent uses a joint multiagent plan.

Imagine a scenario where a vehicle has landed on a planet for the purpose of exploration and sample collection, for example as in the Pathfinder mission to Mars. Like the Pathfinder, there is a lander (called agent "L") from which a mobile rover emerges. However, in this case there are two rovers: the far ("F") rover for distant exploration, and the intermediary ("I") rover for transferring data and samples from F to L.

We assume an agent designer has developed the initial plans for F, I, and L, shown in Figures 2 and 3. These are simplified, rather than realistic, plans – for the purpose of illustration. Basically, rover F is either collecting samples/data (in state COLLECTING) or it is delivering them to rover I (when F is in its state DELIVERING). Rover I can either be receiving samples/data from rover F (when I is in its RECEIVING state) or it can deliver them to lander L (when it is in its DELIVERING state). If L is in its RECEIVING state,

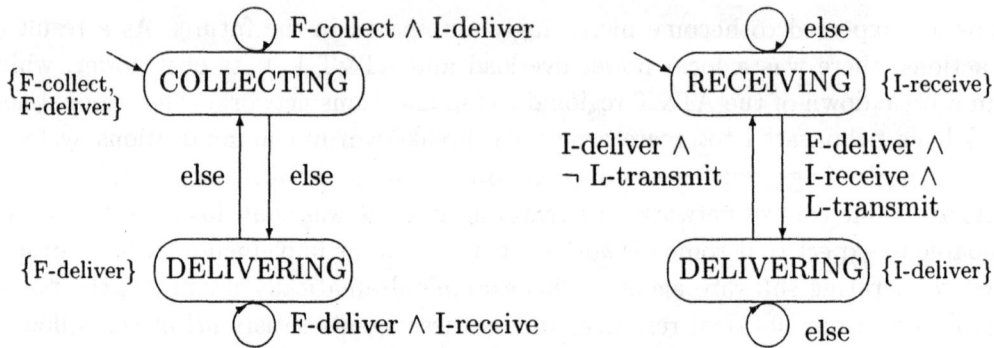

Figure 2: Plans for rovers F (left) and I (right).

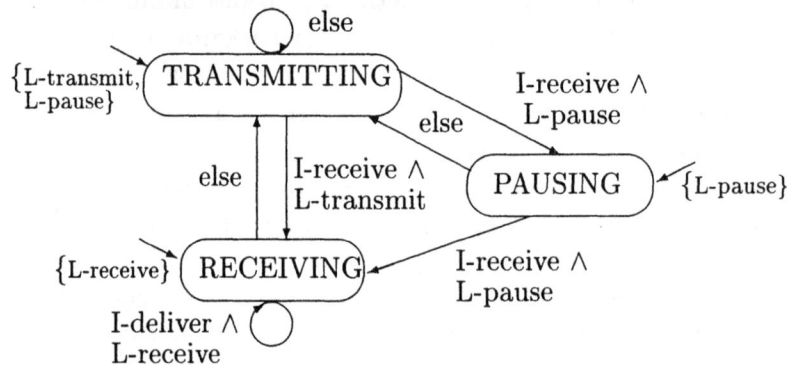

Figure 3: Plan for the lander L.

then it can receive the samples/data from I. Otherwise, L could be busy transmitting data to Earth (in state TRANSMITTING) or pausing between actions (in state PAUSING).

As mentioned above, plans are represented using FSAs. An FSA has a finite set of states (i.e., the vertices) and allowable state-to-state transitions (i.e., the directed edges between vertices). The purpose of having states is to divide the agent's overall task into subtasks. A state with an incoming arrow not from any other state is an *initial state*. Plan execution begins in an initial state.

Plan execution occurs as the agent takes actions, such as agent F taking action F-collect or F-deliver. Each agent has a repertoire of possible actions, a subset of which may be taken from each of its states. A plan designer can specify this subset for each state. The choice of a particular action from this subset is modeled in the FSA as nondeterministic. It is assumed that further criteria, not specified here, are used to make the final run-time choice of a single action from a state.

Let us specify the set of actions for each of the agents (F, I, L) in our example. F has two possible actions: F-collect and F-deliver. The first action means that F collects samples and/or data, and the second action means that it delivers these items to I. Rover I also has two actions: I-receive and I-deliver. The first action means I receives samples/data from F, and the second means that it delivers these items to L. L has three actions: L-transmit, L-pause, and L-receive. The first action means L transmits data to Earth, the second that it pauses between operations, and the third that it receives samples/data from I. For each FSA, the set of allowable actions from each state is specified in Figures 2 and 3 in small font next to the state. For example, rover F can only take action F-deliver from its DELIVERING state.

The *transition conditions* (i.e., the logical expressions labeling the edges) in an FSA plan describe the set of actions that enable a state-to-state transition to occur. The operator ∧ means "AND," ∨ means "OR," and ¬ means "NOT." The condition "else" will be defined shortly. The transition conditions of one agent can refer to the actions of one or more other agents. This is because each agent is assumed to be reactive to what it has observed other agents doing. If not visible, agents communicate their action choice.

Once an agent's action repertoire and its allowable actions from each state have been defined, "else" can be defined. The transition condition "else" labeling an outgoing edge from a state is an abbreviation denoting the set of all remaining actions that may be taken from the state that are not already covered by other transition conditions. For example, in Figure 3, L's three transition conditions from state TRANSMITTING are (I-receive ∧ L-transmit), (I-receive ∧ L-pause), and "else." L can only take L-transmit or L-pause from this state. However, rover I could take I-deliver instead of I-receive. Therefore, in this case "else" is equivalent to ((I-deliver ∧ L-transmit) ∨ (I-deliver ∧ L-pause)).

An FSA plan represents a set of allowable action sequences. In particular, a plan is the set of all action sequences that begin in an initial state and obey the transition conditions. An example action sequence allowed by F's plan is ((F-collect ∧ I-deliver), (F-collect ∧ I-receive), (F-deliver ∧ I-receive), ...) where F takes its actions and observes I's actions at each step in the sequence.

At run-time, these FSA plans are interpreted in the following manner. At every discrete time step, every agent (F, I, L) is at one of the states in its plan, and it selects the next action to take. Agents choose their actions independently. They do not need to synchronize on action choice. The choice of action might be based, for example, on sensory inputs from the environment. Although a complete plan would include the basis for action choice, as mentioned above, here we leave it unspecified in the FSA plans. Our rationale for doing this is that that the focus of this paper is on the verification of properties about correct action sequences. The basis for action choice is irrelevant to these properties.

Once each agent has chosen an action, all agents are assumed to observe the actions of the other agents that are mentioned in its FSA transition conditions. For example, F's transition conditions mention I's actions, so F needs to observe what I did. Based on its own action and those of the other relevant agent(s), an agent knows the next state to which it will transition. There is only one possible next state because the FSAs are assumed to be deterministic. For example, if F is in its COLLECTING state, and it chooses action F-collect, and it observes I taking action I-deliver, then it will stay in its COLLECTING state. The process of being in a state, choosing an action, observing the actions of other agents, then moving to a next state, is repeated indefinitely.

So far, we have been assuming $SIT_{multplans}$ where each agent has its own individual plan. If we assume SIT_{1plan}, then each agent uses the same multiagent plan to decide its actions. A multiagent plan is formed by taking a "product" (defined in Subsection 3.1) of the plans for F, I, and L. This product models the synchronous behavior of the agents, where "synchronous" means that at each time step every agent takes an action, observes actions of other agents, and then transitions to a next state. The product plan is formed, essentially, by taking the Cartesian product of the individual automaton states and the in-

101

tersection of the transition conditions. Multiagent actions enable state-to-state transitions in the product plan. For example, if the agents jointly take the actions F-deliver and I-receive and L-transmit, then all agents will transition from the joint state (COLLECTING, RECEIVING, TRANSMITTING) to the joint state (DELIVERING, DELIVERING, RECEIVING) represented by triples of states in the FSAs for F, I, and L. A multiagent plan consists of the set of all action sequences that begin in a joint initial state of the product plan and obey the transition conditions.

Whether the situation is $SIT_{multplans}$ or SIT_{1plan}, a multiagent plan needs to be formed to verify global multiagent coordination properties (see step 2 of Figure 1). Verification of global properties consists of asking whether *all* of the action sequences allowed by the product plan satisfy the property.

One class of (global) properties of particular importance, which is addressed here, is that of forbidden multiagent actions that we want our agents to always avoid, called *Invariance* properties. An example is property P1: ¬(I-deliver ∧ L-transmit), which states that it should always be the case that I does not deliver at the same time that L is transmitting. This property prevents problems that may arise from the lander simultaneously receiving new data from I while transmitting older data to Earth. The second important class addressed here is *Response* properties. These properties state that if a particular multiagent action (the "trigger") has occurred, then eventually another multiagent action (the necessary "response") will occur. An example is property P2: If F-deliver has occurred, then eventually L will execute L-receive.

If the plans in Figures 2 and 3 are combined into a multiagent plan, will this multiagent plan satisfy properties P1 and P2? Answering this question is probably difficult or impossible for most readers if the determination is based on visual inspection of the FSAs. Yet there are only a couple of very small, simple FSAs in this example! This illustrates how even a few simple agents, when interacting, can exhibit complex global behaviors, thereby making global agent behavior difficult to predict. Clearly there is a need for rigorous behavioral guarantees, especially as the number and complexity of agents increases. Model checking fully automates this process. According to our model checker, the product plan for F, I, and L satisfies properties P1 and P2.

Rigorous guarantees are also needed after learning. Suppose lander L's transmitter gets damaged. Then one learning operator that could be applied is to delete L's action L-transmit, which thereafter prevents this action from being taken from state TRANSMITTING. After applying a learning operator, reverification may be required. For this particular operator (deleting an action), no reverification is needed (see Section 4).

In a multiagent situation, what gets modified by learning? Who forms and verifies the product FSA? And who performs repairs if verification fails, and what is repaired? The answers to these questions depend on whether it is SIT_{1plan} or $SIT_{multplans}$. If SIT_{1plan}, the agent with the greatest computational power, e.g., lander L in our example, maintains the product plan by applying learning to it, verifying it, repairing it as needed, and then sending a copy of it to all of the agents to use. If $SIT_{multplans}$, an agent applies learning to its own individual plan. The individual plans are then sent to the computationally powerful agent, who forms the product and verifies that properties are satisfied. If repairs are needed, one or more agents repair their own individual plans.

It is assumed here that machine learning operators are applied one-at-a-time per agent rather than in batch and, if $SIT_{multiplans}$, the agents co-evolve plans by taking turns learning (Potter, 1997). Beyond these assumptions, this paper does not focus on the learning operators per se (other than to define them). It focuses instead on the outcome resulting from the application of a learning operator. In particular, we address the reverification issue. The next section gives useful background definitions needed for understanding reverification.

3. Preliminary Definitions

This section provides definitions of FSAs, properties, verification, and machine learning operators. For a clear, unambiguous understanding of the results in this paper, many of these definitions are formal.

3.1 Automata for Agents' Plans

FSAs have at least four advantages over classical plans (Nilsson, 1980; Dean & Wellman, 1991). For one, unlike classical plans, the type of finite-state automaton plans used here allows potentially infinite (indeterminate) length action sequences.[6] This provides a good model of embedded agents that are continually responsive to their environment without any artificial termination to their behavior. Execution and learning may be interleaved in a natural manner. Another advantage is that FSA plans have states, and the plan designer can use these states to represent subtasks of the overall task. This subdivides the plan into smaller units, thereby potentially increasing the comprehensibility of the plans. States also enable different action choices at different times, even if the sensory inputs are the same. A third advantage of FSA plans is that they are particularly well-suited to modeling the concurrent behavior of multiple agents. An arbitrary number of single-agent plans can be developed independently and then composed into a synchronous multiagent plan (for which global properties may be tested) in a straightforward manner. Finally, FSA plans can be verified using the very popular and effective *automata-theoretic* model checking methods, e.g., see Kurshan (1994).

A disadvantage of FSA plans as opposed to classical plans is that there is a great deal of research that has been done on automatically forming classical plans, e.g., see Dean and Wellman (1991). It is unclear how much of this might be applicable to FSAs. On the other hand, evolutionary algorithms can be used to evolve FSA plans (Fogel, 1996). A disadvantage of FSA plans as opposed to plans composed of rule sets is that the latter may express a plan more succinctly. Nevertheless for plans that require formal verification, FSAs are preferable because the complex interactions that can occur between rules make them very hard to verify. Formal verification for FSAs is quite sophisticated and widely used in safety-critical industrial applications.

This subsection, which is based on Kurshan (1994), briefly summarizes the basics of the FSAs used to model agent plans. Figures 2 and 3 illustrate the definitions. This paper focuses on FSAs that model agents with a potentially infinite lifetime, represented as an infinite-length "string" (i.e., a sequence of actions).

---

6. Results for agents with finite lifetimes may be found in Gordon (1998, 1999).

Before beginning our discussion of automata, we briefly digress to define Boolean algebra. Examples throughout this paper have automaton transition conditions expressed in Boolean algebra, because Boolean algebra succinctly summarizes these transition conditions. Boolean algebra is also useful for succinctly expressing the properties. Furthermore, it is easier for us to describe two of the incremental reverification algorithms if we use Boolean algebra notation. Therefore, we briefly summarize the basics of Boolean algebra.

A Boolean algebra $\mathcal{K}$ is a set of elements with distinguished elements 0 and 1, closed under the Boolean $\wedge$, $\vee$, and $\neg$ operations, and satisfying the standard properties (Sikorski, 1969). For elements x and y of $\mathcal{K}$, $x \wedge y$ is called the *meet* of x and y, $x \vee y$ is called the *join* of x and y, and $\neg x$ is called the *complement* of x. For those readers who are unfamiliar with Boolean algebras and who want some intuition for these operations, it may help to imagine that each element of $\mathcal{K}$ is itself a set, e.g., a set of actions. Meet, join, and complement would then be set intersection, union, and complement, respectively. Elements 0 and 1, in this case, would be the empty set ($\emptyset$) and the set of all elements in the universe (U), respectively.

The Boolean algebras are assumed to be finite. There is a partial order among the elements, $\preceq$, which is defined as $x \preceq y$ if and only if $x \wedge y = x$. It may help to think of $\preceq$ as analogous to $\subseteq$ for sets. The elements 0 and 1 are defined as $\forall x \in \mathcal{K}$, $0 \preceq x$, and $\forall x \in \mathcal{K}$, $x \preceq 1$. The *atoms* (analogous to single-element sets) of $\mathcal{K}$, $\Gamma(\mathcal{K})$, are the nonzero elements of $\mathcal{K}$ minimal with respect to $\preceq$. In the rovers example, agents F, I, and L each have their own Boolean algebra with its atoms. The atoms of F's Boolean algebra are its actions F-collect and F-deliver; the atoms of I's algebra are I-receive and I-deliver; the atoms of L's algebra are L-transmit, L-pause, and L-receive. The element (F-collect $\vee$ F-deliver) of F's Boolean algebra describes the set of actions {F-collect, F-deliver}.

A Boolean algebra $\mathcal{K}_i$ is a *subalgebra* of $\mathcal{K}$ if $\mathcal{K}_i$ is a nonempty subset of $\mathcal{K}$ that is closed under the operations $\wedge$, $\vee$, and $\neg$, and also has the distinguished elements 0 and 1. $\prod \mathcal{K}_i$ is the *product algebra* of subalgebras $\mathcal{K}_i$. An atom of the product algebra is the meet of the atoms of the subalgebras. For example, if $a_1, ..., a_n$ are atoms of subalgebras $\mathcal{K}_1, ..., \mathcal{K}_n$, respectively, then $a_1 \wedge ... \wedge a_n$ is an atom of $\prod_{i=1}^{n} \mathcal{K}_i$.

The Boolean algebra $\mathcal{K}_F$ for agent F's actions is the smallest one containing the atoms of F's algebra. It contains all Boolean elements formed from F's atoms using the Boolean operators $\wedge$, $\vee$, and $\neg$, including 0 and 1. These same definitions hold for I and L's algebras $\mathcal{K}_I$ and $\mathcal{K}_L$. $\mathcal{K}_F \mathcal{K}_I \mathcal{K}_L$ is the product algebra used for all transition conditions in the multiagent plan (i.e., the product of the F, I, and L FSAs). One atom of the product algebra $\mathcal{K}_F \mathcal{K}_I \mathcal{K}_L$ is (F-collect $\wedge$ I-receive $\wedge$ L-pause). This is the form of actions taken simultaneously by the three agents. Algebras $\mathcal{K}_F$, $\mathcal{K}_I$, and $\mathcal{K}_L$ are subalgebras of the product algebra $\mathcal{K}_F \mathcal{K}_I \mathcal{K}_L$.

Let us return now to automata. Formally, an FSA of the type considered here is a three-tuple $S = (V(S), M_\mathcal{K}(S), I(S))$ where $V(S)$ is the set of vertices (states) of S, $\mathcal{K}$ is the Boolean algebra corresponding to S, $M_\mathcal{K}(S) : V(S) \times V(S) \to \mathcal{K}$ is the matrix of transition conditions which are elements of $\mathcal{K}$, and $I(S) \subseteq V(S)$ are the initial states.[7] Also, $E(S) = \{e \in V(S) \times V(S) \mid M_\mathcal{K}(e) \neq 0\}$ is the set of directed edges connecting pairs of vertices of S. $M_\mathcal{K}(e)$, which is an abbreviation for $M_\mathcal{K}(S)(e)$, is the transition condition of

---

7. There should also be an *output subalgebra*, as in Kurshan (1994). This would help distinguish an agent's own actions from those of other agents. However it is omitted here for notational simplicity.

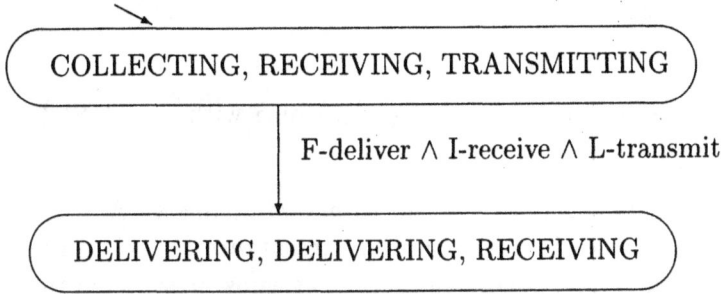

Figure 4: Part of the product plan for agents F, I, and L.

$M_{\mathcal{K}}(S)$ corresponding to edge e. Note that we omit edges labeled "0." By our definition, an edge whose transition condition is 0 does not exist. We can alternatively denote $M_{\mathcal{K}}(e)$ as $M_{\mathcal{K}}(v_i, v_j)$ for the transition condition corresponding to the edge going from vertex v_i to vertex v_j. For example, in Figure 3, $M_{\mathcal{K}}((\text{TRANSMITTING, PAUSING}))$ is (I-receive $\wedge$ L-pause).

Figures 2 and 3 illustrate these FSA definitions. There are FSA plans for three agents, F, I, and L with vertices, edges, and transition conditions. An incoming arrow to a state, not from any other state, signifies that this is an initial state.

A multiagent plan is formed from single agent plans by taking the *tensor product* (also called the "synchronous product" or simply "product") of the FSAs corresponding to the individual plans. Formally, the tensor product is defined as:

$$\otimes_{i=1}^{n} S_i = (\times V(S_i), \otimes_i M(S_i), \times I(S_i))$$

where $\times$ is the Cartesian product, and the tensor product $M(S_i) \otimes ... \otimes M(S_n)$ of n transition matrices is defined as $M(S_1) \otimes ... \otimes M(S_n)((v_1, v_1'), ..., (v_n, v_n')) = M(S_1)(v_1, v_1') \wedge ... \wedge M(S_n)(v_n, v_n')$ for $(v_1, v_1') \in E(S_1), ..., (v_n, v_n') \in E(S_n)$. In words, the product FSA is formed by taking the Cartesian product of the vertices and the intersection of the transition conditions. Initial states of the product FSA are tuples formed from the initial states of the individual FSAs.

The product FSA models a set of synchronous FSAs. The Boolean algebra corresponding to the product FSA is the product algebra. For Figures 2 and 3, to formulate the FSA S modeling the entire multiagent plan, we take the tensor product S = F $\otimes$ I $\otimes$ L of the three FSAs. For this tensor product, $I(S) = \{(\text{COLLECTING, RECEIVING, TRANS-MITTING}), (\text{COLLECTING, RECEIVING, PAUSING}), (\text{COLLECTING, RECEIVING, RECEIVING})\}$. Part of the tensor product FSA is shown in Figure 4.

Next we define the *language* of an FSA, which is the set of all action sequences permitted by the FSA plan. To do this, we first define a *string*, which is a sequence of actions (atoms). Formally, a string $\mathbf{x}$ is an infinite-dimensional vector, $(x_0, ...) \in \Gamma(\mathcal{K})^{\omega}$, i.e., a string is an infinite (ω) length sequence of actions (where $\mathcal{K}$ is the Boolean algebra used by S). A *run* $\mathbf{v}$ *of string* $\mathbf{x}$ is a sequence $(v_0, ...)$ of vertices such that $\forall i, \; x_i \wedge M_{\mathcal{K}}(v_i, v_{i+1}) \neq 0$, i.e., $x_i \preceq M_{\mathcal{K}}(v_i, v_{i+1})$ because the x_i are atoms. In other words, a run of a string is the sequence of vertices visited in an FSA when the string satisfies the transition conditions along the edges.

The language of FSA S is defined as:

$$\mathcal{L}(S) = \{\mathbf{x} \in \Gamma(\mathcal{K})^{\omega} \mid \mathbf{x} \text{ has a run } \mathbf{v} = (v_0, \ldots) \text{ in } S \text{ with } v_0 \in I(S)\}$$

Such a run is called an *accepting run*, and S is said to *accept* string $\mathbf{x}$. Any requirement on accepting runs of an FSA are what is called the FSA *acceptance criterion*. In this case, the acceptance criterion consists of one condition: accepting runs must begin in an initial state. The verification literature calls these FSAs, which accept infinite-length strings, ω-*automata* (Kurshan, 1994).

A few more definitions are needed. An FSA is *complete* if, for each state $v \in V(S)$, $\sum_{w \in V(S)} M_{\mathcal{K}}(v, w) = 1$. In other words, an FSA is complete if it specifies what state-to-state transition the agent should make for all possible actions taken by the other agents. This is a very reasonable assumption to make because otherwise the agent would not know what to do in some circumstances. An FSA is *deterministic* at state v if $w \neq w' \Rightarrow M_{\mathcal{K}}(v, w)$ $\wedge M_{\mathcal{K}}(v, w') = 0$. In other words, the choice of action uniquely determines which edge will be taken from a state. An FSA is deterministic if it is deterministic at each of its states. Unless otherwise stated, it is assumed here that all FSAs are complete and deterministic. The restriction to deterministic FSAs is not a major problem because for every nondeterministic FSA there is a deterministic one accepting the same language (Kurshan, 1994).

We also need the definition of a *cycle* in a graph. Model checking typically consists of looking for cycles, as described in Section 3.3. A *path* in FSA S is a sequence of vertices $\mathbf{v} = (v_0, \ldots, v_n) \in V(S)^{n+1}$, for $n \geq 1$ such that $(v_i, v_{i+1}) \in E(S)$ for $i = 0, \ldots, n-1$, i.e., $M_{\mathcal{K}}(v_i, v_{i+1}) \neq 0$. If $v_n = v_0$, then $\mathbf{v}$ is a cycle. Each cycle in an FSA plan allows the possibility that the agent can infinitely often, or as long as desired, revisit the vertices of the cycle. It also implies that a substring can be repeated indefinitely.

We next illustrate some of these definitions. An example string in the language of FSA S, the multiagent FSA that is the product of F, I, and L, is

((F-collect ∧ I-receive ∧ L-transmit),

(F-deliver ∧ I-receive ∧ L-receive),

(F-deliver ∧ I-receive ∧ L-transmit),

(F-deliver ∧ I-deliver ∧ L-receive), ...).

This is a sequence of atoms of S. A run of this string is

((COLLECTING, RECEIVING, TRANSMITTING),

(DELIVERING, RECEIVING, RECEIVING),

(DELIVERING, RECEIVING, TRANSMITTING),

(DELIVERING, DELIVERING, RECEIVING),

(COLLECTING, RECEIVING, RECEIVING), ...).

All FSAs in Figures 2 and 3 are complete and deterministic. For example, in Figure 2, rover I can only take action I-deliver from its DELIVERING state. However every possible action choice of L determines a unique next state for I from DELIVERING. For example, if L takes L-transmit then I must stay in state DELIVERING, and if L takes L-receive or L-pause then I must go to state RECEIVING.

3.2 Properties

Now that we have presented the FSA formalism used for agent plans, we can address the question of how to formalize properties. For verification, properties are typically expressed either as FSAs (for automata-theoretic verification) or in temporal logic. Here, we assume *linear* temporal logic. In other words, we assume that time proceeds linearly and we do not consider simultaneous possible futures. Using the algorithm of Vardi and Wolper (1986), one can convert any linear temporal logic formula into an automaton (because automata are more expressive than linear temporal logic). Both representations are used here. To simplify our proofs in Section 4, properties are expressed in temporal logic. For some of the incremental reverification methods in Section 6, we use automata-theoretic methods with an FSA representation for the property.

Let us begin by defining temporal logic properties. Many of the definitions are based on Manna and Pnueli (1991). To bridge the gap between automata (for plans) and temporal logic (for properties), we need to define a *computational state* (*c-state*). A computation is an infinite sequence of temporally-ordered atoms, i.e., a string. A c-state is an atom in a computation. In other words, it is a (single or multiagent) action that occurs at a single time step in a computation. We continue to refer to an automaton state as simply a "state."

P is a property that is true (false) for an FSA S. $S \models P$ ($S \not\models P$), if and only if P is true for every string in the language $\mathcal{L}(S)$ (false for some string in $\mathcal{L}(S)$). The notation $\mathbf{x} \models P$ ($\mathbf{x} \not\models P$) means string $\mathbf{x}$ satisfies (does not satisfy) property P, i.e., the property holds (does not hold) for $\mathbf{x}$. Before defining what it means for properties to be true (i.e., hold) for a string, we first define what it means for a formula that is a Boolean expression to be true at a c-state. A *c-state formula* p is true (false) at c-state x_i, i.e., $x_i \models p$ ($x_i \not\models p$) if and only if $x_i \preceq p$ ($x_i \not\preceq p$), i.e., $x_i \wedge p \neq 0$ ($= 0$) because p is a Boolean expression with no variables on the same Boolean algebra used by FSA S, and x_i is an atom of that algebra. For example, F-collect $\models$ (F-collect $\vee$ F-deliver) for c-state F-collect and c-state formula (F-collect $\vee$ F-deliver). One can also talk about a c-state formula being true or false for an atom, since a c-state is an atom.

A c-state formula p is true or false in particular c-states of a string. Property P is defined in terms of p, and is true or false of an entire string. In particular, $\mathbf{x} \models P$ or $\mathbf{x} \not\models P$ for the string $\mathbf{x}$.

We focus on two property classes that are among those most frequently encountered in the verification literature: Invariance and Response properties. Invariance and Response properties are likely to be useful for agents. For the case of a single agent (SIT_{1agent}), Invariance properties can express the requirement that a particular action never be executed.[8] Response properties are also useful for a single agent. They can be used to verify that a pair of the agent's actions will occur in the correct order (i.e., a "response" always follows a "trigger") in the plan. In the context of multiple agents (SIT_{1plan} or $SIT_{multplans}$) Invariance properties express the need for parallel multiagent coordination. In particular, they express that multiple agents should not simultaneously perform some conflicting set of

---

8. This could alternatively be implemented as a run-time check, but then there would be no assurance that the plan without the action is a good one, for example, in terms of how well the revised plan satisfies the agent's goals (perhaps captured in a "fitness function"). Alternatively, the action (atom) could be omitted from the set of actions $\Gamma(\mathcal{K})$. But in general one may not wish to rule out actions, in case the situation and/or properties might change.

actions. Response properties express the need for sequential multiagent coordination. For example, they can express the requirement that one agent's action must follow in response to a particular "triggering" action of another agent.

Here, we only present informal definitions of these properties; the formal definitions are in Appendix B. An Invariance property $P = \Box \neg p$ ("Invariant not p") is true of a string if p is "never" true, i.e., if p is not true in any c-state of the string. $P = \Box(p \to \Diamond q)$ is a Response property, where $\Diamond$ means "eventually." We call p the "trigger" and q the "response." A Response formula states that every trigger is eventually (in finite time) followed by a response.

To illustrate these property types, we continue the rovers and lander example. The property P1 from Section 2, which states that it should always be the case that I does not deliver at the same time that L is transmitting, is formally expressed as an Invariance property P1 defined as: P1 $= \Box$ ($\neg$(I-deliver $\wedge$ L-transmit)). Property P2 from Section 2, which states that if F-deliver has occurred then eventually L will execute L-receive, is an example of a Response property. This is expressed in temporal logic as P2 $= \Box$ (F-deliver $\to \Diamond$ L-receive).

Next consider the FSA representation for properties. As will be explained in Section 3.3 on verification, what we really need to express for automata-theoretic verification is the negation of the property, i.e., $\neg P$. Strings in the language of FSA $\neg P$ violate property P. In this paper, we assume that $\neg P$ is expressed using the popular Büchi ω-automaton (Büchi, 1962). We decided to use the Büchi FSA because one of the simplest and most elegant model checking algorithms in the literature assumes this type of FSA for the property, and we use that algorithm (see Subsections 3.3 and 6.1). A Büchi automaton is defined to be a four-tuple $S = (V(S), M_{\mathcal{K}}(S), I(S), B(S))$, where $B(S) \subseteq V(S)$ is a set of "bad" states. To define the language of a Büchi automaton, we require the following preliminary definition. For a run $\mathbf{v}$ of FSA S, $\mu(\mathbf{v}) = \{v \in V(S) \mid v_i = v$ for infinitely many v_is in run $\mathbf{v}\}$. In other words, $\mu(\mathbf{v})$ equals the set of all vertices of S that occur infinitely often in the run $\mathbf{v}$. Then for a Büchi automaton S, $\mathcal{L}(S) = \{\mathbf{x} \in \Gamma(K)^\omega \mid \mathbf{x}$ has a run $\mathbf{v} = (v_0, ...)$ in S with $v_0 \in I(S)$ and $\mu(\mathbf{v}) \cap B(S) \neq \emptyset\}$. In other words, the Büchi automaton has an acceptance criterion that requires visiting some bad state infinitely often, as well as beginning in an initial state.

An example deterministic Büchi FSA for $\neg$P1, where Invariance property P1 $= \Box$ $\neg$(I-deliver $\wedge$ L-transmit), is in Figure 5 (on the left) with $B(\neg$P1$) = \{2\}$. Note that visiting a state in $B(\neg$P1$)$ infinitely often implies Büchi acceptance, and because the FSA expresses the negation of the property, visiting a "bad" state in $B(\neg$P1$)$ infinitely often is undesirable. From Figure 5 we can see that any string that includes (I-deliver $\wedge$ L-transmit) will visit state 2 infinitely often, and $B(\neg$P1$) = \{2\}$. Thus any string that starts in state 1 and includes (I-deliver $\wedge$ L-transmit) is in $\mathcal{L}(\neg$P1$)$ and therefore violates property P1.

Next consider Response properties of the form $\Box(p \to \Diamond q)$. For this paper, the only type of FSA that we need for verifying Response properties is the very simple deterministic Büchi FSA for the negation of a "First-Response" property.[9] (Determinism is needed for our efficient internal representation. See Subsection 6.1.) A First-Response property checks

---

9. A straightforward inductive argument shows that it is not possible to construct a deterministic Büchi automaton with a finite number of states for the negation of the full Response property $\Box(p \to \Diamond q)$ (Mahesh Viswanathan, personal communication).

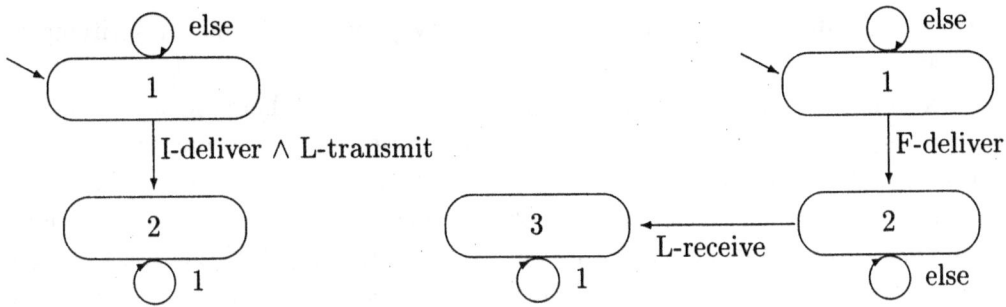

Figure 5: Invariance property ¬P1 (left) and the First-Response version of property ¬P2 (right) as Büchi FSAs, where $B(S) = \{2\}$ for both automata.

whether the *first* trigger p in every string is followed by a response q. Figure 5 (on the right) shows a Büchi FSA for the First-Response property corresponding to ¬P2, where property P2 = □ (F-deliver → ◇ L-receive). For this FSA, $B(\neg P2) = \{2\}$. Any string whose accepting run visits state 2 infinitely often will include the first trigger and not the response that should follow it. As discussed in Subsection 6.5, verifying First-Response properties can in some circumstances (including all of our experiments) be equivalent to verifying the full Response property $\Box(p \to \Diamond q)$. Henceforth, when we use the term "Response" this is assumed to include both the full Response and the First-Response versions.

3.3 Model Checking for Verification

Now that we have our representations for plans and properties, it is possible to describe model checking, i.e., for plan S and property P determining whether $S \models P$. First, however, we need to begin with two essential definitions of accessibility: accessibility of one vertex from another, and accessibility of an atom from a vertex.

Definition 1 Vertex v_n is *accessible from* vertex v_0 if and only if there exists a path from v_0 to v_n.

Definition 2 Atom $a_{n-1} \in \Gamma(\mathcal{K})$ is *accessible from* vertex v_0 if and only if there exists a path from v_0 to v_n and $a_{n-1} \preceq M_{\mathcal{K}}(v_{n-1}, v_n)$.

Accessibility from initial states is central to model checking. The reason is the following. Recall from Section 3.2 that property P is true (false) for an FSA S, (i.e., $S \models P$ ($S \not\models P$)), if and only if P is true for every string in the language $\mathcal{L}(S)$ (false for some string in $\mathcal{L}(S)$). By definition, every string in the language has an accepting run. Therefore, it is only necessary to verify the property for strings that have an accepting run. By definition, every accepting run begins with an initial state. Therefore, every state in an accepting run is accessible from an initial state, and every atom (c-state) in a string of the language is accessible from an initial state. Clearly, the only states and atoms that need to be involved in verification are those accessible from initial states.

Invariance properties can be re-expressed in terms of accessibility. Invariance property $\Box \neg p$ could be restated as saying that there does not exist any atom a, where $a \preceq p$, that is accessible from an initial state. It is much more difficult to express Response properties succinctly using accessibility. Nevertheless, accessibility plays a key role in verifying all properties, as will be seen shortly.

There are a number of ways to perform model checking, but here we focus on two. The first method is specifically tailored for one class of properties; the second is sufficiently general for use in verifying many classes of properties. The rationale for choosing a specific and a general algorithm is that this allows for a comparison to determine the computational efficiency gained by property-specific tailoring (see Subsection 6.5). In this section, we give high-level sketches of these two model checking algorithms. The full algorithms are in Section 6.

The first algorithm is a very simple and efficient method tailored for Invariance properties $P = \Box \neg p$. For every initial state v_i, this method begins at v_i and visits every atom a_j accessible from v_i. If this atom has not already been checked, it checks to see whether $a_j \preceq p$. If $a_j \preceq p$, then this is considered a verification failure. If there are no failures, verification succeeds.

The second method, automata-theoretic (AT) model checking, is very popular in the verification literature (e.g, see Vardi and Wolper, 1986) and can be used to verify *any* property expressible as a finite-state automaton. It is used here for First-Response properties. In AT model checking, asking whether $S \models P$ is equivalent to asking whether $\mathcal{L}(S) \subseteq \mathcal{L}(P)$ for property P. This is equivalent to $\mathcal{L}(S) \cap \overline{\mathcal{L}(P)} = \emptyset$ (where $\overline{\mathcal{L}(P)}$ denotes the complement of $\mathcal{L}(P)$), which is algorithmically tested by first taking the tensor product of the plan FSA S and the FSA corresponding to $\neg P$ (i.e., $S \otimes \neg P$). The FSA corresponding to $\neg P$ accepts $\overline{\mathcal{L}(P)}$. The tensor product implements language intersection. The algorithm then determines whether $\mathcal{L}(S \otimes \neg P) \neq \emptyset$, which implies $\mathcal{L}(S) \cap \overline{\mathcal{L}(P)} \neq \emptyset$ ($S \not\models P$). This determination is implemented as a check for cycles in the product FSA $S \otimes \neg P$ that are accessible from some initial state and that satisfy any other conditions in the FSA acceptance criterion. Recall that a cycle is a sequence of vertices $(v_0, ..., v_n)$ such that $v_n = v_0$. A cycle is accessible from an initial state if one of its vertices is accessible from the initial state. A cycle that is accessible from an initial state and that satisfies the FSA acceptance criterion implies a nonempty language. This is because a string is in the language of an FSA if it is an infinite-length sequence of actions satisfying the FSA acceptance criterion, which always includes the requirement that its accepting run must begin in an initial state. All infinite behavior eventually ends up in a cycle because the FSA has a finite number of states.

Therefore, to be certain that the language is nonempty, it is necessary to determine whether any accessible cycle satisfies the FSA acceptance criterion. The criterion of interest is the Büchi criterion, for the following reason. It is assumed here that the negation of the property ($\neg P$) is expressed as a Büchi automaton. This implies that the FSA being searched, i.e., $S \otimes \neg P$, is also a Büchi automaton, because taking the tensor product preserves this criterion. The final check of this algorithm is whether an accessible cycle in $S \otimes \neg P$ satisfies the Büchi acceptance criterion, because in that case the language is not empty. A product state s is in $B(S \otimes \neg P)$ whenever it has a component state in $B(\neg P)$, e.g., (COLLECTING, RECEIVING, RECEIVING, 2) is in $B(S \otimes \neg P2)$ for property P2 because its fourth component is state 2 of $B(\neg P2)$. According to the Büchi acceptance criterion, visiting a state $v \in B(S \otimes \neg P)$ infinitely often (assuming v is accessible from an initial state) implies $\mathcal{L}(S \otimes \neg P) \neq \emptyset$. This will happen if v is part of an accessible cycle. In that case, $S \not\models P$ and verification fails. Otherwise, if no accessible product state

$v \in B(S \otimes \neg P)$ is visited infinitely often (i.e., it is not in a cycle), then $\mathcal{L}(S \otimes \neg P) = \emptyset$ and therefore $\mathcal{L}(S) \subseteq \mathcal{L}(P)$, i.e., $S \models P$ and verification succeeds. A relatively efficient algorithm for AT verification from the literature is presented in Section 6.

3.4 Machine Learning to Adapt Plans

Given plan S and property P, model checking determines whether $S \models P$. Next we consider the case of learning, which is a change to S. This subsection addresses the issue of how a learning operator can affect a plan S to generate a new plan S'.

We begin by presenting a taxonomy of FSA learning operators. It is likely that any learning method for complete deterministic FSAs will be composed of one or more of these operators. Nothing about our approach requires evolutionary learning per se; however to make the discussion concrete, this is the form of learning that is assumed here. In the context of evolutionary algorithms, the FSA learning operators are perturbations, such as mutations, applied to the FSAs.

```
Procedure EA
t = 0; /* initial generation */
initialize_population(t);
evaluate_fitness(t);
until termination-criterion do
        t = t + 1; /* next generation */
        select_parents(t);
        perturb(t);
        evaluate_fitness(t);
enduntil
end procedure
```

Figure 6: The outline of an evolutionary algorithm.

We assume that learning occurs in two phases: the offline and online phases (see Figure 1). During the offline phase, each agent starts with a randomly initialized population of candidate FSA plans. This population is evolved using the evolutionary algorithm outlined in Figure 6. The main loop of this algorithm consists of selecting parent plans from the population, applying perturbation operators to the parents to produce offspring, evaluating the fitness of the offspring, and then returning the offspring to the population if they are sufficiently fit. After this evolution, verification and repair are done to these initially generated plans.

At the start of the online phase, each agent selects one "best" (according to its "fitness function") plan from its population for execution. The agents are then fielded and plan execution is interleaved with learning (adaptation), reverification, and plan repair as needed. The purpose of learning during the online phase is to fine-tune the plan and adapt it to keep pace with a gradually shifting environment, since normally real-world environments are not static. The evolutionary algorithm of Figure 6 is also used during this phase, but the assumption is a population size of one and incremental learning (i.e., one learning operator applied per FSA per generation). This is practical for situations in which the environment changes gradually, rather than radically.

Formally, a machine learning operator $o : S \to S'$ changes a (product or individual) FSA S to post-learning FSA S'. A mapping between two automata S and S' is defined as a mapping between their elements (Bavel, 1983). At the highest level, we can subdivide the learning operators according to the elements of the FSA that they alter:

- One class of operators adds, deletes, or moves edge transition conditions. In other words, $o : M_{\mathcal{K}}(S) \to M_{\mathcal{K}}(S')$.

- Another class of operators adds, deletes, or moves edges, i.e., $o : E(S) \to E(S')$.

- The third class of operators adds or deletes vertices, along with their edges, i.e., $o : V(S) \to V(S')$ and $o : E(S) \to E(S')$.

- The fourth class of operators changes the Boolean algebra used in the transition conditions, i.e., $o : \mathcal{K} \to \mathcal{K}'$.

Here, we do not define operators that add or delete states. In other words, we do not address the third class of operators. The reason is that with the type of FSAs used here, adding or deleting a state does not, in itself, affect properties. It is what we do with the edges to/from a state and their transition conditions that can alter whether a property is true or false for a plan. This is because properties are true or false for comp-states (atoms) rather than for FSA states. Furthermore, this paper does not address changes to the Boolean algebra, which is the fourth class of operators. This class of operators, which includes abstractions, is addressed in Gordon (1998).

Therefore we are focusing on the first and second classes of operators. We define operator schemas, rather than operators. A machine learning operator schema applies to unspecified (variable) vertices, edges, and transition conditions. When instantiated with particular vertices, edges, and transition conditions, it becomes a machine learning operator. In order to avoid tedium, the operator schema definitions consider only the relevant parts of the FSA, e.g., those parts that get altered. There is an implicit assumption that all unspecified parts of the FSA remain the same after operator application. There is also an assumption that the learner ensures that all operators keep the automaton complete and deterministic.

The operators can be seen in the taxonomy (partition) of Figure 7. We define each of the corresponding operator schemas as follows, beginning with the most general one, called o_{change}, which changes edge transition conditions:

Operator Schema 1 (o_{change}) *Let S be an FSA with Boolean algebra $\mathcal{K}$, and let o_{change} : $S \to S'$. Then we define $o_{change} : M_{\mathcal{K}}(S) \to M_{\mathcal{K}}(S')$. In particular, suppose $z \preceq M_{\mathcal{K}}(v_1, v_2)$, $z \neq 0$, for $(v_1, v_2) \in E(S)$ and $z \npreceq M_{\mathcal{K}}(v_1, v_3)$ for $(v_1, v_3) \in E(S)$. Then $o_{change}(M_{\mathcal{K}}(v_1, v_2))$ $= M_{\mathcal{K}}(v_1, v_2) \wedge \neg z$ (step 1) and/or $o_{change}(M_{\mathcal{K}}(v_1, v_3)) = M_{\mathcal{K}}(v_1, v_3) \vee z$ (step 2). In other words, o_{change} may consist of two steps: the first to remove condition z from edge (v_1, v_2), and the second to add (the same) condition z to edge (v_1, v_3). Alternatively, o_{change} may consist of only one of these two steps.*

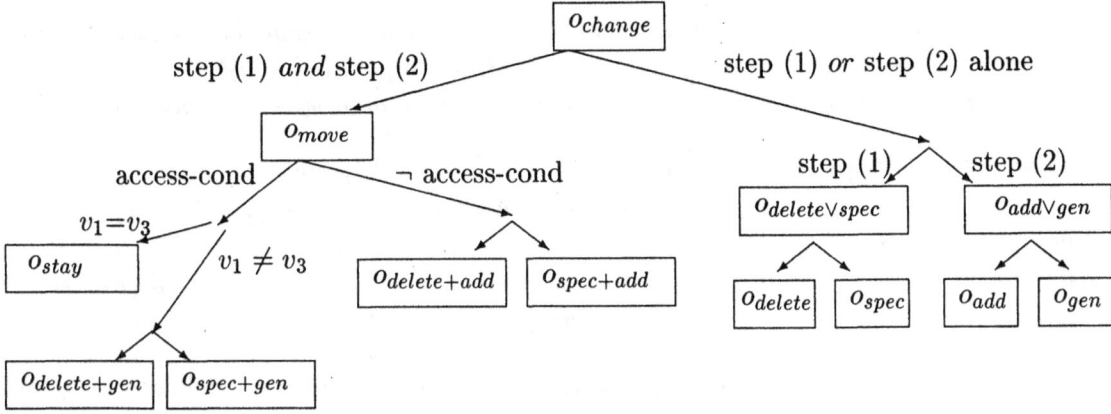

Figure 7: Taxonomy (partition) of learning operators.

All of the remaining operators are easier to describe in terms of a set of four primitive operators. Therefore, we next define these four primitives, which are one-step operators that are special cases of o_{change} and appear at the bottom right as leaves in the hierarchy of Figure 7. The first two primitive operators delete (o_{delete}) and add (o_{add}) edges. We define o_{delete} to delete edge (v_1, v_2) with the operator schema:

Operator Schema 2 (o_{delete}) *Let S be an FSA with Boolean algebra $\mathcal{K}$, and let o_{delete} : $S \to S'$ be defined with o_{delete} : $E(S) \to E(S) \setminus \{(v_1, v_2)\}$ for deleted edge (v_1, v_2) of S. Recall that a nonexistent edge has transition condition 0. Operator o_{delete} could therefore be considered a special case of o_{change} that consists only of step (1) and an additional condition that must be met, namely, that $o_{delete}(M_{\mathcal{K}}(v_1, v_2)) = (M_{\mathcal{K}}(v_1, v_2) \wedge \neg z) = 0$.*

We define o_{add} to add edge (v_1, v_3) with the operator schema:

Operator Schema 3 (o_{add}) *Let S be an FSA with Boolean algebra $\mathcal{K}$, and let o_{add} : $S \to S'$ be defined with o_{add} : $E(S) \to E(S) \cup \{(v_1, v_3)\}$ for added edge (v_1, v_3) of S. Operator o_{add} could be considered a special case of o_{change} that consists only of step (2) and the additional condition that $M_{\mathcal{K}}(v_1, v_3) = 0$ prior to applying o_{add}.*

The other two primitive operators are specialization (o_{spec}) and generalization (o_{gen}). Specialization and generalization are operators commonly found in the machine learning literature, e.g., see Michalski (1983). In the context of an FSA, specialization lowers the level of a particular state-to-state transition condition in the partial order $\preceq$, whereas generalization raises it, as in Mitchell's Version Spaces (Mitchell, 1978). In particular, a transition condition can be specialized with a meet and can be generalized with a join, which is analogous to adding a conjunct to specialize and a disjunct to generalize as in Michalski (1983).

Formally, we define specialization and generalization, respectively, as follows:

Operator Schema 4 (o_{spec}) *Let S be an FSA with Boolean algebra $\mathcal{K}$, and let o_{spec} : $S \to S'$. Then we can define o_{spec} : $M_{\mathcal{K}}(S) \to M_{\mathcal{K}}(S')$, where $o_{spec}(M_{\mathcal{K}}(v_1, v_2)) = M_{\mathcal{K}}(v_1, v_2) \wedge$*

$\neg z$, for some $z \in \mathcal{K}$, $z \neq 0$. Operator o_{spec} could be considered a special case of o_{change} that consists only of step (1) and the additional two conditions $o_{spec}(M_{\mathcal{K}}(v_1, v_2)) = (M_{\mathcal{K}}(v_1, v_2) \wedge \neg z) \neq 0$ (i.e., $o_{spec} \neq o_{delete}$), and $M_{\mathcal{K}}(v_1, v_2) \neq \neg z$ (since otherwise o_{spec} has no effect).

Operator Schema 5 (o_{gen}) *Let S be an FSA with Boolean algebra $\mathcal{K}$, and let $o_{gen} : S \rightarrow S'$. Then we can define $o_{gen} : M_{\mathcal{K}}(S) \rightarrow M_{\mathcal{K}}(S')$, where $o_{gen}(M_{\mathcal{K}}(v_1, v_3)) = M_{\mathcal{K}}(v_1, v_3) \vee z$, for some $z \in \mathcal{K}$, $z \neq 0$. Operator o_{gen} could be considered a special case of o_{change} that consists only of step (2) and the two additional conditions that $M_{\mathcal{K}}(v_1, v_3) \neq 0$ (i.e., $o_{gen} \neq o_{add}$) and $(M_{\mathcal{K}}(v_1, v_3) \wedge z) = 0$ (because otherwise z adds redundancy) prior to o_{gen}.*

Next, 10 learning operators are defined from these four primitives. Below o_{change} in the operator hierarchy of Figure 7 are two subtrees. The right subtree consists of one-step operators, and the left subtree consists of two-step operators. We define the two one-step operators just below o_{change} first (since we just defined the primitive operators below them):

Operator Schema 6 ($o_{delete \vee spec}$) *This operator consists of applying either of the primitive operators o_{delete} or o_{spec}.*

Operator Schema 7 ($o_{add \vee gen}$) *This operator consists of applying either of the primitive operators o_{add} or o_{gen}.*

It is relevant at this point to introduce two more operators that are not in the hierarchy of Figure 7. They are not in the hierarchy because they are merely minor variants of $o_{delete \vee spec}$ and $o_{add \vee gen}$ and they do not belong strictly below our most general operator o_{change}. These operators are introduced here because they are very useful and also because they are guaranteed to preserve completeness of FSAs. In other words, if the FSA is complete prior to applying these operators then it will be complete after applying them. Recall from Section 2 that each FSA state is associated with a set of allowable actions that may be taken from that state. These operators delete or add an action from the set of allowable actions from a state:

Operator Schema 8 ($o_{delete-action}$) *Delete an allowable action from a state v_1 by one or more applications of operator $o_{delete \vee spec}$. Each application may be to a different outgoing edge from v_1.*

Operator Schema 9 ($o_{add-action}$) *Add an allowable action from a state v_1 by one or more applications of operator $o_{add \vee gen}$. Each application may be to a different outgoing edge from v_1.*

To understand why $o_{delete-action}$ consists of one or more applications of $o_{delete \vee spec}$, consider the following example. In Figure 2, deleting F-collect as an allowable action from F's COLLECTING state results in F-deliver being the only allowable action from that state. Furthermore, this results in the edge (COLLECTING, COLLECTING) being deleted and the edge (COLLECTING, DELIVERING) being specialized. The reasoning is similar for why $o_{add-action}$ is one or more applications of $o_{add \vee gen}$.

The remaining operators, which are all of the operators on the left subtree of o_{change} in Figure 7, consist of two steps: the first to remove condition z from edge (v_1, v_2), and the

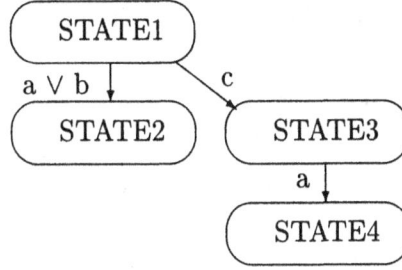

Figure 8: Moving transition conditions between edges.

second to add (the same) condition z to edge (v_1, v_3). The first step consists of applying one primitive operator, and the second step consists of applying another primitive operator. Every one of the following operators preserves determinism and completeness of the FSAs. In other words, if the FSA is deterministic and complete prior to operator application then it will be deterministic and complete afterwards.

Operator Schema 10 ($o_{\mathbf{move}}$) *This operator schema is identical to that of o_{change}, with one exception. Replace "and/or" with "and" in the definition. In other words, we have $o_{move}(M_\mathcal{K}(v_1, v_2)) = M_\mathcal{K}(v_1, v_2) \land \neg z$ and $o_{move}(M_\mathcal{K}(v_1, v_3)) = M_\mathcal{K}(v_1, v_3) \lor z$ for some $(v_1, v_2), (v_1, v_3) \in E(S)$. Therefore o_{move} moves z from one edge to another.*

All of the remaining operators are special cases of o_{move}. We begin with the right subtree of o_{move}:

Operator Schema 11 ($o_{\mathbf{delete+add}}$) *Apply o_{delete} to edge (v_1, v_2) and then apply o_{add} to edge (v_1, v_3).*

An example of $o_{delete+add}$, using Figure 8, is to delete edge (STATE1, STATE3) (i.e., make $M_\mathcal{K}$ (STATE1, STATE3) = 0) and add a new edge (STATE1, STATE1) with transition condition $M_\mathcal{K}$ (STATE1, STATE1) = c.

Operator Schema 12 ($o_{\mathbf{spec+add}}$) *Apply o_{spec} to edge (v_1, v_2) and then apply o_{add} to edge (v_1, v_3).*

For example, using Figure 8, we can move "b" from edge (STATE1, STATE2) to a newly created edge (STATE1, STATE1) to make $M_\mathcal{K}$ (STATE1, STATE2) = a $\land \neg$b and $M_\mathcal{K}$ (STATE1, STATE1) = b. This is specialization of the condition on edge (STATE1, STATE2) followed by addition of edge (STATE1, STATE1).

Next consider the left subtree of o_{move}. At this point, it is relevant to examine the reason for the split into the two subtrees of o_{move}. All of the operators in the left subtree satisfy a condition that is called the "accessibility condition." This condition states that prior to learning (and also after learning), if vertex v_1 is accessible from some initial state then vertex v_3 is guaranteed to also be accessible from that initial state. The reason for this partition will become clear in Subsection 4.2, where we show that a theorem holds for the two-step operators if and only if the accessibility condition is true. The reason that the two operators in the right subtree of o_{move} fail to satisfy the accessibility condition is due to their having o_{add} as their second step. The definition of o_{add} states that $M_{\mathcal{K}}(v_1, v_3) = 0$ prior to operator application, and therefore we have no guarantee of v_3's accessibility, given that v_1 is accessible from an initial state. The following are the definitions of the operators for which the accessibility condition is true:

Operator Schema 13 ($o_{\text{delete+gen}}$) *Apply o_{delete} to edge (v_1, v_2) and then apply o_{gen} to edge (v_1, v_3).*

As an example, in Figure 8, we can move the condition "a ∨ b" from edge (STATE1, STATE2) to edge (STATE1, STATE3) to make $M_{\mathcal{K}}$ (STATE1, STATE2) = 0 and to make $M_{\mathcal{K}}$ (STATE1, STATE3) = c ∨ a ∨ b. This is deletion of edge (STATE1, STATE2) followed by generalization of the transition condition on edge (STATE1, STATE3).

Operator Schema 14 ($o_{\text{spec+gen}}$) *Apply o_{spec} to edge (v_1, v_2) and then apply o_{gen} to edge (v_1, v_3).*

As an example, in Figure 8, we can move the disjunct "b" from edge (STATE1, STATE2) to edge (STATE1, STATE3) to make $M_{\mathcal{K}}$ (STATE1, STATE2) = a ∧ ¬b and $M_{\mathcal{K}}$ (STATE1, STATE3) = c ∨ b. This is a specialization of the transition condition on edge (STATE1, STATE2) followed by a generalization of the transition condition on edge (STATE1, STATE3).

Operator Schema 15 (o_{stay}) *The definition is the same as that of o_{move}, with one exception. Replace vertex v_3 with vertex v_1 everywhere. In other words, the operator consists of moving a condition from edge (v_1, v_2) to edge (v_1, v_1).*

Note that each operator *instantiation* of the schema for o_{stay} will be a special case of one of the following: $o_{delete+add}$, $o_{spec+add}$, $o_{delete+gen}$, or $o_{spec+gen}$. It is considered o_{stay} if and only if on the second step of the operator the transition condition is moved to edge (v_1, v_1). For example, using Figure 8, when we applied operator $o_{spec+add}$ (in the example above) to move the disjunct "b" from edge (STATE1, STATE2) to edge (STATE1, STATE1) to make $M_{\mathcal{K}}$ (STATE1, STATE2) = a ∧ ¬b and $M_{\mathcal{K}}$ (STATE1, STATE1) = b, this could be considered an instantiation of o_{stay}, as well as $o_{spec+add}$. Likewise when we applied $o_{delete+add}$ to delete edge (STATE1, STATE3) and add edge (STATE1, STATE1) with "c" as the transition condition, this could also be considered an instantiation of o_{stay}.

Operator o_{stay} is an especially useful operator. It makes the reasonable assumption that when an agent no longer wants to transition to another state (e.g., an edge is deleted), the agent just stays in its current state. In other words, the condition for transitioning to another state is transferred to the edge leading back to the current state. For example, suppose rover I becomes stuck at the lander and cannot rendezvous with F for an indeterminate period of time. It could generate a temporary plan (see Figure 2) that keeps I in its DELIVERING state by deleting edge (DELIVERING, RECEIVING) and making $M_{\mathcal{K}}$(DELIVERING, DELIVERING) = 1 (and DELIVERING would have to become an initial state).

Recall that accessibility is a key issue for verification. Now that we have a set of operator schemas, let us consider how these operators affect accessibility from initial states.

Clarifying this will be relevant for understanding both the a priori proofs about property preservation, and the motivation for the incremental reverification algorithms. There are two fundamental ways that our learning operators may affect accessibility: *locally* (abbreviated "L"), i.e., by directly altering the accessibility of atoms or states, or *globally* (abbreviated "G"), i.e., by altering accessibility of states or atoms that could be visited *after* the part of the FSA modified by the learning operator. In particular, any change to the accessibility of v_1, v_2, v_3 or atoms in $M_\mathcal{K}(v_1, v_2)$ or $M_\mathcal{K}(v_1, v_3)$, referenced in the operator definition, is considered local. Changes to accessibility of any other states or atoms is considered global.

As an example of an L (local) change to accessibility, using Figure 8, suppose the agent discovers a new action "d" that it can take. It adds "d" to its action repertoire, as well as to the set of allowable actions from one of the states in its FSA. In particular, the agent decides to allow "d" from STATE1 and decides to apply o_{gen} to the transition condition for (STATE1, STATE3) to get condition "c ∨ d." Then atom "d" was not previously accessible from any initial state, but if we assume STATE1 is accessible from an initial state then the application of o_{gen} made the atom "d" accessible. Using Figure 8 to illustrate a G (global) change to accessibility, suppose we delete edge (STATE1, STATE3) in that figure. Then STATE4, which was previously accessible (because we assume STATE1 is accessible) is no longer accessible. On the other hand, the fact that STATE3 is no longer accessible is a local change.

Now we are ready to summarize what the learning operators can do to accessibility. First, we introduce one more notational convenience. The symbols ↑ and ↓ denote "can increase" and "can decrease," respectively, and $\not\uparrow$ and $\not\downarrow$ denote "cannot increase" and "cannot decrease," respectively. We use these symbols with G and L, e.g., ↑ G means that a learning operator can (but does not necessarily) increase global accessibility, and $\not\downarrow$ L means that an operator cannot decrease local accessibility.

The results for the primitive operators are intuitively obvious:

- o_{delete}: ↓ G ↓ L $\not\uparrow$ G $\not\uparrow$ L

- o_{spec}: $\not\downarrow$ G ↓ L $\not\uparrow$ G $\not\uparrow$ L

- o_{add}: $\not\downarrow$ G $\not\downarrow$ L ↑ G ↑ L

- o_{gen}: $\not\downarrow$ G $\not\downarrow$ L $\not\uparrow$ G ↑ L

The primitive operators provide answers about changes in accessibility for all of the one-step operators. For the two-step operators (i.e., o_{move} and all operators below it in the hierarchy of Figure 7), we need to consider the *net* effect. For the results in this paper, we only need to focus on one distinction – the difference in the net effect for those operators that satisfy the accessibility condition (i.e., the left subtree of o_{move}) versus the net effect for those operators that do not satisfy this condition (i.e., the right subtree). The net effect of those operators that satisfy the accessibility condition is that accessibility (global and local) will never be increased, i.e., $\not\uparrow$ G and $\not\uparrow$ L. The reason is as follows. By looking at the results for the primitive operators, it is apparent that the first step in these two-step operators can never increase accessibility, because the first step is always o_{delete} or o_{spec}. Therefore, to understand the intuition behind this result we need to examine the second step. Consider

$o_{delete+gen}$ and $o_{spec+gen}$. Note that o_{gen} does not increase global accessibility ($\not\uparrow$ G), but it can increase local accessibility ($\uparrow$ L). Is $\uparrow$ L a net effect due to the generalization step? Because atoms are being transferred from one outgoing edge of some vertex v_1 to another outgoing edge of v_1 with these two operators, by definition the local accessibility of those atoms from an initial state will not be increased as a net effect. In other words, the atoms are accessible from an initial state if and only if v_1 is, and these two learning operators do not increase the accessibility of v_1. Furthermore, by definition $M_K(v_1, v_3) \neq 0$ prior to learning, so the accessibility of v_3 is not increased. We conclude that $\not\uparrow$ L is a net effect.

A similar line of reasoning explains why operator o_{stay} will not increase local accessibility. Operator o_{stay} cannot increase global accessibility, even if it adds an edge, because the only edge that this operator could add is (v_1, v_1). In conclusion, all three operators that satisfy the accessibility condition have a net effect of *not* increasing accessibility ($\not\uparrow$ G and $\not\uparrow$ L). On the other hand, because operators $o_{delete+add}$ and $o_{spec+add}$ have o_{add} as their second step, they can increase accessibility.

Results from lower in the hierarchy of Figure 7 are inherited up the tree. For example, because $o_{delete+add}$ can increase global accessibility, o_{move} can as well. The following is a summary of the relevant results we have so far about how the two-step learning operators can change accessibility. To avoid overwhelming the reader, we present only those results necessary for understanding this paper.

- o_{stay}, $o_{delete+gen}$, $o_{spec+gen}$: $\not\uparrow$ G $\not\uparrow$ L

- $o_{delete+add}$, $o_{spec+add}$, o_{move}, o_{change}: $\uparrow$ G

Before concluding this section, we briefly consider a different partition of the learning operators than that reflected in the taxonomy of Figure 7. This different partition is necessary for understanding the a priori proofs about the preservation of Response properties (in Section 4). For this partition, we wish to distinguish those operators that can introduce at least one new string with an infinitely repeating substring (e.g., (a,b,c,d,e,d,e,d,e,...) where the ellipsis represents infinite repetition of d followed by e) into the FSA language versus those that cannot. Any operator that can add atoms to the transition condition for an edge in a cycle, add an edge to an existing cycle, or add an edge to create a new cycle belongs to the first class (the class that can add such substrings). Thus this first class includes our operators that can create new cycles (e.g., o_{stay} because it can add a new edge (v_1, v_1)), as well as our operators that can generalize the transition condition along some edge of a cycle (e.g., $o_{delete+gen}$ because it can generalize $M_K(v_1, v_1)$). The operators are divided between these two classes as follows:

1. o_{add}, o_{gen}, $o_{add \lor gen}$, $o_{add-action}$, o_{stay}, $o_{delete+gen}$, $o_{spec+gen}$, $o_{delete+add}$, $o_{spec+add}$, o_{move}, o_{change}

2. o_{delete}, o_{spec}, $o_{delete \lor spec}$, $o_{delete-action}$

It is important to note that *all* of the two-step operators are in the first class.

At this point we have defined a set of useful operators (via their operator schemas) that one could apply to an FSA plan for adaptation. With these operators, it is possible to improve the effectiveness of a plan, and to adapt it to handle previously unforeseen external and internal conditions. To ensure the usefulness of these learning operators, the learner needs to check that it has not generated a useless plan (i.e., $\mathcal{L}(S) \neq \emptyset$). Although not addressed in this paper, we are currently developing efficient methods for making this check using the knowledge of the learning that was done.

The particular choice of learning operators presented here was motivated by four factors. First, these operators translate into easy-to-implement perturbations of entries in a table, which is the representation of FSAs used in our implementation (see Section 6). Second, these operators were inspired by the literature. For example, generalization and specialization operators are considered fundamental for inductive inference (Michalski, 1983), and deleting/adding FSA edges are effective for evolving FSAs (Fogel, 1996). Third, these operators made practical sense in the context of applications that were considered. Fourth, the particular taxonomies presented here facilitate powerful theoretical and empirical results for reducing the time complexity of reverification, as shown in the remainder of this paper.

4. A Priori Results about the Safety of Machine Learning Operators

Subsection 3.4 defined several useful learning operator schemas to modify automaton edges $(o : E(S) \rightarrow E(S'))$ and the transition conditions along edges $(o : M_{\mathcal{K}}(S) \rightarrow M_{\mathcal{K}}(S'))$. The results in this section establish which of these operator schemas o are a priori guaranteed to preserve two property classes of interest (Invariance and Response). This section assumes that all learning operators are applied to a single FSA plan, i.e., SIT_{1agent} or SIT_{1plan}. Section 5 addresses the translation of the operators applied to a single plan into their effect on a product plan (for $SIT_{multiplans}$), and how this affects the results. We begin by formally defining what we mean by "safe machine learning operator."

4.1 "Safe" Online Machine Learning

Our objective is to lower the time complexity of reverification. The ideal solution is to identify *safe machine learning* methods (SMLs), which are machine learning operators that are a priori guaranteed to preserve properties (also called "correctness preserving mappings") and require no run-time reverification. For a plan S and property P, suppose verification has succeeded prior to learning, i.e., $\forall \mathbf{x}$, $\mathbf{x} \in \mathcal{L}(S)$ implies $\mathbf{x} \models P$ (i.e., $S \models P$). Then a machine learning operator $o(S)$ is an SML if and only if verification is guaranteed to succeed after learning. In other words, if $S' = o(S)$, then $S \models P$ implies $S' \models P$.

Subsection 4.2 provides results about the a priori safety of machine learning operators. Some of the results in Subsection 4.2 are negative. Nevertheless, although we do not have an a priori guarantee for these learning operators, Section 6 shows that we can perform reverification more efficiently than total reverification from scratch.

4.2 Theoretical Results

Let us begin by considering the primitive operators. The results for all primitive operators are corollaries of two fundamental theorems, Theorems 1 and 2, which may not be immediately intuitive. For example, it seems reasonable to suspect that if an edge is deleted somewhere along the path from a trigger to a response, then this could cause failure of a Response property to hold because the response is no longer accessible. In fact, this is not true. What actually happens is that deletions reduce the number of strings in the language. If the original language satisfies the property then so does is the smaller language. Theorem 1 formalizes this.

Theorem 1 *Let S' be an FSA with Boolean algebra $\mathcal{K}$. Let S be identical to S', but with additional edges, i.e., $o : S' \to S$ is defined as $o : E(S') \to E(S)$, where $E(S') \subseteq E(S)$. Then $\mathcal{L}(S') \subseteq \mathcal{L}(S)$.*

Proof. The language may be enlarged by the addition of new edges that have newly learned transition conditions. On the other hand, because every accepting run remains an accepting run regardless of new edges, $\mathbf{x} \in \mathcal{L}(S')$ implies $\mathbf{x} \in \mathcal{L}(S)$, and we are never reducing the size of the language. Therefore, $\mathcal{L}(S') \subseteq \mathcal{L}(S)$. $\square$

The results about the machine learning operator schemas o_{delete} and o_{add} follow as corollaries:

Corollary 1 *o_{delete} is an SML with respect to any property P.*

Proof. Assume $S \models P$. Then $\forall \mathbf{x}$, $\mathbf{x} \in \mathcal{L}(S)$ implies $\mathbf{x} \models P$. Define $o_{delete}(S) = S'$. By Theorem 1, $\mathcal{L}(S') \subseteq \mathcal{L}(S)$. Therefore, $\forall \mathbf{x}$, $\mathbf{x} \in \mathcal{L}(S')$ implies $\mathbf{x} \models P$. We conclude that $S' \models P$, i.e., $o_{delete}(S) \models P$. $\square$

To be consistent with Theorem 1, in Corollary 2 only (but not in the rest of the paper), we use S' for the pre-o_{add} FSA and S for the post-o_{add} FSA, i.e., $o_{add}(S') = S$.

Corollary 2 *o_{add} is not necessarily an SML for any property, including Invariance and Response properties.*

Proof. Assume $S' \models P$. Then $\forall \mathbf{x}$, $\mathbf{x} \in \mathcal{L}(S')$ implies $\mathbf{x} \models P$. By Theorem 1, $\mathcal{L}(S') \subseteq \mathcal{L}(S)$. Then we cannot be certain that $S \models P$, i.e., that $o_{add}(S') \models P$. For instance, a counterexample for Invariance property $\square \neg p$ occurs if we add an accessible edge with transition condition p. $\square$

Now we consider a priori results for o_{spec} and o_{gen}. Again, we begin with a relevant theorem for operator schema o.

Theorem 2 *Let S' be an FSA with Boolean algebra $\mathcal{K}$, and let $o : S' \to S$ be defined as $o : M_{\mathcal{K}}(S') \to M_{\mathcal{K}}(S)$ where $\exists z \in \mathcal{K}$, $z \neq 0$, $(v_1, v_3) \in E(S')$, such that $o(M_{\mathcal{K}}(v_1, v_3)) = M_{\mathcal{K}}(v_1, v_3) \vee z$. Then $\mathcal{L}(S') \subseteq \mathcal{L}(S)$.*

Proof. Similar to the proof of Theorem 1. $\square$

Corollary 3 *o_{spec} is an SML for any property.*

Proof. Similar to the proof of Corollary 1 of Theorem 1. $\square$

Corollary 4 *o_{gen} is not necessarily an SML for any property, including Invariance and Response properties.*

Proof. Similar to the proof of Corollary 2 of Theorem 1. $\square$

We can draw the following conclusions from the theorems and corollaries just presented:

- Of the one-step learning operators, those that are guaranteed to be SMLs for any property are o_{delete}, o_{spec}, and $o_{delete \lor spec}$ (which implies that $o_{delete-action}$ is also an SML for any property).

- We need never be concerned with the first step in a two-step operator. It is guaranteed to be an SML (because o_{delete} or o_{spec} is always the first step).

Next consider theorems that are needed to address the two-step operators. Although we found results for the one-step operators that were general enough to address *any* property, we were unable to do likewise for the two-step operators. Our results for the two-step operators determine whether these operators are necessarily SMLs for Invariance or Response properties in particular. Future work will consider other property classes. The theorems are quite intuitive. The first theorem distinguishes those learning operators that will satisfy Invariance properties from those that will not:

Theorem 3 *A machine learning operator is guaranteed to be an SML with respect to any Invariance property P if and only if $\not\uparrow G$ and $\not\uparrow L$ are both true (which, for our two-step operators, implies that the operator satisfies the accessibility condition).*

Proof. Suppose $\not\uparrow G$ and $\not\uparrow L$ are both true. Let Invariance property $P = \square \neg p$. Assume P is true of FSA S prior to learning. Then for every string $\mathbf{y} \in \mathcal{L}(S)$, it must be the case that $\neg p$ is true in every c-state of $\mathbf{y}$. If accessibility of atoms is not increased (i.e., $\not\uparrow G$ and $\not\uparrow L$), then it must be the case that every c-state of every string $\mathbf{x} \in \mathcal{L}(S')$, where $S' = o(S)$, is also a c-state of some string in $\mathcal{L}(S)$. Therefore, for every string $\mathbf{x} \in \mathcal{L}(S')$, it must be the case that $\neg p$ is true in every c-state of $\mathbf{x}$. In other words, moving transition conditions around in an FSA without increasing accessibility will not alter the truth of an Invariance property, which holds in every c-state of every string in the language of the FSA.

Suppose $\uparrow G$ or $\uparrow L$. Increasing accessibility of atoms implies the possibility of introducing a c-state in some string $\mathbf{x} \in \mathcal{L}(S')$, where $S' = o(S)$, that was not in any string of $\mathcal{L}(S)$. This can cause violation of an Invariance property, as in the counterexample in the proof of Corollary 2. Knowing that $\neg p$ is true in every c-state of every string of $\mathcal{L}(S)$ provides no guarantee that $\neg p$ is true in every c-state of every string of $\mathcal{L}(S')$. $\square$

Since we already have results to cover the one-step operators, we need only consider the two-step operators.

Corollary 5 *The machine learning operator schemas $o_{delete+gen}$, $o_{spec+gen}$, and o_{stay} are guaranteed to be SMLs with respect to any Invariance property P because for all of these operators $\not\uparrow G$ and $\not\uparrow L$.*

Corollary 6 *The machine learning operator schemas $o_{delete+add}$, $o_{spec+add}$, o_{move}, and o_{change} are not necessarily SMLs with respect to any Invariance property P because for all of these operators $\uparrow G$.*

121

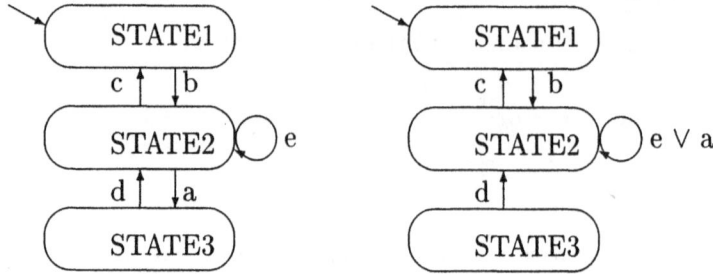

Figure 9: The automata S1 (left) and S1' (right).

The next theorem characterizes those learning operators that cannot be guaranteed to be SMLs with respect to Response properties.

Theorem 4 *Any machine learning operator schema that can introduce a new string with an infinitely repeating substring into the FSA language cannot be guaranteed to be an SML for Response properties.*

Proof. Assume FSA S satisfies a Response property prior to learning. Therefore every string accepted by S satisfies the property. For each accepted string, every instance (or the first instance if it is a First-Response property) of the trigger is eventually followed by a response. Suppose the machine learning operator introduces a new string with an infinitely repeating substring into the language. Then it is possible that the prefix of this string before the infinitely repeating substring includes a trigger and no response, and the infinitely repeating substring does not include a response. □

Since we already have results to cover the one-step operators, we need only consider the two-step operators.

Corollary 7 *All of the two-step learning operators cannot be guaranteed to be SMLs with respect to Response properties because they are in the first class in the partition related to this theorem, i.e., they may introduce strings with infinitely repeating substrings.*

Consider a couple of illustrative examples of Theorem 4 and its corollary, using Figure 9. Prior to learning (the FSA on the left of Figure 9), $\forall \mathbf{x}$, where $\mathbf{x} \in \mathcal{L}(S1)$, $\mathbf{x} \models$ P3, for Response property P3 $= \Box$ (a $\rightarrow \Diamond$ d). Assume operator o_{stay}: S1 $\rightarrow$ S1' deletes edge (STATE2, STATE3) and generalizes the transition condition on edge (STATE2, STATE2) to "e $\lor$ a" (see Figure 9 on the right). Then the string consisting of b followed by infinitely many a's (b,a,a,a,...) $\in \mathcal{L}(S1')$ but $\not\models$ P3. This helps us to see why o_{stay} is not necessarily an SML for Response properties. The same example illustrates why $o_{delete+gen}$ cannot be guaranteed to be an SML for Response properties. For $o_{spec+gen}$, suppose the condition for (STATE2, STATE3) is "f $\lor$ a" in S1, and "f $\land\neg$ a" in S1' but everything else is the same as in Figure 9. Again, we can see the problem for Response properties.

We conclude by summarizing the positive a priori results:

- o_{delete}, o_{spec}, $o_{delete \lor spec}$ and $o_{delete-action}$ are SMLs for any property (expressible in temporal logic).

- $o_{delete+gen}$, $o_{spec+gen}$ and o_{stay} are SMLs for Invariance properties.

and the negative a priori results:

- o_{add}, o_{gen}, $o_{add\lor gen}$, $o_{add-action}$, $o_{spec+add}$, $o_{delete+add}$, o_{move} and o_{change} are not necessarily SMLs for Invariance or Response properties.

- $o_{delete+gen}$, $o_{spec+gen}$ and o_{stay} are not necessarily SMLs for Response properties.

The fact that all three learning operators that satisfy the accessibility condition are guaranteed to be SMLs for Invariance properties is significant, because Invariance properties are extremely useful and common for verifying systems and many important applications need only test properties of this class (Heitmeyer et al., 1998).

Finally, from Theorems 1 and 2 we learned that the heart of the problem for all of the negative results is either an o_{gen} step or an o_{add} step. Later in this paper we address these troublesome steps by finding more efficient methods for dealing with them than total reverification from scratch. However, first, in the next section, we consider how our a priori results are translated from a single to a product FSA for $SIT_{multplans}$.

5. Translating Learning Operators to a Product Automaton

In this section we address $SIT_{multplans}$ where each agent maintains and uses its own individual FSA, but for verification the product FSA needs to be formed and verified. For $SIT_{multplans}$, a learning operator is applied to an individual agent FSA and then the product is formed. Therefore, it is necessary to consider the translation of each learning operator from individual to product FSA, and how that affects the a priori SML results presented above.

For operators $o_{spec+gen}$, $o_{delete+gen}$, $o_{spec+add}$, and $o_{delete+gen}$, we consider only the translations of the primitive operators. This is because the translations of these operators are simply translations of their primitive components. The remaining translations are:

- o_{spec} translates to o_{spec} and/or o_{delete}.

- o_{delete} translates to o_{spec} and/or o_{delete}.

- o_{gen} translates to o_{gen} and/or o_{add}.

- o_{add} translates to o_{gen} and/or o_{add}.

- o_{stay} translates to o_{stay} and/or o_{move}.

- o_{move} translates to o_{move}.

- o_{change} translates to o_{change}.

It may not be intuitive to the reader how o_{gen} can translate to o_{add}. To illustrate, we use Figure 10, where the transition conditions, such as $(a \lor c)$, denote sets of *multiagent* actions. Suppose o_{gen} is applied to edge $(1, 2)$ in the leftmost FSA so that the transition condition is now $(d \lor b)$. Then a new edge $(11', 21')$ is added to the product FSA (rightmost

PRODUCT

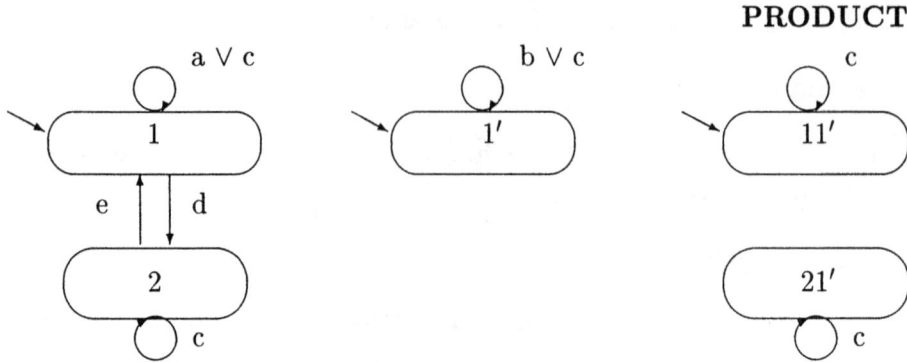

Figure 10: Generalization can become addition in product.

in Figure 10) with the transition condition b. Recall that to form the product FSA we take the Cartesian product of the vertices and the intersection of the transition conditions. Likewise, o_{spec} translates to either o_{spec} or o_{delete} in the product FSA.

To illustrate why o_{stay} can become o_{move} in the product, we use Figure 3. Suppose we delete the edge (TRANSMITTING, RECEIVING) and move the transition condition to edge (TRANSMITTING, TRANSMITTING). Then the global state (DELIVERING, DELIVERING, TRANSMITTING) becomes accessible from initial state (COLLECTING, RECEIVING, TRANSMITTING) by taking multiagent action (F-deliver $\land$ I-receive $\land$ L-transmit). Previously, that multiagent action forced the product FSA to go to (DELIVERING, DELIVERING, RECEIVING).

What implications do these translations have for the safety of the learning operators for the product FSA? The positive a priori results for $o_{delete+gen}$, $o_{spec+gen}$, and o_{stay} for preserving Invariance properties become negative for the product. This is because o_{gen} may become o_{add} and o_{stay} may become o_{move}. On the other hand, the positive a priori results for o_{delete}, o_{spec}, $o_{delete \lor spec}$ and $o_{delete-action}$ preserving all properties remain positive for the product. For o_{delete}, o_{spec}, $o_{delete \lor spec}$, and $o_{delete-action}$, this implies that the product FSA never needs to be formed, reverification does not have to be done, and thus there is *no* run-time cost, even for multiple agents learning autonomously. As mentioned above, the troublesome parts of all operators are due to their o_{gen} or o_{add} component. In the next section we develop methods for reducing the complexity of reverification over total reverification from scratch when these operators have been applied.

6. Incremental Reverification

Recall that operators o_{spec} and o_{delete} cannot cause problems with the safety of learning, whereas o_{gen} and o_{add} are risky (i.e., are not a priori guaranteed to be SMLs). Furthermore, o_{gen} and o_{add} can cause problems when they are the second step in a two-step operator. Fortunately, we have developed incremental reverification algorithms for these operators that can significantly decrease the time complexity over total reverification from scratch.

Recall that there are two ways that operators can alter accessibility: globally (G) or locally (L). Furthermore, recall that o_{add} can increase accessibility either way ($\uparrow$ G $\uparrow$ L), whereas o_{gen} can only increase accessibility locally ($\not\uparrow$ G $\uparrow$ L). We say that o_{gen} has only a "localized" effect on accessibility, whereas the effects of o_{add} may ripple through many parts of the FSA. The implication is that we can have very efficient incremental methods for reverification tailored for o_{gen}, whereas we cannot do likewise for o_{add}. In other words, a more localized effect on accessibility implies that it is easier to localize reverification to gain speed. This is also true for both two-step operators that have o_{gen} as their second step, i.e., $o_{delete+gen}$ and $o_{spec+gen}$ are amenable to incremental (localized) reverification. Because no advantage is gained by considering o_{add} per se, we develop incremental reverification algorithms for the most general operator o_{change}. These algorithms apply to o_{add} and all other special cases of o_{change}.

We have developed two types of incremental reverification algorithms: those that follow the application of o_{gen}, and those that follow the application of o_{change}. For each of our learning operators, one or more of these algorithms is applicable. Before presenting the incremental algorithms, Subsection 6.1 presents two algorithms for total reverification from scratch, namely, one for Invariance properties and the other for all properties expressible as FSAs, as well as an algorithm for taking the tensor product of the FSAs. These algorithms apply to SIT_{1agent}, SIT_{1plan}, or $SIT_{multplans}$. Subsection 6.2 gives incremental versions of all the algorithms in Subsection 6.1. These algorithms are applicable when the learning operator is o_{change} or any of its special cases. Furthermore, they apply to any of SIT_{1agent}, SIT_{1plan}, or $SIT_{multplans}$. Subsection 6.3 has incremental algorithms for SIT_{1agent} and SIT_{1plan}, learning operator o_{gen}, and Invariance and full Response properties in particular. The section concludes with theoretical and empirical results comparing the time complexity of the incremental algorithms with the time complexity of the corresponding total version (as well as with each other).

The goal in developing all of the incremental reverification algorithms is maximal efficiency. These algorithms make the assumption that $S \models P$ prior to learning, which means that any errors found on previous verification(s) have already been fixed. Then learning occurs ($o(S) = S'$), followed by the incremental reverification algorithm (see Figure 1). Next let us consider the *soundness* and *completeness* of the algorithms, where we assume normal termination. All of the incremental reverification algorithms presented here are sound (i.e., whenever they conclude that reverification succeeds, it is in fact true that $S' \models P$) for "downstream" properties and "directionless" properties for which the negation is expressible as a Büchi FSA. Downstream properties (which include Response) check sequences of events in temporal order, e.g., whether every p is followed by a q. In contrast, "upstream" properties check for events in reverse temporal order, e.g., whether every q is preceded by a p.[10] Directionless properties, such as Invariance, impose no order for checking. Some of the incremental algorithms are also complete, i.e., whenever they conclude that reverification fails, it is in fact true that $S' \not\models P$. (The reader should avoid confusing "complete algorithm" with "complete FSA.")

When reverification fails, it does so because of one or more errors, where an "error" implies there is a property violation ($S' \not\models P$). There are two ways to resolve such errors. Either return to the prelearning FSA(s) and choose another learning operator and reverify again, or keep the results of learning but repair the FSA(s) in some other way to fix the error. With one exception, the complete algorithms in this section find *all* true errors

---

10. William Spears (personal communication) identified the upstream/downstream distinction as being relevant to the applicability of the incremental algorithms described here.

	crt	crr	crp	cdt	cdr	cdp	drt	drr	drp	ddt	ddr	ddp
T	R	0	P	T	0	T	R	0	P	T	0	T
R	0	T	0	0	R	0	0	T	0	0	R	0
P	0	0	R	0	0	T	0	0	R	0	0	T

Table 1: The transition function for agent L's FSA plan. The rows correspond to states and the columns correspond to multiagent actions.

introduced by learning. The algorithms that are not complete may also find false errors. Any algorithm that finds all and only true errors can resolve these errors in either of the two ways. An algorithm that does not find all errors or finds false ones requires more restricted error resolution. In particular, it can only be used with the first method for resolving errors, which consists of choosing another learning operator. The algorithms that are sound but not complete (can find false errors) are overly cautious. In other words, they may recommend avoiding a learning operator when in fact the operator may be safe to apply.

Before presenting the incremental algorithms, we first present algorithms for total reverification from scratch. These algorithms do not assume that learning has occurred, and they apply to all situations. They are more general (not tailored for learning), but less efficient, than our incremental algorithms.

6.1 Product and Total (Re)verification Algorithms for All Situations

For implementation efficiency, all of our algorithms assume that FSAs are represented using a table of the transition function $\delta(v_1, a) = v_2$, which means that for state v_1, taking action a leads to next state v_2, as shown in Table 1. Rows correspond to states and columns correspond to multiagent actions. This representation is equivalent to the more visually intuitive representation of Figures 2 and 3. In particular, Table 1 is equivalent to the FSA in Figure 3 for the lander agent L. In Table 1, states are abbreviated by their first letter, and the multiagent actions are abbreviated by their first letters. For example, "crt" means agent F takes action (F-collect), I takes (I-receive), and L takes (L-transmit). The table consists of entries for the next state, i.e., it corresponds to the transition function. A "0" in the table means that there is no possible transition for this state-action pair. One situation in which this occurs is when an action is not allowed from a state. Consider an example use of the table format for finite-state automata. According to the first (upper leftmost) entry in Table 1, if L is in state TRANSMITTING ("T") and F takes action F-collect, I takes I-receive, and L takes L-transmit (which together is multiagent action "crt"), then L will transition to its RECEIVING ("R") state, i.e., $\delta(T, crt) = R$. With this tabular representation, o_{change} is implemented as a perturbation (mutation) operator that changes a table entry to another randomly chosen value for the next state. Operator o_{gen} is a perturbation operator that changes a 0 entry to a next state already appearing in that row. For example, generalizing the transition condition along edge (T,R) can be accomplished by changing one of the 0s to an R in the first row of Table 1. This is because the transition condition associated with edge (T,R) is the set of all multiagent actions that transition from

Suppose there are n agents, and $1 \leq j_k \leq$ the number of states in the FSA for agent k. Then the algorithm forms all product states $v = (v_{j_1}, .., v_{j_n})$ and specifies their transitions:

Procedure product
for each product state $v = (v_{j_1}, .., v_{j_n})$ do
    if all $v_{j_k}, 1 \leq k \leq n$, are initial states, then v is a product initial state
    endif
    for each multiagent action a_i do
        if $(\delta(v_{j_k}, a_i) == 0)$ for some k, $1 \leq k \leq n$, then $\delta(v, a_i) = 0$
        else $\delta(v, a_i) = (\delta(v_{j_1}, a_i), ..., \delta(v_{j_n}, a_i))$; endif
    endfor
endfor
end procedure

Figure 11: $Total_{prod}$ product algorithm.

T to R, i.e., {crt, drt} in Table 1. This set is expressed in Boolean algebra as (I-receive $\wedge$ L-transmit) (see Figure 3).

For SIT_{1plan} or $SIT_{multplans}$, prior to verification the multiagent product FSA S needs to be formed from the individual agent FSAs (see Figure 1). We can implement the algorithm $Total_{prod}$ for generating the product FSA using the data structure of Table 1 as shown in Figure 11. In the product FSA, an example product state and transition is $\delta(CRT, drt)$ = DDR because $\delta(C, drt) = D$, $\delta(R, drt) = D$, and $\delta(T, drt) = R$ for agents F, I, and L, respectively. The initial states of the product FSA are formed by testing whether every individual state of the product is an initial state. For example, if D, D, and R are initial states for F, I, and L, respectively, then DDR will be an initial state for F $\otimes$ I $\otimes$ L. After forming the product states and specifying which are initial, the algorithm of Figure 11 specifies the δ transition for every product state and multiagent action.

Note that the algorithm in Figure 11 forms the product FSA S for testing Invariance properties. To test First-Response properties using AT verification, we need to form the product FSA $S \otimes \neg P$. To do this simply requires considering $\neg P$ to be the $(n+1)$st agent. The algorithm in Figure 11 is modified by changing n to $n+1$ everywhere. It is also important to note that in *all* situations (including SIT_{1agent}), $Total_{prod}$ must be executed to form the product $S \otimes \neg P$ if AT verification is to be done. In SIT_{1agent}, S is just the single agent FSA and n is 1. For SIT_{1plan}, $n = 1$ also. In other words, for SIT_{1plan} the multiagent plan, once formed, is never subdivided and therefore it could be considered like a single agent plan. In both of these cases, if AT verification is done the product is taken of the single plan FSA and the property FSA.

Given that the product FSA has been formed if needed, then the final (multi)agent FSA can be verified. We first consider a very simple model checking algorithm, called $Total_I$, tailored specifically for verifying Invariance properties of the form $\square \neg p$. The algorithm, shown in Figure 12, consists of a depth-first search of S beginning in each initial state. Any accessible atom a_i that is part of a transition condition, where $a_i \preceq p$, violates the property. (We store the set of all atoms $a_i \preceq p$ for rapid access.)

```
Procedure verify
      for each state v ∈ V(S) do
            visited(v) = 0
      endfor
      for each initial state v ∈ I(S) do
            if (visited(v) == 0) then dfs(v); endif
      endfor
end procedure
Procedure dfs(v)
      visited(v) = 1;
      for each atom a_i ∈ Γ(K), a_i ⪯ p, do
            if δ(v, a_i) ≠ 0 then print "Verification error"; endif
      endfor
      for each atom a_i ∈ Γ(K) set w = δ(v, a_i) and do
            if (w ≠ 0) and (visited(w) == 0) then dfs(w); endif
      endfor
end procedure
```

Figure 12: $Total_I$ verification algorithm.

Next we consider an algorithm for verifying *any* property whose negation is expressible as a Büchi FSA, including First-Response properties. The reader may wish to review the high-level description of this AT model checking algorithm presented in Subsection 3.3 before continuing. Figure 13 gives a basic version of this algorithm from Courcoubetis et al. (1992) and Holzmann et al. (1996).[11] We call this algorithm $Total_{AT}$ because it is total automata-theoretic verification. Recall that in AT model checking, the property is represented as an FSA, and asking whether $S \models P$ is equivalent to asking whether $\mathcal{L}(S) \subseteq \mathcal{L}(P)$ for property P. This is equivalent to $\mathcal{L}(S) \cap \overline{\mathcal{L}(P)} = \emptyset$, which is algorithmically tested by taking the tensor product of the plan FSA and the FSA corresponding to $\neg P$. If $\mathcal{L}(S \otimes \neg P) = \emptyset$ then $\mathcal{L}(S) \subseteq \mathcal{L}(P)$, i.e., $S \models P$ and verification succeeds; otherwise, $S \not\models P$ and verification fails. The algorithm of Figure 13 assumes that the negation of the property ($\neg P$) is expressed as a Büchi automaton and the FSA being searched is $S \otimes \neg P$.

Algorithm $Total_{AT}$, in Figure 13, actually checks whether $S \not\models P$ for any property P. To check if $S \not\models P$, we can determine whether $\mathcal{L}(S \otimes \neg P) \neq \emptyset$. This is true if there is some "bad" state in $B(S \otimes \neg P)$ reachable from an initial state and reachable from itself, i.e., part of an accessible cycle and therefore visited infinitely often. The algorithm of Figure 13 performs this check using a nested depth-first search on the product FSA $S \otimes \neg P$. The first depth-first search begins at initial states and visits all accessible states. Whenever a state $s \in B(S \otimes \neg P)$ is discovered, it is called a "seed," and a nested search begins to look for a cycle that returns to the seed. If there is a cycle, this implies the $B(S \otimes \neg P)$ (seed) state can be visited infinitely often, and therefore the language is nonempty (i.e., there is some action sequence in the plan that does not satisfy the property) and verification fails.

---

11. This algorithm is used in the well-known Spin system (Holzmann, 1991). A modification was made to the published algorithm for readability, as well as for efficiency, for the case where it is desirable to halt after the first verification error. This modification makes the nested call first in procedure dfs.

```
Procedure verify
      for each state v ∈ V(S ⊗ ¬P) do
            visited(v) = 0
      endfor
      for each initial state v ∈ I(S ⊗ ¬P) do
            if (visited(v) == 0) then dfs(v); endif
      endfor
end procedure
Procedure dfs(v)
      visited(v) = 1;
      if v ∈ B(S ⊗ ¬P) then
            seed = v;
            for each state v ∈ V(S ⊗ ¬P) do
                  visited2(v) = 0
            endfor
            ndfs(v)
      endif
      for each successor (i.e., next state) w of v do
            if (visited(w) == 0) then dfs(w); endif
      endfor
end procedure
Procedure ndfs(v)  /* the nested search */
      visited2(v) = 1;
      for each successor (i.e., next state) w of v do
            if (w == seed) then print "Bad cycle. Verification error";
            break
            else if (visited2(w) == 0) then ndfs(w); endif
            endif
      endfor
end procedure
```

Figure 13: $Total_{AT}$ verification algorithm.

Suppose there are n agents, and agent i was modified, $1 \leq i \leq n$.

Operator o_{change} modified $\delta(v_i, a_{adapt})$ to be w_i' for state v_i and multiagent action a_{adapt}.

$1 \leq j_k \leq$ the number of states in the FSA for agent k.

Then the algorithm is:

> Procedure product
> for each product state $v = (v_{j_1}, ..., v_i, ..., v_{j_n})$ formed from state v_i do
>   if $(\delta(v_{j_k}, a_{adapt}) == 0)$ for some k, $1 \leq k \leq n$, then $\delta(v, a_{adapt}) = 0$
>   else $\delta(v, a_{adapt}) = (\delta(v_{j_1}, a_{adapt}), ..., w_i', ..., \delta(v_{j_n}, a_{adapt}))$; endif
> endfor
> end procedure

Figure 14: Inc_{prod} product algorithm.

$Total_I$ and $Total_{AT}$ are sound and complete (for *any* property whose negation is expressible as a Büchi FSA), and they find all verification errors. Before elaborating on this, first note that the term "verification error" has a different connotation for $Total_I$ and $Total_{AT}$. For $Total_I$ an error is an accessible bad atom (i.e., an atom $a \preceq p$ where the property is $\Box \neg p$). For $Total_{AT}$ it is an accessible bad state that is part of a cycle. The reason $Total_I$ is sound is that it flags as errors only those atoms $a \preceq p$. It is complete and finds all errors because it does exhaustive search and testing of all accessible atoms. $Total_{AT}$ is also sound and complete, for analogous reasons. Because $Total_I$ and $Total_{AT}$ find all errors, they can be used with either method of error resolution (i.e., choose another operator or fix the FSA).

6.2 Incremental Algorithms for o_{change} and All Situations

All of the algorithms in the previous subsection can be streamlined given that it is known that a learning operator (in this case, o_{change}) has been applied. For simplicity, all of our algorithms assume o_{change} is applied to a single atom (multiagent action). For example, we assume that if $\delta(v_i, a_{adapt}) = w_i$, then $o_{change}(\delta(v_i, a_{adapt})) = w_i'$ where w_i and w_i' are states (or 0, implying no next state), and a_{adapt} is a multiagent action. Since we use the tabular representation, this translates to changing one table entry.

Figure 14 shows an incremental version of $Total_{prod}$, called Inc_{prod}, which is tailored for re-forming the product FSA after o_{change} has been applied. The algorithm of Figure 14 is for Invariance properties; for AT verification change n to $n+1$ in the algorithm and assume $\neg P$ is the $(n+1)$st agent. Although Inc_{prod} is applicable in all situations when taking the product with the property FSA, the primary motivation for developing this algorithm was the multiagent $SIT_{multplans}$. Recall that in this situation, every time learning is applied to an individual agent FSA, the product must be *re*-formed to verify global properties. The wasted cost of doing this motivated the development of this algorithm.

Algorithm Inc_{prod} assumes that the product was formed originally (before learning) using $Total_{prod}$. Inc_{prod} capitalizes on the knowledge of what (individual or multiagent) state (v_i) and multiagent action (a_{adapt}) transition to a new next state as specified by operator o_{change}. This algorithm assumes that the prelearning product FSA is stored. Then the only product FSA states whose next state needs to be modified are those states that

Procedure product
$I(S) = \emptyset$;
for each product state $v = (v_{j_1}, ..., v_i, ..., v_{j_n})$ formed from state v_i do
    if visited(v) then $I(S) = I(S) \cup \{v\}$; endif
    if $(\delta(v_{j_k}, a_{adapt}) == 0)$ for some k, $1 \le k \le n$, then $\delta(v, a_{adapt}) = 0$
    else $\delta(v, a_{adapt}) = (\delta(v_{j_1}, a_{adapt}), ..., w_i', ..., \delta(v_{j_n}, a_{adapt}))$; endif
endfor
end procedure

Figure 15: $Inc_{prod-NI}$ product algorithm: a variation of Inc_{prod} that gets new initial states.

---

include v_i and transition on action a_{adapt}. The method for reverification that is assumed to follow Inc_{prod} is total reverification, i.e., $Total_I$ or $Total_{AT}$.

Next, consider another pair of product and reverification algorithms that is expected to be, overall, potentially even more efficient. The goal is to streamline reverification after o_{change}. This requires a few simple changes to the algorithms. The motivation for these changes is that when model checking downstream properties, o_{change} has only "downstream effects," i.e., it only affects the accessibility of vertices and atoms altered by o_{change} or those that would be visited by verification *after* those altered by o_{change}.

Consider the changes. We start by building a set of the Cartesian product states $v = (v_{j_1}, ..., v_i, ..., v_{j_n})$ that are formed from the state v_i that was affected by learning. The first way that we can shorten reverification is by using these states as the new initial states for reverification. In fact, we need only select those that were visited during the original verification (i.e., are accessible from the original initial states). In other words, suppose for agent i, o_{change} modified $\delta(v_i, a_{adapt})$. Then we reinitialize the set of initial states to be $\emptyset$ and add all product states formed from v_i that were marked "visited" during previous verification. This can be done by modifying the product algorithm of Figure 14 as shown in Figure 15. The algorithm of Figure 15 is to form the product FSA for verifying Invariance properties. To form the product for AT verification, substitute $I(S \otimes \neg P)$ for $I(S)$ and $(n + 1)$ for n in Figure 15. We call this incremental product algorithm $Inc_{prod-NI}$, where "NI" denotes the fact that we are getting new initial states.

The second way to streamline reverification is by only considering a transition on action a_{adapt}, the action whose δ value was modified by learning, from these new initial states. Thereafter, incremental reverification proceeds exactly like total (re)verification. With these changes, $Total_I$ becomes Inc_{I-NI}, shown in Figure 16. Likewise, with these changes $Total_{AT}$ becomes Inc_{AT-NI}, as shown in Figure 17. Figure 17 shows only changes to procedures dfs and verify; ndfs is the same as in Figure 13. One final streamlining added to Inc_{I-NI}, but not Inc_{AT-NI}, is that only the new initial states have "visited" reinitialized to 0. This can be done for Invariance properties because they are not concerned with the order of atoms in strings.[12]

---

12. Suppose o_{change} adds a new edge (v_1, v_3). If v_3 was visited on previous verification of an Invariance property (from a state other than v_1), then all atoms that can be visited after v_3 would already have been tested for the property. On the other hand, when testing First-Response properties the order of

```
Procedure verify
      for each new initial state v ∈ I(S) do
            visited(v) = 0
      endfor
      for each new initial state v ∈ I(S) do
            if (visited(v) == 0) then dfs(v); endif
      endfor
end procedure
Procedure dfs(v)
      visited(v) = 1;
      if v ∈ I(S) and w ≠ 0, where w = δ(v, a_adapt), then
            if (a_adapt ⪯ p) then print "Verification error"; endif
            if (visited(w) == 0) then dfs(w); endif
      else
            for each atom a_i ∈ Γ(K), a_i ⪯ p, do
                  if δ(v, a_i) ≠ 0 then print "Verification error"; endif
            endfor
            for each atom a_i ∈ Γ(K) set w = δ(v, a_i) and do
                  if (w ≠ 0) and (visited(w) == 0) then dfs(w); endif
            endfor
      endif
end procedure
```

Figure 16: Inc_{I-NI} reverification algorithm.

Inc_{I-NI} is sound for Invariance properties, and Inc_{AT-NI} is sound for any downstream or directionless property whose negation is expressible as a Büchi FSA, including First-Response and Invariance. Assuming $S \models P$ prior to applying o_{change} to form S', if these incremental reverification algorithms conclude that $S' \models P$, then total reverification would also conclude that $S' \models P$. Recall that total reverification is sound. Therefore, the same is true for these incremental algorithms. Furthermore, these incremental reverification algorithms will find all of the new violations of the property introduced by o_{change}. The reason the algorithms are sound and find all new errors (for downstream or directionless properties) is that there are only two ways that accessibility can be modified by any of our learning operators, including o_{change}: locally or globally. Recall that local change alters the accessibility of atom a_{adapt} or the state $δ(v_i, a_{adapt})$, and a global change alters the accessibility of states or atoms that would be visited *after* $δ(v_i, a_{adapt})$. In neither case (local or global) will the learning operator modify accessibility of atoms or states visited before, but not after, a_{adapt}. Our algorithms reverify exhaustively (i.e., they reverify as much as total reverification would) for all atoms and states visited at or after a_{adapt}. Since these incremental algorithms perform reverification exactly the same way as their total versions

---

atoms is relevant. Even if v_3 was previously visited, since it might not have been visited from v_1, the addition of (v_1, v_3) could add a new string with a new atom order that might violate the First-Response property. Therefore, v_3 needs to be revisited for First-Response properties, but not for Invariance properties.

```
Procedure verify
    for each state v ∈ V(S ⊗ ¬P) do
        visited(v) = 0
    endfor
    for each new initial state v ∈ I(S ⊗ ¬P) do
        if (visited(v) == 0) then dfs(v); endif
    endfor
end procedure
Procedure dfs(v)
    visited(v) = 1;
    if v ∈ B(S ⊗ ¬P) then
        seed = v;
        for each state v ∈ V(S ⊗ ¬P) do
            visited2(v) = 0
        endfor
        ndfs(v)
    endif
    if v ∈ I(S ⊗ ¬P) and w ≠ 0 and (visited(w) == 0),
    where w = δ(v, a_adapt), then dfs(w)
    else
        for each successor (i.e., next state) w of v do
            if (visited(w) == 0) then dfs(w); endif
        endfor
    endif
end procedure
```

Figure 17: Procedures verify and dfs of the Inc_{AT-NI} reverification algorithm.

do after the part of the FSA that was modified by learning, they will find all new errors introduced by learning.

Inc_{I-NI} is complete for Invariance properties because it flags errors using the same method as $Total_I$, and because Invariance properties are directionless and are therefore impervious to the location of atoms in a string. On the other hand, Inc_{AT-NI} is not complete for all downstream properties. For example, it is not complete for properties that check for the *first* occurrence of a pattern in a string, e.g., First-Response properties. Because Inc_{AT-NI} does not identify whether the new initial states are before or after the first occurrence, there is no way to know if the first occurrence is being checked after learning. Nevertheless, this lack of completeness for First-Response properties actually turns out to be a very useful trait, as we will discover in Subsection 6.5.

6.3 Incremental Algorithms for o_{gen} and $SIT_{1agent/1plan}$

We next present our final two incremental reverification algorithms, which are applicable only in SIT_{1agent} and SIT_{1plan}, when there is one FSA to reverify. These are powerful algorithms in terms of their capability to reduce the complexity of reverification. However, their soundness relies on the assumption that the learning operator's effect on accessibility

```
Procedure check-invariance-property
if v₁ was not previously visited, then output "Verification succeeds."
else
        if (z ⊨ ¬p) then output "Verification succeeds."
        else output "Avoid this instance of o_gen."; endif
endif
end procedure
```

Figure 18: Inc_{gen-I} reverification algorithm.

is localized, i.e., that it is o_{gen} with SIT_{1agent} or SIT_{1plan} but not $SIT_{multplans}$ (where o_{gen} might become o_{add}). An important advantage of these algorithms is that they never require forming a product FSA, not even $S \otimes \neg P$, regardless of whether the property is type Response. The algorithms gain efficiency by being *both* tailored to a specific property type *and* to a specific learning operator. The objective in developing these algorithms was maximal efficiency and therefore they sacrifice completeness and/or the ability to find all errors.

These two incremental algorithms are tailored for reverification after operator o_{gen}. Assume that property P holds for S prior to learning, i.e., $S \models P$. Now we generalize the transition condition $M_{\mathcal{K}}(v_1, v_3) = y$ to form S' via $o_{gen} (M_{\mathcal{K}}(v_1, v_3)) = y \vee z$, where $y \wedge z = 0$. We want to verify that $S' \models P$.

One additional definition is needed before presenting our algorithms. We previously defined what it means for a c-state formula p to be true at a c-state, but to simplify the algorithms we also define what it means for a c-state formula to be true of a transition condition. A c-state formula p is defined to be true of a transition condition y, i.e., "$y \models p$," if and only if $y \preceq p$ (which can be implemented by testing whether for every atom $a \preceq y$, $a \preceq p$.)

Let us begin with the algorithm Inc_{gen-I} (which consists of two very simple tests) tailored for o_{gen} and Invariance properties, shown in Figure 18. Recall that $M_{\mathcal{K}}(v_1, v_3) = y$ and $o_{gen}(M_{\mathcal{K}}(v_1, v_3)) = y \vee z$. Inc_{gen-I}, which tests "$z \models \neg p$," localizes reverification to a restricted portion of the FSA. (For efficiency, $z \models \neg p$ is implemented as a test for $z \preceq p$ rather than $z \preceq \neg p$ because p is typically expected to be more succinct than $\neg p$.) Assume the Invariance property is $P = \Box \neg p$ and $S \models P$. Then every string $\mathbf{x}$ in $\mathcal{L}(S)$ satisfies Invariance property P, so for each $\mathbf{x}$, $\neg p$ is true of every atom in $\mathbf{x}$. This implies $y \models \neg p$. This statement is based on our assumption that v_1 is accessible from an initial state. If not, reverification is not needed. The generalization will not violate P. Therefore, the algorithm begins by testing whether v_1 was visited on previous verification. If not, the output is "success." (Note that o_{gen} does not alter the accessibility of v_1.)

Inc_{gen-I} is sound and complete for Invariance properties. Generalization of $M_{\mathcal{K}}(v_1, v_3)$ is application of $o_{gen} (M_{\mathcal{K}}(v_1, v_3)) = y \vee z$ to form S'. This operator o_{gen} preserves Invariance property P if and only if $S' \models P$, which is true if and only if $z \models \neg p$. The reason for this is that we know S satisfies P from our original verification, and therefore $\neg p$ is true for all atoms in all strings in $\mathcal{L}(S)$. The only possible new atoms in $\mathcal{L}(S')$ but not in $\mathcal{L}(S)$ are in z. If $z \models \neg p$, then $\neg p$ is true for all atoms in $\mathcal{L}(S')$, which implies that every string in

```
Procedure check-response-property
if y ⊨ q then
        if (z ⊨ q and z ⊨ ¬p) then output "Verification succeeds."
        else output "Avoid this instance of o_gen"; endif
else
        if (z ⊨ ¬p) then output "Verification succeeds."
        else output "Avoid this instance of o_gen"; endif
endif
end procedure
```

Figure 19: Inc_{gen-R} reverification algorithm.

$\mathcal{L}(S')$ satisfies P. In other words, $S' \models P$. Therefore, Inc_{gen-I} is sound. We also know that it is complete because if $\exists a$, $a \preceq z$, $a \not\preceq p$, then it must be the case that $S' \not\models P$. In conclusion, Inc_{gen-I}, which consists of the test "$z \models \neg p$," is sound and complete. For maximal efficiency, our implementation of Inc_{gen-I} halts after the first error, although it is simple to modify it to find all errors (and this does not significantly affect the empirical time complexity results of Subsection 6.5, nor does it affect the worst-case time complexity). Inc_{gen-I} is incremental because it is localized to just checking whether the property holds of the newly added atoms in z, rather than all atoms in $\mathcal{L}(S')$. Finally, this algorithm only needs to be executed for o_{gen}, but not for $o_{spec+gen}$ or $o_{delete+gen}$, because o_{gen} is the only version that can add *new* atoms via generalization. Recall that $o_{spec+gen}$ and $o_{delete+gen}$ are SMLs for Invariance properties.

As an example of Inc_{gen-I}, suppose a, b, c, d, and e are atoms, and the transition condition y between STATE1 and STATE2 equals a. Let (a, b, b, d, d,...), where the ellipsis indicates infinite repetition of d, be a string in $\mathcal{L}(S)$ that includes STATE1 and STATE2 as the first two vertices in its accepting run. The property is $P = \Box\neg$ e. Assume the fact that this string satisfies $\neg$ e was proved in the original verification. Suppose o_{gen} generalizes $M_\mathcal{K}(\text{STATE1}, \text{STATE2})$ from a to (a $\lor$ c) (i.e., it adds a new allowable action c from STATE1), which adds the string (c, b, b, d, d,...) to $\mathcal{L}(S')$. Then rather than test whether all of the elements of { a, b, c, d } are $\preceq \neg$ e, we really only need to test whether c $\preceq \neg$ e, because c is the only newly added atom.

The next algorithm, Inc_{gen-R}, is for generalization and full Response properties (and is nothing more than some simple tests). Like Inc_{gen-I}, Inc_{gen-R} localizes reverification to a restricted portion of the FSA. Assume the Response property is $P = \Box(p \rightarrow \Diamond q)$, where p is the trigger and q is the response for c-state formulae p and q. Assume property P holds for S prior to learning ($S \models P$). Now we generalize $M_\mathcal{K}(v_1, v_3) = y$ to form S' by applying $o_{gen}\ (M_\mathcal{K}(v_1, v_3)) = y \lor z$, where $y \land z = 0$. We need to verify that $S' \models P$.

Inc_{gen-R} for o_{gen} and full Response properties is in Figure 19. (Inc_{gen-R} is also applicable for $o_{delete+gen}$ and $o_{spec+gen}$.) The algorithm first checks whether a response could be required of the transition condition $M_\mathcal{K}(v_1, v_3)$. A response is required if, for at least one string in $\mathcal{L}(S)$ whose run includes (v_1, v_3), the prefix of this string before visiting vertex v_1 includes the trigger p not followed by response q, and the string suffix after v_3 does not include q either. Such a string satisfies the property if and only if $y \models q$. Thus if $y \models q$

135

and the property is true prior to learning (i.e., for S), then it is possible that a response is required. In this situation (i.e., $y \models q$), the only way to be sure we are safe ($S' \models P$) is if the newly added condition z also has the response, i.e., $z \models q$. If not, then there could be new strings in $\mathcal{L}(S')$ whose accepting runs include (v_1, v_3) but do not satisfy the property. For example, suppose a, b, c, and d are atoms, and the transition condition y between STATE4 and STATE5 equals d. Let $\mathbf{x} = (a, b, b, d, ...)$ be a string in $\mathcal{L}(S)$ that includes STATE4 and STATE5 as the fourth and fifth vertices in its accepting run. The property is $P = \Box$ (a $\rightarrow$ $\Diamond$ d), and therefore $y \models q$ and $\mathbf{x} \models P$. Suppose o_{gen} generalizes $M_{\mathcal{K}}$(STATE4, STATE5) from d to (d $\vee$ c), where z is c, which adds the string $\mathbf{x}' = (a, b, b, c, ...)$ to $\mathcal{L}(S')$. Then $z \not\models q$. If the string suffix after (a, b, b, c) does not include d, then there is now a string that includes the trigger but does not include the response. In other words, $\mathbf{x}' \not\models P$. Finally, if $y \models q$ and $z \models q$, an extra check is made to be sure $z \models \neg p$ because an atom could be both a response and a trigger. New triggers should be avoided.

The second part of the algorithm states that if $y \not\models q$ and no new triggers are introduced by generalization, then the operator is "safe" to do. It is guaranteed to be safe ($S' \models P$) in this case because if $y \not\models q$, then a response *cannot* be required here. In other words, because $S \models P$, for every string in $\mathcal{L}(S)$ whose accepting run includes (v_1, v_3), either no trigger occurred prior to visiting v_1, or every trigger was followed by a response prior to visiting v_1, or a response occurred after visiting v_3.

Inc_{gen-R} is sound but not complete for full Response properties. Its soundness is based on the fact that o_{gen} does not increase accessibility of vertices or atoms visited after state v_3 (i.e., globally) and therefore reverification can be localized to only $M_{\mathcal{K}}(v_1, v_3)$. Inc_{gen-R} is not complete because it may output "Avoid this instance of o_{gen}" when in fact o_{gen} is safe to do. For example, if $y \models q$ but $z \not\models q$, the algorithm will output "Avoid this instance of o_{gen}." Yet it may be the case that $S' \models P$ if no trigger p precedes response q in $\mathcal{L}(S')$, or if a response is after v_3. When Inc_{gen-R} outputs verification failure, it does not supply sufficient information for FSA repair. Errors must be resolved by selecting another learning operator. Note that "error" has a different connotation for Inc_{gen-R} than for the AT verification algorithms. Any "Avoid..." output is considered an error.

Another disadvantage of Inc_{gen-R} is that it does not allow generalizations that add triggers. If it is desirable to add new triggers during generalization, then one needs to modify Inc_{gen-R} to call Inc_{AT} when reverification with Inc_{gen-R} fails, instead of outputting "Avoid this instance of o_{gen}." This modification also fixes the false error problem, *and* preserves the enormous time savings (see Section 6.5) when reverification succeeds.

6.4 Theoretical Worst-Case Time Complexity Analysis

Recall that one of our primary objectives is timely agent responses. This section compares the worst-case time complexity of the algorithms. Let us begin with the time complexity of $Total_{prod}$. This is $O((\prod_{i=1}^{n} |V(S_i)|) * |\Gamma(\mathcal{K})| * n)$ to form the product of the individual agent FSAs for Invariance property verification, and $O((\prod_{i=1}^{n} |V(S_i)|) * |P| * |\Gamma(\mathcal{K})| * n)$ to form the product for AT verification. Here n is the number of agents, $|V(S_i)|$ is the number of states in single agent FSA S_i, $|P|$ is the number of states in the property FSA P, and $|\Gamma(\mathcal{K})|$ is the total number of atoms (multiagent actions). The reason for this complexity result is that there are $\prod_{i=1}^{n} |V(S_i)|$ product states for Invariance property verification, and

$(\prod_{i=1}^{n} |V(S_i)|) * |P|$ product states for AT verification. The outer loop of $Total_{prod}$ iterates through all product states. The inner loop of $Total_{prod}$ iterates through all $|\Gamma(\mathcal{K})|$ atoms. Note that $(\prod_{i=1}^{n} |V(S_i)|) * |\Gamma(\mathcal{K})|$ and $(\prod_{i=1}^{n} |V(S_i)|) * |P| * |\Gamma(\mathcal{K})|$ are the sizes of the product FSA transition function tables built for $Total_I$ and $Total_{AT}$, respectively. $Total_{prod}$ does at most n lookups for each table entry.

By comparison, our incremental algorithm Inc_{prod} for generating the product FSA has time complexity $O((\prod_{1=1}^{n-1} |V(S_i)|) * n)$ or $O((\prod_{i=1}^{n-1} |V(S_i)|) * |P| * n)$ to modify the product FSA for Invariance property reverification or AT reverification, respectively. This is because the total number of revised product states is $(\prod_{i=1}^{n-1} |V(S_i)|)$ or $(\prod_{i=1}^{n-1} |V(S_i)|) * |P|$, and only one atom is considered (because we assume o_{change} changes the next state for a single atom a_{adapt}). The time complexity of $Inc_{prod-NI}$ is the same as that of Inc_{prod}.

Next consider the worst-case time complexity of total (re)verification after the product has been formed. It is $O((\prod_{i=1}^{n} |V(S_i)|) * |\Gamma(\mathcal{K})|)$ for $Total_I$. This is because, in the worst case, every product state is accessible and therefore every entry in the product FSA transition function table is visited. Assuming $|B|$ is the number of "bad" (in the Büchi sense) states in the product FSA, then the worst-case time complexity of $Total_{AT}$ is $O((|B|+1) * (\prod_{i=1}^{n} |V(S_i)|) * |P| * |\Gamma(\mathcal{K})|)$. This is because, in the worst case, every entry in the product FSA transition function table is visited once on the depth-first search and, for each bad state, again on the nested depth-first search. Unfortunately, the worst-case time complexity of Inc_{I-NI} and Inc_{AT-NI} are the same as that of $Total_I$ and $Total_{AT}$, respectively. This is because, in the worst case, every product state is still accessible. The restriction to transition only on a_{adapt} at first does not reduce the "big O" complexity.

Finally, we consider the worst-case complexity of Inc_{gen-I} and Inc_{gen-R}. First, we define for any Boolean expression x, $|x|$ is the number of elements in $\{a \mid a \in \Gamma(\mathcal{K}) \text{ and } a \preceq x\}$. For Invariance properties P of the form $\Box \neg p$, $|P|$ equals $|p|$ since we test for each atom a whether $a \models p$ rather than $a \models \neg p$, because we expect $|p| < |\neg p|$ in general. Then Inc_{gen-I} requires time $O(|z| * |p|)$ to determine whether $z \models \neg p$. (Checking whether v_1 was visited requires constant time.) Assuming $|p| < \prod_{i=1}^{n} |V(S_i)|$ (which should be true except under bizarre circumstances), and since $|z| \leq \Gamma(\mathcal{K})$, Inc_{gen-I} saves time over $Total_I$. Inc_{gen-R} requires time $O((|y| * |q|) + (|z| * (|p| + |q|)))$ to determine whether $y \models q$, and then to determine whether $z \models q$ and $z \models \neg p$.[13] Clearly $(|y|+|z|) \leq |\Gamma(\mathcal{K})|$ because by the definition of o_{gen}, $y \wedge z = 0$. Therefore, assuming $(|p| + |q|) < ((|B|+1) * |\prod_{i=1}^{n} |V(S_i)| * |P|)$ (which, again, should be true except in bizarre circumstances), the worst-case time complexity of Inc_{gen-R} is lower than that of $Total_{AT}$.

6.5 Empirical Time Complexity Comparisons

Worst-case time complexity is not always a useful measure. Therefore we supplement the worst-case analyses with empirical results on cpu time. Our primary objective in these experiments is to compare the incremental algorithms with total reverification, as well as with each other, for the context of evolving behaviorally correct FSAs. The time required

---

13. Determining whether $z \models \neg p$ can be done by determining whether $z \preceq p$. Also, for Inc_{gen-R}, an additional time $O(|\Gamma(\mathcal{K})| - (|y| + |z|))$ is needed to identify y when using the representation of Table 1. This does not affect our complexity comparisons or conclusions.

for reverification is significant to address if we want timely agent responses, because reverification occurs after *every* learning operator application.

Before describing the experimental results, let us consider the experimental methodology. All code was written in C and run on a Sun Ultra 10 workstation. In our experiments, FSAs were randomly initialized, subject to certain restrictions. The reason for randomness is that this is a typical way to initialize individuals in a population for an evolutionary algorithm. There are two restrictions on the FSAs. First, although determinism and completeness of FSAs are execution, rather than verification, issues and therefore need not be enforced for these experiments, our choice of tabular representation of the FSAs (see Table 1) restricts the FSAs to being deterministic. Second, because the incremental algorithms assume $S \models P$ prior to learning, we restrict the FSAs to comply with this. There are two alternative methods for enforcing this in the experiments: (1) use sparse FSAs (i.e., with many 0s) and keep generating new FSAs until total verification succeeds (which does not take long with sparse FSAs), or (2) use dense FSAs engineered to guarantee property satisfaction. In particular, dense FSAs are forced to satisfy Invariance properties $\Box \neg p$ by inserting 0s in every column of the transition function table (such as Table 1) labeled with an atom $a \preceq p$. Dense FSAs are forced to satisfy First-Response properties with trigger p and response q by inserting 0s in every column labeled with an atom $a \preceq p$. This eliminates triggers initially. Note that either of these methods is a viable way to initialize a population of FSAs for evolution because it ensures early success in satisfying the property. This paper presents only the results with dense FSAs. See Gordon (1999) for the results with sparse FSAs.[14]

Another experimental design decision was to show scaleup in the size of the FSAs. Throughout the experiments there were assumed to be three agents, each with the same 12 multiagent actions. Each individual agent FSA had 25 or 45 states.[15] With 45 states the transition table contains $45^3 * 12$ entries.

A suite of five Invariance and five Response properties was used, which is in Appendix C. Invariance properties were expressed by storing the set of all atoms $a \preceq p$ for property $\Box \neg p$. This suffices for all of our algorithms tailored for Invariance properties. For AT verification, Response properties were expressed with a First-Response Büchi FSA for the negation of the property. An explanation of why this is adequate for our experiments is below. For Inc_{gen-R}, trigger p, and response q, all atoms $a_i \preceq p$ and $a_j \preceq q$ were stored. Six independent experiments were performed to verify each of the properties. In other words, every reverification algorithm was tested with 30 runs – six runs for each of five Invariance or five Response properties. For every one of these runs, a different random seed was used for generating the three FSAs. However, it is important to point out that all algorithms being compared with each other saw the *same* FSAs. For example, in Table 2 we compare Inc_{prod} (row 1), $Inc_{prod-NI}$ (row 4), and $Total_{prod}$ (row 7). They all input the same three FSAs. Furthermore, the learning operator (specific instantiation of the operator schema) was the same for all algorithms being compared.

---

14. Sparse FSAs have an additional advantage, assuming they remain relatively sparse after evolution. The advantage is their succinctness for efficient execution, as in multientity models (Tennenholtz & Moses, 1989).

15. The sparse FSAs had 25, 45, or 65 states. To get accurate timing results with the dense FSAs, though, 65 states required a cpu free of any interfering processes for an unreasonably long time.

Let us consider the results in Tables 2 and 3. In both of these tables, each row corresponds to an algorithm. Rows are numbered for later reference. The entries give performance results, to be described shortly. Table 2 compares the performance of total reverification with the algorithms of Subsection 6.2, which were designed for o_{change} and *all* situations. The situation assumed for these experiments was $SIT_{multplans}$. Three dense random (subject to the above-mentioned restrictions) FSAs were generated, and then the product was formed. The result was a product FSA satisfying the property. Operator o_{change} was then applied, which consisted of a random (but points to a state instead of 0) change to a randomly chosen table entry in the FSA transition table for a random choice of one of the three agents. Finally, the product FSA was re-formed and reverification done.

The methodology for generating Table 3 was similar to that for Table 2, except that o_{gen} was the learning operator and the situation was assumed to be SIT_{1plan}. In other words, the product FSA was formed, and then o_{gen} applied to the *product* FSA of the three agents, the product was taken with the property FSA if needed for AT verification, and then reverification performed. Operator o_{gen} consisted of choosing a random state s_i and a random action a_i for which $\delta(s_i, a_i) = s_k$, and choosing a random action a_j for which $\delta(s_i, a_j) = 0$, and then setting $\delta(s_i, a_j) = s_k$.

Any column in Tables 2 or 3 labeled "sec" gives a mean, over 30 runs, of the cpu time of the algorithm. Columns labeled "spd" give the speedup over total, i.e., the cpu time of the incremental algorithm in that row divided by the cpu time of the corresponding total algorithm. For example, the "spd" entry for Inc_{prod} in row 1 gives its cpu time divided by the cpu time of $Total_{prod}$ in row 7. Columns labeled "err" show the average number of verification errors over 30 runs. This is important to monitor because, for example, the cpu time is most strongly correlated with the number of states "visited" during dfs, and "visited2" during ndfs when AT verification is used. Every property error causes ndfs to be called with a nested search, which may be quite time-consuming. Also, it is important to note that we did not force any verification errors to occur. It was our objective to monitor cpu time under natural circumstances for evolving FSAs. When errors arose they were the natural result of applying a learning operator. The "err" columns are missing from Table 2 because the values are all 0, i.e., no errors occurred during the experiments due to applying o_{change}, although we have observed errors to occur with this operator not during the experiments. The lack of errors in the experiments resulted from the particular random FSAs that happened to be generated during the experiments. Errors are quite common with the specific o_{gen} version of o_{change}, as can be seen in Table 3. Note that "N/A" is in the "err" column for anything other than a verification algorithm because "err" refers to verification errors.

The algorithms (rows) should be considered in triples "p," "v," and "b," or else as a single item "v+b." A "p" next to an algorithm name in Table 2 or 3 denotes it is a product algorithm, a "v" that it is a verification algorithm, and a "b" that it is the sum of the "p" and "v" entries, i.e., the time for *both* re-forming the product and reverifying. For example, Inc_I (b) is considered to be an algorithm pair consisting of Inc_{prod} (p) followed by $Total_I$ (v) (see rows 1-3 of Table 2). If no product needs to be formed, then the "b" version of the algorithm is identical to the "v" version, in which case there is only one row labeled "v+b."

Tables 4, 5, and 6 *re*-present a subset (cpu time only) of the data from Tables 2 and 3 in a format that facilitates some comparisons. In other words, Tables 4, 5, and 6 contain no new data, only reformatted data from Tables 2 and 3. In Tables 4, 5, and 6, results are grouped by "p," "v," or "b."

Let us elaborate on one more interesting issue before listing our experimental hypotheses. Recall that we are using a First-Response property FSA and that this FSA checks only that the *first* trigger in every string is followed by a response. For our evolutionary paradigm (with dense FSA initialization) when using Inc_{AT-NI}, verifying a First-Response property is equivalent to verifying the full Response property. The false errors found by Inc_{AT-NI} due to its incompleteness are in fact violations of the full Response property.[16] Therefore for Inc_{AT-NI}, First-Response FSAs are entirely adequate for reverification of full Response properties. Because we used the evolutionary paradigm in these experiments, and because Inc_{AT-NI} found the same number of errors as $Total_{AT}$ (i.e., Inc_{AT-NI} found no false errors), for the FSAs in these experiments testing First-Response properties was equivalent to testing full Response properties.

For our experiments, five hypotheses were tested:

H1: Algorithms tailored specifically for Invariance properties are faster than those for AT verification, because the latter are general-purpose (and the product algorithms include an additional FSA).

H2: The incremental algorithms are faster than the total algorithms for both product and reverification. This is expected to be true because they were tailored for learning.

H3: The "NI" versions of the incremental algorithms are faster than their counterparts, which do not find new initial states. This is expected because of the increase in streamlining.

H4: Inc_{gen-I} and Inc_{gen-R} are the fastest of all the algorithms, because they are tailored for a less generic learning operator (i.e., o_{gen} rather than o_{change}), *plus* they are also tailored for one specific property type, and they sacrifice finding all errors.

H5: Inc_{gen-I} and Inc_{gen-R} will have the best scaleup properties. They will not take more time as FSA size increases. This latter expectation comes from the worst-case time complexity analysis.

Subsidiary issues we examine are the percentage of wrong predictions (for Inc_{AT-NI} and Inc_{gen-R}, which are not complete algorithms), and the maximum observed speedup.

The results are the following (unless stated otherwise, look at the "sec" columns):

H1: To see the results, in Table 2 look at rows 1 through 9 and compare each row r in this set with row $r+9$. In other words, compare row 1 with row 10, row 2 with row 11, and so on. Rows 1 through 9 are algorithms for Invariance properties, and

---

16. The reason is the following. Dense FSA initialization creates FSAs with no triggers. A learning operator is then applied. After learning, Inc_{AT-NI} begins reverification at *every* state from which a new trigger could have been added by learning. Thus *every* trigger in the FSA will be checked to see if it is followed by a response. At every generation of our evolutionary learning paradigm, at most one learning operator is applied per FSA, and this is immediately followed by reverification and error resolution (if needed). Therefore every new trigger will be caught by Inc_{AT-NI} and, if not followed by a response, the problem will be immediately resolved.

		25-state FSAs		45-state FSAs	
		sec	spd	sec	spd
1	Inc_{prod} **p**	.000157	.00497	.000492	.00255
2	$Total_I$ **v**	.023798	.95663	.206406	.97430
3	Inc_I **b**	.023955	.07023	.206898	.51133
4	$Inc_{prod-NI}$ **p**	.000206	.00652	.000617	.00320
5	Inc_{I-NI} **v**	.000169	.00680	.000528	.00320
6	Inc_{I-NI} **b**	.000375	.00110	.001762	.00435
7	$Total_{prod}$ **p**	.031594	1.0	.192774	1.0
8	$Total_I$ **v**	.024877	1.0	.211851	1.0
9	$Total_I$ **b**	.340817	1.0	.404625	1.0
10	Inc_{prod} **p**	.000493	.00507	.001521	.00259
11	$Total_{AT}$ **v**	.021103	.98903	.177665	.96869
12	Inc_{AT} **b**	.024798	.20022	.180707	.23441
13	$Inc_{prod-NI}$ **p**	.000574	.00590	.001786	.00304
14	Inc_{AT-NI} **v**	.009011	.37450	.090824	.49520
15	Inc_{AT-NI} **b**	.009585	.07900	.092824	.12013
16	$Total_{prod}$ **p**	.097262	1.0	.587496	1.0
17	$Total_{AT}$ **v**	.024062	1.0	.183409	1.0
18	$Total_{AT}$ **b**	.121324	1.0	.770905	1.0

Table 2: Average performance over 30 runs (5 properties, 6 runs each) with operator o_{change} and dense FSAs. Rows 1 through 9 are for reverification of Invariance properties and rows 10 through 18 are for AT reverification of Response properties.

		25-state FSAs			45-state FSAs		
		sec	spd	err	sec	spd	err
1	Inc_{gen-I} **v+b**	.000001	4.25e-5	.20	.000002	9.75e-6	.07
2	Inc_{I-NI} **v+b**	.000002	8.51e-5	.20	.000003	1.46e-5	.07
3	$Total_I$ **v+b**	.023500	1.0	.20	.205082	1.0	.07
4	Inc_{gen-R} **v+b**	.000007	7.23e-8	.73	.000006	2.09e-9	.73
5	$Inc_{prod-NI}$ **p**	.000006	5.22e-5	N/A	.000006	8.51e-6	N/A
6	Inc_{AT-NI} **v**	94.660700	.98099	3569.33	2423.550000	.84442	12553.40
7	Inc_{AT-NI} **b**	94.660706	.97982	N/A	2423.550006	.84421	N/A
8	$Total_{prod}$ **p**	.114825	1.0	N/A	.704934	1.0	N/A
9	$Total_{AT}$ **v**	96.495400	1.0	3569.33	2870.080000	1.0	12553.40
10	$Total_{AT}$ **b**	96.610225	1.0	N/A	2870.784934	1.0	N/A

Table 3: Average performance over 30 runs (5 properties, 6 runs each) with operator o_{gen} and dense FSAs. Rows 1 through 3 are for reverification of Invariance properties and rows 4 through 10 are for reverification of Response properties.

		25-state FSAs	45-state FSAs
1	Inc_{prod} **p**	.000157	.000492
2	$Inc_{prod-NI}$ **p**	.000206	.000617
3	$Total_{prod}$ **p**	.031594	.192774
4	$Total_I$ **v**	.023798	.206406
5	Inc_{I-NI} **v**	.000169	.000528
6	$Total_I$ **v**	.024877	.211851
7	Inc_I **b**	.023955	.206898
8	Inc_{I-NI} **b**	.000375	.001762
9	$Total_I$ **b**	.340817	.404625

Table 4: Average cpu time (in seconds) over 30 runs with operator o_{change} and five Invariance properties. This table is a duplication of some of the material in Table 2.

		25-state FSAs	45-state FSAs
1	Inc_{prod} **p**	.000493	.001521
2	$Inc_{prod-NI}$ **p**	.000574	.001786
3	$Total_{prod}$ **p**	.097262	.587496
4	$Total_{AT}$ **v**	.021103	.177665
5	Inc_{AT-NI} **v**	.009011	.090824
6	$Total_{AT}$ **v**	.024062	.183409
7	Inc_{AT} **b**	.024798	.180707
8	Inc_{AT-NI} **b**	.009585	.092824
9	$Total_{AT}$ **b**	.121324	.770905

Table 5: Average cpu time (in seconds) over 30 runs with operator o_{change} and five Response properties. This table is a duplication of some of the material in Table 2.

		25-state FSAs	45-state FSAs
1	Inc_{gen-R} **p**	0	0
2	Inc_{prod} **p**	.000006	.000006
3	$Total_{prod}$ **p**	.114825	.704934
4	Inc_{gen-R} **v**	.000007	.000006
5	Inc_{AT} **v**	94.660700	2423.550000
6	$Total_{AT}$ **v**	96.495400	2870.080000
7	Inc_{gen-R} **b**	.000007	.000006
8	Inc_{AT} **b**	94.660706	2423.550006
9	$Total_{AT}$ **b**	96.610225	2870.784934

Table 6: Average cpu time (in seconds) over 30 runs with operator o_{gen} and five Response properties. This table is a duplication of some of the material in Table 3.

rows 10 through 18 are algorithms for AT verification. In Table 3, rows 1 through 3 are algorithms for Invariance properties, and rows 5 through 10 are algorithms for AT verification. Compare row 2 with 7, and 3 with 10. (Rows 1 and 4 cannot be compared because row 4 has an algorithm tailored for Response properties.) Note that these comparisons are between a "v+b" and a "b." Since "v+b" means "v" or "b," this is a correct comparison. **These results show that H1 is mostly, but not completely, confirmed.** It is confirmed for all results in Table 3. On the other hand, the results are mixed for Table 2.

H2: The easiest way to compare is to examine Tables 4, 5, and 6. In these cases the comparison is between the first two rows labeled "p" (or "v" or "b") versus the third row of that same label. The reason for making these comparisons is that the first two rows of a given label correspond to an incremental algorithm (except for row 4 of Tables 4 and 5) and the third row of a given label corresponds to a total algorithm. Alternatively, one could examine Tables 2 and 3. In Table 2, rows 1 through 6 (other than 2) and 10 through 15 (other than 11) are incremental algorithms, and rows 2, 11, 7 through 9, and 16 through 18 are total reverification algorithms. The appropriate comparisons are between rows 1 and 7, 4 and 7, 5 and 8, 3 and 9, 6 and 9, 10 and 16, 13 and 16, 14 and 17, 12 and 18, and 15 and 18. In Table 3, rows 1, 2, and 4 through 7 are incremental algorithms, and rows 3 and 8 through 10 are total. The appropriate comparisons are between rows 1 and 3, 2 and 3, 4 and 10, 5 and 8, 6 and 9, and 7 and 10. **All results confirm H2.** The statistical significance of the comparisons in Tables 2 and 3 were tested. Using an exact Wilcoxon rank-sum test, all comparisons relevant to hypothesis H2 in Table 2 are statistically significant ($p < 0.01$ and, in most cases, $p < 0.0001$). In Table 3, however, the differences between Inc_{AT-NI} and $Total_{AT}$ (both the (v) and (b) versions) are not statistically significant at the $p < 0.01$ level. All other comparisons in Table 3 are significant at the $p < 0.01$ level.

H3: This hypothesis does not apply to the algorithms for re-forming the product FSA because, obviously, it will require more time to get the new initial states for the "NI" versions. We wish to test the *overall* time savings of the "NI" versions, so we concentrate on the rows labeled "b." The relevant comparisons are row 7 versus 8 in Table 4 and row 7 versus 8 in Table 5. (Alternatively, one could compare row 3 versus 6, and row 12 versus 15 in Table 2.) Each of these comparisons is between an "NI" version and a counterpart version of the algorithm that is the same as the "NI" version except that it does not find new initial states. Tables 3 and 6 are not relevant because they only have the "NI" versions but not their counterparts. (We only saw the need to make one comparison between all "NI" versions and their counterparts, which is reflected in Table 2.) **All results confirm hypothesis H3.** After testing the statistical significance, it is found that the results are significant ($p < 0.01$).

H4: To determine H4 requires considering Table 3 but not Table 2. This is because we only need to compare algorithms for which o_{gen} has been applied. Compare row 1 versus 2, 1 versus 3, 4 versus 7, and 4 versus 10 to see the results. All results show Inc_{gen-I} (row 1) and Inc_{gen-R} (row 4) to be at least as fast as the other algorithms. **Therefore H4 is confirmed.** In all cases other than Inc_{gen-I} (row 1) versus Inc_{I-NI} (row 2), there is a noticeable speedup. In most cases, the speedup is quite dramatic. All noticeable speedups are statistically significant ($p < 0.0001$).

H5: To test H5, compare the first "spd" column (for 25-state FSAs) with the second column with this label (for 45-state FSAs). A more desirable scaleup shows a lower value for "spd" as the size of the FSA increases. It implies that the ratio of the cpu time of the incremental algorithm to the cpu time of the total algorithm decreases more (or increases less) as the FSA size increases. One should make this two-column comparison for rows 1 through 6 (but not 2) and 10 through 15 (but not 11) of Table 2, and rows 1 and 2, and 4 through 7 of Table 3 because these are all the incremental algorithms. (We don't care about the total algorithms because "spd" is, by definition, always 1.0 for them.)[17] If one considers the results of algorithms appearing in both tables (e.g., Inc_{I-NI} shows different scaleup properties in the two tables, but we need to consider both sets of results), then clearly Inc_{gen-I} (row 1) and Inc_{gen-R} (row 4) in Table 3 show the best scaleup of all the incremental algorithms. **H5 is confirmed.** It is apparent from the "sec" columns that the time complexity of these two algorithms does not increase (other than minor fluctuations) as FSA size increases (see Table 3).

A couple of subsidiary issues are now addressed. For one, recall that Inc_{AT-NI} and Inc_{gen-R} are not complete. Therefore, it is relevant to consider the percentage of incorrect predictions (i.e., false errors) they made. Inc_{AT-NI} made none. For the results in Table 3, 33% of Inc_{gen-R}'s predictions were wrong (i.e., false errors) for the size 25 FSAs, and 50% were wrong for the size 45 FSAs.

Finally, consider the maximum observable speedup. Inc_{gen-R} shows a $\frac{1}{2}$-*billion-fold speedup* over $Total_{AT}$ on size 45 FSA problems (averaged over 30 runs)! This alleviates much of the concern about Inc_{gen-R}'s false error rate. For example, given the rapid reverification time of Inc_{gen-R}, an agent could use it to reverify a long sequence of learning operators culminating in one that satisfies the property in considerably less time than it takes $Total_{AT}$ to reverify one learning operator.

We conclude this section by summarizing, in Table 7, the fastest algorithm (based on our results) for every operator, situation, and property type. In Table 7, it is assumed that a First-Response FSA is used for AT verification of Response properties. Operator $o_{add-action}$ is omitted from this table because it is not clear at this time whether it would be faster to apply total reverification or perform multiple applications of the incremental algorithm (one for each primitive operator application). Section 8 considers an alternative solution as future work. In Table 7, "None" means no reverification is required, i.e., the learning operator is a priori guaranteed to be an SML for this situation and property class.

7. Related Work

There has been a great deal of recent research on model checking, and even on model checking of distributed systems (Holzmann, 1991). Nevertheless, there is very little in the literature about model checking applied to systems that change. Two notable exceptions are the research of Sokolsky and Smolka (1994) on incremental reverification and that of

---

17. If "spd" $\neq 1.0$ for a total algorithm, this is due to the statistical variation in run time.

	$SIT_{1agent/1plan}$ and Invariance	$SIT_{1agent/1plan}$ and Response	$SIT_{multplans}$ and Invariance	$SIT_{multplans}$ and Response
O_{change}	Inc_{I-NI}	Inc_{AT-NI}	Inc_{I-NI}	Inc_{AT-NI}
O_{delete}	$None$	$None$	$None$	$None$
O_{spec}	$None$	$None$	$None$	$None$
O_{add}	Inc_{I-NI}	Inc_{AT-NI}	Inc_{I-NI}	Inc_{AT-NI}
O_{gen}	Inc_{gen-I} or Inc_{I-NI}	Inc_{gen-R}	Inc_{I-NI}	Inc_{AT-NI}
$O_{delete \vee spec}$	$None$	$None$	$None$	$None$
$O_{delete-action}$	$None$	$None$	$None$	$None$
$O_{add \vee gen}$	Inc_{I-NI}	Inc_{AT-NI}	Inc_{I-NI}	Inc_{AT-NI}
O_{move}	Inc_{I-NI}	Inc_{AT-NI}	Inc_{I-NI}	Inc_{AT-NI}
$O_{delete+add}$	Inc_{I-NI}	Inc_{AT-NI}	Inc_{I-NI}	Inc_{AT-NI}
$O_{spec+add}$	Inc_{I-NI}	Inc_{AT-NI}	Inc_{I-NI}	Inc_{AT-NI}
$O_{delete+gen}$	$None$	Inc_{gen-R}	Inc_{I-NI}	Inc_{AT-NI}
$O_{spec+gen}$	$None$	Inc_{gen-R}	Inc_{I-NI}	Inc_{AT-NI}
O_{stay}	$None$	Inc_{AT-NI}	Inc_{I-NI}	Inc_{AT-NI}

Table 7: Learning operators with the fastest reverification method.

Sekar et al. (1994). Both of these papers are about reverification of software after user edits rather than adaptive agents. Nevertheless the work is related. Sokolsky and Smolka use the modal μ-calculus to express Invariance and Liveness properties. They present an incremental version of a model checker that does block-by-block global computations of fixed points, rather than AT or property-specific model checking as we do. The learning operators assumed by their algorithm are edge deletions/additions on a representation similar to FSAs called LTS (but unlike our multiagent work, they assume a single LTS). The worst-case time complexity of their algorithm is the same as that of total reverification, although their empirical results are good. Note that we have a priori results for edge deletion. However we do not have an incremental algorithm specifically tailored for edge addition (for multiple agents and AT or property-specific model checking); thus this may be a fruitful direction for future research. Sekar et al.'s approach consists of converting rule sets to FSAs, then generating and testing functions that map from the post- to the prelearning FSA and property. If the desired function can be found, they apply a theorem from Kurshan (1994), which guarantees that the learning is "safe." Although no complexity results are provided, the generate-and-test approach that they describe appears to be computationally expensive. In contrast to Sekar et al., we have proofs and empirical evidence that our methods are efficient and, in some cases, that they are substantially more efficient than total reverification from scratch.

There is also related research in the field of classical planning. In particular, Weld and Etzioni (1994) have a method to incrementally test an agent's plan to decide whether to add new actions to the plan. Actions are added only when their effects do not violate a certain type of Invariance property. Their method has some similarities with our Inc_{gen-I} algorithm. One difference is that our method is for reactive rather than projective plans.

Another is that our verification method is expressed using the formal foundations in the model checking literature.

As mentioned in the introduction of this paper, FSAs have been shown to be effective representations of reactive agent plans/strategies (Burkhard, 1993; Kabanza, 1995; Carmel & Markovitch, 1996; Fogel, 1996). FSA plans have been used both for multiagent competition and coordination. For example, Fogel's (1996) co-evolving FSA agents for competitive game playing were mentioned above. A similarity with our work is that Fogel assumes agents' plans are expressed as ω-automata. Nevertheless, Fogel never discusses verification of these plans. Goldman and Rosenschein (1994) present a method for multiagent coordination that assumes FSA plans. Multiple agents cooperate by taking actions to favorably alter their environment. The cooperation strategy is implemented by a plan developer who manually edits the FSAs. The relationship to the work here is that they present FSA transformations that ensure multiagent coordination. Likewise, in our research, a learning operator that is a priori guaranteed "safe" for some multiagent coordination property transforms the FSA while ensuring coordination. Although both their method and ours guarantee this coordination, their solution is manual whereas ours is entirely automated.

Some of the more recent research on agent coordination applies formal verification methods. For example, Lee and Durfee (1997) model their agents' semantics with a formalism similar to Petri nets (rather than FSAs). They verify synchronization (Invariance) properties, which prevent deadlock, using model checking. Furthermore, Lee and Durfee suggest recovery from failed verification using two methods: concept learning, and a method analogous to that used by Ramadge and Wonham (1989). Burkhard (1993) and Kabanza (1995) assume agent plans are represented as ω-automata, and they address issues of model checking temporal logic properties of the joint (multiagent) plans. Thus there is a growing precedent for addressing multiagent coordination by expressing plans as ω-automata and verifying them with model checking. Our work builds on this precedent, and also extends it, because none of this previous research addresses efficient *re*verification for agents that learn.

Finally, there are alternative methods for constraining the behavior of agents, which are complementary to reverification and self-repair. For example, Shoham and Tennenholtz (1995) design agents that obey social laws, e.g., safety conventions, by restricting the agents' actions. Nevertheless, the plan designer may not be able to anticipate and engineer all laws into the agents beforehand, especially if the agents have to adapt. One solution is to use laws that allow maximum flexibility (Fitoussi & Tennenholtz, 1998). However this solution does not allow for certain changes in the plan, such as the addition or deletion of actions. An appealing alternative would be to couple initial engineering of social laws with efficient reverification after learning.

A method for ensuring physically bounded behavior of agents is "artificial physics" (Spears & Gordon, 1999). With artificial physics, multiagent behavior is restricted by artificial forces between the agents. Nevertheless, when encountering severe unanticipated circumstances, artificial physics needs to be complemented with reverification and "steering" for self-repair (Gordon et al., 1999).

8. Summary and Future Work

Agent technology is growing rapidly in popularity. To handle real-world domains and interactions with people, agents must be adaptable, predictable, *and* rapidly responsive. An approach to resolving these potentially conflicting requirements is presented here. In summary, we have shown that certain machine learning operators are a priori (with no run-time reverification) safe to perform. In other words, when certain desirable properties hold prior to learning, they are guaranteed to hold post-learning. The property classes considered here are Invariance and Response. Learning operators o_{delete}, o_{spec}, $o_{delete \vee spec}$, and $o_{delete-action}$ were found to preserve properties in either of these classes. For SIT_{1agent} and SIT_{1plan}, where there is a single (multi)agent FSA plan, $o_{delete+gen}$, $o_{spec+gen}$ and o_{stay} were found to preserve Invariance properties. All of the a priori results are independent of the size of the FSA and are therefore applicable to any FSA that has been model checked originally.

We then discussed transformations of learning operators and their corresponding a priori results to a product plan. This addresses $SIT_{multplans}$, where multiple agents each have their own plan but the multiagent plan must be re-formed and reverified to determine whether multiagent properties are preserved. It was discovered that only o_{delete}, o_{spec}, $o_{delete \vee spec}$, and $o_{delete-action}$ preserve their a priori results for this situation.

Finally, we presented novel incremental reverification algorithms for all cases in which the a priori results are negative. It was shown in both theoretical and empirical comparisons that these algorithms can substantially improve the time complexity of reverification over total reverification from scratch. Empirical results showed as much as a $\frac{1}{2}$-billion-fold speedup. These are initial results, but continued research along these lines will likely be applicable to a wide range of important problems, including a variety of agent domains as well as more general software applications.

When learning is required, we suggest that the a priori results should be consulted first. If no positive results (i.e., the learning operator is an SML) exist, then incremental reverification proceeds.

To test our overall framework, we have implemented the rovers example of this paper as co-evolving agents assuming $SIT_{multplans}$, i.e., multiple agents each with its own plan. By using the a priori results and incremental algorithms, we achieved significant speedups. We have also developed a more sophisticated application that uses reverification during evolution. Two agents compete in a board game, and one of the agents evolves its strategy to improve it. The key lesson that has been learned from this implementation is that although the types of FSAs and learning operators are slightly different from those presented in this paper, and the property is quite different (it is a check for a certain type of cyclic behavior on the board), initial experiences show that the methodology and basic results here could potentially be easily extended to a variety of multiagent applications.

Future work will focus primarily on extending the a priori results to other learning operators/methods and property classes, developing other incremental reverification algorithms, and exploring plan repair to recover from reverification failures. One way in which the a priori results might be extended is by discovering when learning operators will make a property true, even if it was not true before learning.

A question that was not addressed here is whether the incremental methods are useful if multiple machine learning operators are applied in batch (e.g., as one might wish to do with operator $o_{add-action}$). In the future we would like to explore how to handle this situation – is it more efficient to treat the operators as having been done one-at-a-time and use incremental reverification for each? Or is total reverification from scratch preferable? Or, better yet, can we develop efficient incremental algorithms for *sets* of learning operators?

Plan repair was not discussed in this paper and is an important future direction. The research of De Raedt and Bruynooghe (1994), which uses counterexamples to guide the revision of theories subject to *integrity constraints*, may provide some ideas. There are also plan repair methods in the classical planning literature that might be relevant to our approach (Joslin & Pollack, 1994; Weld & Etzioni, 1994). It would be interesting to compare the time to repair plans versus trying another learning operator and reverifying.

A limitation of our approach is that it does not handle stochastic plans or properties with time limits, e.g., a Response property for which the response must occur within a specified time after the trigger. We would like to extend this research to stochastic FSAs (Tzeng, 1992) and timed FSAs/properties (Alur & Dill, 1994; Kabanza, 1995), as well as other common agent representations besides FSAs. Another direction for future work would be to extend our results to symbolic model checking, which uses binary decision diagrams (BDDs) so that the full state space need not be explicitly explored during model checking (Burch et al., 1994). In some cases, symbolic model checking can produce dramatic speedup. However, none of the current research on symbolic model checking addresses adaptive systems.

Additionally, the ideas here are applicable to some of the FSA-based control theory work. For example, Ramadge and Wonham (1989) assume FSA representations for both the plant (which is assumed to be a discrete-event system) and the supervisor (which controls the actions of the plant). We are currently applying some of the principles of efficient reverification to change the supervisor in response to changes in the plant in a manner that preserves properties (Gordon & Kiriakidis, 2000).

Finally, future work should focus on studying how to operationalize Asimov's Laws for intelligent agents. What sorts of properties best express these laws? Weld and Etzioni (1994) provide some initial suggestions, but much more remains to be done.

Acknowledgments

This research is supported by the Office of Naval Research (N0001499WR20010) in conjunction with the "Semantic Consistency" MURI. I am grateful to William Spears, Joseph Gordon, Stan Sadin, Chitoor Srinivasan, Ramesh Bharadwaj, Dan Hoey, and the anonymous reviewers for useful suggestions and advice. The presentation of the material in this paper was enormously improved thanks to William Spears' suggestions.

Appendix A. Glossary of Notation

$\models$	Models (satisfies)
model checking	A verification method entailing brute-force search
AT	Automata-theoretic model checking
SIT_{1agent}	Single agent situation
SIT_{1plan}	Multiagent situation where each agent uses a multiagent plan
$SIT_{multplans}$	Multiagent situation where each agent uses an individual plan
FSA	Finite-state automaton
$V(S)$	The set of states (vertices) of FSA S
$E(S)$	The set of state-to-state transitions (edges) of FSA S
transition condition	Logical description of the set of actions enabling a transition
$\mathcal{K}$	A Boolean algebra
$\preceq$	Boolean algebra partial order; $x \preceq y$ iff $x \wedge y = x$
$M_{\mathcal{K}}(S)$	The matrix of transition conditions of FSA S
$M_{\mathcal{K}}(v_i, v_j)$	Transition condition associated with edge (v_i, v_j)
$I(S)$	The set of initial states of FSA S
atoms	Primitive elements of a Boolean algebra; atoms are actions
string	Sequence of actions (atoms)
$\mathcal{L}(S)$	The language of (set of strings accepted by) FSA S
ω-automaton	An FSA that accepts infinite-length strings
run	The sequence of FSA vertices visited by a string
accepting run	The run of a string in the FSA language
acceptance criterion	A requirement of accepting runs of an FSA
$\otimes$	The tensor (synchronous) product of FSAs
complete FSA	Specifies a transition for every possible action
deterministic FSA	The choice of action uniquely determines the next state
path	Sequence of vertices connected by edges
cycle	A path with start and end vertices identical
c-state	Computational state; an action occurring in a computation
accessible from	There exists a path from
$\Box$	Temporal logic "invariant"
$\Diamond$	Temporal logic "eventually"
Invariance property	$\Box \neg p$, i.e., "Invariant not p"
Response property	$\Box(p \rightarrow \Diamond q)$, i.e., "Every p is eventually followed by q"
First-Response property	The first p (trigger) is followed by a q (response)
$B(S)$	The set of "bad" (to be avoided) states of FSA S
$\uparrow$	Can increase accessibility
$\nshortuparrow$	Cannot increase accessibility
$\downarrow$	Can decrease accessibility
$\nshortdownarrow$	Cannot decrease accessibility
SML	Safe machine learning operator, i.e., preserves properties
sound algorithm	One that is correct when it states that $S \models P$
complete algorithm	One that is correct when it states that $S \not\models P$
δ	The FSA transition function

Appendix B. Temporal logic properties

This appendix, which is based on Manna and Pnueli (1991), formally defines Invariance and Response properties in temporal logic. We begin by defining the basic temporal operator $\mathcal{U}$ (Until). We assume a string $(x_0, ...)$ of c-states of FSA S, where $0 \leq i, j, k$. Then for c-state formulae p and q, we define Until as $x_j \models p \, \mathcal{U} \, q \Leftrightarrow$ for some $k \geq j$, $x_k \models q$, and for every i such that $j \leq i < k$, $x_i \models p$.

Invariance properties are defined in terms of Eventually properties, so we define Eventually first. For c-state formula p and FSA S, we define property $P = \Diamond p$ ("Eventually p") as a property that is true (false) for a string if it is true (false) at the initial c-state x_0 of the string. Formally, if $\mathbf{x} = (x_0, ...)$ is a string of FSA S, then $\mathbf{x} \models \Diamond p \Leftrightarrow x_0 \models true \, \mathcal{U} \, p$, i.e., "eventually p." A property $P = \Box \neg p$ ("Invariant not p") is defined as $\mathbf{x} \models \Box \neg p \Leftrightarrow \mathbf{x} \models \neg \Diamond p$, i.e., "never p." Finally, a Response formula is of the form $\Box(p \to \Diamond q)$, where p is called the "trigger" and q the "response." A Response formula states that every trigger is eventually followed by a response.

Appendix C. Properties for Experiments

The following five Invariance properties were used in the test suite:

$\Box \, (\neg(\text{I-deliver} \wedge \text{L-transmit}))$

$\Box \, (\neg(\text{I-deliver} \wedge \text{L-pause}))$

$\Box \, (\neg(\text{F-collect} \wedge \text{I-deliver}))$

$\Box \, (\neg(\text{F-collect} \wedge \text{I-deliver} \wedge \text{L-receive}))$

$\Box \, (\neg(\text{F-deliver} \wedge \text{I-receive} \wedge \text{L-pause}))$

The following five Response properties were used in the test suite:

$\Box \, (\text{F-deliver} \to \Diamond \, \text{L-receive})$

$\Box \, (\text{F-deliver} \to \Diamond \, \text{I-receive})$

$\Box \, (\text{F-collect} \to \Diamond \, \text{L-transmit})$

$\Box \, ((\text{F-collect} \wedge \text{I-deliver}) \to \Diamond \, \text{L-receive})$

$\Box \, (\text{F-deliver} \to \Diamond \, (\text{I-receive} \wedge \text{L-receive}))$

References

Alur, R., & Dill, D. (1994). A theory of timed automata. *Theoretical Computer Science*, *126*, 183–235.

Asimov, I. (1950). *I, Robot*. Greenwich, CT: Fawcett Publications, Inc.

Bavel, Z. (1983). *Introduction to the Theory of Automata*. Reston, VA: Prentice-Hall.

Büchi, J. (1962). On a decision method in restricted second-order arithmetic. In *Methodology and Philosophy of Science, Proceedings of the Stanford International Congress*, pp. 1–11. Stanford, CA: Stanford University Press.

Burch, J., Clarke, E., Long, D., McMillan, K., & Dill, D. (1994). Symbolic model checking for sequential circuit verification. *IEEE Transactions on Computer-Aided Design of Integrated Circuits and Systems, 13(4)*, 401–424.

Burkhard, H. (1993). Liveness and fairness properties in multi-agent systems. In *Proceedings of the Thirteenth International Joint Conference on Artificial Intelligence (IJCAI)*, pp. 325–330. Chambery, France.

Carmel, D., & Markovitch, S. (1996). Learning models of intelligent agents. In *Proceedings of the Thirteenth National Conference on Artificial Intelligence (AAAI)*, pp. 62–67. Portland, OR.

Clarke, E., & Wing, J. (1997). Formal methods: State of the art and future directions. *ACM Computing Surveys, 28(4)*, 626–643.

Courcoubetis, C., Vardi, M., Wolper, P., & Yannakakis, M. (1992). Memory-efficient algorithms for the verification of temporal properties. *Formal Methods in System Design, 1*, 257–288.

De Raedt, L., & Bruynooghe, M. (1994). Interactive theory revision. In Michalski, R., & Tecuci, G. (Eds.), *Machine Learning IV*, pp. 239–264. San Mateo, CA: Morgan Kaufmann.

Dean, T., & Wellman, M. (1991). *Planning and Control*. San Mateo, CA: Morgan Kaufmann.

Elseaidy, W., Cleaveland, R., & Baugh, J. (1994). Verifying an intelligent structure control system: A case study. In *Proceedings of the Real-Time Systems Symposium*, pp. 271–275. San Juan, Puerto Rico.

Fitoussi, D., & Tennenholtz, M. (1998). Minimal social laws. In *Proceedings of the Fifteenth National Conference on Artificial Intelligence*, pp. 26–31. Madison, WI.

Fogel, D. (1996). On the relationship between duration of an encounter and the evolution of cooperation in the iterated prisoner's dilemma. *Evolutionary Computation, 3(3)*, 349–363.

Goldman, S., & Rosenschein, J. (1994). Emergent coordination through the use of cooperative state-changing rules. In *Proceedings of the Twelfth National Conference on Artificial Intelligence*, pp. 408–413. Seattle, WA.

Gordon, D. (1998). Well-behaved borgs, bolos, and berserkers. In *Proceedings of the Fifteenth International Conference on Machine Learning (ICML)*, pp. 224–232. Madison, WI.

Gordon, D. (1999). Re-verification of adaptive agents' plans. Tech. rep., Navy Center for Applied Research in Artificial Intelligence.

Gordon, D., & Kiriakidis, K. (2000). Adaptive supervisory control of interconnected discrete event systems. In *Proceedings of the International Conference on Control Applications (ICCA)*, pp. 50–56. Anchorage, AK.

Gordon, D., Spears, W., Sokolsky, O., & Lee, I. (1999). Distributed spatial control, global monitoring and steering of mobile physical agents. In *Proceedings of the IEEE International Conference on Information, Intelligence, and Systems (ICIIS)*, pp. 681–688. Washington, D.C.

Grefenstette, J., & Ramsey, C. (1992). An approach to anytime learning. In *Proceedings of Ninth International Workshop on Machine Learning*, pp. 189–195. Aberdeen, Scotland.

Heitmeyer, C., Kirby, J., Labaw, B., Archer, M., & Bharadwaj, R. (1998). Using abstraction and model checking to detect safety violations in requirements specifications. *IEEE Transactions on Software Engineering, 24(11)*, 927–948.

Holzmann, G., Peled, D., & Yannakakis, M. (1996). On nested depth-first search. In *Proceedings of the Second Spin Workshop*, pp. 81–89. Rutgers, NJ.

Holzmann, G. J. (1991). *Design and Validation of Computer Protocols*. NJ: Prentice-Hall.

Joslin, D., & Pollack, M. (1994). Least-cost flaw repair: A plan refinement strategy for partial-order planning. In *Proceedings of the Twelfth International Conference on Artificial Intelligence*, pp. 1004–1009. Seattle, WA.

Kabanza, F. (1995). Synchronizing multiagent plans using temporal logic specifications. In *Proceedings of the First International Conference on Multiagent Systems (ICMAS)*, pp. 217–224. San Francisco, CA.

Kurshan, R. (1994). *Computer Aided Verification of Coordinating Processes*. Princeton, NJ: Princeton University Press.

Lee, J., & Durfee, E. (1997). On explicit plan languages for coordinating multiagent plan execution. In *Proceedings of the Fourth International Workshop on Agent Theories, Architectures, and Languages (ATAL)*, pp. 113–126. Providence, RI.

Manna, Z., & Pnueli, A. (1991). Completing the temporal picture. *Theoretical Computer Science, 83(1)*, 97–130.

Michalski, R. (1983). A theory and methodology of inductive learning. In Michalski, R., Carbonell, J., & Mitchell, T. (Eds.), *Machine Learning I*, pp. 83–134. Palo Alto, CA: Tioga.

Mitchell, T. (1978). *Version Space: An Approach to Concept Learning*. Ph.D. thesis, Stanford University.

Nilsson, N. (1980). *Principles of Artificial Intelligence*. Palo Alto, CA: Tioga.

Potter, M. (1997). *The Design and Analysis of a Computational Model of Cooperative Coevolution*. Ph.D. thesis, George Mason University.

Ramadge, P., & Wonham, W. (1989). The control of discrete event systems. *Proceedings of the IEEE, 1*, 81–98.

Sekar, R., Lin, Y.-J., & Ramakrishnan, C. (1994). Modeling techniques for evolving distributed applications. In *Proceedings of Formal Description Techniques (FORTE)*, pp. 22–29. Berne, Switzerland.

Shoham, Y., & Tennenholz, M. (1995). On social laws for artificial agent societies: Off-line design. *Artificial Intelligence, 73(1-2)*, 231–252.

Sikorski, R. (1969). *Boolean Algebras*. New York, NY: Springer-Verlag.

Sokolsky, O., & Smolka, S. (1994). Incremental model checking in the modal mu-calculus. In *Proceedings of Computer-Aided Verification (CAV)*, pp. 351–363. Stanford, CA.

Spears, W., & Gordon, D. (1999). Using artificial physics to control agents. In *Proceedings of the IEEE International Conference on Information, Intelligence, and Systems*, pp. 281–288. Washington, D.C.

Tennenholtz, M., & Moses, Y. (1989). On cooperation in a multi-entity model. In *Proceedings of the Eleventh International Joint Conference on Artificial Intelligence*, pp. 918–923.

Tzeng, W. (1992). Learning probabilistic automata and markov chains via queries. *Machine Learning, 8*, 151–166.

Vardi, M., & Wolper, P. (1986). An automata-theoretic approach to automatic program verification. In *Proceedings of the First Annual Symposium on Logic in Computer Science (LICS)*, pp. 332–345. Cambridge, MA.

Weld, D., & Etzioni, O. (1994). The first law of robotics. In *Proceedings of the Twelfth National Conference on Artificial Intelligence*, pp. 1042–1047. Seattle, WA.

Journal of Artificial Intelligence Research 13 (2000) 155-188   Submitted 6/00; published 10/00

AIS-BN: An Adaptive Importance Sampling Algorithm for Evidential Reasoning in Large Bayesian Networks

Jian Cheng   JCHENG@SIS.PITT.EDU
Marek J. Druzdzel   MAREK@SIS.PITT.EDU
Decision Systems Laboratory
School of Information Sciences and Intelligent Systems Program
University of Pittsburgh, Pittsburgh, PA 15260 USA

Abstract

Stochastic sampling algorithms, while an attractive alternative to exact algorithms in very large Bayesian network models, have been observed to perform poorly in evidential reasoning with extremely unlikely evidence. To address this problem, we propose an adaptive importance sampling algorithm, AIS-BN, that shows promising convergence rates even under extreme conditions and seems to outperform the existing sampling algorithms consistently. Three sources of this performance improvement are (1) two heuristics for initialization of the importance function that are based on the theoretical properties of importance sampling in finite-dimensional integrals and the structural advantages of Bayesian networks, (2) a smooth learning method for the importance function, and (3) a dynamic weighting function for combining samples from different stages of the algorithm.

We tested the performance of the AIS-BN algorithm along with two state of the art general purpose sampling algorithms, likelihood weighting (Fung & Chang, 1989; Shachter & Peot, 1989) and self-importance sampling (Shachter & Peot, 1989). We used in our tests three large real Bayesian network models available to the scientific community: the CPCS network (Pradhan et al., 1994), the PATHFINDER network (Heckerman, Horvitz, & Nathwani, 1990), and the ANDES network (Conati, Gertner, VanLehn, & Druzdzel, 1997), with evidence as unlikely as 10^{-41}. While the AIS-BN algorithm always performed better than the other two algorithms, in the majority of the test cases it achieved orders of magnitude improvement in precision of the results. Improvement in speed given a desired precision is even more dramatic, although we are unable to report numerical results here, as the other algorithms almost never achieved the precision reached even by the first few iterations of the AIS-BN algorithm.

1. Introduction

Bayesian networks (Pearl, 1988) are increasingly popular tools for modeling uncertainty in intelligent systems. With practical models reaching the size of several hundreds of variables (e.g., Pradhan et al., 1994; Conati et al., 1997), it becomes increasingly important to address the problem of feasibility of probabilistic inference. Even though several ingenious exact algorithms have been proposed, in very large models they all stumble on the theoretically demonstrated NP-hardness of inference (Cooper, 1990). The significance of this result can be observed in practice — exact algorithms applied to large, densely connected practical networks require either a prohibitive amount of memory or a prohibitive amount of computation and are unable to complete. While approximating inference to any desired precision has been shown to be NP-hard as well (Dagum & Luby, 1993), it is for very complex networks the only alternative that will produce any result at all. Furthermore, while obtaining the result is crucial in all applications, precision guarantees may not be critical for some types of problems and can be traded off against the speed of computation.

A prominent subclass of approximate algorithms is the family of stochastic sampling algorithms (also called *stochastic simulation* or *Monte Carlo* algorithms). The precision obtained by stochastic sampling generally increases with the number of samples generated and is fairly unaffected by the network size. Execution time is fairly independent of the topology of the network and is linear in the number of samples. Computation can be interrupted at any time, yielding an anytime property of the algorithms, important in time-critical applications.

While stochastic sampling performs very well in predictive inference, diagnostic reasoning, i.e., reasoning from observed evidence nodes to their ancestors in the network often exhibits poor convergence. When the number of observations increases, especially if these observations are unlikely a-priori, stochastic sampling often fails to converge to reasonable estimates of the posterior probabilities. Although this problem has been known since the very first sampling algorithm was proposed by Henrion (1988), little has been done to address it effectively. Furthermore, various sampling algorithms proposed were tested on simple and small networks, or networks with special topology, without the presence of extremely unlikely evidence and the practical significance of this problem has been underestimated. Given a typical number of samples used in real-time that are feasible on today's hardware, say 10^6 samples, the behavior of a stochastic sampling algorithm will be drastically different for different size networks. While in a network consisting of 10 nodes and a few observations, it may be possible to converge to exact probabilities, in very large networks only a negligibly small fraction of the total sample space will be probed. One of the practical Bayesian network models that we used in our tests, a subset of the CPCS network (Pradhan et al., 1994), consists of 179 nodes. Its total sample space is larger than 10^{61}. With 10^6 samples, we can sample only 10^{-55} fraction of the sample space.

We believe that it is crucial (1) to study the feasibility and convergence properties of sampling algorithms on very large practical networks, and (2) to develop sampling algorithms that will show good convergence under extreme, yet practical conditions, such as evidential reasoning given extremely unlikely evidence. After all, small networks can be updated using any of the existing exact algorithms — it is precisely the very large networks where stochastic sampling can be most useful. As to the likelihood of evidence, we know that stochastic sampling will generally perform well when it is high (Henrion, 1988). So, it is important to look at those cases in which evidence is very unlikely. In this paper, we test two existing state of the art stochastic sampling algorithms for Bayesian networks, likelihood weighting (Fung & Chang, 1989; Shachter & Peot, 1989) and self-importance sampling (Shachter & Peot, 1989), on a subset of the CPCS network with extremely unlikely evidence. We show that they both exhibit similarly poor convergence rates. We propose a new sampling algorithm, that we call the *adaptive importance sampling* for Bayesian networks (AIS-BN), which is suitable for evidential reasoning in large multiply-connected Bayesian networks. The AIS-BN algorithm is based on importance sampling, which is a widely applied method for variance reduction in simulation that has also been applied in Bayesian networks (e.g., Shachter & Peot, 1989). We demonstrate empirically on three large practical Bayesian network models that the AIS-BN algorithm consistently outperforms the other two algorithms. In the majority of the test cases, it achieved over two orders of magnitude improvement in convergence. Improvement in speed given a desired precision is even more dramatic, although we are unable to report numerical results here, as the other algorithms never achieved the precision reached even by the first few iterations of the AIS-BN algorithm. The main sources of improvement are: (1) two heuristics for the initialization of the importance function that are based on the theoretical properties of importance sampling in finite-dimensional integrals and the structural advantages of Bayesian networks, (2) a smooth learning method for updating the importance function, and (3) a dynamic weighting function for combining samples from different stages of the algorithm. We study the value of the two heuristics used in the AIS-BN algorithm: (1) initialization of the probability distributions of parents of evidence nodes to uniform distribution and (2) adjusting very small probabilities in the conditional probability tables, and show that they both play an important role in the AIS-BN algorithm but only a moderate role in the existing algorithms.

The remainder of this paper is structured as follows. Section 2 first gives a general introduction to importance sampling in the domain of finite-dimensional integrals, where it was originally proposed. We show how importance sampling can be used to compute probabilities in Bayesian networks and how it can draw additional benefits from the graphical structure of the network. Then we develop a generalized sampling scheme that will aid us in reviewing the previously proposed sampling algorithms and in describing the AIS-BN algorithm. Section 3 describes the AIS-BN algorithm. We propose two heuristics for initialization of the importance function and discuss their theoretical foundations. We describe a smooth learning method for the importance function and a dynamic weighting function for combining samples from different stages of the algorithm. Section 4 describes the empirical evaluation of the AIS-BN algorithm. Finally, Section 5 suggests several possible improvements to the AIS-BN algorithm, possible applications of our learning scheme, and directions for future work.

2. Importance Sampling Algorithms for Bayesian Networks

We feel that it is useful to go back to the theoretical roots of importance sampling in order to be able to understand the source of speedup of the AIS-BN algorithm relative to the existing state of the art importance sampling algorithms for Bayesian networks. We first review the general idea of importance sampling in finite-dimensional integrals and how it can reduce the sampling variance. We then discuss the application of importance sampling to Bayesian networks. Readers interested in more details are directed to literature on Monte Carlo methods in computation of finite integrals, such as the excellent exposition by Rubinstein (1981) that we are essentially following in the first section.

2.1 Mathematical Foundations

Let $g(\mathbf{X})$ be a function of m variables $\mathbf{X} = (X_1, ..., X_m)$ over a domain $\Omega \subset R^m$, such that computing $g(\mathbf{X})$ for any $\mathbf{X}$ is feasible. Consider the problem of approximate computation of the integral

$$I = \int_\Omega g(\mathbf{X}) \, d\mathbf{X} \ . \tag{1}$$

Importance sampling approaches this problem by writing the integral (1) as

$$I = \int_\Omega \frac{g(\mathbf{X})}{f(\mathbf{X})} f(\mathbf{X}) \, d\mathbf{X} \, ,$$

where $f(\mathbf{X})$, often referred to as the *importance function*, is a probability density function over Ω. $f(\mathbf{X})$ can be used in importance sampling if there exists an algorithm for generating samples from $f(\mathbf{X})$ and if the importance function is zero only when the original function is zero, i.e., $g(\mathbf{X}) \neq 0 \implies f(\mathbf{X}) \neq 0$.

After we have independently sampled n points $\mathbf{s}_1, \mathbf{s}_2, \ldots, \mathbf{s}_n, \mathbf{s}_i \in \Omega$, according to the probability density function $f(\mathbf{X})$, we can estimate the integral I by

$$\hat{I}_n = \frac{1}{n} \sum_{i=1}^{n} \frac{g(\mathbf{s}_i)}{f(\mathbf{s}_i)} \tag{2}$$

and estimate the variance of $\hat{I}_n$ by

$$\hat{\sigma}^2(\hat{I}_n) = \frac{1}{n \cdot (n-1)} \sum_{i=1}^{n} \left(\frac{g(\mathbf{s}_i)}{f(\mathbf{s}_i)} - \hat{I}_n \right)^2 . \tag{3}$$

It is straightforward to show that this estimator has the following properties:

1. $E(\hat{I}_n) = I$

2. $\lim_{n\to\infty} \hat{I}_n = I$

3. $\sqrt{n} \cdot (\hat{I}_n - I) \overset{n\to\infty}{\Longrightarrow} \text{Normal}(0, \sigma_{f(\mathbf{X})}^2)$, where

$$\sigma_{f(\mathbf{X})}^2 = \int_\Omega \left(\frac{g(\mathbf{X})}{f(\mathbf{X})} - I \right)^2 f(\mathbf{X}) \, d\mathbf{X} \tag{4}$$

4. $E\left(\hat{\sigma}^2(\hat{I}_n) \right) = \sigma^2(\hat{I}_n) = \sigma_{f(\mathbf{X})}^2 / n$

The variance of $\hat{I}_n$ is proportional to $\sigma_{f(\mathbf{X})}^2$ and inversely proportional to the number of samples. To minimize the variance of $\hat{I}_n$, we can either increase the number of samples or try to decrease $\sigma_{f(\mathbf{X})}^2$. With respect to the latter, Rubinstein (1981) reports the following useful theorem and corollary.

Theorem 1 *The minimum of $\sigma_{f(\mathbf{X})}^2$ is equal to*

$$\sigma_{f(\mathbf{X})}^2 = \left(\int_\Omega |g(\mathbf{X})| \, d\mathbf{X} \right)^2 - I^2$$

and occurs when $\mathbf{X}$ is distributed according to the following probability density function

$$f(\mathbf{X}) = \frac{|g(\mathbf{X})|}{\int_\Omega |g(\mathbf{X})| \, d\mathbf{X}} \, .$$

158

Corollary 1 *If $g(\mathbf{X}) > 0$, then the optimal probability density function is*

$$f(\mathbf{X}) = \frac{g(\mathbf{X})}{I}$$

and $\sigma^2_{f(\mathbf{X})} = 0$.

Although in practice sampling from precisely $f(\mathbf{X}) = g(\mathbf{X})/I$ will occur rarely, we expect that functions that are close enough to it can still reduce the variance effectively. Usually, the closer the shape of the function $f(\mathbf{X})$ is to the shape of the function $g(\mathbf{X})$, the smaller is $\sigma^2_{f(\mathbf{X})}$. In high-dimensional integrals, selection of the importance function, $f(\mathbf{X})$, is far more critical than increasing the number of samples, since the former can dramatically affect $\sigma^2_{f(\mathbf{X})}$. It seems prudent to put more energy in choosing an importance function whose shape is as close as possible to that of $g(\mathbf{X})$ than to apply the brute force method of increasing the number of samples.

It is worth noting here that if $f(\mathbf{X})$ is uniform, importance sampling becomes a general Monte Carlo sampling. Another noteworthy property of importance sampling that can be derived from Equation 4 is that we should avoid $f(\mathbf{X}) \ll |g(\mathbf{X}) - I \cdot f(\mathbf{X})|$ in any part of the domain of sampling, even if $f(\mathbf{X})$ matches well $g(\mathbf{X})/I$ in important regions. If $f(\mathbf{X}) \ll |g(\mathbf{X}) - I \cdot f(\mathbf{X})|$, the variance can become very large or even infinite. We can avoid this by adjusting $f(\mathbf{X})$ to be larger in unimportant regions of the domain of $\mathbf{X}$.

While in this section we discussed importance sampling for continuous variables, the results stated are valid for discrete variables as well, in which case integration should be substituted by summation.

2.2 A Generic Importance Sampling Algorithm for Bayesian Networks

In the following discussion, all random variables used are multiple-valued, discrete variables. Capital letters, such as A, B, or C, denote random variables. Bold capital letters, such as $\mathbf{A}$, $\mathbf{B}$, or $\mathbf{C}$, denote sets of variables. Bold capital letter $\mathbf{E}$ will usually be used to denote the set of evidence variables. Lower case letters a, b, c denote particular instantiations of variables A, B, and C respectively. Bold lower case letters, such as $\mathbf{a}$, $\mathbf{b}$, $\mathbf{c}$, denote particular instantiations of sets $\mathbf{A}$, $\mathbf{B}$, and $\mathbf{C}$ respectively. Bold lower case letter $\mathbf{e}$, in particular, will be used to denote the observations, i.e., instantiations of the set of evidence variables $\mathbf{E}$. $\text{Anc}(A)$ denotes the set of ancestors of node A. $\text{Pa}(A)$ denotes the set of parents (direct ancestors) of node A. $\text{pa}(A)$ denotes a particular instantiation of $\text{Pa}(A)$. \ denotes set difference. $\text{Pa}(\mathbf{A})|_{\mathbf{E}=\mathbf{e}}$ denotes that we use the extended vertical bar to indicate substitution of $\mathbf{e}$ for $\mathbf{E}$ in $\mathbf{A}$.

We know that the joint probability distribution over all variables of a Bayesian network model, $\Pr(\mathbf{X})$, is the product of the probability distributions over each of the nodes conditional on their parents, i.e.,

$$\Pr(\mathbf{X}) = \prod_{i=1}^{n} \Pr(X_i | \text{Pa}(X_i)) \, . \tag{5}$$

In order to calculate $\Pr(\mathbf{E} = \mathbf{e})$, we need to sum over all $\Pr(\mathbf{X} \backslash \mathbf{E}, \mathbf{E} = \mathbf{e})$.

$$\Pr(\mathbf{E} = \mathbf{e}) = \sum_{\mathbf{X} \backslash \mathbf{E}} \Pr(\mathbf{X} \backslash \mathbf{E}, \mathbf{E} = \mathbf{e}) \tag{6}$$

We can see that Equation 6 is almost identical to Equation 1 except that integration is replaced by summation and the domain Ω is replaced by $\mathbf{X}\backslash\mathbf{E}$. The theoretical results derived for the importance sampling that we reviewed in the previous section can thus be directly applied to computing probabilities in Bayesian networks.

While there has been previous work on importance sampling-based algorithms for Bayesian networks, we will postpone the discussion of this work until the next section. Here we will present a generic stochastic sampling algorithm that will help us in both reviewing the prior work and in presenting our algorithm.

The posterior probability $\Pr(\mathbf{a}|\mathbf{e})$ can be obtained by first computing $\Pr(\mathbf{a}, \mathbf{e})$ and $\Pr(\mathbf{e})$ and then combining these based on the definition of conditional probability

$$\Pr(\mathbf{a}|\mathbf{e}) = \frac{\Pr(\mathbf{a}, \mathbf{e})}{\Pr(\mathbf{e})} \ . \tag{7}$$

In order to increase the accuracy of results of importance sampling in computing the posterior probabilities over different network variables given evidence, we should in general use different importance functions for $\Pr(\mathbf{a}, \mathbf{e})$ and for $\Pr(\mathbf{e})$. Doing so increases the computation time only linearly while the gain in accuracy may be significant given that obtaining a desired accuracy is exponential in nature. Very often, it is a common practice to use the same importance function (usually for $\Pr(\mathbf{e})$) to sample both probabilities. If the difference

---

1. Order the nodes according to their topological order.

2. Initialize importance function $\Pr^0(\mathbf{X}\backslash\mathbf{E})$, the desired number of samples m, the updating interval l, and the score arrays for every node.

3. $k \leftarrow 0, T \leftarrow \emptyset$

4. **for** $i \leftarrow 1$ **to** m **do**

5.   **if** $(i \bmod l == 0)$ **then**

6. $k \leftarrow k + 1$

7.   Update importance function $\Pr^k(\mathbf{X}\backslash\mathbf{E})$ based on T.
    end if

8. $\mathbf{s}_i \leftarrow$ generate a sample according to $\Pr^k(\mathbf{X}\backslash\mathbf{E})$

9. $T \leftarrow T \cup \{\mathbf{s}_i\}$

10.   Calculate $\mathrm{Score}(\mathbf{s}_i, \Pr(\mathbf{X}\backslash\mathbf{E}, \mathbf{e}), \Pr^k(\mathbf{X}\backslash\mathbf{E}))$ and add it to the corresponding entry of every score array according to the instantiated states.
   end for

11. Normalize the score arrays for every node.

Figure 1: A generic importance sampling algorithm.

between the optimal importance functions for these two quantities is large, the performance may deteriorate significantly. Although $\widehat{\Pr}(\mathbf{a}, \mathbf{e})$ and $\widehat{\Pr}(\mathbf{e})$ are unbiased estimators according to Property 1 (Section 2.1), $\widehat{\Pr}(\mathbf{a}|\mathbf{e})$ obtained by means of Equation 7 is not an unbiased estimator. However, as the number of samples increases, the bias decreases and can be ignored altogether when the sample size is large enough (Fishman, 1995).

Figure 1 presents a generic stochastic sampling algorithm that captures most of the existing sampling algorithms. Without the loss of generality, we restrict ourselves in our description to so-called *forward sampling*, i.e., generation of samples in the topological order of the nodes in the network. The forward sampling order is accomplished by the initialization performed in Step 1, where parents of each node are placed before the node itself. In forward sampling, Step 8 of the algorithm, the actual generation of samples, works as follows. (*i*) each evidence node is instantiated to its observed state and is further omitted from sample generation; (*ii*) each root node is randomly instantiated to one of its possible states, according to the importance prior probability of this node, which can be derived from $\Pr^k(\mathbf{X}\backslash\mathbf{E})$; (*iii*) each node whose parents are instantiated is randomly instantiated to one of its possible states, according to the importance conditional probability distribution of this node given the values of the parents, which can also be derived from $\Pr^k(\mathbf{X}\backslash\mathbf{E})$; (*iv*) this procedure is followed until all nodes are instantiated. A complete instantiation $\mathbf{s}_i$ of the network based on this method is one sample of the joint importance probability distribution $\Pr^k(\mathbf{X}\backslash\mathbf{E})$ over all variables of the network. The scoring of Step 10 amounts to calculating $\Pr(\mathbf{s}_i, \mathbf{e})/\Pr^k(\mathbf{s}_i)$, as required by Equation 2. The ratio between the total score sum and the number of samples is an unbiased estimator of $\Pr(\mathbf{e})$. In Step 10, if we also count the score sum under the condition $\mathbf{A} = \mathbf{a}$, i.e., that some unobserved variables $\mathbf{A}$ have the values $\mathbf{a}$, the ratio between this score sum and the number of samples is an unbiased estimator of $\Pr(\mathbf{a}, \mathbf{e})$.

Most existing algorithms focus on the posterior probability distributions of individual nodes. As we mentioned above, for the sake of efficiency they count the score sum corresponding to $\Pr(A = a, \mathbf{e})$, $A \in \mathbf{X}\backslash\mathbf{E}$, and record it in an score array for node A. Each entry of this array corresponds to a specified state of A. This method introduces additional variance, as opposed to using the importance function derived from $\Pr^k(\mathbf{X}\backslash\mathbf{E})$ to sample $\Pr(A = a, \mathbf{e})$, $A \in \mathbf{X}\backslash\mathbf{E}$, directly.

2.3 Existing Importance Sampling Algorithms for Bayesian Networks

The main difference between various stochastic sampling algorithms is in how they process Steps 2, 7, and 8 in the generic importance sampling algorithm of Figure 1.

Probabilistic logic sampling (Henrion, 1988) is the simplest and the first proposed sampling algorithm for Bayesian networks. The importance function is initialized in Step 2 to $\Pr(\mathbf{X})$ and never updated (Step 7 is null). Without evidence, $\Pr(\mathbf{X})$ is the optimal importance function for the evidence set, which is empty anyway. It escapes most authors that $\Pr(\mathbf{X})$ may be not the optimal importance function for $\Pr(A = a)$, $A \in \mathbf{X}$, when A is not a root node. A mismatch between the optimal and the actually used importance function may result in a large variance. The sampling process with evidence is the same as without evidence except that in Step 10 we do not count the scores for those samples that are inconsistent with the observed evidence, which amounts to discarding them. When the evidence is very unlikely, there is a large difference between $\Pr(\mathbf{X})$ and the optimal importance function. Effectively, most samples are discarded and the performance of logic sampling deteriorates badly.

Likelihood weighting (LW) (Fung & Chang, 1989; Shachter & Peot, 1989) enhances the logic sampling in that it never discards samples. In likelihood weighting, the importance function in Step 2 is

$$\Pr(\mathbf{X}\backslash\mathbf{E}) = \prod_{x_i \notin \mathbf{e}} \Pr(x_i|\mathrm{Pa}(X_i))\bigg|_{\mathbf{E}=\mathbf{e}} .$$

Likelihood weighting does not update the importance function in Step 7. Although likelihood weighting is an improvement on logic sampling, its convergence rate can be still very slow when there is large difference between the optimal importance function and $\Pr(\mathbf{X}\backslash\mathbf{E})$, again especially in situations when evidence is very unlikely. Because of its simplicity, the likelihood weighting algorithm has been the most commonly used simulation method for Bayesian network inference. It often matches the performance of other, more sophisticated schemes because it is simple and able to increase its precision by generating more samples than other algorithms in the same amount of time.

Backward sampling (Fung & del Favero, 1994) changes Step 1 of our generic algorithm and allows for generating samples from evidence nodes in the direction that is opposite to the topological order of nodes in the network. In Step 2, backward sampling uses the likelihood of some of the observed evidence and some instantiated nodes to calculate $\Pr^0(\mathbf{X}\backslash\mathbf{E})$. Although Fung and del Favero mentioned the possibility of dynamic node ordering, they did not propose any scheme for updating the importance function in Step 7. Backward sampling suffers from problems that are similar to those of likelihood weighting, i.e., a possible mismatch between its importance function and the optimal importance function can lead to poor convergence.

Importance sampling (Shachter & Peot, 1989) is the same as our generic sampling algorithm. Shachter and Peot introduced two variants of importance sampling: *self-importance* (SIS) and *heuristic importance*. The importance function used in the first step of the self-importance algorithm is

$$\Pr^0(\mathbf{X}\backslash\mathbf{E}) = \prod_{x_i \notin \mathbf{e}} \Pr(x_i|\mathrm{Pa}(X_i))\bigg|_{\mathbf{E}=\mathbf{e}} .$$

This function is updated in Step 7. The algorithm tries to revise the conditional probability tables (CPTs) periodically in order to make the sampling distribution gradually approach the posterior distribution. Since the same data are used to update the importance function and to compute the estimator, this process introduces bias in the estimator. Heuristic importance first removes edges from the network until it becomes a polytree, and then uses a modified version of the polytree algorithm (Pearl, 1986) to compute the likelihood functions for each of the unobserved nodes. $\Pr^0(\mathbf{X}\backslash\mathbf{E})$ is a combination of these likelihood functions with $\Pr(\mathbf{X}\backslash\mathbf{E}, \mathbf{e})$. In Step 7 heuristic importance does not update $\Pr^k(\mathbf{X}\backslash\mathbf{E})$. As Shachter and Peot (1989) point out, this heuristic importance function can still lead to a bad approximation of the optimal importance function. There exist also other algorithms such as a combination of self-importance and heuristic importance (Shachter & Peot, 1989;

Shwe & Cooper, 1991). Although some researchers suggested that this may be a promising direction for the work on sampling algorithms, we have not seen any results that would follow up on this.

A separate group of stochastic sampling methods is formed by so-called *Markov Chain Monte Carlo (MCMC)* methods that are divided into Gibbs sampling, Metropolis sampling, and Hybrid Monte Carlo sampling (Geman & Geman, 1984; Gilks, Richardson, & Spiegelhalter, 1996; MacKay, 1998). Roughly speaking, these methods draw random samples from an unknown target distribution $f(\mathbf{X})$ by biasing the search for this distribution towards higher probability regions. When applied to Bayesian networks (Pearl, 1987; Chavez & Cooper, 1990) this approach determines the sampling distribution of a variable from its previous sample given its Markov blanket (Pearl, 1988). This corresponds to updating $\Pr^k(\mathbf{X}\backslash\mathbf{E})$ when sampling every node. $\Pr^k(\mathbf{X}\backslash\mathbf{E})$ will converge to the optimal importance function for $\Pr(\mathbf{e})$ if $\Pr^0(\mathbf{X}\backslash\mathbf{E})$ satisfies some ergodic properties (York, 1992). Since the convergence to the limiting distribution is very slow and calculating updates of the sampling distribution is costly, these algorithms are not used in practice as often as the simple likelihood weighting scheme.

There are also some other simulation algorithms, such as bounded variance algorithm (Dagum & Luby, 1997) and the AA algorithm (Dagum et al., 1995), which are essentially based on the LW algorithm and the Stopping-Rule Theorem (Dagum et al., 1995). Cano et al. (1996) proposed another importance sampling algorithm that performed somewhat better than LW in cases with extreme probability distributions, but, as the authors state, in general cases it "produced similar results to the likelihood weighting algorithm." Hernandez et al. (1998) also applied importance sampling and reported a moderate improvement on likelihood weighting.

2.4 Practical Performance of the Existing Sampling Algorithms

The largest network that has been tested using sampling algorithms is QMR-DT (Quick Medical Reference — Decision Theoretic) (Shwe et al., 1991; Shwe & Cooper, 1991), which contains 534 adult diseases and 4,040 findings, with 40,740 arcs depicting disease-to-finding dependencies. The QMR-DT network belongs to a class of special bipartite networks and its structure is often referred to as BN2O (Henrion, 1991), because of its two-layer composition: disease nodes in the top layer and finding nodes in the bottom layer. Shwe and colleagues used an algorithm combining self-importance and heuristic importance and tested its convergence properties on the QMR-DT network. But since the heuristic method *iterative tabular Bayes* (ITB) that makes use of a version of Bayes' rule is designed for the BN2O networks, it cannot be generalized to arbitrary networks. Although Shwe and colleagues concluded that Markov blanket scoring and self-importance sampling significantly improve the convergence rate in their model, we cannot extend this conclusion to general networks. The computation of Markov blanket scoring is more complex in a general multi-connected network than in a BN2O network. Also, the experiments conducted lacked a gold-standard posterior probability distribution that could serve to judge the convergence rate.

Pradhan and Dagum (1996) tested an efficient version of the LW algorithm — bounded variance algorithm (Dagum & Luby, 1997) and the AA algorithm (Dagum et al., 1995) on a 146 node, multiply connected medical diagnostic Bayesian network. One limitation in their tests is that the probability of evidence in the cases selected for testing was rather high. Although over 10% of the cases had the probability of evidence on the order of 10^{-8} or smaller, a simple calculation based on the reported mean $\mu = 34.5$ number of evidence nodes, shows that the average probability of an observed state of an evidence node conditional on its direct predecessors was on the order of $(10^{-8})^{1/34.5} \approx 0.59$. Given that their algorithm is essentially based on the LW algorithm, based on our tests we suspect that the performance will deteriorate on cases where the evidence is very unlikely. Both algorithms focus on the marginal probability of one hypothesis node. If there are many queried nodes, the efficiency may deteriorate.

We have tested the algorithms discussed in Section 2.3 on several large networks. Our experimental results show that in cases with very unlikely evidence, none of these algorithms converges to reasonable estimates of the posterior probabilities within a reasonable amount of time. The convergence becomes worse as the number of evidence nodes increases. Thus, when using these algorithms in very large networks, we simply cannot trust the results. We will present results of tests of the LW and SIS algorithms in more detail in Section 4.

3. AIS-BN: Adaptive Importance Sampling for Bayesian Networks

The main reason why the existing stochastic sampling algorithms converge so slowly is that they fail to learn a good importance function during the sampling process and, effectively, fail to reduce the sampling variance. When the importance function is optimal, such as in probabilistic logic sampling without any evidence, each of the algorithms is capable of converging to fairly good estimates of the posterior probabilities within relatively few samples. For example, assuming that the posterior probabilities are not extreme (i.e., larger than say 0.01), as few as 1,000 samples may be sufficient to obtain good estimates. In this section, we present the adaptive importance sampling algorithm for Bayesian networks (AIS-BN) that, as we will demonstrate in the next section, performs very well on most tests. We will first describe the details of the algorithm and prove two theorems that are useful in learning the optimal importance sampling function.

3.1 Basic Algorithm — AIS-BN

Compared with importance sampling used in normal finite-dimensional integrals, importance sampling used in Bayesian networks has several significant advantages. First, the network joint probability distribution $\Pr(\mathbf{X})$ is decomposable and can be factored into component parts. Second, the network has a clear structure, which represents many conditional independence relationships. These properties are very helpful in estimating the optimal importance function.

The basic AIS-BN algorithm is presented in Figure 2. The main differences between the AIS-BN algorithm and the basic importance sampling algorithm in Figure 1 is that we introduce a monotonically increasing weight function w^k and two effective heuristic initialization methods in Step 2. We also introduce a special learning component in Step 7 to let the updating process run more smoothly, avoiding oscillation of the parameters. The

---

1. Order the nodes according to their topological order.

2. Initialize importance function $\Pr^0(\mathbf{X} \backslash \mathbf{E})$ using some heuristic methods, initialize weight w^0, set the desired number of samples m and the updating interval l, initialize the score arrays for every node.

3. $k \leftarrow 0$, $T \leftarrow \emptyset$, $w_{TScore} \leftarrow 0$, $w_{sum} \leftarrow 0$

4. **for** $i \leftarrow 1$ **to** m **do**

5.   **if** $(i \bmod l == 0)$ **then**

6. $k \leftarrow k + 1$

7.   Update the importance function $\Pr^k(\mathbf{X} \backslash \mathbf{E})$ and w^k based on T.
     end if

8. $\mathbf{s}_i \leftarrow$ generate a sample according to $\Pr^k(\mathbf{X} \backslash \mathbf{E})$

9. $T \leftarrow T \cup \{\mathbf{s}_i\}$

10. $w_{iScore} \leftarrow$ Score $(\mathbf{s}_i, \Pr(\mathbf{X} \backslash \mathbf{E}, \mathbf{e}), \Pr^k(\mathbf{X} \backslash \mathbf{E}), w^k)$

11. $w_{TScore} \leftarrow w_{TScore} + w_{iScore}$
     (Optional: add w_{iScore} to the corresponding entry of every score array)

12. $w_{sum} \leftarrow w_{sum} + w^k$
     end for

13. Output estimate of $\Pr(\mathbf{E})$ as w_{TScore}/w_{sum}
    (Optional: Normalize the score arrays for every node)

Figure 2: The adaptive importance sampling for Bayesian Networks (AIS-BN) algorithm.

score processing in Step 10 is

$$w_{iScore} = w^k \frac{\Pr(\mathbf{s}_i, \mathbf{e})}{\Pr^k(\mathbf{s}_i)} \,.$$

Note that in this respect the algorithm in Figure 1 becomes a special case of AIS-BN when $w^k = 1$. The reason why we use w^k is that we want to give different weights to the sampling results obtained at different stages of the algorithm. As each stage updates the importance function, they will all have different distance from the optimal importance function. We recommend that $w^k \propto 1/\hat{\sigma}^k$, where $\hat{\sigma}^k$ is the standard deviation estimated in stage k using Equation 3.[1] In order to keep w^k monotonically increasing, if w^k is smaller than w^{k-1}, we adjust its value to w^{k-1}. This weighting scheme may introduce bias into

---

1. A similar weighting scheme based on variance was apparently developed independently by Ortiz and Kaelbling (2000), who recommend the weight $w^k \propto 1/(\hat{\sigma}^k)^2$.

the final result. Since the initial importance sampling functions are often inefficient and introduce big variance into the results, we also recommend that $w^k = 0$ in the first few stages of the algorithm. We have designed this weighting scheme to reflect the fact that in practice estimates with very small estimated variance are usually good estimates.

3.2 Modifying the Sampling Distribution in AIS-BN

Based on the theoretical considerations of Section 2.1, we know that the crucial element of the algorithm is converging on a good approximation of the optimal importance function. In what follows, we first give the optimal importance function for calculating $\Pr(\mathbf{E} = \mathbf{e})$ and then discuss how to use the structural advantages of Bayesian networks to approximate this function. In the sequel, we will use the symbol ρ to denote the importance sampling function and ρ^* to denote the optimal importance sampling function.

Since $\Pr(\mathbf{X}\backslash\mathbf{E}, \mathbf{E} = \mathbf{e}) > 0$, from Corollary 1 we have

$$\rho(\mathbf{X}\backslash\mathbf{E}) = \frac{\Pr(\mathbf{X}\backslash\mathbf{E}, \mathbf{E} = \mathbf{e})}{\Pr(\mathbf{E} = \mathbf{e})} = \Pr(\mathbf{X}|\mathbf{E} = \mathbf{e}) \ .$$

The following corollary captures this result.

Corollary 2 *The optimal importance sampling function $\rho^*(\mathbf{X}\backslash\mathbf{E})$ for calculating $\Pr(\mathbf{E} = \mathbf{e})$ in Equation 6 is $\Pr(\mathbf{X}|\mathbf{E} = \mathbf{e})$.*

Although we know the mathematical expression for the optimal importance sampling function, it is difficult to obtain this function exactly. In our algorithm, we use the following importance sampling function

$$\rho(\mathbf{X}\backslash\mathbf{E}) = \prod_{i=1}^{n} \Pr(X_i|\mathrm{Pa}(X_i), \mathbf{E}) \ . \tag{8}$$

This function partially considers the effect of all the evidence on every node during the sampling process. When the network structure is the same as that of the network which has absorbed the evidence, this function is the optimal importance sampling function. It is easy to learn and, as our experimental results show, it is a good approximation to the optimal importance sampling function. Theoretically, when the posterior structure of the model changes drastically as the result of observed evidence, this importance sampling function may perform poorly. We have tried to find practical networks where this would happen, but to the day have not encountered a drastic example of this effect.

From Section 2.2, we know that the score sums corresponding to $\{x_i, \mathrm{pa}(X_i), \mathbf{e}\}$ can yield an unbiased estimator of $\Pr(x_i, \mathrm{pa}(X_i), \mathbf{e})$. According to the definition of conditional probability, we can get an estimator of $\Pr'(x_i|\mathrm{pa}(X_i), \mathbf{e})$. This can be achieved by maintaining an updating table for every node, the structure of which mimicks the structure of the CPT. Such tables allow us to decompose the above importance function into components that can be learned individually. We will call these tables the *importance conditional probability tables* (ICPT).

Definition 1 *An* importance conditional probability table (ICPT) *of a node X is a table of posterior probabilities $\Pr(X|\mathrm{Pa}(X), \mathbf{E} = \mathbf{e})$ conditional on the evidence and indexed by its immediate predecessors, $\mathrm{Pa}(X)$.*

The ICPT tables will be modified during the process of learning the importance function. Now we will prove a useful theorem that will lead to considerable savings in the learning process.

Theorem 2

$$X_i \in \mathbf{X}, X_i \notin \text{Anc}(\mathbf{E}) \Rightarrow \Pr(X_i|\text{Pa}(X_i), \mathbf{E}) = \Pr(X_i|\text{Pa}(X_i)) \,. \qquad (9)$$

Proof: Suppose we have set the values of all the parents of node X_i to pa(X_i). Node X_i is dependent on evidence $\mathbf{E}$ given pa(X_i) only when X_i is d-connecting with $\mathbf{E}$ given pa(X_i) (Pearl, 1988). According to the definition of d-connectivity, this happens only when there exists a member of X_i's descendants that belongs to the set of evidence nodes $\mathbf{E}$. In other words $X_i \notin \text{Anc}(\mathbf{E})$. $\qquad\qquad\square$

Theorem 2 is very important for the AIS-BN algorithm. It states essentially that the ICPT tables of those nodes that are not ancestors of the evidence nodes are equal to the CPT tables throughout the learning process. We only need to learn the ICPT tables for the ancestors of the evidence nodes. Very often this can lead to significant savings in computation. If, for example, all evidence nodes are root nodes, we have our ICPT tables for every node already and the AIS-BN algorithm becomes identical to the likelihood weighting algorithm. Without evidence, the AIS-BN algorithm becomes identical to the probabilistic logic sampling algorithm.

It is worth pointing out that for some X_i, $\Pr(X_i|P_a(X_i), \mathbf{E})$ (i.e., the ICPT table for X_i), can be easily calculated using exact methods. For example, when X_i is the only parent of an evidence node E_j and E_j is the only child of X_i, the posterior probability distribution of X_i is straightforward to compute exactly. Since the focus of the current paper is on

---

Input: Initialized importance function $\Pr^0(\mathbf{X} \backslash \mathbf{E})$, learning rate $\eta(k)$.
Output: An estimated importance function $\Pr^S(\mathbf{X} \backslash \mathbf{E})$.
for stage $k \leftarrow 0$ **to** S **do**

1. Sample l points $\mathbf{s}_1^k$, $\mathbf{s}_2^k$, ..., $\mathbf{s}_l^k$ independently according to the current importance function $\Pr^k(\mathbf{X} \backslash \mathbf{E})$.

2. For every node X_i such that $X_i \in \mathbf{X} \backslash \mathbf{E}$ and $X_i \notin \text{Anc}(\mathbf{E})$ count score sums corresponding to $\{x_i, \text{pa}(X_i), \mathbf{e}\}$ and estimate $\Pr'(x_i|\text{pa}(X_i), \mathbf{e})$ based on $\mathbf{s}_1^k$, $\mathbf{s}_2^k$, ..., $\mathbf{s}_l^k$.

3. Update $\Pr^k(\mathbf{X} \backslash \mathbf{E})$ according to the following formula:

$$\Pr^{k+1}(x_i|\text{pa}(X_i), \mathbf{e}) = $$
$$\Pr^k(x_i|\text{pa}(X_i), \mathbf{e}) + \eta(k) \cdot \Big(\Pr'(x_i|\text{pa}(X_i), \mathbf{e}) - \Pr^k(x_i|\text{pa}(X_i), \mathbf{e})\Big)$$

end for

Figure 3: The AIS-BN algorithm for learning the optimal importance function.

sampling, the test results reported in this paper do not include this improvement of the AIS-BN algorithm.

Figure 3 lists an algorithm that implements Step 7 of the basic AIS-BN algorithm listed in Figure 2. When we estimate $\Pr'(x_i|\text{pa}(X_i), \mathbf{e})$, we only use the samples obtained at the current stage. One reason for this is that the information obtained in previous stages has been absorbed by $\Pr^k(\mathbf{X}\backslash\mathbf{E})$. The other reason is that in principle, each successive iteration is more accurate than the previous one and the importance function is closer to the optimal importance function. Thus, the samples generated by $\Pr^{k+1}(\mathbf{X}\backslash\mathbf{E})$ are better than those generated by $\Pr^k(\mathbf{X}\backslash\mathbf{E})$. $\Pr'(X_i|\text{pa}(X_i), \mathbf{e}) - \Pr^k(X_i|\text{pa}(X_i), \mathbf{e})$ corresponds to the vector of first partial derivatives in the direction of the maximum decrease in the error. $\eta(k)$ is a positive function that determines the *learning rate*. When $\eta(k) = 0$ (lower bound), we do not update our importance function. When $\eta(k) = 1$ (upper bound), at each stage we discard the old function. The convergence speed is directly related to $\eta(k)$. If it is small, the convergence will be very slow due to the large number of updating steps needed to reach a local minimum. On the other hand, if it is large, convergence rate will be initially very fast, but the algorithm will eventually start to oscillate and thus may not reach a minimum. There are many papers in the field of neural network learning that discuss how to choose the learning rate and let estimated importance function converge quickly to the destination function. Any method that can improve learning rate should be applicable to this algorithm. Currently, we use the following function proposed by Ritter et al. (1991)

$$\eta(k) = a \left(\frac{b}{a}\right)^{k/k_{\max}}, \tag{10}$$

where a is the initial learning rate and b is the learning rate in the last step. This function has been reported to perform well in neural network learning (Ritter et al., 1991).

3.3 Heuristic Initialization in AIS-BN

The dimensionality of the problem of Bayesian network inference is equal to the number of variables in a network, which in the networks considered in this paper can be very high. As a result, the learning space of the optimal importance function is very large. Choice of the initial importance function $\Pr^0(\mathbf{X}\backslash\mathbf{E})$ is an important factor affecting the learning — an initial value of the importance function that is close to the optimal importance function can greatly affect the speed of convergence. In this section, we present two heuristics that help to achieve this goal.

Due to their explicit encoding of the structure of a decomposable joint probability distribution, Bayesian networks offer computational advantages compared to finite-dimensional integrals. A possible first approximation of the optimal importance function is the prior probability distribution over the network variables, $\Pr(\mathbf{X})$. We propose an improvement on this initialization. We know that the effect of evidence nodes on a node will be attenuated as the path length of that node to evidence nodes is increased (Henrion, 1989) and the most affected nodes are the direct ancestors of the evidence nodes. Initializing the ICPT tables of the parents of the evidence nodes to uniform distributions in our experience improves the convergence rate. Furthermore, the CPT tables of the parents of an evidence node E may be not favorable to the observed state e if the probability of $E = e$ without any condition is less than a small value, such as $\Pr(E = e) < 1/(2 \cdot n_E)$, where n_E is the number of outcomes of node E. Based on this observation, we change the CPT tables of the parents of an evidence node E to uniform distributions in our experiment only when $\Pr(E = e) < 1/(2 \cdot n_E)$, otherwise we leave them unchanged. This kind of initialization involves the knowledge of $\Pr(E = e)$, the marginal probability without evidence. Probabilistic logic sampling (Henrion, 1988) enhanced by Latin hypercube sampling (Cheng & Druzdzel, 2000b) or quasi-Monte Carlo methods (Cheng & Druzdzel, 2000a) will produce a very good estimate of $\Pr(E = e)$. This is an one-time effort that can be made at the model building stage and is worth pursuing to any desired precision.

Another serious problem related to sampling are extremely small probabilities. Suppose there exists a root node with a state s that has the prior probability $\Pr(s) = 0.0001$. Let the posterior probability of this state given evidence be $\Pr(s|\mathbf{E}) = 0.8$. A simple calculation shows that if we update the importance function every $1,000$ samples, we can expect to hit s only once every 10 updates. Thus s's convergence rate will be very slow. We can overcome this problem by setting a threshold θ and replacing every probability $p < \theta$ in the network by θ.[2] At the same time, we subtract $(\theta - p)$ from the largest probability in the same conditional probability distribution. For example, the value of $\theta = 10/l$, where l is the updating interval, will allow us to sample 10 times more often in the first stage of the algorithm. If this state turns out to be more likely (having a large weight), we can increase its probability even more in order to converge to the correct answer faster. Considering that we should avoid $f(\mathbf{X}) \ll |g(\mathbf{X}) - I \cdot f(\mathbf{X})|$ in an unimportant region as discussed in Section 2.1, we need to make this threshold larger. We have found that the convergence rate is quite sensitive to this threshold. Based on our empirical tests, we suggest to use $\theta = 0.04$ in networks whose maximum number of outcomes per node does not exceed five. A smaller threshold might lead to fast convergence in some cases but slow convergence in others. If one threshold does not work, changing it in a specific network will usually improve convergence rate.

3.4 Selection of Parameters

There are several tunable parameters in the AIS-BN algorithm. We base the choice of these parameters on the Central Limit Theorem (CLT). According to CLT, if Z_1, Z_2, ..., Z_n are independent and identically distributed random variables with $E(Z_i) = \mu_Z$ and $\text{Var}(Z_i) = \sigma_Z^2$, $i = 1, ..., n$, then $\overline{Z} = (Z_1 + ... + Z_n)/n$ is approximately normally distributed when n is sufficiently large. Thus,

$$\lim_{n \to \infty} P\left(\frac{\left|\overline{Z} - \mu_z\right|}{\mu_z} \geq \frac{\sigma_Z/\sqrt{n}}{\mu_z} \cdot t\right) = \frac{2}{\sqrt{2\pi}} \int_t^\infty e^{-x^2/2} dx \,. \tag{11}$$

Although this approximation holds when n approaches infinity, CLT is known to be very robust and lead to excellent approximations even for small n. The formula of Equation 11 is an *(ε_r, δ) Relative Approximation*, which is an estimate $\overline{\mu}$ of μ that satisfies

$$P\left(\frac{|\overline{\mu} - \mu|}{\mu} \geq \varepsilon_r\right) \leq \delta \,.$$

---

2. This initialization heuristic was apparently developed independently by Ortiz and Kaelbling (2000).

If δ has been fixed,

$$\varepsilon_r = \frac{\sigma_Z/\sqrt{n}}{\mu_z} \cdot \Phi_Z^{-1}\left(\frac{\delta}{2}\right),$$

where $\Phi_Z(z) = \frac{1}{\sqrt{2\pi}} \int_z^\infty e^{-x^2/2} dx$. Since in our sampling problem, μ_z (corresponding to $\Pr(\mathbf{E})$ in Figure 2) has been fixed, setting ε_r to a smaller value amounts to letting $\sigma_Z/\sqrt{n}$ be smaller. So, we can adjust the parameters based on $\sigma_Z/\sqrt{n}$, which can be estimated using Equation 3. It is also the theoretical intuition behind our recommendation $w^k \propto 1/\hat{\sigma}^k$ in Section 3.1. While we expect that this should work well in most networks, no guarantees can be given here — there exist always some extreme cases in sampling algorithms in which no good estimate of variance can be obtained.

3.5 A Generalization of AIS-BN: The Problem of Estimating $\Pr(a|e)$

A typical focus of systems based on Bayesian networks is the posterior probability of various outcomes of individual variables given evidence, $\Pr(a|e)$. This can be generalized to the computation of the posterior probability of a particular instantiation of a set of variables given evidence, i.e., $\Pr(\mathbf{A} = \mathbf{a}|e)$. There are two methods that are capable of performing this computation. The first method is very efficient at the expense of precision. The second method is less efficient, but offers in general better convergence rates. Both methods are based on Equation 7.

The first method reuses the samples generated to estimate $\Pr(\mathbf{e})$ in estimating $\Pr(\mathbf{a}, \mathbf{e})$. Estimation of $\Pr(\mathbf{a}, \mathbf{e})$ amounts to counting the scored sum under the condition $\mathbf{A} = \mathbf{a}$. The main advantage of this method is its efficiency — we can use the same set of samples to estimate the posterior probability of any state of a subset of the network given evidence. Its main disadvantage is that the variance of the estimated $\Pr(\mathbf{a}, \mathbf{e})$ can be large, especially when the numerical value of $\Pr(\mathbf{a}|\mathbf{e})$ is extreme. This method is the most widely used approach in the existing stochastic sampling algorithms.

The second method, used much more rarely (e.g., Cano et al., 1996; Pradhan & Dagum, 1996; Dagum & Luby, 1997), calls for estimating $\Pr(\mathbf{e})$ and $\Pr(\mathbf{a}, \mathbf{e})$ separately. After estimating $\Pr(\mathbf{e})$, an additional call to the algorithm is made for each instantiation $\mathbf{a}$ of the set of variables of interest $\mathbf{A}$. $\Pr(\mathbf{a}, \mathbf{e})$ is estimated by sampling the network with the set of observations $\mathbf{e}$ extended by $\mathbf{A} = \mathbf{a}$. The main advantage of this method is that it is much better at reducing variance than the first method. Its main disadvantage is the computational cost associated with sampling for possibly many combinations of states of nodes of interest.

Cano et al. (1996) suggested a modified version of the second method. Suppose that we are interested in the posterior distribution $\Pr(\mathbf{a}_i|\mathbf{e})$ for all possible values $\mathbf{a}_i$ of $\mathbf{A}$, $i = 1$, $2, \ldots, k$. We can estimate $\Pr(\mathbf{a}_i, \mathbf{e})$ for each $i = 1, \ldots, k$ separately, and use the value $\sum_{i=1}^k \Pr(\mathbf{a}_i, \mathbf{e})$ as an estimate for $\Pr(\mathbf{e})$. The assumption behind this approach is that the estimate of $\Pr(\mathbf{e})$ will be very accurate because of the large sample from which it is drawn. However, even if we can guarantee small variance in every $\Pr(\mathbf{a}_i, \mathbf{e})$, we cannot guarantee that their sum will also have a small variance. So, in the AIS-BN algorithm we only use the pure form of each of the methods. The algorithm listed in Figure 2 is based on the first method when the optional computations in Steps 12 and 13 are performed. An algorithm corresponding to the second method skips the optional steps and calls the basic AIS-BN algorithm twice to estimate $\Pr(\mathbf{e})$ and $\Pr(\mathbf{a}, \mathbf{e})$ separately.

The first method is very attractive because of its simplicity and possible computational efficiency. However, as we have shown in Section 2.2, the performance of a sampling algorithm that uses just one set of samples (as in the first method above) to estimate $\Pr(\mathbf{a}|\mathbf{e})$ will deteriorate if the difference between the optimal importance functions for $\Pr(\mathbf{a},\mathbf{e})$ and $\Pr(\mathbf{e})$ is large. If the main focus of the computation is high accuracy of the posterior probability distribution of a small number of nodes, we strongly recommend to use the algorithm based on the second method. Also, this algorithm can be easily used to estimate confidence intervals of the solution.

4. Experimental Results

In this section, we first describe the experimental method used in our tests. Our tests focus on the CPCS network, which is one of the largest and most realistic networks available and for which we know precisely which nodes are observable. We were, therefore, able to generate very realistic test cases. Since the AIS-BN algorithm uses two initialization heuristics, we designed an experiment that studies the contribution of each of these two heuristics to the performance of the algorithm. To probe the extent of AIS-BN algorithm's excellent performance, we test it on several real and large networks.

4.1 Experimental Method

We performed empirical tests comparing the AIS-BN algorithm to the likelihood weighting (LW) and the self-importance sampling (SIS) algorithms. The two algorithms are basically the state of the art general purpose belief updating algorithms. The AA (Dagum et al., 1995) and the bounded variance (Dagum & Luby, 1997) algorithms, which were suggested by a reviewer, are essentially enhanced special purpose versions of the basic LW algorithm. Our implementation of the three algorithms relied on essentially the same code with separate functions only when the algorithms differed. It is fair to assume, therefore, that the observed differences are purely due to the theoretical differences among the algorithms and not due to the efficiency of implementation. In order to make the comparison of the AIS-BN algorithm to LW and SIS fair, we used the first method of computation (Section 3.5), i.e., one that relies on single sampling rather than calling the basic AIS-BN algorithm twice.

We measured the accuracy of approximation achieved by the simulation in terms of the Mean Square Error (MSE), i.e., square root of the sum of square differences between $\Pr'(x_{ij})$ and $\Pr(x_{ij})$, the sampled and the exact marginal probabilities of state j $(j = 1, 2, \ldots, n_i)$ of node i, such that $X_i \notin \mathbf{E}$. More precisely,

$$MSE = \sqrt{\frac{1}{\sum_{X_i \in \mathbf{N} \backslash \mathbf{E}} n_i} \sum_{X_i \in \mathbf{N} \backslash \mathbf{E}} \sum_{j=1}^{n_i} (\Pr'(x_{ij}) - \Pr(x_{ij}))^2} \ ,$$

where $\mathbf{N}$ is the set of all nodes, $\mathbf{E}$ is the set of evidence nodes, and n_i is the number of outcomes of node i. In all diagrams, the reported MSE is averaged over 10 runs. We used the clustering algorithm (Lauritzen & Spiegelhalter, 1988) to compute the gold standard results for our comparisons of the mean square error. We performed all experiments on a Pentium II, 333 MHz Windows computer.

While *MSE* is not perfect, it is the simplest way of capturing error that lends itself to further theoretical analysis. For example, it is possible to derive analytically the idealized convergence rate in terms of *MSE*, which, in turn, can be used to judge the quality of the algorithm. *MSE* has been used in virtually all previous tests of sampling algorithms, which allows interested readers to tie the current results to the past studies. A reviewer offered an interesting suggestion of using cross-entropy or some other technique that weights small changes near zero much more strongly than the equivalent size change in the middle of the $[0, 1]$ interval. Such measure would penalize the algorithm for imprecisions of possibly several orders of magnitude in very small probabilities. While this idea is interesting, we are not aware of any theoretical reasons as to why this measure would make a difference in comparisons between AIS-BN, LW and SIS algorithms. The *MSE*, as we mentioned above, will allow us to compare the empirically determined convergence rate to the theoretically derived ideal convergence rate. Theoretically, the *MSE* is inversely proportional to the square root of the sample size.

Since there are several tunable parameters used in the AIS-BN algorithm, we list the values of the parameters used in our test: $l = 2,500$; $w^k = 0$ for $k \leq 9$ and $w^k = 1$ otherwise. We stopped the updating process in Step 7 of Figure 2 after $k \geq 10$. In other words, we used only the samples collected in the last step of the algorithm. The learning parameters used in our algorithm are $k_{\max} = 10$, $a = 0.4$, and $b = 0.14$ (see Equation 10). We used an empirically determined value of the threshold $\theta = 0.04$ (Section 3.3). We only change the CPT tables of the parents of a special evidence node A to uniform distributions when $\Pr(A = a) < 1/(2 \cdot n_A)$. Some of the parameters are a matter of design decision (e.g., the number of samples in our tests), others were chosen empirically. Although we have found that these parameters may have different optimal values for different Bayesian networks, we used the above values in all our tests of the AIS-BN algorithm described in this paper. Since the same set of parameters led to spectacular improvement in accuracy in all tested networks, it is fair to say that the superiority of the AIS-BN algorithm to the other algorithms is not too sensitive to the values of the parameters.

For the SIS algorithm, $w^k = 1$ by the design of the algorithm. We used $l = 2,500$. The updating function in Step 7 of Figure 1 is that of (Shwe et al., 1991; Cousins, Chen, & Frisse, 1993):

$$\Pr^k_{new}(x_i|\mathrm{pa}(X_i), \mathbf{e}) = \frac{\Pr(x_i|\mathrm{pa}(X_i)) + k \cdot \widehat{\Pr}_{current}(x_i|\mathrm{pa}(X_i), \mathbf{e})}{1 + k} ,$$

where $\Pr(x_i|\mathrm{pa}(X_i))$ is the original sampling distribution, $\widehat{\Pr}_{current}(x_i|\mathrm{pa}(X_i), \mathbf{e})$ is an equivalent of our ICPT tables estimator based on all currently available information, and k is the updating step.

4.2 Results for the CPCS Network

The main network used in our tests is a subset of the CPCS (Computer-based Patient Case Study) model (Pradhan et al., 1994), a large multiply-connected multi-layer network consisting of 422 multi-valued nodes and covering a subset of the domain of internal medicine.

Among the 422 nodes, 14 nodes describe diseases, 33 nodes describe history and risk factors, and the remaining 375 nodes describe various findings related to the diseases. The CPCS network is among the largest real networks available to the research community at the present time. The CPCS network contains many extreme probabilities, typically on the order of 10^{-4}. Our analysis is based on a subset of 179 nodes of the CPCS network, created by Max Henrion and Malcolm Pradhan. We used this smaller version in order to be able to compute the exact solution for the purpose of measuring approximation error in the sampling algorithms.

The AIS-BN algorithm has some learning overhead. The following comparison of execution time vs. number of samples may give the reader an idea of this overhead. Updating the CPCS network with 20 evidence nodes on our system takes the AIS-BN algorithm a total of 8.4 seconds to learn. It generates subsequently 3,640 samples per second, while the SIS algorithm generates 2,631 samples per second, and the LW algorithm generates 4,167 samples per second. In order to remain conservative towards the AIS-BN algorithm, in all our experiments we fixed the execution time of the algorithms (our limit was 60 seconds) rather than the number of samples. In the CPCS network with 20 evidence nodes, in 60 seconds, AIS-BN generates about 188,000 samples, SIS generates about 158,000 samples and LW generates about 250,000 samples.

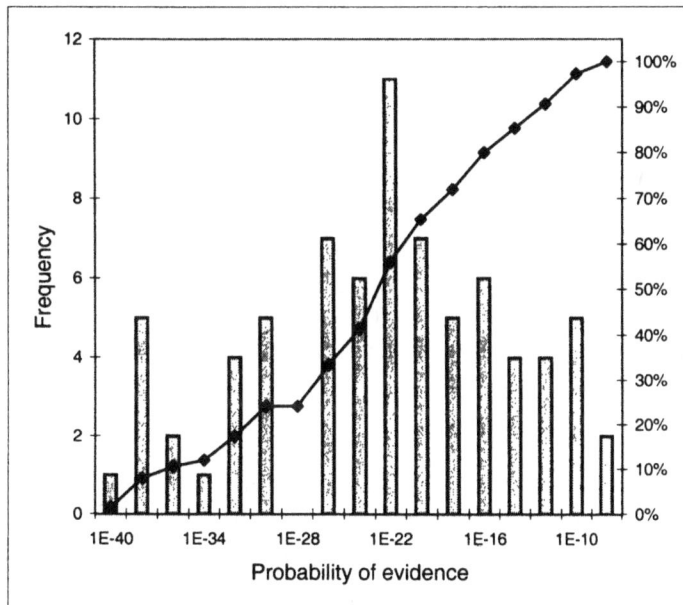

Figure 4: The probability distribution of evidence $\Pr(\mathbf{E} = \mathbf{e})$ in our experiments.

We generated a total of 75 test cases consisting of five sequences of 15 test cases each. We ran each test case 10 times, each time with a different setting of the random number seed. Each sequence had a progressively higher number of evidence nodes: 15, 20, 25, 30, and 35 evidence nodes respectively. The evidence nodes were chosen randomly (equiprobable sampling without replacement) from those nodes that described various plausible medical findings. Almost all of these nodes were leaf nodes in the network. We believe that this constituted very realistic test cases for the algorithms. The distribution of the prior probability of evidence, $\Pr(\mathbf{E} = \mathbf{e})$, across all test runs of our experiments is shown in Figure 4. The least likely evidence was 5.54×10^{-42}, the most likely evidence was 1.37×10^{-9}, and the median was 7×10^{-24}.

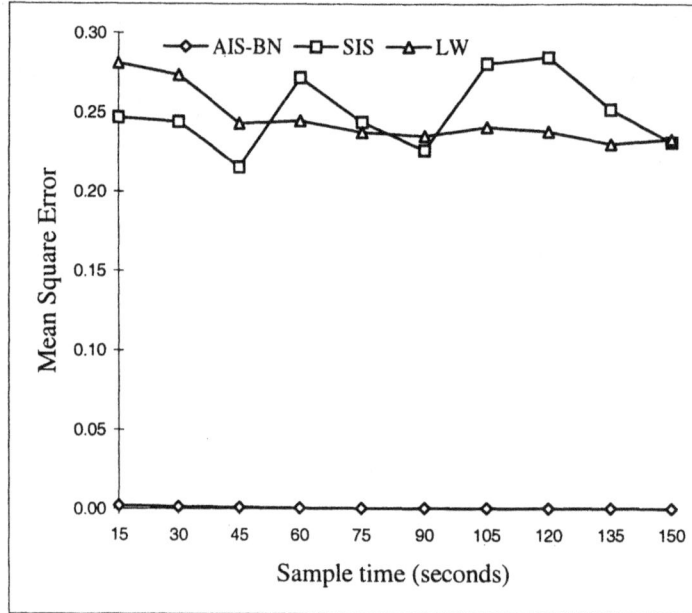

Figure 5: A typical plot of convergence of the tested sampling algorithms in our experiments — Mean Square Error as a function of the execution time for a subset of the CPCS network with 20 evidence nodes chosen randomly among plausible medical observations ($\Pr(\mathbf{E} = \mathbf{e}) = 3.33 \times 10^{-26}$ in this particular case) for the AIS-BN, the SIS, and the LW algorithms. The curve for the AIS-BN algorithm is very close to the horizontal axis.

Figures 5 and 6 show a typical plot of convergence of the tested sampling algorithms in our experiments. The case illustrated involves updating the CPCS network with 20 evidence nodes. We plot the *MSE* after the initial 15 seconds during which the algorithms start converging. In particular, the learning step of the AIS-BN algorithm is usually completed within the first 9 seconds. We ran the three algorithms in this case for 150 seconds rather than the 60 seconds in the actual experiment in order to be able to observe a wider range of convergence. The plot of the *MSE* for the AIS-BN algorithm almost touches the X axis in Figure 5. Figure 6 shows the same plot in a finer scale in order to show more detail in the AIS-BN convergence curve. It is clear that the AIS-BN algorithm dramatically improves the convergence rate. We can also see that the results of AIS-BN converge to exact results very fast as the sampling time increases. In the case captured in Figures 5 and 6, a tenfold increase in the sampling time (after subtracting the overhead for the AIS-BN algorithm, it corresponds to a 21.5-fold increase in the number of samples) results in a 4.55-fold decrease

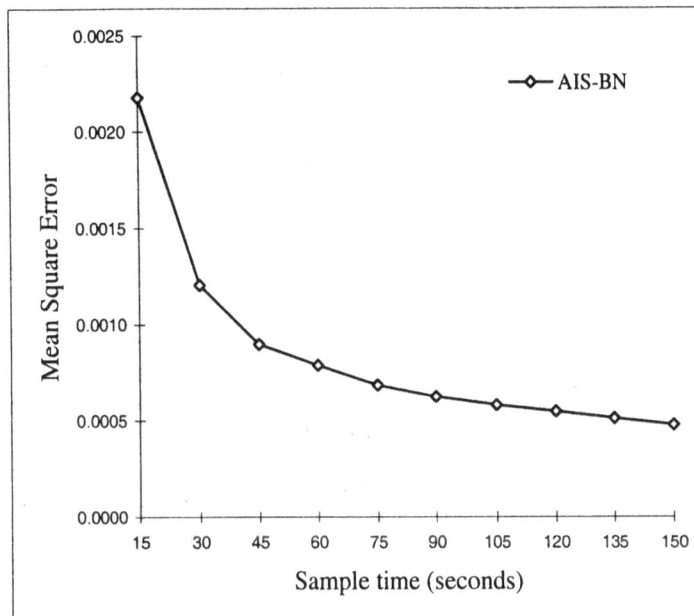

Figure 6: The lower part of the plot of Figure 5 showing the convergence of the AIS-BN algorithm to correct posterior probabilities.

of the *MSE* (to *MSE*≤ 0.00048). The observed convergence of both SIS and LW algorithms was poor. A tenfold increase in sampling time had practically no effect on accuracy. Please note that this is a very typical case observed in our experiments.

	Original CPT	Exact ICPT	Learned ICPT
"Absent"	0.99631	0.0037	0.015
"Mild"	0.00183	0.1560	0.164
"Moderate"	0.00093	0.1190	0.131
"Severe"	0.00093	0.7213	0.690

Table 1: A fragment of the conditional probability table of a node of the CPCS network (node *gasAcute*, parents *hepAcute=Mild* and *wbcTotTho=False*) in Figure 6.

Figure 7 illustrates the ICPT learning process of the AIS-BN algorithm for the sample case shown in Figure 6. The displayed conditional probabilities belong to the node *gasAcute* which is a parent of two evidence nodes, *difInfGasMuc* and *abdPaiExaMea*. The node *gasAcute* has four states: "absent," "mild," "moderate," and "severe", and two parents. We randomly chose a combination of its parents' states as our displayed configuration. The original CPT for this configuration without evidence, the exact ICPT with evidence and the learned ICPT with evidence are summarized numerically in Table 1. Figure 7 illustrates that the learned importance conditional probabilities begin to converge to the exact results

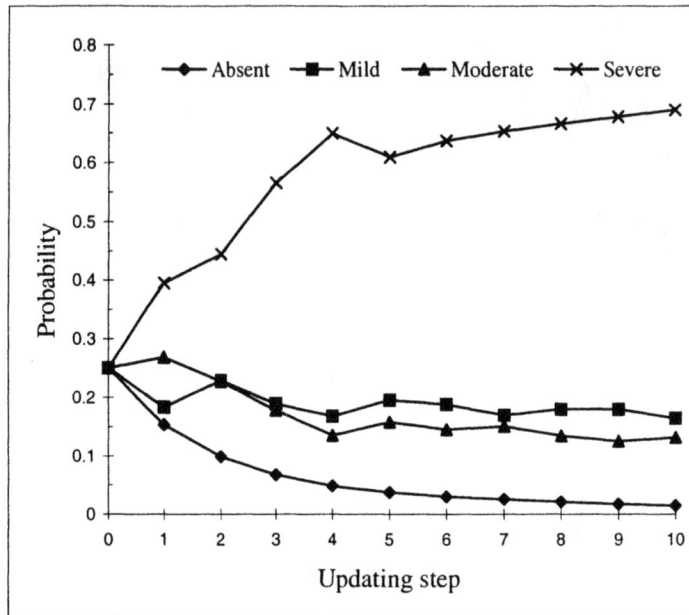

Figure 7: Convergence of the conditional probabilities during the example run of the AIS-BN algorithm captured in Figure 6. The displayed fragment of the conditional probability table belongs to node *gasAcute* which is a parent of one of the evidence nodes.

stably after three updating steps. The learned probabilities in Step 10 are close to the exact results. In this example, the difference between $\Pr(x_i|\mathrm{pa}(X_i), \mathbf{e})$ and $\Pr(x_i|\mathrm{pa}(X_i))$ is very large. Sampling from $\Pr(x_i|\mathrm{pa}(X_i))$ instead of $\Pr(x_i|\mathrm{pa}(X_i), \mathbf{e})$ would introduce large variance into our results.

	AIS-BN	SIS	LW
μ	0.00082	0.110	0.148
σ	0.00022	0.076	0.093
min	0.00049	0.0016	0.0031
median	0.00078	0.105	0.154
max	0.00184	0.316	0.343

Table 2: Summary of the simulation results for all of the 75 simulation cases on the CPCS network. Figure 8 shows each of the 75 cases graphically.

Figure 8 shows the *MSE* for all 75 test cases in our experiments with the summary statistics in Table 2. A paired one-tailed t-test resulted in statistically highly significant differences between the AIS-BN and SIS algorithms ($p < 3.1 \times 10^{-20}$), and also between the SIS and LW algorithms ($p < 1.7 \times 10^{-8}$). As far as the magnitude of difference is

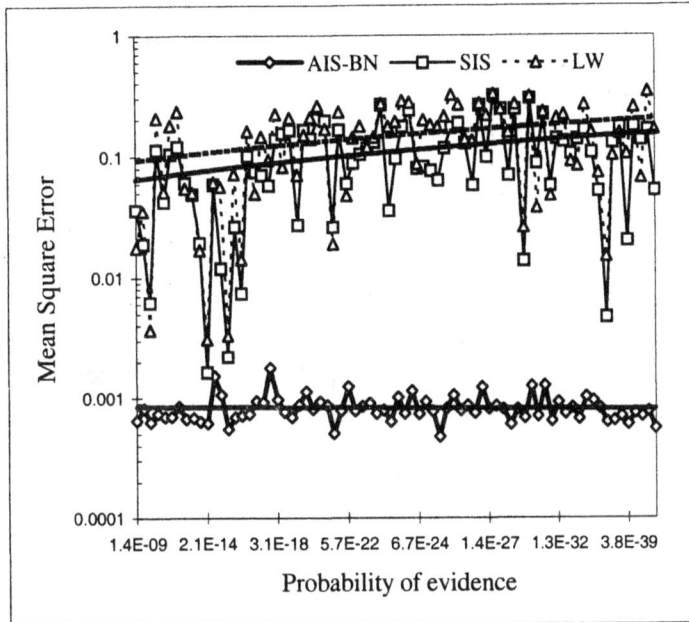

Figure 8: Performance of the AIS-BN, SIS, and LW algorithms: Mean Square Error for each of the 75 individual test cases plotted against the probability of evidence. The sampling time is 60 seconds.

concerned, AIS-BN was significantly better than SIS. SIS was better than LW, but the difference was small. The mean *MSE*s of SIS and LW algorithms were both greater than 0.1, which suggests that neither of these algorithms is suitable for large Bayesian networks.

The graph in Figure 9 shows the *MSE* ratio between the AIS-BN and SIS algorithms. We can see that the percentage of the cases whose ratio was greater than 100 (two orders of magnitude improvement!) is 60%. In other words, we obtained two orders of magnitude improvement in *MSE* in more than half of the cases. In 80% cases, the ratio was greater than 50. The smallest ratio in our experiments was 2.67, which happened when posterior probabilities were dominated by the prior probabilities. In that case, even though the LW and SIS algorithms converged very fast, their *MSE* was still far larger than that of AIS-BN.

Our next experiment aimed at showing how close the AIS-BN algorithm can approach the best possible sampling results. If we know the optimal importance sampling function, the convergence of the AIS-BN algorithm should be the same as that of forward sampling without evidence. In other words, the results of the probabilistic logic sampling algorithm without evidence approach the limit of how well stochastic sampling can perform. We ran the logic sampling algorithm on the CPCS network without evidence mimicking the test runs of the AIS-BN algorithm, i.e., 5 blocks of 15 runs, each repeated 10 times with a different random number seed. The number of samples generated was equal to the average number of samples generated by the AIS-BN algorithm for each series of 15 test runs. We obtained the average *MSE* $\mu = 0.00057$, with $\sigma = 0.000025$, min $= 0.00052$, and

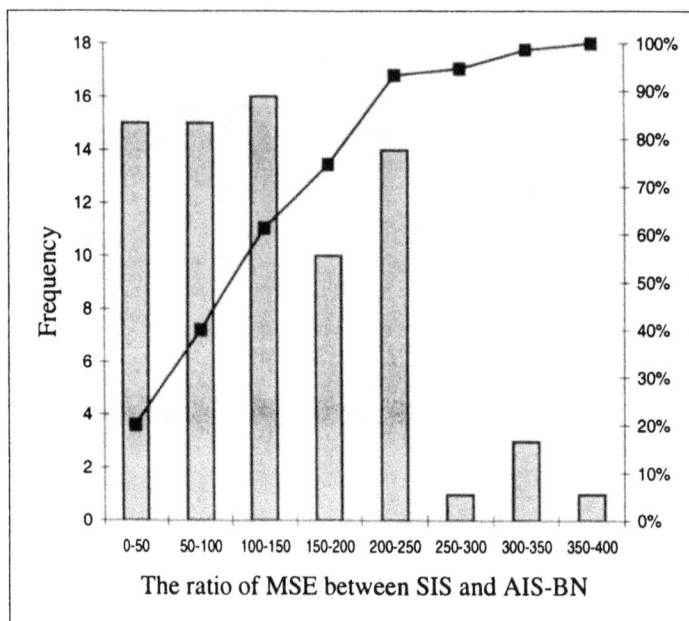

Figure 9: The ratio of *MSE* between SIS and AIS-BN versus percentage.

max = 0.00065. The best results should be around this range. From Table 2, we can see that the minimum *MSE* for the AIS-BN algorithm was 0.00049, within the range of the optimal result. The mean *MSE* in AIS-BN is 0.00082, not too far from the optimal results. The standard deviation, σ, is significantly larger in the AIS-BN algorithm, but this is understandable given that the process of learning the optimal importance function is heuristic in nature. It is not difficult to understand that there exist a difference between the AIS-BN results and the optimal results. First, the AIS-BN algorithm in our tests updated the sampling distribution only 10 times, which may be too few times to let it converge to the optimal importance distribution. Second, even if the algorithm has converged to the optimal importance distribution, the sampling algorithm will still let the parameter oscillate around this distribution and there will be always small differences between the two distributions.

Figure 10 shows the convergence rate for all tested cases for a four-fold increase in sampling time (between 15 and 60 seconds). We adjusted the convergence ratio of the AIS-BN algorithm by dividing it by a constant. According to Equation 3, the theoretically expected convergence ratio for a four-fold increase in the number of samples should be around two. There are about 96% cases among the AIS-BN runs whose ratio lays in the interval (1.75, 2.25], in a sharp contrast to 11% and 13% cases in the SIS and LW algorithms. The ratios of the remaining 4% cases in AIS-BN lay in the interval [2.25, 2.5]. In the SIS and LW algorithms, the percentage of cases whose ratio were smaller than 1.5 was 71% and 77% respectively. Less than 1.5 means that the number of samples was too small to estimate variance and the results cannot be trusted. The ratio greater than 2.25

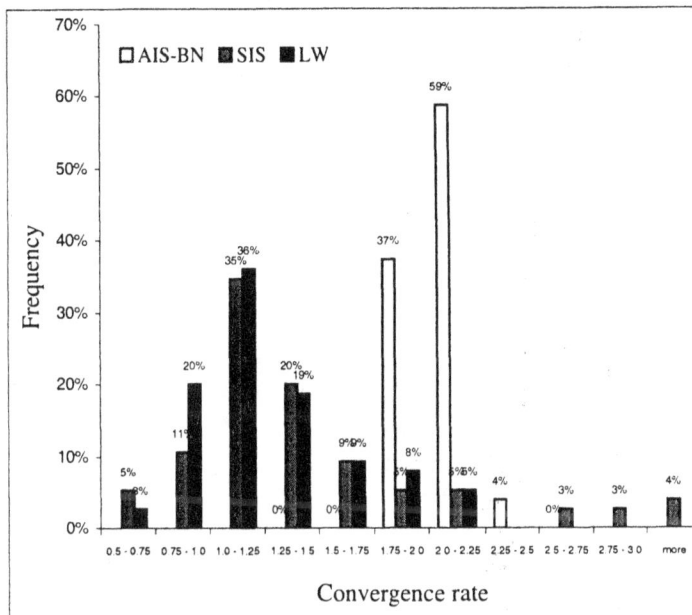

Figure 10: The distribution of the convergence ratio of the AIS-BN, SIS, and LW algorithms when the number of samples increases four times.

means possibly that 60 seconds was long enough to estimate the variance, but 15 seconds was too short.

4.3 The Role of AIS-BN Heuristics in Performance Improvement

From the above experimental results we can see that the AIS-BN algorithm can improve the sampling performance significantly. Our next series of tests focused on studying the role of the two AIS-BN initialization heuristics. The first is initializing the ICPT tables of the parents of evidence to uniform distributions, denoted by U. The second is adjusting small probabilities, denoted by S. We denote AIS-BN without any heuristic initialization method to be the AIS algorithm. AIS+U+S equals AIS-BN. We compared the following versions of the algorithms: SIS, AIS, SIS+U, AIS+U, SIS+S, AIS+S, SIS+U+S, AIS+U+S. All algorithms with SIS used the same number of samples as SIS. All algorithms with AIS used the same number of samples as AIS-BN. We tested these algorithms on the same 75 test cases used in the previous experiment. Figure 11 shows the *MSE* for each of the sampling algorithms with the summary statistics in Table 3. Even though the AIS algorithm is better than the SIS algorithm, the difference is not as large as in case of the AIS+U, AIS+S, and AIS-BN algorithms. It seems that heuristic initialization methods help much. The results for the SIS+S, SIS+U, SIS+U+S algorithms suggest that although heuristic initialization methods can improve performance, they alone cannot improve too much. It is fair to say that significant performance improvement in the AIS-BN algorithm is coming from the combination of AIS with heuristic methods, not any method alone. It is not difficult to understand that, as only with good heuristic initialization methods is it possible to let the learning process quickly exit oscillation areas. Although both S and U methods alone can improve the performance, the improvement is moderate compared to the combination of the two.

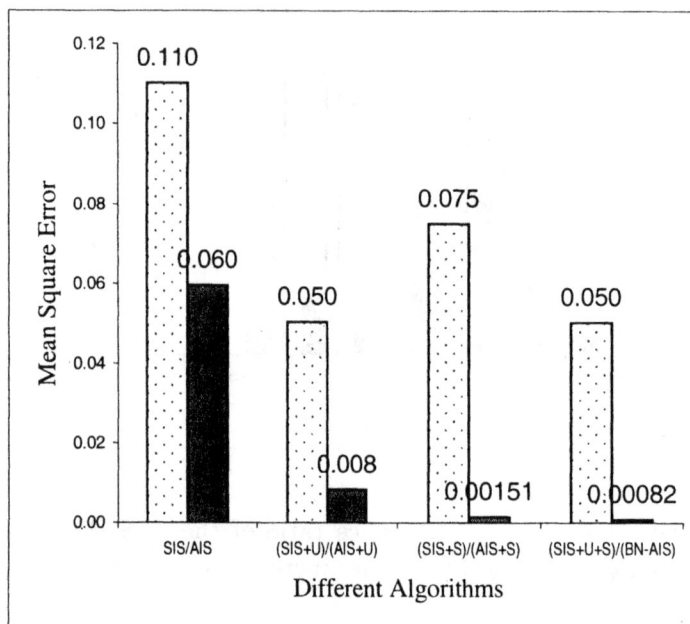

Figure 11: A comparison of different algorithms in the CPCS network. Each bar is based on 75 test cases. The dotted bar shows the *MSE* for the SIS algorithm while the gray bar shows the *MSE* for the AIS algorithm.

	SIS	AIS	SIS+U	AIS+U	SIS+S	AIS+S	SIS+U+S	AIS-BN
μ	0.110	0.060	0.050	0.0084	0.075	0.0015	0.050	0.00082
σ	0.076	0.049	0.052	0.025	0.074	0.0016	0.059	0.00022
min	0.0016	0.00074	0.0011	0.00058	0.00072	0.00056	0.00086	0.00049
median	0.105	0.045	0.031	0.0014	0.052	0.00087	0.028	0.00078
max	0.316	0.207	0.212	0.208	0.279	0.0085	0.265	0.0018

Table 3: Summary of the simulation results for different algorithms in the CPCS network.

4.4 Results for Other Networks

In order to make sure that the AIS-BN algorithm performs well in general, we tested it on two other large networks.

The first network that we used in our tests is the PATHFINDER network (Heckerman et al., 1990), which is the core element of an expert system that assists surgical pathologists with the diagnosis of lymph-node diseases. There are two versions of this network. We used the larger version, consisting of 135 nodes. In contrast to the CPCS network, PATHFINDER contains many conditional probabilities that are equal to 1, which reflects deterministic relationships in certain settings. To make the sampling challenging, we randomly selected 20 evidence nodes from among the leaf nodes. Each of these was an observable node (David Heckerman, personal communication). We verified in each case that the probability of so selected evidence was not equal to zero.

We fixed the execution time of the algorithms to be 60 seconds. The learning overhead for the AIS-BN algorithm in the PATHFINDER network was about 3.5 seconds. In 60 seconds, AIS-BN generated about 366,000 samples, SIS generated about 250,000 samples and LW generated about 2,700,000 samples. The reason why LW could generate more than 10 times as many samples as SIS within the same amount of time is that the LW algorithm terminates sample generation at a very early stage in many samples, when the weight of a sample becomes zero. This is a result of determinism in the probability tables, mentioned above. We will see that LW benefits greatly from generating more samples. The other parameters used in AIS-BN were the same as those used in the CPCS network.

We tested 20 cases, each with randomly selected 20 evidence nodes. The reported *MSE* for each case was averaged over 10 runs. Some of the runs of the SIS and LW algorithms did not manage to generate any effective samples (the weight score sum was equal to zero). SIS had only 75% effective runs and LW had only 89% effective runs, which means that in some runs SIS and LW were unable to yield any information about the posterior distributions. In all those cases, we discarded the run and only averaged over the effective runs. All runs in the AIS-BN algorithm were effective. We report our experimental results with the summary statistics in Table 4. From these data, we can see that the AIS-BN algorithm is still significantly better than the SIS and LW algorithms. Since the LW algorithm can generate more than ten times the number of samples than the SIS algorithm, its performance is better than that of the SIS algorithm.

	AIS-BN	SIS	LW
μ	0.00050	0.166	0.089
σ	0.00037	0.107	0.0707
min	0.00025	0.00116	0.00080
median	0.00037	0.184	0.0866
max	0.0017	0.467	0.294
effective runs	200	150	178

Table 4: Summary of the simulation results for all of the 20 simulation cases on the PATHFINDER network.

The second network that we tested was one of the ANDES networks (Conati et al., 1997). ANDES is an intelligent tutoring system for classical Newtonian physics that is being developed by a team of researchers at the Learning Research and Development Center at the University of Pittsburgh and researchers at the United States Naval Academy. The student model in ANDES uses a Bayesian network to do long–term knowledge assessment, plan recognition, and prediction of students' actions during problem solving. We selected the largest ANDES network that was available to us, consisting of 223 nodes.

In contrast to the previous two networks, the depth of the ANDES network was significantly larger and so was its connectivity. There were only 22 leaf nodes. It is quite predictable that this kind of networks will pose difficulties to learning. We selected 20 evidence nodes randomly from the potential evidence nodes and tested 20 cases. All parameters were the same as those used in the CPCS network. We fixed the execution time of the algorithms to be 60 seconds. The learning overhead for the AIS-BN algorithm in the ANDES network was 13.4 seconds. In 60 seconds, AIS-BN generated about 114,000 samples, SIS generated about 98,000 samples and LW generated about 180,000 samples. In this network, LW still can generate almost two times the number of samples generated by the SIS algorithm.

We report our experimental results with the summary statistics in Table 5. The results show that also in the ANDES network the AIS-BN algorithm was significantly better than the SIS and LW algorithms. Since LW generated almost two times the number of samples that were generated by the SIS algorithm, its performance was better than that of the SIS algorithm.

	AIS-BN	SIS	LW
μ	0.0059	0.0628	0.0404
σ	0.0049	0.102	0.0539
min	0.0023	0.0028	0.0028
median	0.0045	0.0190	0.0198
max	0.0237	0.321	0.221

Table 5: Summary of the simulation results for all of the 20 simulation cases on the ANDES network.

While the AIS-BN algorithm is on the average an order of magnitude more precise than the other two algorithms, the performance improvement is smaller than in the other two networks. The reason why the performance improvement of the AIS-BN algorithm over the SIS and LW algorithms in the ANDES network is smaller compared to that in the CPCS and PATHFINDER networks is that: (1) The ANDES network used in our tests was apparently not challenging enough for sampling algorithms in general. In the ANDES network, SIS and LW also can perform well in some cases. The minimum *MSE* of SIS and LW in our tested cases is almost the same as that of AIS-BN. (2) The number of samples generated by AIS-BN in this network is significantly smaller than that in the previous two networks and AIS-BN needs more time to learn. Although increasing the number of samples will improve the performance of all three algorithms, it improves the performance of AIS-BN more since the convergence ratio of the AIS-BN algorithm is usually larger than that of SIS and LW (see Figure 10). (3) The parameters that we used in this network were tuned for the CPCS network. (4) The large depth and fewer leaf nodes of the ANDES network pose some difficulties to learning.

5. Discussion

There is a fundamental trade-off in the AIS-BN algorithm between the time spent on learning the importance function and the time spent on sampling. Our current approach, which we believe to be reasonable, is to stop learning at the point when the importance function is good enough. In our experiments we stopped learning after 10 iterations.

There are several ways of improving the initialization of the conditional probability tables at the outset of the AIS-BN algorithm. In the current version of the algorithm, we initialize the ICPT table of every parent N of an evidence node E ($N \in \mathrm{Pa}(E)$, $E \in \mathbf{E}$) to the uniform distribution when $\Pr(E = e) < 1/(2 \cdot n_E)$. This can be improved further. We can extend the initialization to those nodes that are severely affected by the evidence. They can be identified by examining the network structure and local CPTs.

We can view the learning process of the AIS-BN algorithm as a network rebuilding process. The algorithm constructs a new network whose structure is the same as the original network (except that we delete the evidence nodes and corresponding arcs). The constructed network models the joint probability distribution $\rho(\mathbf{X} \backslash \mathbf{E})$ in Equation 8, which approaches the optimal importance function. We use the learned ρ' to approximate this distribution. If ρ' approximates $\Pr(\mathbf{X}|\mathbf{E})$ accurately enough, we can use this new network to solve other approximate tasks, such as the problem of computing the Maximum A-Posterior assignment (MAP) (Pearl, 1988), finding k most likely scenarios (Seroussi & Golmard, 1994), etc. A large advantage of this approach is that we can solve each of these problems as if the network had no evidence nodes.

We know that Markov blanket scoring can improve convergence rates in some sampling algorithms (Shwe & Cooper, 1991). It may also be applied to the AIS-BN algorithm to improve its convergence rate. According to Property 4 (Section 2.1), any technique that can reduce the variance $\sigma^2_{\Pr(\mathbf{e})}$ will reduce the variance of $\widehat{\Pr}(\mathbf{e})$ and correspondingly improve the sampling performance. Since the variance of stratified sampling (Rubinstein, 1981) is never much worse than that of random sampling, and can be much better, it can improve the convergence rate. We expect some other variance reduction methods in statistics, such as: (i) the expected value of a random variable; (ii) antithetic variants correlations (stratified sampling, Latin hypercube sampling, etc.); and (iii) systematic sampling, will also improve the sampling performance.

Current learning algorithm used a simple approach. Some heuristic learning methods, such as adjusting learning rates according to changes of the error (Jacobs, 1988), should also be applicable to our algorithm. There are several tunable parameters in the AIS-BN algorithm. Finding the optimal values of these parameters for any given network is another interesting research topic.

It is worth observing that the plots presented in Figure 8 are fairly flat. In other words, in our tests the convergence of the sampling algorithms did not depend too strongly on the probability of evidence. This seems to contradict the common belief that forward sampling schemes suffer from unlikely evidence. AIS-BN for one shows a fairly flat plot. The convergence of the SIS and LW algorithms seems to decrease slightly with unlikely evidence. It is possible that all three algorithms will perform much worse when the probability of evidence drops below some threshold value, which our tests failed to approach. Until this relationship has been studied carefully, we conjecture that the probability of evidence is not a good measure of difficulty of approximate inference.

Given that the problem of approximating probabilistic inference is NP-hard, there exist networks that will be challenging for any algorithm and we have no doubt that even the AIS-BN algorithm will perform poorly on them. To the day, we have not found such networks. There is one characteristic of networks that may be challenging to the AIS-BN algorithm. In general, when the number of parameters that need to be learned by the AIS-BN algorithm increases, its performance will deteriorate. Nodes with many parents, for example, are challenging to the AIS-BN learning algorithm, as it has to update the ICPT tables under all combinations of the parent nodes. It is possible that conditional probability distributions with causal independence properties, such as Noisy-OR distributions (Pearl, 1988; Henrion, 1989; Diez, 1993; Srinivas, 1993; Heckerman & Breese, 1994), common in very large practical networks, can be treated differently and lead to considerable savings in the learning time.

One direction of testing approximate algorithms, suggested to us by a reviewer, is to use very large networks for which exact solution cannot be computed at all. In this case, one can try to infer from the difference in variance at various stages of the algorithm whether it is converging or not. This is a very interesting idea that is worth exploring, especially when combined with theoretical work on stopping criteria in the line of the work of Dagum and Luby (1997).

6. Conclusion

Computational complexity remains a major problem in application of probability theory and decision theory in knowledge-based systems. It is important to develop schemes that improve the performance of updating algorithms — even though the theoretically demonstrated worst case will remain NP–hard, many practical cases may become tractable.

In this paper, we studied importance sampling in Bayesian networks. After reviewing the most important theoretical results related to importance sampling in finite-dimensional integrals, we proposed a new algorithm for importance sampling in Bayesian networks that we call *adaptive importance sampling* (AIS-BN). While the process of learning the optimal importance function for the AIS-BN algorithm is computationally intractable, based on the theory of importance sampling in finite-dimensional integrals we proposed several heuristics that seem to work very well in practice. We proposed heuristic methods for initializing the importance function that we have shown to accelerate the learning process, a smooth learning method for updating importance function using the structural advantages of Bayesian networks, and a dynamic weighting function for combining samples from different stages of the algorithm. All these methods help the AIS-BN algorithm to get fairly accurate estimates of the posterior probabilities in a limited time. Of the two applied heuristics, adjustment of small probabilities, seems to lead to the largest improvement in performance, although the largest decrease in *MSE* is achieved by a combination of the two heuristics with the AIS-BN algorithm.

The AIS-BN algorithm can lead to a dramatic improvement in the convergence rates in large Bayesian networks with evidence compared to the existing state of the art algorithms. We compared the performance of the AIS-BN algorithm to the performance of likelihood weighting and self-importance sampling on a large practical model, the CPCS network, with evidence as unlikely as 5.54×10^{-42} and typically 7×1.0^{-24}. In our experiments, we observed that the AIS-BN algorithm was always better than likelihood weighting and self-importance sampling and in over 60% of the cases it reached over two orders of magnitude improvement in accuracy. Tests performed on the other two networks, PATHFINDER and ANDES, yielded similar results.

Although there may exist other approximate algorithms that will prove superior to AIS-BN in networks with special structure or distribution, the AIS-BN algorithm is simple and robust for general evidential reasoning problems in large multiply-connected Bayesian networks.

Acknowledgments

We thank anonymous referees for several insightful comments that led to a substantial improvement of the paper. This research was supported by the National Science Foundation under Faculty Early Career Development (CAREER) Program, grant IRI-9624629, and by the Air Force Office of Scientific Research grants F49620-97-1-0225 and F49620-00-1-0112. An earlier version of this paper has received the 2000 School of Information Sciences Robert R. Korfhage Award, University of Pittsburgh. Malcolm Pradhan and Max Henrion of the Institute for Decision Systems Research shared with us the CPCS network with a kind permission from the developers of the INTERNIST system at the University of Pittsburgh. We thank David Heckerman for the PATHFINDER network and Abigail Gerner for the ANDES network used in our tests. All experimental data have been obtained using SMILE, a Bayesian inference engine developed at the Decision Systems Laboratory and available at `http://www2.sis.pitt.edu/~genie`.

References

Cano, J. E., Hernandez, L. D., & Moral, S. (1996). Importance sampling algorithms for the propagation of probabilities in belief networks. *International Journal of Approximate Reasoning, 15*, 77–92.

Chavez, M. R., & Cooper, G. F. (1990). A randomized approximation algorithm for probabilistic inference on Bayesian belief networks. *Networks, 20*(5), 661–685.

Cheng, J., & Druzdzel, M. J. (2000a). Computational investigations of low-discrepancy sequences in simulation algorithms for Bayesian networks. In *Proceedings of the Sixteenth Annual Conference on Uncertainty in Artificial Intelligence (UAI-2000)*, pp. 72–81 San Francisco, CA. Morgan Kaufmann Publishers.

Cheng, J., & Druzdzel, M. J. (2000b). Latin hypercube sampling in Bayesian networks. In *Proceedings of the 13th International Florida Artificial Intelligence Research Symposium Conference (FLAIRS-2000)*, pp. 287–292 Orlando, Florida.

Conati, C., Gertner, A. S., VanLehn, K., & Druzdzel, M. J. (1997). On-line student modeling for coached problem solving using Bayesian networks. In *Proceedings of the Sixth*

International Conference on User Modeling (UM-96), pp. 231–242 Vienna, New York. Springer Verlag.

Cooper, G. F. (1990). The computational complexity of probabilistic inference using Bayesian belief networks. *Artificial Intelligence, 42*(2–3), 393–405.

Cousins, S. B., Chen, W., & Frisse, M. E. (1993). A tutorial introduction to stochastic simulation algorithm for belief networks. In *Artificial Intelligence in Medicine*, chap. 5, pp. 315–340. Elsevier Science Publishers B.V.

Dagum, P., Karp, R., Luby, M., & Ross, S. (1995). An optimal algorithm for Monte Carlo estimation (extended abstract). In *Proceedings of the 36th IEEE Symposium on Foundations of Computer Science*, pp. 142–149 Portland, Oregon.

Dagum, P., & Luby, M. (1993). Approximating probabilistic inference in Bayesian belief networks is NP-hard. *Artificial Intelligence, 60*(1), 141–153.

Dagum, P., & Luby, M. (1997). An optimal approximation algorithm for Bayesian inference. *Artificial Intelligence, 93*, 1–27.

Diez, F. J. (1993). Parameter adjustment in Bayes networks. The generalized noisy OR-gate. In *Proceedings of the Ninth Annual Conference on Uncertainty in Artificial Intelligence (UAI-93)*, pp. 99–105 San Francisco, CA. Morgan Kaufmann Publishers.

Fishman, G. S. (1995). *Monte Carlo: concepts, algorithms, and applications*. Springer-Verlag.

Fung, R., & Chang, K.-C. (1989). Weighing and integrating evidence for stochastic simulation in Bayesian networks. In *Uncertainty in Artificial Intelligence 5*, pp. 209–219 New York, N. Y. Elsevier Science Publishing Company, Inc.

Fung, R., & del Favero, B. (1994). Backward simulation in Bayesian networks. In *Proceedings of the Tenth Annual Conference on Uncertainty in Artificial Intelligence (UAI-94)*, pp. 227–234 San Francisco, CA. Morgan Kaufmann Publishers.

Geman, S., & Geman, D. (1984). Stochastic relaxations, Gibbs distributions and the Bayesian restoration of images. *IEEE Transactions on Pattern Analysis and Machine Intelligence, 6*(6), 721–742.

Gilks, W., Richardson, S., & Spiegelhalter, D. (1996). *Markov chain Monte Carlo in practice*. Chapman and Hall.

Heckerman, D., & Breese, J. S. (1994). A new look at causal independence. In *Proceedings of the Tenth Annual Conference on Uncertainty in Artificial Intelligence (UAI-94)*, pp. 286–292 San Mateo, CA. Morgan Kaufmann Publishers, Inc.

Heckerman, D. E., Horvitz, E. J., & Nathwani, B. N. (1990). Toward normative expert systems: The Pathfinder project. Tech. rep. KSL-90-08, Medical Computer Science Group, Section on Medical Informatics, Stanford University, Stanford, CA.

Henrion, M. (1988). Propagating uncertainty in Bayesian networks by probabilistic logic sampling. In *Uncertainty in Artificial Intellgience 2*, pp. 149–163 New York, N. Y. Elsevier Science Publishing Company, Inc.

Henrion, M. (1989). Some practical issues in constructing belief networks. In Kanal, L., Levitt, T., & Lemmer, J. (Eds.), *Uncertainty in Artificial Intelligence 3*, pp. 161–173. Elsevier Science Publishers B.V., North Holland.

Henrion, M. (1991). Search-based methods to bound diagnostic probabilities in very large belief nets. In *Proceedings of the Seventh Annual Conference on Uncertainty in Artificial Intelligence (UAI-91)*, pp. 142–150 San Mateo, California. Morgan Kaufmann Publishers.

Hernandez, L. D., Moral, S., & Antonio, S. (1998). A Monte Carlo algorithm for probabilistic propagation in belief networks based on importance sampling and stratified simulation techniques. *International Journal of Approximate Reasoning, 18*, 53–91.

Jacobs, R. A. (1988). Increased rates of convergence through learning rate adaptation. *Neural Networks, 1*, 295–307.

Lauritzen, S. L., & Spiegelhalter, D. J. (1988). Local computations with probabilities on graphical structures and their application to expert systems. *Journal of the Royal Statistical Society, Series B (Methodological), 50*(2), 157–224.

MacKay, D. (1998). Intro to Monte Carlo methods. In Jordan, M. I. (Ed.), *Learning in Graphical Models*. The MIT Press, Cambridge, Massachusetts.

Ortiz, L. E., & Kaelbling, L. P. (2000). Adaptive importance sampling for estimation in structured domains. In *Proceedings of the Sixteenth Annual Conference on Uncertainty in Artificial Intelligence (UAI-2000)*, pp. 446–454 San Francisco, CA. Morgan Kaufmann Publishers.

Pearl, J. (1986). Fusion, propagation, and structuring in belief networks. *Artificial Intelligence, 29*(3), 241–288.

Pearl, J. (1987). Evidential reasoning using stochastic simulation of causal models. *Artifical Intelligence, 32*, 245–257.

Pearl, J. (1988). *Probabilistic Reasoning in Intelligent Systems: Networks of Plausible Inference*. Morgan Kaufmann Publishers, Inc., San Mateo, CA.

Pradhan, M., & Dagum, P. (1996). Optimal Monte Carlo inference. In *Proceedings of the Twelfth Annual Conference on Uncertainty in Artificial Intelligence (UAI-96)*, pp. 446–453 San Francisco, CA. Morgan Kaufmann Publishers.

Pradhan, M., Provan, G., Middleton, B., & Henrion, M. (1994). Knowledge engineering for large belief networks. In *Proceedings of the Tenth Annual Conference on Uncertainty in Artificial Intelligence (UAI-94)*, pp. 484–490 San Francisco, CA. Morgan Kaufmann Publishers.

Ritter, H., Martinetz, T., & Schulten, K. (1991). *Neuronale Netze*. Addison-Wesley, München.

Rubinstein, R. Y. (1981). *Simulation and the Monte Carlo Method*. John Wiley & Sons.

Seroussi, B., & Golmard, J. L. (1994). An algorithm directly finding the K most probable configurations in Bayesian networks. *International Journal of Approximate Reasoning, 11*, 205–233.

Shachter, R. D., & Peot, M. A. (1989). Simulation approaches to general probabilistic inference on belief networks. In *Uncertainty in Artificial Intelligence 5*, pp. 221–231 New York, N. Y. Elsevier Science Publishing Company, Inc.

Shwe, M. A., & Cooper, G. F. (1991). An empirical analysis of likelihood-weighting simulation on a large, multiply-connected medical belief network. *Computers and Biomedical Research, 24*(5), 453–475.

Shwe, M., Middleton, B., Heckerman, D., Henrion, M., Horvitz, E., & Lehmann, H. (1991). Probabilistic diagnosis using a reformulation of the INTERNIST–1/QMR knowledge base: I. The probabilistic model and inference algorithms. *Methods of Information in Medicine, 30*(4), 241–255.

Srinivas, S. (1993). A generalization of the noisy-OR model. In *Proceedings of the Ninth Annual Conference on Uncertainty in Artificial Intelligence (UAI–93)*, pp. 208–215 San Francisco, CA. Morgan Kaufmann Publishers.

York, J. (1992). Use of the Gibbs sampler in expert systems. *Artificial Intelligence, 56*, 115–130.

Journal of Artificial Intelligence Research 13 (2000) 189-226   Submitted 6/99; published 10/00

OBDD-based Universal Planning for Synchronized Agents in Non-Deterministic Domains

Rune M. Jensen   RUNEJ@CS.CMU.EDU

Manuela M. Veloso   MMV@CS.CMU.EDU

Computer Science Department, Carnegie Mellon University

Pittsburgh, PA 15213-3891, USA

Abstract

Recently model checking representation and search techniques were shown to be efficiently applicable to planning, in particular to non-deterministic planning. Such planning approaches use Ordered Binary Decision Diagrams (OBDDs) to encode a planning domain as a non-deterministic finite automaton and then apply fast algorithms from model checking to search for a solution. OBDDs can effectively scale and can provide universal plans for complex planning domains. We are particularly interested in addressing the complexities arising in non-deterministic, multi-agent domains. In this article, we present UMOP, a new universal OBDD-based planning framework for non-deterministic, multi-agent domains. We introduce a new planning domain description language, *NADL*, to specify non-deterministic, multi-agent domains. The language contributes the explicit definition of controllable agents and uncontrollable environment agents. We describe the syntax and semantics of *NADL* and show how to build an efficient OBDD-based representation of an *NADL* description. The UMOP planning system uses *NADL* and different OBDD-based universal planning algorithms. It includes the previously developed strong and strong cyclic planning algorithms. In addition, we introduce our new optimistic planning algorithm that relaxes optimality guarantees and generates plausible universal plans in some domains where no strong nor strong cyclic solution exists. We present empirical results applying UMOP to domains ranging from deterministic and single-agent with no environment actions to non-deterministic and multi-agent with complex environment actions. UMOP is shown to be a rich and efficient planning system.

1. Introduction

Classical planning involves the automatic generation of actions to traverse a state space to achieve specific goal states. Various algorithms have been developed to address the state-action representation and the search for actions. Traditionally these algorithms have been classified according to their search space representation as either state-space planners (e.g., PRODIGY, Veloso et al., 1995) or plan-space planners (e.g., UCPOP, Penberthy & Weld, 1992).

A new research trend has been to develop new encodings of planning problems in order to adopt efficient algorithms from other research areas, leading to significant developments in planning algorithms, as surveyed by Weld (1999). This class of planning algorithms includes GRAPHPLAN (Blum & Furst, 1997) that uses a flow-graph encoding to constrain the search and SATPLAN (Kautz & Selman, 1996) that encodes the planning problem as a satisfiability problem and uses fast model satisfaction algorithms to find a solution.

Recently, another new planner MBP (Cimatti et al., 1997) was introduced that encodes a planning domain as a non-deterministic finite automaton (NFA) represented by an Ordered Binary Decision Diagram (OBDD, Bryant, 1986). In contrast to the previous algorithms, MBP effectively extends to non-deterministic domains producing universal plans as robust solutions. Due to the scalability of the underlying model checking representation and search techniques, it can be shown to be a very efficient non-deterministic planner (Cimatti et al., 1998a, 1998b).

One of our main research objectives is to develop planning systems suitable for planning in uncertain, single, or multi-agent environments (Haigh & Veloso, 1998; Veloso et al., 1998; Stone & Veloso, 1998). The universal planning approach, as originally developed (Schoppers, 1987), is appealing for this type of environments. A universal plan is a set of state-action rules that aim at covering the possible multiple situations in the non-deterministic environment. A universal plan is executed by interleaving the selection of an action in the plan and observing the resulting effects in the world. Universal planning resembles the outcome of reinforcement learning (Sutton & Barto, 1998), in that the state-action model captures the uncertainty of the world. Universal planning is a precursor approach,[1] where all planning is done prior to execution, building upon the assumption that a non-deterministic model of the execution environment can be acquired, and leading therefore to a sound and complete planning approach.

However, universal planning has been criticized (e.g., Ginsberg, 1989), due to a potential exponential growth of the universal plan size with the number of propositions defining a domain state. An important contribution of MBP is thus the use of OBDDs to represent universal plans. In the worst case, this representation may also grow exponentially with the number of domain propositions, but because OBDDs are very compact representations of boolean functions, this is often not the case for domains with a regular structure (Cimatti et al., 1998a). Therefore, OBDD-based planning seems to be a promising approach to universal planning.

MBP specifies a planning domain in the action description language $\mathcal{AR}$ (Giunchiglia et al., 1997) and translates it to a corresponding NFA, hence limited to planning problems with finite state spaces. The transition relation of the automaton is encoded as an OBDD that allows for the use of efficient breadth-first search techniques developed for model checking (McMillan, 1993). MBP includes two algorithms for universal planning. The *strong planning* algorithm tries to generate a plan that is guaranteed to achieve the goal for all of the possible outcomes of the non-deterministic actions. If no such strong solution exists, the algorithm fails. The *strong cyclic planning* algorithm returns a strong solution, if one exists, or otherwise tries to generate a plan that may contain loops but is guaranteed to achieve the goal, given that all cyclic executions eventually terminate. If no such strong cyclic solution exists, the strong cyclic planning algorithm fails.

In this article we present our OBDD-based planning system, UMOP (Universal Multi-agent OBDD-based Planner), that uses a new OBDD-based encoding, generates universal plans in multi-agent non-deterministic domains, and includes a new "optimistic" planning algorithm.

---

1. The term *precursor* originates in Dean et al. (1995) in contrast to *recurrent* approaches that replan to recover from execution failures.

Our overall approach for designing an OBDD-based planner is similar to the approach developed for MBP. Our main contribution is an efficient encoding of a new front end domain description language, *NADL* (Non-deterministic Agent Domain Language). *NADL* has more resemblance with previous planning languages than the action description language $\mathcal{AR}$ currently used by MBP. It has powerful action descriptions that can perform arithmetic operations on numerical domain variables. Domains comprised of synchronized agents can be modelled by introducing concurrent actions based on a multi-agent decomposition of the domain.

In addition, *NADL* introduces a separate and explicit environment model defined as a set of *uncontrollable* agents, i.e., agents whose actions cannot be a part of the generated plan. *NADL* has been carefully designed to allow for efficient OBDD-encoding. Thus, UMOP contributes a partitioned transition relation representation of the NFA that is known from model checking to scale up well (Burch et al., 1991; Ranjan et al., 1995). Our empirical experiments suggest that this is also the case for UMOP.

UMOP includes the previously developed algorithms for OBDD-based universal planning. In addition, we introduce a new "optimistic" planning algorithm that relaxes optimality guarantees and generates plausible universal plans in domains where no strong nor strong cyclic solution exists.

The article is organized as follows. Section 2 discusses previous approaches to planning in non-deterministic domains. Section 3 gives a brief overview of OBDDs and NFA encodings. It may be skipped by readers already familiar with the subject. Section 4 introduces *NADL*, shows how to encode a planning problem, and formally describes the syntax and semantics of this description language in terms of an NFA. We also discuss the properties of the language based on an example and argue for our design choices. Section 5 presents the OBDD representation of *NADL* domain descriptions. Section 6 describes the different algorithms that have been used for OBDD-based planning and introduces our optimistic planning algorithm. Section 7 presents empirical results in several planning domains, ranging from single-agent and deterministic ones to multi-agent and non-deterministic ones. We experiment with previously used domains and introduce two new ones, namely a power plant and a soccer domain, as non-deterministic, multi-agent planning problems. Finally, Section 8 draws conclusions and discusses directions for future work.

2. Related Work

Recurrent approaches performing planning interleaved or in parallel with execution have been widely used in non-deterministic robotic domains (e.g., Georgeff & Lansky, 1987; Gat, 1992; Wilkins et al., 1994; Haigh & Veloso, 1998). A group of planners suitable for recurrent planning is action selectors based on heuristic search (Koenig & Simmons, 1995; Bonet et al., 1997). The min-max LRTA* algorithm (Koenig & Simmons, 1995; Smirnov et al., 1996) can generate suboptimal plans in non-deterministic domains through a search and execution iteration. The search is based on a heuristic goal distance function that must be provided for a specific problem. The ASP algorithm (Bonet et al., 1997) uses a similar approach and further defines a heuristic function for STRIPS-like (Fikes & Nilsson, 1971) action representations. In contrast to min-max LRTA*, ASP does not assume a non-deterministic environment, but is robust to non-determinism caused by action perturbations (i.e., that another action than the planned action is chosen with some probability).

In general, recurrent approaches are incomplete because acting on an incomplete plan can make the goal unachievable. Precursor approaches perform all decision making prior to execution and thus may be able to generate complete plans by taking all possible effects of actions into account. However, they rely on a complete model of the world's uncertainty.

The precursor approaches include conditional (Etzioni et al., 1992; Peot & Smith, 1992; Blythe & Veloso, 1997), probabilistic (Drummond & Bresina, 1990; Dean et al., 1995; Blythe, 1998) and universal planning (Schoppers, 1987; Cimatti et al., 1998a, 1998b; Kabanza et al., 1997). For example, the CNLP partial order, conditional planner handles non-determinism by constructing a conditional plan that accounts for each possible situation or contingency that could arise (Peot & Smith, 1992). At execution time it is determined which part of the plan to execute by performing sensing actions that are included in the plan to test for the appropriate conditions.

Probabilistic planners try to maximize the probability of goal satisfaction, given conditional actions with probabilistic effects. Drummond and Bresina (1990) represent plans as a set of Situated Control Rules (SCRs) (Drummond, 1989) mapping situations to actions. The planning algorithm begins by adding SCRs corresponding to the most probable execution path that achieves the goal. It then continues adding SCRs for less probable paths and may end with a complete plan taking all possible paths into account.

Universal plans differ from conditional and probabilistic plans by specifying appropriate actions for every possible state in the domain. Like conditional and probabilistic plans, universal plans require the world to be accessible in order to execute the plan.

Universal planning was introduced by Schoppers (1987) who used decision trees to represent plans. Recent approaches include Kabanza et al. (1997) and Cimatti et al. (1998a, 1998b). Kabanza et al. (1997) represents universal plans also as a set of Situated Control Rules. Their algorithm incrementally adds SCRs to a final plan in a way similar to Drummond and Bresina (1990). The goal is a formula in temporal logic that must hold on any valid sequence of actions.

Reinforcement Learning (RL) (Sutton & Barto, 1998) can also be regarded as universal planning. In RL the goal is represented by a reward function in a Markov Decision Process (MDP) model of the domain. In the precursor version of RL, the MDP is assumed to be known and a control policy maximizing the expected reward is found prior to execution. The policy can either be represented explicitly in a table or implicitly by a function (e.g., a neural network). Because RL is a probabilistic approach, its domain representation is more complex than the domain representation used by a non-deterministic planner. Thus, we may expect non-deterministic planners to be able to handle domains with a larger state space than RL. But RL may produce policies with a higher quality than a universal plan generated by a non-probabilistic, non-deterministic planner. Moreover, in the recurrent version, RL learns the world model during execution and thus does not require a complete world model prior to execution. Though, in theory it needs infinite execution examples to converge to the optimal universal plan.

All previous approaches to universal planning, except Cimatti et al. (1998a, 1998b), use an explicit representation of the universal plan (e.g., SCRs). Thus, in the general case, an exponential size of the plan in the number of propositions defining a domain state must be expected, as argued by Ginsberg (1989).

The compact and implicit representation of universal plans obtained with OBDDS does not necessarily grow exponentially for regularly structured domains as shown by Cimatti et al. (1998a). Further, the OBDD-based representation of the NFA of a non-deterministic domain enables the application of efficient search algorithms from model checking capable of handling very large state spaces.

3. Introduction to OBDDs

An Ordered Binary Decision Diagram (Bryant, 1986) is a canonical representation of a boolean function with n linear ordered arguments $x_1, x_2, ..., x_n$.

An OBDD is a rooted, directed acyclic graph with one or two terminal nodes of out-degree zero labeled 1 or 0, and a set of variable nodes u of out-degree two. The two outgoing edges are given by the functions $high(u)$ and $low(u)$. Each variable node is associated with a propositional variable in the boolean function the OBDD represents. The graph is ordered in the sense that all paths in the graph respect the ordering of the variables.

An OBDD representing the function $f(x_1, x_2) = x_1 \wedge x_2$ is shown in Figure 1. Given an assignment of the arguments x_1 and x_2, the value of f is determined by a path starting at the root node and iteratively following the high edge, if the associated variable is true, and the low edge, if the associated variable is false. The value of f is *True* or *False* if the label of the reached terminal node is 1 or 0, respectively.

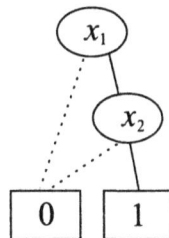

Figure 1: An OBDD representing the function $f(x_1, x_2) = x_1 \wedge x_2$. High and low edges are drawn as solid and dotted lines, respectively.

An OBBD graph is reduced so that no two distinct nodes u and v have the same variable name and low and high successors (Figure 2a), and no variable node u has identical low and high successors (Figure 2b).

The OBDD representation has two major advantages: First, it is an efficient representation of boolean functions because the number of nodes often is much smaller than the number of truth assignments of the variables. The number of nodes can grow exponential with the number of variables, but most commonly encountered functions have a reasonable representation. Second, any operation on two OBDDs, corresponding to a boolean operation on the functions they represent, has a low complexity bounded by the product of their node counts (Bryant, 1986).

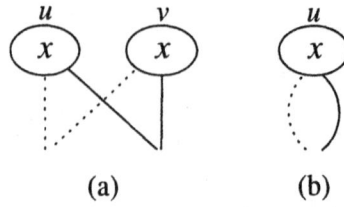

Figure 2: Reductions of OBDDs. (a) nodes associated to the same variable with equal low and high successors will be converted to a single node. (b) nodes causing redundant tests on a variable are eliminated.

A disadvantage of OBDDs is that the size of an OBDD representing some function is very dependent on the ordering of the variables. To find an optimal variable ordering is a co-NP-complete problem in itself, but as illustrated in Figure 3 a good heuristic for choosing an ordering is to locate related variables near each other (Clarke et al., 1999).

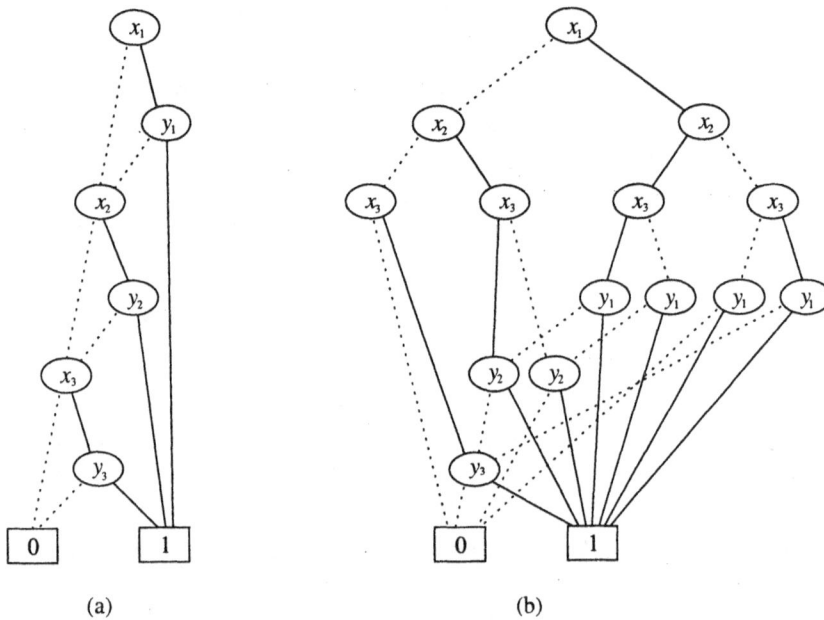

Figure 3: This Figure shows the effect of variable ordering for the expression $(x_1 \wedge y_1) \vee (x_2 \wedge y_2) \vee (x_3 \wedge y_3)$. The OBDD in (a) only grows linearly with the number of variables in the expression, while the OBDD in (b) has an exponential growth. The example illustrates that placing related variables near to each other in the ordering often is a good heuristic.

OBDDs have been successfully applied to model checking. In model checking the behavior of a system is modelled by a finite state automaton with the transition relation represented as an OBDD. Desirable properties are checked by using OBDD manipulations to analyze the state space of the system (Clarke et al., 1986; McMillan, 1993).

Interestingly, a similar approach can be used for solving non-deterministic planning problems. As an example, consider the NFA representation of a non-deterministic planning domain shown in Figure 4a. In this domain there are four states given by the four possible value assignments of the two boolean state variables x_1 and x_2. Inputs to the NFA denote actions in the domain and are defined by the boolean variable a. The OBDD representing the transition relation $T(a, x_1, x_2, x_1', x_2')$ of the NFA is shown in Figure 4b. The definition of T is straightforward: for some assignment of its arguments, T is true iff action a causes a transition from the current state given by the value of x_1 and x_2 to the next state given by the value of x_1' and x_2'.[2] Note that the OBDD representing T for the example turns out not to depend on x_2'.

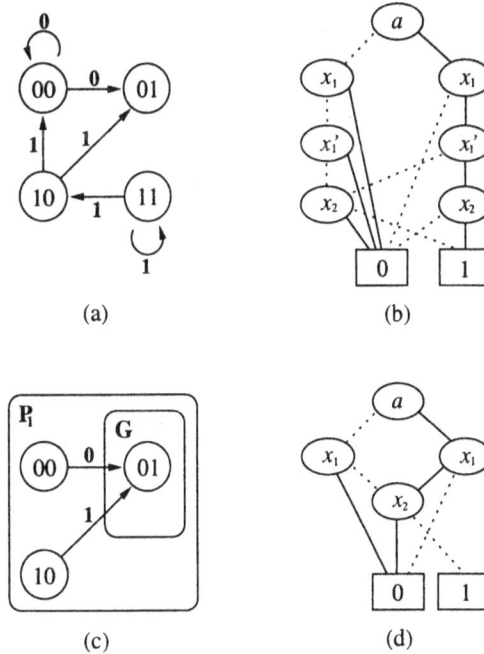

(a)

(b)

(c)

(d)

Figure 4: A planning domain represented as an NFA is shown in (a). States are defined by boolean state variables x_1 and x_2, and the action input to the NFA is given by the boolean variable a. The symbolic representation of the transition relation of the NFA is shown in (b). In (c), P_1 is the set of state action pairs for which, execution of the action can lead to the goal. The symbolic representation of P_1 is shown in (d). It is obtained from the transition relation by restricting the next state to 01.

Assume that the state 01 is a goal state G. A key operation, when generating a universal plan for achieving G, is to find all the state action pairs (s, a) such that G can be reached from s by executing a. This set is labeled P_1 in Figure 4c. To find P_1 from T we constrain x_1' to *False* and x_2' to *True* in T. This reduces T to the OBDD shown in Figure 4d. The resulting OBDD represents P_1 with the states described in the current state variables x_1

---

2. Another notation like x_t and x_{t+1} could have been used for current and next state variables. We have chosen the quote notation because it is the common notation in model checking.

and x_2. Logically we performed the operation $\exists x_1', x_2' . \neg x_1' \wedge x_2' \wedge T$ to obtain the OBDD representing P_1.

4. The *NADL* Description Language

In this section, we first discuss the properties of *NADL* based on an informal definition of the language and a domain encoding example. We then describe the formal syntax and semantics of *NADL*.

An *NADL* domain description consists of: a definition of *state variables*, a description of *system* and *environment agents*, and a specification of an *initial* and *goal condition*.

The set of state variable assignments defines the state space of the domain. An agent's description is a set of *actions*. The agents change the state of the world by performing actions that are assumed to be executed synchronously and to have a fixed and equal duration. At each step, all of the agents perform exactly one action, and the resulting action tuple is a *joint action*. The system agents model the behavior of the agents controllable by the planner, while the environment agents model the uncontrollable world. A valid domain description requires that the system and environment agents constrain a disjoint set of variables.

An action has three parts: a set of *state variables*, a *precondition* formula, and an *effect* formula. Intuitively the action takes responsibility of constraining the values of the state variables in the next state. It further has exclusive access to these variables during execution. In order for the action to be applicable, the precondition formula must be satisfied in the current state. The effect of the action is defined by the effect formula that must be satisfied in the next state. To allow conditional effects, the effect expression can refer to both current and next state variables, where the next state variables need to be a part of the set of constrained variables of the action. All next state variables not constrained by any action in a joint action maintain their value.

The initial and goal condition are formulas that must be satisfied in the initial state and the final state, respectively.

There are two causes for non-determinism in *NADL* domains: (1) actions not restricting all their constrained variables to a specific value in the next state, and (2) the non-deterministic selection of environment actions.

A simple example of an *NADL* domain description is shown in Figure 5. The domain describes a planning problem for Schoppers' (1987) robot-baby domain. The domain has two state variables: a numerical one, position *pos* with range $\{0, 1, 2, 3\}$ and a propositional one, *robot_works*. The robot is the only system agent and it has two actions *Lift-Block* and *Lower-Block*. The *Lift-Block* (and *Lower-Block*) action has a conditional effect described by an if-then-else operator ($\rightarrow$): if *robot_works* is true then *Lift-Block* increases the block position by one else the block position is unchanged. The baby is the only environment agent and it has one action *Hit-Robot*. Because each agent must perform exactly one action at each step, there are two joint actions (*Lift-Block,Hit-Robot*) and (*Lower-Block,Hit-Robot*). Initially *robot_works* is assumed to be true, the robot is assumed to hold a block at Position 0, and its task is to lift it up to Position 3.

The variable *robot_works* can be made false by the baby. The baby's action *Hit-Robot* is non-deterministic, as it only constrains *robot_works* by the effect expression $\neg robot\_works \Rightarrow$

196

```
variables
  nat(4) pos
  bool robot_works
system
  agt: Robot
    Lift-Block
      con: pos
      pre: pos < 3
      eff: robot_works → pos' = pos + 1, pos' = pos
    Lower-Block
      con: pos
      pre: pos > 0
      eff: robot_works → pos' = pos - 1, pos' = pos
environment
  agt: Baby
    Hit-Robot
      con: robot_works
      pre: true
      eff: ¬robot_works ⇒ ¬robot_works'
initially
  pos = 0 ∧ robot_works
goal
  pos = 3
```

Figure 5: An *NADL* domain description.

¬*robot_works'*. Thus, when *robot_works* is true in the current state, the effect expression of *Hit-Robot* does not apply, and *robot_works* can either be true or false in the next state. On the other hand, if *robot_works* is false in the current state, *Hit-Robot* keeps it false in the next state. The *Hit-Robot* action models an aspect of the environment not controlled by the robot agent, in this case a baby, by its effects on *robot_works*. In the example above, *robot_works* stays false when it has become false, reflecting that the robot cannot spontaneously be fixed by a hit of the baby, or any other action in the environment.

An NFA representing the domain is shown in Figure 6. The calculation of the next state value of *pos* in the *Lift-Block* action shows that numerical variables can be updated by an arithmetic expression on the current state variables. The update expression of *pos* and the use of the if-then-else operator further demonstrate the advantage of using explicit references to current state and next state variables in effect expressions. *NADL* does not restrict the representation by enforcing a structure separating current state and next state expressions. The if-then-else operator has been added to support complex conditional effects that often are efficiently and naturally represented as a set of nested if-then-else operators.

The explicit representation of constrained state variables enables any non-deterministic or deterministic effect of an action to be represented, as the constrained variables can be assigned to any value in the next state that satisfies the effect formula. It further turns out to have a clear intuitive meaning, as the action takes the "responsibility" of specifying the values of the constrained variables in the next state.

robot_works

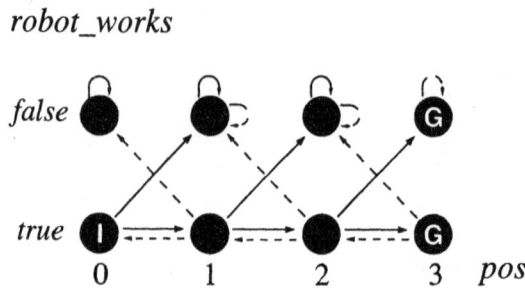

Figure 6: The NFA of the robot-baby domain (see Figure 5). There is one propositional and one numerical state variable: *robot_works* and *pos*. The (*Lift-Block,Hit-Robot*) and (*Lower-Block,Hit-Robot*) joint actions are drawn with solid and dashed arrows, respectively. States marked with "I" and "G" are initial and goal states.

Compared to the action description language $\mathcal{A}$ (Gelfond & Liftschitz, 1993) and $\mathcal{AR}$ that are the only prior languages used for OBDD-based planning (Di Manzo et al., 1998; Cimatti et al., 1998a, 1998b, 1997), *NADL* introduces an explicit environment model, a multi-agent decomposition, and numerical state variables. It can further be shown that *NADL* can be used to model any domain that can be modelled by $\mathcal{AR}$ (see Appendix A).

The concurrent actions in *NADL* are assumed to be synchronously executed and to have fixed and equal duration. A general representation allowing partially overlapping actions and actions with different durations has been avoided, as it requires more complex temporal planning (see e.g., O-PLAN or PARCPLAN, Currie & Tate, 1991; Lever & Richards, 1994). Our joint action representation has more resemblance with $\mathcal{A_C}$ (Baral & Gelfond, 1997) and $\mathcal{C}$ (Giunchiglia & Lifschitz, 1998), where sets of actions are performed at each time step. In contrast to these approaches, though, we model multi-agent domains.

An important issue to address when introducing concurrent actions is synergetic effects between simultaneously executing actions (Lingard & Richards, 1998). A common example of destructive synergetic effects is when two or more actions require exclusive use of a single resource or when two actions have inconsistent effects like $pos' = 3$ and $pos' = 2$.

In *NADL* actions cannot be performed concurrently in the following two conditions: 1) they have inconsistent effects, or 2) they constrain an overlapping set of state variables. The first condition is due to the fact that state knowledge is expressed in a monotonic logic that cannot represent inconsistent knowledge. The second condition addresses the problem of sharing resources. Consider for example two agents trying to drink the same glass of water. If only the first condition defined interfering actions, both agents could simultaneously empty the glass, as the effect *glass_empty* of the two actions would be consistent. With the second condition added, these actions are interfering and cannot be performed concurrently.

The current version of *NADL* only avoids destructive synergetic effects. It does not include ways of representing constructive synergetic effects between simultaneous acting agents. A constructive synergetic effect is illustrated in Baral and Gelfond (1997), where an agent spills soup from a bowl when trying to lift it up with one hand, but not when lifting it up with both hands. In $\mathcal{C}$ and $\mathcal{A_C}$ this kind of synergetic effects can be represented by explicitly stating the effect of a compound action. A similar approach could be used in *NADL* but is currently not supported.

4.1 Syntax

Formally, an *NADL* description is a 7-tuple $D = (SV, S, E, Act, d, I, G)$, where:

- $SV = PVar \cup NVar$ is a finite set of state variables comprised of a finite set of propositional variables, $PVar$, and a finite set of numerical variables, $NVar$.

- S is a finite, nonempty set of system agents.

- E is a finite set of environment agents.

- Act is a set of action descriptions (c, p, e) where c is the set of state variables constrained by the action, p is a precondition state formula in the set *SForm* and e is an effect formula in the set *Form*. Thus $(c, p, e) \in Act \subset 2^{SV} \times SForm \times Form$. The sets *SForm* and *Form* are defined below.

- $d : Agt \to 2^{Act}$ is a function mapping agents ($Agt = S \cup E$) to their actions. Because an action belongs to exactly one agent, d must satisfy the following conditions:

$$\bigcup_{\alpha \in Agt} d(\alpha) = Act$$

$$\forall \alpha_1, \alpha_2 \in Agt \,.\, \alpha_1 \neq \alpha_2 \Rightarrow d(\alpha_1) \cap d(\alpha_2) = \emptyset$$

- $I \in SForm$ is the initial condition.

- $G \in SForm$ is the goal condition.

For a valid domain description, we require that actions of system agents are independent of actions of environment agents:

$$\bigcup_{\substack{e \in E \\ a \in d(e)}} c(a) \ \cap \ \bigcup_{\substack{s \in S \\ a \in d(s)}} c(a) = \emptyset,$$

where $c(a)$ is the set of constrained variables of action a.

The set of formulas *Form* is constructed from the following alphabet of symbols:

- A finite set of current state v and next state v' variables, where $v, v' \in SV$.

- The natural numbers $\mathbf{N}$.

- The arithmetic operators $+, -, /, *$ and *mod*.

- The relation operators $>, <, \leq, \geq, =$ and $\neq$.

- The boolean operators $\neg, \vee, \wedge, \Rightarrow, \Leftrightarrow$ and $\to$.

- The special symbols *true*, *false*, parentheses and comma.

The set of arithmetic expressions is constructed from the following rules:

1. Every numerical state variable $v \in NVar$ is an arithmetic expression.

2. A natural number is an arithmetic expression.

3. If e_1 and e_2 are arithmetic expressions and $\oplus$ is an arithmetic operator, then $e_1 \oplus e_2$ is an arithmetic expression.

Finally, the set of formulas *Form* is generated by the rules:

1. *true* and *false* are formulas.

2. Propositional state variables $v \in PVar$ are formulas.

3. If e_1 and e_2 are arithmetic expressions and $\mathcal{R}$ is a relation operator, then $e_1 \ \mathcal{R} \ e_2$ is a formula.

4. If f_1, f_2 and f_3 are formulas, so are $(\neg f_1)$, $(f_1 \vee f_2)$, $(f_1 \wedge f_2)$, $(f_1 \Rightarrow f_2)$, $(f_1 \Leftrightarrow f_2)$ and $(f_1 \rightarrow f_2, f_3)$.

Parentheses have their usual meaning and operators have their usual priority and associativity with the if-then-else operator "$\rightarrow$" given lowest priority.

SForm $\subset$ *Form* is a subset of the formulas only referring to current state variables. These formulas are called *state formulas*.

4.2 Semantics

All of the symbols in the alphabet of formulas have their usual meaning with the if-then-else operator $f_1 \rightarrow f_2, f_3$ being an abbreviation for $(f_1 \wedge f_2) \vee (\neg f_1 \wedge f_3)$. Each numerical state variable $v \in NVar$ has a finite range $rng(v) = \{0, 1, \cdots, t_v\}$, where $t_v > 0$.

The formal semantics of a domain description $D = (SV, S, E, Act, d, I, G)$ is given in terms of an NFA M:

Definition 1 (NFA) *A Non-deterministic Finite Automaton is a 3-tuple, $M = (Q, \Sigma, \delta)$, where Q is a set of states, Σ is a set of input values, and $\delta : Q \times \Sigma \rightarrow 2^Q$ is a next state function.*

In the following construction of M, we express the next state function as a transition relation. Let $\mathcal{B}$ denote the set of boolean values $\{True, False\}$. Further, let the *characteristic function* $A: \mathcal{B} \rightarrow \mathcal{B}$ associated to a set $A \subseteq \mathcal{B}$ be defined by $A(x) = (x \in A)$.[3] Given an NFA M we define its *transition relation* $T \subseteq Q \times \Sigma \times Q$ as a set of triples with characteristic function $T(s, i, s') = (s' \in \delta(s, i))$.

The set of states Q of M equals the set of all possible variable assignments $Q = (PVar \rightarrow \mathcal{B}) \times (Nvar \rightarrow \mathbf{N})$. The input Σ of M is the set of joint actions of system agents represented

---

3. Note: the characteristic function has the same name as the set.

as sets. That is, $\{a_1, a_2, \cdots, a_{|S|}\} \in \Sigma$ if and only if $(a_1, a_2, \cdots, a_{|S|}) \in \prod_{\alpha \in S} d(\alpha)$, where $|S|$ denotes the number of elements in S.

We define the transition relation $T : Q \times \Sigma \times Q \to \mathcal{B}$ of M by:

$$T(s, i, s') = \exists j \in J \,.\, i \subseteq j \wedge t(s, j, s'),$$

where $t : Q \times J \times Q \to \mathcal{B}$ is the transition relation for joint actions J of both system and environment agents. The existential quantification makes the actions of environment agents uncontrollable, since $T(s, i, s')$ is true, if there exists some joint action of environment agents i_e such that the combined joint action $j = i \cup i_e$ makes $t(s, j, s')$ true.

The transition relation t is a conjunction of three relations A, F and I, $t(s, j, s') = A(s, j, s') \wedge F(s, j, s') \wedge I(j)$. Given an action $a = (c, p, e)$, a current state s and next state s', let $P_a(s)$ and $E_a(s, s')$ denote the value of the precondition formula p and effect formula e of a, respectively.

$A : Q \times J \times Q \to \mathcal{B}$ is then defined by:

$$A(s, j, s') = \bigwedge_{a \in j} \Big(P_a(s) \wedge E_a(s, s') \Big).$$

A defines the constraints on the current state and next state of joint actions. A further ensures that actions with inconsistent effects cannot be performed concurrently, as A reduces to false if any pair of actions in a joint action has inconsistent effects. Thus, A also states the first condition (see Section 4) for avoiding interference between concurrent actions.

$F : Q \times J \times Q \to \mathcal{B}$ is a frame relation ensuring that unconstrained variables maintain their value. Let $c(a)$ denote the set of constrained variables of action a. We then have:

$$F(s, j, s') = \bigwedge_{v \in SV \setminus C} (v = v'),$$

where $C = \bigcup_{a \in j} c(a)$.

$I : J \to \mathcal{B}$ ensures that concurrent actions constrain a non overlapping set of variables and thus states the second condition for avoiding interference between concurrent actions:

$$I(j) = \bigwedge_{(a_1, a_2) \in j^2} \Big(c(a_1) \cap c(a_2) = \emptyset \Big),$$

where j^2 denotes the set $\{(a_1, a_2) \mid (a_1, a_2) \in j \times j \wedge a_1 \neq a_2\}$.

5. OBDD Representation of NADL Descriptions

To build an OBDD $\tilde{T}$ representing the transition relation $T(s, i, s')$ of the NFA of a domain description $D = (SV, S, E, Act, d, I, G)$, we must define a set of boolean variables to represent the current state s, the joint action input i, and the next state s'. As in Section 4.2 we first build a transition relation with the joint actions of both system and environment agents as input and then reduce it to a transition relation with only joint actions of system agents as input.

Joint action inputs are represented in the following way: assume action a is identified by a number p and can be performed by agent α. a is then defined to be the action of agent α, if the number expressed in binary by a set of boolean variables A_α, used to represent the actions of α, is equal to p. Propositional state variables are represented by a single boolean variable, while numerical state variables are represented in binary by a set of boolean variables.

Let $A_{e_1}, \ldots, A_{e_{|E|}}$ and $A_{s_1}, \ldots, A_{s_{|S|}}$ denote sets of boolean variables used to represent the joint action of environment and system agents. Further, let $x_{v_j}^k$ and $x'^k_{v_j}$ denote the kth boolean variable used to represent state variable $v_j \in SV$ in the current and next state. The boolean variables are ordered with the input variables first, followed by an interleaving of the boolean variables of current state and next state variables:

$$A_{e_1} \prec \cdots \prec A_{e_{|E|}} \prec A_{s_1} \prec \cdots \prec A_{s_{|S|}}$$
$$\prec x_{v_1}^1 \prec x'^1_{v_1} \prec \cdots \prec x_{v_1}^{m_1} \prec x'^{m_1}_{v_1}$$
$$\cdots$$
$$\prec x_{v_n}^1 \prec x'^1_{v_n} \prec \cdots \prec x_{v_n}^{m_n} \prec x'^{m_n}_{v_n},$$

where m_i is the number of boolean variables used to represent state variable v_i and n is equal to $|SV|$. The construction of $\tilde{T}$ is quite similar to the construction of T in Section 4.2. An OBDD representing a logical expression is built in the standard way (Bryant, 1986). Arithmetic expressions are represented as lists of OBDDs defining the corresponding binary number. They collapse to single OBDDs when related by arithmetic relations.

To build an OBDD $\tilde{A}$ defining the constraints of the joint actions, we need to refer to the values of the boolean variables representing the actions. Let $i(\alpha)$ be the function that maps an agent α to the value of the boolean variables representing its action and let $b(a)$ be the identifier value of action a. Further let $\tilde{P}(a)$ and $\tilde{E}(a)$ denote OBDD representations of the precondition and effect formula of an action a. $\tilde{A}$ is then given by:

$$\tilde{A} = \bigwedge_{\substack{\alpha \in Agt \\ a \in d(\alpha)}} \left(i(\alpha) = b(a) \Rightarrow \tilde{P}(a) \wedge \tilde{E}(a) \right).$$

Note that logical operators now denote the corresponding OBDD operators.

An OBDD representing the frame relation $\tilde{F}$ changes in a similar way:

$$\tilde{F} = \bigwedge_{v \in SV} \left(\left(\bigwedge_{\substack{\alpha \in Agt \\ a \in d(\alpha)}} (i(\alpha) = b(a) \Rightarrow v \notin c(a)) \right) \Rightarrow s'_v = s_v \right),$$

where $c(a)$ is the set of constrained variables of action a and $s_v = s'_v$ expresses that all current and next state boolean variables representing v are pairwise equal. The expression $v \notin c(a)$ evaluates to *True* or *False* and is represented by the OBDD for *True* or *False*. The action interference constraint $\tilde{I}$ is given by:

$$\tilde{I} = \bigwedge_{\substack{(\alpha_1, \alpha_2) \in S^2 \\ (a_1, a_2) \in c(\alpha_1, \alpha_2)}} \left(i(\alpha_1) = b(a_1) \Rightarrow i(\alpha_2) \neq b(a_2) \right) \wedge$$

$$\bigwedge_{\substack{(\alpha_1, \alpha_2) \in E^2 \\ (a_1, a_2) \in c(\alpha_1, \alpha_2)}} \Big(i(\alpha_1) = b(a_1) \Rightarrow i(\alpha_2) \neq b(a_2)\Big),$$

where $c(\alpha_1, \alpha_2) = \{(a_1, a_2) \mid (a_1, a_2) \in d(\alpha_1) \times d(\alpha_2) \wedge c(a_1) \cap c(a_2) \neq \emptyset\}$.

Finally the OBDD representing the transition relation $\tilde{T}$ is the conjunction of $\tilde{A}$, $\tilde{F}$ and $\tilde{I}$ with action variables of the environment agents existentially quantified:

$$\tilde{T} = \exists A_{e_1}, \cdots, A_{e_{|E|}} . \tilde{A} \wedge \tilde{F} \wedge \tilde{I}.$$

5.1 Partitioning the Transition Relation

The algorithms we use for generating universal plans all consist of a backward search from the states satisfying the goal condition to the states satisfying the initial condition. Empirical studies in model checking have shown that the most complex operation for this kind of algorithms normally is to find the *preimage* of a set of visited states V (Ranjan et al., 1995).

Definition 2 (Preimage) *Given an NFA $M = (Q, \Sigma, \delta)$ and a set of states $V \subseteq Q$, the preimage of V is the set of states $\{s \mid s \in Q \wedge \exists i \in \Sigma, s' \in \delta(s, i) . s' \in V\}$.*

A preimage is said to exist, if it is nonempty. Note that states already belonging to V can also be a part of the preimage of V. Assume that the set of visited states are represented by an OBDD expression $\tilde{V}$ on next state variables and that, for iteration purposes, we want to generate the preimage $\tilde{P}$ also expressed in next state variables. For a monolithic transition relation $\tilde{T}$ we then calculate:

$$\begin{aligned} \tilde{U} &= (\exists \vec{x}' . \tilde{T} \wedge \tilde{V})[\vec{x}/\vec{x}'] \\ \tilde{P} &= \exists \vec{i} . \tilde{U} \end{aligned}$$

where $\vec{i}$, $\vec{x}$ and $\vec{x}'$ denote input, current state and next state variables, and $[\vec{x}/\vec{x}']$ denotes the substitution of current state variables with next state variables. The set expressed by $\tilde{U}$ consists of state input pairs (s, i), for which the state s belongs to the preimage of V and the input i may cause a transition from s to a state in V. The input of an NFA representing a planning domain is a set of actions. Thus, for a planning domain the elements in $\tilde{U}$ are state-action pairs. The generated universal plans of the universal planning algorithms presented in the next section are sets of these state-action pairs. We refer to the state-action pairs as *state-action rules*, because they associate states to actions that can be performed in these states.

The OBDD representing the transition relation $\tilde{T}$ and the set of visited states $\tilde{V}$ tends to be large, and a more efficient computation can be obtained by performing the existential quantification of next state variables early in the calculation (Burch et al., 1991; Ranjan et al., 1995). To do this, the transition relation has to be split into a conjunction of partitions $\tilde{T} = \tilde{T}_1 \wedge \cdots \wedge \tilde{T}_n$ allowing the modified calculation:

$$\begin{aligned} \tilde{U} &= (\exists \vec{x}'_n . \tilde{T}_n \wedge \cdots (\exists \vec{x}'_2 . \tilde{T}_2 \wedge (\exists \vec{x}'_1 . \tilde{T}_1 \wedge \tilde{V})) \cdots)[\vec{x}/\vec{x}'] \\ \tilde{P} &= \exists \vec{i} . \tilde{U} \end{aligned}$$

That is, $\tilde{T}_1$ can refer to all variables, $\tilde{T}_2$ can refer to all variables except $\vec{x}_1'$, $\tilde{T}_3$ can refer to all variables except $\vec{x}_1'$ and $\vec{x}_2'$ and so on.

As shown by Ranjan et al. (1995) the computation time used to calculate the preimage is a convex function of the number of partitions. The reason for this is that, for some number of partitions, a further subdivision of the partitions will not reduce the total complexity, because the complexity introduced by the larger number of OBDD operations is higher than the reduction of the complexity of each OBDD operation.

The representation of the logical expression for each relation A, F and I has been carefully chosen such that it consists of a conjunction of subexpressions that only refer to a small subset of next state variables. This representation allows us to sort out the subexpressions in conjunctive partitions with near optimal sizes that satisfy the above requirements.

6. OBDD-based Universal Planning Algorithms

We first describe two prior algorithms for OBDD-based universal planning and discuss which kind of domains they are suitable for. We then present a new algorithm called *optimistic planning* that is suitable for some domains not covered by the prior algorithms.

The three universal planning algorithms discussed are all based on an iteration of preimage calculations. The iteration corresponds to a parallel backward breadth-first search starting at the goal states and ending when all initial states are included in the set of visited states (see Figure 7). The main difference between the algorithms is the way the preimage is defined.

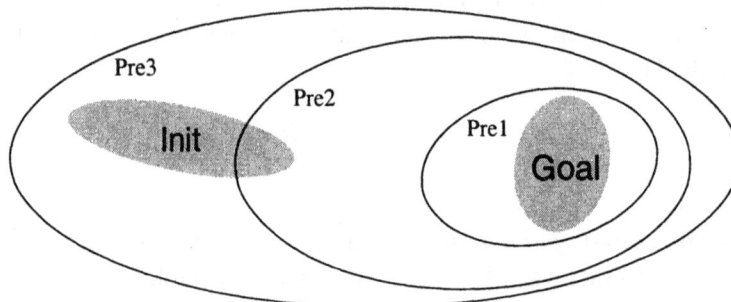

Figure 7: An illustration of the parallel backward breadth-first search used by OBDD-based universal planning algorithms, computing preimages Pre1, Pre2 and Pre3.

6.1 Strong and Weak Preimages

Cimatti et al. (1998a) introduces two different kinds of preimages called *strong* and *weak* preimages. A strong preimage is defined by:

Definition 3 (Strong Preimage) *Given an NFA $M = (Q, \Sigma, \delta)$ and a set of states $V \subseteq Q$, the strong preimage of V is the set of states $\{s \mid s \in Q \wedge \exists i \in \Sigma . \delta(s, i) \subseteq V\}$.*

Thus, for a state s belonging to the strong preimage of a set of states V, there exists at least one action i where all the transitions from s associated with i lead into V. Consider the example shown in Figure 8. The dots and arrows in this figure denote states and transitions for an NFA with a single non-deterministic action. For the set of states GS shown in the figure, the three states having a transition into GS are the strong preimage of GS (indicated by a solid ellipse and labelled pre1), as all transitions from these states lead into GS.

A **weak preimage** is equal to an ordinary preimage as defined in Definition 2. Thus, in Figure 8 all the strong preimages are also weak preimages, but the preimages shown by dashed ellipses are only weak preimages, as the dashed transitions do not satisfy the strong preimage definition.

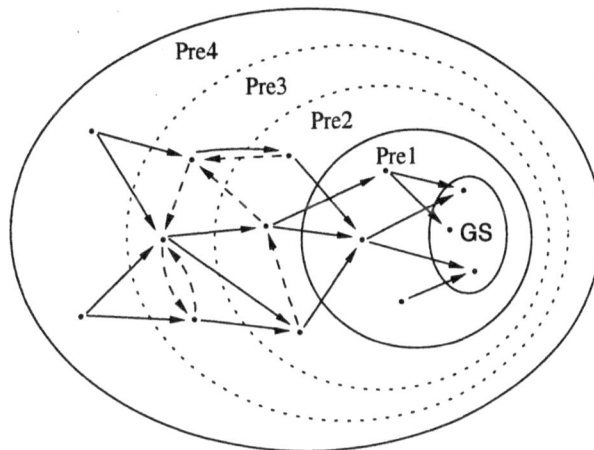

Figure 8: Strong and weak preimage calculations. Solid ellipses denote preimages that are both strong and weak, while dashed ellipses denote preimages that are only weak. Only one action is assumed to exist in the domain. Transitions causing a state to belong to a weak preimage rather than a strong preimage are drawn dashed. The set of goal states is marked "GS".

6.2 Strong and Strong Cyclic Planning

A strong or strong cyclic plan is the union of the state-action rules U found when calculating the preimages necessary for covering the set of initial states (U is defined in Section 5).

Strong planning only considers strong preimages. If a sequence of strong preimages starting at the set of goal states can be calculated, such that the set of initial states is covered, strong planning succeeds and returns the universal plan consisting of the union of all the state-action rules of the calculated strong preimages. Otherwise it fails (Cimatti et al., 1998b).

Consider the example in Figure 8. As depicted in the figure, a strong preimage can be found in the first preimage calculation, but only a weak preimage can be found in the second calculation. Thus, strong planning only succeeds in this example, if the set of initial states is covered by the first preimage and the set of goal states GS.

Strong planning is complete with respect to strong solutions. If a strong plan exists for some planning problem the strong planning algorithm will return it, otherwise, it returns that no solution exists. Strong planning is also optimal due to the breadth-first search. Thus, a strong plan with the fewest number of steps in the worst case is returned.

Strong cyclic planning is a relaxed version of strong planning, because it also considers weak preimages. Strong cyclic planning finds a strong plan, if it exists. Otherwise, when unable to find a strong preimage the algorithm adds a weak preimage. It then tries to prune this preimage by removing all states that have transitions leading out of the preimage and the set of visited states V. If it succeeds, the remaining states in the preimage are added to V and it again tries to add strong preimages. If it fails, it adds a new, weak preimage and repeats the pruning process (Cimatti et al., 1998a).

Consider again the example in Figure 8. The shown sequence of preimage calculations could have been computed by the strong cyclic planning algorithm. The algorithm prefers strong preimages, if they exist, so the first added preimage (Pre1) is strong. No strong second preimage exists and the weak preimage (Pre2) cannot be pruned to only contain states not having transitions leading out of the preimage and the set of visited states. Thus, the strong cyclic algorithm looks for another weak preimage. This preimage (Pre3) has no outgoing transitions, which means that the sequence of weak preimages can be terminated and the algorithm can return to look for strong preimages (Pre4). If the set of initial states after adding preimage Pre4 covers the set of initial states the algorithm succeeds, otherwise it continues until either no strong or pruned weak preimage can be found (in which case the algorithm fails) or the set of visited states covers the set of initial states (in which case the algorithm succeeds).

A strong cyclic plan only guarantees progress towards the goal in the strong parts. In the weak parts, cycles can occur. To ensure that the plan length is finite, we must assume that transitions leading out of the weak parts eventually will be taken. The algorithm is complete with respect to strong solutions, as a strong solution will be returned, if it exists.

6.3 Strengths and Limitations of Strong and Strong Cyclic Planning

An important reason for studying universal planning is that universal planning algorithms can provide state-action rules to completely handle a non-deterministic environment. Thus, if a plan exists for painting the floor, an agent executing a universal plan will always avoid painting itself into the corner or reach any other unrecoverable dead-end. Strong planning and strong cyclic planning algorithms contribute by providing complete OBDD-based algorithms for universal planning.

Unfortunately, real-world domains can have dead-ends that are not always avoidable. Consider, for example, Schoppers' robot-baby domain described in Section 4. As depicted in Figure 6, no universal plan represented by a set of state-action rules can guarantee the goal to be reached in a finite or infinite number of steps, as all relevant actions may lead to an unrecoverable dead-end.

A more interesting example is how to generate a universal plan for a system that can be in a bad state, good state or an unrecoverable failed state (dead-end). Assume that actions can be executed that can bring the system from any bad state to a good state, but environment actions unfortunately can also make the system stay in a bad state or even change to an unrecoverable failed state (see Figure 9). No strong nor strong cyclic solution can be found, because an unrecoverable state can be reached from any initial state. An example of such a domain (a power plant) is studied in Section 7.1.2.

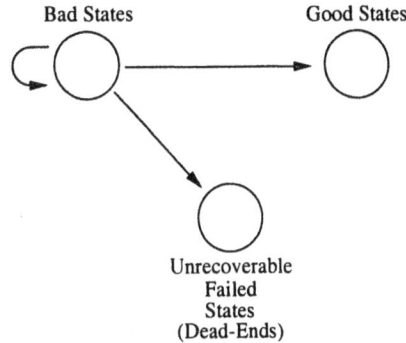

Figure 9: Abstract description of the NFA of a system with unrecoverable states.

Another limitation of strong and strong cyclic planning is the inherent pessimism of these algorithms. Consider for example the domain (Domain 1) illustrated in Figure 10. The domain consists of $n + 1$ states and two different actions (dashed and solid).

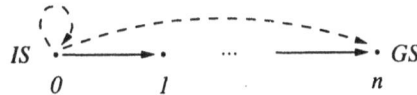

Figure 10: Domain 1. The NFA of a domain with two actions (drawn as solid and dashed arrows) illustrating the possible loss of short plan lengths when preferring strong solutions. IS and GS are the initial and goal state, respectively.

The strong cyclic algorithm returns a strong plan $\{(0, solid), (1, solid), \cdots, (n-1, solid)\}$. This plan would have a best and worst-case length of n. But a strong cyclic plan $\{(0, dashed), (n-1, solid)\}$ also exists and could be preferable because the best-case length of 1 of the cyclic solution may have a much higher probability than the infinite worst-case length. Strong cyclic planning will always prefer to return a strong plan, if it exists, even though a strong cyclic plan may exist with a shorter, best-case plan length.

By adding an unrecoverable dead-end for the dashed action and making solid actions non-deterministic (see Domain 2, Figure 11), strong cyclic planning now returns the strong cyclic plan $\{(0, solid), (1, solid), \cdots, (n-1, solid)\}$. But we might still be interested in the plan $\{(0, dashed), (n-1, solid)\}$ even though the goal is not guaranteed to be achieved.

6.4 Optimistic Planning

The analysis in the previous section shows that there are domains and planning problems for which we may want to use a fully relaxed algorithm that always includes the best-case plan and returns a solution even if it includes dead-ends that cannot be guaranteed to be avoided. We introduce an algorithm similar to the strong planning algorithm that adds an ordinary preimage in each iteration has these properties. Because state-action rules leading to unrecoverable dead-ends may be added to the universal plan, we call this algorithm *optimistic*

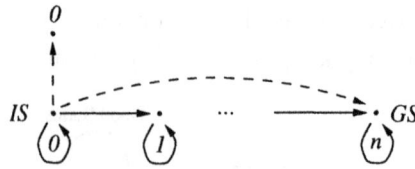

Figure 11: Domain 2. The NFA of a domain with two actions (drawn as solid and dashed arrows) illustrating the possible loss short plan lengths when preferring strong cyclic solutions. IS and GS are the initial and goal state, respectively.

planning. The algorithm is shown in Figure 12. The function Preimage(*VisitedStates*) returns the set of state-action rules U associated with the preimage of the visited states. Prune(*StateActions, VisitedStates*) removes the state-action rules, where the state already is included in the set of visited states, and StatesOf(*PrunedStateActions*) returns the set of states of the pruned state-action rules. UMOP includes the optimistic planning algorithm. The optimistic planning algorithm is incomplete with respect to strong solutions, because it

```
procedure OptimisticPlanning(Init, Goal)
    VisitedStates := Goal
    UniversalPlan := ∅
    while (Init ⊄ VisitedStates)
        StateActions := Preimage(VisitedStates)
        PrunedStateActions := Prune(StateActions, VisitedStates)
        if PrunedStateActions ≠ ∅ then
            UniversalPlan := UniversalPlan ∪ PrunedStateActions
            VisitedStates := VisitedStates ∪ StatesOf(PrunedStateActions)
        else
            return "No optimistic plan exists"
    return UniversalPlan
```

Figure 12: The optimistic planning algorithm.

does not necessarily return a strong solution, if one exists. Intuitively, optimistic planning only guarantees that there exists some effect of a plan action leading to the goal, where strong planning guarantees that all effects of plan actions lead to the goal.

The purpose of optimistic planning is not to substitute strong or strong cyclic planning. These algorithms should be used in domains where strong or strong cyclic plans can be found and goal achievement has the highest priority. Optimistic planning might be the better choice in domains where goal achievement cannot be guaranteed or the shortest plan should be included in the universal plan.

Consider again, as an example, the robot-baby domain described in Section 4. For this problem the optimistic solution makes the robot try to lift the block when the position of the block is less than 3 and the robot is working. This seems to be the only reasonable strategy, even though no guarantee for goal achievement can be given. It is worthwhile

Domain	Strong		Strong Cyclic		Optimistic	
	best	worst	best	worst	best	worst
1	n	n	1	∞	1	∞
2	-	-	n	∞	1	∞_D

Table 1: The best and worst-case plan length of possible strong, strong cyclic and optimistic plans in Domains 1 and 2 (see Figures 10 and 11).(-) means that no solution exists. (∞_D) indicates that the plan length is infinite, and an unrecoverable dead-end is reached.

constructing an optimistic plan for this kind of domains since the alternative is no plan at all.

A similar optimistic plan is generated for the domain shown in Figure 9. For all bad states, the optimistic plan associates an action that brings the system to a good state in one step. This continues as long as the environment keeps the system in a bad state. Because no strategy can be used to prevent the environment from bringing the system to an unrecoverable dead-end, the optimistic solution is quite sensible.

For Domains 1 and 2 shown in Figures 10 and 11, optimistic planning returns a universal plan $\{(0, dotted), (n - 1, solid)\}$. For both domains this is a universal plan with the shortest best-case length. Compared to the strong cyclic solution the cost in the first domain is that the plan may have an infinite length, while the cost in the second domain is that a dead-end may be reached. The results of strong, strong cyclic, and optimistic planning in Domains 1 and 2 are summarized in Table 1.

7. Empirical Results

The input to UMOP is an *NADL* description[4] and a specification of which planning algorithm to use. This description is then converted to a set of OBDDs representing the partitioned transition relation as described in Section 5. The OBDD representation is used by a set of planning algorithms to generate a plan. The output of UMOP is a universal plan or sequential plan depending on the planning algorithm. A universal plan is represented by an OBDD. It defines for each domain state a set of joint actions that the system agents must execute synchronously in order to achieve the goal. The implemented planning algorithms are:

1. Strong planning.

2. Strong cyclic planning.

3. Optimistic planning.

4. Classical deterministic planning.

---

4. The *NADL* description accepted by the current implementation includes all logical operators but only the arithmetic operators + and −. An implementation of the remaining operators is straightforward and is part of our current work.

Deterministic planning can be viewed as a special case of non-deterministic planning. In UMOP, we used the optimistic planning algorithm for the backward search of classical deterministic planning. (The strong or strong cyclic algorithm could also have been used, as all the described non-deterministic algorithms behave similarly in deterministic domains.) The only new feature of the deterministic algorithm is that a sequential plan is generated from the universal plan by choosing an initial state and iteratively adding an action from the universal plan until a goal state is reached. The deterministic planning algorithm has been implemented to verify the performance of UMOP compared to other classical planners. It has not been our intention in this work, though, to develop a fast OBDD-based classical planning algorithm like Di Manzo et al. (1998). Our main interest is non-deterministic, multi-agent universal planning.

The UMOP planning system is implemented in C/C++ and uses the BUDDY package (Lind-Nielsen, 1999) for OBDD manipulations. During planning the dynamic variable re-ordering facility of the BUDDY package is used to find a better ordering of the OBDD variables.

In the following four subsections we present results obtained with the UMOP planning system in nine different domains ranging from deterministic and single-agent with no environment actions to non-deterministic and multi-agent with complex environment actions. All experiments were carried out on a 450 MHz Pentium PC with 1 GByte RAM running Red Hat Linux 4.2. A more detailed description of the experiments including the complete description of the *NADL* domains can be found in Jensen (1999).

7.1 Non-Deterministic Domains

We first test UMOP's performance for some of the non-deterministic domains solved by MBP. Next, we present a power plant domain and finally, we show results from a multi-agent soccer domain.

7.1.1 DOMAINS TESTED BY MBP

One of the domains solved by MBP is a non-deterministic transportation domain. The domain consists of a set of locations and a set of actions like drive-truck, drive-train and fly to move between the locations. Non-determinism is caused by non-deterministic actions (e.g., after a drive action a truck may or may not have fuel left) and environmental changes (e.g., fog at airports, Cimatti et al., 1998a). We defined the two domain examples tested by MBP for strong and strong cyclic planning in *NADL* and ran UMOP using strong and strong cyclic planning. Both examples were solved in less than 0.05 seconds. Similar results were obtained with MBP. A general version of the hunter and prey or "Pursuit" domain (Benda et al., 1986) and a beam walk domain have also been tested by MBP. The generalization of the hunter and prey domain is not described in detail in (Cimatti et al., 1998a). Thus, we have not been able to make an *NADL* implementation of this domain for a meaningful comparison.

The problem in the beam walk domain is for an agent to walk from one end of a beam to the other without falling down. If the agent falls, it has to walk back to the end of the beam and try again. The finite state machine of the domain is shown in Figure 13. The edges denote the outcome of a walk action. When the agent is on the beam, the walk action can either move it one step further on the beam or make it fall to a location under the beam.

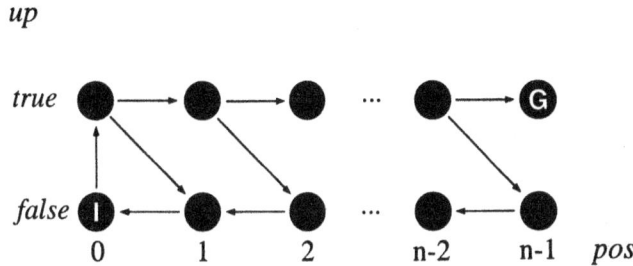

Figure 13: The beam walk domain. The *NADL* encoding of the beam walk domain has one propositional state variable *up* that is true if the agent is on the beam and false otherwise, and a numerical state variable *pos* that denotes the position of the agent either on the beam or on the ground. "I" and "G" are the initial state and goal state respectively.

We implemented a generator program for *NADL* descriptions of beam walk domains and produced domains with 4 to 4096 positions. Because the domain only contains two state variables, UMOP cannot exploit a partitioned transition relation for this domain, but has to use a monolithic representation.

The performance of UMOP and MBP is shown in Figure 14. Discounting that MBP was run on a slower machine,[5] the performance of UMOP and MBP is quite similar in this domain. For domains where UMOP can exploit a partitioned representation, we would expect it to be able to solve larger problems than MBP, since MBP currently can only use a monolithic representation. Further comparisons between UMOP and MBP are on our research agenda.

7.1.2 The Power Plant Domain

The purpose of the remaining experiments in non-deterministic domains is to show universal planning results for domains where the multi-agent and environment modelling features of *NADL* have been used.

The power plant domain demonstrates a multi-agent domain with an environment model and further exemplifies optimistic planning. It consists of reactors, heat exchangers, turbines and valves. A domain example is shown in Figure 15.

In the power plant domain each controllable unit is associated with an agent such that all control actions can be performed simultaneously. The environment consists of a single agent that at any time can fail a number of heat exchanges and turbines and also ensures that already failed units remain failed. A failed heat exchanger leaks water from the internal to the external water loop and must be closed by a block action *b*. The energy production from the reactor can be controlled by *p* to fit the demand *f*, but the reactor will always produce one energy unit. To transport the energy from the reactor away from the plant at least one heat exchanger and one turbine must be working. Otherwise the plant is in an unrecoverable failed state, where the reactor will overheat.

---

5. A 266MHz Pentium II with 96 MBytes RAM was used to generate the results for MBP.

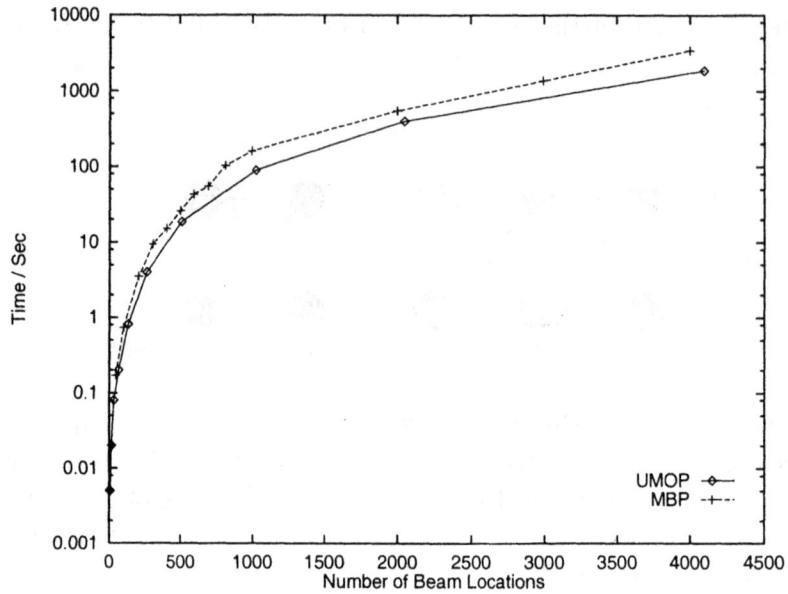

Figure 14: Planning time of UMOP and MBP in the beam walk domain. The MBP data has been extracted with possible loss of accuracy from (Cimatti et al., 1998a).

The state space of the power plant can be divided into three disjoint sets: good, bad and failed states. In the good states, therefore the goal states, the power plant satisfies its safety and activity requirements. In our example the safety requirements ensure that energy can be transported away from the plant, and that failed units are shut down:

```
% energy can be transported away from the plant
(okh1 \/ okh2 \/ okh3 \/ okh4) /\
(okt1 \/ okt2 \/ okt3 \/ okt4) /\

% heat exchangers blocked if failed
(~okh1 => b1) /\
(~okh2 => b2) /\
(~okh3 => b3) /\
(~okh4 => b4) /\

% turbines stopped if failed
(~okt1 => s1) /\
(~okt2 => s2) /\
(~okt3 => s3) /\
(~okt4 => s4)
```

The activity requirements state that the energy production equals the demand and that all valves to working turbines are open:

```
% power production equals demand
p = f /\

% turbine valve is open if turbine is ok
(okt1 => v1) /\
(okt2 => v2) /\
(okt3 => v3) /\
(okt4 => v4)
```

In a bad state, the plant does not satisfy the safety and activity requirements but is not unrecoverably failed. In a failed state all heat exchangers or turbines are failed.

The universal planning task is to generate a universal plan to get from any bad state to some good state without ending in a failed state. Assuming that no units fail during execution, it is obvious that only one joint action is needed. Unfortunately, the environment can fail any number of units during execution, thus, as described in Section 6.2, for any bad state the resulting joint action may loop back to a bad state or cause the plant to end in a failed state (see Figure 9). For this reason no strong or strong cyclic solution exist.

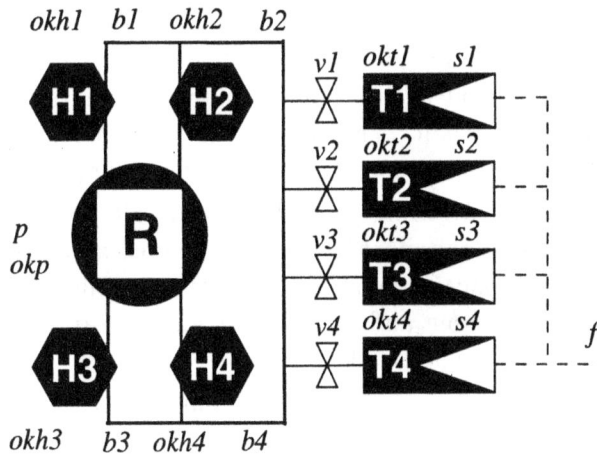

Figure 15: A power plant domain example. The reactor R is surrounded by four heat exchangers H1, H2, H3 and H4. The heat exchangers produce high pressure steam to four electricity generating turbines T1, T2, T3 and T4. A failed heat exchanger Hi must be closed by a block action bi. For a failed turbine Ti the stop action si must be carried out. The energy production of the reactor is p and can be controlled to fit the demand f. Each turbine Ti can be closed by a valve vi. The ok variables capture the working status of the units.

An optimistic solution simply ignores that joint actions can loop back to a bad state or lead to a failed state and finds a solution to the problem after one preimage calculation. Intuitively, the optimistic plan assumes that no units will fail during execution and always chooses joint actions that lead directly from a bad state to a good state. The optimistic plan is an optimal control strategy, because it always chooses the shortest plan to a good state and no other strategy exists that can avoid looping back to a bad state or end in a failed state.

The size of the state space of the above power plant domain is 2^{24}. An optimistic solution was generated by UMOP in 0.92 seconds and contained 37619 OBDD nodes. As an example, a joint action was extracted from the plan for a bad state where H3 and H4 were failed and energy demand f was 2 energy units, while the energy production p was only 1 unit. The extraction time was 0.013 seconds and, as expected, the set of joint actions included a single joint action changing $b3$ and $b4$ to true and setting p to 2.

7.1.3 THE SOCCER DOMAIN

The purpose of the soccer domain is to demonstrate a multi-agent domain with a more elaborate environment model than the power plant domain. It consists of two teams of players that can move in a grid world and pass a ball to each other. At each time step a player either moves in one of the four major directions or passes the ball to another team player. The task is to generate a universal plan for one of the teams that can be applied to score a goal whenever the team possesses the ball.

A simple *NADL* description of the soccer domain models the team possessing the ball as system agents that can move and pass the ball independent of each other. Thus, a player possessing the ball can always pass to any other team player. The opponent team is modelled as a set of environment agents that can move in the four major directions but have no actions for handling the ball. The goal of the universal plan is to have a player with the ball in front of the opponent goal without having any opponents in the goal area.

It is impossible to generate a strong plan that covers all possible initial states. For instance an initial state with an opponent located in the goal area has no strong solution. But a strong plan covering as many initial states as possible is still useful, because it defines all the "scoring" states of the game and further provides a plan for scoring the goal no matter the actions, the opponent players choose.

We implemented an *NADL* generator for soccer domains with different field sizes and numbers of agents. The multi-agent graph in Figure 16 shows UMOP's planning time using the strong planning algorithm in soccer domains with 64 locations and one to six players on each team. The planning time seems to grow exponentially with the number of players. This is not surprising as not only the state space but also the number of joint actions grow exponentially with the number of agents. To investigate the complexity introduced by joint actions we constructed a version of the soccer domain with only a single system and environment agent and ran UMOP again. The single-agent graph in Figure 16 shows the dramatic decrease in computation time. It is not obvious though, that using more agents increases the computational load, as this normally also reduces the number of preimage calculations, because a larger number of states is reached in each iteration. Indeed, in a version of the power plant domain with deterministic actions, we found the planning time to decrease (see the power plant graph in Figure 16), when more agents were added (Jensen, 1999). Again we measured the time for extracting actions from the generated universal plans. For the multi-agent version of the five player soccer domain the two joint actions achieving the goal shown in Figure 17 were extracted from the universal plan in less than 0.001 seconds.

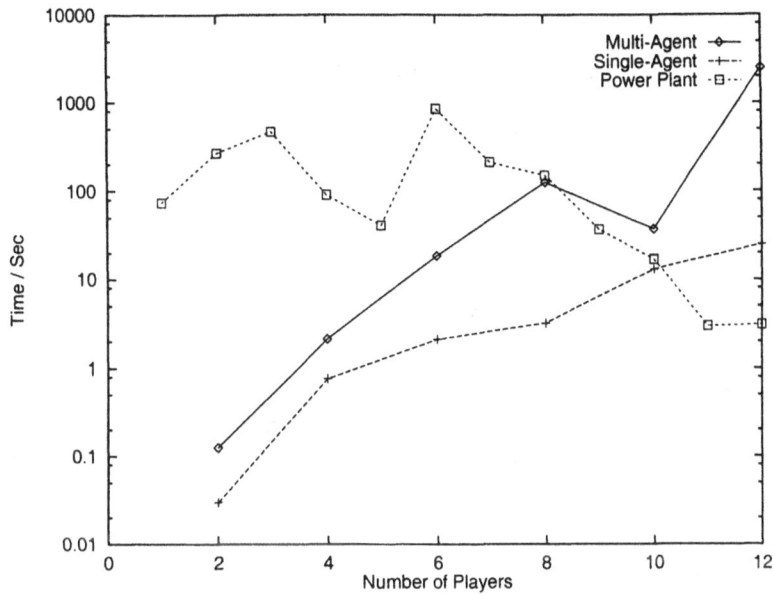

Figure 16: Planning time of UMOP for generating strong universal plans in soccer domains with one to six players on each team. For the multi-agent experiment each player was associated with an agent, while only a single system and environment agent was used in the single-agent experiment. The power plant graph shows planning time for a deterministic version of the power plant domain using 1 to 12 system agents.

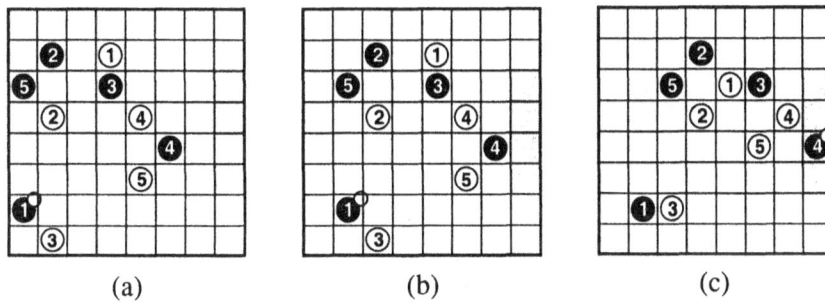

Figure 17: Plan execution sequence. The three states show a hypothetical attack based on a universal plan. The state (a) is a "scoring" state, because the attackers (black) can extract a nonempty set of joint actions from the universal plan. Choosing some joint actions from the plan, the attackers can enter the goal area (shaded) with the ball within two time steps (state (b) and (c)) no matter what actions, the opponent players choose.

7.2 Deterministic Domains

A number of experiments have been carried out in deterministic domains in order to verify UMOP's performance and illustrate the generality of universal plans versus classical, sequential plans. We compare run time results obtained with UMOP in some of the AIPS'98 competition domains to the results of the competition planners (McDermott, 1999). We then show that a universal plan in a deterministic domain is more general than a classical sequential plan, because a large number of classical sequential plans are contained in the universal plan.

7.2.1 AIPS'98 COMPETITION DOMAINS

Four planning systems BLACKBOX (Kautz & Selman, 1999), IPP (Koehler et al., 1997), STAN (Long & Fox, 1998) and HSP (Haslum & Geffner, 2000)[6] competed in the three domains we have studied. BLACKBOX is based on SATPLAN, while IPP and STAN are graphplan-based planners. HSP uses a heuristic search approach based on a preprocessing of the domain. The AIPS'98 planners were run on 233 MHz (or 400MHz)[7] Pentium PCs with 128 MBytes RAM equipped with Linux.

The Gripper Domain. The gripper domain consists of two rooms A and B, a robot with a left and right gripper and a number of balls that can be moved by the robot. The task is to move all the balls from room A to room B with the robot initially in room A. The state variables of the *NADL* encoding of the domain are the position of the robot and the position of the balls. The position of the robot is either 0 (room A) or 1 (room B), while the position of a ball can be 0 (room A), 1 (room B), 2 (in left gripper) or 3 (in right gripper). For the AIPS'98 gripper problems the number of plan steps in an optimal plan grows linearly with the problem number. Problem 1 contains 4 balls, and the number of balls grows by two for each problem. The result of the experiment is shown in Table 2 together with the results of the planners in the AIPS'98 competition. A graphical representation of the planning time in the table is shown in Figure 18. UMOP generates minimum-length plans due to its parallel breadth-first search algorithm. As depicted in Figure 18, it avoids the exponential growth of the planning time that characterizes all of the competition planners except HSP. When using a partitioned transition relation UMOP is the only planner capable of generating optimal plans for all the problems. For this domain the transition relation of an *NADL* description can be divided into $n + 1$ basic partitions, where n is the number of balls. As discussed in Section 5, the optimal number of partitions is not necessarily the largest number of partitions. For the results in Table 2 each partition consisted of a conjunction of 10 basic partitions. Compared to the monolithic transition relation representation the results obtained with the partitioned transition relation were significantly better on the larger problems. The memory usage of problem 20 with a partitioned transition relation was 87 MBytes, while it exceeded the limit of 128 MBytes at problem 17 for the monolithic transition relation.

The Movie Domain. In the movie domain the task is to get chips, dip, pop, cheese and crackers, rewind a movie and set the counter to zero. The only interference between

---

6. PRODIGY4.0 also successfully ran in some of the domains, but was not an official entry in the competition.
7. Unfortunately, no exact record has been kept on the machines and there is some disagreement about their clock frequency. According to Drew McDermott, who chaired the competition, they were 233 MHz Pentiums, but Derek Long (STAN) believes that they were at least 400 MHz Pentiums, as STAN performed worse on a 300 MHz Pentium than in the competition.

Problem	UMOP Part.			UMOP Mono.		STAN		HSP		IPP		BLACKBOX	
1	20	11	1	20	11	46	11	2007	13	50	15	113	11
2	150	17	1	130	17	1075	17	2150	21	380	23	7820	17
3	710	23	1	740	23	54693	23	2485	31	3270	31	-	-
4	1490	29	2	2230	29	3038381	29	3060	37	26680	39	-	-
5	3600	35	2	6040	35	-	-	3320	47	226460	47	-	-
6	7260	41	2	11840	41	-	-	3779	53	-	-	-	-
7	13750	47	2	24380	47	-	-	4797	63	-	-	-	-
8	23840	53	2	38400	53	-	-	5565	71	-	-	-	-
9	36220	59	3	68750	59	-	-	6675	79	-	-	-	-
10	56200	65	3	95140	65	-	-	7583	85	-	-	-	-
11	84930	71	3	145770	71	-	-	9060	93	-	-	-	-
12	127870	77	3	216110	77	-	-	10617	101	-	-	-	-
13	197170	83	3	315150	83	-	-	12499	109	-	-	-	-
14	290620	89	4	474560	89	-	-	15050	119	-	-	-	-
15	411720	95	4	668920	95	-	-	16886	125	-	-	-	-
16	549610	101	4	976690	101	-	-	20084	135	-	-	-	-
17	746920	107	4	-	-	-	-	23613	143	-	-	-	-
18	971420	113	4	-	-	-	-	26973	151	-	-	-	-
19	1361580	119	5	-	-	-	-	29851	157	-	-	-	-
20	1838110	125	5	-	-	-	-	33210	165	-	-	-	-

Table 2: Gripper domain results. Column one and two for each planner show the planning time in milliseconds and the plan length. UMOP Part. and UMOP Mono. show the planning time for UMOP using a partitioned and a monolithic transition relation, respectively. For UMOP with partitioned transition relation the third column shows the number of partitions. (-) means that the planner used more than 128 MBytes of memory or was terminated before returning a solution. Only results for executions using less than 128 MBytes are shown for UMOP.

the subgoals is that the movie must be rewound, before the counter can be set to zero. The problems in the movie domain only differ by the number of objects of each type of food. The number of objects increases linearly from 5 for Problem 1 to 34 for Problem 30.

Our *NADL* description of the movie domain represents each type of food as a numerical state variable with a range equal to the number of objects of that type of food. Table 3 shows the planning time for UMOP and the competition planners for the movie domain problems. In this experiment and the remaining experiments UMOP used its default partitioning of the transition relation. For every problem all the planners find the optimal solution. Like most of the competition planners UMOP has a low computation time, but it is the only planner not showing any increase in computation time even though, the size of the state space of its encoding increases from 2^{24} to 2^{39}.

The Logistics Domain. The logistics domain (Veloso, 1994) consists of cities, trucks, airplanes and packages. Trucks can only move between locations in the same city. Airplanes can only move between airport locations in different cities. The task is to move packages to specific locations. Problems differ by the number of packages, cities, airplanes and trucks. The logistics domain is hard, and only Problem 1,2,5,7 and 11 of the 30 problems were solved by any planner in the AIPS'98 competition (see Table 4). The *NADL* description

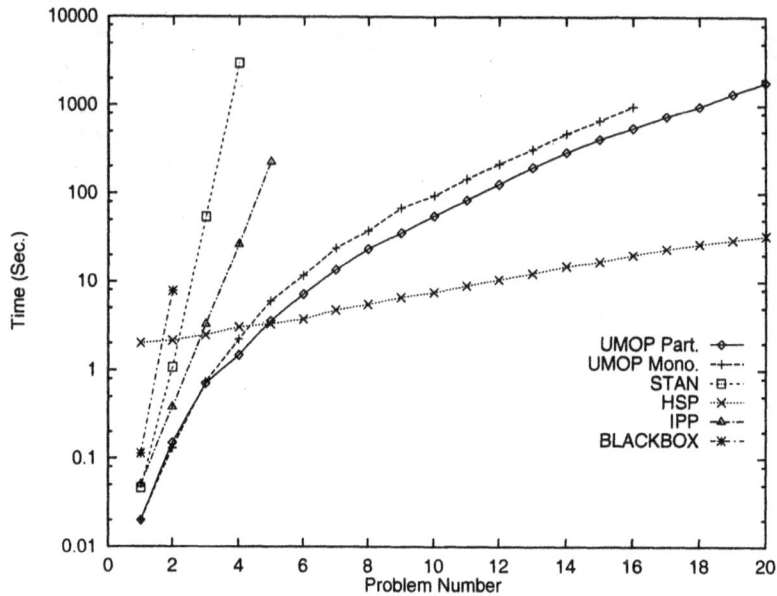

Figure 18: Planning time for UMOP and the AIPS'98 competition planners for the gripper domain problems. UMOP Part. and UMOP Mono. show the planning time for UMOP using a partitioned and a monolithic transition relation, respectively.

of the logistics domain uses numerical state variables to represent locations of packages, where trucks and airplanes are treated as special locations. Even though the state space of the small problems is moderate, UMOP fails to solve any of the problems in the domain. It succeeds to generate the transition relation but fails to finish the preimage calculations.

We have studied the logistics domain extensively, recently focusing on OBDD-based deterministic planning. The logistics domain seems to be hard using a plain OBDD-based approach, as the sizes of the preimages grow too fast. To address this complexity, we have developed an abstraction technique for OBDD-based deterministic planning. In a nutshell, a problem is first solved using an abstract transition system, where each transition corresponds to a set of serializable actions. Then the steps in the abstract plan are serialized using an ordinary transition system. With this new algorithm, we have been able to solve several of the complex AIPS'98 competition logistics problems (Jensen et al., 2000).

7.2.2 THE OBSTACLE DOMAIN

The obstacle domain has been constructed to demonstrate the generality of universal plans. It consists of a grid world with 2^5 cells, n obstacles and a robot agent. The positions of the obstacles are not defined. The goal position of the robot is the upper right corner of the grid, and the task for the robot is to move from any position in the grid to the goal position. Because the initial locations of obstacles are unknown, the universal plan must take any possible position of obstacles into account, which gives $2^{5(n+1)} - 2^{5n}$ initial states. For a specific initial state a sequential plan can be generated from the universal plan. Thus, $2^{5(n+1)} - 2^{5n}$ sequential plans are comprised in one universal plan. Note that a universal

Problem	UMOP	STAN	HSP	IPP	BLACKBOX
1	14	19	2121	10	11
2	12	18	2104	10	12
3	14	19	2144	10	14
4	4	20	2188	10	16
5	14	21	2208	10	18
6	16	22	2617	10	20
7	14	22	2316	20	22
8	12	23	2315	20	24
9	14	25	2357	-	26
10	14	26	2511	10	29
11	14	27	2427	30	30
12	4	28	2456	30	32
13	16	29	3070	20	36
14	14	31	2573	30	35
15	16	32	2577	30	38
16	14	34	2699	10	39
17	16	35	2645	30	41
18	14	37	2686	10	43
19	16	39	2727	30	45
20	12	40	2787	20	47
21	16	42	2834	20	49
22	14	45	2834	20	51
23	16	48	2866	20	53
24	14	50	3341	20	55
25	16	52	2997	30	57
26	16	54	3013	40	58
27	16	57	3253	50	60
28	4	62	3049	40	63
29	18	64	3384	50	64
30	16	67	3127	40	66

Table 3: Movie domain results. The table shows the run time in milliseconds for each planner. (-) means that the planner used more than 128 MBytes of memory or was terminated before returning a solution. All planners generated optimal plans of length 7. UMOP used far less than 128 MBytes for any problem in this domain.

plan with n obstacles includes any universal plan with 1 to n obstacles, as obstacles can be placed at the same location. Note moreover, that the universal plans never cover all initial states, because obstacles can be placed at the goal position, and obstacles can block the robot.

A universal plan for an obstacle domain with 5 obstacles was generated with UMOP in 420 seconds and contained 488296 OBDD nodes (13.3 MBytes). Sequential plans were extracted from the universal plan for a specific position of the obstacles. Figure 19 shows the extraction time of sequential plans for an increasing number of steps in the plan. Even though the OBDD representing the universal plan is large, the extraction is very fast and only grows linearly with the plan length.

The set of actions associated with a state s in a universal plan p is extracted by computing the conjunction of the OBDD representation of s and p. As described in Section 3, this operation has an upper bound complexity of $O(|s||p|)$. For the universal plan in the

Problem	UMOP		STAN		HSP		IPP		BLACKBOX	
1	-	-	767	27	79682	43	900	26	2062	27
2	-	-	4319	32	97114	44	-	-	6436	32
5	-	-	364932	29	144413	26	2400	24	-	-
7	-	-	-	-	788914	112	-	-	-	-
11	-	-	12806	34	86195	30	6940	33	6544	32

Table 4: Logistics domain results. For each planner column one and two show the run time in milliseconds and the plan length. (-) means that the planner used more than 128 MBytes of memory or was terminated before returning a solution.

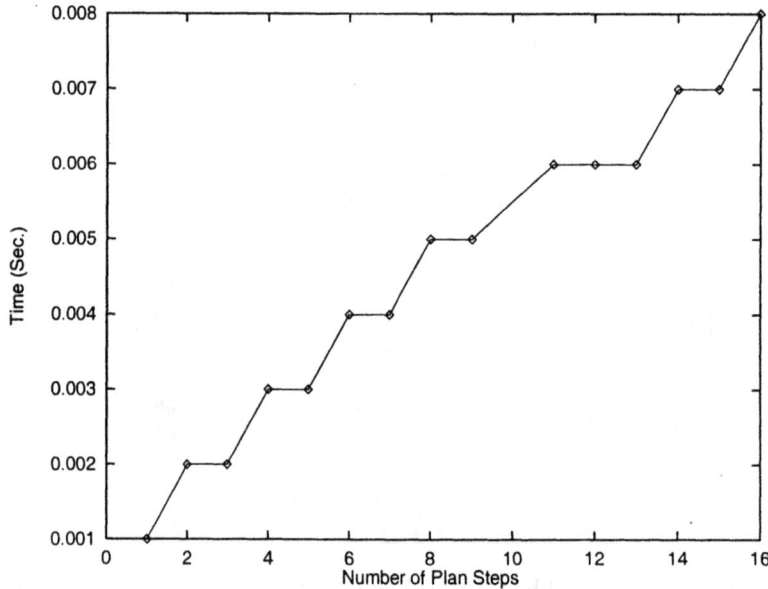

Figure 19: Time for extracting sequential plans from a universal plan for the obstacle domain with 5 obstacles.

obstacle domain with five obstacles, this computation was fast (less than one millisecond) and would allow an executing robot to meet low reaction time constraints.

8. Conclusion and Future Work

In this article we have presented a new OBDD-based planning system, UMOP, for planning in non-deterministic, multi-agent domains. An expressive domain description language, *NADL* , has been developed and an efficient OBDD representation of its NFA semantics has been described. We have analyzed previous planning algorithms for OBDD-based planning and deepened the understanding of when these planning algorithms are appropriate. Finally, we have proposed an optimistic planning algorithm for finding sensible solutions in some domains where no strong or strong cyclic solution exists. The results obtained with UMOP are encouraging, as UMOP has a good performance compared to some of the fastest classical planners known today.

Our research has drawn our attention to a number of open questions that we would like to address in the future. In particular we wonder how well our encoding of planning problems scales compared to the encoding used by MBP. Currently MBP's encoding does not support a partitioned representation of the transition relation, but the encoding may have other properties that, despite the monolithic representation, may make it a better choice. The two systems may also have an equal performance when both are using a monolithic representation (as in the beam walk example), which should give UMOP an advantage in domains where a partitioning of the transition relation can be defined.

Another interesting question is to investigate which kind of planning domains is suitable for OBDD-based planning. It was surprising for us that the logistics domain turned out to be so hard for UMOP. Recently we have studied this domain thoroughly. Using an abstraction technique we have now been able to solve several of the logistics problems in the AIPS'98 competition (Jensen et al., 2000).

The current definition of *NADL* is powerful but should be extended to enable modelling of constructive synergetic effects as described in Section 4. Also, we envision more experiments comparing multi-agent and single-agent domains to investigate the complexity of *NADL*'s representation of concurrent actions.

Several planners, in particular PRODIGY (Veloso et al., 1995), have shown that domain knowledge should be used by a planning system in order to scale up to real-world problems. Also (Bacchus & Kabanza, 1996) show how the search tree of a forward chaining planner can be efficiently pruned by stating the goal as a formula in temporal logic on the sequence of actions leading to the goal. In this way the goal can include knowledge about the domain (e.g., that towers in the blocks world must be built from bottom to top). A similar approach for reducing the complexity of OBDD-based planning seems promising, especially because techniques for testing temporal formulas already have been developed in model checking.

Other future challenges include introducing abstraction in OBDD-based planning and defining specialized planning algorithms for multi-agent domains (e.g., algorithms using the least number of agents for solving a problem).

Acknowledgments

Special thanks to Paolo Traverso, Marco Roveri and the other members of the IRST group for introducing us to MBP and for many rewarding discussions on OBDD-based planning and model checking. We also wish to thank Randal E. Bryant, Edmund Clarke, Henrik R. Andersen, Jørn Lind-Nielsen and Lars Birkedal for advice on OBDD issues and formal representation. Finally, we thank the anonymous reviewers for their comments that greatly improved the presentation of this article.

This work was carried out while the first author was visiting Carnegie Mellon University from the Technical University of Denmark. The research is sponsored in part by McKinsey & Company, Selmer & Trane's Fond, the Defense Advanced Research Projects Agency (DARPA) and the Air Force Research Laboratory (AFRL) under agreement number F30602-97-2-0250. The views and conclusions contained herein are those of the authors and should not be interpreted as necessarily representing the official policies or endorsements, either expressed or implied, of the Defense Advanced Research Projects Agency (DARPA), the Air Force Research Laboratory (AFRL) or the U.S. Government.

Appendix A. *NADL* includes the $\mathcal{AR}$ Family

Theorem 1 *If A is a domain description in some $\mathcal{AR}$ language, then there exists a domain description D in NADL with the same semantics as A.*

Proof: Let $M_a = (Q, \Sigma, \delta)$ denote the NFA (see Definition 1) corresponding to the semantics of A as defined by Giunchiglia et al. (1997). An *NADL* domain description D with semantics equal to M_a can be constructed in the following way: Let D be a single-agent domain where all fluents are encoded as numerical state variables and there is an action for each element in the alphabet Σ of M_a. Consider the action a associated to input $i \in \Sigma$. Let the set of constrained state variables of a equal the set of state variables in D. The precondition of a is an expression that defines the set of states having an outgoing transition for input i. The effect condition of a is a conjunction of conditional effects $(P_s \Rightarrow N_s)$. There is one conditional effect for each state that has an outgoing transition for input i. P_s in the conditional effect associated with state s is the characteristic expression for s and N_s is a characteristic expression for the set of next states $\delta(s, i)$. $\square$

References

Bacchus, F., & Kabanza, F. (1996). Using temporal logic to control search in a forward chaining planner. In Ghallab, M., & Milani, A. (Eds.), *New directions in AI planning*, pp. 141–153. ISO Press.

Baral, C., & Gelfond, M. (1997). Reasoning about effects of concurrent actions. *The Journal of Logic Programming*, 85–117.

Benda, M., Jagannathan, V., & Dodhiawala, R. (1986). On optimal cooperation of knowledge sources - an empirical investigation. Tech. rep. BCS–G2010–28, Boeing Advanced Technology Center, Boeing Computing Services.

Blum, A., & Furst, M. L. (1997). Fast planning through planning graph analysis. *Artificial Intelligence*, *90*, 281–300.

Blythe, J. (1998). *Planning under uncertainty in dynamic domains*. Ph.D. thesis, Computer Science Department, Carnegie Mellon University. CMU-CS-98-147.

Blythe, J., & Veloso, M. M. (1997). Analogical replay for efficient conditional planning. In *Proceedings of the 14th National Conference on Artificial Intelligence (AAAI'97)*, pp. 668–673. AAAI Press.

Bonet, B., Loerincs, G., & Geffner, H. (1997). A robust and fast action selection mechanism for planning. In *Proceedings of the 14th National Conference on Artificial Intelligence (AAAI'97)*, pp. 714–719. AAAI Press.

Bryant, R. E. (1986). Graph-based algorithms for boolean function manipulation. *IEEE Transactions on Computers*, *8*, 677–691.

Burch, J., Clarke, E., & Long, D. (1991). Symbolic model checking with partitioned transition relations. In *International Conference on Very Large Scale Integration*, pp. 49–58. North-Holland.

Cimatti, A., Giunchiglia, E., Giunchiglia, F., & Traverso, P. (1997). Planning via model checking: A decision procedure for $\mathcal{AR}$. In *Proceedings of the 4th European Conference on Planning (ECP'97)*, Lecture Notes in Artificial Intelligence, pp. 130–142. Springer-Verlag.

Cimatti, A., Roveri, M., & Traverso, P. (1998a). Automatic OBDD-based generation of universal plans in non-deterministic domains. In *Proceedings of the 15th National Conference on Artificial Intelligence (AAAI'98)*, pp. 875–881. AAAI Press.

Cimatti, A., Roveri, M., & Traverso, P. (1998b). Strong planning in non-deterministic domains via model checking. In *Proceedings of the 4th International Conference on Artificial Intelligence Planning System (AIPS'98)*, pp. 36–43. AAAI Press.

Clarke, E., Grumberg, O., & Peled, D. (1999). *Model Checking*. MIT Press.

Clarke, E. M., Emerson, E. A., & Sistla, A. P. (1986). Automatic verification of finite-state concurrent systems using temporal logic specifications. *ACM Transactions on Programming Languages and Systems, 8*(2), 244–263.

Currie, K., & Tate, A. (1991). O-plan: the open planning architecture. *Artificial Intelligence, 52*, 49–86.

Dean, T., Kaelbling, L. P., Kirman, J., & Nicholson, A. (1995). Planning under time constraints in stochastic domains. *Artificial Intelligence, 76*, 35–74.

Di Manzo, M., Giunchiglia, E., & Ruffino, S. (1998). Planning via model checking in deterministic domains: Preliminary report. In *Proceedings of the 8th International Conference on Artificial Intelligence: Methodology, Systems and Applications (AIMSA'98)*, pp. 221–229. Springer-Verlag.

Drummond, M. (1989). Situated control rules. In *Proceedings of the 1'st International Conference on Principles of Knowledge Representation and Reasoning (KR'89)*, pp. 103–113. Morgan Kaufmann.

Drummond, M., & Bresina, J. (1990). Anytime synthetic projection: Maximizing the probability of goal satisfaction. In *Proceedings of the 8th Conference on Artificial Intelligence*, pp. 138–144. AAAI Press.

Etzioni, O., Hanks, S., Weld, D., Draper, D., Lesh, N., & Williamson, M. (1992). An approach for planning with incomplete information. In *Proceedings of the 3'rd International Conference on Principles of Knowledge Representation and Reasoning*.

Fikes, R. E., & Nilsson, N. J. (1971). STRIPS: A new approach to the application of theorem proving to problem solving. *Artificial Intelligence, 2*, 189–208.

Gat, E. (1992). Integrating planning and reacting in a heterogeneous asynchronous architecture for controlling real-world mobile robots. In *Proceedings of the 10th National Conference on Artificial Intelligence (AAAI'92)*, pp. 809–815. AAAI Press.

Gelfond, M., & Liftschitz, V. (1993). Representing action and change by logic programs. *The Journal of Logic Programming, 17*, 301–322.

Georgeff, M. P., & Lansky, A. L. (1987). Reactive reasoning and planning. In *Proceedings of the 6th National Conference on Artificial Intelligence (AAAI'87)*, pp. 677–682. Morgan Kaufmann.

Ginsberg, M. L. (1989). Universal planning: An (almost) universal bad idea. *AI Magazine, 10*(4), 40–44.

Giunchiglia, E., Kartha, G. N., & Lifschitz, Y. (1997). Representing action: Indeterminacy and ramifications. *Artificial Intelligence, 95*, 409–438.

Giunchiglia, E., & Lifschitz, V. (1998). An action language based on causal explanation: Preliminary report. In *Proceedings of the 15th National Conference on Artificial Intelligence (AAAI'98)*, pp. 623–630. AAAI Press.

Haigh, K. Z., & Veloso, M. M. (1998). Planning, execution and learning in a robotic agent. In *Proceedings of the 4th International Conference on Artificial Intelligence Planning Systems (AIPS'98)*, pp. 120–127. AAAI Press.

Haslum, P., & Geffner, H. (2000). Admissible heuristics for optimal planning. In *Proceedings of the 5th International Conference on Artificial Intelligence Planning System (AIPS'00)*, pp. 140–149. AAAI Press.

Jensen, R. M. (1999). OBDD-based universal planning in multi-agent, non-deterministic domains. Master's thesis, Technical University of Denmark, Department of Automation. IAU99F02.

Jensen, R. M., Veloso, M., & Bryant, R. E. (2000). Abstraction techniques for OBDD-based planning. Forthcoming.

Kabanza, F., Barbeau, M., & St-Denis, R. (1997). Planning control rules for reactive agents. *Artificial Intelligence, 95*, 67–113.

Kautz, H., & Selman, B. (1996). Pushing the envelope: Planning, propositional logic and stochastic search. In *Proceedings of the 13th National Conference on Artificial Intelligence (AAAI'96)*, Vol. 2, pp. 1194–1201. AAAI Press.

Kautz, H., & Selman, B. (1999). Unifying SAT-based and graph-based planning. In *Proceedings of the 16th International Joint Conference on Artificial Intelligence (IJCAI-99)*, Vol. 1, pp. 318–325. Morgan Kaufmann.

Koehler, J., Nebel, B., Hoffmann, J., & Dimopoulos, Y. (1997). Extending planning graphs to an ADL subset. In *Proceedings of the 4th European Conference on Planning (ECP'97)*, pp. 273–285. Springer-Verlag.

Koenig, S., & Simmons, R. G. (1995). Real-time search in non-deterministic domains. In *Proceedings of the 14th International Joint Conference on Artificial Intelligence (IJCAI-95)*, pp. 1660–1667. Morgan Kaufmann.

Lever, J., & Richards, B. (1994). *Parcplan: a planning architecture with parallel actions and constraints*. In *Lecture Notes in Artificial Intelligence*, pp. 213–222. ISMIS'94, Springer-Verlag.

Lind-Nielsen, J. (1999). BuDDy - A Binary Decision Diagram Package. Tech. rep. IT-TR: 1999-028, Institute of Information Technology, Technical University of Denmark. http://cs.it.dtu.dk/buddy.

Lingard, A. R., & Richards, E. B. (1998). Planning parallel actions. *Artificial Intelligence*, *99*, 261–324.

Long, D., & Fox, M. (1998). Domain independent planner compilation. In *AIPS'98 Workshop: Knowledge Engineering and Acquisition for Planning: Bridging Theory and Practice*. AAAI technical Report WS-98-03.

McDermott, D. (1999). The 1998 AI planning system competition. *Artificial Intelligence Magazine*. (submitted).

McMillan, K. L. (1993). *Symbolic Model Checking*. Kluwer Academic Publ.

Penberthy, J. S., & Weld, D. S. (1992). UCPOP: A sound, complete, partial order planner for ADL. In *Proceedings of the 3'rd International Conference on Principles of Knowledge Representation and Reasoning*, pp. 103–114. Morgan Kaufmann.

Peot, M., & Smith, D. (1992). Conditional nonlinear planning. In *Proceedings of the 1'st International Conference on Artificial Intelligence Planning Systems (AIPS'92)*, pp. 189–197. Morgan Kaufmann.

Ranjan, R. K., Aziz, A., Brayton, R. K., Plessier, B., & Pixley, C. (1995). Efficient BDD algorithms for FSM synthesis and verification. In *IEEE/ACM Proceedings of the International Workshop on Logic Synthesis*.

Schoppers, M. J. (1987). Universal plans for reactive robots in unpredictable environments. In *Proceedings of the 10th International Joint Conference on Artificial Intelligence (IJCAI-87)*, pp. 1039–1046. Morgan Kaufmann.

Smirnov, Y., Koenig, S., Veloso, M., & Simmons, R. (1996). Efficient goal-directed exploration. In *Proceedings , the Thirteenth National Conference on Artificial Intelligence (AAAI'96)*, pp. 292–297. AAAI Press.

Stone, P., & Veloso, M. M. (1998). Towards collaborative and adversarial learning: A case study in robotic soccer. *International Journal of Human-Computer Studies (IJHCS)*.

Sutton, R. S., & Barto, A. G. (1998). *Reinforcement learning: an introduction*. MIT Press.

Veloso, M., Carbonell, J., Pérez, A., Borrajo, D., Fink, E., & Blythe, J. (1995). Integrating planning and learning: The PRODIGY architecture. *Journal of Experimental and Theoretical Artificial Intelligence*, 7(1), 81–120.

Veloso, M. M. (1994). *Planning and learning by analogical reasoning*. Springer-Verlag.

Veloso, M. M., Pollack, M. E., & Cox, M. T. (1998). Rationale-based monitoring for planning in dynamic environments. In *Proceedings of the 4th International Conference on Artificial Intelligence Planning Systems (AIPS'98)*, pp. 171–179. AAAI Press.

Weld, D. (1999). Recent advances in AI planning. *Artificial Intelligence Magazine*, 93–123.

Wilkins, D. E., Myers, K. L., Lowrance, J. D., & Wesley, L. P. (1994). Planning and reacting in uncertain and dynamic environments. *Journal of Experimental and Theoretical Artificial Intelligence*, 6, 197–227.

Journal of Artificial Intelligence Research 13 (2000) 227-303   Submitted 11/99; published 11/00

Hierarchical Reinforcement Learning with the MAXQ Value Function Decomposition

Thomas G. Dietterich   TGD@CS.ORST.EDU
Department of Computer Science, Oregon State University
Corvallis, OR 97331

Abstract

This paper presents a new approach to hierarchical reinforcement learning based on decomposing the target Markov decision process (MDP) into a hierarchy of smaller MDPs and decomposing the value function of the target MDP into an additive combination of the value functions of the smaller MDPs. The decomposition, known as the MAXQ decomposition, has both a procedural semantics—as a subroutine hierarchy—and a declarative semantics—as a representation of the value function of a hierarchical policy. MAXQ unifies and extends previous work on hierarchical reinforcement learning by Singh, Kaelbling, and Dayan and Hinton. It is based on the assumption that the programmer can identify useful subgoals and define subtasks that achieve these subgoals. By defining such subgoals, the programmer constrains the set of policies that need to be considered during reinforcement learning. The MAXQ value function decomposition can represent the value function of any policy that is consistent with the given hierarchy. The decomposition also creates opportunities to exploit state abstractions, so that individual MDPs within the hierarchy can ignore large parts of the state space. This is important for the practical application of the method. This paper defines the MAXQ hierarchy, proves formal results on its representational power, and establishes five conditions for the safe use of state abstractions. The paper presents an online model-free learning algorithm, MAXQ-Q, and proves that it converges with probability 1 to a kind of locally-optimal policy known as a recursively optimal policy, even in the presence of the five kinds of state abstraction. The paper evaluates the MAXQ representation and MAXQ-Q through a series of experiments in three domains and shows experimentally that MAXQ-Q (with state abstractions) converges to a recursively optimal policy much faster than flat Q learning. The fact that MAXQ learns a representation of the value function has an important benefit: it makes it possible to compute and execute an improved, non-hierarchical policy via a procedure similar to the policy improvement step of policy iteration. The paper demonstrates the effectiveness of this non-hierarchical execution experimentally. Finally, the paper concludes with a comparison to related work and a discussion of the design tradeoffs in hierarchical reinforcement learning.

1. Introduction

The area of Reinforcement Learning (Bertsekas & Tsitsiklis, 1996; Sutton & Barto, 1998) studies methods by which an agent can learn optimal or near-optimal plans by interacting directly with the external environment. The basic methods in reinforcement learning are based on the classical dynamic programming algorithms that were developed in the late 1950s (Bellman, 1957; Howard, 1960). However, reinforcement learning methods offer two important advantages over classical dynamic programming. First, the methods are online. This permits them to focus their attention on the parts of the state space that are important and to ignore the rest of the space. Second, the methods can employ function approximation algorithms (e.g., neural networks) to represent their knowledge. This allows them to generalize across the state space so that the learning time scales much better.

Despite recent advances in reinforcement learning, there are still many shortcomings. The biggest of these is the lack of a fully satisfactory method for incorporating hierarchies into reinforcement learning algorithms. Research in classical planning has shown that hierarchical methods such as hierarchical task networks (Currie & Tate, 1991), macro actions (Fikes, Hart, & Nilsson, 1972; Korf, 1985), and state abstraction methods (Sacerdoti, 1974; Knoblock, 1990) can provide exponential reductions in the computational cost of finding good plans. However, all of the basic algorithms for probabilistic planning and reinforcement learning are "flat" methods—they treat the state space as one huge flat search space. This means that the paths from the start state to the goal state are very long, and the length of these paths determines the cost of learning and planning, because information about future rewards must be propagated backward along these paths.

Many researchers (Singh, 1992; Lin, 1993; Kaelbling, 1993; Dayan & Hinton, 1993; Hauskrecht, et al., 1998; Parr & Russell, 1998; Sutton, Precup, & Singh, 1998) have experimented with different methods of hierarchical reinforcement learning and hierarchical probabilistic planning. This research has explored many different points in the design space of hierarchical methods, but several of these systems were designed for specific situations. We lack crisp definitions of the main approaches and a clear understanding of the relative merits of the different methods.

This paper formalizes and clarifies one approach and attempts to understand how it compares with the other techniques. The approach, called the MAXQ method, provides a hierarchical decomposition of the given reinforcement learning problem into a set of subproblems. It simultaneously provides a decomposition of the value function for the given problem into a set of value functions for the subproblems. Hence, it has both a declarative semantics (as a value function decomposition) and a procedural semantics (as a subroutine hierarchy).

The decomposition into subproblems has many advantages. First, policies learned in subproblems can be shared (reused) for multiple parent tasks. Second, the value functions learned in subproblems can be shared, so when the subproblem is reused in a new task, learning of the overall value function for the new task is accelerated. Third, if state abstractions can be applied, then the overall value function can be represented compactly as the sum of separate terms that each depends on only a subset of the state variables. This more compact representation of the value function will require less data to learn, and hence, learning will be faster.

Previous research shows that there are several important design decisions that must be made when constructing a hierarchical reinforcement learning system. To provide an overview of the results in this paper, let us review these issues and see how the MAXQ method approaches each of them.

The first issue is how to specify subtasks. Hierarchical reinforcement learning involves breaking the target Markov decision problem into a hierarchy of subproblems or subtasks. There are three general approaches to defining these subtasks. One approach is to define each subtask in terms of a fixed policy that is provided by the programmer (or that has been learned in some separate process). The "option" method of Sutton, Precup, and Singh (1998) takes this approach. The second approach is to define each subtask in terms of a non-deterministic finite-state controller. The Hierarchy of Abstract Machines (HAM) method of Parr and Russell (1998) takes this approach. This method permits the programmer to provide a "partial policy" that constrains the set of permitted actions at each point, but does not specify a complete policy for each subtask. The third approach is to define each subtask in terms of a termination predicate and a local reward function. These define what it means for the subtask to be completed and what the final reward should be for completing the subtask. The MAXQ method described in this paper follows this approach, building upon previous work by Singh (1992), Kaelbling (1993), Dayan and Hinton (1993), and Dean and Lin (1995).

An advantage of the "option" and partial policy approaches is that the subtask can be defined in terms of an amount of effort or a course of action rather than in terms of achieving a particular goal condition. However, the "option" approach (at least in the simple form described in this paper), requires the programmer to provide complete policies for the subtasks, which can be a difficult programming task in real-world problems. On the other hand, the termination predicate method requires the programmer to guess the relative desirability of the different states in which the subtask might terminate. This can also be difficult, although Dean and Lin show how these guesses can be revised automatically by the learning algorithm.

A potential drawback of all hierarchical methods is that the learned policy may be suboptimal. The hierarchy constrains the set of possible policies that can be considered. If these constraints are poorly chosen, the resulting policy will be suboptimal. Nonetheless, the learning algorithms that have been developed for the "option" and partial policy approaches guarantee that the learned policy will be the best possible policy consistent with these constraints.

The termination predicate method suffers from an additional source of suboptimality. The learning algorithm described in this paper converges to a form of local optimality that we call *recursive optimality*. This means that the policy of each subtask is locally optimal given the policies of its children. But there might exist better hierarchical policies where the policy for a subtask must be locally suboptimal so that the overall policy is optimal. For example, a subtask of buying milk might be performed suboptimally (at a more distant store) because the larger problem also involves buying film (at the same store). This problem can be avoided by careful definition of termination predicates and local reward functions, but this is an added burden on the programmer. (It is interesting to note that this problem of recursive optimality has not been noticed previously. This is because previous work focused on subtasks with a single terminal state, and in such cases, the problem does not arise.)

The second design issue is whether to employ state abstractions within subtasks. A subtask employs state abstraction if it ignores some aspects of the state of the environment. For example, in many robot navigation problems, choices about what route to take to reach a goal location are independent of what the robot is currently carrying. With few exceptions, state abstraction has not been explored previously. We will see that the MAXQ method creates many opportunities to exploit state abstraction, and that these abstractions can have a huge impact in accelerating learning. We will also see that there is an important design tradeoff: the successful use of state abstraction requires that subtasks be defined in terms of termination predicates rather than using the option or partial policy methods. This is why the MAXQ method must employ termination predicates, despite the problems that this can create.

The third design issue concerns the non-hierarchical "execution" of a learned hierarchical policy. Kaelbling (1993) was the first to point out that a value function learned from a hierarchical policy could be evaluated incrementally to yield a potentially much better non-hierarchical policy. Dietterich (1998) and Sutton, et al. (1999) generalized this to show how arbitrary subroutines could be executed non-hierarchically to yield improved policies. However, in order to support this non-hierarchical execution, extra learning is required. Ordinarily, in hierarchical reinforcement learning, the only states where learning is required at the higher levels of the hierarchy are states where one or more of the subroutines could terminate (plus all possible initial states). But to support non-hierarchical execution, learning is required in all states (and at all levels of the hierarchy). In general, this requires additional exploration as well as additional computation and memory. As a consequence of the hierarchical decomposition of the value function, the MAXQ method is able to support either form of execution, and we will see that there are many problems where the improvement from non-hierarchical execution is worth the added cost.

The fourth and final issue is what form of learning algorithm to employ. An important advantage of reinforcement learning algorithms is that they typically operate online. However, finding online algorithms that work for general hierarchical reinforcement learning has been difficult, particularly within the termination predicate family of methods. Singh's method relied on each subtask having a unique terminal state; Kaelbling employed a mix of online and batch algorithms to train her hierarchy; and work within the "options" framework usually assumes that the policies for the subproblems are given and do not need to be learned at all. The best previous online algorithms are the HAMQ Q learning algorithm of Parr and Russell (for the partial policy method) and the Feudal Q algorithm of Dayan and Hinton. Unfortunately, the HAMQ method requires "flattening" the hierarchy, and this has several undesirable consequences. The Feudal Q algorithm is tailored to a specific kind of problem, and it does not converge to any well-defined optimal policy.

In this paper, we present a general algorithm, called MAXQ-Q, for fully-online learning of a hierarchical value function. This algorithm enables all subtasks within the hierarchy to be learned simultaneously and online. We show experimentally and theoretically that the algorithm converges to a recursively optimal policy. We also show that it is substantially faster than "flat" (i.e., non-hierarchical) Q learning when state abstractions are employed.

The remainder of this paper is organized as follows. After introducing our notation in Section 2, we define the MAXQ value function decomposition in Section 3 and illustrate it with a simple example Markov decision problem. Section 4 presents an analytically tractable version of the MAXQ-Q learning algorithm called the MAXQ-0 algorithm and proves its convergence to a recursively optimal policy. It then shows how to extend MAXQ-0 to produce the MAXQ-Q algorithm, and shows how to extend the theorem similarly. Section 5 takes up the issue of state abstraction and formalizes a series of five conditions under which state abstractions can be safely incorporated into the MAXQ representation. State abstraction can give rise to a hierarchical credit assignment problem, and the paper briefly discusses one solution to this problem. Finally, Section 7 presents experiments with three example domains. These experiments give some idea of the generality of the MAXQ representation. They also provide results on the relative importance of temporal and state abstractions and on the importance of non-hierarchical execution. The paper concludes with further discussion of the design issues that were briefly described above, and in particular, it addresses the tradeoff between the method of defining subtasks (via termination predicates) and the ability to exploit state abstractions.

Some readers may be disappointed that MAXQ provides no way of learning the structure of the hierarchy. Our philosophy in developing MAXQ (which we share with other reinforcement learning researchers, notably Parr and Russell) has been to draw inspiration from the development of Belief Networks (Pearl, 1988). Belief networks were first introduced as a formalism in which the knowledge engineer would describe the structure of the networks and domain experts would provide the necessary probability estimates. Subsequently, methods were developed for learning the probability values directly from observational data. Most recently, several methods have been developed for learning the structure of the belief networks from data, so that the dependence on the knowledge engineer is reduced.

In this paper, we will likewise require that the programmer provide the structure of the hierarchy. The programmer will also need to make several important design decisions. We will see below that a MAXQ representation is very much like a computer program, and we will rely on the programmer to design each of the modules and indicate the permissible ways in which the modules can invoke each other. Our learning algorithms will fill in "implementations" of each module in such a way that the overall program will work well. We believe that this approach will provide a practical tool for solving large real-world MDPs. We also believe that it will help us understand the structure of hierarchical learning algorithms. It is our hope that subsequent research will be able to automate most of the work that we are currently requiring the programmer to do.

2. Formal Definitions

We begin by introducing definitions for Markov Decision Problems and Semi-Markov Decision Problems.

2.1 Markov Decision Problems

We employ the standard definition for Markov Decision Problems (also known as Markov decision processes). In this paper, we restrict our attention to situations in which an agent is interacting with a fully-observable stochastic environment. This situation can be modeled as a Markov Decision Problem (MDP) $\langle S, A, P, R, P_0 \rangle$ defined as follows:

- S: the finite set of states of the environment. At each point in time, the agent can observe the complete state of the environment.

- A: a finite set of actions. Technically, the set of available actions depends on the current state s, but we will suppress this dependence in our notation.

- P: When an action $a \in A$ is performed, the environment makes a probabilistic transition from its current state s to a resulting state s' according to the probability distribution $P(s'|s, a)$.

- R: Similarly, when action a is performed and the environment makes its transition from s to s', the agent receives a real-valued (possibly stochastic) reward r whose expected value is $R(s'|s, a)$. To simplify the notation, it is customary to treat this reward as being given at the time that action a is initiated, even though it may in general depend on s' as well as on s and a.

- P_0: The starting state distribution. When the MDP is initialized, it is in state s with probability $P_0(s)$.

A *policy*, π, is a mapping from states to actions that tells what action $a = \pi(s)$ to perform when the environment is in state s.

We will consider two settings: episodic and infinite-horizon.

In the episodic setting, all rewards are finite and there is at least one zero-cost absorbing terminal state. An absorbing terminal state is a state in which all actions lead back to the same state with probability 1 and zero reward. For technical reasons, we will only consider problems where all deterministic policies are "proper"—that is, all deterministic policies have a non-zero probability of reaching a terminal state when started in an arbitrary state. (We believe this condition can be relaxed, but we have not verified this formally.) In the episodic setting, the goal of the agent is to find a policy that maximizes the expected cumulative reward. In the special case where all rewards are non-positive, these problems are referred to as stochastic shortest path problems, because the rewards can be viewed as costs (i.e., lengths), and the policy attempts to move the agent along the path of minimum expected cost.

In the infinite horizon setting, all rewards are also finite. In addition, there is a discount factor γ, and the agent's goal is to find a policy that minimizes the infinite discounted sum of future rewards.

The value function V^π for policy π is a function that tells, for each state s, what the expected cumulative reward will be of executing policy π starting in state s. Let r_t be a random variable that tells the reward that the agent receives at time step t while following policy π. We can define the value function in the episodic setting as

$$V^\pi(s) = E\left\{r_t + r_{t+1} + r_{t+2} + \cdots | s_t = s, \pi\right\}.$$

In the discounted setting, the value function is

$$V^\pi(s) = E\left\{r_t + \gamma r_{t+1} + \gamma^2 r_{t+2} + \cdots \bigg| s_t = s, \pi\right\}.$$

We can see that this equation reduces to the previous one when $\gamma = 1$. However, in infinite-horizon MDPs this sum may not converge when $\gamma = 1$.

The value function satisfies the Bellman equation for a fixed policy:

$$V^\pi(s) = \sum_{s'} P(s'|s, \pi(s)) \left[R(s'|s, \pi(s)) + \gamma V^\pi(s') \right].$$

The quantity on the right-hand side is called the *backed-up value* of performing action a in state s. For each possible successor state s', it computes the reward that would be received and the value of the resulting state and then weights those according to the probability of ending up in s'.

The optimal value function V^* is the value function that simultaneously maximizes the expected cumulative reward in all states $s \in S$. Bellman (1957) proved that it is the unique solution to what is now known as the Bellman equation:

$$V^*(s) = \max_a \sum_{s'} P(s'|s, a) \left[R(s'|s, a) + \gamma V^*(s') \right]. \tag{1}$$

There may be many optimal policies that achieve this value. Any policy that chooses a in s to achieve the maximum on the right-hand side of this equation is an optimal policy. We will denote an optimal policy by π^*. Note that all optimal policies are "greedy" with respect to the backed-up value of the available actions.

Closely related to the value function is the so-called *action-value function*, or Q function (Watkins, 1989). This function, $Q^\pi(s, a)$, gives the expected cumulative reward of performing action a in state s and then following policy π thereafter. The Q function also satisfies a Bellman equation:

$$Q^\pi(s, a) = \sum_{s'} P(s'|s, a) \left[R(s'|s, a) + \gamma Q^\pi(s', \pi(s')) \right].$$

The optimal action-value function is written $Q^*(s, a)$, and it satisfies the equation

$$Q^*(s, a) = \sum_{s'} P(s'|s, a) \left[R(s'|s, a) + \gamma \max_{a'} Q^*(s', a') \right]. \tag{2}$$

Note that any policy that is greedy with respect to Q^* is an optimal policy. There may be many such optimal policies—they differ only in how they break ties between actions with identical Q^* values.

An *action order*, denoted ω, is a total order over the actions within an MDP. That is, ω is an anti-symmetric, transitive relation such that $\omega(a_1, a_2)$ is true iff a_1 is strictly preferred to a_2. An *ordered greedy policy*, π_ω is a greedy policy that breaks ties using ω. For example, suppose that the two best actions at state s are a_1 and a_2, that $Q(s, a_1) = Q(s, a_2)$, and that $\omega(a_1, a_2)$. Then the ordered greedy policy π_ω will choose a_1: $\pi_\omega(s) = a_1$. Note that although there may be many optimal policies for a given MDP, the ordered greedy policy, π_ω^*, is unique.

2.2 Semi-Markov Decision Processes

In order to introduce and prove some of the properties of the MAXQ decomposition, we need to consider a simple generalization of MDPs—the semi-Markov decision process.

A discrete-time *semi-Markov Decision Process* (SMDP) is a generalization of the Markov Decision Process in which the actions can take a variable amount of time to complete. In particular, let the random variable N denote the number of time steps that action a takes when it is executed in state s. We can extend the state transition probability function to be the joint distribution of the result states s' and the number of time steps N when action a is performed in state s: $P(s', N|s, a)$. Similarly, the expected reward can be changed to be $R(s', N|s, a)$.[1]

It is straightforward to modify the Bellman equation to define the value function for a fixed policy π as

$$V^\pi(s) = \sum_{s', N} P(s', N|s, \pi(s)) \left[R(s', N|s, \pi(s)) + \gamma^N V^\pi(s') \right].$$

The only change is that the expected value on the right-hand side is taken with respect to both s' and N, and γ is raised to the power N to reflect the variable amount of time that may elapse while executing action a.

Note that because expectation is a linear operator, we can write each of these Bellman equations as the sum of the expected reward for performing action a and the expected value of the resulting state s'. For example, we can rewrite the equation above as

$$V^\pi(s) = \overline{R}(s, \pi(s)) + \sum_{s', N} P(s', N|s, \pi(s)) \gamma^N V^\pi(s'). \tag{3}$$

where $\overline{R}(s, \pi(s))$ is the expected reward of performing action $\pi(s)$ in state s, and the expectation is taken with respect to s' and N.

All of the results given in this paper can be generalized to apply to discrete-time semi-Markov Decision Processes. A consequence of this is that whenever this paper talks of executing a primitive action, it could just as easily talk of executing a hand-coded open-loop "subroutine". These subroutines would not be learned, and nor could their execution be interrupted as discussed below in Section 6. But in many applications (e.g., robot control with limited sensors), open-loop controllers can be very useful (e.g., to hide partial-observability). For an example, see Kalmár, Szepesvári, and A. Lörincz (1998).

Note that for the episodic case, there is no difference between a MDP and a Semi-Markov Decision Process, because the discount factor γ is 1, and therefore neither the optimal policy nor the optimal value function depend on the amount of time each action takes.

2.3 Reinforcement Learning Algorithms

A reinforcement learning algorithm is an algorithm that tries to construct an optimal policy for an unknown MDP. The algorithm is given access to the unknown MDP via the following

---

1. This formalization is slightly different from the standard formulation of SMDPs, which separates $P(s'|s, a)$ and $F(t|s, a)$, where F is the cumulative distribution function for the probability that a will terminate in t time units, and t is real-valued rather than integer-valued. In our case, it is important to consider the joint distribution of s' and N, but we do not need to consider actions with arbitrary real-valued durations.

reinforcement learning protocol. At each time step t, the algorithm is told the current state s of the MDP and the set of actions $A(s) \subseteq A$ that are executable in that state. The algorithm chooses an action $a \in A(s)$, and the MDP executes this action (which causes it to move to state s') and returns a real-valued reward r. If s is an absorbing terminal state, the set of actions $A(s)$ contains only the special action reset, which causes the MDP to move to one of its initial states, drawn according to P_0.

In this paper, we will make use of two well-known learning algorithms: Q learning (Watkins, 1989; Watkins & Dayan, 1992) and SARSA(0) (Rummery & Niranjan, 1994). We will apply these algorithms to the case where the action value function $Q(s, a)$ is represented as a table with one entry for each pair of state and action. Every entry of the table is initialized arbitrarily.

In Q learning, after the algorithm has observed s, chosen a, received r, and observed s', it performs the following update:

$$Q_t(s, a) := (1 - \alpha_t)Q_{t-1}(s, a) + \alpha_t[r + \gamma \max_{a'} Q_{t-1}(s', a')],$$

where α_t is a learning rate parameter.

Jaakkola, Jordan and Singh (1994) and Bertsekas and Tsitsiklis (1996) prove that if the agent follows an "exploration policy" that tries every action in every state infinitely often and if

$$\lim_{T \to \infty} \sum_{t=1}^{T} \alpha_t = \infty \quad \text{and} \quad \lim_{T \to \infty} \sum_{t=1}^{T} \alpha_t^2 < \infty \tag{4}$$

then Q_t converges to the optimal action-value function Q^* with probability 1. Their proof holds in both settings discussed in this paper (episodic and infinite-horizon).

The SARSA(0) algorithm is very similar. After observing s, choosing a, observing r, observing s', and choosing a', the algorithm performs the following update:

$$Q_t(s, a) := (1 - \alpha_t)Q_{t-1}(s, a) + \alpha_t[r + \gamma Q_{t-1}(s', a')],$$

where α_t is a learning rate parameter. The key difference is that the Q value of the chosen action a', $Q(s', a')$, appears on the right-hand side in the place where Q learning uses the Q value of the best action. Singh, et al. (1998) provide two important convergence results: First, if a fixed policy π is employed to choose actions, SARSA(0) will converge to the value function of that policy provided α_t decreases according to Equations (4). Second, if a so-called GLIE policy is employed to choose actions, SARSA(0) will converge to the value function of the optimal policy, provided again that α_t decreases according to Equations (4). A GLIE policy is defined as follows:

Definition 1 *A GLIE (Greedy in the Limit with Infinite Exploration) policy is any policy satisfying*

    1. Each action is executed infinitely often in every state that is visited infinitely often.

    2. In the limit, the policy is greedy with respect to the Q-value function with probability 1.

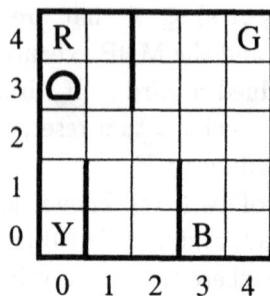

Figure 1: The Taxi Domain.

3. The MAXQ Value Function Decomposition

At the center of the MAXQ method for hierarchical reinforcement learning is the MAXQ value function decomposition. MAXQ describes how to decompose the overall value function for a policy into a collection of value functions for individual subtasks (and subsubtasks, recursively).

3.1 A Motivating Example

To make the discussion concrete, let us consider the following simple example. Figure 1 shows a 5-by-5 grid world inhabited by a taxi agent. There are four specially-designated locations in this world, marked as R(ed), B(lue), G(reen), and Y(ellow). The taxi problem is episodic. In each episode, the taxi starts in a randomly-chosen square. There is a passenger at one of the four locations (chosen randomly), and that passenger wishes to be transported to one of the four locations (also chosen randomly). The taxi must go to the passenger's location (the "source"), pick up the passenger, go to the destination location (the "destination"), and put down the passenger there. (To keep things uniform, the taxi must pick up and drop off the passenger even if he/she is already located at the destination!) The episode ends when the passenger is deposited at the destination location.

There are six primitive actions in this domain: (a) four navigation actions that move the taxi one square North, South, East, or West, (b) a Pickup action, and (c) a Putdown action. There is a reward of −1 for each action and an additional reward of +20 for successfully delivering the passenger. There is a reward of −10 if the taxi attempts to execute the Putdown or Pickup actions illegally. If a navigation action would cause the taxi to hit a wall, the action is a no-op, and there is only the usual reward of −1.

To simplify the examples throughout this section, we will make the six primitive actions deterministic. Later, we will make the actions stochastic in order to create a greater challenge for our learning algorithms.

We seek a policy that maximizes the total reward per episode. There are 500 possible states: 25 squares, 5 locations for the passenger (counting the four starting locations and the taxi), and 4 destinations.

This task has a simple hierarchical structure in which there are two main sub-tasks: Get the passenger and Deliver the passenger. Each of these subtasks in turn involves the subtask of navigating to one of the four locations and then performing a Pickup or Putdown action.

This task illustrates the need to support temporal abstraction, state abstraction, and subtask sharing. The temporal abstraction is obvious—for example, the process of navigating to the passenger's location and picking up the passenger is a temporally extended action that can take different numbers of steps to complete depending on the distance to the target. The top level policy (get passenger; deliver passenger) can be expressed very simply if these temporal abstractions can be employed.

The need for state abstraction is perhaps less obvious. Consider the subtask of getting the passenger. While this subtask is being solved, the destination of the passenger is completely irrelevant—it cannot affect any of the nagivation or pickup decisions. Perhaps more importantly, when navigating to a target location (either the source or destination location of the passenger), only the target location is important. The fact that in some cases the taxi is carrying the passenger and in other cases it is not is irrelevant.

Finally, support for subtask sharing is critical. If the system could learn how to solve the navigation subtask once, then the solution could be shared by both the "Get the passenger" and "Deliver the passenger" subtasks. We will show below that the MAXQ method provides a value function representation and learning algorithm that supports temporal abstraction, state abstraction, and subtask sharing.

To construct a MAXQ decomposition for the taxi problem, we must identify a set of individual subtasks that we believe will be important for solving the overall task. In this case, let us define the following four tasks:

- Navigate(t). In this subtask, the goal is to move the taxi from its current location to one of the four target locations, which will be indicated by the formal parameter t.

- Get. In this subtask, the goal is to move the taxi from its current location to the passenger's current location and pick up the passenger.

- Put. The goal of this subtask is to move the taxi from the current location to the passenger's destination location and drop off the passenger.

- Root. This is the whole taxi task.

Each of these subtasks is defined by a subgoal, and each subtask terminates when the subgoal is achieved.

After defining these subtasks, we must indicate for each subtask which other subtasks or primitive actions it should employ to reach its goal. For example, the Navigate(t) subtask should use the four primitive actions North, South, East, and West. The Get subtask should use the Navigate subtask and the Pickup primitive action, and so on.

All of this information can be summarized by a directed acyclic graph called the *task graph*, which is shown in Figure 2. In this graph, each node corresponds to a subtask or a primitive action, and each edge corresponds to a potential way in which one subtask can "call" one of its child tasks. The notation *formal/actual* (e.g., $t/source$) tells how a formal parameter is to be bound to an actual parameter.

Now suppose that for each of these subtasks, we write a policy (e.g., as a computer program) to achieve the subtask. We will refer to the policy for a subtask as a "subroutine", and we can view the parent subroutine as invoking the child subroutine via ordinary

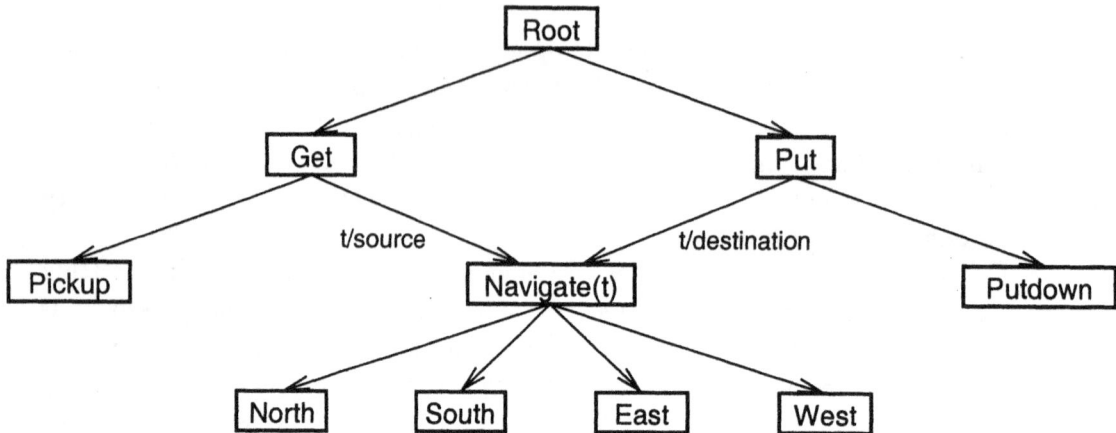

Figure 2: A task graph for the Taxi problem.

subroutine-call-and-return semantics. If we have a policy for each subtask, then this gives us an overall policy for the Taxi MDP. The Root subtask executes its policy by calling subroutines that are policies for the Get and Put subtasks. The Get policy calls subroutines for the Navigate(t) subtask and the Pickup primitive action. And so on. We will call this collection of policies a *hierarchical policy*. In a hierarchical policy, each subroutine executes until it enters a terminal state for its subtask.

3.2 Definitions

Let us formalize the discussion so far.

The MAXQ decomposition takes a given MDP M and decomposes it into a finite set of subtasks $\{M_0, M_1, \ldots, M_n\}$ with the convention that M_0 is the root subtask (i.e., solving M_0 solves the entire original MDP M).

Definition 2 *An* unparameterized subtask *is a three-tuple, $\langle T_i, A_i, \tilde{R}_i \rangle$, defined as follows:*

1. *T_i is a termination predicate that partitions S into a set of active states, S_i, and a set of terminal states, T_i. The policy for subtask M_i can only be executed if the current state s is in S_i. If, at any time that subtask M_i is being executed, the MDP enters a state in T_i, then M_i terminates immediately (even if it is still executing a subtask, see below).*

2. *A_i is a set of actions that can be performed to achieve subtask M_i. These actions can either be primitive actions from A, the set of primitive actions for the MDP, or they can be other subtasks, which we will denote by their indexes i. We will refer to these actions as the "children" of subtask i. The sets A_i define a directed graph over the subtasks $M_0, \ldots, M_n$, and this graph may not contain any cycles. Stated another way, no subtask can invoke itself recursively either directly or indirectly.*

   If a child subtask M_j has formal parameters, then this is interpreted as if the subtask occurred multiple times in A_i, with one occurrence for each possible tuple of actual values that could be bound to the formal parameters. The set of actions A_i may differ from one state to another and from one set of actual parameter values to another, so technically, A_i is a function of s and the actual parameters. However, we will suppress this dependence in our notation.

3. $\tilde{R}_i(s')$ is the pseudo-reward function, which specifies a (deterministic) pseudo-reward for each transition to a terminal state $s' \in T_i$. This pseudo-reward tells how desirable each of the terminal states is for this subtask. It is typically employed to give goal terminal states a pseudo-reward of 0 and any non-goal terminal states a negative reward. By definition, the pseudo-reward $\tilde{R}_i(s)$ is also zero for all non-terminal states s. The pseudo-reward is only used during learning, so it will not be mentioned further until Section 4.

Each primitive action a from M is a primitive subtask in the MAXQ decomposition such that a is always executable, it always terminates immediately after execution, and its pseudo-reward function is uniformly zero.

If a subtask has formal parameters, then each possible binding of actual values to the formal parameters specifies a distinct subtask. We can think of the values of the formal parameters as being part of the "name" of the subtask. In practice, of course, we implement a parameterized subtask by parameterizing the various components of the task. If b specifies the actual parameter values for task M_i, then we can define a parameterized termination predicate $T_i(s, b)$ and a parameterized pseudo-reward function $\tilde{R}_i(s', b)$. To simplify notation in the rest of the paper, we will usually omit these parameter bindings. However, it should be noted that if a parameter of a subtask takes on a large number of possible values, this is equivalent to creating a large number of different subtasks, each of which will need to be learned. It will also create a large number of candidate actions for the parent task, which will make the learning problem more difficult for the parent task as well.

Definition 3 *A* hierarchical policy, *π, is a set containing a policy for each of the subtasks in the problem: $\pi = \{\pi_0, \ldots, \pi_n\}$.*

Each subtask policy π_i takes a state and returns the name of a primitive action to execute or the name of a subroutine (and bindings for its formal parameters) to invoke. In the terminology of Sutton, Precup, and Singh (1998), a subtask policy is a deterministic "option", and its probability of terminating in state s (which they denote by $\beta(s)$) is 0 if $s \in S_i$, and 1 if $s \in T_i$.

In a parameterized task, the policy must be parameterized as well so that π takes a state and the bindings of formal parameters and returns a chosen action and the bindings (if any) of its formal parameters.

Table 1 gives a pseudo-code description of the procedure for executing a hierarchical policy. The hierarchical policy is executed using a stack discipline, similar to ordinary programming languages. Let K_t denote the contents of the pushdown stack at time t. When a subroutine is invoked, its name and actual parameters are pushed onto the stack. When a subroutine terminates, its name and actual parameters are popped off the stack. Notice (line 16) that if *any* subroutine on the stack terminates, then all subroutines below

Table 1: Pseudo-Code for Execution of a Hierarchical Policy.

Procedure EXECUTEHIERARCHICALPOLICY(π)

1   s_t is the state of the world at time t

2   K_t is the state of the execution stack at time t

3   Let $t = 0$; K_t = empty stack; observe s_t

4   push $(0, nil)$ onto stack K_t (invoke the root task with no parameters)

5   **repeat**

6   **while** $top(K_t)$ is not a primitive action

7   Let $(i, f_i) := top(K_t)$, where

8   i is the name of the "current" subroutine, and

9   f_i gives the parameter bindings for i

10   Let $(a, f_a) := \pi_i(s, f_i)$, where

11   a is the action and f_a gives the parameter bindings chosen by policy π_i

12   push (a, f_a) onto the stack K_t

13   **end** // while

14   Let $(a, nil) := pop(K_t)$ be the primitive action on the top of the stack.

15   Execute primitive action a, observe s_{t+1}, and receive reward $R(s_{t+1}|s_t, a)$

16   If any subtask on K_t is terminated in s_{t+1} then

17   Let M' be the terminated subtask that is highest (closest to the root) on the stack.

18   while $top(K_t) \neq M'$ do $pop(K_t)$

19        $pop(K_t)$

20    $K_{t+1} := K_t$ is the resulting execution stack.

21   **until** K_{t+1} is empty

end EXECUTEHIERARCHICALPOLICY

---

it are immediately aborted, and control returns to the subroutine that had invoked the terminated subroutine.

It is sometimes useful to think of the contents of the stack as being an additional part of the state space for the problem. Hence, a hierarchical policy implicitly defines a mapping from the current state s_t and current stack contents K_t to a primitive action a. This action is executed, and this yields a resulting state s_{t+1} and a resulting stack contents K_{t+1}. Because of the added state information in the stack, the hierarchical policy is non-Markovian with respect to the original MDP.

Because a hierarchical policy maps from states s and stack contents K to actions, the value function for a hierarchical policy must assign values to combinations of states s and stack contents K.

Definition 4 *A hierarchical value function, denoted $V^\pi(\langle s, K \rangle)$, gives the expected cumulative reward of following the hierarchical policy π starting in state s with stack contents K.*

This hierarchical value function is exactly what is learned by Ron Parr's (1998b) HAMQ algorithm, which we will discuss below. However, in this paper, we will focus on learning only the *projected value functions* of each of the subtasks $M_0, \ldots, M_n$ in the hierarchy.

Definition 5 *The* projected value function *of hierarchical policy π on subtask M_i, denoted $V^\pi(i, s)$, is the expected cumulative reward of executing π_i (and the policies of all descendents of M_i) starting in state s until M_i terminates.*

The purpose of the MAXQ value function decomposition is to decompose $V(0, s)$ (the projected value function of the root task) in terms of the projected value functions $V(i, s)$ of all of the subtasks in the MAXQ decomposition.

3.3 Decomposition of the Projected Value Function

Now that we have defined a hierarchical policy and its projected value function, we can show how that value function can be decomposed hierarchically. The decomposition is based on the following theorem:

Theorem 1 *Given a task graph over tasks $M_0, \ldots, M_n$ and a hierarchical policy π, each subtask M_i defines a semi-Markov decision process with states S_i, actions A_i, probability transition function $P_i^\pi(s', N | s, a)$, and expected reward function $\overline{R}(s, a) = V^\pi(a, s)$, where $V^\pi(a, s)$ is the projected value function for child task M_a in state s. If a is a primitive action, $V^\pi(a, s)$ is defined as the expected immediate reward of executing a in s: $V^\pi(a, s) = \sum_{s'} P(s' | s, a) R(s' | s, a)$.*

Proof: Consider all of the subroutines that are descendents of task M_i in the task graph. Because all of these subroutines are executing fixed policies (specified by hierarchical policy π), the probability transition function $P_i^\pi(s', N | s, a)$ is a well defined, stationary distribution for each child subroutine a. The set of states S_i and the set of actions A_i are obvious. The interesting part of this theorem is the fact that the expected reward function $\overline{R}(s, a)$ of the SMDP is the projected value function of the child task M_a.

To see this, let us write out the value of $V^\pi(i, s)$:

$$V^\pi(i, s) = E\{r_t + \gamma r_{t+1} + \gamma^2 r_{t+2} + \cdots | s_t = s, \pi\} \tag{5}$$

This sum continues until the subroutine for task M_i enters a state in T_i.

Now let us suppose that the first action chosen by π_i is a subroutine a. This subroutine is invoked, and it executes for a number of steps N and terminates in state s' according to $P_i^\pi(s', N | s, a)$. We can rewrite Equation (5) as

$$V^\pi(i, s) = E\left\{\sum_{u=0}^{N-1} \gamma^u r_{t+u} + \sum_{u=N}^{\infty} \gamma^u r_{t+u} \middle| s_t = s, \pi\right\} \tag{6}$$

The first summation on the right-hand side of Equation (6) is the discounted sum of rewards for executing subroutine a starting in state s until it terminates, in other words, it is $V^\pi(a, s)$, the projected value function for the child task M_a. The second term on the right-hand side of the equation is the value of s' for the current task i, $V^\pi(i, s')$, discounted by γ^N, where s' is the current state when subroutine a terminates. We can write this in the form of a Bellman equation:

$$V^\pi(i, s) = V^\pi(\pi_i(s), s) + \sum_{s', N} P_i^\pi(s', N | s, \pi_i(s)) \gamma^N V^\pi(i, s') \tag{7}$$

This has the same form as Equation (3), which is the Bellman equation for an SMDP, where the first term is the expected reward $\overline{R}(s, \pi(s))$. **Q.E.D.**

To obtain a hierarchical decomposition of the projected value function, let us switch to the action-value (or Q) representation. First, we need to extend the Q notation to handle the task hierarchy. Let $Q^\pi(i, s, a)$ be the expected cumulative reward for subtask M_i of performing action a in state s and then following hierarchical policy π until subtask M_i terminates. Action a may be either a primitive action or a child subtask. With this notation, we can re-state Equation (7) as follows:

$$Q^\pi(i, s, a) = V^\pi(a, s) + \sum_{s', N} P_i^\pi(s', N | s, a) \gamma^N Q^\pi(i, s', \pi(s')), \tag{8}$$

The right-most term in this equation is the expected discounted reward of *completing* task M_i after executing action a in state s. This term only depends on i, s, and a, because the summation marginalizes away the dependence on s' and N. Let us define $C^\pi(i, s, a)$ to be equal to this term:

Definition 6 *The completion function, $C^\pi(i, s, a)$, is the expected discounted cumulative reward of completing subtask M_i after invoking the subroutine for subtask M_a in state s. The reward is discounted back to the point in time where a begins execution.*

$$C^\pi(i, s, a) = \sum_{s', N} P_i^\pi(s', N | s, a) \gamma^N Q^\pi(i, s', \pi(s')) \tag{9}$$

With this definition, we can express the Q function recursively as

$$Q^\pi(i, s, a) = V^\pi(a, s) + C^\pi(i, s, a). \tag{10}$$

Finally, we can re-express the definition for $V^\pi(i, s)$ as

$$V^\pi(i, s) = \begin{cases} Q^\pi(i, s, \pi_i(s)) & \text{if } i \text{ is composite} \\ \sum_{s'} P(s' | s, i) R(s' | s, i) & \text{if } i \text{ is primitive} \end{cases} \tag{11}$$

We will refer to equations (9), (10), and (11) as the *decomposition equations* for the MAXQ hierarchy under a fixed hierarchical policy π. These equations recursively decompose the projected value function for the root, $V^\pi(0, s)$ into the projected value functions for the individual subtasks, $M_1, \ldots, M_n$ and the individual completion functions $C^\pi(j, s, a)$ for $j = 1, \ldots, n$. The fundamental quantities that must be stored to represent the value function decomposition are just the C values for all non-primitive subtasks and the V values for all primitive actions.

To make it easier for programmers to design and debug MAXQ decompositions, we have developed a graphical representation that we call the *MAXQ graph*. A MAXQ graph for the Taxi domain is shown in Figure 3. The graph contains two kinds of nodes, Max nodes and Q nodes. The Max nodes correspond to the subtasks in the task decomposition—there is one Max node for each primitive action and one Max node for each subtask (including the Root) task. Each primitive Max node i stores the value of $V^\pi(i, s)$. The Q nodes correspond to the actions that are available for each subtask. Each Q node for parent task i, state s

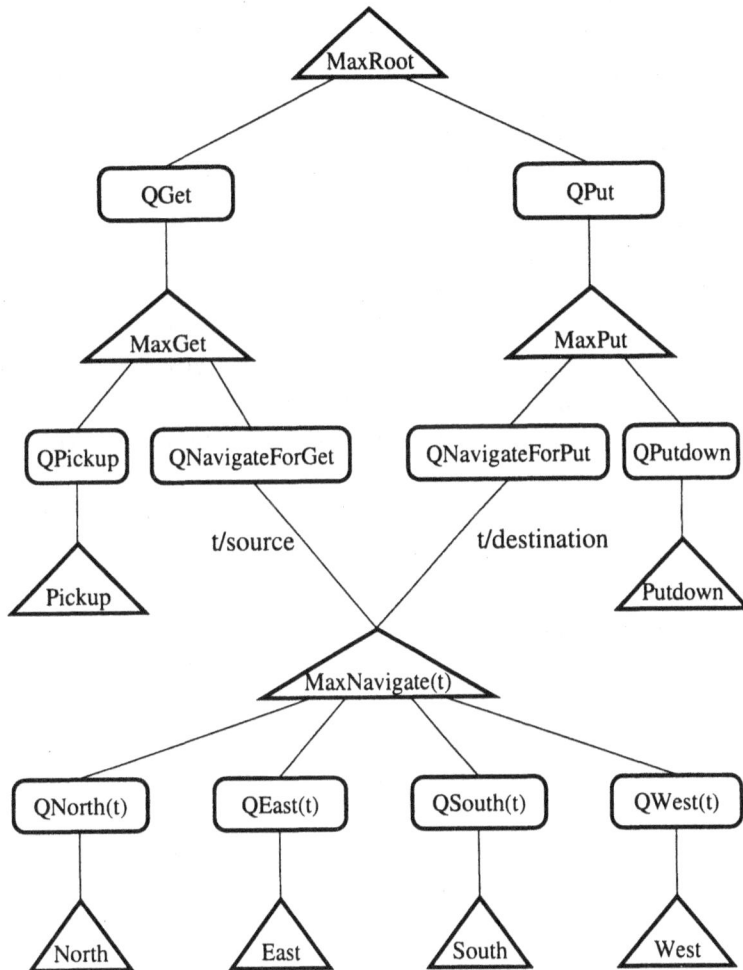

Figure 3: A MAXQ graph for the Taxi Domain.

and subtask a stores the value of $C^\pi(i, s, a)$. The children of any node are *unordered*—that is, the order in which they are drawn in Figure 3 does not imply anything about the order in which they will be executed. Indeed, a child action may be executed multiple times before its parent subtask is completed.

In addition to storing information, the Max nodes and Q nodes can be viewed as performing parts of the computation described by the decomposition equations. Specifically, each Max node i can be viewed as computing the projected value function $V^\pi(i, s)$ for its subtask. For primitive Max nodes, this information is stored in the node. For composite Max nodes, this information is obtained by "asking" the Q node corresponding to $\pi_i(s)$. Each Q node with parent task i and child task a can be viewed as computing the value of $Q^\pi(i, s, a)$. It does this by "asking" its child task a for its projected value function $V^\pi(a, s)$ and then adding its completion function $C^\pi(i, s, a)$.

As an example, consider the situation shown in Figure 1, which we will denote by s_1. Suppose that the passenger is at R and wishes to go to B. Let the hierarchical policy we are evaluating be an optimal policy denoted by π (we will omit the superscript * to reduce the clutter of the notation). The value of this state under π is 10, because it will cost 1 unit to move the taxi to R, 1 unit to pickup the passenger, 7 units to move the taxi to B, and 1 unit to putdown the passenger, for a total of 10 units (a reward of -10). When the passenger is delivered, the agent gets a reward of $+20$, so the net value is $+10$.

Figure 4 shows how the MAXQ hierarchy computes this value. To compute the value $V^\pi(\text{Root}, s_1)$, MaxRoot consults its policy and finds that $\pi_{\text{Root}}(s_1)$ is Get. Hence, it "asks" the Q node, QGet to compute $Q^\pi(\text{Root}, s_1, \text{Get})$. The completion cost for the Root task after performing a Get, $C^\pi(\text{Root}, s_1, \text{Get})$, is 12, because it will cost 8 units to deliver the customer (for a net reward of $20 - 8 = 12$) after completing the Get subtask. However, this is just the reward *after* completing the Get, so it must ask MaxGet to estimate the expected reward of performing the Get itself.

The policy for MaxGet dictates that in s_1, the Navigate subroutine should be invoked with t bound to R, so MaxGet consults the Q node, QNavigateForGet to compute the expected reward. QNavigateForGet knows that after completing the Navigate(R) task, one more action (the Pickup) will be required to complete the Get, so $C^\pi(\text{MaxGet}, s_1, \text{Navigate}(R)) = -1$. It then asks MaxNavigate(R) to compute the expected reward of performing a Navigate to location R.

The policy for MaxNavigate chooses the North action, so MaxNavigate asks QNorth to compute the value. QNorth looks up its completion cost, and finds that $C^\pi(\text{Navigate}, s_1, \text{North})$ is 0 (i.e., the Navigate task will be completed after performing the North action). It consults MaxNorth to determine the expected cost of performing the North action itself. Because MaxNorth is a primitive action, it looks up its expected reward, which is -1.

Now this series of recursive computations can conclude as follows:

- $Q^\pi(\text{Navigate}(R), s_1, \text{North}) = -1 + 0$

- $V^\pi(\text{Navigate}(R), s_1) = -1$

- $Q^\pi(\text{Get}, s_1, \text{Navigate}(R)) = -1 + -1$
  (-1 to perform the Navigate plus -1 to complete the Get.

- $V^\pi(\text{Get}, s_1) = -2$

- $Q^\pi(\text{Root}, s_1, \text{Get}) = -2 + 12$
  (-2 to perform the Get plus 12 to complete the Root task and collect the final reward).

The end result of all of this is that the value of $V^\pi(\text{Root}, s_1)$ is decomposed into a sum of C terms plus the expected reward of the chosen primitive action:

$$
\begin{aligned}
V^\pi(\text{Root}, s_1) &= V^\pi(\text{North}, s_1) + C^\pi(\text{Navigate}(R), s_1, \text{North}) + \\
&\quad\ C^\pi(\text{Get}, s_1, \text{Navigate}(R)) + C^\pi(\text{Root}, s_1, \text{Get}) \\
&= -1 + 0 + -1 + 12 \\
&= 10
\end{aligned}
$$

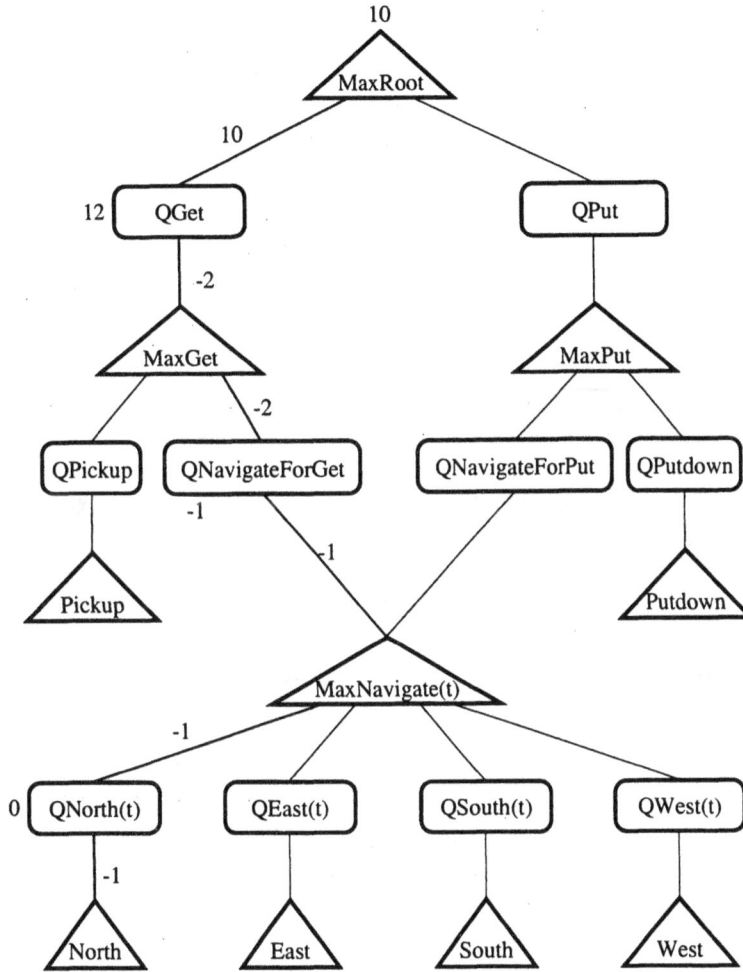

Figure 4: Computing the value of a state using the MAXQ hierarchy. The C value of each Q node is shown to the left of the node. All other numbers show the values being returned up the graph.

In general, the MAXQ value function decomposition has the form

$$V^\pi(0, s) = V^\pi(a_m, s) + C^\pi(a_{m-1}, s, a_m) + \ldots + C^\pi(a_1, s, a_2) + C^\pi(0, s, a_1), \quad (12)$$

where $a_0, a_1, \ldots, a_m$ is the "path" of Max nodes chosen by the hierarchical policy going from the Root down to a primitive leaf node. This is summarized graphically in Figure 5.

We can summarize the presentation of this section by the following theorem:

Theorem 2 *Let $\pi = \{\pi_i; i = 0, \ldots, n\}$ be a hierarchical policy defined for a given MAXQ graph with subtasks $M_0, \ldots, M_n$, and let $i = 0$ be the root node of the graph. Then there exist values for $C^\pi(i, s, a)$ (for internal Max nodes) and $V^\pi(i, s)$ (for primitive, leaf Max*

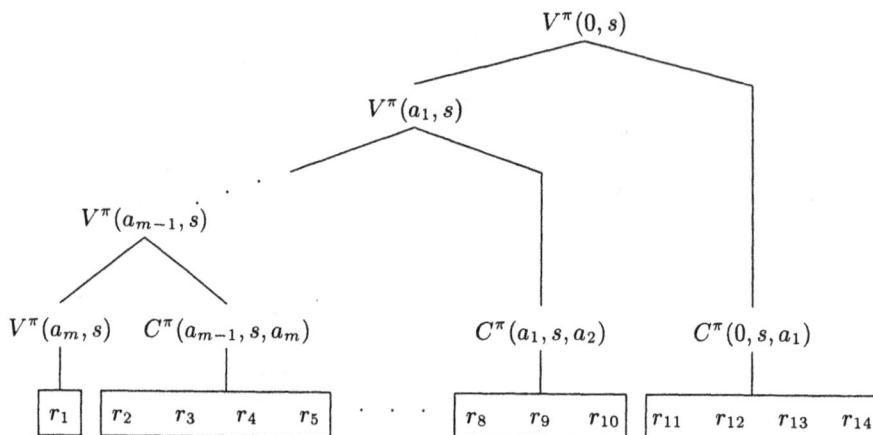

Figure 5: The MAXQ decomposition; $r_1, \ldots, r_{14}$ denote the sequence of rewards received from primitive actions at times $1, \ldots, 14$.

nodes) such that $V^\pi(0, s)$ (as computed by the decomposition equations (9), (10), and (11)) is the expected discounted cumulative reward of following policy π starting in state s.

Proof: The proof is by induction on the number of levels in the task graph. At each level i, we compute values for $C^\pi(i, s, \pi(s))$ (or $V^\pi(i, s)$, if i is primitive) according to the decomposition equations. We can apply the decomposition equations again to compute $Q^\pi(i, s, \pi(s))$ and apply Equation (8) and Theorem 1 to conclude that $Q^\pi(i, s, \pi(s))$ gives the value function for level i. When $i = 0$, we obtain the value function for the entire hierarchical policy. **Q. E. D.**

It is important to note that this representation theorem does not mention the pseudo-reward function, because the pseudo-reward is used only during learning. This theorem captures the *representational power* of the MAXQ decomposition, but it does not address the question of whether there is a learning algorithm that can find a given policy. That is the subject of the next section.

4. A Learning Algorithm for the MAXQ Decomposition

This section presents the central contributions of the paper. First, we discuss what optimality criteria should be employed in hierarchical reinforcement learning. Then we introduce the MAXQ-0 learning algorithm, which can learn value functions (and policies) for MAXQ hierarchies in which there are no pseudo-rewards (i.e., the pseudo-rewards are zero). The central theoretical result of the paper is that MAXQ-0 converges to a recursively optimal policy for the given MAXQ hierarchy. This is followed by a brief discussion of ways of accelerating MAXQ-0 learning. The section concludes with a description of the MAXQ-Q learning algorithm, which handles non-zero pseudo-reward functions.

4.1 Two Kinds of Optimality

In order to develop a learning algorithm for the MAXQ decomposition, we must consider exactly what we are hoping to achieve. Of course, for any MDP M, we would like to find an optimal policy π^*. However, in the MAXQ method (and in hierarchical reinforcement learning in general), the programmer imposes a hierarchy on the problem. This hierarchy constrains the space of possible policies so that it may not be possible to represent the optimal policy or its value function.

In the MAXQ method, the constraints take two forms. First, within a subtask, only some of the possible primitive actions may be permitted. For example, in the taxi task, during a Navigate(t), only the North, South, East, and West actions are available—the Pickup and Putdown actions are not allowed. Second, consider a Max node M_j with child nodes $\{M_{j_1}, \ldots, M_{j_k}\}$. The policy learned for M_j must involve executing the learned policies of these child nodes. When the policy for child node M_{j_i} is executed, it will run until it enters a state in T_{j_i}. Hence, any policy learned for M_j must pass through some subset of these terminal state sets $\{T_{j_1}, \ldots, T_{j_k}\}$.

The HAM method shares these same two constraints and in addition, it imposes a partial policy on each node, so that the policy for any subtask M_i must be a deterministic refinement of the given non-deterministic initial policy for node i.

In the "option" approach, the policy is even further constrained. In this approach, there are only two non-primitive levels in the hierarchy, and the subtasks at the lower level (i.e., whose children are all primitive actions) are given complete policies by the programmer. Hence, any learned policy at the upper level must be constructed by "concatenating" the given lower level policies in some order.

The purpose of imposing these constraints on the policy is to incorporate prior knowledge and thereby reduce the size of the space that must be searched to find a good policy. However, these constraints may make it impossible to learn the optimal policy.

If we can't learn the optimal policy, the next best target would be to learn the best policy that is consistent with (i.e., can be represented by) the given hierarchy.

Definition 7 *A* hierarchically optimal policy *for MDP M is a policy that achieves the highest cumulative reward among all policies consistent with the given hierarchy.*

Parr (1998b) proves that his HAMQ learning algorithm converges with probability 1 to a hierarchically optimal policy. Similarly, given a fixed set of options, Sutton, Precup, and Singh (1998) prove that their SMDP learning algorithm converges to a hierarchically optimal value function. Incidentally, they also show that if the primitive actions are also made available as "trivial" options, then their SMDP method converges to the optimal policy. However, in this case, it is hard to say anything formal about how the options speed the learning process. They may in fact hinder it (Hauskrecht et al., 1998).

Because the MAXQ decomposition can represent the value function of any hierarchical policy, we could easily construct a modified version of the HAMQ algorithm and apply it to learn hierarchically optimal policies for the MAXQ hierarchy. However, we decided to pursue an even weaker form of optimality, for reasons that will become clear as we proceed. This form of optimality is called recursive optimality.

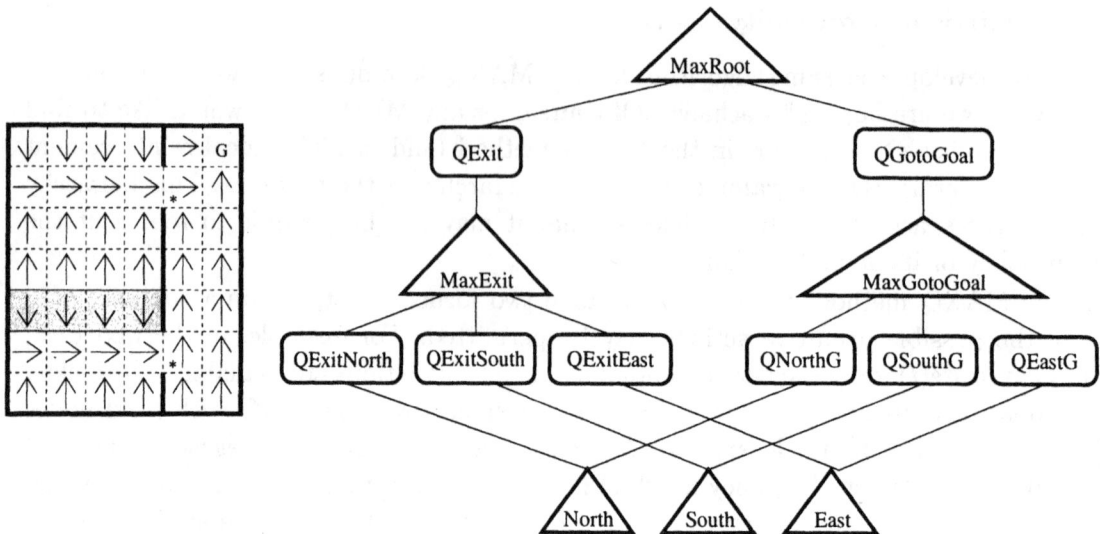

Figure 6: A simple MDP (left) and its associated MAXQ graph (right). The policy shown in the left diagram is recursively optimal but not hierarchically optimal. The shaded cells indicate points where the locally-optimal policy is not globally optimal.

Definition 8 *A recursively optimal policy for Markov decision process M with MAXQ decomposition* $\{M_0, \ldots, M_k\}$ *is a hierarchical policy* $\pi = \{\pi_0, \ldots, \pi_k\}$ *such that for each subtask* M_i, *the corresponding policy* π_i *is optimal for the SMDP defined by the set of states* S_i, *the set of actions* A_i, *the state transition probability function* $P^\pi(s', N|s, a)$, *and the reward function given by the* sum *of the original reward function* $R(s'|s, a)$ *and the pseudo-reward function* $\tilde{R}_i(s')$.

Note that the state transition probability distribution, $P^\pi(s', N|s, a)$ for subtask M_i is defined by the locally optimal policies $\{\pi_j\}$ of all subtasks that are descendents of M_i in the MAXQ graph. Hence, recursive optimality is a kind of local optimality in which the policy at each node is optimal given the policies of its children.

The reason to seek recursive optimality rather than hierarchical optimality is that recursive optimality makes it possible to solve each subtask without reference to the context in which it is executed. This context-free property makes it easier to share and re-use subtasks. It will also turn out to be essential for the successful use of state abstraction.

Before we proceed to describe our learning algorithm for recursive optimality, let us see how recursive optimality differs from hierarchical optimality.

It is easy to construct examples of policies that are recursively optimal but not hierarchically optimal (and vice versa). Consider the simple maze problem and its associated MAXQ graph shown in Figures 6. Suppose a robot starts somewhere in the left room, and it must reach the goal G in the right room. The robot has three actions, North, South, and East, and these actions are deterministic. The robot receives a reward of -1 for each move. Let us define two subtasks:

- Exit. This task terminates when the robot exits the left room. We can set the pseudo-reward function $\tilde{R}$ to be 0 for the two terminal states (i.e., the two states indicated by *'s).

- GotoGoal. This task terminates when the robot reaches the goal G.

The arrows in Figure 6 show the locally optimal policy within each room. The arrows on the left seek to exit the left room by the shortest path, because this is what we specified when we set the pseudo-reward function to 0. The arrows on the right follow the shortest path to the goal, which is fine. However, the resulting policy is neither hierarchically optimal nor optimal.

There exists a hierarchical policy that would always exit the left room by the upper door. The MAXQ value function decomposition can represent the value function of this policy, but such a policy would not be locally optimal (because, for example, the states in the "shaded" region would not follow the shortest path to a doorway). Hence, this example illustrates both a recursively optimal policy that is not hierarchically optimal and a hierarchically optimal policy that is not recursively optimal.

If we consider for a moment, we can see a way to fix this problem. The value of the upper starred state under the optimal hierarchical policy is -2 and the value of the lower starred state is -6. Hence, if we changed $\tilde{R}$ to have these values (instead of being zero), then the recursively-optimal policy would be hierarchically optimal (and globally optimal). In other words, if the programmer can guess the right values for the terminal states of a subtask, then the recursively optimal policy will be hierarchically optimal.

This basic idea was first pointed out by Dean and Lin (1995). They describe an algorithm that makes initial guesses for the values of these starred states and then updates those guesses based on the computed values of the starred states under the resulting recursively-optimal policy. They proved that this will converge to a hierarchically optimal policy. The drawback of their method is that it requires repeated solution of the resulting hierarchical learning problem, and this does not always yield a speedup over just solving the original, flat problem.

Parr (1998a) proposed an interesting approach that constructs a *set* of different $\tilde{R}$ functions and computes the recursively optimal policy under each of them for each subtask. His method chooses the $\tilde{R}$ functions in such a way that the hierarchically optimal policy can be approximated to any desired degree. Unfortunately, the method is quite expensive, because it relies on solving a series of linear programming problems each of which requires time polynomial in several parameters, including the number of states $|S_i|$ within the subtask.

This discussion suggests that while, in principle, it is possible to learn good values for the pseudo-reward function, in practice, we must rely on the programmer to specify a single pseudo-reward function, $\tilde{R}$, for each subtask. If the programmer wishes to consider a small number of alternative pseudo-reward functions, they can be handled by defining a small number of subtasks that are identical except for their $\tilde{R}$ functions, and permitting the learning algorithm to choose the one that gives the best recursively-optimal policy.

In our experiments, we have employed the following simplified approach to defining $\tilde{R}$. For each subtask M_i, we define two predicates: the termination predicate, T_i, and a goal predicate, G_i. The goal predicate defines a subset of the terminal states that are "goal states", and these have a pseudo-reward of 0. All other terminal states have a fixed constant pseudo-reward (e.g., -100) that is set so that it is always better to terminate in a goal state than in a non-goal state. For the problems on which we have tested the MAXQ method, this worked very well.

In our experiments with MAXQ, we have found that it is easy to make mistakes in defining T_i and G_i. If the goal is not defined carefully, it is easy to create a set of subtasks that lead to infinite looping. For example, consider again the problem in Figure 6. Suppose we permit a fourth action, West, in the MDP and let us define the termination and goal predicates for the right hand room to be satisfied iff either the robot reaches the goal or it exits the room. This is a very natural definition, since it is quite similar to the definition for the left-hand room. However, the resulting locally-optimal policy for this room will attempt to move to the nearest of these three locations: the goal, the upper door, or the lower door. We can easily see that for all but a few states near the goal, the only policies that can be constructed by MaxRoot will loop forever, first trying to leave the left room by entering the right room, and then trying to leave the right room by entering the left room. This problem is easily fixed by defining the goal predicate G_i for the right room to be true if and only if the robot reaches the goal G. But avoiding such "undesired termination" bugs can be hard in more complex domains.

In the worst case, it is possible for the programmer to specify pseudo-rewards such that the recursively optimal policy can be made arbitrarily worse than the hierarchically optimal policy. For example, suppose that we change the original MDP in Figure 6 so that the state immediately to the left of the upper doorway gives a large negative reward $-L$ whenever the robot visits that square. Because rewards everywhere else are -1, the hierarchically-optimal policy exits the room by the lower door. But suppose the programmer has chosen instead to force the robot to exit by the upper door (e.g., by assigning a pseudo-reward of $-10L$ for leaving via the lower door). In this case, the recursively-optimal policy will leave by the upper door and suffer the large $-L$ penalty. By making L arbitrarily large, we can make the difference between the hierarchically-optimal policy and the recursively-optimal policy arbitrarily large.

4.2 The MAXQ-0 Learning Algorithm

Now that we have an understanding of recursively optimal policies, we present two learning algorithms. The first one, called MAXQ-0, applies only in the case when the pseudo-reward function $\tilde{R}$ is always zero. We will first prove its convergence properties and then show how it can be extended to give the second algorithm, MAXQ-Q, which works with general pseudo-reward functions.

Table 2 gives pseudo-code for MAXQ-0. MAXQ-0 is a recursive function that executes the current exploration policy starting at Max node i in state s. It performs actions until it reaches a terminal state, at which point it returns a count of the total number of primitive actions that have been executed. To execute an action, MAXQ-0 calls itself recursively (line 9). When the recursive call returns, it updates the value of the completion function for node i. It uses the count of the number of primitive actions to appropriately discount the value of the resulting state s'. At leaf nodes, MAXQ-0 updates the estimated one-step expected reward, $V(i, s)$. The value $\alpha_t(i)$ is a "learning rate" parameter that should be gradually decreased to zero in the limit.

Table 2: The MAXQ-0 learning algorithm.

---

function MAXQ-0(MaxNode i, State s)

```
1     if i is a primitive MaxNode
2          execute i, receive r, and observe result state s′
3          V_{t+1}(i, s) := (1 − α_t(i)) · V_t(i, s) + α_t(i) · r_t
4          return 1
5     else
6          let count = 0
7          while T_i(s) is false do
8               choose an action a according to the current exploration policy π_x(i, s)
9               let N = MAXQ-0(a, s) (recursive call)
10              observe result state s′
11              C_{t+1}(i, s, a) := (1 − α_t(i)) · C_t(i, s, a) + α_t(i) · γ^N V_t(i, s′)
12              count := count + N
13              s := s′
14         end
15         return count
      end MAXQ-0


16    // Main program
17    initialize V(i, s) and C(i, s, j) arbitrarily
18    MAXQ-0(root node 0, starting state s_0)
```

There are three things that must be specified in order to make this algorithm description complete.

First, to keep the pseudo-code readable, Table 2 does not show how "ancestor termination" is handled. Recall that after each action, the termination predicates of all of the subroutines on the calling stack are checked. If the termination predicate of any one of these is satisfied, then the calling stack is unwound up to the highest terminated subroutine. In such cases, no C values are updated in any of the subroutines that were interrupted except as follows. If subroutine i had invoked subroutine j, and j's termination condition is satisfied, then subroutine i can update the value of $C(i, s, j)$.

Second, we must specify how to compute $V_t(i, s')$ in line 11, since it is not stored in the Max node. It is computed by the following modified versions of the decomposition equations:

$$V_t(i, s) = \begin{cases} \max_a Q_t(i, s, a) & \text{if } i \text{ is composite} \\ V_t(i, s) & \text{if } i \text{ is primitive} \end{cases} \tag{13}$$

$$Q_t(i, s, a) = V_t(a, s) + C_t(i, s, a). \tag{14}$$

These equations reflect two important changes compared with Equations (10) and (11). First, in Equation (13), $V_t(i, s)$ is defined in terms of the Q value of the *best* action a, rather than of the action chosen by a fixed hierarchical policy. Second, there are no π superscripts, because the current value function, $V_t(i, s)$, is not based on a fixed hierarchical policy π.

To compute $V_t(i, s)$ using these equations, we must perform a complete search of all paths through the MAXQ graph starting at node i and ending at the leaf nodes. Table 3

Table 3: Pseudo-code for Greedy Execution of the MAXQ Graph.

---

function EVALUATEMAXNODE(i, s)

1	if i is a primitive Max node
2	return $\langle V_t(i, s), i \rangle$
3	else
4	for each $j \in A_i$,
5	let $\langle V_t(j, s), a_j \rangle = $ EVALUATEMAXNODE(j, s)
6	let $j^{hg} = \mathrm{argmax}_j\ V_t(j, s) + C_t(i, s, j)$
7	return $\langle V_t(j^{hg}, s), a_{j^{hg}} \rangle$

end // EVALUATEMAXNODE

---

gives pseudo-code for a recursive function, EVALUATEMAXNODE, that implements a depth-first search. In addition to returning $V_t(i, s)$, EVALUATEMAXNODE also returns the action at the leaf node that achieves this value. This information is not needed for MAXQ-0, but it will be useful later when we consider non-hierarchical execution of the learned recursively-optimal policy.

This search can be computationally expensive, and a problem for future research is to develop more efficient methods for computing the best path through the graph. One approach is to perform a best-first search and use bounds on the values within subtrees to prune useless paths through the MAXQ graph. A better approach would be to make the computation incremental, so that when the state of the environment changes, only those nodes whose values have changed as a result of the state change are re-considered. It should be possible to develop an efficient bottom-up method similar to the RETE algorithm (and its successors) that is used in the SOAR architecture (Forgy, 1982; Tambe & Rosenbloom, 1994).

The third thing that must be specified to complete our definition of MAXQ-0 is the exploration policy, π_x. We require that π_x be an ordered GLIE policy.

Definition 9 *An ordered GLIE policy is a GLIE policy (Greedy in the Limit with Infinite Exploration) that converges in the limit to an ordered greedy policy, which is a greedy policy that imposes an arbitrary fixed order ω on the available actions and breaks ties in favor of the action a that appears earliest in that order.*

We need this property in order to ensure that MAXQ-0 converges to a uniquely-defined recursively optimal policy. A fundamental problem with recursive optimality is that in general, each Max node i will have a choice of many different locally optimal policies given the policies adopted by its descendent nodes. These different locally optimal policies will all achieve the same locally optimal value function, but they can give rise to different probability transition functions $P(s', N|s, i)$. The result will be that the Semi-Markov Decision Problems defined at the next level above node i in the MAXQ graph will differ depending on which of these various locally optimal policies is chosen by node i. These differences may lead to better or worse policies at higher levels of the MAXQ graph, even though they make no difference inside subtask i. In practice, the designer of the MAXQ graph will need to design the pseudo-reward function for subtask i to ensure that all locally optimal policies are equally valuable for the parent subroutine. But to carry out our formal analysis, we will just rely on an arbitrary tie-breaking mechanism.[2] If we establish a fixed ordering over the Max nodes in the MAXQ graph (e.g., a left-to-right depth-first numbering), and break ties in favor of the lowest-numbered action, then this defines a unique policy at each Max node. And consequently, by induction, it defines a unique policy for the entire MAXQ graph. Let us call this policy π_r^*. We will use the r subscript to denote recursively optimal quantities under an ordered greedy policy. Hence, the corresponding value function is V_r^*, and C_r^* and Q_r^* denote the corresponding completion function and action-value function. We now prove that the MAXQ-0 algorithm converges to π_r^*.

Theorem 3 *Let $M = \langle S, A, P, R, P_0 \rangle$ be either an episodic MDP for which all deterministic policies are proper or a discounted infinite horizon MDP with discount factor γ. Let H be a MAXQ graph defined over subtasks $\{M_0, \ldots, M_k\}$ such that the pseudo-reward function $\tilde{R}_i(s')$ is zero for all i and s'. Let $\alpha_t(i) > 0$ be a sequence of constants for each Max node i such that*

$$\lim_{T \to \infty} \sum_{t=1}^{T} \alpha_t(i) = \infty \quad and \quad \lim_{T \to \infty} \sum_{t=1}^{T} \alpha_t^2(i) < \infty \tag{15}$$

Let $\pi_x(i, s)$ be an ordered GLIE policy at each node i and state s and assume that the immediate rewards are bounded. Then with probability 1, algorithm MAXQ-0 converges to π_r^*, the unique recursively optimal policy for M consistent with H and π_x.

Proof: The proof follows an argument similar to those introduced to prove the convergence of Q learning and $SARSA(0)$ (Bertsekas & Tsitsiklis, 1996; Jaakkola et al., 1994). We will employ the following result from stochastic approximation theory, which we state without proof:

Lemma 1 *(Proposition 4.5 from Bertsekas and Tsitsiklis, 1996) Consider the iteration*

$$r_{t+1}(i) := (1 - \alpha_t(i))r_t(i) + \alpha_t(i)((Ur_t)(i) + w_t(i) + u_t(i)).$$

Let $\mathcal{F}_t = \{r_0(i), \ldots, r_t(i), w_0(i), \ldots, w_{t-1}(i), \alpha_0(i), \ldots, \alpha_t(i), \forall i\}$ be the entire history of the iteration.
If

(a) *The $\alpha_t(i) \geq 0$ satisfy conditions (15)*

(b) *For every i and t, the noise terms $w_t(i)$ satisfy $E[w_t(i)|\mathcal{F}_t] = 0$*

(c) *Given any norm $\| \cdot \|$ on $\mathcal{R}^n$, there exist constants A and B such that $E[w_t^2(i)|\mathcal{F}_t] \leq A + B\|r_t\|^2$.*

(d) *There exists a vector r^*, a positive vector ξ, and a scalar $\beta \in [0, 1)$, such that for all t,*

$$\|Ur_t - r^*\|_\xi \leq \beta \|r_t - r^*\|_\xi$$

---

2. Alternatively, we could break ties by using a stochastic policy that chose randomly among the tied actions.

(e) *There exists a nonnegative random sequence θ_t that converges to zero with probability 1 and is such that for all t*

$$|u_t(i)| \leq \theta_t(\|r_t\|_\xi + 1)$$

then r_t converges to r^* with probability 1. The notation $\|\cdot\|_\xi$ denotes a weighted maximum norm

$$\|A\|_\xi = \max_i \frac{|A(i)|}{\xi(i)}.$$

The structure of the proof of Theorem 3 will be inductive, starting at the leaves of the MAXQ graph and working toward the root. We will employ a different time clock at each node i to count the number of update steps performed by MAXQ-0 at that node. The variable t will always refer to the time clock of the current node i.

To prove the base case for any primitive Max node, we note that line 3 of MAXQ-0 is just the standard stochastic approximation algorithm for computing the expected reward for performing action a in state s, and therefore it converges under the conditions given above.

To prove the recursive case, consider any composite Max node i with child node j. Let $P_t(s', N|s, j)$ be the transition probability distribution for performing child action j in state s at time t (i.e., while following the exploration policy in all descendent nodes of node j). By the inductive assumption, MAXQ-0 applied to j will converge to the (unique) recursively optimal value function $V_r^*(j, s)$ with probability 1. Furthermore, because MAXQ-0 is following an ordered GLIE policy for j and its descendents, they will all converge to executing a greedy policy with respect to their value functions, so $P_t(s', N|s, j)$ will converge to $P_r^*(s', N|s, j)$, the unique transition probability function for executing child j under the locally optimal policy π_r^*. What remains to be shown is that the update assignment for C (line 11 of the MAXQ-0 algorithm) converges to the optimal C_r^* function with probability 1.

To prove this, we will apply Lemma 1. We will identify the x in the lemma with a state-action pair (s, a). The vector r_t will be the completion-cost table $C_t(i, s, a)$ for all s, a and fixed i after t update steps. The vector r^* will be the optimal completion-cost $C_r^*(i, s, a)$ (again, for fixed i). Define the mapping U to be

$$(UC)(i, s, a) = \sum_{s'} P_r^*(s', N|s, a)\gamma^N \left(\max_{a'}[C(i, s', a') + V_r^*(a', s')] \right)$$

This is a C update under the MDP M_i assuming that all descendent value functions, $V_r^*(a, s)$, and transition probabilities, $P_r^*(s', N|s, a)$, have converged.

To apply the lemma, we must first express the C update formula in the form of the update rule in the lemma. Let $\bar{s}$ be the state that results from performing a in state s. Line 11 can be written

$$
\begin{aligned}
C_{t+1}(i, s, a) \quad &:= \quad (1 - \alpha_t(i)) \cdot C_t(i, s, a) + \alpha_t(i) \cdot \gamma^{\bar{N}} \left(\max_{a'}[C_t(i, \bar{s}, a') + V_t(a', \bar{s})] \right) \\
&:= \quad (1 - \alpha_t(i)) \cdot C_t(i, s, a) + \alpha_t(i) \cdot [(UC_t)(i, s, a) + w_t(i, s, a) + u_t(i, s, a)]
\end{aligned}
$$

where

$$
\begin{aligned}
w_t(i, s, a) &= \gamma^{\overline{N}} \left(\max_{a'}[C_t(i, \overline{s}, a') + V_t(a', \overline{s})] \right) - \\
&\quad \sum_{s', N} P_t(s', N | s, a) \gamma^N \left(\max_{a'}[C_t(i, s', a') + V_t(a', s')] \right) \\
u_t(i, s, a) &= \sum_{s', N} P_t(s', N | s, a) \gamma^N \left(\max_{a'}[C_t(i, s', a') + V_t(a', s')] \right) - \\
&\quad \sum_{s', N} P_r^*(s', N | s, a) \gamma^N \left(\max_{a'}[C_t(i, s', a') + V_r^*(a', s')] \right)
\end{aligned}
$$

Here $w_t(i, s, a)$ is the difference between doing an update at node i using the single *sample point* $\overline{s}$ drawn according to $P_t(s', N | s, a)$ and doing an update using the full distribution $P_t(s', N | s, a)$. The value of $u_t(i, s, a)$ captures the difference between doing an update using the current probability transitions $P_t(s', N | s, a)$ and current value functions of the children $V_t(a', s')$ and doing an update using the optimal probability transitions $P_r^*(s', N | s, a)$ and the optimal values of the children $V_r^*(a', s')$.

We now verify the conditions of Lemma 1.

Condition (a) is assumed in the conditions of the theorem with $\alpha_t(s, a) = \alpha_t(i)$.

Condition (b) is satisfied because $\overline{s}$ is sampled from $P_t(s', N | s, a)$, so the expected value of the difference is zero.

Condition (c) follows directly from the fact that $|C_t(i, s, a)|$ and $|V_t(i, s)|$ are bounded. We can show that these are bounded for both the episodic case and the discounted case as follows. In the episodic case, we have assumed all policies are proper. Hence, all trajectories terminate in finite time with a finite total reward. In the discounted case, the infinite sum of future rewards is bounded if the one-step rewards are bounded. The values of C and V are computed as temporal averages of the cumulative rewards received over a finite number of (bounded) updates, and hence, their means, variances, and maximum values are all bounded.

Condition (d) is the condition that U is a weighted max norm pseudo-contraction. We can derive this by starting with the weighted max norm for Q learning. It is well known that Q is a weighted max norm pseudo-contraction (Bertsekas & Tsitsiklis, 1996) in both the episodic case where all deterministic policies are proper (and the discount factor $\gamma = 1$) and in the infinite horizon discounted case (with $\gamma < 1$). That is, there exists a positive vector ξ and a scalar $\beta \in [0, 1)$, such that for all t,

$$
\|TQ_t - Q^*\|_\xi \le \beta \|Q_t - Q^*\|_\xi, \tag{16}
$$

where T is the operator

$$
(TQ)(s, a) = \sum_{s', N} P(s', N | s, a) \gamma^N [R(s' | s, a) + \max_{a'} Q(s', a')].
$$

Now we will show how to derive the pseudo-contraction for the C update operator U. Our plan is to show first how to express the U operator for learning C in terms of the T operator for updating Q values. Then we will replace TQ in the pseudo-contraction equation for Q

learning with UC, and show that U is a weighted max-norm pseudo-contraction under the same weights ξ and the same β.

Recall from Eqn. (10) that $Q(i, s, a) = C(i, s, a) + V(a, s)$. Furthermore, the U operator performs its updates using the optimal value functions of the child nodes, so we can write this as $Q_t(i, s, a) = C_t(i, s, a) + V^*(a, s)$. Now once the children of node i have converged, the Q-function version of the Bellman equation for MDP M_i can be written as

$$Q(i, s, a) = \sum_{s', N} P_r^*(s', N | s, a) \gamma^N [V_r^*(a, s) + \max_{a'} Q(i, s', a')].$$

As we have noted before, $V_r^*(a, s)$ plays the role of the immediate reward function for M_i. Therefore, for node i, the T operator can be rewritten as

$$(TQ)(i, s, a) = \sum_{s', N} P_r^*(s' | s, a) \gamma^N [V_r^*(a, s) + \max_{a'} Q(i, s', a')].$$

Now we replace $Q(i, s, a)$ by $C(i, s, a) + V_r^*(a, s)$, and obtain

$$(TQ)(i, s, a) = \sum_{s', N} P_r^*(s', N | s, a) \gamma^N (V_r^*(a, s) + \max_{a'} [C(i, s', a') + V_r^*(a', s')]).$$

Note that $V_r^*(a, s)$ does not depend on s' or N, so we can move it outside the expectation and obtain

$$
\begin{aligned}
(TQ)(i, s, a) &= V_r^*(a, s) + \sum_{s', N} P_r^*(s', N | s, a) \gamma^N (\max_{a'} [C(i, s', a') + V_r^*(a', s')]) \\
&= V_r^*(a, s) + (UC)(i, s, a)
\end{aligned}
$$

Abusing notation slightly, we will express this in vector form as $TQ(i) = V_r^* + UC(i)$. Similarly, we can write $Q_t(i, s, a) = C_t(i, s, a) + V_r^*(a, s)$ in vector form as $Q_t(i) = C_t(i) + V_r^*$.

Now we can substitute these two formulas into the max norm pseudo-contraction formula for T, Eqn. (16) to obtain

$$\|V_r^* + UC_t(i) - (C_r^*(i) + V_r^*)\|_\xi \leq \beta \|V_r^* + C_t(i) - (C_r^*(i) + V_r^*)\|_\xi.$$

Thus, U is a weighted max-norm pseudo-contraction,

$$\|UC_t(i) - C_r^*(i)\|_\xi \leq \beta \|C_t(i) - C_r^*(i)\|_\xi,$$

and condition (d) is satisfied.

Finally, it is easy to verify (e), the most important condition. By assumption, the ordered GLIE policies in the child nodes converge with probability 1 to locally optimal policies for the children. Therefore $P_t(s', N | s, a)$ converges to $P_r^*(s', N | s, a)$ for all $s', N, s,$ and a with probability 1 and $V_t(a, s)$ converges with probability 1 to $V_r^*(a, s)$ for all child actions a. Therefore, $|u_t|$ converges to zero with probability 1. We can trivially construct a sequence $\theta_t = |u_t|$ that bounds this convergence, so

$$|u_t(s, a)| \leq \theta_t \leq \theta_t(\|C_t(s, a)\|_\xi + 1).$$

We have verified all of the conditions of Lemma 1, so we can conclude that $C_t(i)$ converges to $C_r^*(i)$ with probability 1. By induction, we can conclude that this holds for all nodes in the MAXQ including the root node, so the value function represented by the MAXQ graph converges to the unique value function of the recursively optimal policy π_r^*. **Q.E.D.**

The most important aspect of this theorem is that it proves that Q learning can take place at all levels of the MAXQ hierarchy simultaneously—the higher levels do not need to wait until the lower levels have converged before they begin learning. All that is necessary is that the lower levels eventually converge to their (locally) optimal policies.

4.3 Techniques for Speeding Up MAXQ-0

Algorithm MAXQ-0 can be extended to accelerate learning in the higher nodes of the graph by a technique that we call "all-states updating". When an action a is chosen for Max node i in state s, the execution of a will move the environment through a sequence of states $s = s_1, \ldots, s_N, s_{N+1} = s'$. Because all of our subroutines are Markovian, the same resulting state s' would have been reached if we had started executing action a in state s_2, or s_3, or any state up to and including s_N. Hence, we can execute a version of line 11 in MAXQ-0 for each of these intermediate states as shown in this replacement pseudo-code:

11a	**for** j **from** 1 **to** N **do**
11b	$C_{t+1}(i, s_j, a) := (1 - \alpha_t(i)) \cdot C_t(i, s_j, a) + \alpha_t(i) \cdot \gamma^{(N+1-j)} max_{a'} Q_t(i, s', a')$
11c	**end** // **for**

In our implementation, as each composite action is executed by MAXQ-0, it constructs a linked list of the sequence of primitive states that were visited. This list is returned when the composite action terminates. The parent Max node can then process each state in this list as shown above. The parent Max node concatenates the state lists that it receives from its children and passes them to its parent when it terminates. All experiments in this paper employ all-states updating.

Kaelbling (1993) introduced a related, but more powerful, method for accelerating hierarchical reinforcement learning that she calls "all-goals updating." To understand this method, suppose that for each primitive action, there are several composite tasks that could have invoked that primitive action. In all-goals updating, whenever a primitive action is executed, the equivalent of line 11 of MAXQ-0 is applied in every composite task that could have invoked that primitive action. Sutton, Precup, and Singh (1998) prove that each of the composite tasks will converge to the optimal Q values under all-goals updating. Furthermore, they point out that the exploration policy employed for choosing the primitive actions can be different from the policies of *any* of the subtasks being learned.

It is straightforward to implement a simple form of all-goals updating within the MAXQ hierarchy for the case where composite tasks invoke primitive actions. Whenever one of the primitive actions a is executed in state s, we can update the $C(i, s, a)$ value for all parent tasks i that can invoke a.

However, additional care is required to implement all-goals updating for non-primitive actions. Suppose that by executing the exploration policy, the following sequence of world states and actions has been obtained: $s_0, a_0, s_1, \ldots, a_{k-1}, s_{k-1}, a_k, s_{k+1}$. Let j be a composite task that is terminated in state s_{k+1}, and let $s_{k-n}, a_{k-n}, \ldots, a_{k-1}, a_k$ be a sequence of actions that *could have been executed* by subtask j and its children. In other words, suppose it is possible to "parse" this state-action sequence in terms of a series of subroutine calls and returns for one invocation of subtask j. Then for each possible parent task i that invokes j, we can update the value of $C(i, s_{k-n}, j)$. Of course, in order for these updates to be useful, the exploration policy must be an ordered GLIE policy that will converge to the recursively optimal policy for subtask j and its descendents. We cannot follow an arbitrary exploration policy, because this would not produce accurate samples of result states drawn according to $P^*(s', N|s, j)$. Hence, unlike the simple case described by Sutton, Precup, and Singh, the exploration policy cannot be different from the policies of the subtasks being learned.

Although this considerably reduces the usefulness of all-goals updating, it does not completely eliminate it. A simple way of implementing non-primitive all-goals updating would be to perform MAXQ-Q learning as usual, but whenever a subtask j was invoked in state s and returned, we could update the value of $C(i, s, j)$ for all potential calling subtasks i. We have not implemented this, however, because of the complexity involved in identifying the possible actual parameters of the potential calling subroutines.

4.4 The MAXQ-Q Learning Algorithm

Now that we have shown the convergence of MAXQ-0, let us design a learning algorithm that can work with arbitrary pseudo-reward functions, $\tilde{R}_i(s')$. We could just add the pseudo-reward into MAXQ-0, but this would have the effect of changing the MDP M to have a different reward function. The pseudo-rewards "contaminate" the values of all of the completion functions computed in the hierarchy. The resulting learned policy will not be recursively optimal for the original MDP.

This problem can be solved by learning one completion function for use "inside" each Max node and a separate completion function for use "outside" the Max node. The quantities used "inside" a node will be written with a tilde: $\tilde{R}$, $\tilde{C}$, and $\tilde{Q}$. The quantities used "outside" a node will be written without the tilde.

The "outside" completion function, $C(i, s, a)$ is the completion function that we have been discussing so far in this paper. It computes the expected reward for completing task M_i after performing action a in state s and then following the learned policy for M_i. It is computed without any reference to $\tilde{R}_i$. This completion function will be used by parent tasks to compute $V(i, s)$, the expected reward for performing action i starting in state s.

The second completion function $\tilde{C}(i, s, a)$ is a completion function that we will use only "inside" node i in order to discover the locally optimal policy for task M_i. This function will incorporate rewards both from the "real" reward function, $R(s'|s, a)$, and from the pseudo-reward function, $\tilde{R}_i(s')$. It will also be used by EVALUATEMAXNODE in line 6 to choose the best action j^{hg} to execute. Note, however, that EVALUATEMAXNODE will still return the "external" value $V_t(j^{hg}, s)$ of this chosen action.

We will employ two different update rules to learn these two completion functions. The $\tilde{C}$ function will be learned using an update rule similar to the Q learning rule in line 11 of MAXQ-0. But the C function will be learned using an update rule similar to SARSA(0)— its purpose is to learn the value function for the policy that is discovered by optimizing $\tilde{C}$. Pseudo-code for the resulting algorithm, MAXQ-Q is shown in Table 4.

The key step is at lines 15 and 16. In line 15, MAXQ-Q first updates $\tilde{C}$ using the value of the greedy action, a^*, in the resulting state. This update includes the pseudo-reward $\tilde{R}_i$.

Table 4: The MAXQ-Q learning algorithm.

---

function MAXQ-Q(MaxNode i, State s)

1   **let** $seq = ()$ be the sequence of states visited while executing i
2   **if** i is a primitive MaxNode
3   execute i, receive r, and observe result state s'
4        $V_{t+1}(i, s) := (1 - \alpha_t(i)) \cdot V_t(i, s) + \alpha_t(i) \cdot r_t$
5   push s onto the beginning of seq
6   **else**
7   **let** $count = 0$
8   **while** $T_i(s)$ is false **do**
9   choose an action a according to the current exploration policy $\pi_x(i, s)$
10   **let** $childSeq = $ MAXQ-Q(a, s), where $childSeq$ is the sequence of states visited
             while executing action a. (in reverse order)
11   observe result state s'
12   **let** $a^* = \mathrm{argmax}_{a'} \, [\tilde{C}_t(i, s', a') + V_t(a', s')]$
13   **let** $N = 1$
14   **for each** s in $childSeq$ **do**
15           $\tilde{C}_{t+1}(i, s, a) := (1 - \alpha_t(i)) \cdot \tilde{C}_t(i, s, a) + \alpha_t(i) \cdot \gamma^N[\tilde{R}_i(s') + \tilde{C}_t(i, s', a^*) + V_t(a^*, s)]$
16           $C_{t+1}(i, s, a) := (1 - \alpha_t(i)) \cdot C_t(i, s, a) + \alpha_t(i) \cdot \gamma^N[C_t(i, s', a^*) + V_t(a^*, s')]$
17           $N := N + 1$
18   **end** // for
19   **append** $childSeq$ onto the front of seq
20       $s := s'$
21   **end** // while
22   **end** // else
23   **return** seq
    end MAXQ-Q

Then in line 16, MAXQ-Q updates C using this *same greedy action* a^*, even if this would not be the greedy action according to the "uncontaminated" value function. This update, of course, does not include the pseudo-reward function.

It is important to note that whereever $V_t(a, s)$ appears in this pseudo-code, it refers to the "uncontaminated" value function of state s when executing the Max node a. This is computed recursively in exactly the same way as in MAXQ-0.

Finally, note that the pseudo-code also incorporates all-states updating, so each call to MAXQ-Q returns a list of all of the states that were visited during its execution, and the updates of lines 15 and 16 are performed for each of those states. The list of states is ordered most-recent-first, so the states are updated starting with the last state visited and working backward to the starting state, which helps speed up the algorithm.

When MAXQ-Q has converged, the resulting recursively optimal policy is computed at each node by choosing the action a that maximizes $\tilde{Q}(i, s, a) = \tilde{C}(i, s, a) + V(a, s)$ (breaking ties according to the fixed ordering established by the ordered GLIE policy). It is for this reason that we gave the name "Max nodes" to the nodes that represent subtasks (and learned policies) within the MAXQ graph. Each Q node j with parent node i stores both $\tilde{C}(i, s, j)$ and $C(i, s, j)$, and it computes both $\tilde{Q}(i, s, j)$ and $Q(i, s, j)$ by invoking its child Max node j. Each Max node i takes the maximum of these Q values and computes either $V(i, s)$ or computes the best action, a^* using $\tilde{Q}$.

Corollary 1 *Under the same conditions as Theorem 3, MAXQ-Q converges to the unique recursively optimal policy for MDP M defined by MAXQ graph H, pseudo-reward functions $\tilde{R}$, and ordered GLIE exploration policy π_x.*

Proof: The argument is identical to, but more tedious than, the proof of Theorem 3. The proof of convergence of the $\tilde{C}$ values is identical to the original proof for the C values, but it relies on proving convergence of the "new" C values as well, which follows from the same weighted max norm pseudo-contraction argument. **Q.E.D.**

5. State Abstraction

There are many reasons to introduce hierarchical reinforcement learning, but perhaps the most important reason is to create opportunities for state abstraction. When we introduced the simple taxi problem in Figure 1, we pointed out that within each subtask, we can ignore certain aspects of the state space. For example, while performing a MaxNavigate(t), the taxi should make the same navigation decisions regardless of whether the passenger is in the taxi. The purpose of this section is to formalize the conditions under which it is safe to introduce such state abstractions and to show how the convergence proofs for MAXQ-Q can be extended to prove convergence in the presence of state abstraction. Specifically, we will identify five conditions that permit the "safe" introduction of state abstractions.

Throughout this section, we will use the taxi problem as a running example, and we will see how each of the five conditions will permit us to reduce the number of distinct values that must be stored in order to represent the MAXQ value function decomposition. To establish a starting point, let us compute the number of values that must be stored for the taxi problem *without* any state abstraction.

The MAXQ representation must have tables for each of the C functions at the internal nodes and the V functions at the leaves. First, at the six leaf nodes, to store $V(i, s)$, we must store 500 values at each node, because there are 500 states; 25 locations, 4 possible destinations for the passenger, and 5 possible current locations for the passenger (the four special locations and inside the taxi itself). Second, at the root node, there are two children, which requires $2 \times 500 = 1000$ values. Third, at the MaxGet and MaxPut nodes, we have 2 actions each, so each one requires 1000 values, for a total of 2000. Finally, at MaxNavigate(t), we have four actions, but now we must also consider the target parameter t, which can take four possible values. Hence, there are effectively 2000 combinations of states and t values for each action, or 8000 total values that must be represented. In total, therefore, the MAXQ representation requires 14,000 separate quantities to represent the value function.

To place this number in perspective, consider that a flat Q learning representation must store a separate value for each of the six primitive actions in each of the 500 possible states, for a total of 3,000 values. Hence, we can see that without state abstraction, the MAXQ representation requires more than four times the memory of a flat Q table!

5.1 Five Conditions that Permit State Abstraction

We now introduce five conditions that permit the introduction of state abstractions. For each condition, we give a definition and then prove a lemma which states that if the condition is satisfied, then the value function for some corresponding class of policies can be represented abstractly (i.e., by abstract versions of the V and C functions). For each condition, we then provide some rules for identifying when that condition can be satisfied and give examples from the taxi domain.

We begin by introducing some definitions and notation.

Definition 10 *Let M be a MDP and H be a MAXQ graph defined over M. Suppose that each state s can be written as a vector of values of a set of state variables. At each Max node i, suppose the state variables are partitioned into two sets X_i and Y_i, and let χ_i be a function that projects a state s onto only the values of the variables in X_i. Then H combined with χ_i is called a* state-abstracted MAXQ graph.

In cases where the state variables can be partitioned, we will often write $s = (x, y)$ to mean that a state s is represented by a vector of values for the state variables in X and a vector of values for the state variables in Y. Similarly, we will sometimes write $P(x', y', N | x, y, a)$, $V(a, x, y)$, and $\tilde{R}_a(x', y')$ in place of $P(s', N | s, a)$, $V(a, s)$, and $\tilde{R}_a(s')$, respectively.

Definition 11 (Abstract Policy) *An abstract hierarchical policy for MDP M with state-abstracted MAXQ graph H and associated abstraction functions χ_i, is a hierarchical policy in which each policy π_i (corresponding to subtask M_i) satisfies the condition that for any two states s_1 and s_2 such that $\chi_i(s_1) = \chi_i(s_2)$, $\pi_i(s_1) = \pi_i(s_2)$. (When π_i is a stochastic policy, such as an exploration policy, this is interpreted to mean that the probability distributions for choosing actions are the same in both states.)*

In order for MAXQ-Q to converge in the presence of state abstractions, we will require that at all times t its (instantaneous) exploration policy is an abstract hierarchical policy. One way to achieve this is to construct the exploration policy so that it only uses information from the relevant state variables in deciding what action to perform. Boltzmann exploration based on the (state-abstracted) Q values, ϵ-greedy exploration, and counter-based exploration based on abstracted states are all abstract exploration policies. Counter-based exploration based on the full state space is not an abstract exploration policy.

Now that we have introduced our notation, let us describe and analyze the five abstraction conditions. We have identified three different kinds of conditions under which abstractions can be introduced. The first kind involves eliminating irrelevant variables within a subtask of the MAXQ graph. Under this form of abstraction, nodes toward the leaves of the MAXQ graph tend to have very few relevant variables, and nodes higher in the graph have more relevant variables. Hence, this kind of abstraction is most useful at the lower levels of the MAXQ graph.

The second kind of abstraction arises from "funnel" actions. These are macro actions that move the environment from some large number of initial states to a small number of resulting states. The completion cost of such subtasks can be represented using a number of values proportional to the number of resulting states. Funnel actions tend to appear higher in the MAXQ graph, so this form of abstraction is most useful near the root of the graph.

The third kind of abstraction arises from the structure of the MAXQ graph itself. It exploits the fact that large parts of the state space for a subtask may not be reachable because of the termination conditions of its ancestors in the MAXQ graph.

We begin by describing two abstraction conditions of the first type. Then we will present two conditions of the second type. And finally, we describe one condition of the third type.

5.1.1 CONDITION 1: MAX NODE IRRELEVANCE

The first condition arises when a set of state variables is irrelevant to a Max node.

Definition 12 (Max Node Irrelevance) *Let M_i be a Max node in a MAXQ graph H for MDP M. A set of state variables Y is irrelevant for node i if the state variables of M can be partitioned into two sets X and Y such that for any stationary abstract hierarchical policy π executed by the descendents of i, the following two properties hold:*

- *the state transition probability distribution $P^\pi(s', N|s, a)$ at node i can be factored into the product of two distributions:*

$$P^\pi(x', y', N|x, y, a) = P^\pi(y'|x, y, a) \cdot P^\pi(x', N|x, a), \qquad (17)$$

  where y and y' give values for the variables in Y, and x and x' give values for the variables in X.

- *for any pair of states $s_1 = (x, y_1)$ and $s_2 = (x, y_2)$ such that $\chi(s_1) = \chi(s_2) = x$, and any child action a, $V^\pi(a, s_1) = V^\pi(a, s_2)$ and $\tilde{R}_i(s_1) = \tilde{R}_i(s_2)$.*

Note that the two conditions must hold for all stationary abstract policies π executed by all of the descendents of the subtask i. We will discuss below how these rather strong requirements can be satisfied in practice. First, however, we prove that these conditions are sufficient to permit the C and V tables to be represented using state abstractions.

Lemma 2 *Let M be an MDP with full-state MAXQ graph H, and suppose that state variables Y_i are irrelevant for Max node i. Let $\chi_i(s) = x$ be the associated abstraction function that projects s onto the remaining relevant variables X_i. Let π be any abstract hierarchical policy. Then the action-value function Q^π at node i can be represented compactly, with only one value of the completion function $C^\pi(i, s, j)$ for each equivalence class of states s that share the same values on the relevant variables.*

Specifically $Q^\pi(i, s, j)$ can be computed as follows:

$$Q^\pi(i, s, j) = V^\pi(j, \chi_i(s)) + C^\pi(i, \chi_i(s), j)$$

where

$$C^\pi(i, x, j) = \sum_{x', N} P^\pi(x', N|x, j) \cdot \gamma^N [V^\pi(\pi(x'), x') + \tilde{R}_i(x') + C^\pi(i, x', \pi(x'))],$$

where $V^\pi(j', x') = V^\pi(j', x', y_0)$, $\tilde{R}_i(x') = \tilde{R}_i(x', y_0)$, and $\pi(x) = \pi(x, y_0)$ for some arbitrary value y_0 for the irrelevant state variables Y_i.

Proof: Define a new MDP $\chi_i(M_i)$ at node i as follows:

- States: $X = \{x \mid \chi_i(s) = x, \text{ for some } s \in S\}$.

- Actions: A.

- Transition probabilities: $P^\pi(x', N | x, a)$

- Reward function: $V^\pi(a, x) + \tilde{R}_i(x')$

Because π is an abstract policy, its decisions are the same for all states s such that $\chi_i(s) = x$ for some x. Therefore, it is also a well-defined policy over $\chi_i(M_i)$. The action-value function for π over $\chi_i(M_i)$ is the unique solution to the following Bellman equation:

$$Q^\pi(i, x, j) = V^\pi(j, x) + \sum_{x', N} P^\pi(x', N | x, j) \cdot \gamma^N [\tilde{R}_i(x') + Q^\pi(i, x', \pi(x'))] \qquad (18)$$

Compare this to the Bellman equation over M_i:

$$Q^\pi(i, s, j) = V^\pi(j, s) + \sum_{s', N} P^\pi(s', N | s, j) \cdot \gamma^N [\tilde{R}_i(s') + Q^\pi(i, s', \pi(s'))] \qquad (19)$$

and note that $V^\pi(j, s) = V^\pi(j, \chi(s)) = V^\pi(j, x)$ and $\tilde{R}_i(s') = \tilde{R}_i(\chi(s')) = \tilde{R}_i(x')$. Furthermore, we know that the distribution P^π can be factored into separate distributions for Y_i and X_i. Hence, we can rewrite (19) as

$$Q^\pi(i, s, j) = V^\pi(j, x) + \sum_{y'} P(y' | x, y, j) \sum_{x', N} P^\pi(x', N | x, j) \cdot \gamma^N [\tilde{R}_i(x') + Q^\pi(i, s', \pi(s'))]$$

The right-most sum does not depend on y or y', so the sum over y' evaluates to 1, and can be eliminated to give

$$Q^\pi(i, s, j) = V^\pi(j, x) + \sum_{x', N} P^\pi(x', N | x, j) \cdot \gamma^N [\tilde{R}_i(x') + Q^\pi(i, s', \pi(s'))]. \qquad (20)$$

Finally, note that equations (18) and (20) are identical except for the expressions for the Q values. Since the solution to the Bellman equation is unique, we must conclude that

$$Q^\pi(i, s, j) = Q^\pi(i, \chi(s), j).$$

We can rewrite the right-hand side to obtain

$$Q^\pi(i, s, j) = V^\pi(j, \chi(s)) + C^\pi(i, \chi(s), j),$$

where

$$C^\pi(i, x, j) = \sum_{x', N} P(x', N | x, j) \cdot \gamma^N [V^\pi(\pi(x'), x') + \tilde{R}_i(x') + C^\pi(i, x', \pi(x'))].$$

Q.E.D.

Of course we are primarily interested in being able to discover and represent the *optimal* policy at each node i. The following corollary shows that the optimal policy is an abstract policy, and hence, that it can be represented abstractly.

Corollary 2 *Consider the same conditions as Lemma 2, but with the change that the abstract hierarchical policy π is executed only by the descendents of node i, but not by node i. Let ω be an ordering over actions. Then the optimal ordered policy π^*_ω at node i is an abstract policy, and its action-value function can be represented abstractly.*

Proof: Define the policy ρ^*_ω to be the optimal ordered policy over the abstract MDP $\chi(M)$, and let $Q^*(i, x, j)$ be the corresponding optimal action-value function. Then by the same argument given above, Q^* is also a solution to the optimal Bellman equation for the original MDP. This means that the policy π^*_ω defined by $\pi^*_\omega(s) = \rho^*(\chi(s))$ is an optimal ordered policy, and by construction, it is an abstract policy. **Q.E.D.**

As stated, the Max node irrelevance condition appears quite difficult to satisfy, since it requires that the state transition probability distribution factor into X and Y components for all possible abstract hierarchical policies. However, in practice, this condition is often satisfied.

For example, let us consider the Navigate(t) subtask. The source and destination of the passenger are irrelevant to the achievement of this subtask. Any policy that successfully completes this subtask will have the same value function regardless of the source and destination locations of the passenger. By abstracting away the passenger source and destination, we obtain a huge savings in space. Instead of requiring 8000 values to represent the C functions for this task, we require only 400 values (4 actions, 25 locations, 4 possible values for t).

The advantages of this form of abstraction are similar to those obtained by Boutilier, Dearden and Goldszmidt (1995) in which belief network models of actions are exploited to simplify value iteration in stochastic planning. Indeed, one way of understanding the conditions of Definition 12 is to express them in the form of a decision diagram, as shown in Figure 7. The diagram shows that the irrelevant variables Y do not affect the rewards either directly or indirectly, and therefore, they do not affect either the value function or the optimal policy.

One rule for noticing cases where this abstraction condition holds is to examine the subgraph rooted at the given Max node i. If a set of state variables is irrelevant to the leaf state transition probabilities and reward functions and also to all pseudo-reward functions and termination conditions in the subgraph, then those variables satisfy the Max Node Irrelevance condition:

Lemma 3 *Let M be an MDP with associated MAXQ graph H, and let i be a Max node in H. Let X_i and Y_i be a partition of the state variables for M. A set of state variables Y_i is irrelevant to node i if*

- *For each primitive leaf node a that is a descendent of i,*

$$P(x', y'|x, y, a) = P(y'|x, y, a)P(x'|x, a) \text{ and}$$
$$R(x', y'|x, y, a) = R(x'|x, a),$$

- *For each internal node j that is equal to node i or is a descendent of i , $\tilde{R}_j(x', y') = \tilde{R}_j(x')$ and the termination predicate $T_j(x', y')$ is true iff $T_j(x')$.*

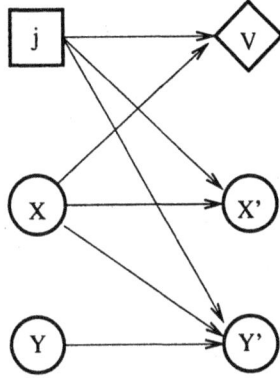

Figure 7: A dynamic decision diagram that represents the conditions of Definition 12. The probabilistic nodes X and Y represent the state variables at time t, and the nodes X' and Y' represent the state variables at a later time $t + N$. The square action node j is the chosen child subroutine, and the utility node V represents the value function $V(j, x)$ of that child action. Note that while X may influence Y', Y cannot affect X', and therefore, it cannot affect V.

Proof: We must show that any abstract hierarchical policy will give rise to an SMDP at node i whose transition probability distribution factors and whose reward function depends only on X_i. By definition, any abstract hierarchical policy will choose actions based only upon information in X_i. Because the primitive probability transition functions factor into an independent component for X_i and since the termination conditions at all nodes below i are based only on the variables in X_i, the probability transition function $P_i(x', y', N|x, y, a)$ must also factor into $P_i(y'|x, y, a)$ and $P_i(x', N|x, a)$. Similarly, all of the reward functions $V(j, x, y)$ must be equal to $V(j, x)$, because all rewards received within the subtree (either at the leaves or through pseudo-rewards) depend only on the variables in X_i. Therefore, the variables in Y_i are irrelevant for Max node i. **Q.E.D.**

In the Taxi task, the primitive navigation actions, North, South, East, and West only depend on the location of the taxi and not on the location of the passenger. The pseudo-reward function and termination condition for the MaxNavigate(t) node only depend on the location of the taxi (and the parameter t). Hence, this lemma applies, and the passenger source and destination are irrelevant for the MaxNavigate node.

5.1.2 Condition 2: Leaf Irrelevance

The second abstraction condition describes situations under which we can apply state abstractions to leaf nodes of the MAXQ graph. For leaf nodes, we can obtain a stronger result than Lemma 2 by using a slightly weaker definition of irrelevance.

Definition 13 (Leaf Irrelevance) *A set of state variables Y is irrelevant for a primitive action a of a MAXQ graph if for all states s the expected value of the reward function,*

$$V(a, s) = \sum_{s'} P(s'|s, a) R(s'|s, a)$$

does not depend on any of the values of the state variables in Y. In other words, for any pair of states s_1 and s_2 that differ only in their values for the variables in Y,

$$\sum_{s_1'} P(s_1'|s_1, a) R(s_1'|s_1, a) = \sum_{s_2'} P(s_2'|s_2, a) R(s_2'|s_2, a).$$

If this condition is satisfied at leaf a, then the following lemma shows that we can represent its value function $V(a, s)$ compactly.

Lemma 4 *Let M be an MDP with full-state MAXQ graph H, and suppose that state variables Y are irrelevant for leaf node a. Let $\chi(s) = x$ be the associated abstraction function that projects s onto the remaining relevant variables X. Then we can represent $V(a, s)$ for any state s by an abstracted value function $V(a, \chi(s)) = V(a, x)$.*

Proof: According to the definition of Leaf Irrelevance, any two states that differ only on the irrelevant state variables have the same value for $V(a, s)$. Hence, we can represent this unique value by $V(a, x)$. **Q.E.D.**

Here are two rules for finding cases where Leaf Irrelevance applies. The first rule shows that if the probability distribution factors, then we have Leaf Irrelevance.

Lemma 5 *Suppose the probability transition function for primitive action a, $P(s'|s, a)$, factors as $P(x', y'|x, y, a) = P(y'|x, y, a) P(x'|x, a)$ and the reward function satisfies $R(s'|s, a) = R(x'|x, a)$. Then the variables in Y are irrelevant to the leaf node a.*

Proof: Plug in to the definition of $V(a, s)$ and simplify.

$$
\begin{aligned}
V(a, s) &= \sum_{s'} P(s'|s, a) R(s'|s, a) \\
&= \sum_{x', y'} P(y'|x, y, a) P(x'|x, a) R(x'|x, a) \\
&= \sum_{y'} P(y'|x, y, a) \sum_{x'} P(x'|x, a) R(x'|x, a) \\
&= \sum_{x'} P(x'|x, a) R(x'|x, a)
\end{aligned}
$$

Hence, the expected reward for the action a depends only on the variables in X and not on the variables in Y. **Q.E.D.**

The second rule shows that if the reward function for a primitive action is constant, then we can apply state abstractions even if $P(s'|s, a)$ does not factor.

Lemma 6 *Suppose $R(s'|s, a)$ (the reward function for action a in MDP M) is always equal to a constant r_a. Then the entire state s is irrelevant to the primitive action a.*

Proof:

$$
\begin{aligned}
V(a, s) &= \sum_{s'} P(s'|s, a) R(s'|s, a) \\
&= \sum_{s'} P(s'|s, a) r_a \\
&= r_a.
\end{aligned}
$$

This does not depend on s, so the entire state is irrelevant to the primitive action a. **Q.E.D.**

This lemma is satisfied by the four leaf nodes North, South, East, and West in the taxi task, because their one-step reward is a constant (-1). Hence, instead of requiring 2000 values to store the V functions, we only need 4 values—one for each action. Similarly, the expected rewards of the Pickup and Putdown actions each require only 2 values, depending on whether the corresponding actions are legal or illegal. Hence, together, they require 4 values, instead of 1000 values.

5.1.3 CONDITION 3: RESULT DISTRIBUTION IRRELEVANCE

Now we consider a condition that results from "funnel" actions.

Definition 14 (Result Distribution Irrelevance). *A set of state variables Y_j is irrelevant for the result distribution of action j if, for all abstract policies π executed by node j and its descendents in the MAXQ hierarchy, the following holds: for all pairs of states s_1 and s_2 that differ only in their values for the state variables in Y_j,*

$$
P^{\pi}(s', N|s_1, j) = P^{\pi}(s', N|s_2, j)
$$

for all s' and N.

If this condition is satisfied for subtask j, then the C value of its parent task i can be represented compactly:

Lemma 7 *Let M be an MDP with full-state MAXQ graph H, and suppose that the set of state variables Y_j is irrelevant to the result distribution of action j, which is a child of Max node i. Let χ_{ij} be the associated abstraction function: $\chi_{ij}(s) = x$. Then we can define an abstract completion cost function $C^{\pi}(i, \chi_{ij}(s), j)$ such that for all states s,*

$$
C^{\pi}(i, s, j) = C^{\pi}(i, \chi_{ij}(s), j).
$$

Proof: The completion function for fixed policy π is defined as follows:

$$
C^{\pi}(i, s, j) = \sum_{s', N} P(s', N|s, j) \cdot \gamma^N Q^{\pi}(i, s'). \tag{21}
$$

Consider any two states s_1 and s_2, such that $\chi_{ij}(s_1) = \chi_{ij}(s_2) = x$. Under Result Distribution Irrelevance, their transition probability distributions are the same. Hence, the right-hand sides of (21) have the same value, and we can conclude that

$$
C^{\pi}(i, s_1, j) = C^{\pi}(i, s_2, j).
$$

Therefore, we can define an abstract completion function, $C^\pi(i, x, j)$ to represent this quantity. **Q.E.D.**

In undiscounted cumulative reward problems, the definition of result distribution irrelevance can be weakened to eliminate N, the number of steps. All that is needed is that for all pairs of states s_1 and s_2 that differ only in the irrelevant state variables, $P^\pi(s'|s_1, j) = P^\pi(s'|s_2, j)$ (for all s'). In the undiscounted case, Lemma 7 still holds under this revised definition.

It might appear that the result distribution irrelevance condition would rarely be satisfied, but we often find cases where the condition is true. Consider, for example, the Get subroutine for the taxi task. No matter what location the taxi has in state s, the taxi will be at the passenger's starting location when the Get finishes executing (i.e., because the taxi will have just completed picking up the passenger). Hence, the starting location is irrelevant to the resulting location of the taxi, and $P(s'|s_1, \mathsf{Get}) = P(s'|s_2, \mathsf{Get})$ for all states s_1 and s_2 that differ only in the taxi's location.

Note, however, that if we were maximizing discounted reward, the taxi's location would not be irrelevant, because the probability that Get will terminate in exactly N steps would depend on the location of the taxi, which could differ in states s_1 and s_2. Different values of N will produce different amounts of discounting in (21), and hence, we cannot ignore the taxi location when representing the completion function for Get.

But in the undiscounted case, by applying Lemma 7, we can represent $C(\mathsf{Root}, s, \mathsf{Get})$ using 16 distinct values, because there are 16 equivalence classes of states (4 source locations times 4 destination locations). This is much less than the 500 quantities in the unabstracted representation.

Note that although state variables Y may be irrelevant to the result distribution of a subtask j, they may be important *within* subtask j. In the Taxi task, the location of the taxi is critical for representing the value of $V(\mathsf{Get}, s)$, but it is irrelevant to the result state distribution for Get, and therefore it is irrelevant for representing $C(\mathsf{Root}, s, \mathsf{Get})$. Hence, the MAXQ decomposition is essential for obtaining the benefits of result distribution irrelevance.

"Funnel" actions arise in many hierarchical reinforcement learning problems. For example, abstract actions that move a robot to a doorway or that move a car onto the entrance ramp of a freeway have this property. The Result Distribution Irrelevance condition is applicable in all such situations as long as we are in the undiscounted setting.

5.1.4 CONDITION 4: TERMINATION

The fourth condition is closely related to the "funnel" property. It applies when a subtask is guaranteed to cause its parent task to terminate in a goal state. In a sense, the subtask is funneling the environment into the set of states described by the goal predicate of the parent task.

Lemma 8 (Termination). *Let M_i be a task in a MAXQ graph such that for all states s where the goal predicate $G_i(s)$ is true, the pseudo-reward function $\tilde{R}_i(s) = 0$. Suppose there is a child task a and state s such that for all hierarchical policies π,*

$$\forall s'\; P_i^\pi(s', N|s, a) > 0 \;\Rightarrow\; G_i(s').$$

(i.e., every possible state s' that results from applying a in s will make the goal predicate, G_i, true.)

Then for any policy executed at node i, the completion cost $C(i, s, a)$ is zero and does not need to be explicitly represented.

Proof: When action a is executed in state s, it is guaranteed to result in a state s' such that $G_i(s)$ is true. By definition, goal states also satisfy the termination predicate $T_i(s)$, so task i will terminate. Because $G_i(s)$ is true, the terminal pseudo-reward will be zero, and hence, the completion function will always be zero. **Q.E.D.**

For example, in the Taxi task, in all states where the taxi is holding the passenger, the Put subroutine will succeed and result in a goal terminal state for Root. This is because the termination predicate for Put (i.e., that the passenger is at his or her destination location) implies the goal condition for Root (which is the same). This means that $C(\text{Root}, s, \text{Put})$ is uniformly zero, for all states s where Put is not terminated.

It is easy to detect cases where the Termination condition is satisfied. We only need to compare the termination predicate T_a of a subtask with the goal predicate G_i of the parent task. If the first implies the second, then the termination lemma is satisfied.

5.1.5 Condition 5: Shielding

The shielding condition arises from the structure of the MAXQ graph.

Lemma 9 (Shielding). *Let M_i be a task in a MAXQ graph and s be a state such that in all paths from the root of the graph down to node M_i there is a subtask j (possibly equal to i) whose termination predicate $T_j(s)$ is true, then the Q nodes of M_i do not need to represent C values for state s.*

Proof: In order for task i to be executed in state s, there must exist some path of ancestors of task i leading up to the root of the graph such that all of those ancestor tasks are not terminated. The condition of the lemma guarantees that this is false, and hence that task i cannot be executed in state s. Therefore, no C values need to be represented. **Q.E.D.**

As with the Termination condition, the Shielding condition can be verified by analyzing the structure of the MAXQ graph and identifying nodes whose ancestor tasks are terminated.

In the Taxi domain, a simple example of this arises in the Put task, which is terminated in all states where the passenger is not in the taxi. This means that we do not need to represent $C(\text{Root}, s, \text{Put})$ in these states. The result is that, when combined with the Termination condition above, we do not need to explicitly represent the completion function for Put at all!

5.1.6 Dicussion

By applying these five abstraction conditions, we obtain the following "safe" state abstractions for the Taxi task:

- North, South, East, and West. These terminal nodes require one quantity each, for a total of four values. (Leaf Irrelevance).

- Pickup and Putdown each require 2 values (legal and illegal states), for a total of four. (Leaf Irrelevance.)

- QNorth(t), QSouth(t), QEast(t), and QWest(t) each require 100 values (four values for t and 25 locations). (Max Node Irrelevance.)

- QNavigateForGet requires 4 values (for the four possible source locations). (The passenger destination is Max Node Irrelevant for MaxGet, and the taxi starting location is Result Distribution Irrelevant for the Navigate action.)

- QPickup requires 100 possible values, 4 possible source locations and 25 possible taxi locations. (Passenger destination is Max Node Irrelevant to MaxGet.)

- QGet requires 16 possible values (4 source locations, 4 destination locations). (Result Distribution Irrelevance.)

- QNavigateForPut requires only 4 values (for the four possible destination locations). (The passenger source and destination are Max Node Irrelevant to MaxPut; the taxi location is Result Distribution Irrelevant for the Navigate action.)

- QPutdown requires 100 possible values (25 taxi locations, 4 possible destination locations). (Passenger source is Max Node Irrelevant for MaxPut.)

- QPut requires 0 values. (Termination and Shielding.)

This gives a total of 632 distinct values, which is much less than the 3000 values required by flat Q learning. Hence, we can see that by applying state abstractions, the MAXQ representation can give a much more compact representation of the value function.

A key thing to note is that with these state abstractions, the value function is decomposed into a sum of terms such that no single term depends on the entire state of the MDP, even though the value function as a whole does depend on the entire state of the MDP. For example, consider again the state described in Figures 1 and 4. There, we showed that the value of a state s_1 with the passenger at R, the destination at B, and the taxi at (0,3) can be decomposed as

$$
\begin{aligned}
V(\mathsf{Root}, s_1) \;=\; & V(\mathsf{North}, s_1) + C(\mathsf{Navigate}(R), s_1, \mathsf{North}) + \\
& C(\mathsf{Get}, s_1, \mathsf{Navigate}(R)) + C(\mathsf{Root}, s_1, \mathsf{Get})
\end{aligned}
$$

With state abstractions, we can see that each term on the right-hand side only depends on a subset of the features:

- $V(\mathsf{North}, s_1)$ is a constant

- $C(\mathsf{Navigate}(R), s_1, \mathsf{North})$ depends only on the taxi location and the passenger's source location.

- $C(\mathsf{Get}, s_1, \mathsf{Navigate}(R))$ depends only on the source location.

- $C(\mathsf{Root}, s_1, \mathsf{Get})$ depends only on the passenger's source and destination.

Without the MAXQ decomposition, no features are irrelevant, and the value function depends on the entire state.

What prior knowledge is required on the part of a programmer in order to identify these state abstractions? It suffices to know some qualitative constraints on the one-step reward functions, the one-step transition probabilities, and termination predicates, goal predicates, and pseudo-reward functions within the MAXQ graph. Specifically, the Max Node Irrelevance and Leaf Irrelevance conditions require simple analysis of the one-step transition function and the reward and pseudo-reward functions. Opportunities to apply the Result Distribution Irrelevance condition can be found by identifying "funnel" effects that result from the definitions of the termination conditions for operators. Similarly, the Shielding and Termination conditions only require analysis of the termination predicates of the various subtasks. Hence, applying these five conditions to introduce state abstractions is a straightforward process, and once a model of the one-step transition and reward functions has been learned, the abstraction conditions can be checked to see if they are satisfied.

5.2 Convergence of MAXQ-Q with State Abstraction

We have shown that state abstractions can be safely introduced into the MAXQ value function decomposition under the five conditions described above. However, these conditions only guarantee that the value function of any fixed *abstract* hierarchical policy can be represented—they do not show that recursively optimal policies can be represented, nor do they show that the MAXQ-Q learning algorithm will find a recursively optimal policy when it is forced to use these state abstractions. The goal of this section is to prove these two results: (a) that the ordered recursively-optimal policy is an abstract policy (and, hence, can be represented using state abstractions) and (b) that MAXQ-Q will converge to this policy when applied to a MAXQ graph with safe state abstractions.

Lemma 10 *Let M be an MDP with full-state MAXQ graph H and abstract-state MAXQ graph $\chi(H)$ where the abstractions satisfy the five conditions given above. Let ω be an ordering over all actions in the MAXQ graph. Then the following statements are true:*

- *The unique ordered recursively-optimal policy π_r^* defined by M, H, and ω is an abstract policy (i.e., it depends only on the relevant state variables at each node; see Definition 11),*

- *The C and V functions in $\chi(H)$ can represent the projected value function of π_r^*.*

Proof: The five abstraction lemmas tell us that if the ordered recursively-optimal policy is abstract, then the C and V functions of $\chi(H)$ can represent its value function. Hence, the heart of this lemma is the first claim. The last two forms of abstraction (Shielding and Termination) do not place any restrictions on abstract policies, so we ignore them in this proof.

The proof is by induction on the levels of the MAXQ graph, starting at the leaves. As a base case, let us consider a Max node i all of whose children are primitive actions. In this case, there are no policies executed *within* the children of the Max node. Hence if variables Y_i are irrelevant for node i, then we can apply our abstraction lemmas to represent the value function of any policy at node i—not just abstract policies. Consequently, the value function of any optimal policy for node i can be represented, and it will have the property that

$$Q^*(i, s_1, a) = Q^*(i, s_2, a) \qquad (22)$$

for any states s_1 and s_2 such that $\chi_i(s_1) = \chi_i(s_2)$.

Now let us impose the action ordering ω to compute the optimal *ordered* policy. Consider two actions a_1 and a_2 such that $\omega(a_1, a_2)$ (i.e., ω prefers a_1), and suppose that there is a "tie" in the Q^* function at state s_1 such that the values

$$Q^*(i, s_1, a_1) = Q^*(i, s_1, a_2)$$

and they are the only two actions that maximize Q^* in this state. Then the optimal ordered policy must choose a_1. Now in all other states s_2 such that $\chi_i(s_1) = \chi_i(s_2)$, we have just established in (22) that the Q^* values will be the same. Hence, the same tie will exist between a_1 and a_2, and hence, the optimal ordered policy must make the same choice in all such states. Hence, the optimal ordered policy for node i is an abstract policy.

Now let us turn to the recursive case at Max node i. Make the inductive assumption that the ordered recursively-optimal policy is abstract within all descendent nodes and consider the locally optimal policy at node i. If Y is a set of state variables that are irrelevant to node i, Corollary 2 tells us that $Q^*(i, s_1, j) = Q^*(i, s_2, j)$ for all states s_1 and s_2 such that $\chi_i(s_1) = \chi_i(s_2)$. Similarly, if Y is a set of variables irrelevant to the result distribution of a particular action j, then Lemma 7 tells us the same thing. Hence, by the same ordering argument given above, the ordered optimal policy at node i must be abstract. By induction, this proves the lemma. **Q.E.D.**

With this lemma, we have established that the combination of an MDP M, an abstract MAXQ graph H, and an action ordering defines a unique recursively-optimal ordered abstract policy. We are now ready to prove that MAXQ-Q will converge to this policy.

Theorem 4 *Let $M = \langle S, A, P, R, P_0 \rangle$ be either an episodic MDP for which all deterministic policies are proper or a discounted infinite horizon MDP with discount factor $\gamma < 1$. Let H be an unabstracted MAXQ graph defined over subtasks $\{M_0, \ldots, M_k\}$ with pseudo-reward functions $\tilde{R}_i(s')$. Let $\chi(H)$ be a state-abstracted MAXQ graph defined by applying state abstractions χ_i to each node i of H under the five conditions given above. Let $\pi_x(i, \chi_i(s))$ be an abstract ordered GLIE exploration policy at each node i and state s whose decisions depend only on the "relevant" state variables at each node i. Let π_r^* be the unique recursively-optimal hierarchical policy defined by π_x, M, and $\tilde{R}$. Then with probability 1, algorithm MAXQ-Q applied to $\chi(H)$ converges to π_r^* provided that the learning rates $\alpha_t(i)$ satisfy Equation (15) and the one-step rewards are bounded.*

Proof: Rather than repeating the entire proof for MAXQ-Q, we will only describe what must change under state abstraction. The last two forms of state abstraction refer to states whose values can be inferred from the structure of the MAXQ graph, and therefore do not need to be represented at all. Since these values are not updated by MAXQ-Q, we can ignore them. We will now consider the first three forms of state abstraction in turn.

We begin by considering primitive leaf nodes. Let a be a leaf node and let Y be a set of state variables that are Leaf Irrelevant for a. Let $s_1 = (x, y_1)$ and $s_2 = (x, y_2)$ be two states that differ only in their values for Y. Under Leaf Irrelevance, the probability transitions $P(s_1'|s_1, a)$ and $P(s_2'|s_2, a)$ need not be the same, but the expected reward of performing a in both states must be the same. When MAXQ-Q visits an abstract state x, it does not "know" the value of y, the part of the state that has been abstracted away. Nonetheless, it draws a sample according to $P(s'|x, y, a)$, receives a reward $R(s'|x, y, a)$, and updates its estimate of $V(a, x)$ (line 4 of MAXQ-Q). Let $P_t(y)$ be the probability that MAXQ-Q is visiting (x, y) given that the unabstracted part of the state is x. Then Line 4 of MAXQ-Q is computing a stochastic approximation to

$$\sum_{s', N, y} P_t(y) P_t(s', N|x, y, a) R(s'|x, y, a).$$

We can write this as

$$\sum_y P_t(y) \sum_{s', N} P_t(s', N|x, y, a) R(s'|x, y, a).$$

According to Leaf Irrelevance, the inner sum has the same value for all states s such that $\chi(s) = x$. Call this value $r_0(x)$. This gives

$$\sum_y P_t(y) r_0(x),$$

which is equal to $r_0(x)$ for any distribution $P_t(y)$. Hence, MAXQ-Q converges under Leaf Irrelevance abstractions.

Now let us turn to the two forms of abstraction that apply to internal nodes: Max Node Irrelevance and Result Distribution Irrelevance. Consider the SMDP defined at each node i of the abstracted MAXQ graph at time t during MAXQ-Q. This would be an ordinary SMDP with transition probability function $P_t(x', N|x, a)$ and reward function $V_t(a, x) + \tilde{R}_i(x')$ except that when MAXQ-Q draws samples of state transitions, they are drawn according to the distribution $P_t(s', N|s, a)$ over the original state space. To prove the theorem, we must show that drawing (s', N) according to this second distribution is equivalent to drawing (x', N) according to the first distribution.

For Max Node Irrelevance, we know that for all abstract policies applied to node i and its descendents, the transition probability distribution factors as

$$P(s', N|s, a) = P(y'|x, y, a) P(x', N|x, a).$$

Because the exploration policy is an abstract policy, $P_t(s', N|s, a)$ factors in this way. This means that the Y_i components of the state cannot affect the X_i components, and hence, sampling from $P_t(s', N|s, a)$ and discarding the Y_i values gives samples for $P_t(x', N|x, a)$. Therefore, MAXQ-Q will converge under Max Node Irrelevance abstractions.

Finally, consider Result Distribution Irrelevance. Let j be a child of node i, and suppose Y_j is a set of state variables that are irrelevant to the result distribution of j. When the SMDP at node i wishes to draw a sample from $P_t(x', N|x, j)$, it does not "know" the current value of y, the irrelevant part of the current state. However, this does not matter, because Result Distribution Irrelevance means that for all possible values of y, $P_t(x', y', N|x, y, j)$ is the same. Hence, MAXQ-Q will converge under Result Distribution Irrelevance abstractions.

In each of these three cases, MAXQ-Q will converge to a locally-optimal ordered policy at node i in the MAXQ graph. By Lemma 10, this produces a locally-optimal ordered policy for the unabstracted SMDP at node i. Hence, by induction, MAXQ-Q will converge to the unique ordered recursively optimal policy π_r^* defined by MAXQ-Q H, MDP M, and ordered exploration policy π_x. **Q.E.D.**

5.3 The Hierarchical Credit Assignment Problem

There are still some situations where we would like to introduce state abstractions but where the five properties described above do not permit them. Consider the following modification of the taxi problem. Suppose that the taxi has a fuel tank and that each time the taxi moves one square, it costs one unit of fuel. If the taxi runs out of fuel before delivering the passenger to his or her destination, it receives a reward of −20, and the trial ends. Fortunately, there is a filling station where the taxi can execute a Fillup action to fill the fuel tank.

To solve this modified problem using the MAXQ hierarchy, we can introduce another subtask, Refuel, which has the goal of moving the taxi to the filling station and filling the tank. MaxRefuel is a child of MaxRoot, and it invokes Navigate(t) (with t bound to the location of the filling station) to move the taxi to the filling station.

The introduction of fuel and the possibility that we might run out of fuel means that we must include the current amount of fuel as a feature in representing every C value (for internal nodes) and V value (for leaf nodes) throughout the MAXQ graph. This is unfortunate, because our intuition tells us that the amount of fuel should have no influence on our decisions inside the Navigate(t) subtask. That is, either the taxi will have enough fuel to reach the target t (in which case, the chosen navigation actions do not depend on the fuel), or else the taxi will not have enough fuel, and hence, it will fail to reach t regardless of what navigation actions are taken. In other words, the Navigate(t) subtask should not need to worry about the amount of fuel, because even if there is not enough fuel, there is no action that Navigate(t) can take to get more fuel. Instead, it is the top-level subtasks that should be monitoring the amount of fuel and deciding whether to go refuel, to go pick up the passenger, or to go deliver the passenger.

Given this intuition, it is natural to try abstracting away the "amount of remaining fuel" within the Navigate(t) subtask. However, this doesn't work, because when the taxi runs out of fuel and a −20 reward is given, the QNorth, QSouth, QEast, and QWest nodes cannot "explain" why this reward was received—that is, they have no consistent way of setting their C tables to predict when this negative reward will occur, because their C values ignore the amount of fuel in the tank. Stated more formally, the difficulty is that the Max Node Irrelevance condition is not satisfied because the one-step reward function $R(s'|s, a)$ for these actions depends on the amount of fuel.

We call this the *hierarchical credit assignment problem*. The fundamental issue here is that in the MAXQ decomposition all information about rewards is stored in the leaf nodes of the hierarchy. We would like to separate out the basic rewards received for navigation (i.e., −1 for each action) from the reward received for exhausting fuel (−20). If we make the reward at the leaves only depend on the location of the taxi, then the Max Node Irrelevance condition will be satisfied.

One way to do this is to have the programmer manually decompose the reward function and indicate which nodes in the hierarchy will "receive" each reward. Let $R(s'|s,a) = \sum_i R(i,s'|s,a)$ be a decomposition of the reward function, such that $R(i,s'|s,a)$ specifies that part of the reward that must be handled by Max node i. In the modified taxi problem, for example, we can decompose the reward so that the leaf nodes receive all of the original penalties, but the out-of-fuel rewards must be handled by MaxRoot. Lines 15 and 16 of the MAXQ-Q algorithm are easily modified to include $R(i,s'|s,a)$.

In most domains, we believe it will be easy for the designer of the hierarchy to decompose the reward function. It has been straightforward in all of the problems we have studied. However, an interesting problem for future research is to develop an algorithm that can solve the hierarchical credit assignment problem autonomously.

6. Non-Hierarchical Execution of the MAXQ Hierarchy

Up to this point in the paper, we have focused exclusively on representing and learning hierarchical policies. However, often the optimal policy for a MDP is not strictly hierarchical. Kaelbling (1993) first introduced the idea of deriving a non-hierarchical policy from the value function of a hierarchical policy. In this section, we exploit the MAXQ decomposition to generalize her ideas and apply them recursively at all levels of the hierarchy. We will describe two methods for non-hierarchical execution.

The first method is based on the dynamic programming algorithm known as policy iteration. The policy iteration algorithm starts with an initial policy π^0. It then repeats the following two steps until the policy converges. In the *policy evaluation* step, it computes the value function V^{π_k} of the current policy π_k. Then, in the *policy improvement step*, it computes a new policy, π_{k+1} according to the rule

$$\pi_{k+1}(s) := \operatorname*{argmax}_a \sum_{s'} P(s'|s,a)[R(s'|s,a) + \gamma V^{\pi_k}(s')]. \tag{23}$$

Howard (1960) proved that if π_k is not an optimal policy, then π_{k+1} is guaranteed to be an improvement. Note that in order to apply this method, we need to know the transition probability distribution $P(s'|s,a)$ and the reward function $R(s'|s,a)$.

If we know $P(s'|s,a)$ and $R(s'|s,a)$, we can use the MAXQ representation of the value function to perform one step of policy iteration. We start with a hierarchical policy π and represent its value function using the MAXQ hierarchy (e.g., π could have been learned via MAXQ-Q). Then, we can perform one step of policy improvement by applying Equation (23) using $V^\pi(0,s')$ (computed by the MAXQ hierarchy) to compute $V^\pi(s')$.

Corollary 3 Let $\pi^g(s) = \operatorname{argmax}_a \sum_{s'} P(s'|s,a)[R(s'|s,a) + \gamma V^\pi(0,s)]$, where $V^\pi(0,s)$ is the value function computed by the MAXQ hierarchy and a is a primitive action. Then, if π was not an optimal policy, π^g is strictly better for at least one state in S.

Proof: This is a direct consequence of Howard's policy improvement theorem. **Q.E.D.**

Unfortunately, we can't iterate this policy improvement process, because the new policy, π^g is very unlikely to be a hierarchical policy (i.e., it is unlikely to be representable in

Table 5: The procedure for executing the one-step greedy policy.

---

procedure EXECUTEHGPOLICY(s)

1   **repeat**
2   Let $\langle V(0,s), a \rangle := $ EVALUATEMAXNODE$(0, s)$
3   execute primitive action a
4   Let s be the resulting state
    end // EXECUTEHGPOLICY

---

terms of local policies for each node of the MAXQ graph). Nonetheless, one step of policy improvement can give very significant improvements.

This approach to non-hierarchical execution ignores the internal structure of the MAXQ graph. In effect, the MAXQ hierarchy is just viewed as a way to represent V^{π}—any other representation would give the same one-step improved policy π^g.

The second approach to non-hierarchical execution borrows an idea from Q learning. One of the great beauties of the Q representation for value functions is that we can compute one step of policy improvement without knowing $P(s'|s, a)$, simply by taking the new policy to be $\pi^g(s) := \operatorname{argmax}_a Q(s, a)$. This gives us the same one-step greedy policy as we computed above using one-step lookahead. With the MAXQ decomposition, we can perform these policy improvement steps *at all levels of the hierarchy*.

We have already defined the function that we need. In Table 3 we presented the function EVALUATEMAXNODE, which, given the current state s, conducts a search along all paths from a given Max node i to the leaves of the MAXQ graph and finds the path with the best value (i.e., with the maximum sum of C values along the path, plus the V value at the leaf). This is equivalent to computing the best action greedily at each level of the MAXQ graph. In addition, EVALUATEMAXNODE returns the primitive action a at the end of this best path. This action a would be the first primitive action to be executed if the learned hierarchical policy were executed starting in the current state s. Our second method for non-hierarchical execution of the MAXQ graph is to call EVALUATEMAXNODE in each state, and execute the primitive action a that is returned. The pseudo-code is shown in Table 5.

We will call the policy computed by EXECUTEHGPOLICY the *hierarchical greedy policy*, and denote it π^{hg*}, where the superscript * indicates that we are computing the greedy action at each time step. The following theorem shows that this can give a better policy than the original, hierarchical policy.

Theorem 5 *Let G be a MAXQ graph representing the value function of hierarchical policy π (i.e., in terms of $C^{\pi}(i, s, j)$, computed for all i, s, and j). Let $V^{hg}(0, s)$ be the value computed by* EXECUTEHGPOLICY *(line 2), and let π^{hg*} be the resulting policy. Define V^{hg*} to be the value function of π^{hg*}. Then for all states s, it is the case that*

$$V^{\pi}(s) \leq V^{hg}(0, s) \leq V^{hg*}(s). \tag{24}$$

Proof: (sketch) The left inequality in Equation (24) is satisfied by construction by line 6 of EVALUATEMAXNODE. To see this, consider that the original hierarchical policy, π, can

276

be viewed as choosing a "path" through the MAXQ graph running from the root to one of the leaf nodes, and $V^\pi(0, s)$ is the sum of the C^π values along this chosen path (plus the V^π value at the leaf node). In contrast, EVALUATEMAXNODE performs a traversal of *all* paths through the MAXQ graph and finds the *best* path, that is, the path with the largest sum of C^π (and leaf V^π) values. Hence, $V^{hg}(0, s)$ must be at least as large as $V^\pi(0, s)$.

To establish the right inequality, note that by construction $V^{hg}(0, s)$ is the value function of a policy, call it π^{hg}, that chooses one action greedily at each level of the MAXQ graph (recursively), and then follows π thereafter. This is a consequence of the fact that line 6 of EVALUATEMAXNODE has C^π on its right-hand side, and C^π represents the cost of "completing" each subroutine by following π, not by following some other, greedier, policy. (In Table 3, C^π is written as C_t.) However, when we execute EXECUTEHGPOLICY (and hence, execute π^{hg*}), we have an opportunity to improve upon π and π^{hg} at each time step. Hence, $V^{hg}(0, s)$ is an underestimate of the actual value of π^{hg*}. **Q.E.D.**

Note that this theorem only works in one direction. It says that if we can find a state where $V^{hg}(0, s) > V^\pi(s)$, then the greedy policy, π^{hg*}, will be strictly better than π. However, it could be that π is not an optimal policy and yet the structure of the MAXQ graph prevents us from considering an action (either primitive or composite) that would improve π. Hence, unlike the policy improvement theorem of Howard (where all primitive actions are always eligible to be chosen), we do not have a guarantee that if π is suboptimal, then the hierarchically greedy policy is a strict improvement.

In contrast, if we perform one-step policy improvement as discussed at the start of this section, Corollary 3 guarantees that we will improve the policy. So we can see that in general, neither of these two methods for non-hierarchical execution is always better than the other. Nonetheless, the first method only operates at the level of individual primitive actions, so it is not able to produce very large improvements in the policy. In contrast, the hierarchical greedy method can obtain very large improvements in the policy by changing which actions (i.e., subroutines) are chosen near the root of the hierarchy. Hence, in general, hierarchical greedy execution is probably the better method. (Of course, the value functions of both methods could be computed, and the one with the better estimated value could be executed.)

Sutton, et al. (1999) have simultaneously developed a closely-related method for non-hierarchical execution of macros. Their method is equivalent to EXECUTEHGPOLICY for the special case where the MAXQ hierarchy has only one level of subtasks. The interesting aspect of EXECUTEHGPOLICY is that it permits greedy improvements at all levels of the tree to influence which action is chosen.

Some care must be taken in applying Theorem 5 to a MAXQ hierarchy whose C values have been learned via MAXQ-Q. Being an online algorithm, MAXQ-Q will not have correctly learned the values of *all* states at all nodes of the MAXQ graph. For example, in the taxi problem, the value of $C(\text{Put}, s, \text{QPutdown})$ will not have been learned very well except at the four special locations R, G, B, and Y. This is because the Put subtask cannot be executed until the passenger is in the taxi, and this usually means that a Get has just been completed, so the taxi is at the passenger's source location. During exploration, both children of Put will be tried in such states. The PutDown will usually fail (and receive a negative reward), whereas the Navigate will eventually succeed (perhaps after lengthy exploration) and take the taxi to the destination location. Now because of all-states updating, the values for $C(\text{Put}, s, \text{Navigate}(t))$ will have been learned at all of the states along the path to the passenger's destination, but the C values for the Putdown action will only be learned for the passenger's source and destination locations. Hence, if we train the MAXQ representation using hierarchical execution (as in MAXQ-Q), and then switch to hierarchically-greedy execution, the results will be quite bad. In particular, we need to introduce hierarchically-greedy execution early enough so that the exploration policy is still actively exploring. (In theory, a GLIE exploration policy never ceases to explore, but in practice, we want to find a good policy quickly, not just asymptotically).

Of course an alternative would be to use hierarchically-greedy execution from the very beginning of learning. However, remember that the higher nodes in the MAXQ hierarchy need to obtain samples of $P(s', N|s, a)$ for each child action a. If the hierarchical greedy execution interrupts child a before it has reached a terminal state (i.e., because at some state along the way, another subtask appears better to EVALUATEMAXNODE), then these samples cannot be obtained. Hence, it is important to begin with purely hierarchical execution during training, and make a transition to greedy execution at some point.

The approach we have taken is to implement MAXQ-Q in such a way that we can specify a number of primitive actions L that can be taken hierarchically before the hierarchical execution is "interrupted" and control returns to the top level (where a new action can be chosen greedily). We start with L set very large, so that execution is completely hierarchical—when a child action is invoked, we are committed to execute that action until it terminates. However, gradually, we reduce L until it becomes 1, at which point we have hierarchical greedy execution. We time this so that it reaches 1 at about the same time our Boltzmann exploration cools to a temperature of 0.1 (which is where exploration effectively has halted). As the experimental results will show, this generally gives excellent results with very little added exploration cost.

7. Experimental Evaluation of the MAXQ Method

We have performed a series of experiments with the MAXQ method with three goals in mind: (a) to understand the expressive power of the value function decomposition, (b) to characterize the behavior of the MAXQ-Q learning algorithm, and (c) to assess the relative importance of temporal abstraction, state abstraction, and non-hierarchical execution. In this section, we describe these experiments and present the results.

7.1 The Fickle Taxi Task

Our first experiments were performed on a modified version of the taxi task. This version incorporates two changes to the task described in Section 3.1. First, each of the four navigation actions is noisy, so that with probability 0.8 it moves in the intended direction, but with probability 0.1 it instead moves to the right (of the intended direction) and with probability 0.1 it moves to the left. The purpose of this change is to create a more realistic and more difficult challenge for the learning algorithms. The second change is that after the taxi has picked up the passenger and moved one square away from the passenger's source location, the passenger changes his or her destination location with probability 0.3. The purpose of this change is to create a situation where the optimal policy is not a hierarchical policy so that the effectiveness of non-hierarchical execution can be measured.

We compared four different configurations of the learning algorithm: (a) flat Q learning, (b) MAXQ-Q learning without any form of state abstraction, (c) MAXQ-Q learning with state abstraction, and (d) MAXQ-Q learning with state abstraction and greedy execution. These configurations are controlled by many parameters. These include the following: (a) the initial values of the Q and C functions, (b) the learning rate (we employed a fixed learning rate), (c) the cooling schedule for Boltzmann exploration (the GLIE policy that we employed), and (d) for non-hierarchical execution, the schedule for decreasing L, the number of steps of consecutive hierarchical execution. We optimized these settings separately for each configuration with the goal of matching or exceeding (with as few primitive training actions as possible) the best policy that we could code by hand. For Boltzmann exploration, we established an initial temperature and then a cooling rate. A separate temperature is maintained for each Max node in the MAXQ graph, and its temperature is reduced by multiplying by the cooling rate each time that subtask terminates in a goal state.

The process of optimizing the parameter settings for each algorithm is time-consuming, both for flat Q learning and for MAXQ-Q. The most critical parameter is the schedule for cooling the temperature of Boltzmann exploration: if this is cooled too rapidly, then the algorithms will converge to a suboptimal policy. In each case, we tested nine different cooling rates. To choose the different cooling rates for the various subtasks, we started by using fixed policies (e.g., either random or hand-coded) for all subtasks except the subtasks closest to the leaves. Then, once we had chosen schedules for those subtasks, we allowed their parent tasks to learn their policies while we tuned their cooling rates, and so on. One nice effect of our method of cooling the temperature only when a subtask terminates is that it naturally causes the subtasks higher in the MAXQ graph to cool more slowly. This meant that good results could often be obtained just by using the same cooling rate for all Max nodes.

The choice of learning rate is easier, since it is determined primarily by the degree of stochasticity in the environment. We only tested three or four different rates for each configuration. The initial values for the Q and C functions were set based on our knowledge of the problems—no experiments were required.

We took more care in tuning these parameters for these experiments than one would normally take in a real application, because we wanted to ensure that each method was compared under the best possible conditions. The general form of the results (particularly the speed of learning) is the same for wide ranges of the cooling rate and learning rate parameter settings.

The following parameters were selected based on the tuning experiments. For flat Q learning: initial Q values of 0.123 in all states, learning rate 0.25, and Boltzmann exploration with an initial temperature of 50 and a cooling rate of 0.9879. (We use initial values that end in .123 as a "signature" during debugging to detect when a weight has been modified.)

For MAXQ-Q learning without state abstraction, we used initial values of 0.123, a learning rate of 0.50, and Boltzmann exploration with an initial temperature of 50 and cooling rates of 0.9996 at MaxRoot and MaxPut, 0.9939 at MaxGet, and 0.9879 at MaxNavigate.

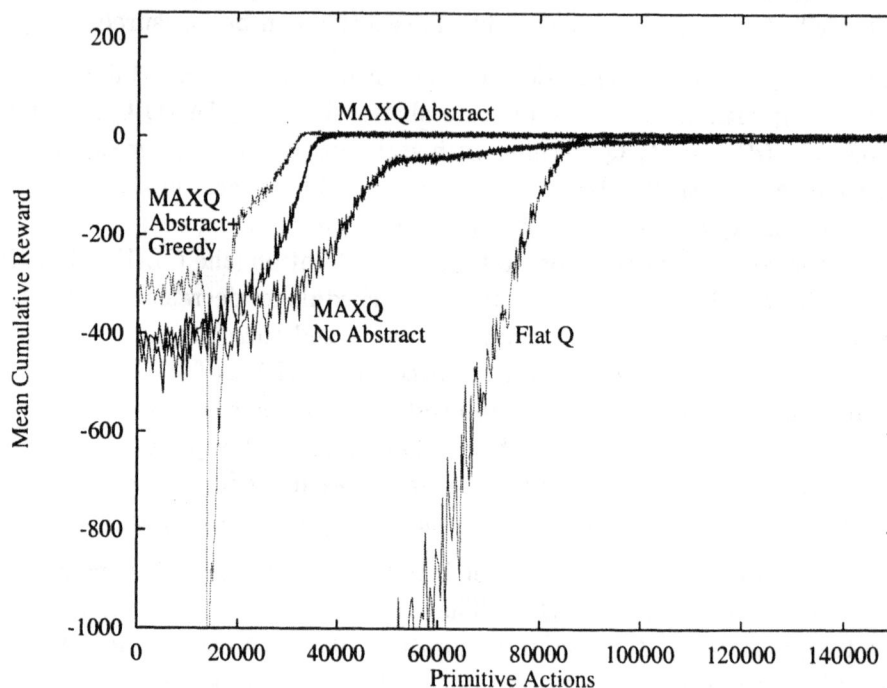

Figure 8: Comparison of performance of hierarchical MAXQ-Q learning (without state abstractions, with state abstractions, and with state abstractions combined with hierarchical greedy evaluation) to flat Q learning.

For MAXQ-Q learning with state abstraction, we used initial values of 0.123, a learning rate of 0.25, and Boltzmann exploration with an initial temperature of 50 and cooling rates of 0.9074 at MaxRoot, 0.9526 at MaxPut, 0.9526 at MaxGet, and 0.9879 at MaxNavigate.

For MAXQ-Q learning with non-hierarchical execution, we used the same settings as with state abstraction. In addition, we initialized L to 500 and decreased it by 10 with each trial until it reached 1. So after 50 trials, execution was completely greedy.

Figure 8 shows the averaged results of 100 training runs. Each training run involves performing repeated trials until convergence. Because the different trials execute different numbers of primitive actions, we have just plotted the number of primitive actions on the horizontal axis rather than the number of trials.

The first thing to note is that all forms of MAXQ learning have better initial performance than flat Q learning. This is because of the constraints introduced by the MAXQ hierarchy. For example, while the agent is executing a Navigate subtask, it will never attempt to pickup or putdown the passenger, because those actions are not available to Navigate. Similarly, the agent will never attempt to putdown the passenger until it has first picked up the passenger (and vice versa) because of the termination conditions of the Get and Put subtasks.

The second thing to notice is that without state abstractions, MAXQ-Q learning actually takes longer to converge, so that the Flat Q curve crosses the MAXQ/no abstraction curve. This shows that without state abstraction, the cost of learning the huge number of parameters in the MAXQ representation is not really worth the benefits. We suspect this is a consequence of the model-free nature of the MAXQ-Q algorithm. The MAXQ decomposition represents some information redundantly. For example, the cost of performing a Put subtask is computed both as $C(\text{Root}, s, \text{Get})$ and also as $V(\text{Put}, s)$. A model-based algorithm could compute both of these from a learned model, but MAXQ-Q must learn each of them separately from experience.

The third thing to notice is that with state abstractions, MAXQ-Q converges very quickly to a hierarchically optimal policy. This can be seen more clearly in Figure 9, which focuses on the range of reward values in the neighborhood of the optimal policy. Here we can see that MAXQ with abstractions attains the hierarchically optimal policy after approximately 40,000 steps, whereas flat Q learning requires roughly twice as long to reach the same level. However, flat Q learning, of course, can continue onward and reach optimal performance, whereas with the MAXQ hierarchy, the best hierarchical policy is slow to respond to the "fickle" behavior of the passenger when he/she changes the destination.

The last thing to notice is that with greedy execution, the MAXQ policy is also able to attain optimal performance. But as the execution becomes "more greedy", there is a temporary drop in performance, because MAXQ-Q must learn C values in new regions of the state space that were not visited by the recursively optimal policy. Despite this drop in performance, greedy MAXQ-Q recovers rapidly and reaches hierarchically optimal performance faster than purely-hierarchical MAXQ-Q learning. Hence, there is no added cost—in terms of exploration—for introducing greedy execution.

This experiment presents evidence in favor of three claims: first, that hierarchical reinforcement learning can be much faster than flat Q learning; second, that state abstraction is required by MAXQ-Q learning for good performance; and third, that non-hierarchical execution can produce significant improvements in performance with little or no added exploration cost.

7.2 Kaelbling's HDG Method

The second task that we will consider is a simple maze task introduced by Leslie Kaelbling (1993) and shown in Figure 11. In each trial of this task, the agent starts in a randomly-chosen state and must move to a randomly-chosen goal state using the usual North, South, East, and West operators (we employed deterministic operators). There is a small cost for each move, and the agent must minimize the undiscounted sum of these costs.

Because the goal state can be in any of 100 different locations, there are actually 100 different MDPs. Kaelbling's HDG method starts by choosing an arbitrary set of landmark states and defining a Voronoi partition of the state space based on the Manhattan distances to these landmarks (i.e., two states belong to the same Voronoi cell iff they have the same nearest landmark). The method then defines one subtask for each landmark l. The subtask is to move from any state in the current Voronoi cell *or in any neighboring Voronoi cell* to the landmark l. Optimal policies for these subtasks are then computed.

Once HDG has the policies for these subtasks, it can solve the abstract Markov Decision Problem of moving from each landmark state to any other landmark state using the subtask solutions as macro actions (subroutines). So it computes a value function for this MDP.

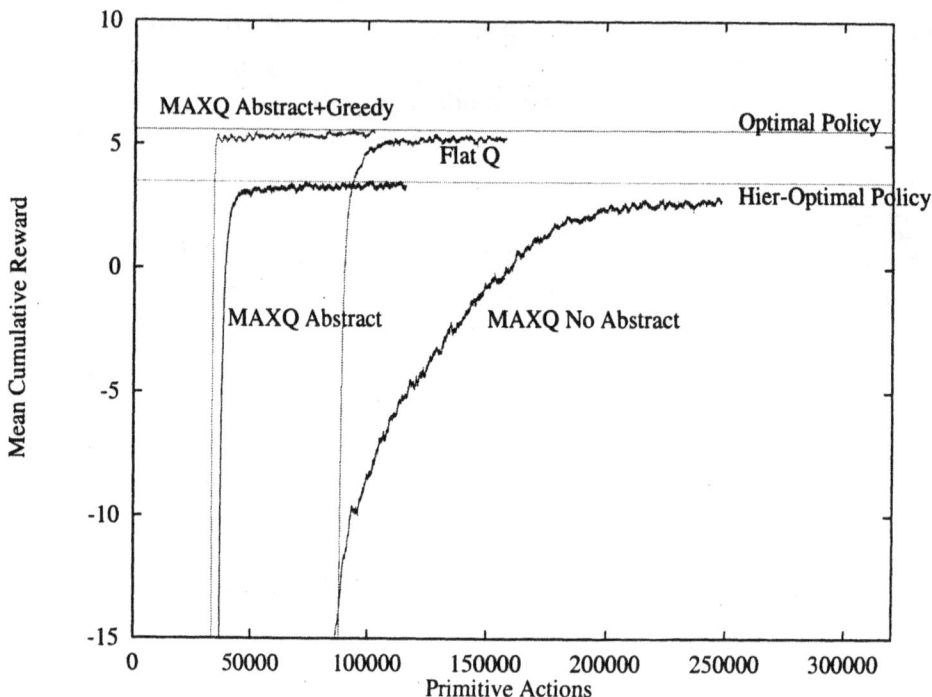

Figure 9: Close-up view of the previous figure. This figure also shows two horizontal lines indicating optimal performance and hierarchically optimal performance in this domain. To make this figure more readable, we have applied a 100-step moving average to the data points (which are themselves the average of 100 runs).

Finally, for each possible destination location g within a Voronoi cell for landmark l, the HDG method computes the optimal policy of getting from l to g.

By combining these subtasks, the HDG method can construct a good approximation to the optimal policy as follows. In addition to the value functions discussed above, the agent maintains two other functions: $NL(s)$, the name of the landmark nearest to state s, and $N(l)$, a list of the landmarks of the cells that are immediate neighbors of cell l. By combining these, the agent can build a list for each state s of the current landmark and the landmarks of the neighboring cells. For each such landmark, the agent computes the sum of three terms:

(t1) the expected cost of reaching that landmark,

(t2) the expected cost of moving from that landmark to the landmark in the goal cell, and

(t3) the expected cost of moving from the goal-cell landmark to the goal state.

Note that while terms (t1) and (t3) can be exact estimates, term (t2) is computed using the landmark subtasks as subroutines. This means that the corresponding path must pass through the intermediate landmark states rather than going directly to the goal landmark.

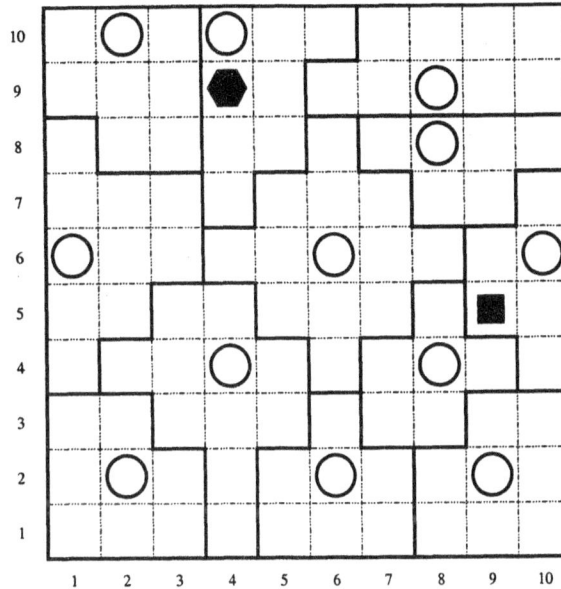

Figure 10: Kaelbling's 10-by-10 navigation task. Each circled state is a landmark state, and the heavy lines show the boundaries of the Voronoi cells. In each episode, a start state and a goal state are chosen at random. In this figure, the start state is shown by the black square, and the goal state is shown by the black hexagon.

Hence, term (t2) is typically an overestimate of the required distance. (Also note that (t3) is the same for all choices of the intermediate landmarks, so it does not need to be explicitly included in the computation of the best action until the agent enters the cell containing the goal.)

Given this information, the agent then chooses to move toward the best of the landmarks (unless the agent is already in the goal Voronoi cell, in which case the agent moves toward the goal state). For example, in Figure 10, term (t1) is the cost of reaching the landmark in row 6, column 6, which is 4. Term (t2) is the cost of getting from row 6, column 6 to the landmark at row 1 column 4 (by going from one landmark to another). In this case, the best landmark-to-landmark path is to go directly from row 6 column 6 to row 1 column 4. Hence, term (t2) is 6. Term (t3) is the cost of getting from row 1 column 4 to the goal, which is 1. The sum of these is $4 + 6 + 1 = 11$. For comparison, the optimal path has length 9.

In Kaelbling's experiments, she employed a variation of Q learning to learn terms (t1) and (t3), and she computed (t2) at regular intervals via the Floyd-Warshall all-sources shortest paths algorithm.

Figure 11 shows a MAXQ approach to solving this problem. The overall task Root, takes one argument g, which specifies the goal cell. There are three subtasks:

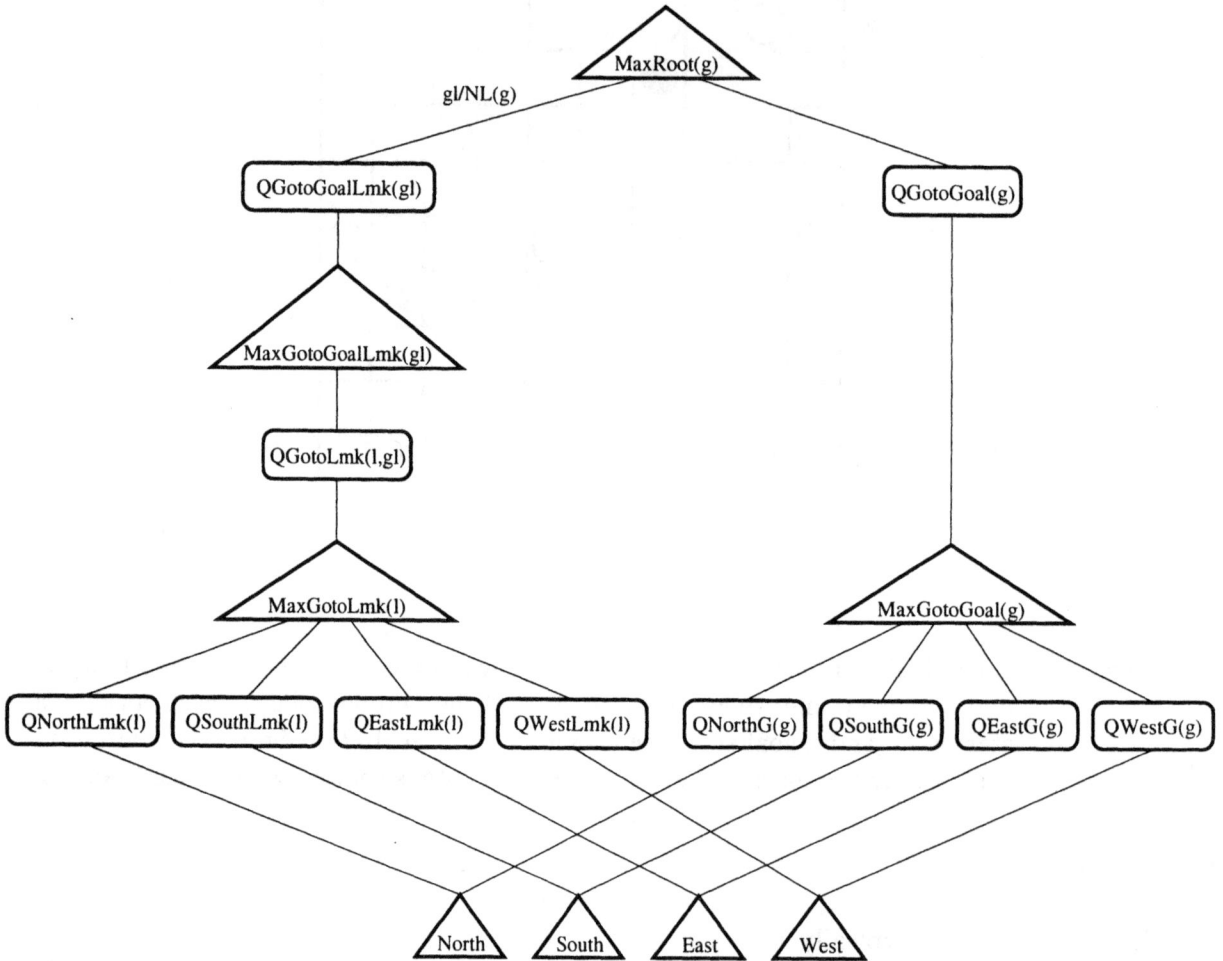

Figure 11: A MAXQ graph for the HDG navigation task.

- GotoGoalLmk, go to the landmark nearest to the goal location. The termination predicate for this subtask is true if the agent reaches the landmark nearest to the goal. The goal predicate is the same as the termination predicate.

- GotoLmk(l), go to landmark l. The termination predicate for this is true if either (a) the agent reaches landmark l or (b) the agent is outside of the region defined by the Voronoi cell for l and the neighboring Voronoi cells, $N(l)$. The goal predicate for this subtask is true only for condition (a).

- GotoGoal(g), go to the goal location g. The termination predicate for this subtask is true if either the agent is in the goal location or the agent is outside of the Voronoi cell $NL(g)$ that contains g. The goal predicate for this subtask is true if the agent is in the goal location.

The MAXQ decomposition is essentially the same as Kaelbling's method, but somewhat redundant. Consider a state where the agent is not inside the same Voronoi cell as the goal g. In such states, HDG decomposes the value function into three terms (t1), (t2), and (t3). Similarly, MAXQ also decomposes it into these same three terms:

- $V(\textsf{GotoLmk}(l), s, a)$ the cost of getting to landmark l. This is represented as the sum of $V(a, s)$ and $C(\textsf{GotoLmk}(l), s, a)$.

- $C(\textsf{GotoGoalLmk}(gl), s, \textsf{MaxGotoLmk}(l))$ the cost of getting from landmark l to the landmark gl nearest the goal.

- $C(\textsf{Root}, s, \textsf{GotoGoalLmk}(gl))$ the cost of getting to the goal location after reaching gl (i.e., the cost of completing the Root task after reaching gl).

When the agent is inside the goal Voronoi cell, then again HDG and MAXQ store essentially the same information. HDG stores $Q(\textsf{GotoGoal}(g), s, a)$, while MAXQ breaks this into two terms: $C(\textsf{GotoGoal}(g), s, a)$ and $V(a, s)$ and then sums these two quantities to compute the Q value.

Note that this MAXQ decomposition stores some information twice—specifically, the cost of getting from the goal landmark gl to the goal is stored both as $C(\textsf{Root}, s, \textsf{GotoGoalLmk}(gl))$ and as $C(\textsf{GotoGoal}(g), s, a) + V(a, s)$.

Let us compare the amount of memory required by flat Q learning, HDG, and MAXQ. There are 100 locations, 4 possible actions, and 100 possible goal states, so flat Q learning must store 40,000 values.

To compute quantity (t1), HDG must store 4 Q values (for the four actions) for each state s with respect to its own landmark and the landmarks in $N(NL(s))$. This gives a total of 2,028 values that must be stored.

To compute quantity (t2), HDG must store, for each landmark, information on the shortest path to every other landmark. There are 12 landmarks. Consider the landmark at row 6, column 1. It has 5 neighboring landmarks which constitute the five macro actions that the agent can perform to move to another landmark. The nearest landmark to the goal cell could be any of the other 11 landmarks, so this gives a total of 55 Q values that must be stored. Similar computations for all 12 landmarks give a total of 506 values that must be stored.

Finally, to compute quantity (t3), HDG must store information, for each square inside each Voronoi cell, about how to get to each of the other squares inside the same Voronoi cell. This requires 3,536 values.

Hence, the grand total for HDG is 6,070, which is a huge savings over flat Q learning. Now let's consider the MAXQ hierarchy with and without state abstractions.

- $V(a, s)$: This is the expected reward of each primitive action in each state. There are 100 states and 4 primitive actions, so this requires 400 values. However, because the reward is constant (-1), we can apply Leaf Irrelevance to store only a single value.

- $C(\textsf{GotoLmk}(l), s, a)$, where a is one of the four primitive actions. This requires the same amount of space as (t1) in Kaelbling's representation—indeed, combined with $V(a, s)$, this represents exactly the same information as (t1). It requires 2,028 values. No state abstractions can be applied.

- $C(\mathsf{GotoGoalLmk}(gl), s, \mathsf{GotoLmk}(l))$: This is the cost of completing the GotoGoalLmk task after going to landmark l. If the primitive actions are deterministic, then GotoLmk(l) will always terminate at location l, and hence, we only need to store this for each pair of l and gl. This is exactly the same as Kaelbling's quantity (t2), which requires 506 values. However, if the primitive actions are stochastic—as they were in Kaelbling's original paper—then we must store this value for each possible terminal state of each GotoLmk action. Each of these actions could terminate at its target landmark l or in one of the states bordering the set of Voronoi cells that are the neighbors of the cell for l. This requires 6,600 values. When Kaelbling stores values only for (t2), she is effectively making the assumption that GotoLmk(l) will never fail to reach landmark l. This is an approximation which we can introduce into the MAXQ representation by our choice of state abstraction at this node.

- $C(\mathsf{GotoGoal}, s, a)$: This is the cost of completing the GotoGoal task after executing one of the primitive actions a. This is the same as quantity (t3) in the HDG representation, and it requires the same amount of space: 3,536 values.

- $C(\mathsf{Root}, s, \mathsf{GotoGoalLmk})$: This is the cost of reaching the goal once we have reached the landmark nearest the goal. MAXQ must represent this for all combinations of goal landmarks and goals. This requires 100 values. Note that these values are the same as the values of $C(\mathsf{GotoGoal}(g), s, a) + V(a, s)$ for each of the primitive actions. This means that the MAXQ representation stores this information twice, whereas the HDG representation only stores it once (as term (t3)).

- $C(\mathsf{Root}, s, \mathsf{GotoGoal})$. This is the cost of completing the Root task after we have executed the GotoGoal task. If the primitive action are deterministic, this is always zero, because GotoGoal will have reached the goal. Hence, we can apply the Termination condition and not store any values at all. However, if the primitive actions are stochastic, then we must store this value for each possible state that borders the Voronoi cell that contains the goal. This requires 96 different values. Again, in Kaelbling's HDG representation of the value function, she is ignoring the probability that GotoGoal will terminate in a non-goal state. Because MAXQ is an exact representation of the value function, it does not ignore this possibility. If we (incorrectly) apply the Termination condition in this case, the MAXQ representation becomes a function approximation.

In the stochastic case, without state abstractions, the MAXQ representation requires 12,760 values. With safe state abstractions, it requires 12,361 values. With the approximations employed by Kaelbling (or equivalently, if the primitive actions are deterministic), the MAXQ representation with state abstractions requires 6,171 values. These numbers are summarized in Table 6. We can see that, with the unsafe state abstractions, the MAXQ representation requires only slightly more space than the HDG representation (because of the redundancy in storing $C(\mathsf{Root}, s, \mathsf{GotoGoalLmk})$.

This example shows that for the HDG task, we can start with the fully-general formulation provided by MAXQ and impose assumptions to obtain a method that is similar to HDG. The MAXQ formulation guarantees that the value function of the hierarchical policy will be represented exactly. The assumptions will introduce approximations into the

Table 6: Comparison of the number of values that must be stored to represent the value function using the HDG and MAXQ methods.

HDG item	MAXQ item	HDG values	MAXQ no abs	MAXQ safe abs	MAXQ unsafe abs
	$V(a, s)$	0	400	1	1
(t1)	$C(\text{GotoLmk}(l), s, a)$	2,028	2,028	2,028	2,028
(t2)	$C(\text{GotoGoalLmk}, s, \text{GotoLmk}(l))$	506	6,600	6,600	506
(t3)	$C(\text{GotoGoal}(g), s, a)$	3,536	3,536	3,536	3,536
	$C(\text{Root}, s, \text{GotoGoalLmk})$	0	100	100	100
	$C(\text{Root}, s, \text{GotoGoal})$	0	96	96	0
Total Number of Values Required		6,070	12,760	12,361	6,171

value function representation. This might be useful as a general design methodology for building application-specific hierarchical representations. Our long-term goal is to develop such methods so that each new application does not require inventing a new set of techniques. Instead, off-the-shelf tools (e.g., based on MAXQ) could be specialized by imposing assumptions and state abstractions to produce more efficient special-purpose systems.

One of the most important contributions of the HDG method was that it introduced a form of non-hierarchical execution. As soon as the agent crosses from one Voronoi cell into another, the current subtask of reaching the landmark in that cell is "interrupted", and the agent recomputes the "current target landmark". The effect of this is that (until it reaches the goal Voronoi cell), the agent is always aiming for a landmark outside of its current Voronoi cell. Hence, although the agent "aims for" a sequence of landmark states, it typically does not visit many of these states on its way to the goal. The states just provide a convenient set of intermediate targets. By taking these "shortcuts", HDG compensates for the fact that, in general, it has overestimated the cost of getting to the goal, because its computed value function is based on a policy where the agent goes from one landmark to another.

The same effect is obtained by hierarchical greedy execution of the MAXQ graph (which was directly inspired by the HDG method). Note that by storing the NL (nearest landmark) function, Kaelbling's HDG method can detect very efficiently when the current subtask should be interrupted. This technique only works for navigation problems in a space with a distance metric. In contrast, EXECUTEHGPOLICY performs a kind of "polling", because it checks after each primitive action whether it should interrupt the current subroutine and invoke a new one. An important goal for future research on MAXQ is to find a general purpose mechanism for avoiding unnecessary "polling"—that is, a mechanism that can discover efficiently-evaluable interrupt conditions.

Figure 12 shows the results of our experiments with HDG using the MAXQ-Q learning algorithm. We employed the following parameters: for Flat Q learning, initial values of 0.123, a learning rate of 1.0, initial temperature of 50, and cooling rate of 0.9074; for MAXQ-Q without state abstractions: initial values of -25.123, learning rate of 1.0, initial

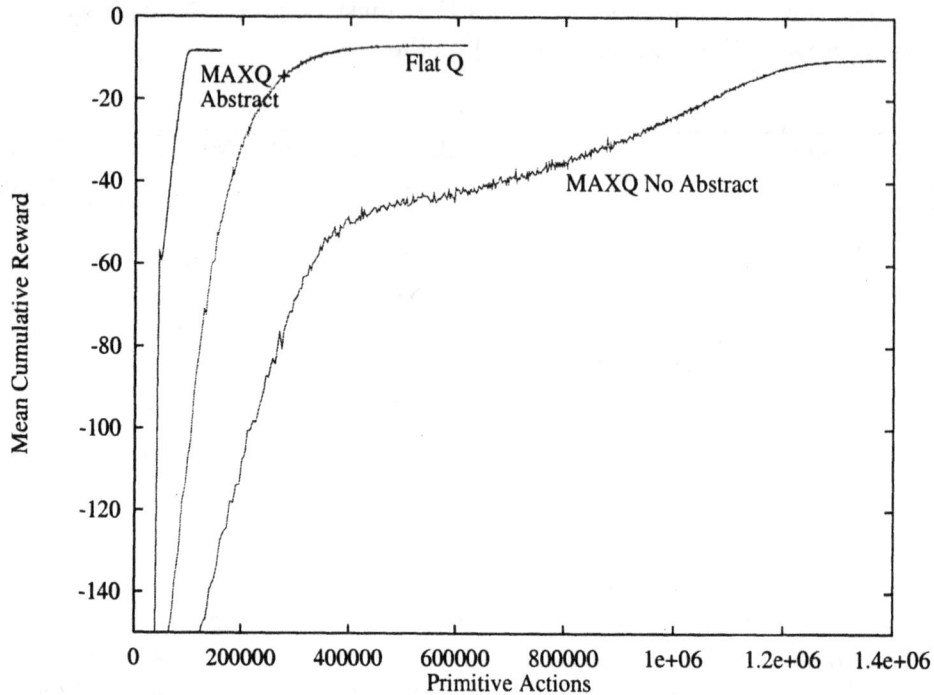

Figure 12: Comparison of Flat Q learning with MAXQ-Q learning with and without state abstraction. (Average of 100 runs.)

temperature of 50, and cooling rates of 0.9074 for MaxRoot, 0.9999 for MaxGotoGoalLmk, 0.9074 for MaxGotoGoal, and 0.9526 for MaxGotoLmk; for MAXQ-Q with state abstractions: initial values of -20.123, learning rate of 1.0, initial temperature of 50, and cooling rates of 0.9760 for MaxRoot, 0.9969 for MaxGotoGoal, 0.9984 for MaxGotoGoalLmk, and 0.9969 for MaxGotoLmk. Hierarchical greedy execution was introduced by starting with 3000 primitive actions per trial, and reducing this every trial by 2 actions, so that after 1500 trials, execution is completely greedy.

The figure confirms the observations made in our experiments with the Fickle Taxi task. Without state abstractions, MAXQ-Q converges much more slowly than flat Q learning. With state abstractions, it converges roughly three times as fast. Figure 13 shows a close-up view of Figure 12 that allows us to compare the differences in the final levels of performance of the methods. Here, we can see that MAXQ-Q with no state abstractions was not able to reach the quality of our hand-coded hierarchical policy—presumably even more exploration would be required to achieve this, whereas with state abstractions, MAXQ-Q is able to do slightly better than our hand-coded policy. With hierarchical greedy execution, MAXQ-Q is able to reach the goal using one fewer action, on the average—so that it approaches the performance of the best hierarchical greedy policy (as computed by value iteration). Notice however, that the best performance that can be obtained by hierarchical greedy execution of the best recursively-optimal policy cannot match optimal performance. Hence, Flat Q

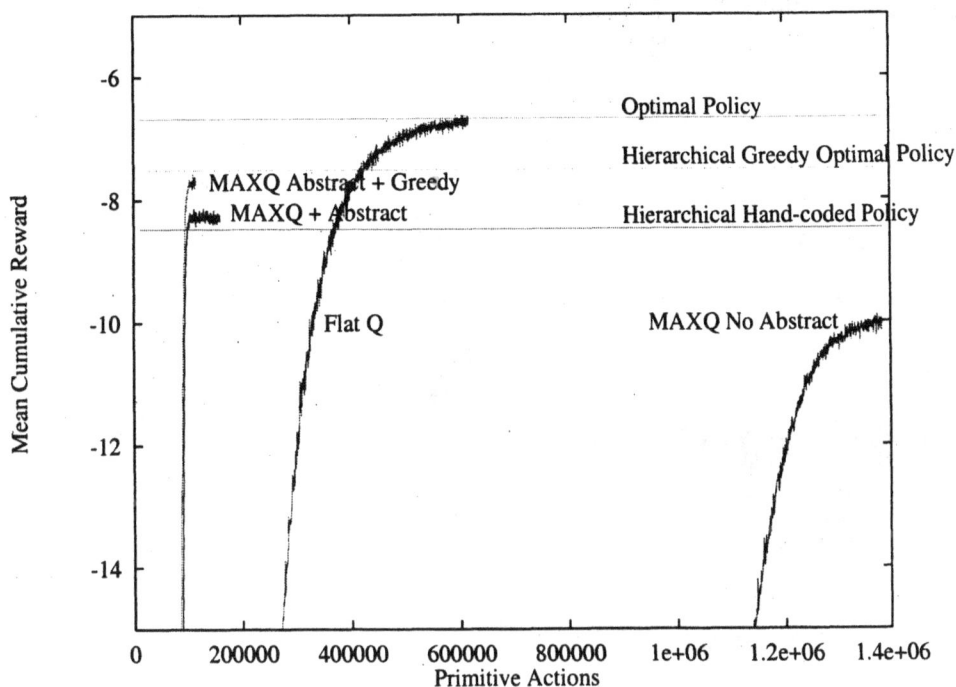

Figure 13: Expanded view comparing Flat Q learning with MAXQ-Q learning with and without state abstraction and with and without hierarchical greedy execution. (Average of 100 runs.)

learning achieves a policy that reaches the goal state, on the average, with about one fewer primitive action. Finally notice that as in the taxi domain, there was no added exploration cost for shifting to greedy execution.

Kaelbling's HDG work has recently been extended and generalized by Moore, Baird and Kaelbling (1999) to any sparse MDP where the overall task is to get from any given start state to any desired goal state. The key to the success of their approach is that each landmark subtask is guaranteed to terminate in a single resulting state. This makes it possible to identify a *sequence* of good intermediate landmark states and then assemble a policy that visits them in sequence. Moore, Baird and Kaelbling show how to construct a hierarchy of landmarks (the "airport" hierarchy) that makes this planning process efficient. Note that if each subtask did not terminate in a single state (as in general MDPs), then the airport method would not work, because there would be a combinatorial explosion of potential intermediate states that would need to be considered.

7.3 Parr and Russell: Hierarchies of Abstract Machines

In his (1998b) dissertation work, Ron Parr considered an approach to hierarchical reinforcement learning in which the programmer encodes prior knowledge in the form of a hierarchy of finite-state controllers called a HAM (Hierarchy of Abstract Machines). The hierarchy

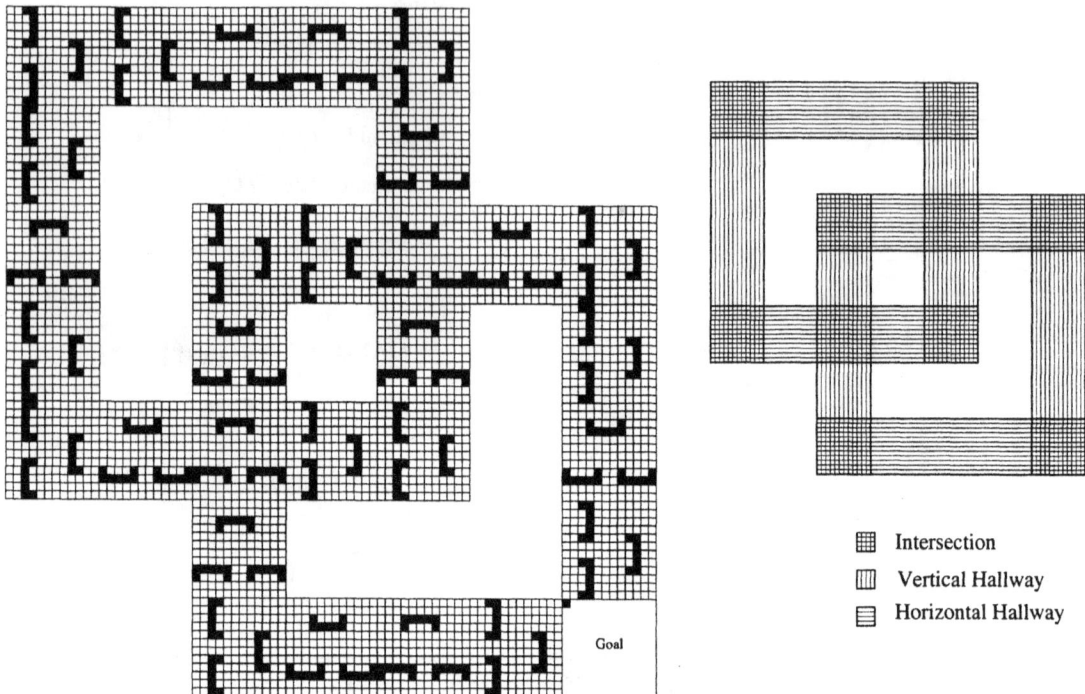

Figure 14: Parr's maze problem (on left). The start state is in the upper left corner, and all states in the lower right-hand room are terminal states. The smaller diagram on the right shows the hallway and intersection structure of the maze.

is executed using a procedure-call-and-return discipline, and it provides a *partial policy* for the task. The policy is partial because each machine can include non-deterministic "choice" machine states, in which the machine lists several options for action but does not specify which one should be chosen. The programmer puts "choice" states at any point where he/she does not know what action should be performed. Given this partial policy, Parr's goal is to find the best policy for making choices in the choice states. In other words, his goal is to learn a hierarchical value function $V(\langle s, m \rangle)$, where s is a state (of the external environment) and m contains all of the internal state of the hierarchy (i.e., the contents of the procedure call stack and the values of the current machine states for all machines appearing in the stack). A key observation is that it is only necessary to learn this value function at choice states $\langle s, m \rangle$. Parr's algorithm does not learn a decomposition of the value function. Instead, it "flattens" the hierarchy to create a new Markov decision problem over the choice states $\langle s, m \rangle$. Hence, it is hierarchical primarily in the sense that the programmer structures the prior knowledge hierarchically. An advantage of this is that Parr's method can find the optimal hierarchical policy subject to constraints provided by the programmer. A disadvantage is that the method cannot be executed "non-hierarchically" to produce a better policy.

Parr illustrated his work using the maze shown in Figure 14. This maze has a large-scale structure (as a series of hallways and intersections), and a small-scale structure (a series of obstacles that must be avoided in order to move through the hallways and intersections).

In each trial, the agent starts in the top left corner, and it must move to any state in the bottom right corner room. The agent has the usual four primitive actions, North, South, East, and West. The actions are stochastic: with probability 0.8, they succeed, but with probability 0.1 the action will move to the "left" and with probability 0.1 the action will move to the "right" instead (e.g., a North action will move east with probability 0.1 and west with probability 0.1). If an action would collide with a wall or an obstacle, it has no effect.

The maze is structured as a series of "rooms", each containing a 12-by-12 block of states (and various obstacles). Some rooms are parts of "hallways", because they are connected to two other rooms on opposite sides. Other rooms are "intersections", where two or more hallways meet.

To test the representational power of the MAXQ hierarchy, we want to see how well it can represent the prior knowledge that Parr is able to represent using the HAM. We begin by describing Parr's HAM for his maze task, and then we will present a MAXQ hierarchy that captures much of the same prior knowledge.[3]

Parr's top level machine, MRoot, consists of a loop with a single choice state that chooses among four possible child machines: MGo(*East*), MGo(*South*), MGo(*West*), and MGo(*North*). The loop terminates when the agent reaches a goal state. MRoot will only invoke a particular machine if there is a hallway in the specified direction. Hence, in the start state, it will only consider MGo(*South*) and MGo(*East*).

The MGo(*d*) machine begins executing when the agent is in an intersection. So the first thing it tries to do is to exit the intersection into a hallway in the specified direction *d*. Then it attempts to traverse the hallway until it reaches another intersection. It does this by first invoking an MExitIntersection(*d*) machine. When that machine returns, it then invokes an MExitHallway(*d*) machine. When that machine returns, MGo also returns.

The MExitIntersection and MExitHallway machines are identical except for their termination conditions. Both machines consist of a loop with one choice state that chooses among four possible subroutines. To simplify their description, suppose that MGo(*East*) has chosen MExitIntersection(*East*). Then the four possible subroutines are MSniff(*East, North*), MSniff(*East, South*), MBack(*East, North*), and MBack(*East, South*).

The MSniff(*d, p*) machine always moves in direction *d* until it encounters a wall (either part of an obstacle or part of the walls of the maze). Then it moves in perpendicular direction *p* until it reaches the end of the wall. A wall can "end" in two ways: either the agent is now trapped in a corner with walls in both directions *d* and *p* or else there is no longer a wall in direction *d*. In the first case, the MSniff machine terminates; in the second case, it resumes moving in direction *d*.

The MBack(*d, p*) machine moves one step backwards (in the direction opposite from *d*) and then moves five steps in direction *p*. These moves may or may not succeed, because the actions are stochastic and there may be walls blocking the way. But the actions are carried out in any case, and then the MBack machine returns.

The MSniff and MBack machines also terminate if they reach the end of a hall or the end of an intersection.

---

3. The author thanks Ron Parr for providing the details of the HAM for this task.

These finite-state controllers define a highly constrained partial policy. The MBack, MSniff, and MGo machines contain no choice states at all. The only choice points are in MRoot, which must choose the direction in which to move, and in MExitIntersection and MExitHall, which must decide when to call MSniff, when to call MBack, and which "perpendicular" direction to tell these machines to try when they cannot move forward.

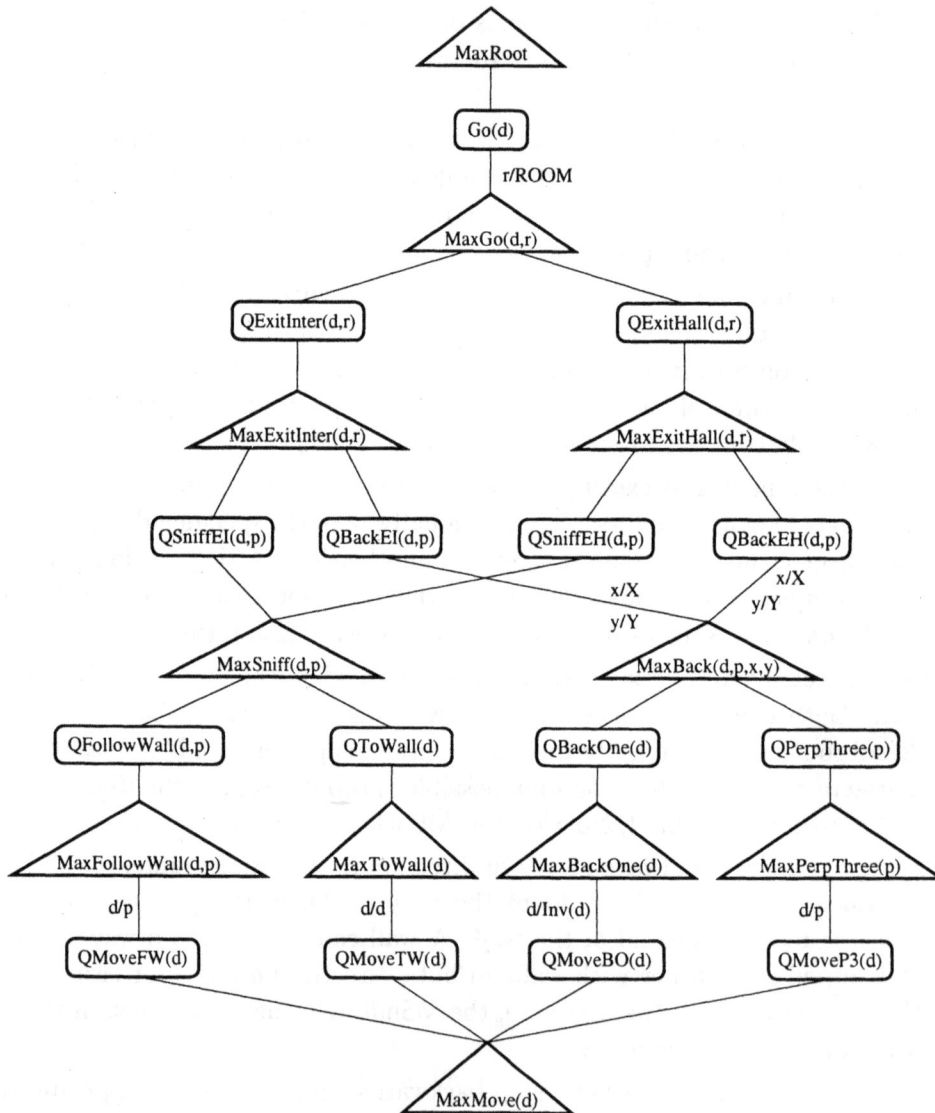

Figure 15: MAXQ graph for Parr's maze task.

Figure 15 shows a MAXQ graph that encodes a similar set of constraints on the policy. The subtasks are defined as follows:

- **Root.** This is exactly the same as the MRoot machine. It must choose a direction d and invoke Go. It terminates when the agent enters a terminal state. This is also its goal condition (of course).

- **Go**(d, r). (Go in direction d leaving room r.) The parameter r is bound to an identification number corresponding to the current 12-by-12 "room" in which the agent is located. Go terminates when the agent enters the room at the end of the hallway in direction d or when it leaves the desired hallway (e.g., in the wrong direction). The goal condition for Go is satisfied only if the agent reaches the desired intersection.

- **ExitInter**(d, r). This terminates when the agent has exited room r. The goal condition is that the agent exit room r in direction d.

- **ExitHall**(d, r). This terminates when the agent has exited the current hall (into some intersection). The goal condition is that the agent has entered the desired intersection in direction d.

- **Sniff**(d, r). This encodes a subtask that is equivalent to the MSniff machine. However, Sniff must have two child subtasks, ToWall and FollowWall, that were simply internal states of MSniff. This is necessary, because a subtask in the MAXQ framework cannot contain any internal state, whereas a finite-state controller in the HAM representation can contain as many internal states as necessary. In particular, it can have one state for when it is moving forward and another state for when it is following a wall sideways.

- **ToWall**(d). This is equivalent to one part of MSniff. It terminates when there is a wall in "front" of the agent in direction d. The goal condition is the same as the termination condition.

- **FollowWall**(d, p). This is equivalent to the other part of MSniff. It moves in direction p until the wall in direction d ends (or until it is stuck in a corner with walls in both directions d and p). The goal condition is the same as the termination condition.

- **Back**(d, p, x, y). This attempts to encode the same information as the MBack machine, but this is a case where the MAXQ hierarchy cannot capture the same information. MBack simply executes a sequence of 6 primitive actions (one step back, five steps in direction p). But to do this, MBack must have 6 internal states, which MAXQ does not allow. Instead, the Back subtask has the subgoal of moving the agent at least one square backwards and at least 3 squares in the direction p. In order to determine whether it has achieved this subgoal, it must remember the x and y position where it started to execute, so these are bound as parameters to Back. Back terminates if it achieves the desired change in position or if it runs into walls that prevent it from achieving the subgoal. The goal condition is the same as the termination condition.

- **BackOne**(d, x, y). This moves the agent one step backwards (in the direction opposite to d. It needs the starting x and y position in order to tell when it has succeeded. It terminates if it has moved at least one unit in direction d or if there is a wall in this direction. Its goal condition is the same as its termination condition.

- PerpThree(p, x, y). This moves the agent three steps in the direction p. It needs the starting x and y positions in order to tell when it has succeeded. It terminates when it has moved at least three units in the direction p or if there is a wall in that direction. The goal condition is the same as the termination condition.

- Move(d). This is a "parameterized primitive" action. It executes one primitive move in direction d and terminates immediately.

From this, we can see that there are three major differences between the MAXQ representation and the HAM representation. First, a HAM finite-state controller can contain internal states. To convert them into a MAXQ subtask graph, we must make a separate subtask for each internal state in the HAM. Second, a HAM can terminate based on an "amount of effort" (e.g., performing 5 actions), whereas a MAXQ subtask must terminate based on some change in the state of the world. It is impossible to define a MAXQ subtask that performs k steps and then terminate regardless of the effects of those steps (i.e., without adding some kind of "counter" to the state of the MDP). Third, it is more difficult to formulate the termination conditions for MAXQ subtasks than for HAM machines. For example, in the HAM, it was not necessary to specify that the MExitHallway machine terminates when it has entered a *different* intersection than the one where the MGo was executed. However, this is important for the MAXQ method, because in MAXQ, each subtask learns its own value function and policy—independent of its parent tasks. For example, without the requirement to enter a *different* intersection, the learning algorithms for MAXQ will always prefer to have MaxExitHall take one step backward and return to the room in which the Go action was started (because that is a much easier terminal state to reach). This problem does not arise in the HAM approach, because the policy learned for a subtask depends on the whole "flattened" hierarchy of machines, and returning to the state where the Go action was started does not help solve the overall problem of reaching the goal state in the lower right corner.

To construct the MAXQ graph for this problem, we have introduced three programming tricks: (a) binding parameters to aspects of the current state (in order to serve as a kind of "local memory" for where the subtask began executing), (b) having a parameterized primitive action (in order to be able to pass a parameter value that specifies which primitive action to perform), and (c) employing "inheritance of termination conditions"—that is, each subtask in this MAXQ graph (but not the others in this paper) inherits the termination conditions of all its ancestor tasks. Hence, if the agent is in the middle of executing a ToWall action when it leaves an intersection, the ToWall subroutine terminates because the ExitInter termination condition is satisfied. This behavior is very similar to the standard behavior of MAXQ. Ordinarily, when an ancestor task terminates, all of its descendent tasks are forced to return *without updating their C values.* With inheritance of termination conditions, on the other hand, the descendent tasks are forced to terminate, but *after updating their C values.* In other words, the termination condition of each child task is the logical disjuntion of all of the termination conditions of its ancestors (plus its own termination condition). This inheritance made it easier to write the MAXQ graph, because the parents did not need to pass down to their children all of the information necessary for the children to define the complete termination and goal predicates.

There are essentially no opportunities for state abstraction in this task, because there are no irrelevant features of the state. There are some opportunities to apply the Shielding and Termination properties, however. In particular, ExitHall(d) is guaranteed to cause its parent task, MaxGo(d), to terminate, so it does not require any stored C values. There are many states where some subtasks are terminated (e.g., Go($East$) in any state where there is a wall on the east side of the room), and so no C values need to be stored.

Nonetheless, even after applying the state elimination conditions, the MAXQ representation for this task requires much more space than a flat representation. An exact computation is difficult, but after applying MAXQ-Q learning, the MAXQ representation required 52,043 values, whereas flat Q learning requires fewer than 16,704 values. Parr states that his method requires only 4,300 values.

To test the relative effectiveness of the MAXQ representation, we compare MAXQ-Q learning with flat Q learning. Because of the very large negative values that some states acquire (particularly during the early phases of learning), we were unable to get Boltzmann exploration to work well—one very bad experience would cause an action to receive such a low Q value, that it would never be tried again. Hence, we experimented with both ϵ-greedy exploration and counter-based exploration. The ϵ-greedy exploration policy is an ordered, abstract GLIE policy in which a random action is chosen with probability ϵ, and ϵ is gradually decreased over time. The counter-based exploration policy keeps track of how many times each action a has been executed in each state s. To choose an action in state s, it selects the action that has been executed the fewest times until all actions have been executed T times. Then it switches to greedy execution. Hence, it is not a genuine GLIE policy. Parr employed counter-based exploration policies in his experiments with this task.

As in the other domains, we conducted several experimental runs (e.g., testing Boltzmann, ϵ-greedy, and counter-based exploration) to determine the best parameters for each algorithm. For Flat Q learning, we chose the following parameters: learning rate 0.50, ϵ-greedy exploration with initial value for ϵ of 1.0, ϵ decreased by 0.001 after each successful execution of a Max node, and initial Q values of -200.123. For MAXQ-Q learning, we chose the following parameters: counter-based exploration with $T = 10$, learning rate equal to the reciprocal of the number of times an action had been performed, and initial values for the C values selected carefully to provide underestimates of the true C values. For example, the initial values for QExitInter were -40.123, because in the worst case, after completing an ExitInter task, it takes about 40 steps to complete the subsequent ExitHall task and hence, complete the Go parent task. Performance was quite sensitive to these initial C values, which is a potential drawback of the MAXQ approach.

Figure 16 plots the results. We can see that MAXQ-Q learning converges about 10 times faster than Flat Q learning. We do not know whether MAXQ-Q has converged to a recursively optimal policy. For comparison, we also show the performance of a hierarchical policy that we coded by hand, but in our hand-coded policy, we used knowledge of contextual information to choose operators, so this policy is surely better than the best recursively optimal policy. HAMQ learning should converge to a policy equal to or slightly better than our hand-coded policy.

This experiment demonstrates that the MAXQ representation can capture most—but not all—of the prior knowledge that can be represented by the HAMQ hierarchy. It also

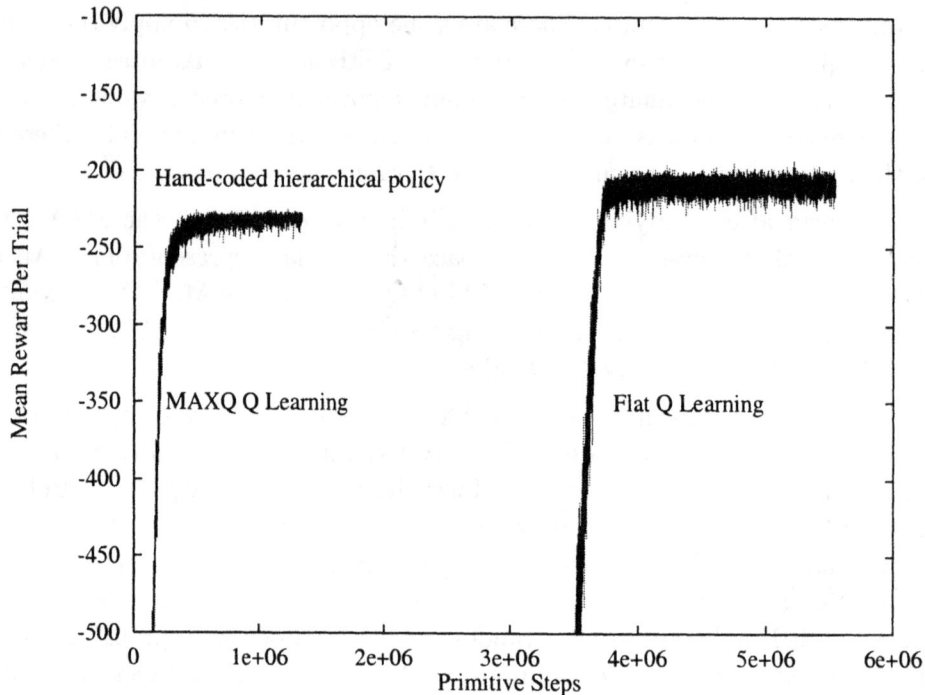

Figure 16: Comparison of Flat Q learning and MAXQ-Q learning in the Parr maze task.

shows that the MAXQ representation requires much more care in the design of the goal conditions for the subtasks.

7.4 Other Domains

In addition to the three domains discussed above, we have developed MAXQ graphs for Singh's (1992) "flag task", the treasure hunter task described by Tadepalli and Dietterich (1997), and Dayan and Hinton's (1993) Feudal-Q learning task. All of these tasks can be easily and naturally placed into the MAXQ framework—indeed, all of them fit more easily than the Parr and Russell maze task.

MAXQ is able to exactly duplicate Singh's work and his decomposition of the value function—while using exactly the same amount of space to represent the value function. MAXQ can also duplicate the results from Tadepalli and Dietterich—however, because MAXQ is not an explanation-based method, it is considerably slower and requires substantially more space to represent the value function.

In the Feudal-Q task, MAXQ is able to give better performance than Feudal-Q learning. The reason is that in Feudal-Q learning, each subroutine makes decisions using only a Q function learned at its own level of the hierarchy—that is, without information about the estimated costs of the actions of its descendents. In contrast, the MAXQ value function decomposition permits each Max node to make decisions based on the sum of its completion function, $C(i, s, j)$, and the costs estimated by its descendents, $V(j, s)$. Of course, MAXQ also supports non-hierarchical execution, which is not possible for Feudal-Q, because it does not learn a value function decomposition.

8. Discussion

Before concluding this paper, we wish to discuss two issues: (a) design tradeoffs in hierarchical reinforcement learning and (b) methods for automatically learning (or at least improving) MAXQ hierarchies.

8.1 Design Tradeoffs in Hierarchical Reinforcement Learning

In the introduction to this paper, we discussed four issues concerning the design of hierarchical reinforcement learning architectures: (a) the method for defining subtasks, (b) the use of state abstraction, (c) non-hierarchical execution, and (d) the design of learning algorithms. In this subsection, we want to highlight a tradeoff between the first two of these issues.

MAXQ defines subtasks using a termination predicate T_i and a pseudo-reward function $\tilde{R}$. There are at least two drawbacks of this method. First, it can be hard for the programmer to define T_i and $\tilde{R}$ correctly, since this essentially requires guessing the value function of the optimal policy for the MDP at all states where the subtask terminates. Second, it leads us to seek a recursively optimal policy rather than a hierarchically optimal policy. Recursively optimal policies may be much worse than hierarchically optimal ones, so we may be giving up substantial performance.

However, in return for these two drawbacks, MAXQ obtains a very important benefit: the policies and value functions for subtasks become *context-free*. In other words, they do not depend on their parent tasks or the larger context in which they are invoked. To understand this point, consider again the MDP shown in Figure 6. It is clear that the *optimal* policy for exiting the left-hand room (the Exit subtask) depends on the location of the goal. If it is at the top of the right-hand room, then the agent should prefer to exit via the upper door, whereas if it is at the bottom of the right-hand room, the agent should prefer to exit by the lower door. However, if we define the subtask of exiting the left-hand room using a pseudo-reward of zero for both doors, then we obtain a policy that is not optimal in either case, but a policy that we can re-use in both cases. Furthermore, this policy *does not depend on the location of the goal*. Hence, we can apply Max node irrelevance to solve the Exit subtask using only the location of the robot and ignore the location of the goal.

This example shows that we obtain the benefits of subtask reuse and state abstraction because we define the subtask using a termination predicate and a pseudo-reward function. The termination predicate and pseudo-reward function provide a barrier that prevents "communication" of value information between the Exit subtask and its context.

Compare this to Parr's HAM method. The HAMQ algorithm finds the best policy consistent with the hierarchy. To achieve this, it must permit information to propagate "into" the Exit subtask (i.e., the Exit finite-state controller) from its environment. But this means that if any state that is reached after leaving the Exit subtask has different values depending on the location of the goal, then these different values will propagate back into the Exit subtask. To represent these different values, the Exit subtask must know the location of the goal. In short, to achieve a hierarchically optimal policy within the Exit subtask, we must (in general) represent its value function using the *entire* state space. State abstractions cannot be employed without losing hierarchical optimality.

We can see, therefore, that there is a direct tradeoff between achieving hierarchical optimality and employing state abstractions. Methods for hierarchical optimality have more freedom in defining subtasks (e.g., using partial policies, as in the HAM approach). But they cannot (safely) employ state abstractions within subtasks, and in general, they cannot reuse the solution of one subtask in multiple contexts. Methods for recursive optimality, on the other hand, must define subtasks using some method (such as pseudo-reward functions for MAXQ or fixed policies for the options framework) that isolates the subtask from its context. But in return, they can apply state abstraction and the learned policy can be reused in many contexts (where it will be more or less optimal).

It is interesting that the iterative method described by Dean and Lin (1995) can be viewed as a method for moving along this tradeoff. In the Dean and Lin method, the programmer makes an initial guess for the values of the terminal states of each subtask (i.e., the doorways in Figure 6). Based on this initial guess, the locally optimal policies for the subtasks are computed. Then the locally optimal policy for the parent task is computed—while holding the subtask policies fixed (i.e., treating them as options). At this point, their algorithm has computed the recursively optimal solution to the original problem, given the initial guesses. Instead of solving the various subproblems sequentially via an offline algorithm as Dean and Lin suggested, we could use the MAXQ-Q learning algorithm.

But the method of Dean and Lin does not stop here. Instead, it computes new values of the terminal states of each subtask based on the learned value function for the entire problem. This allows it to update its "guesses" for the values of the terminal states. The entire solution process can now be repeated to obtain a new recursively optimal solution, based on the new guesses. They prove that if this process is iterated indefinitely, it will converge to the hierarchically optimal policy (provided, of course, that no state abstractions are used within the subtasks).

This suggests an extension to MAXQ-Q learning that adapts the $\tilde{R}$ values online. Each time a subtask terminates, we could update the $\tilde{R}$ function based on the computed value of the terminated state. To be precise, if j is a subtask of i, then when j terminates in state s', we should update $\tilde{R}_j(s')$ to be equal to $\tilde{V}(i, s') = \max_{a'} \tilde{Q}(i, s', a')$. However, this will only work if $\tilde{R}_j(s')$ is represented using the full state s'. If subtask j is employing state abstractions, $x = \chi(s)$, then $\tilde{R}_j(x')$ will need to be the average value of $\tilde{V}(i, s')$, where the average is taken over all states s' such that $x' = \chi(s')$ (weighted by the probability of visiting those states). This is easily accomplished by performing a stochastic approximation update of the form

$$\tilde{R}_j(x') = (1 - \alpha_t)\tilde{R}_j(x') + \alpha_t \tilde{V}(i, s')$$

each time subtask j terminates. Such an algorithm could be expected to converge to the best hierarchical policy consistent with the given state abstractions.

This also suggests that in some problems, it may be worthwhile to first learn a recursively optimal policy using very aggressive state abstractions and then use the learned value function to initialize a MAXQ representation with a more detailed representation of the states. These progressive refinements of the state space could be guided by monitoring the degree to which the values of $\tilde{V}(i, x')$ vary for each abstract state x'. If they have a large variance, this means that the state abstractions are failing to make important distinctions in the values of the states, and they should be refined.

Both of these kinds of adaptive algorithms will take longer to converge than the basic MAXQ method described in this paper. But for tasks that an agent must solve many times in its lifetime, it is worthwhile to have learning algorithms that provide an initial useful solution but then gradually improve that solution until it is optimal. An important goal for future research is to find methods for diagnosing and repairing errors (or sub-optimalities) in the initial hierarchy so that ultimately the optimal policy will be discovered.

8.2 Automated Discovery of Abstractions

The approach taken in this paper has been to rely upon the programmer to design the MAXQ hierarchy including the termination conditions, pseudo-reward functions, and state abstractions. But the results of this paper, particularly concerning state abstraction, suggest ways in which we might be able to automate the construction of the hierarchy.

The main purpose of the hierarchy is to create opportunities for subtask sharing and state abstraction. These are actually very closely related. In order for a subtask to be shared in two different regions of the state space, it must be the case that the value function in those two different regions is identical except for an additive offset. In the MAXQ framework, that additive offset would be the difference in the C values of the parent task. So one way to find reusable subtasks would be to look for regions of state space where the value function exhibits these additive offsets.

A second way would be to search for structure in the one-step probability transition function $P(s'|s, a)$. A subtask will be useful if it enables state abstractions such as Max Node Irrelevance. We can formulate this as the problem of identifying some region of state space such that, conditioned on being in that region, $P(s'|s, a)$ factors according to Equation 17. A top-down divide-and-conquer algorithm similar to decision-tree algorithms might be able to do this.

A third way would be to search for funnel actions by looking for bottlenecks in the state space through which all policies must travel. This would be useful for discovering cases of Result Distribution Irrelevance.

In some ways, the most difficult kinds of state abstractions to discover are those in which arbitrary subgoals are introduced to constrain the policy (and sacrifice optimality). For example, how could an algorithm automatically decide to impose landmarks onto the HDG task? Perhaps by detecting a large region of state space without bottlenecks or variations in the reward function?

The problem of discovering hierarchies is an important challenge for the future, but at least this paper has provided some guidelines for what constitute good state abstractions, and these can serve as objective functions for guiding the automated search for abstractions.

9. Concluding Remarks

This paper has introduced a new representation for the value function in hierarchical reinforcement learning—the MAXQ value function decomposition. We have proved that the MAXQ decomposition can represent the value function of any hierarchical policy under both the finite-horizon undiscounted, cumulative reward criterion and the infinite-horizon discounted reward criterion. This representation supports subtask sharing and re-use, because the overall value function is decomposed into value functions for individual subtasks.

The paper introduced a learning algorithm, MAXQ-Q learning, and proved that it converges with probability 1 to a recursively optimal policy. The paper argued that although recursive optimality is weaker than either hierarchical optimality or global optimality, it is an important form of optimality because it permits each subtask to learn a locally optimal policy while ignoring the behavior of its ancestors in the MAXQ graph. This increases the opportunities for subtask sharing and state abstraction.

We have shown that the MAXQ decomposition creates opportunities for state abstraction, and we identified a set of five properties (Max Node Irrelevance, Leaf Irrelevance, Result Distribution Irrelevance, Shielding, and Termination) that allow us to ignore large parts of the state space within subtasks. We proved that MAXQ-Q still converges in the presence of these forms of state abstraction, and we showed experimentally that state abstraction is important in practice for the successful application of MAXQ-Q learning—at least in the Taxi and HDG tasks.

The paper presented two different methods for deriving improved non-hierarchical policies from the MAXQ value function representation, and it has formalized the conditions under which these methods can improve over the hierarchical policy. The paper verified experimentally that non-hierarchical execution gives improved performance in the Fickle Taxi Task (where it achieves optimal performance) and in the HDG task (where it gives a substantial improvement).

Finally, the paper has argued that there is a tradeoff governing the design of hierarchical reinforcement learning methods. At one end of the design spectrum are "context free" methods such as MAXQ-Q learning. They provide good support for state abstraction and subtask sharing but they can only learn recursively optimal policies. At the other end of the spectrum are "context-sensitive" methods such as HAMQ, the options framework, and the early work of Dean and Lin. These methods can discover hierarchically optimal policies (or, in some cases, globally optimal policies), but their drawback is that they cannot easily exploit state abstractions or share subtasks. Because of the great speedups that are enabled by state abstraction, this paper has argued that the context-free approach is to be preferred—and that it can be relaxed as needed to obtain improved policies.

Acknowledgements

The author gratefully acknowledges the support of the National Science Foundation under grant number IRI-9626584, the Office of Naval Research under grant number N00014-95-1-0557, the Air Force Office of Scientific Research under grant number F49620-98-1-0375, and the Spanish government under their program of Estancias de Investigadores Extranjeros en Regimen de Año Sabatico en España. In addition, the author is indebted to many colleagues for helping develop and clarify the ideas in this paper including Valentina Zubek, Leslie Kaelbling, Bill Langford, Wes Pinchot, Rich Sutton, Prasad Tadepalli, and Sebastian Thrun. I particularly want to thank Eric Chown for encouraging me to study Feudal reinforcement learning, Ron Parr for providing the details of his HAM machines, and Sebastian Thrun for encouraging me to write a single comprehensive paper. I also thank Andrew Moore (the action editor), Valentina Zubek, and the two sets of anonymous reviewers of previous drafts of this paper for their suggestions and careful reading, which have improved the paper immeasurably.

References

Bellman, R. E. (1957). *Dynamic Programming*. Princeton University Press.

Bertsekas, D. P., & Tsitsiklis, J. N. (1996). *Neuro-Dynamic Programming*. Athena Scientific, Belmont, MA.

Boutilier, C., Dearden, R., & Goldszmidt, M. (1995). Exploiting structure in policy construction. In *Proceedings of the Fourteenth International Joint Conference on Artificial Intelligence*, pp. 1104–1111.

Currie, K., & Tate, A. (1991). O-plan: The open planning architecture. *Artificial Intelligence*, *52*(1), 49–86.

Dayan, P., & Hinton, G. (1993). Feudal reinforcement learning. In *Advances in Neural Information Processing Systems, 5*, pp. 271–278. Morgan Kaufmann, San Francisco, CA.

Dean, T., & Lin, S.-H. (1995). Decomposition techniques for planning in stochastic domains. Tech. rep. CS-95-10, Department of Computer Science, Brown University, Providence, Rhode Island.

Dieterich, T. G. (1998). The MAXQ method for hierarchical reinforcement learning. In *Fifteenth International Conference on Machine Learning*, pp. 118–126. Morgan Kaufmann.

Fikes, R. E., Hart, P. E., & Nilsson, N. J. (1972). Learning and executing generalized robot plans. *Artificial Intelligence*, *3*, 251–288.

Forgy, C. L. (1982). Rete: A fast algorithm for the many pattern/many object pattern match problem. *Artificial Intelligence*, *19*(1), 17–37.

Hauskrecht, M., Meuleau, N., Kaelbling, L. P., Dean, T., & Boutilier, C. (1998). Hierarchical solution of Markov decision processes using macro-actions. In *Proceedings of the Fourteenth Annual Conference on Uncertainty in Artificial Intelligence (UAI-98)*, pp. 220–229 San Francisco, CA. Morgan Kaufmann Publishers.

Howard, R. A. (1960). *Dynamic Programming and Markov Processes*. MIT Press, Cambridge, MA.

Jaakkola, T., Jordan, M. I., & Singh, S. P. (1994). On the convergence of stochastic iterative dynamic programming algorithms. *Neural Computation*, *6*(6), 1185–1201.

Kaelbling, L. P. (1993). Hierarchical reinforcement learning: Preliminary results. In *Proceedings of the Tenth International Conference on Machine Learning*, pp. 167–173 San Francisco, CA. Morgan Kaufmann.

Kalmár, Z., Szepesvári, C., & Lörincz, A. (1998). Module based reinforcement learning for a real robot. *Machine Learning, 31*, 55–85.

Knoblock, C. A. (1990). Learning abstraction hierarchies for problem solving. In *Proceedings of the Eighth National Conference on Artificial Intelligence*, pp. 923–928 Boston, MA. AAAI Press.

Korf, R. E. (1985). Macro-operators: A weak method for learning. *Artificial Intelligence, 26*(1), 35–77.

Lin, L.-J. (1993). *Reinforcement learning for robots using neural networks*. Ph.D. thesis, Carnegie Mellon University, Department of Computer Science, Pittsburgh, PA.

Moore, A. W., Baird, L., & Kaelbling, L. P. (1999). Multi-value-functions: Efficient automatic action hierarchies for multiple goal MDPs. In *Proceedings of the International Joint Conference on Artificial Intelligence*, pp. 1316–1323 San Francisco. Morgan Kaufmann.

Parr, R. (1998a). Flexible decomposition algorithms for weakly coupled Markov decision problems. In *Proceedings of the Fourteenth Annual Conference on Uncertainty in Artificial Intelligence (UAI-98)*, pp. 422–430 San Francisco, CA. Morgan Kaufmann Publishers.

Parr, R. (1998b). *Hierarchical control and learning for Markov decision processes*. Ph.D. thesis, University of California, Berkeley, California.

Parr, R., & Russell, S. (1998). Reinforcement learning with hierarchies of machines. In *Advances in Neural Information Processing Systems*, Vol. 10, pp. 1043–1049 Cambridge, MA. MIT Press.

Pearl, J. (1988). *Probabilistic Inference in Intelligent Systems. Networks of Plausible Inference*. Morgan Kaufmann, San Mateo, CA.

Rummery, G. A., & Niranjan, M. (1994). Online Q-learning using connectionist systems. Tech. rep. CUED/FINFENG/TR 166, Cambridge University Engineering Department, Cambridge, England.

Sacerdoti, E. D. (1974). Planning in a hierarchy of abstraction spaces. *Artificial Intelligence, 5*(2), 115–135.

Singh, S., Jaakkola, T., Littman, M. L., & Szepesvári, C. (1998). Convergence results for single-step on-policy reinforcement-learning algorithms. Tech. rep., University of Colorado, Department of Computer Science, Boulder, CO. To appear in *Machine Learning*.

Singh, S. P. (1992). Transfer of learning by composing solutions of elemental sequential tasks. *Machine Learning, 8*, 323–339.

Sutton, R. S., Singh, S., Precup, D., & Ravindran, B. (1999). Improved switching among temporally abstract actions. In *Advances in Neural Information Processing Systems*, Vol. 11, pp. 1066–1072. MIT Press.

Sutton, R., & Barto, A. G. (1998). *Introduction to Reinforcement Learning*. MIT Press, Cambridge, MA.

Sutton, R. S., Precup, D., & Singh, S. (1998). Between MDPs and Semi-MDPs: Learning, planning, and representing knowledge at multiple temporal scales. Tech. rep., University of Massachusetts, Department of Computer and Information Sciences, Amherst, MA. To appear in *Artificial Intelligence*.

Tadepalli, P., & Dietterich, T. G. (1997). Hierarchical explanation-based reinforcement learning. In *Proceedings of the Fourteenth International Conference on Machine Learning*, pp. 358–366 San Francisco, CA. Morgan Kaufmann.

Tambe, M., & Rosenbloom, P. S. (1994). Investigating production system representations for non-combinatorial match. *Artificial Intelligence*, *68*(1), 155–199.

Watkins, C. J. C. H. (1989). *Learning from Delayed Rewards*. Ph.D. thesis, King's College, Oxford. (To be reprinted by MIT Press.).

Watkins, C. J., & Dayan, P. (1992). Technical note Q-Learning. *Machine Learning*, *8*, 279.

Journal of Artificial Intelligence Research 13 (2000) 305-338   Submitted 6/00; published 12/00

Conformant Planning via Symbolic Model Checking

Alessandro Cimatti   CIMATTI@IRST.ITC.IT
ITC-IRST, *Via Sommarive 18, 38055 Povo, Trento, Italy*

Marco Roveri   ROVERI@IRST.ITC.IT
ITC-IRST, *Via Sommarive 18, 38055 Povo, Trento, Italy*
DSI, University of Milano, Via Comelico 39, 20135 Milano, Italy

Abstract

We tackle the problem of planning in nondeterministic domains, by presenting a new approach to conformant planning. Conformant planning is the problem of finding a sequence of actions that is guaranteed to achieve the goal despite the nondeterminism of the domain. Our approach is based on the representation of the planning domain as a finite state automaton. We use Symbolic Model Checking techniques, in particular Binary Decision Diagrams, to compactly represent and efficiently search the automaton. In this paper we make the following contributions. First, we present a general planning algorithm for conformant planning, which applies to fully nondeterministic domains, with uncertainty in the initial condition and in action effects. The algorithm is based on a breadth-first, backward search, and returns conformant plans of minimal length, if a solution to the planning problem exists, otherwise it terminates concluding that the problem admits no conformant solution. Second, we provide a symbolic representation of the search space based on Binary Decision Diagrams (BDDs), which is the basis for search techniques derived from symbolic model checking. The symbolic representation makes it possible to analyze potentially large sets of states and transitions in a single computation step, thus providing for an efficient implementation. Third, we present CMBP (Conformant Model Based Planner), an efficient implementation of the data structures and algorithm described above, directly based on BDD manipulations, which allows for a compact representation of the search layers and an efficient implementation of the search steps. Finally, we present an experimental comparison of our approach with the state-of-the-art conformant planners CGP, QBFPLAN and GPT. Our analysis includes all the planning problems from the distribution packages of these systems, plus other problems defined to stress a number of specific factors. Our approach appears to be the most effective: CMBP is strictly more expressive than QBFPLAN and CGP and, in all the problems where a comparison is possible, CMBP outperforms its competitors, sometimes by orders of magnitude.

1. Introduction

In recent years, there has been a growing interest in planning in nondeterministic domains. Rejecting some fundamental (and often unrealistic) assumptions of classical planning, domains are considered where actions can have uncertain effects, exogenous events are possible, and the initial state can be only partly specified. The challenge is to find a *strong* plan, that is guaranteed to achieve the goal despite the nondeterminism of the domain, regardless of the uncertainty on the initial condition and on the effect of actions. Conditional planning (Cassandra, Kaelbling, & Littman, 1994; Weld, Anderson, & Smith, 1998; Cimatti, Roveri, & Traverso, 1998b) tackles this problem by searching for a conditional course of actions, that depends on information that can be gathered at run-time. In certain domains, however, run-time information gathering may be too expensive or simply impossible. *Conformant planning* (Goldman & Boddy, 1996) is the problem of finding an unconditioned course of actions, i.e. a classical plan, that does not depend on run-time information gathering to guarantee the achievement of the goal. Conformant planning has been recognized as a significant problem in Artificial Intelligence since the work by Michie (1974): the Blind Robot problem requires to program the activity for a sensorless agent, which can be positioned in any location of a given room, so that it will be guaranteed to achieve a given goal. Conformant planning can be also seen as a problem of control for a system with an unobservable and unknown state, such as a microprocessor at power-up, or a software system under black-box testing.

Because of uncertainty, a plan is associated to potentially many different executions, which must be all taken into account in order to guarantee goal achievement. This makes conformant planning significantly harder than classical planning (Rintanen, 1999a; De Giacomo & Vardi, 1999). Despite this increased complexity, several approaches to conformant planning have been recently proposed, based on (extensions of) the main planning techniques for classical planning. The most interesting are CGP (Smith & Weld, 1998) based on GRAPHPLAN, QBFPLAN (Rintanen, 1999a) which extends the SAT-plan approach to QBF, and GPT (Bonet & Geffner, 2000) which encodes conformant planning as heuristic search. In this paper, we propose a new approach to conformant planning, based on Symbolic Model Checking (McMillan, 1993). Symbolic Model Checking is a formal verification technique, which allows one to analyze finite state automata of high complexity, relying on symbolic techniques, Binary Decision Diagrams (BDDs) (Bryant, 1986) in particular, for the compact representation and efficient search of the automaton. Our approach builds on the planning via model checking paradigm presented by Cimatti and his colleagues (1997, 1998b, 1998a), where finite state automata are used to represent complex, nondeterministic planning domains, and planning is based on (extensions of) the basic model checking steps. We make the following contributions.

- First, we present a general algorithm for conformant planning, which applies to any nondeterministic domain with uncertain action effects and initial condition, expressed as a nondeterministic finite-state automaton. The algorithm performs a breadth-first search, exploring plans of increasing length, until a plan is found or no more candidate plans are available. The algorithm is complete, i.e. it returns with failure if and only if the problem admits no conformant solution. If the problem admits a solution, the algorithm returns a conformant plan of minimal length.

- Second, we provide a symbolic representation of the search space based on Binary Decision Diagrams, which allows for the application of search techniques derived from symbolic model checking. The symbolic representation makes it possible to analyze *sets* of transitions in a single computation step. These sets can be compactly represented and efficiently manipulated despite their potentially large cardinality. This way it is possible to overcome the enumerative nature of the other approaches to conformant planning, for which the degree of nondeterminism tends to be a limiting factor.

- Third, we developed CMBP (Conformant Model Based Planner), which is an efficient implementation of the data structures and algorithm described above. CMBP is developed on top of MBP, the planner based on symbolic model checking techniques developed by Cimatti, Roveri and Traveso (1998b, 1998a). CMBP implements several new techniques, directly based on BDD manipulations, to compact the search layers and optimize termination checking.

- Finally, we provide an experimental evaluation of the state-of-the-art conformant planners, comparing CMBP with CGP, QBFPLAN and GPT. Because of the difference in expressivity, not all the problems which can be tackled by CMBP can also be represented in the other planners. However, for the problems where a direct comparison was possible, CMBP outperforms its competitors. In particular, it features a better qualitative behavior, not directly related to the *number* of initial states and uncertain action effects, and more stable with respect to the use of heuristics.

The paper is structured as follows. In Section 2 we review the representation of (nondeterministic) planning domains as finite state automata. In Section 3 we provide the intuitions and a formal definition of conformant planning in this setting. In Section 4 we present the planning algorithm, and in Section 5 we discuss the symbolic representation of the search space, which allows for an efficient implementation. In Section 6 we present the CMBP planner, and in Section 7 we present the experimental results. In Section 8 we discuss some further related work. In Section 9 we draw the conclusions and discuss future research directions.

2. Planning Domains as Finite State Automata

We are interested in complex, nondeterministic planning domains, where actions can have preconditions, conditional effects, and uncertain effects, and the initial state can be only partly specified. In the rest of this paper, we use a very simple though paradigmatic domain for explanatory purposes, a variation of Moore's *bomb in the toilet* domain (McDermott, 1987) (from now on called BTUC — BT with Uncertain Clogging). There are two packages, and one of them contains an armed bomb. It is possible to dunk either package in the toilet (actions $Dunk_1$ and $Dunk_2$), provided that the toilet is not clogged. Dunking either package has the uncertain effect of clogging the toilet. Furthermore, dunking the package containing the bomb has the effect of disarming the bomb. The action *Flush* has the effect of unclogging the toilet.

We represent such domains as finite state automata. Figure 1 depicts the automaton for the BTUC domain. Each state is given a number, and contains all the propositions holding in that state. For instance, state 1 represents the state where the bomb is in package 1, is not defused, and the toilet is not clogged. Given that there is only one bomb, we write In_2 as an abbreviation for the negation of In_1. Arrows between states depict the transitions of the automaton, representing the possible behavior of actions. The transition from state 2 to state 1 labeled by *Flush* represents the fact that the action *Flush*, if executed in state 2, only has the effect of removing the clogging. The execution of $Dunk_1$ in state 1, which has the uncertain effect of clogging the toilet, is represented by the multiple transitions to states 5 and 6. Since there is no transition outgoing from state 2 and labelled by $Dunk_1$,

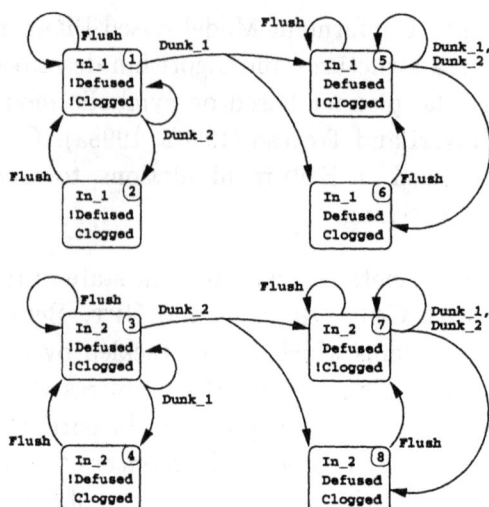

Figure 1: The automaton for the BTUC domain

state 2 does not satisfy the preconditions of action $Dunk_1$, i.e. $Dunk_1$ is not applicable in state 2.

We formally define nondeterministic planning domains as follows.

Definition 1 (Planning Domain) *A Planning Domain is a 4-tuple $\mathcal{D} = (\mathcal{P}, \mathcal{S}, \mathcal{A}, \mathcal{R})$, where $\mathcal{P}$ is the (finite) set of atomic propositions, $\mathcal{S} \subseteq 2^{\mathcal{P}}$ is the set of states, $\mathcal{A}$ is the (finite) set of actions, and $\mathcal{R} \subseteq \mathcal{S} \times \mathcal{A} \times \mathcal{S}$ is the transition relation.*

Intuitively, a proposition is in a state if and only if it holds in that state. In the following we assume that a planning domain $\mathcal{D}$ is given. We use s, s' and s'' to denote states of $\mathcal{D}$, and α to denote actions. $\mathcal{R}(s, \alpha, s')$ holds iff when executing the action α in the state s the state s' is a possible outcome. We say that an action α is applicable in s iff there is at least one state s' such that $\mathcal{R}(s, \alpha, s')$ holds. We say that an action α is deterministic in s iff there is a unique state s' such that $\mathcal{R}(s, \alpha, s')$ holds. An action α has an uncertain outcome in s if there are at least two distinct states s' and s'' such that $\mathcal{R}(s, \alpha, s')$ and $\mathcal{R}(s, \alpha, s'')$ hold. As described by Cimatti and his colleagues (1997), the automaton for a given domain can be efficiently built starting from a compact description given in an expressive high level action language, for instance $\mathcal{AR}$ (Giunchiglia, Kartha, & Lifschitz, 1997).

3. Conformant Planning

Conformant planning (Goldman & Boddy, 1996) can be described as the problem of finding a sequence of actions that is guaranteed to achieve the goal regardless of the nondeterminism of the domain. That is, for *all* possible initial states, and for *all* uncertain action effects, the execution of the plan results in a goal state.

Consider the following problem for the BTUC domain. Initially, the bomb is armed but its position and the status of the toilet are uncertain, i.e. the initial state can be any of the states in $\{1, 2, 3, 4\}$. The goal is to reach a state where the bomb is defused, and the toilet

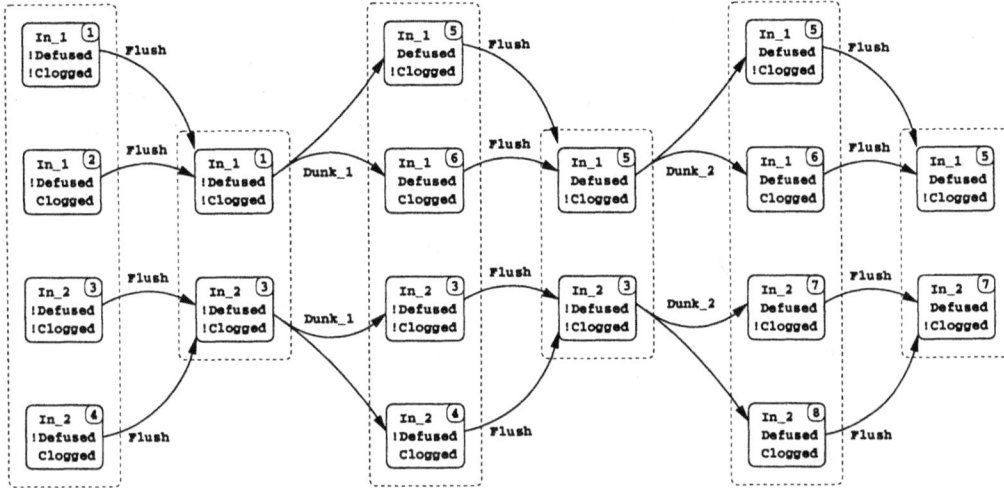

Figure 2: A conformant solution for the BTUC problem

is not clogged, i.e. the set of goal states is $\{5,7\}$. A conformant plan solving this problem is

$$Flush;\ Dunk_1\ ;\ Flush\ ;\ Dunk_2;\ Flush \tag{1}$$

Figure 2 outlines the possible executions of the plan, for all possible initial states and uncertain action effects. The initial uncertainty lies in the fact that the domain might be in any of the states in $\{1, 2, 3, 4\}$. The possible initial states of the planning domain are collected into a set by a dashed line. We call such a set a *belief state*. Intuitively, a belief state expresses a condition of uncertainty about the domain, by collecting together all the states which are indistinguishable from the point of view of an agent reasoning about the domain. The first action, *Flush*, is used to remove the possible clogging. This reduces the uncertainty to the belief state $\{1, 3\}$. Despite the remaining uncertainty (i.e. it is still not known in which package the bomb is), action $Dunk_1$ is now guaranteed to be applicable because its precondition is met in both states. $Dunk_1$ has the effect of defusing the bomb if it is contained in package 1, and has the uncertain effect of clogging the toilet. The resulting belief state is $\{3, 4, 5, 6\}$. The following action, *Flush*, removes the clogging, reducing the uncertainty to the belief state $\{3, 5\}$, and guarantees the applicability of $Dunk_2$. After $Dunk_2$, the bomb is guaranteed to be defused, but the toilet might be clogged again (states 6 and 8 in the belief state $\{5, 6, 7, 8\}$). The final *Flush* reduces the uncertainty to the belief state $\{5, 7\}$, and guarantees the achievement of the goal.

In general, in order for a plan to be a conformant solution, no action must be executed in states which do not satisfy the preconditions, and any state that can result from the execution of the plan (for all the initial states and for all the uncertain action effects) is a goal state. The main difficulty in achieving these conditions is that no information is (assumed to be) available at run-time. Therefore, at planning time we face the problem of reasoning about action execution in a belief state, i.e. under a condition of uncertainty.

Definition 2 (Action Applicability) *Let $Bs \subseteq S$ be a Belief State. The action α is applicable in Bs iff $Bs \neq \emptyset$ and α is applicable in every state $s \in Bs$.*

In order for an action to be applicable in a belief state, we require that its preconditions must be guaranteed notwithstanding the uncertainty. In other words, we reject "reckless" plans, which take the chance of applying an action without the guarantee of its applicability. This choice is strongly motivated in practical domains, where possibly fatal consequences can follow from the attempt to apply an action when its preconditions might not be satisfied (e.g. starting to fix an electrical device without being sure that it is not powered). The effect of action execution from an uncertain condition is defined as follows.

Definition 3 (Action Image) *Let $Bs \subseteq S$ be a belief state, and let α be an action applicable in Bs. The image (also called execution) of α in Bs, written $Image[\alpha](Bs)$, is defined as follows.*

$$Image[\alpha](Bs) \;\doteq\; \{s' \mid \text{there exists } s \in Bs \text{ such that } \mathcal{R}(s, \alpha, s')\}$$

Notice that the image of an action combines the uncertainty in the belief state with the uncertainty on the action effects. (Consider for instance that $Image[Dunk_1](\{1,3\})=\{3,4,5,6\}$.) In the following, we write $Image[\alpha](s)$ instead of $Image[\alpha](\{s\})$.

Plans are elements of $\mathcal{A}^*$, i.e. finite sequences of actions. We use ϵ for the 0-length plan, π and ρ to denote generic plans, and $\pi; \rho$ for plan concatenation. The notions of applicability and image generalize to plans as follows.

Definition 4 (Plan Applicability and Image) *Let $\pi \in \mathcal{A}^*$, and let $Bs \subseteq S$. π is applicable in Bs iff one of the following holds:*

1. $\pi = \epsilon$ and $Bs \neq \emptyset$;

2. $\pi = \alpha; \rho$, α is applicable in Bs, and ρ is applicable in $Image[\alpha](Bs)$.

The image (also called execution) of π in Bs, written $Image[\pi](Bs)$, is defined as:

1. $Image[\epsilon](Bs) \doteq Bs$;

2. $Image[\alpha; \pi](Bs) \doteq Image[\pi](Image[\alpha](Bs))$;

A planning problem is formally characterized by the set of initial and goal states. The following definition captures the intuitive meaning of conformant plan given above.

Definition 5 (Conformant Planning) *Let $\mathcal{D} = (\mathcal{P}, S, \mathcal{A}, \mathcal{R})$ be a planning domain. A Planning Problem for $\mathcal{D}$ is a triple $(\mathcal{D}, \mathcal{I}, \mathcal{G})$, where $\emptyset \neq \mathcal{I} \subseteq S$ and $\emptyset \neq \mathcal{G} \subseteq S$.*

The plan π is a conformant plan for (that is, a conformant solution to) the planning problem $(\mathcal{D}, \mathcal{I}, \mathcal{G})$ iff the following conditions hold:

(i) π is applicable in $\mathcal{I}$;

(ii) $Image[\pi](\mathcal{I}) \subseteq \mathcal{G}$.

In the following, when clear from the context, we omit the domain from the planning problem, and we simply write $(\mathcal{I}, \mathcal{G})$.

4. The Conformant Planning Algorithm

Our conformant planning algorithm is based on the exploration of the space of plans, limiting the exploration to plans which are conformant by construction. The algorithm builds Belief state-Plan (BsP) pairs of the form $\langle Bs \cdot \pi \rangle$, where Bs is a non-empty belief state and π is a plan. The idea is to use a BsP pair to associate each explored plan with the maximal belief state where it is applicable, and from which it is guaranteed to result in goal states. The exploration is based on the basic function $SPreImage[\alpha](Bs)$, that, given a belief state Bs and an action α, returns the belief state containing all the states where α is applicable, and whose image under α is contained in Bs.

Definition 6 (Strong Pre-Image) *Let* $\emptyset \neq Bs \subseteq \mathcal{S}$ *be a belief state and let* α *be an action. The strong pre-image of* Bs *under* α*, written* $SPreImage[\alpha](Bs)$*, is defined as follows.*

$$SPreImage[\alpha](Bs) \doteq \{s \mid \alpha \text{ is applicable in } s, \text{ and } Image[\alpha](s) \subseteq Bs\}$$

If $SPreImage[\alpha](Bs)$ is not empty, then α is applicable in it, and it is a conformant solution to the problem $(SPreImage[\alpha](Bs), Bs)$. Therefore, if the plan π is a conformant solution for the problem $(Bs, \mathcal{G})$, then the plan $\alpha; \pi$ is a conformant solution to the problem $(SPreImage[\alpha](Bs), \mathcal{G})$.

Figure 3 depicts the space of BsP pairs built by the algorithm while solving the BTUC problem. The levels are built from the goal, on the right, towards the initial states, on the left. At level 0, the only BsP pair is $\langle \{5, 7\} \cdot \epsilon \rangle$, composed by the set of goal states indexed by the 0-length plan ϵ. (Notice that ϵ is a conformant solution to every problem with goal set $\{5, 7\}$ and initial states contained in $\{5, 7\}$.) The dashed arrows represent the application of $SPreImage$. At level 1, only the BsP pair $\langle \{5, 6, 7, 8\} \cdot Flush \rangle$ is built, since the strong pre-image of the belief state 0 for the actions $Dunk_1$ and $Dunk_2$ is empty. At level 2, there are three BsP pairs, with (overlapping) belief states Bs_2, Bs_3 and Bs_4, indexed, respectively, by the length 2 plans $Dunk_1; Flush$, $Flush; Flush$ and $Dunk_2; Flush$. (A plan associated with a belief state Bs_i is a sequence of actions labeling the path from Bs_i to Bs_0.) Notice that Bs_3 is equal to Bs_1, and therefore deserves no further expansion. The expansion of belief states 2 and 4 gives the belief states 5 and 6, both obtained by the strong pre-image under $Flush$, while the strong pre-image under actions $Dunk_1$ and $Dunk_2$ returns empty belief states. The further expansion of Bs_5 results in three belief states. The one resulting from the strong pre-image under $Flush$ is not reported, since it is equal to Bs_5. Belief state 7 is also equal to Bs_2, and deserves no further expansion. Belief state 8 can be obtained by expanding both Bs_5 and Bs_6. At level 5, the expansion produces Bs_{10}, which contains all the initial states. Therefore, both of the corresponding plans are conformant solutions to the problem.

The conformant planning algorithm CONFORMANTPLAN is presented in Figure 4. It takes as input the planning problem in the form of the set of states $\mathcal{I}$ and $\mathcal{G}$ (the domain $\mathcal{D}$ is assumed to be globally available). The algorithm performs a backwards breadth-first search, exploring BsP pairs corresponding to plans of increasing length at each step. The status of the search (each level in Figure 3) is represented by a BsP table, i.e. a set of BsP pairs

$$BsPT = \{\langle Bs_1 \cdot \pi_1 \rangle, \ldots, \langle Bs_n \cdot \pi_n \rangle\}$$

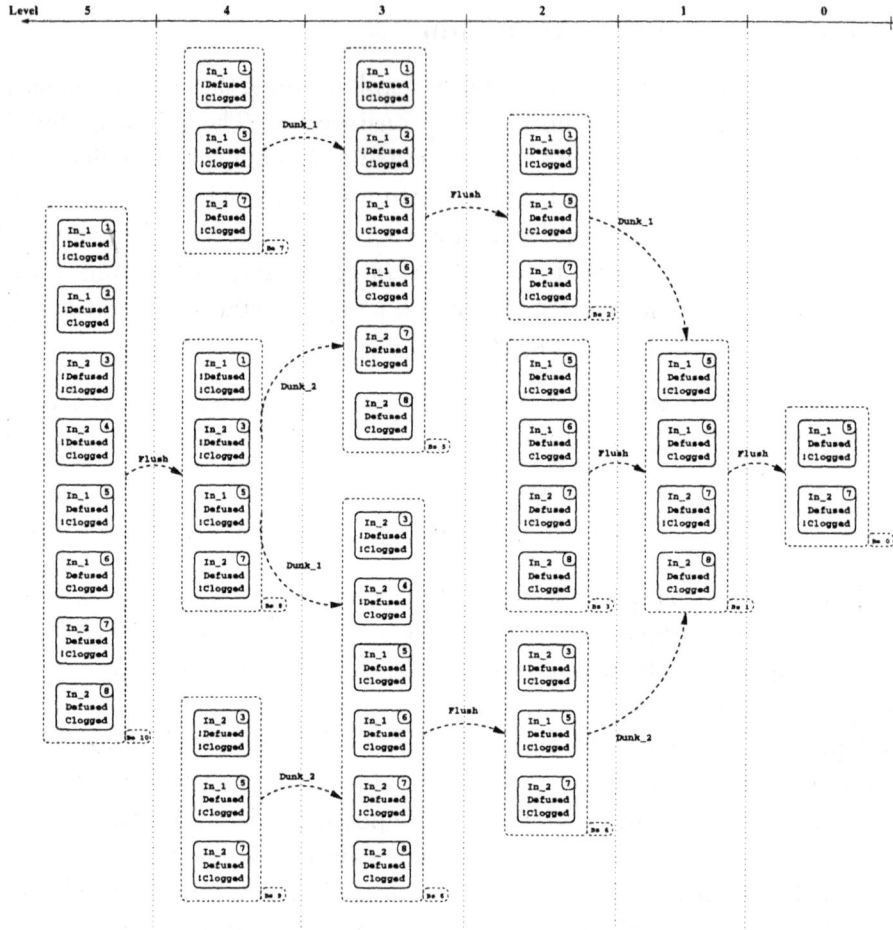

Figure 3: The BsP tables for the BTUC problem

where the π_i are plans of the same length, such that $\pi_i \neq \pi_j$ for all $1 \leq j \neq i \leq n$. We call Bs_i the belief set indexed by π_i. When no ambiguity arises, we write $BsPT(\pi_i)$ for Bs_i. The array *BsPTables* is used to store the BsP tables representing the levels of the search. The algorithm first checks (line 4) if there are plans of length 0, i.e. if ϵ is a solution. If no conformant plan of such length exists $((Plans = \emptyset)$ in line 4), then the while loop is entered. At each iteration, conformant plans of increasing length are explored (lines 5 to 8). The step at line 6 expands the BsP table in $BsPTables[i-1]$ and stores the resulting BsP table in $BsPTables[i]$. BsP pairs which are redundant with respect to the current search are eliminated from $BsPTables[i]$ (line 7). The possible solutions contained in $BsPTables[i]$ are extracted and stored in *Plans* (line 8). The loop terminates if either a plan is found $(Plans \neq \emptyset)$, or the space of conformant plans has been completely explored $(BsPTables[i] = \emptyset)$.

The definitions of the basic functions used in the algorithm are reported in Figure 5. The function EXPANDBSPTABLE expands the BsP table provided as argument, containing conformant plans of length $i-1$, and returns a BsP table with conformant plans of length i. Each BsP in the input BsP table is expanded by EXPANDBSPPAIR. For each possible

```
       function CONFORMANTPLAN(I,G)
0      begin
1          i = 0;
2          BsPTables[0] := { ⟨G . ϵ⟩ };
3          Plans := EXTRACTSOLUTION(I, BsPTables[0]);
4          while ((BsPTables[i] ≠ ∅) ∧ (Plans = ∅)) do
5              i := i + 1;
6              BsPTables[i] := EXPANDBSPTABLE(BsPTables[i-1]);
7              BsPTables[i] := PRUNEBSPTABLE(BsPTables[i], BsPTables, i);
8              Plans := EXTRACTSOLUTION(I, BsPTables[i]);
9          done
10         if (BsPTables[i] = ∅) then
11             return Fail;
12             else return Plans;
13     end
```

Figure 4: The conformant planning algorithm.

action α, the strong pre-image of Bs is computed, and if the resulting belief state Bs' is not empty, i.e. there is a belief state from which α guarantees the achievement of Bs, then the plan π is extended with α and $\langle Bs' . \alpha; \pi \rangle$ is returned. The expansion of a BsP table is the union of the expansions of each BsP pair. The function EXTRACTSOLUTION takes as input a BsP table and returns the (possibly empty) set of plans which index a belief states containing $\mathcal{I}$. PRUNEBSPTABLE takes as input the BsP table to be pruned, an array of previously constructed BsP tables $BsPTables$, and an index of the current step. It removes from the BsP table in the input the plans which are not worth being explored because the corresponding belief states have already been visited.

The algorithm has the following properties. First, it always terminates. This follows from the fact that the set of explored belief sets (stored in $BsPTables$) is monotonically increasing — at each step we proceed only if at least one new belief state is generated. Because of its finiteness (the set of accumulated belief states is contained in 2^S which is finite), a fix point is eventually reached. Second, it is correct, i.e. when a plan is returned it is a conformant solution to the given problem. The correctness of the algorithm follows from the properties of $SPreImage$: each plan is associated with a belief state for which it is conformant, i.e. where it is guaranteed to be applicable and from which it results in a belief state contained in the goal. Third, the algorithm is optimal, i.e. it returns plans of minimal length. This property follows from the breadth-first style of the search. Finally, the algorithm is able to decide whether a problem admits no solution, returning $Fail$ in such cases. Indeed, a conformant solution is always associated with a belief state containing the initial states. $SPreImage$ generates the *maximal* belief state associated with a conformant plan, each new belief state generated in the exploration is compared with the initial states to check if it is a solution, and a plan is pruned only if an equivalent plan has already been explored.

$$\text{EXPANDBsPTABLE}(BsPT) \doteq \bigcup_{\langle Bs \ . \ \pi \rangle \in BsPT} \text{EXPANDBsPPAIR}(\langle Bs \ . \ \pi \rangle)$$

$$\text{EXPANDBsPPAIR}(\langle Bs \ . \ \pi \rangle) \doteq \{\langle Bs' \ . \ \alpha; \pi \rangle | \text{ such that } Bs' = SPreImage[\alpha](Bs) \neq \emptyset\}$$

$$\text{PRUNEBsPTABLE}(BsPT, BsPTables, i) \doteq$$
$$\{\langle Bs \ . \ \pi \rangle \in BsPT \mid \text{ for all } j < i, \text{ there is no } \langle Bs \ . \ \pi' \rangle \in BsPTables[j] \text{ such that } (Bs' = Bs)\}$$

$$\text{EXTRACTSOLUTION}(\mathcal{I}, BsPT) \doteq \{\pi \mid \text{ there exists } \langle Bs \ . \ \pi \rangle \in BsPT \text{ such that } \mathcal{I} \subseteq Bs\}$$

Figure 5: The primitives used by the conformant planning algorithm.

5. Conformant Planning via Symbolic Model Checking

Model checking is a formal verification technique based on the exploration of finite state automata (Clarke, Emerson, & Sistla, 1986). Symbolic model checking (McMillan, 1993) is a particular form of model checking using Binary Decision Diagrams to compactly represent and efficiently analyze finite state automata. The introduction of symbolic techniques into model checking led to a breakthrough in the size of model which could be analyzed (Burch et al., 1992), and made it possible for model checking to be routinely applied in industry, especially in logic circuits design (for a survey see Clarke & Wing, 1996).

In the rest of this section, we will provide an overview of Binary Decision Diagrams, and we will describe the representation of planning domains, based on the BDD-based representation of finite state automata used in model checking. Then, we will discuss the extension which allows to symbolically represent BsP tables and their transformations, thus allowing for an efficient implementation of the algorithm described in the previous section.

5.1 Binary Decision Diagrams

A Reduced Ordered Binary Decision Diagram (Bryant, 1992, 1986) (improperly called BDD) is a directed acyclic graph (DAG). The terminal nodes are either *True* or *False*. Each non-terminal node is associated with a boolean variable, and two BDDs, called left and right branches. Figure 6 (a) depicts a BDD for $(a_1 \leftrightarrow b_1) \wedge (a_2 \leftrightarrow b_2) \wedge (a_3 \leftrightarrow b_3)$. At each non-terminal node, the right [left, respectively] branch is depicted as a solid [dashed, resp.] line, and represents the assignment of the value *True* [*False*, resp.] to the corresponding variable. A BDD represents a boolean function. For a given truth assignment to the variables in the BDD, the value of the function is determined by traversing the graph from the root to the leaves, following each branch indicated by the value assigned to the variables[1]. The

---

1. A path from the root to a leaf can visit nodes associated with a subset of all the variables of the BDD. See for instance the path associated with $a_1, \neg b_1$ in Figure 6(a).

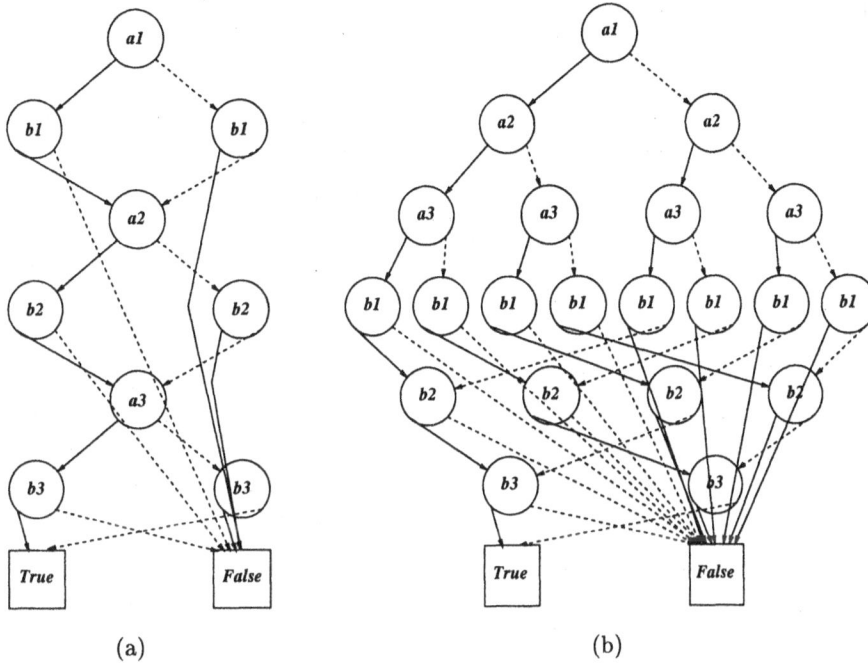

Figure 6: Two BDDs for the formula $(a_1 \leftrightarrow b_1) \wedge (a_2 \leftrightarrow b_2) \wedge (a_3 \leftrightarrow b_3)$.

reached leaf node is labeled with the resulting truth value. If v is a BDD, its size $|v|$ is the number of its nodes. If n is a node, $var(n)$ indicates the variable indexing node n.

BDDs are a canonical representation of Boolean functions. The canonicity follows by imposing a total order $<$ over the set of variables used to label nodes, such that for any node n and respective non-terminal child m, their variables must be ordered, i.e. $var(n) <$ $var(m)$, and requiring that the BDD contains no isomorphic subgraphs.

BDDs can be combined with the usual boolean transformations (e.g. negation, conjunction, disjunction). Given two BDDs, for instance, the conjunction operator builds and returns the BDD corresponding to the conjunction of its arguments. Substitution can also be represented as BDD transformations. In the following, if v is a variable, and Φ and ψ are BDDs, we indicate with $\Phi[v/\psi]$ the BDD resulting from the substitution of v with ψ in Φ. If $\mathbf{v_1}$ and $\mathbf{v_2}$ are vectors of (the same number of) distinct variables, we indicate with $\Phi[\mathbf{v_1}/\mathbf{v_2}]$ the parallel substitution in Φ of the variables in vector $\mathbf{v_1}$ with the (corresponding) variables in $\mathbf{v_2}$.

BDDs also allow for transformations described as quantifications, in the style of Quantified Boolean Formulae (QBF). QBF is a definitional extension to propositional logic, where propositional variables can be universally and existentially quantified. In terms of BDD computations, a quantification corresponds to a tranformation mapping the BDD of Φ and the variable v_i being quantified into the BDD of the resulting (propositional) formula. If Φ is a formula, and v_i is one of its variables, the existential quantification of v_i in Φ, written $\exists v_i.\Phi(v_1, \ldots, v_n)$, is equivalent to $\Phi(v_1, \ldots, v_n)[v_i/False] \vee \Phi(v_1, \ldots, v_n)[v_i/True]$. Analogously, the universal quantification $\forall v_i.\Phi(v_1, \ldots, v_n)$ is equivalent to $\Phi(v_1, \ldots, v_n)[v_i/False] \wedge$

$\Phi(v_1, \ldots, v_n)[v_i/True]$. In QBF, quantifiers can be arbitrarily applied and nested. In general, a QBF formula has an equivalent propositional formula, but the conversion is subject to an exponential blow-up.

The time complexity of the algorithm for computing a truth-functional boolean transformation $f_1 <op> f_2$ is $O(|f_1| \cdot |f_2|)$. As far as quantifications are concerned, the time complexity is quadratic in the size of the BDD being quantified, and linear in the number of variables being quantified, i.e. $O(|\mathbf{v}| \cdot |f|^2)$ (Bryant, 1992, 1986).

BDD *packages* are efficient implementations of such data structures and algorithms (Brace et al., 1990; Somenzi, 1997; Yang et al., 1998; Coudert et al., 1993). Basically, a BDD package deals with a single multi-rooted DAG, where each node represents a boolean function. Memory efficiency is obtained by using a "unique table", and by sharing common subgraphs between BDDs. The unique table is used to guarantee that at each time there are no isomorphic subgraphs and no redundant nodes in the multi-rooted DAG. Before creating a new node, the unique table is checked to see if the node is already present, and only if this is not the case a new node is created and stored in the unique table. The unique table allows to perform the equivalence check between two BDDs in constant time (since two equivalent functions always share the same subgraph) (Brace et al., 1990; Somenzi, 1997). Time efficiency is obtained by maintaining a "computed table", which keeps track of the results of recently computed transformations, thus avoiding the recomputation.

A critical computational factor with BDDs is the order of the variables used. (Figure 6 shows an example of the impact of a change in the variable ordering on the size of a BDD.) For a certain class of boolean functions, the size of the corresponding BDD is exponential in the number of variables for any possible variable ordering (Bryant, 1991). In many practical cases, however, finding a good variable ordering is rather easy. Beside affecting the memory used to represent a Boolean function, finding a good variable ordering can have a big impact on computation times, since the complexity of the transformation algorithms depends on the size of the operands. Most BDD packages provide heuristic algorithms for finding good variable orderings, which can be called to try to reduce the overall size of the stored BDDs. The reordering algorithms can also be activated dynamically by the package, during a BDD computation, when the total number of nodes in the package reaches a predefined threshold (dynamic reoredering).

5.2 Symbolic Representation of Planning Domains

A planning domain $(\mathcal{P}, \mathcal{S}, \mathcal{A}, \mathcal{R})$ can be represented symbolically using BDDs, as follows. A set of (distinct) BDD variables, called *state* variables, is devoted to the representation of the states $\mathcal{S}$ of the domain. Each of these variables has a direct association with a proposition of the domain in $\mathcal{P}$ used in the description of the domain. For instance, for the BTUC domain, each of In_1, $Defused$ and $Clogged$ is associated with a unique BDD variable. In the following we write $\boldsymbol{x}$ for the vector of state variables. Because the particular order is irrelevant but for performance issues, in the rest of this section we will not distinguish a proposition and the corresponding BDD variable.

A state is a set of propositions of $\mathcal{P}$ (specifically, the propositions which are intended to hold in it). For each state s, there is a corresponding assignment to the state variables $\boldsymbol{x}$, i.e. the assignment where each variable corresponding to a proposition $p \in s$ is assigned to *True*, and each other variable is assigned to *False*. We represent s with the BDD $\xi(s)$, having such an assignment as its unique satisfying assignment. For instance, $\xi(6) \doteq (In_1 \wedge Defused \wedge Clogged)$ is the BDD representing state 6, while $\xi(4) \doteq \neg In_1 \wedge \neg Defused \wedge Clogged$ represents state 4, and so on. (Without loss of generality, in the following we do not distinguish a propositional formula from the corresponding BDD.) This representation naturally extends to any *set of states* $Q \subseteq S$ as follows:

$$\xi(Q) \doteq \bigvee_{s \in Q} \xi(s)$$

In other words, we associate a set of states with the generalized disjunction of the BDDs representing each of the states. Notice that the satisfying assignments of the $\xi(Q)$ are exactly the assignment representations of the states in Q. This representation mechanism is very natural. For instance, the BDD $\xi(\mathcal{I})$ representing the the set of initial states of the BTUC $\mathcal{I} \doteq \{1, 2, 3, 4\}$ is $\neg Defused$, while for the set of goal states $\mathcal{G} \doteq \{5, 7\}$ the corresponding BDD is $Defused \wedge \neg Clogged$. A BDD is also used to represent the set S of all the states of the domain automaton. In the BTUC, $\xi(S) = True$ because $S = 2^P$. In a different formulation, where two *independent* propositions In_1 and In_2 are used to represent the position of a bomb, $\xi(S)$ would be the BDD $In_1 \leftrightarrow \neg In_2$.

In general, a BDD represents the set of (states which correspond to) its models. As a consequence, set theoretic transformations are naturally represented by propositional operations, as follows.

$$
\begin{aligned}
\xi(S \backslash Q) &\doteq \xi(S) \wedge \neg \xi(Q) \\
\xi(Q_1 \cup Q_2) &\doteq \xi(Q_1) \vee \xi(Q_2) \\
\xi(Q_1 \cap Q_2) &\doteq \xi(Q_1) \wedge \xi(Q_2)
\end{aligned}
$$

The main efficiency of this symbolic representation lies in the fact that the cardinality of the represented set is not directly related to the size of the BDD. For instance, $\xi(\mathcal{G})$ uses two (non-terminal) nodes to represent two states, while $\xi(\mathcal{I})$ uses one node to represent four states. As limit cases, $\xi(S)$ and $\xi(\{\})$ are (the leaf BDDs) *True* and *False*, respectively. As a further advantage, symbolic representation is extremely efficient in dealing with irrelevant information. Notice, for instance, that only the variable $Defused$ occurs in $\xi(\{5, 6, 7, 8\})$. For this reason, a symbolic representation can have a dramatic improvement over an explicit, enumerative representation. This is what allows symbolic, BDD-based model checkers to handle finite state automata with a very large number of states (see for instance Burch et al., 1992). In the following, we will collapse a set of states and the BDD representing it.

Another set of BDD variables, called *action* variables, written $\boldsymbol{\alpha}$, is used to represent actions. We use one action variable for each possible action in $\mathcal{A}$. Intuitively, a BDD action variable is true if and only if the corresponding action is being executed. If we assume that a sequential encoding is used, i.e. no concurrent actions are allowed, we also use a BDD, $\text{SEQ}(\boldsymbol{\alpha})$, to express that exactly one of the action variables must be true at each time[2]. For

---

2. In the specific case of sequential encoding, an alternative approach using only $\lceil \log |\mathcal{A}| \rceil$ is possible: an assignment to the action variables denotes a specific action to be executed. Two assignments being mutually exclusive, the constraint $\text{SEQ}(\boldsymbol{\alpha})$ needs not to be represented. When the cardinality of the set of actions is not a power of two, the standard solution is to associate more than one assignment to certain values. This optimized solution, which is actually used in the implementation, is not described here for the sake of simplicity.

the BTUC problem, where $\mathcal{A}$ contains three actions, we use the three BDD variables $Dunk_1$, $Dunk_2$ and $Flush$, while we express the serial encoding constraint with the following BDD:

$$\text{SEQ}(\boldsymbol{\alpha}) \doteq (Dunk_1 \vee Dunk_2 \vee Flush) \wedge \neg(Dunk_1 \wedge Dunk_2) \wedge \neg(Dunk_1 \wedge Flush) \wedge \neg(Dunk_2 \wedge Flush)$$

As for state variables, we are referring to BDD action variables with symbolic names for the sake of simplicity. In practice, they will be internally represented as integers, but their position in the ordering of the BDD package is totally irrelevant in logical terms.

A BDD in the variables $\boldsymbol{x}$ and $\boldsymbol{\alpha}$ represents a set of state-action pairs, i.e. a relation between states and actions. For instance, the applicability relation in the BTUC (i.e., all actions are possible in all states, except for dunking actions which require the toilet not to be clogged) is represented by the BDD $\neg(Clogged \wedge (Dunk_1 \vee Dunk_2))$. Notice that it represents a set of 16 state-action pairs, each associating a state with an applicable action.

A transition is a 3-tuple composed of a state (the initial state of the transition), an action (the action being executed), and a state (the resulting state of the transition). To represent transitions, another vector $\boldsymbol{x}'$ of BDD variables, called *next state* variables, is allocated in the BDD package. We write $\xi'(s)$ for the representation of the state s in the next state variables. With $\xi'(Q)$ we denote the construction of the BDD corresponding to the set of states Q, using each variable in the next state vector $\boldsymbol{x}'$ instead of each current state variables $\boldsymbol{x}$. We require that $|\boldsymbol{x}| = |\boldsymbol{x}'|$, and assume that the i-th variable in $\boldsymbol{x}$ and the i-th variable in $\boldsymbol{x}'$ correspond. We define the representation of a set of states in the next variables as follows.

$$\xi'(s) \doteq \xi(s)[\boldsymbol{x}/\boldsymbol{x}']$$

We call the operation $\Phi[\boldsymbol{x}/\boldsymbol{x}']$ "forward shifting", because it transforms the representation of a set of "current" states in the representation of a set of "next" states. The dual operation $\Phi[\boldsymbol{x}'/\boldsymbol{x}]$ is called backward shifting. In the following, we call $\boldsymbol{x}$ *current* state variables to distinguish them from next state variables. A transition is represented as an assignment to $\boldsymbol{x}$, $\boldsymbol{\alpha}$ and $\boldsymbol{x}'$. For the BTUC, the transition corresponding to the application of action $Dunk_1$ in state 1 resulting in state 5 is represented by the following BDD

$$\xi(\langle 1, Dunk_1, 5 \rangle) \doteq \xi(1) \wedge Dunk_1 \wedge \xi'(5)$$

The transition relation $\mathcal{R}$ of the automaton corresponding to a planning domain is simply a set of transitions, and is thus represented by a BDD in the BDD variables $\boldsymbol{x}$, $\boldsymbol{\alpha}$ and $\boldsymbol{x}'$, where each satisfying assignment represents a possible transition.

$$\xi(\mathcal{R}) \doteq \text{SEQ}(\boldsymbol{\alpha}) \wedge \bigvee_{t \in \mathcal{R}} \xi(t)$$

In the rest of this paper, we assume that the BDD representation of a planning domain is given. In particular, we assume as given the vectors of variables $\boldsymbol{x}, \boldsymbol{x}', \boldsymbol{\alpha}$, the encoding functions ξ and ξ', and we simply call $\mathcal{S}$, $\mathcal{R}$, $\mathcal{I}$ and $\mathcal{G}$ the BDD representing the states of the domain, the transition relation, the initial states and the goal states, respectively. We write $\Phi(\mathbf{v})$ to stress that the BDD Φ depends on the variables in $\mathbf{v}$. With this representation, it is possible to reason about plans, simulating symbolically the execution of sets of actions in sets of states, by means of QBF transformations. The BDD representing the applicability relation can be directly obtained with the following computation.

$$\text{APPLICABLE}(\boldsymbol{x}, \boldsymbol{\alpha}) \doteq \exists \boldsymbol{x}'.\mathcal{R}(\boldsymbol{x}, \boldsymbol{\alpha}, \boldsymbol{x}')$$

The resulting BDD, APPLICABLE(x, α), represents the set of state-action pairs such that the action is applicable in the state. The BDD representing the states reachable from Q in one step is obtained with the following computation.

$$\exists x. \exists \alpha. (\mathcal{R}(x, \alpha, x') \wedge Q(x))[x'/x]$$

Notice that, with this single operation, we symbolically simulate the effect of the application of any applicable action in $\mathcal{A}$ to any of the states in Q. Similarly, the following transformation allows to symbolically compute the *SPreImage* of a set of states Q under all possible actions in one single computation:

$$\forall x'. (\mathcal{R}(x, \alpha, x') \rightarrow Q(x)[x/x']) \wedge \text{APPLICABLE}(x, \alpha)$$

The resulting BDD represents all the state-action pairs $\langle x \ . \ \alpha \rangle$ such that α is applicable in x and the execution of α in x results in states in Q.

5.3 Symbolic Search in the Space of Belief States

The main strength of the symbolic approach is that it allows to perform a symbolic breadth-first search, and it provides a way for compactly representing and efficiently expanding the frontier. For instance, plans can be constructed by symbolic breadth-first search in the space of states, repeatedly applying the strong pre-image to the goal states (Cimatti et al., 1998b). However, the machinery presented in the previous section cannot be directly applied to tackle conformant planning. The basic difference is that with conformant planning we are searching in the space of belief states[3], and therefore the frontier of the search is basically a *set of sets of states*. We introduce a way to symbolically represent BsP tables. Basically, this can be seen as a construction on demand, based on the algorithm steps, of increasingly large portions of the space of belief states. The key intuition is that a BsP table

$$\{\langle \{s_1^1, \dots, s_{n_1}^1\} \ . \ \pi_1 \rangle, \dots, \langle \{s_1^k, \dots, s_{n_k}^k\} \ . \ \pi_k \rangle\}$$

is represented as a relation between plans (of the same length) and states, by associating the plan directly with each state in the belief state indexed by the plan, as follows:

$$\{\langle s_1^1 \ . \ \pi_1 \rangle, \dots, \langle s_{n_1}^1 \ . \ \pi_1 \rangle, \dots, \langle s_1^k \ . \ \pi_k \rangle, \dots, \langle s_{n_k}^k \ . \ \pi_k \rangle\} \tag{2}$$

We use additional variables to represent the plans in the BsP tables. In order to represent plans of increasing length, at each step of the algorithm, a vector of new BDD variables, called *plan variables*, is introduced. The vector of plan variables introduced at the i-th step of the algorithm is written $\pi_{[i]}$, with $|\pi_{[i]}| = |\alpha|$, and is used to encode the i-th to last action in the plan[4]. At step one of the algorithm, we introduce the vector of plan variables $\pi_{[1]}$ to represent the action corresponding to each 1-length possible conformant plan. The BsP

---

3. In principle, the machinery for symbolic search could be used to do conformant planning if applied to the determinization of the domain automaton, i.e. an automaton having 2^S as its state space. However, this would require the introduction of an exponential number of state variables, which is impractical even for very small domains.

4. The search being performed backwards, plans need to be reversed once found.

table $BsPT_1$ at level 1 is built by ExpandBsPTable by performing the following Bdd computation starting from the BsP table at level 0, i.e. $\mathcal{G}(x)$:

$$(\forall x'.(\mathcal{R}(x, \alpha, x') \to \mathcal{G}(x)[x/x']) \ \wedge \ \text{Applicable}(x, \alpha))[\alpha/\pi_{[1]}]$$

The computation collects those state-action pairs $\langle x \,.\, \alpha \rangle$ such that (the action represented by) α is applicable in (the state represented by) x, and such that all the resulting (states represented by) x' are goal states. Then we replace the vector of action variables α with the first vector of plan variables $\pi_{[1]}$. The resulting Bdd, $BsPT(x, \pi_{[1]})$, represents a BsP table containing plans of length one in the form of a relation between states and plans as in (2). In the general case, after step $i-1$, the BsP table $BsPT_{i-1}$, associating belief states to plans of length $i-1$, is represented by a Bdd in the state variables x and in the plan variables $\pi_{[i-1]}, \dots, \pi_{[1]}$. The computation performed by ExpandBsPTable at step i is implemented as the following Bdd transformation on $BsPT_{i-1}$

$$(\forall x'.(\mathcal{R}(x, \alpha, x') \to BsPT_{i-1}(x, \pi_{[i-1]}, \dots, \pi_{[1]})[x/x']) \ \wedge \ \text{Applicable}(x, \alpha))[\alpha/\pi_{[i]}] \quad (3)$$

The next state variables in $\mathcal{R}$ and in $BsPT_{i-1}$ (resulting from the forward shifting) disappear because of the universal quantification. The action variables α are renamed to the newly introduced plan variables $\pi_{[i]}$, so that in the next step of the algorithm the construction can be repeated.

ExtractSolution extracts the assignments to plan variables such that the corresponding set contains the initial states. In terms of Bdd transformations, ExtractSolution is implemented as follows:

$$\forall x.(\mathcal{I}(x) \to BsPT_i(x, \pi_{[i]}, \dots, \pi_{[1]})) \quad (4)$$

The result is a Bdd in the plan variables $\pi_{[i]}, \dots, \pi_{[1]}$. If the Bdd is *False*, then there are no solutions of length i. Otherwise, each of the satisfying assignments to the resulting Bdd represents a conformant solution to the problem.

To guarantee the termination of the algorithm, at each step the BsP table returned by ExpandBsPTable is simplified by PruneBsPTable by removing all the belief states which do not deserve further expansion. This requires the comparison of the belief states contained in the BsP table with the belief states contained in each of the BsP tables built at previous levels. This is one of the crucial steps in terms of efficiency. An earlier implementation of this step with logical Bdd transformations, following directly from the set-theoretical definition of PruneBsPTable, was extremely inefficient (Cimatti & Roveri, 1999). Furthermore, we noticed that the serial encoding could yield BsP tables containing a large number of equivalent plans, all indexing exactly the same belief state. Often these equivalent plans only differ in the order of some independent actions, and this is a potential source of combinatorial explosion. This occurs even in the simple version of the BTUC (in Figure 3, two equivalent conformant plans are associated with Bs_8). Therefore, we developed a new implementation which could tackle these two problems by operating directly on the BsP table. The idea is depicted in Figure 7. Initially, the cache contains Bs_1, Bs_2 and Bs_3. The simplification performs a traversal of the Bdd, by accumulating the subtrees representing belief states, comparing them with the ones built at previous levels, and inserting the new ones in the cache (in Figure 7, Bs_4, Bs_5 and Bs_6). Each time a path is identified which

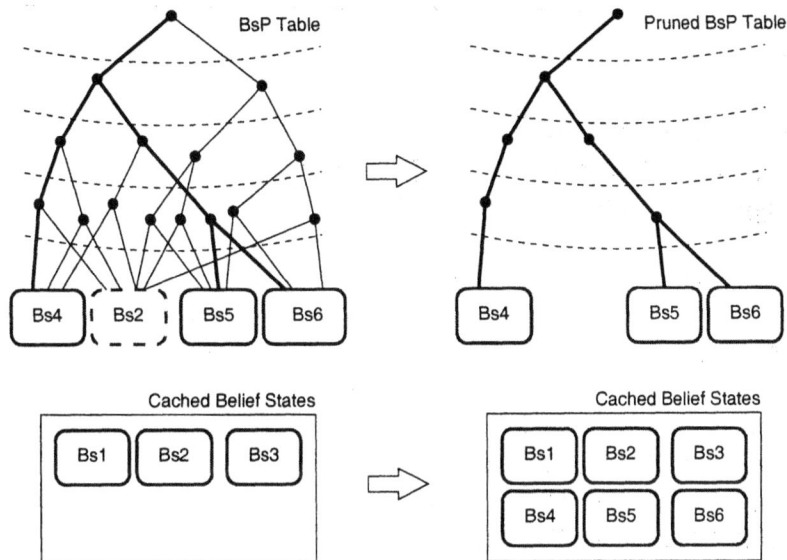

Figure 7: An example of pruning of a BsP table

represents a plan indexing an already cached belief state, the plan is redundant and the corresponding path is pruned[5]. The cost of the simplification is linear in the size of the BsP being simplified and is highly effective in pruning.

6. CMBP: a BDD-based Conformant Planner

CMBP (Conformant Model Based Planner) is a conformant planner implementing the data structures and algorithms for conformant planning described in the previous sections. CMBP inherits the features of MBP (Cimatti et al., 1997, 1998b, 1998a), a planner based on symbolic model checking techniques. MBP is built on top of NuSMV, a symbolic model checker jointly developed by ITC-IRST and CMU (Cimatti et al., 2000), and uses the CUDD (Somenzi, 1997) state-of-the-art BDD package. MBP is a two-stage system. In the first stage, an internal BDD-based representation of the domain is built, while in the second stage planning problems can be solved. Currently, planning domains are described by means of the high-level action language $\mathcal{AR}$ (Giunchiglia et al., 1997). $\mathcal{AR}$ allows to specify (conditional and uncertain) effects of actions by means of high level assertions. For instance, Figure 8 shows the $\mathcal{AR}$ description of the BTUC problem[6]. The semantics of $\mathcal{AR}$ yields a serial encoding, i.e. exactly one action is assumed to be executed at each

---

5. This pruning mechanism is actually weaker than the earlier one (Cimatti & Roveri, 1999). Here we require that the same belief state must not be expanded twice during the search, while in the earlier version we prune belief states *contained* in previously explored ones. This may increase the *number* of explored belief states. However, it allows for a much more efficient implementation, without impacting on the properties of the algorithm.

6. ! and & stand for negation and conjunction, respectively. The description is slightly edited for the sake of readability. In particular, MBP currently does not accept parameterized $\mathcal{AR}$ descriptions. In practice we use a script language to generate ground instances of different complexity from a parameterized problem description.

```
DOMAIN BTUC

ACTIONS Dunk_1, Dunk_2, Flush;
FLUENTS In_1, In_2, Defused, Clogged : boolean;
INERTIAL Clogged, Defused, In_1, In_2;

ALWAYS In_1 <-> !In_2;

Flush CAUSES !Clogged;

for i in [1, 2] {
  Dunk_<i> HAS PRECONDITIONS !Clogged;
  Dunk_<i> CAUSES Defused IF In_<i>;
  Dunk_<i> POSSIBLY CHANGES Clogged;
}

INITIALLY !Defused;
CONFORMANT Defused & !Clogged;
```

Figure 8: An $\mathcal{AR}$ description for the BTUC problem

time. The automaton corresponding to an $\mathcal{AR}$ description is obtained by means of the minimization procedure by Giunchiglia (1996). This procedure solves the frame problem and the ramification problem, and is efficiently implemented in MBP (Cimatti et al., 1997). Because of the separation between the domain construction and the planning phases, MBP is not bound to $\mathcal{AR}$. Standard deterministic domains specified in PDDL (Ghallab et al., 1998) can also be given to MBP by means of a (prototype) compiler. We are also starting to investigate the potential use of the $\mathcal{C}$ action language (Giunchiglia & Lifschitz, 1998), which allows to represent domains with parallel actions.

Different planning algorithms can be applied to the specified planning problems. They operate solely on the automaton representation, and are completely independent of the particular language used to specify the domain. MBP allows for automatic construction of conditional plans under total observability, by implementing the algorithms for strong planning (Cimatti et al., 1998b), and for strong cyclic plannig (Cimatti et al., 1998a; Daniele, Traverso, & Vardi, 1999). In CMBP, we implemented the ideas described in the previous sections. The primitives to construct and prune BsP tables required a lot of tuning, in particular with the ordering of BDD variables. We found a general ordering strategy which works reasonably well: action variables are positioned at the top of the ordering, followed by plan variables, followed by state variables, with current state and next state variables interleaved. The specific ordering within action variables, plan variables, and state variables is determined by the standard mechanism implemented in NuSMV. CMBP implements several algorithms for conformant planning. In addition to the backward algorithm presented in

Section 4, CMBP implements an algorithm based on forward search, which allows to exploit the initial knowledge of the problem, sometimes resulting in significant speed ups (Cimatti & Roveri, 2000). Backward and forward search can also be combined, to tackle the exponential growth of the search time with the depth of search. For all these algorithms, different options enable and disable different versions of the termination check.

7. Experimental Evaluation

In this section we present an experimental evaluation of our approach, which was carried out by comparing CMBP with state-of-the-art conformant planners. We first describe the other conformant planners considered in the analysis, and then we present the experimental comparison that was carried out.

7.1 Other Conformant Planners

CGP (Smith & Weld, 1998) extends the ideas of GRAPHPLAN (Blum & Furst, 1995, 1997) to deal with uncertainty. Basically, a planning graph is built of every possible sequence of possible worlds, and constraints among planning graphs are propagated to ensure conformance. The CGP system takes as input domains described in an extension of PDDL (Ghallab et al., 1998), where it is possible to specify uncertainty in the initial state. CGP inherits from GRAPHPLAN the ability to deal with parallel actions. CGP was the first efficient conformant planner: it was shown to outperform several other planners such as Buridan (Peot, 1998) and UDTPOP (Kushmerick, Hanks, & Weld, 1995). The detailed comparison reported by Smith and Weld (1998) leaves no doubt on the superiority of CGP with respect to these systems. Therefore, we compared CMBP with CGP and did not consider the other systems analyzed by Smith and Weld (1998). CMBP is more expressive than CGP in two respects. First, CGP can only handle uncertainty in the initial state. For instance, CGP cannot analyze the BTUC domain presented in Section 3. Smith and Weld (1998) describe how the approach can be extended to actions with uncertain effects. Second, CGP cannot conclude that a planning problem has no conformant solutions.

QBFPLAN is (our name for) the planning system by Rintanen (1999a). QBFPLAN generalizes the idea of SAT-based planning (Kautz, McAllester, & Selman, 1996; Kautz & Selman, 1996, 1998) to nondeterministic domains, by encoding problems in QBF. The QBFPLAN approach is not limited to conformant planning, but can be used to do conditional planning under uncertainty, also under partial observability: different encodings, corresponding to different structures in the resulting plan, can be synthesized. In this paper, we are only considering encodings which enforce the resulting plan to be a sequence. Given a bound on the length of the plan, first a QBF encoding of the problem is generated, and then a QBF solver (Rintanen, 1999b) is called. If no solution is found, a new encoding for a longer plan must be generated and solved. QBFPLAN is able to handle actions with uncertain effects. This is done by introducing auxiliary (choice) variables, the assignments to which the different possible outcomes of actions correspond. These variables are universally quantified to ensure conformance of the solution. Differently from e.g. BLACKBOX (Kautz & Selman, 1998), QBFPLAN does not have a heuristic to guess the "right" length of the plan. Given a limit in the length of the plan, it generates all the encodings up to the specified length, and repeatedly calls the QBF solver on encodings of increasing length until a plan is found.

As CGP, QBFPLAN cannot conclude that a planning problem has no conformant solutions. Similarly to CMBP, QBFPLAN relies on a symbolic representation of the problem, although QBF transformations are performed by a theorem prover rather than with BDDs.

GPT (Bonet & Geffner, 2000) is a general planning framework, where the conformant planning problem is seen as deterministic search problem in the space of belief states. GPT uses an explicit representation of the search space, where each belief state is represented as a separate data structure. The search is based on the A* algorithm (Nilsson, 1980), driven by domain dependent heuristics which are automatically generated from the problem description. GPT accepts problem descriptions in a syntax based on PDDL, extended to deal with probabilities and uncertainty. It is possible to represent domains with uncertain action effects (although the representation of actions resulting in a large number of different states is rather awkward). As for the planning algorithm, GPT is able to conclude that a given planning problem has no conformant solution by exhaustively exploring the space of belief states.

7.2 Experiments and Results

The evaluation was performed by running the systems on a number of parameterized problem domains. We considered all the problems from the CGP and GPT distributions, plus other problems which were defined to test specific features of the planners. We considered domains with uncertainty limited to the initial state, and domains with uncertain action effects. Besides problems admitting a solution, we also considered problems not admitting a solution, in which case we measured the effectiveness of the plannner in returning with failure.

Given their different expressivity, it was not possible to run all the systems on all the examples. CMBP was run on all the classes of examples, while GPT was run on all but one. CGP was run only on the problems which admit a solution, and with uncertainty limited to the initial condition. QBFPLAN was run on all the examples for which an encoding was already available from the QBFPLAN distribution. This is only a subset of the problems expressible in CGP. The main limiting factor was the low level of the input format of QBFPLAN: problem descriptions must be specified as ML code which generates the QBF encodings. Writing new encodings turned out to be a very difficult task, especially due to the lack of documentation.

We ran CGP, QBFPLAN and CMBP on an Intel 300MHz Pentium-II, 512MB RAM, running Linux. The comparison between CMBP and GPT was run on a Sun Ultra Sparc 270MHz, 128Mb RAM running Solaris (GPT was available as a binary). However, the performance of the two machines is comparable — the run times for CMBP were almost identical. CPU time was limited to 7200 sec (two hours) for each test. To avoid swapping, the memory limit was fixed to the physical memory of the machine. In the following, we write "—" or "≡" for a test that did not complete within the above time and memory limits, respectively. The performance of the systems are reported in tables listing only the search time. This excludes the time needed by QBFPLAN to generate the encodings, the time spent by CMBP to construct the automaton representation into BDD, and the time needed by GPT to generate the source code of its internal representation, and to compile it. Overall, the most significant time ignored is the automaton construction of CMBP.

Currently, the automaton construction is not fully optimized. Even in the most complex examples, however, the construction never required more than a couple of minutes[7].

7.2.1 BOMB IN THE TOILET

Bomb in the Toilet. The first domain we tackled is the classical bomb in the toilet, where there is no notion of clogging. We call the problem BT(p), where the parameter p is the number of packages. The only uncertainty is in the initial condition, where it is not known which package contains the bomb. The goal is to defuse the bomb. The results for the BT problem are shown in Table 1. The columns relative to CMBP are the length of the plan ($|P|$), the number of cached belief states and the number of hits in the cache (#BS and #NBS respectively), the time (expressed in seconds) needed for searching the automaton under Pentium/Linux (Time(L)) and under Sparc/Solaris (Time(S)). In the following, when clear from the context, the execution platform is omitted. The columns relative to CGP are the number of levels in the planning graphs ($|L|$) and the search time. The column relative to GPT is the search time.

		CMBP				CGP		GPT
	$|P|$	#BS/#BSH	Time(L)	Time(S)	$|L|$	Time	Time
BT(2)	2	2 / 2	0.000	0.000	1	0.000	0.074
BT(3)	3	6 / 11	0.000	0.000	1	0.000	0.077
BT(4)	4	14 / 36	0.000	0.000	1	0.000	0.080
BT(5)	5	30 / 103	0.000	0.000	1	0.000	0.087
BT(6)	6	62 / 266	0.010	0.010	1	0.010	0.102
BT(7)	7	126 / 641	0.010	0.030	1	0.010	0.139
BT(8)	8	254 / 1496	0.030	0.030	1	0.020	0.230
BT(9)	9	510 / 3463	0.070	0.070	1	0.020	0.481
BT(10)	10	1022 / 7862	0.150	0.140	1	0.020	1.018

Table 1: Results for the BT problems.

The BT problem is intrinsically parallel, i.e. the depth of the planning graph is always one, because all the packages can be dunked at the same time. CGP inherits from GRAPHPLAN the ability to deal with parallel actions efficiently, and therefore it is almost insensitive to the problem size. For this problem CGP outperforms both CMBP and GPT. Notice that the number of levels explored by CGP is always 1, while the length of the plan produced by CMBP and CGP grows linearly. CMBP performs slightly better than GPT.

Bomb in the Toilet with Clogging. We call BTC(p) the extension of the BT(p) where dunking a package (always) clogs the toilet, flushing can remove the clogging, and no clogging is a precondition for dunking a package. Again, p is the number of packages. The toilet is initially not clogged. With this modification, the problem no longer allows for a parallel solution. The results for this problem are listed in Table 2. The impact of the depth of the plan length becomes significant for all systems. Both CMBP and GPT outperform CGP. In this case CMBP performs better than GPT, especially on large instances (see BTC(16)).

---

7. More precisely, the maximum time in building the automaton was required for the BMTC(10,6) examples (88 secs.), the RING(10) example (77 secs.), the BMTC(9,6) examples (40 secs.), and the BMTC(10,5) examples (41 secs.). For most of the other examples, the time required for the automaton construction was less than 10 seconds.

		CMBP				CGP		GPT
	|P|	#BS/#BSH	Time(L)	Time(S)	|L|	Time	Time	
BTC(2)	3	6 / 8	0.000	0.010	3	0.000		0.074
BTC(3)	5	14 / 23	0.000	0.000	5	0.010		0.077
BTC(4)	7	30 / 61	0.010	0.010	7	0.030		0.082
BTC(5)	9	62 / 150	0.020	0.020	9	0.130		0.094
BTC(6)	11	126 / 347	0.020	0.020	11	0.860		0.113
BTC(7)	13	254 / 796	0.070	0.080	13	2.980		0.166
BTC(8)	15	510 / 1844	0.150	0.160	15	13.690		0.288
BTC(9)	17	1022 / 4149	0.320	0.330	17	41.010		0.607
BTC(10)	19	2046 / 9190	0.710	0.700	19	157.590		1.309
BTC(16)	31	131070 / 921355	99.200	99.800				351.457

QBFPLAN

	BTC(6)		BTC(10)
|P|	Time	|P|	Time
1	0.00	1	0.02
2	0.01	2	0.03
3	0.26	3	0.78
4	0.63	4	2.30
5	1.53	5	4.87
6	2.82	6	8.90
7	6.80	7	22.61
8	14.06	8	52.72
9	35.59	9	156.12
10	93.34	10	410.86
11	(+) 2.48	11	1280.88
		13	3924.96
		14	—
		...	...
		18	—
		19	(+) 16.84

Table 2: Results for the BTC problems.

The comparison with QBFPLAN is limited to the 6 and 10 package instances (the ones available from the distribution package). The performance of QBFPLAN is reported in the left table in Table 2. Each line reports the time needed to decide whether there is a plan of length i. The performance of QBFPLAN is rather good when tackling an encoding admitting a solution (in Table 2 these entries are labeled by (+)). For instance, in the BTC(10) QBFPLAN finds the solution solving the encodings at depth 19 reasonably fast. However, when a solution cannot be found, i.e. the QBF formula admits no model, the performance of QBFPLAN degrades significantly (for the depth 18 encoding, we let the solver run for 10 CPU hours and it did not complete the search). Because of the difference in performance, and the difficulty in writing new domains, in the rest of the comparison we will not consider QBFPLAN.

Bomb in Multiple Toilets. The next domain, called BMTC(p,t), is the generalization of the BTC problem to the case of multiple toilets (p is the number of packages, while t is the number of toilets). The problem becomes more parallelizable when the number of toilets increases. Furthermore, we considered three versions of the problem with increasing uncertainty in the initial states. In the first class of tests ("Low Uncertainty" columns), the only uncertainty is the position of the bomb which is unknown, while toilets are known to be not clogged. The "Mid Uncertainty" and "High Uncertainty" columns show the results in presence of more uncertainty in the initial state. In the second [third, respectively] class of tests, the status of every odd [every, resp.] toilet can be either clogged or not clogged. This increases the number of possible initial states.

The results are reported in Table 3 (for the comparison with CGP) and in Table 4 (for the comparison with GPT). The IS column represents the number of initial states of the corresponding problem. CGP is able to fully exploit the parallelism of the problem. However, CGP is never able to explore more than 9 levels in the planning graph, with depth decreasing with the number of initial states. The results also show that CMBP and GPT are much less sensitive to the number of initial states than CGP. With increasing initial

BMTC (p,t)	IS	|P|	Low CMBP #BS/#BSH	Low CMBP Time	Low CGP |L|	Low CGP Time	Mid IS	Mid CMBP #BS/#BSH	Mid CMBP Time	Mid CGP |L|	Mid CGP Time	High IS	High CMBP #BS/#BSH	High CMBP Time	High CGP |L|	High CGP Time
(2,2)	2	2	10 / 18	0.000	1	0.000	4	12 / 34	0.000	2	0.010	8	12 / 40	0.000	2	0.030
(3,2)	3	4	26 / 84	0.000	3	0.020	6	28 / 106	0.000	3	0.040	12	28 / 112	0.010	4	13.560
(4,2)	4	6	58 / 250	0.020	3	0.030	8	60 / 286	0.020	4	0.020	16	60 / 294	0.010	4	145.830
(5,2)	5	8	122 / 652	0.030	5	1.390	10	124 / 702	0.030	5	0.460	20	124 / 710	0.040	4	—
(6,2)	6	10	250 / 1552	0.070	5	3.490	12	252 / 1614	0.080	5	13,180	24	252 / 1622	0.080		
(7,2)	7	12	506 / 3586	0.180	7	508.510	14	508 / 3662	0.190		—	28	508 / 3670	0.190		
(8,2)	8	14	1018 / 8262	0.400	7	918.960	16	1020 / 8362	0.430			32	1020 / 8372	0.450		
(9,2)	9	16	2042 / 18484	0.940	7	—	18	2044 / 18602	0.960			36	2044 / 18612	0.950		
(10,2)	10	18	4090 / 40676	1.820			20	4092 / 40810	1.990			40	4092 / 40820	2.030		
(2,3)	2	2	18 / 42	0.000	1	0.010	8	24 / 99	0.000	2	0.090	16	24 / 126	0.010	2	0.170
(3,3)	3	3	47 / 202	0.010	1	0.010	12	56 / 349	0.020	2	0.200	24	56 / 373	0.020	2	0.690
(4,3)	4	5	110 / 736	0.030	3	0.110	16	120 / 942	0.040	3	0.990	32	120 / 972	0.040	3	—
(5,3)	5	7	237 / 2034	0.080	3	0.170	20	248 / 2335	0.110		—	40	248 / 2371	0.120		
(6,3)	6	9	492 / 5106	0.230	3	0.340	24	504 / 5520	0.250			48	504 / 5562	0.240		
(7,3)	7	11	1003 / 12128	0.560	5	6248.010	28	101 / 12673	0.590			56	1016 / 12721	0.640		
(8,3)	8	13	2026 / 27836	1.300	4	—	32	204 / 28530	1.350			64	2040 / 28584	1.330		
(9,3)	9	15	4073 / 62470	3.330			36	408 / 63331	3.370			72	4088 / 63391	3.390		
(10,3)	10	17	8168 / 138046	7.280			40	818 / 139092	7.460			80	8184 / 139158	7.430		
(2,4)	2	2	29 / 75	0.010	1	0.000	8	29 / 75	0.000	1	0.020	32	48 / 332	0.020	2	1.610
(3,4)	3	3	92 / 492	0.020	1	0.010	12	108 / 808	0.030	2	0.290	48	112 / 960	0.040	2	8.690
(4,4)	4	4	206 / 1686	0.060	1	0.010	16	236 / 2356	0.080	2	0.730	64	240 / 2532	0.090	2	32.190
(5,4)	5	6	457 / 4987	0.190	3	0.500	20	492 / 5888	0.230	2	—	80	496 / 6092	0.240	3	—
(6,4)	6	8	964 / 12456	0.410	3	1.160	24	1004 / 13648	0.470			96	1008 / 13876	0.470		
(7,4)	7	10	1983 / 29453	1.040	3	2.410	28	2028 / 31004	1.120			112	2032 / 31260	1.160		
(8,4)	8	12	4026 / 68466	2.740	3	8.540	32	4076 / 70584	2.870			128	4080 / 70912	2.910		
(9,4)	9	14	8117 / 153895	6.690	4	—	36	8172 / 15654	6.900			144	8176 / 156904	6.970		
(10,4)	10	16	16304 / 339160	14.420			40	16364 / 34234	14.630			160	16368 / 342736	14.770		
(2,5)	2	2	43 / 117	0.010	1	0.010	16	43 / 117	0.010	1	0.130	64	93 / 751	0.030	2	21.120
(3,5)	3	3	164 / 1031	0.040	1	0.020	24	212 / 2008	0.080	1	3.540	96	224 / 2591	0.120	2	138.430
(4,5)	4	4	416 / 4304	0.150	1	0.040	32	475 / 6375	0.260	2	6.320	128	480 / 6740	0.260	2	551.210
(5,5)	5	5	872 / 11763	0.490	1	0.050	40	987 / 15928	0.700	2	37.959	160	992 / 16393	0.730	2	1523.840
(6,5)	6	7	1875 / 31695	1.300	3	5.920	48	2011 / 37759	1.890	2	—	192	2016 / 38334	1.980	2	—
(7,5)	7	9	3901 / 78009	3.990	3	18.410	56	4059 / 86716	4.480			224	4064 / 87411	4.540		
(8,5)	8	11	7974 / 183036	9.670	3	62.040	64	8155 / 195055	10.590			256	8160 / 195880	10.640		
(9,5)	9	13	16142 / 416333	24.250	3	194.640	72	16347 / 432408	25.600			288	16352 / 433373	25.370		
(10,5)	10	15	32501 / 927329	54.910	3	289.680	80	32731 / 948279	56.420			320	32736 / 948394	56.290		
(2,6)	2	2	60 / 168	0.010	1	0.010	16	60 / 168	0.010	1	0.200	128	171 / 1533	0.040	2	337.604
(3,6)	3	3	270 / 1848	0.070	1	0.010	24	270 / 1848	0.070	1	0.830	192	448 / 6248	0.310	2	1459.110
(4,6)	4	4	786 / 9294	0.300	1	0.040	32	920 / 13810	0.500	2	30.630	256	960 / 16344	0.690	2	5643.450
(5,6)	5	5	1777 / 29075	1.160	1	0.060	40	1958 / 37636	1.940	2	30.140	320	1984 / 39710	2.120	2	—
(6,6)	6	6	3613 / 71123	3.290	1	0.100	48	4005 / 90111	4.080	2	57.300	384	4032 / 92772	4.600		
(7,6)	7	8	7625 / 180127	9.060	3	211.720	56	8100 / 208050	10.130	2	—	448	8128 / 211370	10.400		
(8,6)	8	10	15726 / 429198	20.710	3	1015.160	64	16291 / 469277	22.620			512	16320 / 473328	23.000		
(9,6)	9	12	32012 / 986188	50.610	3	3051.990	72	32674 / 1.04173e+06	53.510			576	32704 / 1.04658e+06	54.010		
(10,6)	10	14	64675 / 2.21106e+06	111.830	2	—	80	65441 / 2.285885e+06	116.440			640	65472 / 2.29158e+06	116.240		

Table 3: Results for the BMTC problems.

BMTC (p,t)	Low Unc.		High Unc.	
	CMBP Time	GPT Time	CMBP Time	GPT Time
(2,2)	0.000	0.079	0.010	0.079
(3,2)	0.010	0.087	0.010	0.091
(4,2)	0.000	0.105	0.020	0.121
(5,2)	0.040	0.146	0.040	0.198
(6,2)	0.080	0.227	0.070	0.376
(7,2)	0.190	0.441	0.200	0.850
(8,2)	0.390	0.922	0.400	1.966
(9,2)	0.910	2.211	0.950	4.743
(10,2)	1.850	5.169	1.900	10.620
(2,4)	0.000	0.109	0.010	0.121
(3,4)	0.010	0.156	0.040	0.284
(4,4)	0.050	0.270	0.100	1.016
(5,4)	0.180	0.616	0.240	3.282
(6,4)	0.370	1.435	0.460	9.374
(7,4)	1.080	3.484	1.190	27.348
(8,4)	2.700	8.767	2.830	72.344
(9,4)	8.970	23.858	6.920	180.039
(10,4)	14.210	59.966	114.690	440.308
(2,6)	0.010	0.303	0.060	0.482
(3,6)	0.050	0.562	0.260	2.471
(4,6)	0.310	1.354	0.620	17.406
(5,6)	1.110	3.257	2.060	74.623
(6,6)	3.400	8.691	4.660	243.113
(7,6)	8.910	25.677	10.430	701.431
(8,6)	21.240	68.427	23.860	=
(9,6)	49.880	289.000	54.190	
(10,6)	113.680	486.969	118.590	

Table 4: Results for the BMTC problems.

uncertainty, CGP is almost unable to solve what were trivial problems. GPT performs better than CGP, but it suffers from the explicit representation of the search space.

Bomb in the Toilet with Uncertain Clogging. The BTUC(p) domain is the domain described in Section 2, where clogging is an uncertain outcome of dunking a package. This kind of problem cannot be expressed in CGP. The results for CMBP and GPT are reported in Table 5. Although CMBP performs better than GPT (by a factor of two to three), there is no significant difference in the behavior. It is interesting to compare the results of CMBP for the BTC and BTUC problems. For GPT a slight difference is noticeable, resulting from the increased branching factor in the search space due to the uncertainties in the effects of action executions. In the performance of CMBP, the number of uncertainties is not a direct factor — for example, in the BTC(16) and BTUC(16), the performance is almost the same.

7.2.2 RING OF ROOMS

Simple Ring of Room. We considered another domain, where a robot can move in a ring of rooms. Each room has a window, which can be either open, closed or locked. The robot can move (either clockwise or counterclockwise), close the window of the room where it is, and lock it if closed. The goal is to have all windows locked.

		CMBP		GPT
	|P|	#BS/#BSH	Time	Time
BTUC(2)	3	6 / 8	0.000	0.076
BTUC(3)	5	14 / 23	0.000	0.078
BTUC(4)	7	30 / 61	0.010	0.085
BTUC(5)	9	62 / 150	0.010	0.098
BTUC(6)	11	126 / 347	0.030	0.128
BTUC(7)	13	254 / 796	0.050	0.205
BTUC(8)	15	510 / 1844	0.170	0.380
BTUC(9)	17	1022 / 4149	0.310	0.812
BTUC(10)	19	2046 / 9190	0.720	1.828
BTUC(16)	31	131070 / 921355	98.270	486.252

Table 5: Results for the BTUC problems.

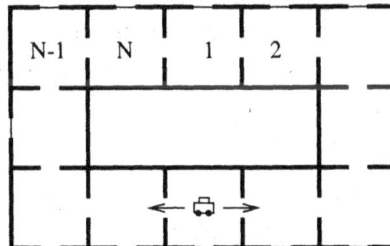

In the problem RING(r), where r is the number of rooms, the uncertainty is only in the initial condition: both the position of the robot and the status of the windows can be uncertain. These problems do not have a parallel solution, and have a large number of initial states ($r * 3^r$), corresponding to full uncertainty on the position of the robot and on the status of each window. The results[8] are reported on the left in Table 6. CMBP outperforms

		CMBP			CGP	GPT
	|P|	#BS/#BSH	Time	|L|	Time	Time
RING(2)	5	8 / 24	0.000	3	0.070	0.085
RING(3)	8	26 / 78	0.020	4	—	0.087
RING(4)	11	80 / 240	0.040			0.392
RING(5)	14	242 / 726	0.120			1.150
RING(6)	17	728 / 2184	0.370			6.620
RING(7)	20	2186 / 6558	1.420			23.636
RING(8)	23	6560 / 19680	4.950			105.158
RING(9)	26	19682 / 59046	27.330			=
RING(10)	29	59048 / 177144	106.870			

CGP on RING(5)				
IS	|L|	Time	|L|	Time
1	5	0.010	9	0.020
2	5	0.060	9	0.140
4	5	0.420	9	1.950
8	5	6.150	9	359.680
16	5	—	9	—

Table 6: The results for the RING problems.

both CGP and GPT, although GPT performs much better than CGP. Both CGP and GPT suffer from the increasing complexity of the problem. On the right in Table 6, we plot (for the RING(5) problem) the dependency of CGP on the number of initial states combined with the number of levels to be explored (different goals were provided which require the exploration of different levels). It is clear that the number of initial states and the depth of the search are both critical factors for CGP.

8. The times reported for CGP refer to a scaled-down version of the problem, where locking is not taken into account, and thus the maximum number of initial states is $r * 2^r$.

Ring of Rooms with Uncertain Action Effects. We considered a variation of the
RING domain, called URING, first introduced by Cimatti and Roveri (1999), which is not
expressible in CGP. If a window is not locked and the robot is not performing an action
which will determine its status (e.g. closing it), then the window can open or close nondeterministically. For instance, while the robot is moving from room 1 to room 2, the windows in
room 3 and 4 could be open or closed by the wind. This domain is clearly designed to stress
the ability of a planner to deal with actions having a large number of resulting states. In the
worst case (e.g. a move action performed when no window is locked), there are 2^r possible
resulting states. Although seemingly artificial, this captures the fact that environments can
be in practice highly nondeterministic. We tried to compare CMBP and GPT on the URING
problem. In principle GPT is able to deal with uncertainty in the action effects. However,
we failed to codify the URING in the GPT language, because it requires a conditional description of uncertain effects. Therefore, we experimented with a variation of the RING
domain featuring a higher degree of nondeterminism, called NDRING in the following. The
NDRING domain contains an increasing number of additional propositions, called in the
following *noninertial* propositions, which are initially unknown and are nondeterministically
altered by each action. If i is the number of noninertial propositions, each action has 2^i

	CMBP			GPT			
	$|P|$	#BS/#BSH	Time (5)	Time (2)	Time (3)	Time (4)	Time (5)
NDRING(2)	5	8 / 24	0.000	0.140	0.384	0.948	4.544
NDRING(3)	8	26 / 78	0.020	0.256	0.679	2.574	13.960
NDRING(4)	11	80 / 240	0.040	1.046	3.025	12.548	67.714
NDRING(5)	14	242 / 726	0.110	4.550	12.960	48.426	=
NDRING(6)	17	728 / 2184	0.350	18.758	57.300	=	
NDRING(7)	20	2186 / 6558	1.350	108.854	=		
NDRING(8)	23	6560 / 19680	4.990	=			
NDRING(9)	26	19682 / 59046	27.060				
NDRING(10)	29	59048 / 177144	103.760				

Table 7: The results for the NDRING problems.

possible outcomes. The results are listed in Table 7, with columns labeled with Time(i).
The growing branching factor during the search has a major impact on the performance of
GPT, while CMBP is insensitive to this kind of uncertainty. (The performance of CMBP for
a lower number of noninertial propositions are not reported because they are basically the
same.)

The URING problem was run only on CMBP. The results are listed in Table 8. It can
be noticed that the performances of CMBP improve significantly with respect to the RING
problem. This can be explained considering that, despite the larger number of transitions,
the number of explored belief states is significantly smaller (see the Bs cache statistics in
Tables 6 and 8).

7.2.3 SQUARE AND CUBE

The following domains are the SQUARE(n) and CUBE(n) from the GPT distribution (Bonet
& Geffner, 2000). These problems consist of a robot navigating in a square or cube of side
n. In both domains there are actions for moving the robot in all the possible directions.
Moving the robot against a boundary leaves the robot in the same position. The original

	CMBP		
	|P|	#BS/#BSH	Time
URING(2)	5	5 / 16	0.000
URING(3)	8	11 / 34	0.010
URING(4)	11	23 / 70	0.020
URING(5)	14	47 / 142	0.040
URING(6)	17	95 / 286	0.080
URING(7)	20	191 / 574	0.190
URING(8)	23	383 / 1150	0.410
URING(9)	26	767 / 2302	0.980
URING(10)	29	1535 / 4606	2.2300

Table 8: Results for the URING problems.

problems, called CORNER in the following, require the robot to reach a corner, starting from a completely unspecified position. We introduced two variations. In the first, called FACE, the initial position is any position of a given side [face] of the square [cube], while the goal is to reach the central position of the opposite side [face]. In the second, called CENTER, the initial position is completely unspecified, and the goal is the center of the square [cube]. For the corner problem, a simple heuristic is to perform only steps towards the corner, thus pruning half of the actions. The variations are designed not to allow for a simple heuristic — for instance, in the CENTER problem, no action can be eliminated.

SQUARE(i)	CORNER				FACE				CENTER			
	CMBP			GPT	CMBP			GPT	CMBP			GPT
	|P|	#BS/#BSH	Time	Time	|P|	#BS/#BSH	Time	Time	|P|	#BS/#BSH	Time	Time
SQUARE(2)	2	2 / 4	0.000	0.074	2	2 / 4	0.000	0.058	2	2 / 4	0.000	0.060
SQUARE(4)	6	15 / 37	0.000	0.080	7	33 / 83	0.000	0.065	8	76 / 190	0.010	0.083
SQUARE(6)	10	35 / 93	0.000	0.092	12	86 / 232	0.020	0.089	14	218 / 592	0.040	0.216
SQUARE(8)	14	63 / 173	0.020	0.115	17	163 / 453	0.040	0.139	20	432 / 1210	0.090	0.695
SQUARE(10)	18	99 / 277	0.030	0.149	22	264 / 746	0.090	0.228	26	718 / 2044	0.190	2.135
SQUARE(12)	22	143 / 405	0.050	0.196	27	389 / 1111	0.150	0.371	32	1076 / 3094	0.360	5.340
SQUARE(14)	26	195 / 557	0.070	0.261	32	538 / 1548	0.230	0.582	38	1506 / 4360	0.560	12.284
SQUARE(16)	30	255 / 733	0.080	0.357	37	711 / 2057	0.320	0.908	44	2008 / 5842	0.820	26.241
SQUARE(18)	34	323 / 933	0.120	0.503	42	908 / 2638	0.540	1.343	50	2582 / 7540	1.330	52.091
SQUARE(20)	38	399 / 1157	0.160	0.638	47	1129 / 3291	0.650	1.883	56	3228 / 9454	1.790	94.204

CUBE(i)	CORNER				FACE				CENTER			
	CMBP			GPT	CMBP			GPT	CMBP			GPT
	|P|	#BS/#BSH	Time	Time	|P|	#BS/#BSH	Time	Time	|P|	#BS/#BSH	Time	Time
CUBE(2)	3	6 / 19	0.000	0.332	3	6 / 19	0.000	0.061	3	6 / 19	0.010	0.061
CUBE(3)	6	26 / 99	0.010	0.168	6	26 / 99	0.000	0.069	6	26 / 99	0.010	0.144
CUBE(4)	9	63 / 261	0.020	0.430	11	319 / 1360	0.050	0.193	12	722 / 3091	0.130	0.569
CUBE(5)	12	124 / 537	0.040	0.276	14	709 / 3095	0.220	0.412	15	1696 / 7402	0.430	2.010
CUBE(6)	15	215 / 957	0.050	0.500	19	1343 / 6116	0.430	1.479	21	3365 / 15432	0.910	10.717
CUBE(7)	18	342 / 1551	0.100	0.567	22	2255 / 10377	0.840	3.323	24	5797 / 26814	1.860	34.074
CUBE(8)	21	511 / 2349	0.160	1.082	27	3519 / 16464	1.400	8.161	30	9248 / 43541	3.520	109.852
CUBE(9)	24	728 / 3381	0.330	1.765	30	5169 / 24331	2.810	16.272	33	13786 / 65237	7.260	701.910
CUBE(10)	27	999 / 4677	0.440	2.068	35	7279 / 34564	4.550	32.226	39	19667 / 93898	9.990	=
CUBE(15)	42	3374 / 16167	1.940	9.207	54	26439 / 127825	28.560	=	60	74041 / 359354	58.930	

Table 9: Results for the SQUARE and CUBE problems.

The results for these problems are reported in Table 9. The tests were run only with CMBP and GPT. The experiments highlight that the efficiency of GPT strongly depends on the quality of the heuristic function. If, as in the first set of experiments, the heuristics are effective, then GPT is almost as good as CMBP. Otherwise, GPT degrades significantly. In general, finding heuristics which are effective in the belief space appears to be a nontrivial problem. CMBP appears to be more stable[9], as it performs a blind, breadth-first search, and relies on the cleverness of the symbolic representation to achieve efficiency.

7.2.4 OMELETTE

Finally, we considered the OMELETTE(i) problem (Levesque, 1996). The goal is to have i good eggs and no bad ones in one of two bowls of capacity i. There is an unlimited number of eggs, each of which can be unpredictably good or bad. The eggs can be grabbed and broken into a bowl. The content of a bowl can be discarded, or poured to the other bowl. Breaking a rotten egg in a bowl has the effect of spoiling the bowl. A bowl can always be cleaned by discarding its content. The problem is originally presented as a partial observability problem, with a sensing action allowing to test if a bowl is spoiled or not. We considered the variation of the problem without sensing action: in this case no conformant solution exists. We used the OMELETTE problems to test the ability of CMBP and GPT to discover that the problem admits no conformant solution. The results are reported in Table 10. The table shows that CMBP is very effective in checking the absence of a conformant solution, and outperforms GPT by several orders of magnitude.

		CMBP			GPT
	# steps	#BS/#BSH	Time		Time
OMELETTE(3)	9	15 / 34	0.020		0.237
OMELETTE(4)	11	19 / 42	0.030		0.582
OMELETTE(5)	13	23 / 50	0.040		1.418
OMELETTE(6)	15	27 / 58	0.050		2.904
OMELETTE(7)	17	31 / 66	0.060		5.189
OMELETTE(8)	19	35 / 74	0.090		10.307
OMELETTE(9)	21	39 / 82	0.110		18.744
OMELETTE(10)	23	43 / 90	0.120		32.623
OMELETTE(15)	33	63 / 130	0.210		225.530
OMELETTE(20)	43	83 / 170	0.440		=
OMELETTE(30)	63	123 / 250	0.890		

Table 10: Results for the OMELETTE problems.

7.3 Summarizing Remarks

Overall, CMBP appears to implement the most effective approach to conformant planning, both in terms of expressivity and performance. CGP is only able to deal with uncertainties in the initial states, and cannot conclude that the problem does not admit a conformant solution. The main problem in CGP seems to be its enumerative approach to uncertainties, and the increased number of initial states severely affects the performance (see Table 3 and Table 6).

QBFPLAN is in principle able to deal with uncertain action effects, but cannot conclude that the problem does not admit a conformant solution. From the small number of ex-

---

9. Consider also that the problems are increasingly more difficult (see for instance the plan length).

periments that we could perform, the approach implemented by QBFPLAN is limited by the SATPLAN style of search: the intermediate results obtained while solving an encoding at depth k are not reused while solving encodings of increasing depth. Furthermore, the solver appears to be specialized in finding a model, rather than in proving unsatisfiability. However, the latter ability is needed in all encodings but the final one.

GPT is a very expressive system, which allows efficiently dealing with a wide class of planning problems. As far as conformant planning is concerned, it is as expressive as CMBP. It allows dealing with uncertain action effects, and can conclude that a problem does not have a conformant solution. However, CMBP appears to outperform GPT in several respects. First, the behaviour of GPT appears to be directly related to the number of possible outcomes in an action. Furthermore, the efficiency of GPT depends on the effectiveness of the heuristic functions, which can be sometimes difficult to devise, and cannot help when the problem does not admit a solution.

The main strength of CMBP is its independence on the *number* of uncertainties, which is achieved with the use of symbolic techniques. Being fully symbolic, CMBP does not exhibit the enumerative behaviour of its competitors. Compared to the original approach described by Cimatti and Roveri (1999), a substantial improvement of the performance has been obtained by the new implementation of the pruning step. A disclaimer is in order. It is well known that BDD based computations are subject to a blow-up in memory requirements when computing certain classes of boolean functions, e.g. multipliers (Bryant, 1986). It would be trivial to make up an example where the performance of CMBP degrades exponentially. However, in none of the examples we considered, which included all the examples in the distribution of CGP and GPT, this phenomenon occurred.

8. Other Related Work

The term *conformant planning* was first introduced by Goldman (1996), while presenting a formalism for constructing conformant plans based on an extension of dynamic logic. Recently, Ferraris and Giunchiglia (2000) presented another conformant planner based on SAT techniques. The system is not available for a direct comparison with CMBP. The effectiveness of the approach is difficult to evaluate, as only a limited testing is described (Ferraris & Giunchiglia, 2000). The performance is claimed to be comparable with CGP. However, the results are reported only for the enconding corresponding to the solution, and the behaviour of QBFPLAN reported in Table 2 suggests that this kind of analysis might be limited.

Several works share the idea of planning based on automata theory. The most closely related are the works in the lines of planning via model checking (Cimatti et al., 1997), upon which our work is based. This approach allows, for instance, to automatically construct universal plans which are guaranteed to achieve the goal in a finite number of steps (Cimatti et al., 1998b), or which implement trial-and-error strategies (Cimatti et al., 1998a; Daniele et al., 1999). These results are obtained under the hypothesis of total observability, while here run-time observation is not available. The main difference is that a substantial extension is required to lift symbolic techniques to search in the space of belief states. De Giacomo and Vardi (1999) analyze several forms of planning in the automata theoretic framework. Goldman, Musliner and Pelican (2000) present a method where model checking in timed automata is interleaved with the plan formation activity, to make sure that the timing constraints are met. Finally, Hoey and his colleagues (1999) use algebraic decision diagrams to tackle the problem of stochastic planning.

9. Conclusions and Future Work

In this paper we presented a new approach to conformant planning, based on the use of Symbolic Model Checking techniques. The algorithm is very general, and applies to complex planning domains, with uncertainty in the initial condition and in action effects, which can be described as finite state automata. The algorithm is based on a breadth-first, backward search, and returns conformant plans of minimal length, if a solution to the planning problem exists. Otherwise, it terminates with failure. The algorithm is designed to take full advantage of the symbolic representation based on BDDs. The implementation of the approach in the CMBP system has been highly optimized, in particular in the crucial step of termination checking. We performed an experimental comparison of our approach with the state of the art conformant planners CGP, QBFPLAN and GPT. CMBP is strictly more expressive than QBFPLAN and CGP. On all the problems for which a comparison was possible, CMBP outperformed its competitors in terms of run times, sometimes by orders of magnitude. Thanks to the use of symbolic data structures, CMBP is able to deal efficiently with problems with large numbers of initial states and action outcomes. On the other hand, the qualitative behavior of CGP and GPT seems to depend heavily on the enumerative nature of their algorithms. Differently from GPT, CMBP is independent of the effectiveness of the heuristic used to drive the search.

The research presented in this paper will be extended in the following directions. First, we are investigating an alternative approach to conformant planning, where the breadth-first style of the search is given up. These techniques appear to be extremely promising — preliminary experiments have led to speed ups of up to two orders of magnitude over the results presented in this paper for problems which admit a solution. Second, we will tackle the problem of conditional planning under partial observability, under the hypothesis that a limited amount of information can be acquired at run time. As conformant planning, this problem can be seen as search in the belief space. However, it appears to be significantly complicated by the need for dealing with run-time observation and conditional plans. Finally, we are considering the extension of the domain construction of the planner with more expressive input language, such as $\mathcal{C}$, and invariant detection techniques.

Acknowledgements

Fausto Giunchiglia provided continuous encouragement and feedback on this work. We thank Piergiorgio Bertoli, Blai Bonet, Marco Daniele, Hector Geffner, Enrico Giunchiglia, Jussi Rintanen, David Smith, Paolo Traverso, Dan Weld for valuable discussions on conformant planning and various comments on this paper. David Smith provided the code of CGP, a large number of examples, and the time-out mechanism used in the experimental evaluation. Jussi Rintanen made QBFPLAN available under Linux.

References

Blum, A. L., & Furst, M. L. (1995). Fast planning through planning graph analysis. In *Proc. Ijcai*.

Blum, A. L., & Furst, M. L. (1997). Fast planning through planning graph analysis. *Artificial Intelligence 1-2, 90*, 279–298.

Bonet, B., & Geffner, H. (2000). Planning with Incomplete Information as Heuristic Search in Belief Space. In Chien, S., Kambhampati, S., & Knoblock, C. (Eds.), 5th *International Conference on Artificial Intelligence Planning and Scheduling*, pp. 52–61. AAAI-Press.

Brace, K., Rudell, R., & Bryant, R. (1990). Efficient Implementation of a BDD Package. In *27th ACM/IEEE Design Automation Conference*, pp. 40–45 Orlando, Florida. ACM/IEEE, IEEE Computer Society Press.

Bryant, R. E. (1986). Graph-Based Algorithms for Boolean Function Manipulation. *IEEE Transactions on Computers, C-35*(8), 677–691.

Bryant, R. E. (1991). On the complexity of VLSI implementations and graph representations of Boolean functions with application to integer multiplication. *IEEE Transactions on Computers, 40*(2), 205–213.

Bryant, R. E. (1992). Symbolic Boolean manipulation with ordered binary-decision diagrams. *ACM Computing Surveys, 24*(3), 293–318.

Burch, J. R., Clarke, E. M., McMillan, K. L., Dill, D. L., & Hwang, L. J. (1992). Symbolic Model Checking: 10^{20} States and Beyond. *Information and Computation, 98*(2), 142–170.

Cassandra, A., Kaelbling, L., & Littman, M. (1994). Acting optimally in partially observable stochastic domains. In *Proc. of AAAI-94*. AAAI-Press.

Cimatti, A., Clarke, E., Giunchiglia, F., & Roveri, M. (2000). NuSMV : a new symbolic model checker. *International Journal on Software Tools for Technology Transfer (STTT), 2*(4).

Cimatti, A., Giunchiglia, E., Giunchiglia, F., & Traverso, P. (1997). Planning via Model Checking: A Decision Procedure for $\mathcal{AR}$. In Steel, S., & Alami, R. (Eds.), *Proceeding of the Fourth European Conference on Planning*, No. 1348 in Lecture Notes in Artificial Intelligence, pp. 130–142 Toulouse, France. Springer-Verlag. Also ITC-IRST Technical Report 9705-02, ITC-IRST Trento, Italy.

Cimatti, A., & Roveri, M. (1999). Conformant Planning via Model Checking. In Biundo, S. (Ed.), *Proceeding of the Fifth European Conference on Planning*, Lecture Notes in Artificial Intelligence Durham, United Kingdom. Springer-Verlag. Also ITC-IRST Technical Report 9908-01, ITC-IRST Trento, Italy.

Cimatti, A., & Roveri, M. (2000). Forward Conformant Planning via Symbolic Model Checking. In *Proceeding of the AIPS2k Workshop on Model-Theoretic Approaches to Planning* Breckenridge, Colorado.

Cimatti, A., Roveri, M., & Traverso, P. (1998a). Automatic OBDD-based Generation of Universal Plans in Non-Deterministic Domains. In *Proceeding of the Fifteenth National Conference on Artificial Intelligence (AAAI-98)* Madison, Wisconsin. AAAI-Press. Also IRST-Technical Report 9801-10, Trento, Italy.

Cimatti, A., Roveri, M., & Traverso, P. (1998b). Strong Planning in Non-Deterministic Domains via Model Checking. In *Proceeding of the Fourth International Conference on Artificial Intelligence Planning Systems (AIPS-98)* Carnegie Mellon University, Pittsburgh, USA. AAAI-Press.

Clarke, E. M., & Wing, J. M. (1996). Formal methods: State of the art and future directions. *ACM Computing Surveys, 28*(4), 626–643.

Clarke, E., Emerson, E., & Sistla, A. (1986). Automatic verification of finite-state concurrent systems using temporal logic specifications. *ACM Transactions on Programming Languages and Systems, 8*(2), 244–263.

Coudert, O., Madre, J. C., & Touati, H. (1993). *TiGeR Version 1.0 User Guide*. Digital Paris Research Lab.

Daniele, M., Traverso, P., & Vardi, M. Y. (1999). Strong Cyclic Planning Revisited. In Biundo, S. (Ed.), *Proceeding of the Fifth European Conference on Planning*, Lecture Notes in Artificial Intelligence Durham, United Kingdom. Springer-Verlag.

De Giacomo, G., & Vardi, M. (1999). Automata-Theoretic Approach to Planning for Temporally Extended Goals. In Biundo, S. (Ed.), *Proceeding of the Fifth European Conference on Planning*, Lecture Notes in Artificial Intelligence Durham, United Kingdom. Springer-Verlag.

Ferraris, P., & Giunchiglia, E. (2000). Planning as satisfiability in nondeterministic domains. In *Proceedings of Seventeenth National Conference on Artificial Intelligence (AAAI'00)* Austin, Texas. AAAI Press.

Ghallab, M., Howe, A., Knoblock, C., McDermott, D., Ram, A., Weld, D., & Wilkins, D. (1998). PDDL — The Planning Domain Definition Language. Tech. rep. CVC TR-98-003/DCS TR-1165, Yale Center for Computational Vision and Control.

Giunchiglia, E. (1996). Determining Ramifications in the Situation Calculus. In *In Fifth International Conference on Principles of Knowledge Representation and Reasoning (KR'96)* Cambridge, Massachusetts. Morgan Kaufmann Publishers.

Giunchiglia, E., Kartha, G. N., & Lifschitz, V. (1997). Representing action: Indeterminacy and ramifications. *Artificial Intelligence, 95*(2), 409–438.

Giunchiglia, E., & Lifschitz, V. (1998). An action language based on causal explanation: Preliminary report. In *Proceedings of the 15th National Conference on Artificial Intelligence (AAAI-98) and of the 10th Conference on Innovative Applications of Artificial Intelligence (IAAI-98)*, pp. 623–630 Menlo Park. AAAI Press.

Goldman, R. P., Musliner, D. J., & Pelican, M. J. (2000). Using Model Checking to Plan Hard Real-Time Controllers. In *Proceeding of the AIPS2k Workshop on Model-Theoretic Approaches to Planning* Breckenridge, Colorado.

Goldman, R., & Boddy, M. (1996). Expressive Planning and Explicit Knowledge. In *Proceedings of the 3rd International Conference on Artificial Intelligence Planning Systems (AIPS-96)*, pp. 110–117. AAAI Press.

Hoey, J., St-Aubin, R., Hu, A., & Boutilier, C. (1999). Spudd: Stochastic planning using decision diagrams. In *Proceedings of the Fifteenth Conference on Uncertainty in Articial Intelligence (1999)*, pp. 279–288. AAAI Press.

Kautz, H., & Selman, B. (1998). BLACKBOX: A New Approach to the Application of Theorem Proving to Problem Solving. In *Working notes of the Workshop on Planning as Combinatorial Search* Pittsburgh, PA, USA.

Kautz, H. A., McAllester, D., & Selman, B. (1996). Encoding Plans in Propositional Logic. In *Proc. KR-96*.

Kautz, H. A., & Selman, B. (1996). Pushing the Envelope: Planning, Propositional Logic, and Stochastic Search. In *Proc. AAAI-96*.

Kushmerick, N., Hanks, S., & Weld, D. S. (1995). An algorithm for probabilistic planning. *Artificial Intelligence, 76*(1-2), 239–286.

Levesque, H. J. (1996). What is planning in the presence of sensing?. In *Proceedings of the Thirteenth National Conference on Artificial Intelligence and the Eighth Innovative Applications of Artificial Intelligence Conference*, pp. 1139–1146 Menlo Park. AAAI Press / MIT Press.

McDermott, D. (1987). A critique of pure reason. *Computational Intelligence, 3*(3), 151–237.

McMillan, K. (1993). *Symbolic Model Checking*. Kluwer Academic Publ.

Michie, D. (1974). Machine Intelligence at Edinburgh. In *On Machine Intelligence*, pp. 143–155. Edinburgh University Press.

Nilsson, N. (1980). *Principles of Artificial Intelligence*. Morgan Kaufmann Publishers, Inc., Los Altos, CA.

Peot, M. (1998). *Decision-Theoretic Planning*. Ph.D. thesis, Dept. Engineering-Economic Systems — Stanford University.

Rintanen, J. (1999a). Constructing conditional plans by a theorem-prover. *Journal of Artificial Intellegence Research, 10*, 323–352.

Rintanen, J. (1999b). Improvements to the Evaluation of Quantified Boolean Formulae. In Dean, T. (Ed.), *16th Iinternational Joint Conference on Artificial Intelligence*, pp. 1192–1197. Morgan Kaufmann Publishers.

Smith, D. E., & Weld, D. S. (1998). Conformant graphplan. In *Proceedings of the 15th National Conference on Artificial Intelligence (AAAI-98) and of the 10th Conference on Innovative Applications of Artificial Intelligence (IAAI-98)*, pp. 889–896 Menlo Park. AAAI Press.

Somenzi, F. (1997). CUDD: CU Decision Diagram package — release 2.1.2. Department of Electrical and Computer Engineering — University of Colorado at Boulder.

Weld, D. S., Anderson, C. R., & Smith, D. E. (1998). Extending graphplan to handle uncertainty and sensing actions. In *Proceedings of the 15th National Conference on Artificial Intelligence (AAAI-98) and of the 10th Conference on Innovative Applications of Artificial Intelligence (IAAI-98)*, pp. 897–904 Menlo Park. AAAI Press.

Yang, B., Bryant, R. E., O'Hallaron, D. R., Biere, A., Coudert, O., Janssen, G., Ranjan, R. K., & Somenzi, F. (1998). A performance study of BDD-based model checking. In *Proceedings of the Formal Methods on Computer-Aided Design*, pp. 255–289.

Author Index